The Emerson Brothers

The Emerson Brothers
A Fraternal Biography in Letters

RONALD A. BOSCO and JOEL MYERSON

OXFORD
UNIVERSITY PRESS

2006

OXFORD
UNIVERSITY PRESS

Oxford University Press, Inc., publishes works that further
Oxford University's objective of excellence
in research, scholarship, and education.

Oxford   New York
Auckland   Cape Town   Dar es Salaam   Hong Kong   Karachi
Kuala Lumpur   Madrid   Melbourne   Mexico City   Nairobi
New Delhi   Shanghai   Taipei   Toronto

With offices in
Argentina Austria Brazil Chile Czech Republic France Greece
Guatemala Hungary Italy Japan Poland Portugal Singapore
South Korea Switzerland Thailand Turkey Ukraine Vietnam

Copyright © 2006 by Oxford University Press, Inc.

Published by Oxford University Press, Inc.
198 Madison Avenue, New York, New York 10016

www.oup.com

Oxford is a registered trademark of Oxford University Press

Library of Congress Cataloging-in-Publication Data
Bosco, Ronald A.
The Emerson brothers : a fraternal biography in letters / Ronald A. Bosco and Joel Myerson.
p. cm.
Includes bibliographical references and index.
ISBN-13 978-0-19-514036-1
ISBN 0-19-514036-2
1. Emerson, Ralph Waldo, 1803–1882—Family.   2. Emerson, Ralph Waldo, 1803–1882—
Correspondence.   3. Authors, American—19th century—Family relationships.   4. Authors,
American—19th century—Correspondence.   5. Brothers—United States—Correspondence.
6. Emerson, Charles Chauncy, 1808–1836.   7. Emerson, Edward Bliss, 1805–1834.
8. Emerson, William, 1801–1868.   9. Emerson family.   I. Myerson, Joel.   II. Title.
PS1631.B625 2005
814'.3—dc22   2004030379

1 3 5 7 9 8 6 4 2

Printed in the United States of America
on acid-free paper

To
Bernadette M. Bosco
and
Greta D. Little

Preface

The Emerson Brothers: A Fraternal Biography in Letters is our narrative and epistolary biography based upon the life-long correspondence exchanged among the four Emerson brothers: Charles Chauncy (1808–1836), Edward Bliss (1805–1834), Ralph Waldo (1803–1882), and William (1801–1868) Emerson.[1] Even though Charles and Edward died relatively young, this is an extensive correspondence: of the surviving letters exchanged among the brothers, there are 259 from Charles (35 to Edward, 43 to Waldo, 181 to William), 141 from Edward (9 to Charles, 42 to Waldo, 90 to William), and 368 from William (7 to Charles, 18 to Edward, 343 to Waldo).[2] In all, there are 621 letters by Charles, 171 by Edward, and 459 by William: 1,251 letters, amounting to more than half a million words.[3]

Because this biography is based on previously inaccessible sources, we believe it will create opportunities for general readers and specialists to approach Waldo's inner life fresh, that is, without any of the preconceptions that traditional scholarship has reinforced that make him a difficult—if not impossible—figure to imagine personally. In addition, because we portray Waldo in relation to his brothers who, on the evidence of the letters, are his intellectual equals, this biography expands on the relational nature of Waldo's intellect and imagination that has been the core of recent biographical and editorial studies of his family. Often composed as "round-robin" exchanges among and between the brothers, these letters document a formidable nineteenth-century fraternal relationship; they complement Waldo's accounts of his intellectual development, his comments on the major events and public concerns of his day, and his remarks on family history found in his letters, journals, and notebooks; and they complete an extraordinary archaeology of intellectual and personal influences circulating within the Emerson family and around Waldo from his early through his mature years.

As one might suspect from most biographical treatments of their famous brother, each of the Emerson brothers aspired to make an intellectual, if not also a social, reputation for himself.[4] Whereas lesser figures might have faltered under the dual burden of having been born an Emerson, with social, political, and ecclesiastic roots extending back to the first century of New England settlement, and of having been raised in reduced circumstances after the death of their father William in 1811, these letters reveal that the brothers were invigorated by their shared sense of origin as well as by a sense of duty to improve upon their father's literary and intellectual work.[5] Particularly in exchanges between Charles, Edward, and William and their Aunt Mary Moody Emerson,[6] but also in the brothers' side of their correspondence with Waldo, these letters illuminate aspects of Waldo's character and personal and intellectual development for the first time. For instance, we learn the extent of Waldo's debt to William for his first serious encounters with German Higher Criticism in the mid-1820s. We also find in the brothers' remarks on the devastation he felt at the death in 1831 of his first wife, Ellen Louisa Tucker, a correction to Waldo's own sometimes underrecorded sense of grief at her passing. As Charles, Edward, and William share thoughts about their respective careers and prospects, and as Charles, William, and Waldo draw from their own meager funds to support Edward in his declining health, and provide for both their mother and their hidden brother Bulkeley who was developmentally challenged,[7] we realize for the first time that Waldo's desire for financial security for himself, his mother, and his brothers was at least as powerful a motivation behind his resignation from Boston's Second Church in 1832 as were Ellen's death and his reservations about the Lord's Supper. And in the body of this correspondence which extends from the early 1820s to William's death in 1868, we mark, through the observations of those closest to him, Waldo's self-conscious and steady progress away from the forms of institutionalized religion toward the career of lecturer, essayist, poet, and social reformer that earned him his reputation as a principal architect of American culture.

The Emerson Brothers: A Fraternal Biography in Letters attempts to bring the brothers' relationship alive by allowing them to speak to the reader through their correspondence, while we provide contextual and interpretive materials to assist the reader to more fully appreciate the wealth of intellectual and factual information contained in our selections.[8] In many ways, our biography is patterned after the "life and letters" format made popular in the nineteenth century, in which extensive quotations from the subject's correspondence are woven into a continuous narrative of the subject's life. Readers interested in viewing the entire correspondence will find it on the Web site of the Ralph Waldo Emerson Society.[9]

However, unlike earlier "life and letters" volumes, we have decided against using a chronological structure. The details of Waldo's life are well known through the many books and articles published on that subject, and the general outlines of the brothers' lives are similarly sketched in these works. Rather, we have chosen to focus on the emotional and intellectual interactions of the four young men, their step-grandfather Ezra Ripley, their mother Ruth Haskins Emerson, and, above all, their Aunt Mary Moody Emerson.[10] In this, we follow Waldo's biographer John McAleer, who successfully divided his biography into chapters exploring various encounters comprised of separate incidents or individual friendships, rather than following him chronologically from birth to death. More important, we also have been guided by Waldo's own dictum for reading, in which he advises to "read for the lustres, as if one should use a fine picture in a chromatic experiment, for its rich colors."[11] We focus on these "lustres"; indeed, it is our contention that the lives of Waldo and his brothers are formed by a series of crucial events and friendships—following Waldo's belief that life is "a train of moods like a string of beads, and, as we pass through them, they prove to be many-colored lenses which paint the world their own hue"[12]—and that these "lustres," when strung together and studied in detail, yield crucial information about the brothers, their relations with each other and with their extended family.[13]

Fortunately for the many generations of scholars who have written on Ralph Waldo Emerson and his family, he was a keeper of family records and manuscripts. None of the great modern editions of writings by Emerson would have been possible had Emerson not kept his journals, notebooks, sermons, letters, lectures, and literary manuscripts together, as well collecting those of family members such as his father and mother, brothers, and Mary Moody Emerson. His children preserved his papers and the papers of their mother, Lidian Jackson Emerson. In turn, subsequent generations of Emersons have ensured that the family's papers survived intact until they could finally be housed at institutions that could properly care for them. The letters used as the basis for this biography have come down through two branches of the Emerson family.

The core collection begun by Ralph Waldo Emerson and added to by his children Ellen Tucker Emerson and Edward Waldo Emerson was for many years kept at Bush, the family home in Concord. Sometime in the 1920s, Sylvester Baxter, a Boston journalist, gained access to the brother's correspondence, and produced a number of drafts of what he called "The Other Emersons: Being an Account of the Three Brilliant and Scholarly Brothers *William, Edward Bliss, and Charles Chauncy Emerson,*" which he hoped the Emerson family might print; however, the project was never completed.[14] When Edward, the last of Lidian and Waldo's children, died in 1930, the family established the Ralph Waldo Emerson Memorial Association to care for the papers, which were kept at Bush, with various family members, and at the Fogg Museum of Harvard University, when Waldo's grandson Edward Waldo Forbes served as director. When the Houghton Library opened in 1942, the family deposited almost all its collections there.[15]

The William Emerson family papers were first collected by Haven Emerson, William's grandson. Haven used the collection for a talk he gave at the

Charaka Club in 1932 and transcribed many of William's earlier letters as part of an unfinished biographical project he worked on as late as 1933.[16] Ralph L. Rusk had access to these materials in preparing his edition of Emerson's *Letters* (1939), where some letters from the brothers are briefly cited in notes, and he microfilmed the papers and deposited the film at Columbia University. Karen Kalinevitch and Henry F. Pommer also used these manuscripts in their studies of Emerson's family.[17]

As this brief history indicates, the manuscripts by Emerson's brothers have not been much used by scholars; indeed, we would estimate that fewer than a dozen letters have been published in their entirety. Thus, our work on this biography owes more to the stewardship of generations of Emersons than to a long line of scholars.

Mr. Myerson made preliminary transcriptions of most of the letters in the William Emerson collection, as well as the ones at Harvard University, during the early 1980s; both authors then completed and perfected the transcriptions. Dr. Ethel Emerson Wortis, William's great-granddaughter, encouraged Mr. Myerson in the early stages of the work, and her son Dr. Michael Wortis and his wife, Ruth Emerson Wortis, helped us as we reached its conclusion. The Wortises have been most generous in sharing the superb collection of William Emerson family papers with scholars (now at the Massachusetts Historical Society).[18] Louis L. Tucker was instrumental in obtaining this collection for the Society, and we thank him, Peter Drummey, and William Fowler for facilitating our access to it. Leslie A. Morris, curator of manuscripts, greatly facilitated our use of the Ralph Waldo Emerson Memorial Association collection at the Houghton Library, and we thank her and the staff there, including Denison Beach, Tom Ford, Susan Halpert, Jennifer Rathbun, Virginia Smyers, Emily Walhout, and Melanie Wisner. Materials from these collections are published by permission of the Ralph Waldo Emerson Memorial Association, the Houghton Library of Harvard University, the Massachusetts Historical Society, Michael Wortis, and Ruth Emerson Wortis. Materials from *The Letters of Ellen Tucker Emerson, The Selected Letters of Mary Moody Emerson,* and *The Letters of Ralph Waldo Emerson* are quoted by permission of the Ralph Waldo Emerson Memorial Association. Materials from *The Journals and Miscellaneous Notebooks of Ralph Waldo Emerson* are quoted by permission of the Belknap Press of Harvard University Press, copyright by the President and Fellows of Harvard College. The miniature of Ellen Louisa Tucker Emerson is reproduced by permission of the Concord Museum, Concord, Massachusetts.

Elizabeth Maxfield-Miller shared unpublished notes from her pioneering work on Elizabeth Hoar with us, as well as assisted us with genealogical research. Nancy Craig Simmons provided us with transcriptions of letters from Mary Moody Emerson to the Emerson brothers that were not included in her edition of *The Selected Letters of Mary Moody Emerson.* Albert J. von Frank shared with us his unpublished comprehensive chronology of Emerson's life, which we have used in preparing the chronology to this work.[19] We have benefited from the assistance and advice of Lawrence Buell, David R. Chesnutt, Phyllis Cole, Francis Dedmond, Rodney Dennis, Travis Gordon, Edith E. W. Gregg, Robert N. Hudspeth, Karen Kalinevitch, Lewis Leary, Kenneth Lohf, Wesley T. Mott, Ralph H. Orth, Robert D. Richardson, Jr., David M. Robinson, Merton M. Sealts, Jr., Eleanor M. Tilton, Leslie Perrin Wilson, and Thomas Wortham.

Mr. Bosco would like to thank Gareth Griffiths, chair of English, former Dean of Arts and Sciences V. Mark Durand and current Dean Joan Wick-Pelletier, Provost Carlos Santiago, former President Karen R. Hitchcock, and Interim President John R. Ryan of the University at Albany, State University of New York, for providing him with the intellectual space to work on this volume. He would also like to acknowledge the conscientious work of his research assistant, Susan H. Kayorie of the University at Albany.

Mr. Myerson would like to thank Alan Brasher, Ward Briggs, Caroline Bokinsky, Bert Dillon, Armida Gilbert, Scott Gwara, Trevor Howard-Hill, Jennifer Hynes, Alfred G. Litton, Michael McLoughlin, Chris Nesmith, Robert Newman, Todd Richardson, Daniel Shealy, Susan Stone, and especially Chris Heafner. Steven Lynn, chair of the Department of English of the University of South Carolina, continues to generously support Mr. Myerson's Emerson research. He is also grateful to the American Philosophical Society for a research grant, the University of South Carolina for a sabbatical leave, and the South Carolina Committee for the Humanities for a summer fellowship to work on this book.

Both Mr. Bosco and Mr. Myerson gratefully acknowledge the Ralph Waldo Emerson Memorial Association, and especially Margaret Emerson Bancroft and Roger L. Gregg, for their financial support of this work. Both authors are grateful to the National Endowment for the Humanities, an independent federal agency, for awarding us a Collaborative Research Program grant to complete this book.

T. Susan Chang brought this book to Oxford University Press, and we appreciate her early enthusiasm and support. Elissa Morris shared Susie's enthusiasm and we thank her for helping us to bring this project to a successful conclusion.

Our wives have been amazingly patient with us as over the past fourteen years we have brought our several projects dealing with the Emerson Family Papers into our homes and casually commandeered whole rooms, hallways, and most recently garages as our newest versions of expanded office space. More often than we would like to remember, together we have made William, Waldo, Edward, and Charles Emerson conversational guests at dinners and family outings both in this country and abroad. Throughout it all, the love, support, and generous good cheer of our wives have made it possible for us to do our work and remain somewhat sane in the process. With profound gratitude to them, we dedicate this fraternal biography to Bernadette M. Bosco and Greta D. Little.

Contents

A photo gallery appears after page 188

Abbreviations

The following abbreviations are employed in this book:

JMN   *The Journals and Miscellaneous Notebooks of Ralph Waldo Emerson,* ed.
        William H. Gilman, Ralph H. Orth, et al., 16 vols. Cambridge, Mass.:
        Harvard University Press, 1960–1982.
L   *The Letters of Ralph Waldo Emerson,* ed. Ralph L. Rusk (vols. 1–6)
        & Eleanor M. Tilton (vols. 7–10), 10 vols. New York: Columbia
        University Press, 1939, 1990–1995.
MH   Houghton Library, Harvard University
MHi   Massachusetts Historical Society
MMEL *The Selected Letters of Mary Moody Emerson,* ed. Nancy Craig
        Simmons. Athens: University of Georgia Press, 1993.

Chronology

1796	25 October	Reverend William Emerson marries Ruth Haskins
1798	9 February	Phoebe Ripley Emerson born
1799	28 November	John Clarke Emerson born
1800	28 September	Phoebe Ripley Emerson dies
1801	31 July	William Emerson born
1802	20 September	Lydia Jackson born
1803	25 May	Ralph Waldo Emerson born
1805	17 April	Edward Bliss Emerson born
1806	Spring	William and Waldo attend Mrs. Whitwell's School
1807	11 April	Robert Bulkeley Emerson born
	26 April	John Clarke Emerson dies
1808	27 November	Charles Chauncy Emerson born
1811	26 February	Mary Caroline Emerson dies
	12 May	Reverend William Emerson dies; the family remains in the parsonage house until 1813, when a new minister for the First Church is appointed
1813	22 January	William delivers an "Essay in English Prose" at the Boston Latin School's "Semi-Annual Visitation"
	8 June	William goes to Waltham to be examined by Sophia Alden Bradford Ripley in preparation for Harvard
1814	14 April	Mary Caroline Emerson dies
	14 July	Elizabeth Sherman Hoar born
	26 August	Waldo is a participant in "A Latin Dialogue, 'Augustus Caesar and Lucius Junius Brutus,' translated from Hughes" at the Boston Latin School Exhibition
	30 September	William enters Harvard College
	1 November?	Ruth Emerson arrives in Concord with her family

1815	25 March?	Emerson family returns to Boston
	25 August	Waldo reads "Poetical Essay—Independence" at a Boston Latin School Exhibition
	Winter	William helps in Samuel Ripley's school in Waltham
1816	21 August	Waldo reads his "Poem on Eloquence" at a Boston Latin School Exhibition
	14 October	Edward enters Phillips Academy in Andover
1817	4 January	Waldo reads his "Poem on Eloquence" at a Boston Latin School Exhibition
	10 October	Waldo enters Harvard College
	12 December	William leaves for Kennebunk, Maine, to keep school
1818	7 January	Waldo assists at the Waltham school of Samuel Ripley
	14 March	Waldo returns to Harvard
	26 August	William participates in a "Conference—Upon architecture, painting, poetry, and music, as tending to produce and perpetuate religious impressions" at the Harvard commencement ceremonies
	16 September	Waldo teaches school in Waltham
1820	25 January	Waldo begins the first of his regular journals, Wide World I
	September	Waldo wins a Bowdoin Prize for his "Dissertation on the Character of Socrates" as well as a Boylston Prize for public speaking
	1 October?	Edward enters Harvard College, rooming with Waldo (a senior)
1821	24 April	Waldo delivers "Indian Superstition" at the College Exhibition
	29 August	Waldo participates in "A Conference, 'On the Character of John Knox, William Penn, and John Wesley'" at the Harvard Commencement
	Summer?	Waldo stays at the Old Manse with Ezra and Sarah Ripley, where he meets and gives Greek lessons to seven-year-old Elizabeth Hoar
	Fall?	William teaches a girls' school in Boston
1822	January	Waldo assists in William's school
	25 May	Waldo and William take a two-week walking tour through Northborough, Milton, and Worcester, Mass.
	13 July	Charles recites an "Extract from North-American Review on English Universities" at a public declamation at the Boston Latin School
	2 August	Charles goes to Kennebunk, Maine, for his health
	21 August	Charles delivers "An English Essay, 'The Settlement of New-England'" at the Boston Latin School Exhibition

	November	"Thoughts on the Religion of the Middle Ages," Waldo's first publication, appears in the *Christian Disciple and Theological Review*
1823	December?	Edward teaches school at Sudbury
	5 December	William sails for Europe; Waldo takes over his school
1824	5 March	William reaches Göttingen
	27 April	Edward presents a mathematic chart "Calculation and projection of a solar eclipse in May, 1836" at the Harvard Exhibition
	June	Edward teaches in a school in Roxbury, where Bulkeley is being boarded out
	8 July	Waldo completes the quarter at William's Boston school
	9 July	Edward wins a Bowdoin prize for his essay "Antiquity, Extent, Cultivation, and Present State of the Empire of China"
	19 September	William, during a walking tour of Germany, meets with Goethe
	October	Bulkeley is boarded out at Waterford, Maine
	November	Bulkeley returns home
	31 December	Waldo closes his school
1825	18 January	Edward enters his name to study law at Daniel Webster's office
	11 February	Waldo enrolls in the Harvard Divinity School
	30 March	William leaves Göttingen
	29 August	William sails from Liverpool, reaching Boston in mid-October
	12 September	Waldo opens a school in Chelmsford, Mass. (closes it at end of year)
	23 October	Edward sails for Europe for his health
	31 December	Bulkeley is boarded out in Roxbury
1826	3 January	Waldo takes over Edward's school in Roxbury (closes it on 28 March)
	1 April	Waldo opens a school in Cambridge (closes it on 23 October)
	30 August	Charles wins a Boylston prize in elocution at the Harvard Commencement
	September	William goes to New York to apprentice as a lawyer
	10 October	Waldo preaches first sermon before Middlesex Association of Ministers and is approbated to preach
	19 October	Edward returns from Europe
	25 November	Waldo sails to Charleston, S.C., and St. Augustine, Fla., for his health

1827	3 June	Waldo returns to Boston
	16 July	Charles delivers "An Oration in English: 'The Value of Letters'" at the Harvard Exhibition
	29 August	Edward gives the English Oration on "The Importance of Efforts for the Diffusion of Knowledge" at the Harvard Commencement; Waldo receives a M.A. degree
	October	Charles publishes "Conversation" in the *Harvard Register*
	October	William contributes to the *New York Journal of Commerce*
	25 December	Waldo meets sixteen-year-old Ellen Louisa Tucker for the first time
1828	1 January	Charles publishes "Friendship" in the *Harvard Register*
	6 March	William lectures on "English Literature" for the New York Athenaeum at the Chapel of Columbia College; other installments are on 13 and 27 March
	29 April	Charles participates in the "Mathematical and Astronomical Exercises" at Harvard
	25 May	Edward suffers a nervous breakdown
	2 July	Edward hospitalized at McLean Asylum
	15 July	Charles delivers Class Day valedictory oration at Harvard
	27 August	Charles delivers an oration on "Public Opinion" at the Harvard Commencement
	4 December	Waldo's first letter to William that includes extensive financial accounts
	6 December	Edward is released from McLean Asylum
	17 December	Waldo is engaged to Ellen Louisa Tucker
1829	9 January	Edward moves to Concord to study law
	19 January	Ellen is attacked with "a bleeding at the lungs"
	11 March	Waldo is ordained junior pastor at the Second Church, Boston
	30 March	Waldo moves to Chardon Street, Boston
	26 August	Charles closes his school
	30 September	Waldo and Ellen are married at Concord, N.H.
	5 October	Waldo and Ellen move to Chardon St., Boston, along with her two sisters and both their mothers
1830	3 February	Charles lectures before Concord Lyceum on "The Constitution of Man as Affected by Outward Circumstances"
	20 May?	The Emersons move to new lodgings in Brookline
	25 September	Bulkeley is at Charlestown
	16 November	Charles has "a little inflammation of the lungs"
	12 December	Edward sails for St. Croix (Santa Cruz) for his health
1831	8 February	Ellen dies
	14 May	Edward settles at the home of Sidney Mason at St. Johns (San Juan), Puerto Rico

	30 May	Waldo and Charles leave for Vermont, returning on 14 June
	31 August	Charles receives his law degree
	19 October	Charles' tuberculosis bothers him again
	7 December	Charles sails for Puerto Rico for his health
	22 December	Charles arrives at St. Johns
1832	29 March	Waldo visits Ellen's tomb and opens the coffin
	10 April?	Charles leaves St. John's, returning on 1 May
	21 June	Waldo travels with Charles to Portsmouth, N.H.; Charles returns alone on 6 July
	13 August	Edward comes to New York for a visit, returning to Puerto Rico on 6 October
	16 August	William announces his engagement to Susan Woodward Haven
	11 September	Waldo resigns from his position at the Second Church
	2 October	Charles is sworn in as an attorney of the Court of Common Pleas and opens his office at 17 Court Street, Boston
	25 December	Waldo sails to Malta, arriving there on 2 February
1833	1 January	Ruth Haskins Emerson and Charles raise $951.68 by auctioning the family's household goods
	9 January	Charles lectures on "One of the West India Islands" at the Concord Lyceum
	7 April	Susan Haven meets Ruth Haskins Emerson and Charles for the first time
	27 June	Charles writes Waldo that his suit over the Tucker estate has been settled in his favor
	2 August	Charles becomes engaged to Elizabeth Hoar this weekend
	26 August	Waldo visits Jane Welsh and Thomas Carlyle in Scotland
	4 September	Waldo sails from Liverpool, arriving in New York on 7 October
	5 November	Waldo delivers his first lecture, "The Uses of Natural History," in Boston
	3 December	William marries Susan Woodward Haven at Portsmouth, N.H.
	10 December	Waldo moves to 276 Washington Street, Boston, where Charles also lives
	18 December	Charles lectures on "The Life, Death, and Character of Socrates" at the Concord Lyceum
1834	1 January	Charles gives Elizabeth a pin with a braid of Ellen Emerson's hair
	March	Waldo meets Lydia Jackson of Plymouth, Mass.
	16 April	Susan meets Waldo for the first time

	13 May	Waldo receives a partial inheritance of $11,600 from Ellen Emerson's estate
	1 July	Ruth Haskins Emerson moves from Newton to the Old Manse to keep house for Ezra Ripley
	1 October	Edward dies in Puerto Rico
	9 October	Waldo moves to Concord, Mass.
	18 October	Waldo learns of Edward's death
	29 October	Charles lectures on "Civil, Political, and Religious Duties" at the Concord Lyceum
1835	9 January	Charles lectures on "Modern Society" at Plymouth, Mass.
	17 January	Charles lectures at Waltham
	20 January	Charles lectures at Plymouth
	22 January	Charles lectures before the Boston Lyceum at Boylston Hall
	24 January	Waldo proposes Lydia Jackson, who accepts on 28 January
	29 January	Squire Hoar offers Charles his Concord law practice while he serves as a Congressman in Washington, which Charles accepts on 12 February
	3 February	Charles lectures at Plymouth
	8 April	Charles lectures on "Socrates" at Lowell
	29 April	Charles completes "Lecture on Slavery"
	18 June	William Emerson, Jr., is born to Susan and William
	7 July	Waldo buys the Coolidge House in Concord, to be called "Bush" by the family
	12 September	Waldo delivers a discourse on Concord's history (published in November)
	14 September	Waldo marries Lydia Jackson (whom he calls "Lidian") in Plymouth
	15 September	Waldo and Lidian return to Concord to live
	15 December	Charles lectures at the Cambridge Lyceum
1836	6 January	Charles rooms with George Partridge Bradford in Boston during the Court sessions
	4 March	Elizabeth stays at the Beacon Hill home of the Reverend David Greene
	21 April	Waldo cancels his lectures at Salem to take Charles to New York
	26 April	Waldo and Charles arrive at William's house at New York, where Ruth Haskins Emerson is staying
	9 May	Charles dies
	10 May	Waldo and Elizabeth set out for New York, arriving the next day, when the funeral takes place
	15 May	Elizabeth comes to Bush to spend a week

	9 August	Waldo is appointed administrator of Charles' estate
	9 September	*Nature* published
	30 October	Waldo Emerson is born to Lidian and Waldo
1837	30 March	Bulkeley visits Concord from Chelmsford
	late July	Waldo receives the remainder of his inheritance (another $11,675) from Ellen Emerson's estate
	31 August	Waldo delivers an address on the "American Scholar" at Harvard (published 23 September)
1838	2 January	Ruth Haskins Emerson visits William in New York
	10 June	Bulkeley is back at the McLean Asylum
	15 July	Waldo delivers an address at the Harvard Divinity School (published 21 August)
	19 July	William moves into his house on Staten Island
	24 July	Waldo delivers an address on "Literary Ethics" at Dartmouth College (published 8 September)
1839	24 February	Ellen Emerson is born to Lidian and Waldo
	28 May	Ruth Haskins Emerson returns to Concord
1840	15 April	John Haven Emerson is born to Susan and William
	late July	Bulkeley comes to Concord for a month's visit before going to Lowell
1841	19 March	*Essays* [*First Series*] published (and in England on 21 August)
	June	William is made a judge of the Richmond County court
	11 August	Waldo delivers "The Method of Nature" at Waterville College, Maine (published 21 October)
	21 September	Ezra Ripley dies
	14 October	Bulkeley is at the McLean Asylum
	22 November	Edith Emerson is born to Lidian and Waldo
	15 December	Charles Emerson is born to Susan and William
1842	27 January	Young Waldo dies
1843	February	William helps arrange Waldo's lectures before the Berean Institute
	7 May	Henry David Thoreau arrives in Staten Island to stay with William and tutor Willie; he returns to Concord on 23 November
1844	10 July	Edward Waldo Emerson is born to Lidian and Waldo
	1 August	Waldo delivers an address on "Emancipation of the Negroes in the British West Indies" at Concord Court House (published 9 September and in England in October)
	19 October	*Essays: Second Series* published (and in England on 9 November)

1845	December	Waldo enlists William's help in publishing a book by Carlyle
	2 December	Waldo purchases forty-one acres at Walden Pond
1846	12 December	*Poems* published in England (and in America on 25 December)
1847	5 October	Waldo sails for Europe, arriving at Liverpool on 22 October
1848	7 May	Waldo arrives in Paris
	2 June	Waldo returns to England
	15 July	Waldo sails from Liverpool, arriving at Boston on 27 July
1849	11 September	*Nature; Addresses, and Lectures* published
	7 December	William asks Waldo, on behalf of the New York Mercantile Library, for one or two lectures in January
1850	1 January	*Representative Men* published (and in England on 5 January)
1853	16 November	Ruth Haskins Emerson dies at Concord
1856	6 August	*English Traits* published (and in England on 6 September)
1858	April	William Emerson, Jr., is engaged to Sarah Gibbons; William becomes the guardian of 13-year-old Emily Jenks
1859	27 May	Bulkeley dies
1860	4 March	William rents out his Staten Island home for three years and boards in New York City
	8 December	*The Conduct of Life* published (and in England on 8 December)
1862	6 May	Thoreau dies
1863	1 May	Mary Moody Emerson dies
	25 November	William Emerson, Jr., is married
1864	29 January	William leases the Whiting house in Concord
	29 February	William Emerson, Jr., dies
1865	Spring	Susan and William are living in Concord
	3 October	Edith Emerson marries William Hathaway Forbes
1866	10 July	Ralph Emerson Forbes, Waldo's first grandchild, born
1867	29 April	*May-Day and Other Pieces* published (and in England on 8 June)
1868	6 February	Susan dies; William returns to New York to live with Haven
	2 June	Haven marries Susan Tompkins

	13 September	Waldo arrives in New York in time to speak to William before he dies
1870	5 March	*Society and Solitude* published (and in England on 5 March)
1872	24 July	Bush is severely damaged by fire
	23 October	Waldo goes to Europe and Egypt with Ellen
1873	26 May	Waldo and Ellen return to America
1874	19 September	Edward Waldo Emerson marries Annie Shepard Keyes
	19 December	*Parnassus* published, a poetry collection edited by Waldo
1875	15 December	*Letters and Social Aims* published (and in England on 8 January 1876)
1878	25 February	Waldo delivers an address on "Fortune of the Republic" in Boston (published 10 August)
	7 April	Elizabeth Hoar dies
1882	20 April	Waldo catches cold
	27 April	Waldo dies
	30 April	Waldo is buried in Sleepy Hollow Cemetery, Concord

The Emerson Brothers

Chapter 1

"What poems are many private lives"
The Emerson Brothers

The world looks poor & mean so long as I think only of its great men; most of them of spotted reputation. But when I remember how many obscure persons I myself have seen possessing gifts that excited wonder, speculation, & delight in me; when I remember that the very greatness of Homer, of Shakspeare, of [Daniel] Webster & [William Ellery] Channing is the truth with which they reflect the mind of all mankind;[1] when I consider that each fine genius that appears is already predicted in our constitution inasmuch as he only makes apparent shades of thought in us of which we hitherto knew not . . . and when I consider the absolute boundlessness of our capacity—no one of us but has the whole untried world of geometry, fluxions, natural philosophy, Ethics, wide open before him.

When I recollect the charms of certain women, what poems are many private lives, each of which can fill our eye if we so will, (as the swan, the eagle, the cedar bird, the canary each seems the type of bird-kind whilst we gaze at it alone,) and then remember how many millions I know not; then I feel the riches of my inheritance in being set down in this world gifted with organs of communication with this accomplished company. (8 December 1834, JMN, 4:353–354)

The combined intellectual and imaginative instincts of a philosopher, a historian, and an idealist steeped in humanistic tradition and possessing the rarest sensibility are required to conceive and then express in so few words a sentiment that acknowledges the poetry residing in the recesses of "many private lives." For Ralph Waldo Emerson, a master of humanistic tradition who

3

possessed the liberal sensibility of one conversant in multiple disciplines, the ability to articulate this sentiment in 1834 meant that he had personally assimilated two fundamental truths about human experience.

The first truth, which he had to witness before he could personalize and assimilate it, was the relatedness of all things in the universe. Waldo experienced this truth first hand in 1833, when, during an extended European tour following the death of his first wife, Ellen Louisa Tucker, in 1831 and his eventual resignation from the pulpit of the Second Church in Boston in 1832, he visited the Jardin des Plantes in Paris over a period of several days. There, on 13 July 1833, he spent the day wandering through the rooms of the Cabinet of Natural History. His account of the thoughts that occurred to him as he studied case after case of specimens preserved in the museum identifies this as the moment he literally saw and fully understood how all objects in the universe were ultimately related. Nature struck him as suddenly and unexpectedly large and thoroughly organic; observer and observed became one as the objects he studied came to life as extensions of the mind that beheld them and as symbols of the imagination that interpreted them. In that moment, Waldo experienced a classic epiphany; seeing the world anew, he discovered that he could access the accumulated wisdom of the ages, comprehend exactly how "each fine genius that appears is already predicted in our constitution," appreciate "the riches of [his] inheritance in being set down in this world . . . with this accomplished company," and then reason toward an ethical and metaphysical doctrine he eventually labeled "the infinitude of the private man" (*JMN, 7*:342). Reflecting a few days later on what he had seen and learned in the Cabinet of Natural History, Waldo wrote in his journal, "How much finer things are in composition than alone."

'Tis wise in man to make Cabinets. When I was come into the Ornithological Chambers, I wished I had come only there. The fancy-coloured vests of these elegant beings make me as pensive as the hues & forms of a cabinet of shells, formerly. It is a beautiful collection & makes the visiter as calm & genial as a bridegroom. The limits of the possible are enlarged, & the real is stranger than the imaginary. . . .

In other rooms I saw amber containing perfect musquitoes, grand blocks of quartz, native gold in all its forms of crystallization, threads, plates, crystals, dust; & silver black as from fire. Ah said I this is philanthropy, wisdom, taste—to form a Cabinet of natural history. . . . Here we are impressed with the inexhaustible riches of nature. The Universe is a more amazing puzzle than ever as you glance along this bewildering series of animated forms . . . & the upheaving principle of life everywhere incipient in the very rock aping organized forms. Not a form so grotesque, so savage, nor so beautiful but is an expression of some property inherent in man the observer,—an occult relation between the very scorpions and man. I feel the centipede in me—cayman, carp, eagle, & fox. I am moved by strange sympathies. (*JMN*, 4:198–200)

Even though he did not acknowledge them as such, the "strange sympathies" Waldo felt moved by while reflecting on his experience in Paris were not entirely new. They were the sympathies he had been quietly feeling and assimilating throughout his life in the private world of family and friends and in the love he shared with Ellen during their seventeen-month marriage. They were sympathies that he knew through the devotion of his parents to their children, as the preparation of a world and identity for him by ancestors and elders whose lives, thoughts, and works represented tangible investments in his own, and as the bond of fraternal love he shared with his brothers, a bond so profound that Waldo often professed that he was complete as a person only to the extent that his brothers constituted, literally, parts of himself.

"Strange sympathies": think of them as forms of love, affection, devotion— but Waldo and his brothers thought of them in terms of their fraternal relationships. Once recognized, once felt, once acknowledged, they served as measures of who they were as individuals, and how, only as extensions of each other, the Emerson brothers could think of themselves as whole. This was the second truth about human experience that Waldo had to witness and assimilate, and although it would not be exactly accurate to say that he and his brothers were "obscure" persons, his and his brothers' ability to excite "wonder, speculation, & delight" in each other for as long as they lived was the principal means through which Waldo understood how "many private lives" were "poems." The existence and importance of wonderful sympathies shared among family, friends, and even strangers was a truth that informed his entire life, and as late as the last years of his active career as a lecturer, Waldo held this truth so dear that he referred to it as "the rule of life":

> You shall not go to the sermons in the churches for the true theology, but talk with artists, naturalists, and other thoughtful men who are interested in verities, and note how the idea of God lies in their minds; not the less, how the sentiment of duty lies in the heart of the "bobbin-woman," of any unspoiled daughter, or matron, in the farmhouse. These are the crucial experiments, these the wells where the coy truth lies hid.
>
> I think, as I go, Life is always rich; spontaneous graces and forces elevate it, in every domestic circle, which are overlooked, whilst we are reading of something less excellent in old authors. I go through the streets; each one of these innumerable houses has its own calendar of domestic saints, its unpublished anecdotes of courage, of patience, of wit, of cheerfulness. For the best, I know, were in the most private corners.

> Everything draws to its kind, and frivolous people will not hear of
> noble traits; but let any good example of this secret virtue come acciden-
> tally to air . . . and you shall hear of parallel examples in every direction.
> From the obscurity and casualty of those which I know, I infer the ob-
> scurity and casualty of the like balm, and consolation, and immortality
> in a thousand homes which I do not know, and all 'round the world. Let
> it lie hid in the shade there from the compliments and praise of foolish
> society: it is safer so. All it seems to demand, is, that we know it, when
> we see it.[2]

Although Waldo Emerson is one of the principal figures in the biography
that follows, in a departure from the direction of virtually all Emerson studies
published since Waldo's death in 1882, he is not *the* principle figure. This is a
"fraternal biography," and as such, he will share the stage as one of four principal figures whose lives "made but one man together."[3] Those other figures
are his older brother William Emerson and his younger brothers Edward Bliss
Emerson and Charles Chauncy Emerson. Under normal circumstances, Robert Bulkeley Emerson (1807–1859), a fifth brother who lived to maturity, also
would have been a central figure in this biography; however, because Bulkeley,
as he was familiarly known within the family, never really entered the relationship shared among his brothers, his presence in this biography is peripheral at
best.

Seemingly normal at the time of his birth and a handsome and cheerful boy
for the first few years of his life, by the time Bulkeley turned nine, he appeared
to be developmentally challenged and incapable of taking his place in the co-
terie of young scholars that was forming around his brothers. All of Waldo's
biographers have labeled him mentally retarded, and then dismissed him from
any further consideration in their studies. However, a growing number of Emersonians have speculated privately that Bulkeley may have been a victim of
what is now known as "Tourette's Syndrome": a disease that manifests itself in
various involuntary "tics," including neck-jerking, shoulder-shrugging, facial
grimacing, barking, hissing, *coprolalia* (the blurting out of, typically, obscene
words), and *palilalia* (the repeating of sounds or words).[4] Unfortunately, because
members of the Emerson family, including Bulkeley's brothers, were never specific in their characterization of his symptoms, it is impossible to determine
the exact form of defect or disease that he endured. In the letters exchanged
among William, Waldo, Edward, and Charles on which this fraternal biography
is largely based, Bulkeley is a shadowy figure. He appears only as the subject
of, at most, a sentence or two, but the substance of those sentences invariably
amounts to a tallying of the costs of his care either in institutions for the insane
such as the McLean Asylum in Charlestown, Massachusetts, to which Bulkeley
was periodically committed by his family, or on local farms in Littleton and

Chelmsford, Massachusetts, where he was boarded out by his brothers as a day laborer. When Bulkeley died on 27 May 1859, Waldo asked Henry David Thoreau to arrange for his brother's funeral and burial in the Emerson family plot in Concord's new Sleepy Hollow Cemetery; on 30 May, the day after the ceremonies, Waldo provided his brother William, who had remained in New York, with the following account of them.

> Yesterday morning [29 May] . . . Bulkeley's body was brought to my house. . . . His face was not much changed by death, but sadly changed by life from the comely boy I can well remember. His expression was now however calm & peaceful. . . . Mr Thoreau kindly undertook the charge of the funeral and Rev Mr Reynolds to whom I explained what I thought necessary,[5] & whom Lidian [Waldo's wife] visited afterwards lest he should not do justice to Bulkeley's virtues, officiated. . . . The afternoon was warm & breezy half in sun half in shade and it did not seem so odious to be laid down there under the oak trees in as perfect an innocency as was Bulkeleys, as to live corrupt & corrupting with thousands. What a happiness, that, with his infirmities, he was clean of all vices! (L, 5:149–150)

A few months later, Waldo had a tombstone placed over Bulkeley's grave on which he ordered this line from Matthew 25:23 to be carved: "Thou has been faithful over a few things."

Three other of the brothers' siblings born to the brothers' parents, the Reverend William and Ruth Haskins Emerson, do not appear in this biography, two having died in infancy and the third as a young boy: Phebe Emerson (1798–1800), John Clarke Emerson (1799–1807), and Mary Caroline Emerson (1811–1814). Although no records survive to state the causes of either Phebe's or Mary Caroline's early deaths, John Clarke's death from what appears to have been complications of tuberculosis in its early stages, together with Bulkeley's infirmities, introduces a difficult subject that dominates all aspects of the Emerson brothers' personal history. The subject, which makes its appearance in the earliest epistolary accounts the brothers' provide of themselves and their relations with each other, involves the presence of tuberculosis, mental disease and defect, and extreme psychological distress in the generation of the immediate family into which they were born.

Because it dominates their narratives about themselves, every chapter that follows deals with one or more aspects of this subject as a recurrent element in our narrative of the brothers' lives. Thus, although this is not the place for an exhaustive treatment of this subject, it is worth observing that prior to their father's death from tuberculosis in 1811, there is no recorded evidence of the disease in the brothers' paternal or maternal family histories. In addition to John

Clarke, each of the Reverend William Emerson's sons suffered from a form of the disease during his life with the exception, so far as we can tell, of Bulkeley.[6] In the 1820s, William, who of all the brothers had consistently enjoyed the most decent health as a young man, created a stir in the family when he confessed that he had experienced tell-tale symptoms of the disease—a prolonged cold accompanied by a severe cough and headaches—in the winter of 1828; although William ultimately died of pneumonia forty years later, his first son, also named William, did die of tuberculosis, and his second son, John Haven, experienced small pulmonary hemorrhages as a young man on two occasions.[7] Edward, who had been ill with precursors of the disease throughout his childhood and early adult years, had major outbreaks of tuberculosis that required him to interrupt his studies and his entrance into the law; these occurred in the winter of 1820, when he had to leave New England for the warmth of Alexandria, Virginia; in the spring of 1822, when he retreated from Boston inland to the drier climate of Worcester, Massachusetts; and in much of the first half of 1825, when he finally accepted his doctors' advice and left New England for Europe for an entire year. Edward eventually died of tuberculosis—or "galloping consumption" as it was called in its terminal phases—in 1834, with his death in Puerto Rico ending a four-year exile from his family. In the 1820s, Waldo, too, exhibited symptoms of the disease both during and after his student years at Harvard.[8] By the middle of the decade, his symptoms had become severe enough to prompt him to seek refuge in Charleston, South Carolina, and St. Augustine, Florida, during the winter of 1826–1827. Although Waldo lived until 1882, dying a relatively serene death that followed several years of declining memory, his letters and journal entries suggest that he was wary of coughs, colds, and sore throats accompanied by hoarseness throughout his life, and he was also concerned about the health of his children. His concern was not misplaced; of his four children, Waldo (1836–1842), Ellen Tucker (1841–1909), Edith (1841–1929), and Edward Waldo (1844–1930), Waldo died suddenly of scarlatina or scarlet fever in January 1842, and Edward had to be withdrawn from Harvard during his freshman year, and spent most of 1861 and 1862 regaining his strength at home and on a purposely slow overland journey to California after what appears to have been an early eruption of tuberculosis.[9] Finally, although he had been in good physical health for much of his life, Charles, the youngest of the brothers, experienced serious symptoms of tuberculosis in the autumn of 1831. When the symptoms became so severe that he and his family worried whether he would survive, Charles left Boston in December 1831, and after spending the next four months with his brother Edward in San Juan, Puerto Rico, he returned home in May 1832 with his health apparently restored. Charles remained in good physical health until the winter of 1835–1836, when his symptoms recurred, and he succumbed to tuberculosis in a few weeks at his brother William's home in New York City on 9 May 1836.

In addition to dealing with a history of tuberculosis in the family that began with their father, which affected them individually and collectively throughout their lives, and extended into the next generation of Emersons as well, the brothers also had to contend with various manifestations of mental and psychological illness from which only William and Waldo appear to have been wholly exempted. The situation the brothers faced with Bulkeley has already been explained, and because of its early onset and extremity, they never had to fear that the condition that plagued Bulkeley might some day plague them too. However, to the extent they genuinely believed that as brothers they together constituted "one man," William, Waldo, and Charles had to face the implications of the extreme display of insanity that required them to temporarily institutionalize Edward at the McLean Asylum in 1828. Moreover, William and Waldo had to face, after Charles's death, their recognition of the depth of depression and despair that their brother had secretly endured for roughly the last six years of his life. An undated poem by Charles, inscribed in his hand and found by Waldo among his brother's papers after his death, suggests the severity of the forms of mental suffering that not only Charles, but also his brother Edward, endured during the last years of their lives.

Thekla's Song.

The woods are sighing, The clouds are flying,
    The maiden is walking the grassy shore;—
And as the waves break with might, with might,
    She sings aloud through the darksome night
    But a tear is in her troubled eye.
For the world feels cold,—and the heart gets old,—
And reflects the bright aspect of nature no more.
    Then take back thy child, Holy Virgin, to thee—
I have plucked the one blossom that hangs on Earth's tree,
    I have lived, & have loved, & die.[10]

As the brothers' history unfolds in this biography, Waldo's belief in the poetry inherent in private lives, which he expressed at the very time Edward was dying and Charles was suffering inward torment while outwardly exhibiting a relatively pleasant and optimistic demeanor, was a truly remarkable expression of faith and idealism on his part.

Our primary resource for developing the Emerson brothers' lives in this biography is the extraordinary archive of previously unpublished letters that over the course of their respective lifetimes they exchanged among themselves and with others in their immediate family. Although the Emerson family has generally been gifted with fair and thorough biographers, lacking access to the complete resource we have had at our disposal, none of them has been able to portray all of the Emerson brothers speaking in their own right. In these letters, we hear the brothers' voices and witness the character and personality of each brother emerge slowly over time, responding to the epistolary thoughts, queries, fancies, and fears of his brothers. The content of these letters runs the gamut of life's comedy and tragedy, and as the last person to have read them in their entirety before we did, Waldo must have felt confirmed that in the epistolary company of his brothers he discovered "the absolute boundlessness of [his own] capacity" and had "the whole untried world of geometry, fluxions, natural philosophy, Ethics, wide open before him" (*JMN*, 4:353). Collectively, the brothers' letters are chatty and gossipy, but also learned in their regular allusions to lines borrowed from a host of classical and contemporary writers, philosophers, and religious thinkers; they demonstrate their authors' capacity for flights of imagination as well as serious introspection, intellectual reasoning, and close attention to those large and small details of life—finances, career prospects and career reversals, births and deaths—that the brothers, like everyone else, had to face every day. Given the time in which they lived, the atmosphere in which they were raised, and the close settings in which they lived even after leaving home, the brothers obviously enjoyed engaging in conversation with each other first and foremost; however, when they could not speak to each other, their letters filled the void. Repeatedly, the brothers end their letters to each other with a hope that a particular letter's recipient will write back soon. Even when they found themselves forced apart by business or pleasure or the pursuit of studies, the brothers' loneliness, which they always expressed in their correspondence as a form of homesickness, was significantly lessened by a letter.

Even though letter writing was the Emerson brothers' second-choice approach to retaining and reinforcing the feeling of fraternal closeness whenever they were apart, and even though on more than one occasion Waldo and Edward grated at the time it took them to engage in extended correspondences, all the brothers were capable of using the medium to great advantage. Waldo eventually constructed a theory that made letter writing in general a truer form of honest personal expression than conversation.[11] Writing to his brother Charles from St. Augustine, Florida, on 23 February 1827, when he was himself feeling homesick during his forced retreat to the south for his health, Waldo remarked,

> I have not yet recd your letters. . . . Write half a dozen. The world is before you for topics & when sense is not to be had, nonsense is a thousandfold better than nothing. You are in the heyday of youth when time is marked not by numbering days but by the intervals of mentality, the flux & reflux of the soul. One day has a solemn complexion the next is cheerful, the south wind makes a third poetic, and another is 'sicklied

oer with a pale cast of thought,"[12] but all are redolent of knowledge &
joy. The river of life with you is yet in its mountain sources bounding &
shouting on its way. . . . Vouchsafe then to give to your poor patriarchal
exhorting brother some of these sweet waters. Write. write. I have heard
men say . . . they had rather have ten words viva voce from a man than
volumes of letters for getting at his opinion.—I had rather converse with
them by the interpreter. Politeness ruins conversation. You get nothing
but the scum & surface of opinions. . . . Men's spoken notions are thus
nothing but outlines & generally uninviting outlines of a subject, & so
general, as to have no traits appropriate & peculiar to the individual.
But when a man writes, he divests himself of his manners & all physical
imperfections & it is the pure intellect that speaks. There can be no
deception here. You get the measure of his soul. Instead of the old verse,
"Speak that I may know thee,"[13] I write 'Speak, that I may suspect thee;
write, that I may *know* thee.' Brandish your pen therefore, & give me the
secret history of that sanctuary you call yourself. (*L,* 1:191)

Ironically, of his brothers, Charles was probably Waldo's worst choice to
instruct and exhort in the virtues of open epistolary exchange; as their letters
reveal, Edward and William were far better candidates to receive Waldo's ex-
hortation, because their own practices confirm that they were already believers
of his theory. But although he was as affected as any of his brothers by their
periods of separation, and as an adult often felt a profound sense of loneliness
when left by himself, Charles seems to have had mixed feelings about how
much of himself to expose in his letters to his brothers. On a page inscribed
on 16 September 1835 and preserved in his secret diary, Charles admitted to
overwhelming personal insecurities, and in doing so, he explained—at least to
himself—his ambivalence toward full epistolary exposure:

Oh God keep me from losing sight of thee. Keep me from the sealed
slumber of the sensual & worldly. If to distrust or even to loathe ones-
self were a sign of grace, my condition how full of hope! But it is quite
otherwise, a mark of a restless, estrayed soul—tending downwards, or
but freshly awakened out of its doltish sleep.
  The days teach me nothing but despair. Men do but repeat over to me
the forumlas of life that I have long since learned. Even Duty contracts
her infinite horizon, & so ineffectual & phenomenal seems my existence,
so sluggish & dull to the motions of the will my moral energy, that I
wonder why the sun continues to rise morning after morning upon such
a thing as I. Were it not for the desire so strong to live . . . I should look
to be blown off the face of this planet to which I have so loose holdings,
as chaff from the threshing floor.

How I dare to write is proof how callous & reckless I have become—This page might tally with the confessions of cells in hospitals & prisons.[14]

Nevertheless, Charles could and often did take his paternal aunt Mary Moody Emerson into his confidence in his letters to her, and he was similarly open in his letters to step-grandfather Ezra Ripley, but he stopped short of granting his brothers complete admission into that "sanctuary" he called himself *except* in conversation. For instance, when Waldo resigned from the Second Church in 1832, Charles was devastated, yet his devastation was not over his brother's decision to leave the pulpit, which he considered an act of intellectual and ethical heroism, but over the effect his decision would have on the pleasant domestic setting that Waldo and he were then sharing with their mother in a house on Chardon Street in Boston. On 10 December 1832, he expressed his feelings in nearly identical terms to their paternal aunt Mary Moody Emerson and step-grandfather Ezra Ripley. "We shall break up housekeeping immediately," he wrote to Ripley, adding, before repeating himself by saying yet again "our household [will soon be] broken up," that though their future plans were still unsettled, he thought Ripley would appreciate hearing the news from him rather than second-hand from someone else.[15] But, barely two months later, when Charles wrote his first letter to Waldo, who by then was in Italy, the real cause of his anxiety over his brother's European journey finally emerged. Not only did Charles miss Waldo's presence, he especially missed his brother's conversation.

You have now been gone so long that I feel better assured in writing to you that my letter will be welcome. If I knew how to be simply eyes & ears for you—& could telegraph to you all good news, I should be glad. But I do not easily fall into that train—& am used when my pen is in my hand to say something from myself—Yet although I would fain believe there is some chamber of my spiritual house wherein you might find a moment's entertainment exploring the imagery on the walls,—I have been so accustomed to talk with you face to face—eye to eye—& conversation between people who understand one another is so elliptic & allusive,—that now I come to write, I seem to introduce myself as a stranger, & widen instead of lessening the distance between us. I often wish like the little Waltham Pyrrhonist 'that I was not I'[16]—that the elements had been differently mixed in me—I think women must be *happier* than men, since it is their *nature* to forget *themselves,* & there live where they have garnered up their hearts. I continually pine & pray for some all absorbing exalting principle, idea, cause, in which I may be bound up & lose this ever wakeful consciousness that is so private & personal. I long for action or contemplation in the energy of which I shall altogether forget that I have any individual stake in the universe. But how coldly am I constituted—And with how many pitiful reserves do I give myself to so many charitable work! I am in much worse plight than the infant philosopher abovementioned—I am ashamed,—yea wo is me, that I am I. How tired of life the selfish man must get to be—And what a mean thing is it to deal with God as a merchant, looking only to secure our own advantage, in the overflowings of his bounty—& to use his Divine indulgence—these ingenious faculties of His inspiration—& all He leads us to know & hope, as the architects only of our own fate, the machinery of a studious self aggrandisement. . . .

It is easier to read than to think, & to think than to write. When I hear men speak what they have written, I wish to take the word out of their mouths—to have guided the pen as they wrote. But to my single self, the desire to write almost never comes & would never so I had the means of delivering the mind by any more expeditious midwifery. Now a days I have scarce any nest wherein to lay the conversational egg.[17]

Although transitions and separations were always disruptive to the bonds that held the Emerson brothers together, unlike their brother Charles, Waldo, Edward, and William were constituted in ways that removed the risk that a disruption of those bonds could lead to a displacement of their fraternal sympathies. In the chapters that follow, it will be apparent that Edward physically and mentally suffered the anxieties of separation as much as any of his brothers. Although Charles had access once again to Waldo's company and conversation when he returned from Europe in October 1833, and William had both a career and, by the mid-1830s, a family of his own in New York, Edward was literally exiled from his family and the comfort of his mother's hearth for the last four years of his life. To his credit, however, and to the credit also of the "strange sympathies" he shared with his brothers, Edward actually became emotionally—if not physically—stronger on his own by, as he explained to Waldo in a letter written from San Juan on 20 January 1833, relying on "our little brotherhood . . . turn[ing] my thoughts homeward & assure[ing] myself of fraternal sympathy."

I am thinking that if the old rule of ama, si vis amari[18] be true nowadays I must be a great pet with my brothers; my affection towards them, perhaps, being as strong as if it had been exhibited in good deeds, instead of arising in so great a degree from gratitude & instinct.

I never read the treatises about friendship which ancients & moderns have written without thinking of our little brotherhood—& when most feeble, most straitened, least esteemed, I feel strong if I can turn my thoughts homeward & assure myself of fraternal sympathy. I don't know why the ancients did not say more about brothers, unless it was taken for granted that these were friends—& so needed not to be set forth in the glowing pictures drawn of "Amicitia" & "amici" in prose & poetry.—Perhaps they had *got "behind"* instinct & common domestic attachments. Be it so—the practical age having come back again, we'll revive the old fashion of brotherly love.—But all this what doth it avail me at the present moment, & what doth it avail you, which is the politer inquiry reading as you may be this letter with the sea between us? But as the Spaniard says "que quiere usted," what do you wish, or "what would you," a frequent expression to signify that all has been done that could be done—; having nothing in the way of adventures either chivalric or mercantile to relate, I have filled the first page without them and now I am so entirely at a loss in respect to your present situation, health, intentions & wishes that I can only half speak to you. . . . I pray for you & hope daily for the best news.—

If you could travel a little while after the fashion of Martiny the French poet, who says, (according to the newspaper) when about visiting Palestine, Greece &c. &c. "I do not calculate on writing much—I go to read before I die some of the beautiful pages of the material creation. If poetry shᵈ find new inspiration & images I shall gather them into the silence of thoughts; they may color what remains of my literary career;" if you could slacken the speed & augment the volume of your powers by a tour in any strange land—it would be most excellent; but if means are wanting, why the feast & the consolation of the Christian still abide—the faith the hope & the Charity which the apostles received they have transmitted.—I will not preach to the preacher.[19]

The focus of this biography is on the lives of the Emerson brothers from the time of eldest brother William's birth in 1801 to the deaths of Edward and Charles in 1834 and 1836, respectively. In the remainder of this chapter, we introduce three important subjects that establish the contexts for much of what follows. The first subject is the influence of the Emerson and Haskins families' past and the extent to which the lives of the Emerson brothers were shaped by assumptions about their place in family history and position in the world-at-large. These assumptions had been developed over nearly two centuries prior to the brothers' birth and were reinforced in the lessons on family history passed down to the brothers by their Aunt Mary and Ezra Ripley. The second subject is the relationship between the brothers and their mother, Ruth Haskins Emerson, and the third introduces the brothers as Harvard men and examines how Edward and Charles, especially, were remembered by others long after their deaths as a means to contrast them with their brothers William and Waldo (who survived them for three and nearly five decades, respectively). Chapter

2 examines William's life and studies in Germany, and his eventual rejection of the ministerial mantle that had been passed to him by several generations of Emerson forebears who had made the family's reputation by serving in New England's pulpits from the earliest days of settlement. Chapter 3 considers the lives of Edward and Charles over the few years they each lived after graduating from Harvard. Chapter 4 examines the brothers' relationship with their Aunt Mary, and recognizes her as the figure who exerted the most considerable and sustained influence on the brothers' personal and psychological development during their formative years. Chapter 5 examines "the brothers in love" by first considering Waldo's marriages to Ellen Louisa Tucker—who remained a force not only in Waldo's life but also in the lives of his brothers for decades after her death in 1831—and Lidia Jackson, who succeeded her, and William's marriage to Susan Woodward Haven, before taking up the intense and extended engagement between Charles and Elizabeth Sherman Hoar, which began in 1833 and lasted until Charles's death three years later. Finally, for the first time in Emerson family studies, chapter 6 examines William and Waldo's oversight of the family's finances.

As opposed to the typical biography of Waldo Emerson in which the subject is surrounded by and developed through reference to a cast of increasingly renowned characters, this fraternal biography maintains its focus by emphasizing the Emerson brothers in relation to each other. Although Waldo took his first steps toward what would become a world-wide audience for his lectures and writings in the 1840s and 1850s when he met figures such as William Wordsworth, Alexander Ireland, and Thomas Carlyle during his journey to Europe in 1833, the persons with whom we are primarily concerned here were neither party to those meetings nor particularly influenced by them. The major figures with whom the Emerson brothers were engaged in study and working relationships were first and foremost each other and members of their immediate family, and then with occasional luminaries of their day such as Daniel Webster, in whose law office Edward briefly worked and whose son he briefly tutored; Edward Everett, one of America's foremost orators of the day, whose public speeches the brothers greatly admired and whose lectures on Greek literature at Harvard Waldo enthusiastically attended;[20] and "Squire" Samuel Hoar, one of the leading citizens of Concord, Massachusetts, who supported the brothers' careers and successfully recruited Charles to his law office after his engagement to the Squire's daughter Elizabeth.[21]

Thus, throughout this fraternal biography, our view is the one to which Waldo himself drew our attention when, in the journal selection that opens this chapter, he remarked on the capacity of essentially "obscure persons" to "excite wonder, speculation, & delight" in him. His mother Ruth, his Aunt Mary and step-grandfather Ezra Ripley, his sons and daughters and a number of his uncles, aunts, cousins, and other relations who will make their appearance in the brothers' letters that follow, and especially his brothers William, Edward, and Charles, were just such persons. Though all were certainly less well known than either Homer and Shakespeare or Daniel Webster and Dr. Channing, the "wonder" that each of these individuals represented for Waldo was that the better he knew them, the more he believed any one or all of them could have spoken to Homer, Shakespeare, Webster, and Channing as equals. The individuals with whom we are most concerned in this fraternal biography confirmed the famous Waldo's moral sense, and the actions they undertook in their obscurity represented for him the noblest aspirations of the human race. In the prime of his intellectual life and public reputation, these were the individuals with whom Waldo himself was most concerned, and as he remembered them as Providence's special gift to him, he conferred on them his choicest praise:

> When a man is born with a profound moral sentiment, preferring truth, justice and the serving of all men to any honors or any gain, men readily feel the superiority. They who deal with him are elevated with joy and hope; he lights up the house or the landscape in which he stands. His actions are poetic and miraculous in their eyes. In his presence, or within his influence, every one believes in the immortality of the soul. . . .
>
> A chief event of life is the day in which we have encountered a mind that startled us by its large scope. I am in the habit of thinking—not, I hope, out of partial experience, but confirmed by what I notice in many lives—that to every serious mind Providence sends from time to time five or six or seven teachers who are of the first importance to him in the lessons they have to impart. The highest of these not so much give particular knowledge, as they elevate by sentiment and by their habitual grandeur of view.[22]

"THE SPIRIT OF OUR FATHERS"
Sons of the Present, Specters of the Past

During the nearly two decades that separate William and Waldo's boyhood years from Edward and Charles's collegiate years at Harvard, the Emerson brothers may well have thought that they were living in two worlds, with each world constantly vying for their attention and allegiance. Their visible world was the bustling environment of early nineteenth-century America, a world in which, as members of the first generation born after the Revolution, the brothers were as much engaged as their contemporaries in negotiating the national and personal terms of American character and identity. But they possessed— and, to borrow a phrase from New England's Calvinist liturgy, they were possessed by—an "invisible world" as well. The brothers' invisible world consisted of their family's past, which was occupied by the specters of heroic ancestors. The men and women from the Emerson and Haskins lines had settled in the New World, and served religion to generations of pre-Revolution Englishmen (as well as native inhabitants) or competed in the spheres of commerce and real estate speculation. The brothers' forbears in commerce had successfully accumulated wealth and land and achieved fair social standing. Each successive generation raised the bar of expectation higher for the next, so that by the time the Reverend William and Ruth Haskins Emerson were married in October 1796 and settled first in the rural town of Harvard, Massachusetts, where the liberal minister and his new wife began their family, and then, in 1799, in Boston, where the proprietors of the First Church had called William to succeed the Reverend John Clarke as their pastor, they and the children they would have were the inheritors of nearly two centuries' worth of increasingly elevated New World piety and ambition.[23]

In nineteenth-century middle- and upper-middle class America, the legacy of a family's past was often transmitted to members of its new generation by family elders. Boys would be schooled in family traditions and directed toward the occupations that seemed most suited to them by their grandfathers, fathers, and uncles, whereas girls would be instructed in their future roles as wives, mothers, and, particularly in the early years of the new Republic, as the guardians of a literate citizenry by their grandmothers, mothers, and aunts. This pattern emerged out of Old World customs, and with little modification, it had served New Englanders well from the earliest days of settlement.

In brief, at the time the Emerson brothers were born, their paternal grandfather, the Reverend William Emerson (1743–1776), pastor of the church in Concord, Massachusetts, had been dead for a quarter of a century; their paternal grandmother, Phebe Bliss Emerson (1741–1825), still resided in Concord, where she had married her late husband's successor, the Reverend Ezra Ripley (1751–1841), and produced a second family with him. The eight children born to Phebe Bliss during her two marriages were all alive at the opening of the nineteenth century. They included the brothers' father William; Aunt Hannah Emerson (1770–1807), who was married to William Farnham of Newburyport, Massachusetts; Aunt Phebe Emerson (1772–1839), who was married to Lincoln Ripley of Waterford, Maine; Aunt Mary Moody Emerson (1774–1863); Aunt Rebecca Emerson (1776–1845), who was married to their maternal uncle Robert Haskins of Waterford, Maine; step-aunt Sarah Ripley (1781–1826), who was unmarried; step-uncle Samuel Ripley of Waltham, Massachusetts, who was married to Sarah Alden Bradford; and step-uncle Daniel Ripley (1784–1825), of Concord, Massachusetts, who was married to Susan Fitts. Of these relations on the brothers' father's side, step-grandfather Ezra Ripley, Aunts Mary Moody and Rebecca Emerson, and step-uncle Samuel Ripley along with his wife Sarah were significant presences in the brothers' lives, and they exerted the most sustained influence on them as boys and young men. More than two dozen first cousins produced by aunts and uncles on their father's side make appearances in their letters from time to time.

On their mother's side, the brothers' grandfather John Haskins (1729–1814), one of Boston's most prominent citizens, who made his fortune as a distiller in the West Indies trade and a speculator in real estate, married Hannah Waite Upham (1734–1819) of Malden, Massachusetts, on 6 May 1752. Their marriage was officiated over by the Reverend Joseph Emerson, the brothers' paternal great-grandfather, and it initiated a friendly association between the Emerson and Haskins families of which William and Ruth's sons were among the beneficiaries. Grandfather John, a pew-holder at King's Chapel and, later, at Trinity Church in Boston, preferred the Episcopal service (as, in fact, did his daughter Ruth for most of her life[24]), whereas grandmother Hannah had come from a long line of Congregationalists, and after their marriage she worshipped—separately from her husband—at Boston's New South Congregational Meeting House. When the thirteen of their sixteen children who survived infancy became old enough to decide on a form of worship for themselves, John Haskins presented them with the choice; roughly half decided to follow their father's preference and the remainder their mother's. John Haskins's democratic application of the principle of religious freedom and the ideal of individual conscience, together with his kindness (which his children universally acknowledged), must have become family lore by the time of his death, for on that occasion his eleven-year-old grandson Waldo Emerson composed this brief elegy on "the aged saint":

> See the calm exit of the aged saint,
> Without a murmur and without complaint;
> While round him gathered, all his children stand,
> And some one holds his withered, pallid hand.
> He bids them trust in God, nor mourn, nor weep;
> He breathes religion, and then falls asleep.
> Then on angelic wings he soars to God.
> Rejoiced to leave his earthly, mortal load;
> His head is covered with a crown of gold,
> His hands, renewed, a harp immortal hold;
> Thus clothed with light, the tuneful spirit sings—
> He sings of mercy and of Heavenly things.[25]

Like the Emersons who, with a few exceptions along the way, were a long-lived line, the Haskins side of the brothers' family was large and its members enjoyed remarkable longevity. In his account of the Haskins family, David Greene

Haskins remarks that at his death on 27 October 1814, grandfather John—or "Honest John Haskins" as he was known about Boston—was survived by the same thirteen children to whom he had put the question of religious preference years before as well as by forty-six grandchildren; Haskins found it further remarkable that John Haskins' death was "the first that had taken place in his immediate family for nearly fifty-three years, and that from Nov. 5, 1761, to Dec. 14, 1822, not a death occurred among the thirteen children who survived him."[26] Of John and Hannah Upham Haskins's thirteen surviving children, six, in addition to the brothers' mother Ruth, would themselves, and in several instances their children, become visible figures in the Emerson brothers' lives and make regular appearances in their correspondence: Uncle John Haskins (1762–1840) of Newton, Massachusetts, who was married to Elizabeth Ladd of Little Compton, Rhode Island; Aunts Elizabeth Haskins (1771–1853) and Fanny Haskins (1777–1854) of Boston, who were unmarried; Uncle Robert Haskins (1773–1855) of Waterford, Maine, who was married to the brothers' maternal Aunt Rebecca Emerson; Uncle Thomas Haskins (1775–1853) of Boston, who was married to Elizabeth Foxcroft; and Uncle Ralph Haskins (1779–1852) of Boston, who was married to Rebecca Greene.

Haskins family history was transmitted to William, Waldo, Edward, and Charles mostly through their mother, her brothers Robert, Thomas, and Ralph, and, especially, her sisters Elizabeth and Fanny, all of whom appear frequently in the brothers' correspondence. The death of their paternal grandfather during the Revolutionary War and of their maternal grandfather when the Ruth and William's sons were still young, together with the various infirmities from which their paternal and their maternal grandmothers suffered, deprived the brothers of some of the more usual sources of instruction in the Emerson or Haskins families' respective pasts. Yet it will become clear that on the Emerson side of the family the place of these elders was admirably filled by two figures who loom large in many of the brothers' letters—including those that they exchanged with persons outside of their fraternal circle—and often in their daily lives as well. They were the boys' step-grandfather Ezra Ripley and their paternal aunt Mary Moody Emerson, and the lessons in Emerson family traditions and ideals they delivered to their young charges were invariably punctuated with a challenge to live up to the ideals of their forefathers, a challenge only moderated by anecdotes of their illustrious ancestors' success in surviving the harsh realities of this world while preparing themselves for the glories of the next. The influence of these two individuals on the brothers' personal, intellectual, and moral development was profound and enduring.

As the brothers' letters reveal, the one constant in all the lessons they received from both Ripley and Aunt Mary during their schooling in Emerson family history was the importance of religion to the emergence of the family's reputation and financial security in the New World. Indeed, religion and the

successful—and visible—ministries held by successive generations of Emersons in New England were *the* central features of the family's identity. For each
of the brothers, that identity served as a source of inspiration to excel in their
own lives and, quite often, as a psychological and professional burden as well.

From the earliest days of the Puritan colony through the beginning of the
nineteenth century, as Calvinism evolved into Congregationalism, and liberal
Congregationalism into Unitarianism, the Emersons supplied New England
with a steady line of ministers to fill her pulpits and provide for the needs of
her faithful. Joseph Emerson (1620–1680), who was born in England and was
the minister of Mendon, Massachusetts, when it was destroyed during King
Philip's War in the 1670s, was the first in this distinguished line. In 1665,
Joseph married Elizabeth Bulkeley (1638–1693), his second wife, who was the
daughter of the Reverend Edward Bulkeley (1614–1696) of Concord, Massachusetts, and the granddaughter of the Reverend Peter Bulkeley (1583–1659),
one of Concord's founders and its first minister. Joseph and Elizabeth Bulkeley
Emerson's son, Edward (1670–1743), who introduced the name Waldo into the
Emerson line when he married Rebecca Waldo (1682–1752) in 1697, was a deacon of the church in Newbury, Massachusetts, and Edward and Rebecca Waldo
Emerson's son, who was named Joseph (1700–1767), married Mary Moody
(1702–1799), the daughter of the Reverend Samuel and Hannah Sewall Moody
of York, Maine, in 1721, and eventually preached in the pulpit at Malden, Massachusetts, formerly occupied by Michael Wigglesworth, colonial America's
premier poet.

The Reverend William Emerson, Sr., the brothers' paternal grandfather, was
the twelfth of thirteen children born to Joseph and Mary Moody Emerson of
Malden, and was one of Joseph's three sons who, after attending Harvard, entered the ministry. On 1 January 1766, this William was ordained minister
of Concord, Massachusetts, and in August 1766 he married Phebe Bliss, the
daughter of Daniel Bliss (1714–1764), who was his predecessor as the minister
of Concord. The brothers' father (also named William) was born to William
and Phebe Bliss Emerson in 1769, and their Aunt Mary was born to them in
1774. Following the elder William Emerson's death in 1776 while trying to
return home from Fort Ticonderoga, where he had served the patriot cause as a
chaplain, his widow—the brothers' grandmother—subsequently married Ezra
Ripley, William's successor in Concord, who was one of the early proponents
for Unitarianism and, until his death in 1841 at the age of ninety, a devoted
step-grandfather and mentor to the Emerson brothers.

The brothers' father, William, continued the family ministerial tradition until his premature death on 12 May 1811, and although the brothers were young
at the time, the family assumed that William and Ruth's oldest surviving son,
William, would resume the family tradition and enter the ministry. But when
William decided against the pulpit in favor of a career in the law, after study-

ing abroad in Germany from 1823 to 1825, the mantle passed to Waldo, who held it perhaps more by default than by disposition until he resigned from his pastorate at Boston's Second Church in 1832. If their Aunt Mary had her way, Edward and Charles, who like their brother William ultimately chose the law as their profession, would have joined their brothers in the family's ministerial line or, at least, after first William and then Waldo had abandoned their visible connection to the Emerson, Bulkeley, Moody, and Bliss family legacy, they would have rescued the family's honor by serving God in the tradition of their fathers.

In their respective correspondences with their step-grandfather Ripley and Aunt Mary, each of the Emerson brothers exhibited the greatest consideration for these couriers of the past. Although Edward and, to a lesser extent, William, openly resisted Mary's insistence on their taking to the pulpits for which she believed they had been born and bred, neither they nor Waldo or Charles ever questioned the sincerity of the motives out of which she and Ripley urged them to adhere to the ministerial legacy that was their most tangible inheritance. In a passage entered in his journal on 4 May 1841, Waldo, speaking as much for his brothers as for himself, drew an interesting distinction between talent and genius, explicitly citing Aunt Mary as the personification of genius, and, without mentioning him by name, implicitly developing Ripley's character as the ideal representation of talent. "The difference between talent & genius is in the direction of the current," he wrote, explaining,

> in genius, it is from within outward; in talent, from without inward. Talent finds its models & methods & ends in society, and goes to the soul only for power to work: genius is its own end & derives its means and the style of its architecture from within. . . . Aunt Mary . . . is Genius always new, subtle, frolicsome, musical, unpredictable. All your learning of all literatures & states of society, Platonistic, Calvinistic, English, or Chinese, would never enable you to anticipate one thought or expression.[27] She is embarrassed by no Moses or Paul, no Angelo or Shakspeare,[28] after whose type she is to fashion her speech: her wit is the wild horse of the desert who snuffs the sirocco & scours the palm-grove without having learned his paces in the Stadium. . . . What liberal, joyful architecture, liberal & manifold as the vegetation from the earth's bosom, or the creations of frost work on the window! Nothing can excel the freedom & felicity of her letters,—such nobility is in this self rule, this absence of all reference to style or standard: it is the march of the mountain winds, the waving of flowers, or the flight of birds. (JMN, 7:442)

Waldo's enthusiasm for Aunt Mary's genius, which he recognized here in the "freedom & felicity of her letters," her whirlwind presence, and her submission of her intellect and imagination to no standard but "self rule," echoes that of his brothers, especially Charles, who enjoyed an unusually close relationship with his aunt. For Waldo and Charles, Mary was a "blind prophetess," and her realms of power were, first, the spiritual world and, second, the past to the extent that it figuratively superseded the present. Writing to his brother William about their aunt on 12 September 1834, Charles exclaimed, "What a link she is to all the Past," adding that he found her so thoroughly connected to the past that "she scarce [made] part of the Present."[29] In a letter to Elizabeth Hoar written a few weeks later, Charles raised the point again: "You should see Aunt Mary—sick, weak, eyeless, but clear & spiritual ever;—you can scarcely think of her as going to sleep—'Flesh & blood so well refined.' . . . A marvelously transparent atmosphere she hath her being in. And people talk . . . of what relates to the five senses. Fools."[30] Yet because in his treatment of Mary Waldo did not place the seeming otherworldliness of genius and the apparent worldliness of talent in opposition to each other, but developed them as varied directions of the same current, it would be a mistake to think that by extolling Mary's genius in so extravagant a manner Waldo (or the brothers for whom he spoke) would have ever diminished Ripley's importance to their lives or discounted the value of the lessons from the past that this country parson drew from the depths of his soul for their edification. Ripley was a man of "talent," according to Waldo's use of the term; he was a man of this world and a shrewd Yankee as well. Following the call by the people of Concord to succeed the brothers' paternal grandfather as the town's minister, his marriage in 1780 to the widow Phebe Bliss Emerson, who was ten years older than he, brought him all the lands and material wealth that had formerly belonged to the Emerson, Bulkeley, and Bliss lines—including the Manse that the senior William Emerson had built in 1770 beside Concord's famed North Bridge. Although young men of a more volatile temperament than the Emerson brothers possessed might well have resented the shadow that Ripley's presence cast over the family's fortunes, there is not the slightest hint of resentment or jealously in any preserved records of the brothers' or their parents' dealings with Ripley. Instead, the brothers followed their father's lead and always treated their step-grandfather with respect, and, in fact, they always addressed or referred to him as "Grandfather."

Waldo represented the depth of affection shared between Ezra Ripley and his step-grandsons whenever he reflected on his influence in Concord, in New England's ecclesiastic circles, or in the Emerson family. When Ripley died on the morning of 21 September 1841, Waldo, who was himself then nearing 40, took his mother to view "the patriarch," who had just been laid out in his casket. Clearly, Waldo's mind and memory were at work during the entire visit to the front parlor of the Manse, for upon returning to his home on the other side of Concord he entered in his journal a long and somewhat romantic reminiscence of the man who had been step-grandfather, spiritual advisor, and professional mentor to the Emerson brothers for virtually their entire lives. Although Ripley's connection to the Emerson, Bulkeley, and Bliss family past was not one based on blood, in spirit it was the next closest thing to a blood relation. It was a connection that Waldo and his brothers cherished, and one that—to the extent Waldo recognized in Ripley the antecedents of the old style religious sensibility that Unitarianism and Transcendentalism emerged first to resist, then to displace—defined crucial aspects of his and his brothers' intellectual ancestry.

Dr. Ripley died this morning. The fall of this oak of ninety years makes some sensation in the forest old & doomed as it was. He has identified himself with the forms at least of the old church of the New England Puritans; his nature was eminently loyal, not in the least adventurous or democratical & his whole being leaned backward on the departed so that he seemed one of the rearguard of this great camp & army which have filled the world with fame & with him passes out of sight almost the last banner & guide's flag of a mighty epoch. For these men however in our last days they have declined into ritualists, solemnized the heyday of their strength by the planting & the liberating of America.

Great, grim, earnest men I belong by natural affinity to other thoughts & schools than yours but my affection hovers respectfully about your retiring footprints. . . . Well the new is only the seed of the old. What is this abolition & non-resistance & temperance[31] but the continuation of Puritanism tho' it operate inevitably the destruction of the church in which it grew, as the new is always making the old superfluous.

Dr R. was a gentleman, no dandy: courtly, hospitable, manly, public spirited: his nature social, his house open to all. . . . To see his friends unloosed his tongue & talents: they were his study. His talk was chiefly narrative: a man of anecdote he told his stories admirably well. Indeed all his speech was form & pertinence itself. . . . In private discourse or in debate of a more public kind the structure of his speech was perfect, so neat, so natural, so terse, no superfluous clause, his words fell like stones. & commonly tho' quite unconscious of it his speech was a satire on the loose, voluminous, draggletail periods of other speakers. . . . E[dward]. B[liss]. E[merson]. used to say that "a man who could tell a story so well was company for kings." . . . His knowledge was an external experience, an Indian wisdom, the observation of such facts as country life for nearly a hundred years could supply. He sympathized with the cow, the horse, the sheep, & the dog whose habits he had watched so long & so friendly. For those who do not separate poetry blend it with things. His eye was always on the horizon. . . . [He] was very good company & counsel, but he never divined, never speculated. . . . He was always sincere, & true to his mark & his mark was never remote. . . . He knew everybody's grandfather. This day has perished more history [and] more local & personal anecdote for this village & vicinity than in any ten men who have died in it before. He was the patriarch of all the tribe and his manners had a natural dignity that comported with his office. . . . Many & many a felicity he had in his prayer now forever lost which eclipsed all the rules of all the rhetoricians. He did not know when he was good in prayer or sermon, . . . [but] he believed & therefore spoke. He was sincere in his attachment to forms & he was the genuine fruit of a ritual church. The incarnation of the platform of the Puritan Church. A modern Israelite, a believer in the Genius or Jehovah of the Jews to the very letter. . . . He was a punctual fulfiller of all duties. What order! what prudence! no waste, & no stint. Always open handed; just & generous. . . .

He was a man very easy to read, for his whole life & conversation was consistent & transparent: all his opinions & actions might be certainly predicted by any one who had good opportunities of seeing him. . . . And now in his old age when all the antique Hebraism & customs are going to pieces it is fit he too should depart, most fit that in the fall of laws a loyal man should die.

Shall I not say in general, of him, that, given his constitution, his life was harmonious & perfect.

His body is a handsome & noble spectacle. My mother was moved just now to call it "the beauty of the dead." He looks like a sachem fallen in the forest, or rather like "a warrior taking his rest with his martial cloak around him."[32] (JMN, 8:53–57)

As opposed to Mary Moody Emerson's "genius," which was, as Waldo observed, "always new, subtle, frolicsome, musical" *and* "unpredictable," Ezra Ripley's "talent"—the candor of his speech, the richness of his store of local and family history and useful anecdote, the "natural dignity" of his manners, his "very good counsel & company" and sincerity, and the Thoreauvian "Indian wisdom" out of which he preached and interacted with his fellow Concordians and their environment—enabled him to live a life that was, as Waldo summarily assessed it, "harmonious & perfect." Whereas the persistent, heavy-handed authoritarianism out of which Aunt Mary spoke and wrote as she directed her nephews' reading, careers, and, ultimately, thought sometimes grated on the brothers' nerves, the amiable social conservatism out of which Ripley interacted with his step-grandsons and supported their professional ambitions was always warmly received. This speaks volumes about Ripley's character as the brothers perceived it, and it suggests that the lessons of the past that he had to impart to them were positively received rather than resisted. Moreover, although Aunt

Mary may have been the primary guide of the brothers' intellectual development, and her repeated invocations of the lives of their fathers were undoubtedly intended to spur them to high purpose in their own lives, Ripley appears
to have been the most effective guide to their practical development of hearts
and social consciences. He may not have been the fiery reformer that Mary was
when subjects such as slavery were on the table, but he was a steady, temperate
reformer, whose own practices, such as his service on Concord's fire brigade
and town committees, his creation of a local lending library, and his subscrip-
tion to all charities that supported local causes, served as models of social responsibility for the brothers to follow.

Ezra Ripley's character, manners, and sense of social responsibility definitely
resonated with the Emerson brothers, and as the comparisons between Aunt
Mary and Ripley developed above suggest, she, rather than he, invariably suffered by any comparison. At the conclusion of his journal eulogy on Ripley,
which from time to time he rewrote into more extensive prose that James Elliot
Cabot arranged after his death as an essay published in the *Atlantic Monthly*
in 1883, Waldo disclosed the secret of his step-grandfather's personal appeal,
observing that although "[a] man is but a little thing in the midst of [the] great
objects of nature"—"the mountains, the clouds, and the cope of the horizon &
the globes of heaven"—yet by his "moral quality" this same man "may abolish
all thoughts of magnitude & in his manners equal the majesty of the world"
(*JMN*, 8:57).[33] Thus, Ripley's "talent" and his "moral quality" amounted to the
same thing in Waldo's eyes, and the affection that he and his brothers felt for
their step-grandfather is most evident in the tone of their letters to him. In fact,
the cordial, respectful tone of their correspondence was set by Ripley himself in
his earliest letters to them. For instance, in his first letter to William, written in
1809, when William was eight years old, Ripley apologized for taking so long to
reply to his letter, and then he wrote to "My dear grandson" much as we might
imagine that he would have spoken to him in person.

It is true, I have long delayed to answer your letter; but it is not
true, that I have forgotten you, or ceased to recollect with pleasure that
expression of your dutiful regards to me. . . .

Your letter, Master William, was a very good one, being your first essay of the kind, it was better than I should have expected from a lad so
young. I sincerely thank you for it. But a little while ago, thought I, William was a little urchin tottling about and learning to go alone; and now,
here is a fine letter in his own handwriting! Time runs away very fast;
and you must take care, that you gain in learning as fast as you grow in
years, lest you should have the years & stature of a man before you have
the knowledge of a man. Your letter, however, is a just presage of something very excellent in some few years to come. Well, go on & increase

in writing, composition, & every thing praise worthy, equally in virtue. My prayer for you is, that you may grow in stature, in knowledge, and in favour with God and man. As you grow older, you must grow better, and strive to excel lads of your age in every thing virtuous. You must set an amiable example before your little brothers. They will look to you, as a pattern in much of their puerile conduct, because you are the oldest. And what a sad thing it would be, if they should learn of you any bad dispositions, or vicious actions! This would be very wicked in you, hurtful to them, and very grievous to your kind and good parents. You must never disobey and grieve your parents. No good child ever does this without being very sorry for it afterwards, and resolving never to do so again.

I would have you write to me again, and often. My letters are so much longer than your's, that you must write two or three to my one.[34]

Good natured, cheerful, and supportive of the Emerson brothers' ambitions—including William, Edward, and Charles's secular ambitions—in ways that no other of their elders seemed able to equal, Ezra Ripley lessened the sting of the unworthiness and sense of personal failure that the brothers felt whenever they measured themselves against their illustrious ancestors and, as in his letter to young William, he made even instruction in righteousness palatable. All evidence suggests that, except for his references to affection and respect, Waldo was not including Ripley or libeling his ministry when he alluded to Ripley's predecessors in his journal eulogy: "Great, grim, earnest men I belong by natural affinity to other thoughts & schools than yours but my affection hovers respectfully about your retiring footprints." Indeed, although they rarely agreed on anything, Waldo and Nathaniel Hawthorne, who rented the Manse for four years after Ripley's death, frequently portrayed Ripley in the same positive light. In the journal eulogy, for example, Waldo remembered him as "[a]lways open handed" and famed for his generosity. He reported that when his "little boy [Waldo] a week ago carried him a peach," he was sent home "with two pears," and he remembered that when he himself carried Ripley a basket full of melons, his step-grandfather sent him home with a basket full of apples (*JMN*, 8:56). Similarly, in the preface to *Mosses from an Old Manse*, a collection of stories that he published in 1846, Hawthorne portrayed Ripley as the Manse's gentle ghost, whose presence provided him relief from the unnerving rustles of his contentious and sulfuric Concord predecessors, Daniel Bliss and the senior William Emerson. Recalling that Ripley had planted an apple orchard on the Manse's grounds, which would supply fruit for generations to come, Hawthorne romanticized the act as placing the minister in a relation to all mankind that also connected him to the important matters of the heart.

Edward Bliss Emerson recognized the positive and romantic quality of Ezra Ripley as well. Like Waldo and Hawthorne, Edward found Ripley the most cosmopolitan, realistic, and even-tempered of all his elders, and from his earliest years, Edward divided his affections between Ripley and Aunt Mary. However, as will be apparent in our treatment of Edward's physical and mental break-down in 1828, which occurred at the Manse and during which he is reported to have kicked, sworn at, and spat on his step–grandfather, Edward's continued affection for his step-grandfather after 1828 is unexpected. Obviously, his affection was a response to Ripley's own kindness toward him during his period of distress, and it follows from Edward's sense that though Aunt Mary considered his illness a Calvinist-style stroke from God for his impiety (a response that created a breach between them for the remainder of Edward's life), Ripley was beyond labeling Edward's breakdown in this way. During Edward's four-year exile in the Caribbean prior to his death in 1834, Ripley exchanged a few letters with his step-grandson. The following letter, which Edward wrote to him from San Juan, Puerto Rico, in October 1831 and in which he described at length the customs of the people he encountered and confessed his surprise at how appealing he found the rituals celebrated by the island's Hispanic Catholics, is indicative of the easy, open relation the two once again enjoyed.

My dear & hon^d Sir,

I thank you for your very kind letter; itself a compliment as coming from you to me,—to say nothing of the affectionate language & the encouragement that filled it.—As to what you have said in it about the matter of [my] seclusion from society &c. you will not wonder that I subscribe to your doctrine, when you recollect how long I had the pleasure of seeing it practised not a thousand miles from your own dwelling. I must however say, in justice to Hermit Low, (whom you seem to suspect of *avarice,*) that I don't know that any treasures of money are at his command, & I intended to mention in my account of him nothing else about his wealth, than that he had the right of being maintained on the spot he occupies.—Upon the main question of commerce with society or retirement, it seems to me that while on earth, a man in common cases, has no more the right than he has the power, to make himself a little solitary heaven beforehand, if I may use the expression. What right has he to please himself with the notion that he is devoting his life to godliness when he is only taking his ease by shunning the worldly? How shall he boast of resisting temptation, who is only fleeing from the devil, instead of putting him to flight?—

You are aware I suppose that this island like a docile child follows the mother country, & rests in the bosom of the Catholic Church.—There are two Convents with churches attached to them & two other churches of considerable size, beside one or two small chapels. In all of these mass & bell & latin & images are found instead of stirring eloquence.—I am told that during Lent some sermons will be preached,—when I shall get a chance perhaps of being rebuked & warned.—At present my Sundays are indeed days of rest; & I confess that I often enjoy the repose & liberty that offers itself here to one from whom no conformity is expected & upon whose conduct not a censorious remark is to be feared, so much that I forget to regret that I am not going to take my seat in the congregation. Every man may learn some thing from every other man, & perhaps every sect much from every other sect. While the Catholics of St Johns [San Juan] might learn in New England to show their respect for the Sabbath by a more general suspension of labor & traffic than is here observed, I think the religionists of the north might also learn in Porto Rico the advantage of admitting relaxation & some amusement to enter into their holy time. Some men here fatigue themselves with secular business or riotous pastime; & some of the Christians of New England do so labor to be, to do, & to suffer good, on the Sabbath, that they certainly fail to obey the commandment "to do no manner of work."—If we could exclude cock fighting, house scouring, occasional drunken frolics some labor in the country required during the mornings, & much of the marketing & shop keeping carried on in the city from the Sundays here, & if on the other hand the third & fourth services, or lectures, the prohibitions laid, by custom or precept, upon innocent diversion or pleasant conversation & the mint & cummin of excessive sobriety which is not seldom exacted at the expense of the good temper & comfort of our youth, could be be removed from the New England Sunday—the Sabbath might be better used & valued in both places.—

You remember, Sir, you always allowed me to talk & so will excuse my meddling in such high matters, as the right & wrong observance of ordinances.—At another time when I have a fresh sheet I will give you some account of one or two of the ceremonies which I have witnessed here.—. . . May each new year be more happy, & each step on the ladder from earth to heaven be more easy.[35]

Much as the Emerson brothers prized their relationship with Ezra Ripley, they never forgot—or at least their Aunt Mary never allowed them to forget—their relation to the sainted "Man of God," grandfather William Emerson, who had died in the service of his country. Interestingly, this William is more often present in letters they exchanged among themselves or with Mary than is his son, their father William, although the brothers never account for the fact other than referring to him as the specter from the past whose idealized legacy they had to measure themselves against. Knowing that no one had ever visited the elder William's grave, and believing that a walking tour to Vermont in search of it might help Waldo out of the depression he had been laboring under since

Ellen's death in February, in the spring of 1831 Charles persuaded Waldo join him on a walking tour in search of their illustrious ancestor's final resting place. Waldo appears to have gone along with the plan only to satisfy his brother. He wrote nothing about their journey and, as he explained to his brother William, he missed out entirely on whatever recuperative benefits it was to have supplied. Writing to William on 19 June 1831 after returning home to Boston, Waldo reported, "My journey was a strange one so pleasant & cheering & yet so sad. My memory was far more busy than if I had staid at home & my memory is a bitter sweet" (L, 1:325). But Charles kept account of their tour, which began on 30 May and ended on 14 June, and he reported on it in several letters to members of the family.

Writing from the road to Aunt Mary, and then finishing his letter to her and composing new ones to his brother Edward and step-grandfather Ripley from Cambridge upon his return home, Charles described the brothers' tour through Vermont and the Lake George and Fort Ticonderoga regions of New York in search of grandfather William's grave. In his three letters that follow, Charles constructed an attachment between the fallen Revolutionary "Man of God" and his daughter Aunt Mary, grandsons, and successor. The connection between past and present is nearly seamless in his prose, and it reveals Charles's assumption that grandfather William, an heroic figure exiled from his family in the cause of freedom and, finally, in death, was never far from any of the recipients' thoughts even as they pursued their everyday affairs. Writing to Mary, for instance, Charles developed an image of his ancestral hero that certainly accorded with her own preferred way of remembering her father: "the pious patriot, collecting about him such as were moved by his earnest & spiritual eloquence, to hear that truth where with Christ has made us free." With a dramatic flair modeled after the Calvinist pedagogy Mary had long practiced on her nephews, Charles fancied his grandfather's last days, "[t]he red spot glow[ing] on his wan cheek, as he mounts above all feeling of bodily disease, and many a faint heart is encouraged, & many a bold sinner is rebuked, by his words of holy fire."[36] Writing to Edward, the family's present generation exile in Puerto Rico, he kept details of the search for the elder William's grave to a minimum and, instead, while concentrating on the journey itself, poeticized the shifting scene of an afternoon sail that Waldo and he took on Lake George into a metaphor for the cycle of the family's past and current fortunes. As sunny skies turned overcast and wind gusts transformed the face of the once serene lake into whipping whitecaps, Charles mused that just as nature had "chased away the romance, the dream of the morning," he learned anew that "we were still Adam's sons & born to a mixed destiny of trouble & delight."[37] Finally, in his letter to Ripley, Charles was less concerned with offering his step-grandfather details about the brothers' quest than he was with chatting about those persons they had met who were also known to Ripley and drawing out a lesson the journey had provided for Waldo as an extended metaphor for the journey of life, a lesson he knew Ripley would approve. With Ellen's death still fresh in everyone's memory, Charles remarked that this walking tour was "every way agreeable & Waldo enjoyed it as much as it was reasonable & natural to suppose he could—he says the blessed companion of his earthly journey is removed from him, & the way seems hard & tedious."[38]

➤ *Charles Chauncy Emerson to Mary Moody Emerson, 12–15 June [1831]*

We have been to Rutland—have diligently sought out & inquired concerning the place where the bones of the man of God repose—but nothing can be ascertained with regard to the precise spot. We visited the old men who were alive & living in the town in '76—But tho' they remembered the circumstances, or had heard them of his death & burial, they knew not much which could satisfy our present curiosity. One noble old fellow we found in his barn shearing sheep, who was a soldier at Ticonderoga, & who well remembered on his return to Rutland, hearing of Mr. Emerson's death, & of his entire resignation in view of that event—Mrs Root, he said, was too much attached to life—& she asked your father whether the prospect of dying was not dreadful to him, but he taught her better things by his faith & hope. I went to the house in which Mr. Root formerly lived; it is however doubtful whether this was the same in which Grandfather died—Some of the old people thought it was probably in a log-house on the same ground.[39] We had no doubt, on the whole, of the burying ground where he was interred—Of course we visited it; & I sent back my thoughts to the hour when few & silent, the little procession entered the yard to lay the stranger's body in the earth—'They left him alone in his glory'—It is pleasant however to find that his ashes sleep in so fine a village & among so good people. Our stay was but one day long; we were kindly treated by Mr. Barrett.[40] He took a good deal of interest (as did all) in the object of our coming, & he was very attentive & hospitable. But not the burial place alone should be visited—One would see & stand upon the ground, which was the scene of the action of a great soul. We went to Ticonderoga—fancied the busy groups of soldiers filling the now deserted entrenchments, & in one spot, a little aside, the pious patriot, collecting about him such as were moved by his earnest & spiritual eloquence, to hear that truth where with Christ has made us free. The red spot glows on his wan cheek, as he mounts above all feeling of bodily disease, and many a faint heart is encouraged, & many a bold sinner is rebuked, by his words of holy fire.

Ticonderoga is a very finely situated place—looks up & down the fair waters of the Champlain. I picked up a bullet from the ground which I brought home as a treasure. I saw a young man in a tavern not more than a mile or two from the old fort, who told me he had often been there to search for a bullet or some memorial of the sort, but had never succeeded.

Cambridge June 15—

Again at home, again retired to that chamber of private meditations & study, where nearly all the progressive journey of the man towards the great ends of life, is begun & completed. It is in this chamber that his widest voyages of discovery will be made—here that his greatest variety of scene will be enjoyed. "Here either we must live or bear no life."[41] I return from every vacation & every ramble, to this chamber with a heavier sense of responsibleness—a more solemn purpose of dedicating myself wholly to the service of God, & a stronger endeavour to strike off every secret selfish reservation from the terms of the surrender. I need prayer to strengthen & guide me.

Waldo is well. I was sorry not to find you still at home. You will write to me often—Waldo too will be very lonely—The same constitution which enables him to be easily amused by society, leaves him I suspect at other times unelastic, & sad. Ah me—How little we are masters of ourselves—How much servants![42]

↠ Charles Chauncy Emerson to Edward Bliss Emerson, 16 June 1831

Waldo & I have just returned from a little tour through Vermont. . . . The country is a little mountain Eden—We liked the land & the dwellers thereon. We visited Rutland & staid there a day in the hope of ascertaining in what spot lay the bones of that man of God our grandfather. We did not succeed in determining anything more precise as to the place of his burial, than that his body was interred in the old burying-ground for there are more than one; this of course we went to see, & it was pleasant to find it in so tidy order & in the midst of such a fine town as Rutland. We got out of the Stage-coach spent a few minutes in exploring the old forts at Ticonderoga. . . .

Lake George we sailed upon, one sunny forenoon—while the sail was up & we skimmed over the jasper floor of the lake, before a western breeze, I stretched myself along the boat & gazed & sniffed the sweet air, & thought how unlike Earth our enjoyment was—But we were to go back—the wind was in our teeth, & after in vain endeavouring to beat our way home, we were obliged to be rowed by the men who went with us, & the sweat which rolled down their faces, & the sense of tardy & difficult progress which forced itself on us, chased away the romance the dream of the morning & I found we were still Adam's sons & born to a mixed destiny of trouble & delight.

You are in Mr. Mason's house & counting room at Porto Rico[43]—& we have sent letters to Havana—I have written many times, but from your seldom mentioning hearing from me, I think my despatches must have missed of you. . . . I study Law as much as I think good for the body & the soul—I doubt sometimes whether I shall ever make a lawyer, but en avant![44] we shall see. Study or life without doubts, were like a summer without cloud or caterpillar; They are the growth of our ignorance as naturally as mists rise from the marsh. We must turn them to good account—use them . . . to water & to quicken good enterprises & efforts. . . .

I hope you find your new employments agreeable to you—they postpone the day of your return, but if they amuse & invigorate you, I will never grumble a word. . . .

We are cut up into various parties in this quarter of the world. There are Masons & Anti-Masons & the Working men's party,[45] now added to the various sectional & political divisions which existed before. . . . If it were not for the heroes & sages now numbered with the dead, & a few a very few—that live, one would cut the strings that tie him to his Country & sail for a hermitage in the Sandwitch Islands[46]—

⤳ Charles Chauncy Emerson to Ezra Ripley, 17 June 1831

Last Tuesday evening Waldo & I got home from our little tour. We were absent a fortnight & a couple of days beyond—We took the stage to Keene from Boston, & the next day went on to Royalton Vt.—the third day would have carried us to Burlington, but we left the stage Wednesday in order to walk through what is called the Gulf road—famous for its fine scenery; Perhaps you have passed through it—it is a valley road winding between two mountain walls on either side, piled up a few yards apart, to the height of a thousand or more feet almost perpendicular. The air is like that of a cavern in the hottest day. It resembles the Notch of the White Mountains somewhat.

On Thursday we got into the Stage-coach again & reached Burlington Thursday Eveg. Burlington is a beautiful town & the waters of Lake Champlain make a fine foreground in the landscape as you look from the hill on which the village is built. We staid at Burlington until Monday following—Waldo preached . . . on the Sabbath.[47] We were very kindly treated by Col. Rice—& made acquaintance with Prest. Marsh of Burlington University & with other pleasant gentlemen.[48] Monday morning we set of for Middlebury, thence went to Lake George & Ticonderoga—This part of our

journey was interesting both from the remarkable beauty of the country we
visited, & from the associations connected with a portion of it. I picked up
a bullet in the old Fort at Ti. which I would fain believe to be one of true
Revolutionary memory. We returned to Middlebury & went from thence to
Rutland. Here we staid a day—going about to ask of all the old people what
they knew & remembered concerning our Grand-father's burial place. As
was to be expected we learned nothing more than in which burying ground
his body was laid. But we were very hospitably received by Mr. Barrett, the
son of Maj. Barrett of Concord, who rode about with us & much facilitated our obtaining the information or rather our making the inquiries we
wished. We took tea at his house & on the next morning, (Friday) took the
stage to Brattleboro & reached Northampton Saturday noon—Here Waldo
preached[49]—we staid at the house of your very kind friends Judge Lyman
& his wife[50]—they detained us through Monday, & Tuesday saw us on our
way to the old City of the Puritans. Our journey was every way agreeable
& Waldo enjoyed it as much as it was reasonable & natural to suppose he
could—he says the blessed companion of his earthly journey is removed
from him, & the way seems hard & tedious—

    Thinking you, Sir, would like to know where we had been & how we
had been, I have written this letter[51]—

Although their journey in search of Grandfather William's final resting place
ended in frustration—the sacred site was never found, nor was Waldo restored
from his grief as Charles had hoped he might be—Waldo and Charles, like
their brothers William and Edward, carried an idealized image of the man in
their minds and imaginations until the day they died. The Reverend William
Emerson personified their relation to the past, and though that relation served
the brothers as a source of family pride and inspiration, it also served them as a
source of anxiety that was especially painful for Charles, but only slightly less
so for his brothers, as in their personal and professional lives they constantly
struggled with the tension they perceived between the reality of their world and
Aunt Mary's idealization of the figure whose death initiated a familial fall. The
memory of their grandfather, particularly as Mary revived it at every opportunity, nagged them about what their financial security and social position might
have been had not the elder's death deprived them of their rightful inheritance.
That memory also brought into stark relief another tension that, as young men
of a generation championing "the new ideas" (as Waldo was fond of character-
izing them), the brothers felt whenever they tried to reconcile their liberal intel-
lectualism and spirituality with the "grim" and "earnest" piety of their ancestral
heritage. In an unusually dark and almost cynical meditation on that tension,
entered in his journal in the fall of 1834 (when he and his mother were residing at the Manse), Waldo portrayed the tension as a meeting of extremes that

seemed to validate the brothers' "misfortunes." While a tempest roared outside the house, symbolizing the tension between past and present that he and each of his brothers had internalized, Waldo wrote,

> Extremes meet. Misfortunes . . . may be so accumulated as to be ludicrous. To be shipwrecked is bad; to be shipwrecked on an iceberg is horrible; to be shipwrecked on an iceberg in a snowstorm, confounds us; to be shipwrecked on an iceberg in a storm and to find a bear on the snow bank to dispute the sailor's landing which is not driven away till he has bitten off a sailor's arm, is rueful to laughter.
>
> Some people smile spite of themselves in communicating the worst news.
>
> "Overturn, Overturn, and overturn," said our aged priest [Ezra Ripley], "until he whose right it is to reign, shall come into his kingdom."
>
> The great willowtree over my roof is the trumpet & accompaniment of the storm & gives due importance to every caprice of the gale and the trees in the avenue announce the same facts with equal din to the front tenants. Hoarse concert: they roar like the rigging of a ship in a tempest. (*JMN*, 4:383–384)

The Emerson family past was indeed a burden that could drive the brothers to levels of distraction sufficient to make them laugh or cry like madmen, and it was also capable of making them physically ill, as happened to Waldo in the last months of 1832, when he suffered from a form of colitis while he was engaged in separating himself from his congregation. Waldo's physical debilitation during this period is only now recognizable because of Charles's comments about it in a few of his letters, and in Charles's account its cause was as much connected with the emotional chaos Waldo experienced at having failed to live up to his ancestors' investment in the ministerial mantle he was now forsaking as it was with the fact that he was leaving a congregation that had been completely supportive of him from the day they first called him to their pulpit. Writing to Ezra Ripley on 1 October 1832, Charles remarked, "Waldo is quite sick & weak—his bowel complaint does not leave him—& he goes up hill & down continually—gaining a little strength & then suffering a relapse."[52] Later in October, Charles wrote to his brother William on the morning after the proprietors of the Second Church formally voted to dissolve their relation with Waldo. Describing the scene that had taken place the night before, Charles told William that the proprietors parted from "their pastor, whom many of them tenderly love, & all respect, with heavy hearts. And Waldo looks very sad"; he then added, "Waldo has last week a return of his tedious complaint, & looks very thin & is very weak."[53] The burden of the Emerson family past was also difficult for Edward and Charles to bear. Although Edward's breakdown in 1828 has been traditionally understood in accounts of Emerson family history as the consequence of his excessive ambition, the source of Edward's ambition was unquestionably tied to his need to succeed in the world in order to appease the spectral figures of ancestors that Aunt Mary held up to him as, ultimately, figures whose idealized lives he found impossible to emulate. Ironically, with the onset of active tuberculosis and his permanent removal from New England to the Caribbean for his health in 1830, Edward was finally freed from the spiritual malaise that had plagued him for most of his life. Charles, however, was never as fortunate as his brother in this respect. Try as he might to weather the tempests of depression and world-weariness that followed his every attempt to live up to the idealized version of his ancestors, until his death Charles believed that because he was never able to equal their model piety in this world, he had good reason to fear for his soul in the next.

The intrusion of those spectral figures into all aspects of his life seemed to mar Charles's every achievement, and arguably they rendered him incapable of enjoying as fully and freely as he ought the love that Elizabeth Hoar offered him during the three years of their courtship prior to his death in 1836. Throughout his last year at Harvard, an inexplicable sense of guilt and shame undermined the pleasure Charles should have felt as he accumulated prizes for his scholastic accomplishments and was repeatedly honored with praise and friendship by his peers. Although William and Waldo's collegiate records were mediocre at best, Edward and Charles rose to the top of their respective classes. Writing to Ruth Haskins Emerson in March 1828 to acknowledge the excitement building in the family as it seemed likely that he would receive highest honors at graduation, Charles cautioned her against being presumptuous, and he asked her to relate his own sermonette on humility to Ezra Ripley, who was very pleased by his step-grandson's success. "Will you return my thanks to Gr.father for the interest he has expressed in my little distinctions," Charles wrote his mother, but, he then added, "remind him of the text, 'Let not him who putteth on the armour, boast himself as he shall taketh it off'[54]—a life of temptation, trial, action, is before me,—God grant I may not degenerate from the purity or fall behind the example of my fathers!"[55] Although he was awarded the Bowdoin Prize for his dissertation on "Whether the Moral Influence of Poetry Has Been on the Whole Beneficial to Mankind" in July and delivered a commencement oration on "Publick Opinion" to his class at graduation in August,[56] Charles felt little joy on either occasion. Earlier, when he wrote to Aunt Mary in April and confessed his unease at the prospect of his success, she quickly identified its source, and that source colored Charles's response to his own hard-earned academic distinctions. "[D]o you propose to be *sufficient to yourself*," Mary asked her nephew. If he did, she said, she would applaud his self-sufficiency as "the only security" in this world, but she reminded him, self-sufficiency "require[d] an uncommon deal of virtue." For that, she remarked, he would have to turn to his ideal parents for inspiration and sustenance—to his Lord in heaven and to his forebears who glorified their Lord there. "*[A]re you pious,*" Mary then rhetorically asked him, answering the question herself in the negative:

> Why not? Love of the world? How much better might you love it & enjoy
> it if you loved its Auther. Neglect of your excellent parent tho' you had
> every other virtue could be a kind of parricide—yet you neglect . . . the
> worship—the adoration of your real & only Parent. . . . The embodying of
> one's feelings in solemn prayer is as nessecarily connected with all virtue
> as any cause & effect. Ah . . . when I think there may be some high office
> for you to fill in a future state this little world appears less than ever. Little
> it must, as yet, appear to one of your understanding, as you have scarsly
> been but a passive recipient of it's hopes & pleasures & advantages.[57]

Of all the brothers, Charles bore the burden of the Emerson family's elevated past with the greatest difficulty. Yet it is fair to say that even when he expressed the anxiety and fear of his darkest moments, anxieties and fears that invariably had to do with his ability to measure up to the ideals of his fathers, Charles spoke for his brothers as well as for himself. The difference between his response to the challenges presented by the past to their identity as men of a new generation and theirs was a matter of degree, and, under Aunt Mary's influence, Charles's response was always the most extreme. William, Waldo, and eventually Edward, who in Puerto Rico was finally freed from the everyday reminders of their burden, appreciated the impossibility of being men of new ideas in a new country while still adhering to the intellectual and spiritual platform of their Calvinist forebears, and they ultimately reconciled themselves to walking a fine line between genuine respect for the past and admiration for the labors of those who had come before them and the necessity of forming and securing their own identities as individuals and as brothers. Even Charles understood the virtue of the position his brothers took, for he recognized that by investing themselves in the opportunities for self-sufficiency afforded them by the democracy into which they were born, they were not repudiating the values of the past, but living as Americans. Homesick in Puerto Rico, where he had traveled to join Edward and recuperate from the bout of tuberculosis that had plagued him the fall of 1831, Charles wrote Waldo a rambling letter between 9 and 14 January 1832 in which he acknowledged the importance of letting go of the past in order that he might search for and savor the pleasures of the present, and he acknowledged that by treasuring the present and being an American, he was not disqualified from one day reposing with "good & wise who have gone to rest before us." "You say," he remarked to his brother,

> keep one eye a patriot & the other an emigrant. So I try to do, but the
> West Indian pupil is apt to contract & its brother mean while to dilate, till

I look all asquint—& the mind runs backward & enjoys the past, instead of searching, enjoying, & treasuring up the present scene.

. . . I have been to take my before-breakfast-walk this morning—but it always damps all I enjoy, to think as I cannot help doing, yes, it is fine—fine for them who were born to it—but I, I have no property in [this] soil—My Fathers never shed a drop of precious blood in its defence—their bones do not repose in its bosom—my boot never will tread lightly over the sod that is guarded by the cannon of . . . [a] monarch over the sea—No Waldo, we will live, or if God so order, die . . . by our own altars & homes,—& our ashes shall mix with the holy dust of the good & wise who have gone to rest before us.[58]

RUTH HASKINS EMERSON AND HER SONS

➤ *Charles Chauncy Emerson to Ruth Haskins Emerson, [December? 1828]*

I was thinking over past years, the other night, & when I remembered what you had gone through since I was old enough to think, & what you must have suffered long before I was a conscious & reflecting being; the troubles you endured in the sickness & death & poverty & labour of those whom you most loved; the hard trials of ministering to the bodily wants of those in whom you had no interest, nor they in you, & the whims & selfish caprices & irreverent manners to which you were daily exposed—when I thought of the difficulties which under such circumstances must have beseiged you in the education of your children, for whose sake you did & suffered all—And then when I considered what had been your success & comfort in them & the friends you had raised up for them, I could not help being more than ever called to thank our kind God whose almighty arm was about you for protection & blessing. He will still be our rock & our consolation—May the choicest blessings of Heaven be showered upon your head, my dear mother in the health & usefulness & honor of my beloved brothers[59]—

Like Ezra Ripley and her sister-in-law Mary Moody Emerson, Ruth Haskins Emerson (1768–1853) was born in colonial America, and she lived to see two full generations that included her own children, grandchildren, nephews, and nieces born and mature in the new American Republic. Ruth was a steady and long-lived figure of the utmost importance in the lives of her sons. However, unlike Ripley and Aunt Mary, whose voices sound clearly in the letters they exchanged with the Emerson brothers, she is the one person among her sons' elders whose voice we rarely hear spoken in its own right. We "hear" Ruth's voice mainly through inferences drawn from remarks directed to or about her that were entered in the correspondences of others. Although Ruth wrote a few letters to her sons, and they sent a few letters of their own to her alone, she was usually one of two or more recipients included in the round-robin exchange of letters in which her sons engaged. Throughout this biography, for instance, numerous letters are cited that one of her sons addressed to one of his brothers as well as to her, and even if the letter was not explicitly addressed to her, Ruth was a constant, almost sainted presence in her sons' correspondence with each other until the day she died. Indeed, she was held in such high esteem by her sons that in all the hundreds of letters exchanged among the Emerson brothers, not a single one discloses family news or personal information that might have a tangential reference to her that the author would have regretted his mother reading. In contrast to the air of confessional secrecy that often surrounded Mary's correspondence with her nephews, the brothers' correspondence to and about their mother was always candid and respectful.

Ezra Ripley's relationship with his step-grandsons was based on mutual respect and affection; Aunt Mary's relationship with her nephews was complex and often trying for all parties; but Ruth's relationship with her sons was based on unqualified love and devotion. To judge by the tone of letters in which she is either addressed or alluded to, Ruth and her sons must have been easy conversationalists in each other's company. For instance, when in the late 1820s and 1830s she visited at William's home in New York, one of her "Boston boys"— Waldo or Charles, or Edward until he left New England for the Caribbean in December 1830—routinely kept her informed of the collegiate or professional activities of all three and gave her regular updates on Bulkeley's condition. And whenever they shared news of their health and studies or of their work or family life with her, her sons were always solicitous about her own health and comfort, as is apparent in the following letter Charles sent to his mother on 11 December 1830, when she had rushed to William's home in New York in order to bring an ailing Edward back to New England, where Ellen was also in such dire straits that caused Waldo to recruit Ezra Ripley to supply his pulpit in his stead. Unaware that Edward had already booked passage for St. Croix, for which he would set sail on 12 December to escape the winter's debilitating effects on his tubercular condition, Charles wrote,

> We your children here at home are behaving very well—looking some-what impatiently for tidings from you & Edw. It would not be worth while for me to put the questions to you which are uppermost in my mind, because they will be answered by a letter from New York long before you receive this. . . . Grandfather has continued with us, & will preach for Waldo, tomorrow afternoon.
> You are now in that big City where you have supposed your sons al-

most lost—I hope you will see enough of it, to be able hereafter to refer William to his own proper place & snug corner, & feel as if he too had his local habitation, & name—

If Edward is gone, you will soon be at home again—& if he has not he will, I hope, come with you. I hope the passage to N.Y. on board the Steam-boat, was so little disagreeable, that you do not dread coming home. Uncle Ralph [Haskins] called today to ask about Edward & you. I put in these matters, because they are pieces of kind attention, & because we have no more important communications to make.

We send a great deal of love to William to Edward, if still with you we say, as did the Father in Scripture to the other son, 'All that we have is yours.'[60] With prayers for yourself & for Edward's better health.[61]

Such filial consideration was deserved. For the forty-two years following her husband William's death in 1811, Ruth lived entirely for her sons. When William's congregation called a successor to his former pulpit, Ruth took in boarders, including John L. Abbot, William's successor, in order to extend the length of her entitlement as the minister's widow to the Summer Street parsonage that was owned by the First Church of Boston. With the assistance of her unmarried sisters, Elizabeth and Fanny, and her sister-in-law Mary, Ruth provided for her five young sons and her infant daughter Mary Caroline, who died in 1814. In the First Church parsonage and later in other houses she occupied in and around Boston, Ruth took in relatives from Maine who needed a place to board while staying in the city, and she took in and nursed relatives and strangers who were ill. She altered each son's clothing so that it could be passed on to his brother next in the line, and without a care for her personal pride, she accepted the charity of her in-laws, Phebe Bliss Emerson Ripley and her husband, who offered her financial support as well as regular invitations to the Manse, which served as a holiday or summer retreat for herself and her sons. She was single-minded in her insistence that each of her sons receive a proper education, and she was instrumental in creating the system whereby William taught school to support Waldo's studies at Harvard, Waldo then taught school to support Edward's studies at Harvard and William's studies in Germany, and Waldo and Edward then taught school to support Charles's studies at Harvard. Under Ruth's tutelage, the brothers learned and then lived the old adage, "charity begins at home," for even when, by 1827, Waldo had begun to preach on a regular basis, William and Edward were embarking on their careers in the law, and Charles was still a student, the brothers always looked out for their mother's and each other's financial security.[62] Finally, unlike Aunt Mary, who, as we shall see, was never shy in arranging and rearranging her nephews' position on a scale that ranged from "favorite"—initially William, then Waldo, then Edward, and finally Charles—to "out of favor"—a rank that each brother held at some point in his relationship with her, Ruth never showed favoritism toward any one of her sons at the expense of the others.

The emphasis of this fraternal biography is on the lives the Emerson brothers shared between their boyhood years and Edward and Charles's deaths in the mid-1830s. The fact that one or more of Ruth's sons lived with her for most of these years helps explain the small number of letters exchanged between the brothers and their mother; moreover, after Waldo moved to Concord in 1834 and permanently settled there in 1835, Ruth lived primarily in his home for the remainder of her life, although she visited William and his growing family in New York on a regular basis. Yet, as Charles's letter to his mother that opens this discussion of Ruth Haskins Emerson's relationship with her sons suggests, the lack of epistolary volume between Ruth and her sons does not mean their relationship somehow lacked feeling or that her sons failed to appreciate all that she had done for them. Charles's remarks, written, we believe, in December 1828—when Edward was being discharged from the McLean Asylum in Charlestown to which he had been committed following his physical and mental breakdown earlier in the year—reflect his and his brothers' sense of their mother's suffering all forms of deprivation and insult while remaining steadfastly devoted to her sons' welfare. Except for their father's death, which Edward and Charles and to a certain extent Waldo were too young to remember in precise detail, and for Edward and Charles's later illnesses and deaths, Edward's breakdown in 1828 was the single greatest catastrophe that Ruth and her sons ever faced together. It was fitting, therefore, that Charles, writing for himself and his brothers after "thinking over past years," would extend himself in so thoughtful and considerate a manner to his mother at that time. In fact, about ten days after Edward was committed to McLean, William also seized the opportunity to express his love and concern to his mother. Pained by the spectacle of her son in torment, a spectacle that she witnessed as she cared for him at the Manse for the month before his commitment, Ruth told Waldo and William that she hoped Edward might find peace in death rather than live any longer in so tortured a condition. Brought to the brink of despair himself by his brother's breakdown, William wrote the following letter to Ruth.

> I must write to you. . . . But having acknowledged this, I am tempted to throw aside my pen. We may grieve together, it is true, & there is certainly a consolation in not grieving alone—but grieve we must, & that deeply, too deeply for words to paint. As far as human power can go, it is an affliction past remedy, as it is past comfort—but the end is
> s   with God, & therefore it is not yet past hope. Do not then, I beseech you, my dear mother, do not again wish that he may die. While there is life there is hope. Greater miracles are within the compass of Almighty Power, greater have been performed, even in what man has called the

ordinary part of Providence, than the restoration of Edward to health & sanity. Let us not despair, my dear mother; one who surveyed the field of creation with an eye of wonderful comprehension has truly said—Spirits are not finely touched, but to fine issues. And till the body begins to grow corrupt in the strong grasp of death, & the light of t   eye as well as the reason is extinguished, I will never believe that the nicely organized frame of Edward's vigorous intellect has answered the purposes of its Divine Contriver. Should he die, it would indeed add a   to the inexplicable mysteries of the operations of God. But while he lives, & I pray God to spare his life, I will not—I cannot abandon my hope for his recovery.

. . . [L]et me beg you, dear mother, to take care of your own health. So much care & anxiety as you have had must, I fear, have injured it. I repeat the request that you will take care & reserve yourself for your children, & for happier days—for they will come.[63]

Born in 1801, William was forced by circumstances to become the man of the Emerson household while he was still a boy. He left home for Harvard in September 1814, assisted his half-uncle Samuel Ripley at his preparatory school in Waltham, Massachusetts, in 1815, interrupted his studies to support the family by teaching in Kennebunk, Maine, from December 1817 to March 1818, graduated in August 1818—Uncle Ripley paying his commencement fees—and opened the School for Young Ladies in Boston, where he taught until the end of 1823. With Waldo's graduation from Harvard in 1821 and Edward's ability to supplement his own income and assist Waldo with Charles's expenses by teaching in Sudbury and Roxbury, Massachusetts, William was finally in a position to leave Boston to study theology at Göttingen in Germany, where, at last, he could prepare himself for the ministerial mantle that had been thrust upon him by two centuries' of Emerson family expectations. However, when he returned home from Germany in October 1825 after taking an extended tour of Europe, William announced that his conscience would not allow him to accept the mantle after all—thus thrusting the mantle onto Waldo's shoulders. Having decided against a career in the ministry, William took over a school in Roxbury in early 1826 for his brother Edward, who left New England in October 1825 for Europe to recover his health. In September of that year William moved to New York City to read law.

William made the metropolitan area his home for virtually the rest of his life, returning regularly to Boston and then to Concord for visits with his family that, as the years passed, consisted mainly of his mother, Aunt Mary, and his brother Waldo. William joined the New York firm of Ketchum and Fessenden, where he practiced real estate and civil law, and in December 1833 he married Susan Woodward Haven (1807–1868) of Portsmouth, New Hampshire, with whom he had three sons: William (1835–1864), who was familiarly known as "Willie," John Haven (1840–1913), who was called Haven, and Charles (1841–1916). William and Susan spent most of their married life either on Staten Island in a home they dubbed the "Snuggery" or in Manhattan. By all accounts, their marriage was a satisfactory one, and the door to their home in New York opened frequently for visits from William's brothers Charles, who died there in 1836, and Waldo, who often stayed with his brother or met him for dinner when he lectured in New York City or one of its boroughs, for Waldo's growing family, and for visits from Aunt Mary and his mother Ruth. In addition to his law practice, William speculated in real estate on Staten Island (with decidedly mixed results), and in May 1841, the New York State Senate confirmed William's appointment by the governor as judge of the Court of Common Pleas in Richmond County.

William's letters to his mother account for the largest number of letters sent to Ruth by any of her sons, and they reveal a close relationship between mother and son. In them, as in his letters to Waldo, William emerges as an earnest, hard-working person and family man, whose principal liability was his attraction to capital ventures that were beyond his own financial means. With the exception of his letters written to Ruth during the two years he studied in Germany (see chapter 2), the letters printed here touch upon some of most of the important events of his life into the 1830s.

For instance, here we will find him discussing the highs and lows of his first year at Harvard in a narrative that sounds almost modern with its references to collegiate studies as well as to the sorts of hazing and joking around that undergraduates indulge in to this day.[64] In one letter he tells his mother that he needs clothes, whereas in another, written when he first arrived in Maine in 1817, he registers his chagrin at having to board in the home of a Calvinist.[65] Nevertheless, a devout person himself, in another letter written from Kennebunk to his mother he acknowledges, "feeling the deepest sense of gratitude to God for the mercies he has showered upon me." Telling her of the sudden death of one of his college classmates with whom he had "breathed the same pestilential air," he notes that because his own "life and health have been preserved," he has been "often induced to reflect upon the peculiar care of Providence" in his personal life.[66] In almost every letter William acknowledges the debt he owes to his mother for her care and labor on his behalf, and in one, written when he hoped to secure a teaching position at the Boston Latin School, he asks her to have Waldo put in a good word for him with Nathaniel Langdon Frothingham, who was a member of the school's governance committee.[67] Finally, in one of the most remarkable sets of letters that he ever wrote to anyone, William recounted for Ruth the splendors of nature that he witnessed during a Fourth of July retreat he made in the Hudson River Valley. Thrilled and awed by the sublime prospect before him everywhere he turned—even more thrilling and awesome, he felt, than some of the natural scenery he had witnessed in Europe—he exclaimed to his mother, "[T]hat prospect! Who can tell its magnificance, or sum up its beauties? How boundless is nature, & how little is man, & man's ambition!"[68] William had previously invited Waldo to join him on this retreat, but Waldo preferred to accompany Charles on a visit to Quincy, Massachusetts, where they heard former President John Quincy Adams deliver a Fourth of July oration. Chiding his brother for making the wrong choice, William described his journey through the Catskills in language that, as do his letters to his mother on this occasion, reveals a stream of rare romantic impulse in his mind and imagination that is completely unexpected given the tendency of Emerson family historians to always portray him as the most "practical" Emerson brother. William told Waldo, "It will duly tantalize you . . . & show you how great a mistake you made in not coming here the other day instead of going thro' the familiar & comparatively tame scenery of N.E." "I can't let you into the marvellous beauty of what surrounds me," he continued, "I can only count a few of the apples of gold, & give you the cold, dead number, while I gaze on the living beauty." In less than sixty hours, William admitted to his brother, "I seem to have lived a month of ordinary time, & many a month must roll by, before I forget the lively pleasure of these few hours."[69]

➤➤ *William Emerson to Ruth Haskins Emerson, 1–[4] October 1814*

[No. 3, Hollis Hall, Cambridge]

Being now pretty thoroughly settled, I sit down to give you a circumstantial account of the 2 or 3 first days of my College life. I arrived here about 11 o'clock yesterday morning, and found that the furniture of the last occupants was still in the room. Indeed it was 3 o'clock before the room was cleared, and I could get into my study. About half past 12 o'clock, the dinner bell rung, and we were ushered into a hall in the new chapel, where we had the pleasure to see others eating, for some time, before we ourselves were employed. At last, however, having obtained some food, we made a very good dinner upon roast-beef and potatoes, (which, by the bye, we were obliged to peel ourselves,) with boiled rice and moderate sauce. After dinner I settled my things, but was obliged to put my Pembroke table into the study, because my other was too wide for the door. At 6 o'clock in the afternoon, we went to Prayers, where the President made a short prayer,[70] then read a chapter in the bible, and closed the service by a long prayer. Immediately after, we went to supper, where we had 8 young men to a table, a biscuit apiece, two Coffee-pots to a table, a bowl of sugar, pitcher of milk, and half a lump of butter. About 8 o'clock in the evening, (for the Sophomores always attempt to trick the Freshmen,) some of the Sophomores dressed themselves in cloaks and surtouts, went into a room round a large table, darkened it by a shade to the lamp, that their faces might not be recognized, sent their messengers all round to the Freshmen, to deceive them. A recital of my adventures will be a good sample of the rest. James Blanchard and myself went to see W D Lamb a few minutes;[71] we were scarcely seated, when some one knocked at the door, and enquired if Mr. Lamb was at home: being answered in the affirmative, he said, that the government had sent, and were waiting, for him. Lamb rose, hesitated, at length took his hat, and walking to the door, looked at the fellow, and asked him, "What government is this"? The Sophomore, finding we knew the trick, bowed and retired. Upon returning from Lamb's room, Jenks called me,[72] and told me the government wished me to follow him directly to them: I looked as calmly at him as I could, and asked, "Who personates the President?" He smiled, and went off.

We went to bed about 9 o'clock, but there was such a continual passing up and down stairs, that I was kept awake till about half past 10 o'clock, when, as we were nearly asleep, we were very much terrified by hearing our windows break by wholesale, as we ascertained in the morning that there were 8 frames broken, and 2 cracked. A pint of water was poured into the crack of our door, when we went to lock it for the night; and our door was kicked at, about a dozen times every quarter of an hour. This morning I obtained an order for them to be mended from Mr. Cogswell, our particular tutor.[73]

Sunday Evening, Oct. 2.

My troubles are not over yet. Last night, after I was asleep, there were two more windows broken: But James B[lanchard]. was sadly treated. He lent his hammer a minute, and wanting it again, went for it; when he returned, he was just entering the room, when he received the entire contents of a pail of water from the top of the stairs; so thoroughly was he wet, that he was obliged to change every article of his clothing. Today and yesterday we attended commons in the morning, and fared the same as at the supper mentioned above. . . .

Today the difference in our dinner was, that we had apple pudding instead of rice. Today I had a lesson set me on "Grotius on the truth of the Christian Religion."[74] He in the first place, proves that there is a God, and answers objections to this truth; secondly, that there can be but one God; 3d, that all perfection resides in him; 4th, that he is an infinite being, 5th, that he is eternal, omnipotent, omniscient, and supremely good; which is the end of my exercise. His arguments are weighty, and he writes in elegant Latin.

Monday Evening.

I recited my lesson in Grotius this morning. We attended Mr Frothingham at 8 o'clock this morning, and were divided for the purpose of
studying rhetoric.[75] At 11, we attended Mr Phillips, who sat an exercise
in Mathematics.[76] This afternoon we recited from Livy's Roman history.[77]
His preface is the hardest piece of latin [I] ever met with.

Tuesday morning.

Last night there were 2 pitchers of water poured through my broken
windows. . . . Love to aunt, Ralph, Edward, whom I expect Thursday, and
Charles. Please send up 25 cts. as a fee to Regents freshman, with a pair
of scissors to trim my Lamp; and a letter would be very acceptable.[78]

↦ *William Emerson to Ruth Haskins Emerson, 12 September* [1817]

[Waltham, Massachusetts]

I have been wishing in vain for a letter from home ever since I have
been here. But my time has passed very pleasantly. I have read considerable, of that which was useful. . . . I begin to feel the want of woolen
clothes, and will thank you to send out my blue pantaloons by uncle Ripley. I hope with them to have the pleasure of receiving a letter from you
or Aunt Mary.—My coat begins to be shabby.[79]

↦ *William Emerson to Ruth Haskins Emerson, 5–19 December 1817*

[Kennebunk, Maine]

I left Boston at 1/2 past 2, with 3 other passengers in company. We
reached Newburyport to breakfast, and dined in Berwick, and reached
this place before seven at night. . . . In the evening I was introduced to
Dr. Dorrance and family, with whom I am to board. He is rather reserved,
says little, but is a very worthy man, and quite attentive to religion. He is a
Calvinist in sentiment, but his wife is a very benevolent, liberal Christian.
They could not get the room in readiness, for the school today, principally
on account of the weather, since it has been hailing, raining or snowing,
ever since I left Boston. I am to have only 15 or 16 scholars, which will
be very pleasant. The school house is so large and inconvenient, that the
committee have made choice of a private room in the neighborhood.

Tuesday evening, Dec. 16, 1817.

Yesterday I commenced my school with 16 scholars, one of whom is
about my age and nearly of my size, but a well disposed boy; the rest are

quite young, 6 girls and the rest boys. You can readily conceive what an agreeable surprise it was to me, to find, among my scholars 4 who are studying Latin, one of whom is reading Virgil.[80] The other 3 are girls, who have been attending to the language for a year or two, so that I am not obliged to drill them in the first rudiments, which would be extremely tedious. Today I had 17 scholars, which will probably be the number which will constantly attend me.[81]

↠ William Emerson to Ruth Haskins Emerson, 1–10 January 1818

[Kennebunk, Maine]

I have again the pleasure of offering you the congratulations of the season. I am at a greater distance from you than at any preceding new year; but, (you will not not accuse me of vanity in quoting what so well expresses my own feelings)

> "My heart, untravelled, fondly turns to thee,
> "Still to my mother turns[82]—

For never did my affections so constantly remind me of my friends at a distance, as since I have been here. You know I have been almost constantly absent from home for these few years past. I have felt happy to hear from home; but, at present, there is a peculiar sensation with regard to home, never experienced before, which renders news and letters from home doubly acceptable. This may be, perhaps, easily accounted for from my distance from you. I hope you will not think me homesick; I am in no danger of it. My situation is so pleasant I could not wish it different. In reviewing the past year, and considering my circumstances at the commencement of the present, can I help feeling the deepest sense of gratitude to God for the mercies he has showered upon me. My life and health have been preserved, and that of my friends in general. But as an individual, I am often induced to reflect upon the peculiar care of Providence. My classmate McCulloch enjoyed an equal, if not greater degree of health than myself, on the day of exhibition, when you were at Cambridge. From that time, we both breathed the same pestilential air; *he* was affected, sickened, and died, as you recollect, only the day after I left Cambridge, and left a most affectionate family to lament his departure; I was scarcely affected with the disorder, was able to prosecute my studies with increased, and, I hope, productive diligence during the last term, and now, at the commencement of a new year, in the enjoyment of perfect health, spending my time both pleasantly and profitably in a place, where, though, a short time since, a land of strangers, God has surrounded me with a host of kind friends and acquaintances, and placed me in a pleasant family, who are but too indulgent to me, who anticipate the most trifling wants, and treat me in the most hospitable manner. Dear mother, ought I not, as an individual, even without taking into consideration the mercies bestowed upon our family, in the continuation of your life and health, (of the most vital consequence to us,) and numerous other blessings upon our family, even exclusive of these, ought I not be very grateful to the Deity for his manifold mercies towards me? It is often, very often, the subject of my grateful meditations, and more particularly, at this season, which, you, and my dear father have been accustomed, to set apart, (and inculcated the duty upon your children,) for serious recollections. May the return of this solemn anniversary often again, (as, I hope, at present,) find you in the enjoyment of health and happiness, and above all, may no misconduct of your sons ever detract from the pleasure with which you witness its recurrence. Please to tell Bulkeley and Charles that I wish them "many a happy new year" and that I wish still more, that every new year may find them making constant improvement in knowledge, and exercising the amiable affections of brotherly love, and fulfilling every duty with cheerfulness and alacrity.

Afternoon of Saturday, January 10th

I have hitherto deferred closing my letter in hopes of receiving one from home, and I have at length received what I have so long wished for. I was very glad that you had committed those thoughts to paper which had occurred to you at the close of another year. I felt happy also in the reflection, that its closing hours, and the beginning of the new year had been devoted by me in a manner which I am confident you approve, although grateful preponderated over painful thoughts in my retrospect. Your advice will always be an acceptable accompaniment to your letters; it will always be received with respect, and acted upon cheerfully. I most sincerely hope and pray that the anxiety which you always feel and express for my "welfare and happiness" will be rewarded by the usefulness and happiness of your children. . . .

I thought you would laugh at my minuteness in my former letter; but you were quite merciful; you only called it "circumstantial." I hope you will not discover my old propensity to take the roundabout road in this letter, if you do, pray mention it. It is a fault which I ought and must correct. The boots fit very well. They are only a little too large, which is a very "*good failing.*" There was some thing singular in my good fortune. It was pleasant and did not snow since I came here till the night of the 9th Jan. Early in the morning of the 10th before I went to school I received them in time to put them on, and your letter, more acceptable than the boots, much as I needed them.

. . . Please to give my love &c to inquiring friends. This letter is the expression of feelings which I intended for you and my brothers only. Therefore, I hope you will not show it to any other friends. From you, my dear mother, I hope never to have cause to conceal my heart, which is now as always most affectionately yours.[83]

↠ *William Emerson to Ruth Haskins Emerson, 23 July 1818*

[Waltham, Massachusetts]

When I arrived the farmers were groaning for want of rain, but the resulting rain of the last few days has entirely altered the appearance of nature, and with it the tone of the farmers.—There are some most beautiful walks in Waltham, especially near the river, where I usually walk after breakfast. My visit is peculiarly well-timed, as the small fruits are just ripening; so that you perceive, my dear mother, that with regard to the pleasures of sense, objects which gratify the eye and the palate, I have no reason to complain. As to intellectual employment I am reading Florian with the greatest pleasure and improvement.[84] I suppose school-keeping, though time renders it to a great degree mechanical, is perhaps to be considered as a mental employment. It has become much pleasanter than formerly and here it is rendered much easier by inflicting corporal punishment myself.—I have this moment received the letter I expected from Kennebunk. The offer is $420 per annum. Although it says nothing of board, I suppose *that* is understood of course; for I have seen, you will know, two of the committee, and informed them that my offer from Maryland was $400 and board; I shall, however, write immediately and ascertain the fact. As my expenses would be 30 or 50 dls less during the year, beside being nearer home, than at Maryland, I should have no hesitation in accepting an equal offer from K.—Since I suppose you would probably hesitate as little, I shall write immediately to signify my acceptance, if board is understood.—There is however a slight prospect of one of the ushers leaving the Latin school; so that I wish Ralph would call on Mr. Frothingham, the next time he comes into town, and desire him to mention my name as a candidate for the place. (I believe Mr. F. is one of the committee.) Mr. Ripley insists upon it that he will bear the expense of Commencement day for me.—My bill, which came out a few days ago, you will be glad to hear, is cancelled. The codicil will not probably amount to many dollars. When do you think it will be in your power [to] pay my last?—How are the boys? Please to give my love to them, and ask them to write; I am so busy, I can hardly write to you.[85]

↠ *William Emerson to Ruth Haskins Emerson, 18 October 1818*

[Kennebunk, Maine]

When I wrote you last, would you believe it, I had not commenced my school. Notwithstanding I had expected to begin on Tuesday or Wednesday after I left you, it was impossible, for it was necessary that the house should undergo a week's repairs, and the former master had not finished his term. They could not procure carpenters to undertake the repairs for a long time, so that I did not begin till Monday, Oct. 5. (A month after I left you. Sept. 17th) I know, that when I wrote, you would suppose I had began, and therefore mentioned the number whose names were on the list for admission, being willing to let you remain under the deception till I knew, what what even then uncertain, the time I should commence. However, the affair is not quite so bad as you might suppose; for the committee, have very politely allowed me to arrange the vacations to suit my own convenience, and I have therefore considered as vacation the three weeks previous to Oct. 5. Consequently my year began Sept. 14.—There are now 28 names upon the list for admission, all of whom I shall probably have by the close of this, or the commencement of the ensuing quarter. I have had but 20 as yet. The school is as pleasant as it was last winter, and the accomodations far superior. The house is within a stone's throw of my boarding place, so that I must take exercise by rising early to walk. I have explored several pleasant walks in the neighborhood. I have as yet, visited but little, finding that I have too much to occupy me at home to indulge myself much in this respect; for I have already perused 4 law books, am engaged upon a 5th & 6th, beside paying considerable attention to French, for I have told my neighbors that I would instruct in that language, and a moderate degree of attention to it enables me to support the character of being perfectly acquainted with it. Such constant employment leaves me no time, even if my situation were not pleasant, to find it out so that you may be perfectly at ease with regard to my lot, for it has certainly fallen in pleasant places.

I am very sorry to have no letter of yours to answer, for more reasons than one, for besides my loss, it proves that your avocations are such as to leave you little time. I hope and trust, dear mother, that you will be very careful of your health, though the wish proceeds partly from the selfish consideration, of the immense importance to us that it should be preserved; it is certainly a cause for gratitude, that it has hitherto been so good. Do your former complaints trouble you now? Do not, I pray you, confine yourself in the house too much.

Edward & Ralph, Bulkeley and Charles, have been very kind in writing. They know not how valuable to me, on every account, is every letter from each of them. I mean if possible to answer their favors. . . . I beg that none but the boys may see this letter, for though it contains those particulars which you would blame me for omitting, yet I fear, to any one else, it would seem that I should say less about myself, and appear to think and feel more for my friends; you, my dear mother, *know* that I am always aff^y your son William.

P.S. If you can understand my confused account of myself, you will perceive that by present arrangements, I shall have lost only a week after leaving home.—This indeed is only loss as it is breaking up my time for I was hard at work upon law, even during that time.[86]

→ *William Emerson to Ruth Haskins Emerson, 4 July 1831*

[Catskill Mountain House, Pine Orchard, New York]

Not being able to write you yesterday, I improve the present moment to tell you of a beautiful excursion of which I am now enjoying the full pleasure. I left New York by the "New Philadelphia" steamboat on Saturday at 5 P.M. & before night closed had 4 hours sail through the delightful & every varying scenery of the Hudson. It then became dark, & I contrived as well as I could to get some sleep; but this was often broken by the noise & crowd, & frequent stoppages to land passengers till at 3 the next morning, (Sunday) we reached Catskill, & about 25 were landed there, having come 110 miles in 10 hours. A stage was immediately engaged for our party, consisting of nine, & by an ascending, difficult road, we arrived at Pine Orchard, on the summit of the mountain, at 8 A.M. The last three miles of the way we found much pleasanter on foot, than we had found the rest in the coach. The elevation of the house where I write (a fine house, & the only house on this part of the mountain) is about 3000 feet above the Hudson, not much less than that of the Monadnoc.[87] And the view is most magnificent—your toil in the ascension is forgotten—it is nothing—to the intense feeling of delight with which you survey the immense landscape spread out at your feet, comprising nearly the whole of 8 large & populous & finely cultivated counties, traversed, in a long winding line of beauty by the Hudson. The season & the weather were both favorable, having sufficient clearness in the atmosphere, & an ample variety of coloring upon the landscape. In the afternoon we threaded the woods by a rustic path to the Cauterskill (or Catskill) falls, which are found in a vast & richly wooded amphitheatre. The fall is double; the first pitch is said to be 175, & the second 80 feet, & the quantity of water, which of course varies with the season, at some times leaving the cascade but the appearance of a white ribbon suspended from the rocks, happens now to be so great as to add much to the beauty & grandeur of the scene, which must be always beautiful & grand. After surveying it from a platform built directly over the fall, we went down to the foot of the first pitch, & four of us went behind the falling sheet of water, to be sure at the expense of a wetting, but from that point the view is singular & beautiful. The changing, semi-lucid mass of water is between you & the light; the roar of the fall is here the loudest, & you are standing in a vast cavern, whose ceiling is the arch of living rock, which, from directly over your head, reaches upward to where the river springs from its edge. From under the principal fall, myself & one companion made our way down with some difficulty to the foot of the second fall, whence the eye could embrace both, together with the noble amphitheatre in a single view, & it was indeed magnificent. I think it fully equal to the much celebrated fall of the Velino, & the scenery around is more rich & harmonious than that which surrounds the Italian fall.—This morning, from 4 to 5 o'clock, presented me with a new field of sublime & pleasing contemplation. The increasing light showed us a mighty & changing sea of clouds beneath our feet, rolling round the mountain side, intercepting our view of a large part of yesterday's landscape, & thinning itself off at the edges into those light, long clouds which we are wont to see floating high above us; at the same moment the waning moon nearly over our heads was set deep in the clear blue sky. The sun rose upon this beautiful scene, & added new beauty to it, changing & brightening the shades into colors, & stealing in cheerful light along the fields & distant woods not covered by the cloudy sea.—I do not find the fresh recollection of these glorious objects to be tedious, yet much I fear that on paper you will have found it so, as most descriptions are. Yet it comes from your affectionate son.[88]

→ *William Emerson to Ruth Haskins Emerson, 10 July 1831*

[New York City]

So vivid is still the impression left on my mind by the sublime scenery of the Catskill, that I don't think I shall rest contented, till at some favorable time, I shall have induced you to bear me company in a second visit. You would hardly believe there was a scene of so much interest within 2 days' journey from Boston, without having been visited by yourself & all your friends. Its beauties are now so well known here, that almost every resident in the city, in the higher classes of course, has been there once or more. For a social party this excursion has the great recommendation that all can keep together throughout the whole circle of interesting objects; instead of leaving the ladies at the foot of the mountain, as is often done in similar tours, they can comfortably ascend to the top in a good coach, & find one of the best hotels in the land at the summit. From the house to the falls you can either ride or walk; & after each excursion the wearied frame may repose itself till strength is recruited, while the eye roves over the vast prospect that is spread out beneath the steep rock on whose brow stands the Mountain house. And that prospect! who can tell its magnificence, or sum up its beauties? How boundless is nature, & how little is man, & man's ambition! There, to call his own three or four of those green & yellow squares on yonder broad chequer-board, how will a man toil & sweat, & spend his days in labor, & his nights in sleepless anxiety! But from this point how little do they look, & how much less, nay invisible in their littleness, the boastful lords of these narrow plots of earth. And that mighty Hudson, which bears fleets upon its bosom, & pours wealth into the lap of thousands, how is it shrunk to a span! it seems but a small canal that traverses the meadow; & the tall sloops on its surface seem so many petty sail-boats, & the large & rapid steamboat, with 500 souls on board is shrunk to the dimensions of a half burnt cigar, & you can scarce be sure it moves. By & bye, however, the judgment corrects the optical delusion, & that which seemed one level plain, with patches of different colors, begins to assume a greater variety of shade & hue, by which you can ascertain the real inequalities of the ground, till at last, without any diminution of the vastness of your prospect, it acquires all the variety which most delights the imagination. I am afraid of tiring you out, and therefore stop.[89]

An important advantage of the Emerson brothers' letters to their mother is that they reveal aspects of the boys' formative years that are otherwise difficult, if not impossible, to identify elsewhere. In addition to their special poignancy, through which we witness the emergence of the brothers' personal humanity as they disclose their love and devotion to their mother as a reflection of her own love and devotion to them, these letters chronicle the brothers' early years of school and work, and without having any particular axe to grind against any one person or institution, they disclose the hardships that Ruth and her sons had to endure after the Reverend William Emerson's death. In these letters, the brothers' distinct personalities begin to emerge, and in that respect, they will provide future Emerson family historians with a way of understanding them as persons in their own right, as opposed to accepting yet again Waldo's later reminiscences of his brothers as young men as the sole available indexes to the formation of their individual character and personality.

William's letters, especially those he wrote to Waldo and his mother from the Catskills, reveal a wholly unexpected and thoroughly appealing side of the man. We have always had relatively full access to Waldo and Charles's formative years, and in any case, Waldo was a worthy chronicler of Charles's life and thought in his journals. But next to Bulkeley, who will always appear as a shadowy figure, identifying "the real" Edward has been a challenge that has frustrated the efforts of every Emerson family historian to create a complete portrait of the brothers' early years and place Edward in it. Our access to Edward's letters to his mother finally answers that challenge.

Of the brothers who survived to maturity, Edward Bliss Emerson was Ruth's middle son. Born in 1805 and sickly as a boy, after his father's death Edward was often assigned to the care of his Aunt Mary or step-grandfather Ripley, who together schooled him in theology, history, philosophy, Latin, and Greek. As the Emerson who achieved the best record of the four brothers at Harvard, where he graduated first in his class and took almost every academic honor available to an undergraduate along the way, Edward's beginning as a scholar was inauspicious. In 1816, he enrolled at the Phillips Academy in Andover, Massachusetts, where, at a considerable expense to Ruth and his brother William, Edward began his preparation for admission to college. At Andover, and later as a student at Samuel Ripley's school in Waltham, he excelled in his studies and demonstrated a degree of intellectual ambition that impressed but also scared his elders. Frequent illnesses during the fall and winter seasons—all harbingers of the tuberculosis that would eventually destroy him—a high-strung disposition and, at times, exceedingly boyish and, where his health was concerned, sometimes irresponsible behavior, and family finances all conspired to delay Edward's admission to Harvard until 1820, when he entered college and roomed with his brother Waldo at No. 9 Hollis Hall.

As we observe in our later extended treatment of Edward and Charles, the two brothers shared so many traits of character and personality that, although it has been easy for us to keep them separate as persons from their brothers William and Waldo, it has been difficult for us to keep them separated as persons from each other. Both Edward and Charles were the brightest of the Emerson brothers, and though it served little purpose other than providing us with moments of intriguing speculation, we have caught ourselves sometimes following the impulse of earlier Emerson family historians who wondered what the ultimate record of the brothers' individual and collective achievements might have been had Edward and Charles lived as long as William and Waldo. Certainly, as the youngest of Ruth's sons to have been destined to find their way to Harvard—since by the time Edward completed his studies at Andover, Bulkeley's developmental disability was already apparent to all in the family, and it took him out of the college preparatory order—both Edward and Charles profited from the considerable intellectual and fiscal labors of William and Waldo who had gone before them. But far more than either William or Waldo, both Edward and Charles were also victims of what Waldo once called "the leprosy" of the Emerson family race—"ill-weaved ambition"—and its counterparts, a too-fragile physical constitution accompanied by a boyish neediness that each carried into manhood.[90]

In Edward's case, the combination of ambition and physical weakness led to a period of intellectual exhaustion and temporary insanity, whereas in Charles's it led to profound but secret self-doubt, despair, and world-weariness that plagued him for much of his adult life; in both cases, only their complete debilitation and death from tuberculosis saved them from additional misery.

As opposed to Charles, whose letters occupy so much of this volume and are the most competent epistolary narratives of those written by the Emerson brothers, as a young man and as an adult, Edward wrote letters in which the narrative invariably falls flat. This is less a function of his ability to write letters than an indication that, like his brother Waldo, Edward did not always like to write them.[91] His letters to his mother and to his brothers are, therefore, notable exceptions to his general rule to avoid letter writing whenever possible. The selection of Edward's letters to Ruth that follows, as well as those that are printed throughout this volume, present a fair balance between letters Edward wrote of necessity (he's feeling overworked and ill, or he needs money for firewood, or he's simply homesick) and those he composed in an attempt to extend into acts of epistolary prose the familiar personal conversations he and his correspondents would otherwise have enjoyed in each other's company.

The following letters were written between October 1816, when Edward took up residence at the Phillips Academy, and May 1822, when he was first advised to travel abroad for his health. Although Edward postponed travel to Europe until October 1825, twice during the period covered by these letters he interrupted his studies and sought refuge for his health, first, in the warmer winter climate of Alexandria, Virginia, in the spring of 1820 and, then, in the dry (relative to Boston) inland setting of Worcester, Massachusetts, in May 1822. His letters from Alexandria and Worcester are the most interesting of the group, and they each exhibit Edward's ability to create and sustain an engaging epistolary narrative based on his surprise that not all communities in America impose New England habits on their citizens, even those that are less than a day's journey from Boston, the New Englander's center of the universe.

For instance, writing between 2 and 7 March 1820 from Alexandria, where he was wintering at his cousin John Haskins Ladd's home, Edward revealed to Ruth his first reactions to race in the South. At the same time, he registered his shock at the fact that, unlike their condition in New England culture, within Southern culture, women did not work. Commenting on the gardening habits of Alexandrians now that spring weather has arrived, he reports, "The inhabitants . . . are busy in their gardens, or rather their negroes are, for nobody else works here," while remarking on what he perceives as Southern women's adversity to work, he writes, "never yet have I seen more than 3 ladies in the town with work in their hands of any kind; nor do I remember having seen any with a book excepting Cousin Eliza[beth]."[92] Two years later, writing home to his mother from Worcester on 15 May 1822, Edward observes that, as his experience while living in Andover had taught him earlier life is much easier, far less hectic, and better for his health in rural Massachusetts towns than it is in the bustling metropolitan area in which he had been raised. Enjoying the Worcester outdoors, Edward also reveals to his mother as well as to us that he did not entirely share William, Waldo, and Charles's unequivocal love of nature as he relates the following tale of a new pastoral exercise he has been enjoying at the expense of his studies. Stating that his days have become "extremely agreeable," he explains that "the weather is so delightful & gunning is such fine *sport* that I *read* not more than 10 or 15 pages in a whole day. Mr Heywood has lent me a beautiful fowling piece & two robins & a yellow-bird have fallen victims to my humanity; before breakfast this morning one of them departed this life. It is a pity to kill them, but they obstruct the prospect, & there are too many of them to enjoy life.—Gunning is excellent exercise."[93]

Apart from his letters to Ruth written from Alexandria and Worcester, the remaining letters that Edward wrote to his mother betray his preoccupations with study, work, and personal finances, the difficult—almost primitive—conditions in which he is living which make firewood, warm clothes, and long-lasting candles his most sought after creature comforts, his dietary habits, including his breakfast and dinner menus and his insatiable lust for oranges, figs, and berries of every kind, and his precarious health. Throughout, his health is consistently foremost in Edward's mind (and, apparently, his mother's as well), and he reports every cold, cough, chill, pair of wet feet, headache, toothache (owing to the fact that he left his toothbrush at home), and night sweat he experiences. Except for his toothache, all the other health-related events that Edward mentions to his mother are significant to note, for they have a direct bearing on his ability to protect himself from a full-blown tubercular attack. On the subject of his recurrent night sweats, which were directly related to his tubercular condition, he wrote to Ruth from Worcester, "I wish there was some medicine to prevent perspiration for every night I am awake for an hour in a very uncomfortable state from violent perspiration, exactly as when at home . . . & *not more violent,* though I call it so because it is so disagreeable."[94]

⤙ *Edward Bliss Emerson to Ruth Haskins Emerson, 19 October 1816*

I am rather closely confined to school [at Andover] but as it is saturday afternoon I have an opportunity of writing to you. Mr. Adams called me to him yesterday and told me to inform you that the committee met the night before, and have determined that I shall stay for three months and that if I bear a good examination at the end of them that they will pay my board from the time I entered for a year.[95] The school in the morning begins at half past eight and ends half past twelve and begins again at half past one and ends a little before six. When we go to school in the morning Mr Adams first prays and then the scholars read the bible in turns then those who go to singing master sing a hymn and as many of the others as choose to join with them, may.

Mr Adams then prays a second time about twenty minutes. At the end of school in the afternoon we have one prayer and a hymn. I shall go to meeting tomorrow in the hall directly over the academy. The persons who generally preach there are the students of the theological institution and Professor Pearson.[96] All the scholars on Monday morning give some account of the sermon to Mr Adams. I find I am very pleasantly in every thing but having such a long walk to school. We shorten it a little by crossing the fields. Mrs Abbot does not supply us with wood or candles.[97] As there are four of us the way the young gentlemen are here, proposed was that one of us should get a pound and the other three pay him their part of the price. I shall use part of the money you left me for that purpose. But I do not know what I shall do about wood. I thought we should set in Mrs Abbots room in the evenings but we have to set in our own rooms. Please give love to all at home.[98]

➝ *Edward Bliss Emerson to Ruth Haskins Emerson, 27 April 1817*

I reciev'd your letter and the oranges, for which I am very much oblig'd to you, on Friday. In the letter, you mention'd that you enclosed a dollar but there was no dollar enclos'd; therefore I suppos'd that you forgot to put it in when you sent the letter.—

Last Wednesday I had a beautiful walk to the mills and to the fish gutter; I went into the room where they were weaving and spinning and into the place where the carding machine was. I saw the mill to grind plaister of paris, and the cotton mill, and paper mill, and grist mill. Near the mills are two handsome falls, not very high but one about six feet. I am oblig'd to study quite hard now though I do not set up late in the evening (for I go to bed about 8 o'clock) but get my lessons in the mornings. As there is generally no fire in the stove, I am not troubled with the head ache, and am quite well.—

The vacation commences three weeks from Tuesday and continues a fortnight. I suppose you would be willing to have me come home if it is pleasant weather.

I am in need of money, for my roommates bought half a cord of wood and paid for my part and they wish the money very much. My part comes to 4/4. I shall need no more for candles this term and have now eighteen cents.

A week or two ago I heard some letters from Mr Gordon Hall the missionary.[99] He sent a picture showing a woman worshipping a heathen god. The picture is to be engraved and sold a three cents a copy. I subscribed for one.[100]

➤ *Edward Bliss Emerson to Ruth Haskins Emerson, 19 December 1817*

Fearful lest you should be anxious about me, I write this time to inform you that I arrived here safely at half past 4 on Saturday and I believe that I caught no cold.[101] The day after, (Sunday) and monday we had a great storm here and I caught cold but I am getting better now.—I have been reckoning up the expenses which I have incurred since I have been at Andover. They amount, exclusively of my board the first six weeks, to eighteen dollars and 33[cts]. We have bought our wood for 4 dollars a cord and as there are three of us my part came to 8 shillings. I expect this wood will last to the end of the term which is eight weeks from last Wednesday. Have you heard from William the schoolmaster?[102]

➤ *Edward Bliss Emerson to Ruth Haskins Emerson, 24 March 1818*

[Waltham?]

I was very much pleased to hear Aunt [Mary] was *at length,* on her way from "Elm vale" to Boston,[103] where I hope you are now enjoying her society. I suppose she intends to come to Waltham soon, perhaps tomorrow, (if you can spare her *yet,*) a day or two.—

You recollect I read Charles' [letter of the] 12th when I was with you. I am now reading it in the French. I devote my leisure time (which indeed is but little,) one week to French, & the next to Latin. Almost every day now increases the play time of the boys. I believe I have plodded through the hardest part of the year and I expect much pleasure here this summer from walking, talking, and the like.

Uncle [Samuel] Ripley has told me since I wrote you last that you have nothing to do with my clothes, and is going to get me a pair made here, I believe, and therefore you need not trouble yourself . . . any longer, as to clothes. Mrs. [Sarah Alden Bradford] Ripley gave me a waistcoat the other day.—

Ralph's shirt is here & Aunt [Ripley] says she recollects seeing, a pocket-handkerchief like the one I lost, but there is none of Ralph's here. I did not go to Newton the day I came up, nor since, and have not engaged Charle's shoes yet. I shall go soon, if there is dry walking. I hope to see *you* here soon, if Aunt Mary stays long with you.[104]

➤ *Edward Bliss Emerson to Ruth Haskins Emerson, 6 April 1818*

[Andover]

Though I wrote you a letter pretty lately yet I hope that *this* letter will not be unacceptable to you,[105] when it comes from your son, and is written only to inform you that he is well, contented, and *almost* happy. I think that I should be happy if I could hear from home, how you do and my brothers. I have not received but one letter and I am very desirous to hear from you, as I do not *know* but what you are all sick though I *suppose* that is not the case or I should have heard. Mr Adams has been to Boston and came back last Saturday, yet still I have no letters. He is going again, I understand, tomorrow to stay a week or fortnight. I wish you would endeavour to send either by him or by Dr. Pearson, or Dr. Porter,[106] who will all be down this week. I shall be very much disappointed if I do not receive a letter by any of them, though I shall endeavour to make myself contented if I do not. I have become so used to disappointments now that I do not mind them quite so much as formerly. I hardly know though whether I can bear it very *patiently* if I do not go to College this year. I wish when you write next you would tell me whether you think I shall go to College or not next Commencement. Will you please give my love to my brothers and ask them to write me some letters. If you can possibly find time will you be so kind as to write me, and send my tooth brush.[107]

↠ *Edward Bliss Emerson to Ruth Haskins Emerson, 10 April 1818*

As there is an opportunity to send to Boston I thought I would write you a line if it were only a request to you to write me. I received Ralph's letter to day and was sorry there was none from you.—

One of my fellow-boarders is very sick indeed and is obliged to have watchers. Mrs. Abbot with whom I board is very attentive to him, and wat[manuscript torn] with him the other night; she gets him every thing which she [manuscript torn] will comfort him and is a very good nurse indeed. I do not know of any place where I had rather be taken sick (home excepted) than here. I have myself been quite unwell with a cold and head ache, I suppose on account of the dampness of the weather. If you have an orange in the house which you can send me to give my fellow boarder, I should be much obliged to you, as the doctor says that they are very good for him; or if you can send me a few figs they would do as well. He can eat nothing but figs boiled or an orange or cracker soaked. There are no oranges to sell in Andover I believe. Will you be so kind as to send me my tooth brush as soon as possible for my teeth are suffering. Please to give my love to my brothers.[108]

↠ *Edward Bliss Emerson to Ruth Haskins Emerson, 17 April 1818*

To day is my birth-day, and I think that a few moments of it cannot be better employed than in writing to you. I received your letter Tuesday

evening together with the oranges and figs for which I am very much
obliged to you. Mr. Bent had some oranges which his mother brought
up that same day; but those you sent up were much the sweetest and he
relished them very much. You wished me to be very particular concerning wet feet and I have been very much so or I think I should have been
sick before now. I am very glad that our prospects about the weather
are a little brightened now, and the sun has reappeared after its long
absence. . . .

. . . I am glad that you *wish* to have me go to College this Commencement; but if it should be impossible I shall endeavour to follow your advice and be resigned to staying another year.

. . . You wished me to have milk if I could where I boarded. I have
spoken to Mrs. Abbot and she says I shall have it very soon; the cows do
not give quite so much now as they will.[109]

➻ Edward Bliss Emerson to Ruth Haskins Emerson, 4 June 1818

Though I was a little tired yet I went to school all day yesterday. In the
morning I gave your letter to the principal and he . . . gave me very readily
permission, to study out.[110] So that I am now perfectly contented. I have
as much reading, writing, and studying for me this term that I have not
had yet, nor do I expect to have an idle moment. I must get up early and
go to bed as late as is consistent with my health. I think I shall be done
with Goldsmith, by next week. My eyes have been rather weak since yesterday morning though they do not pain me much. As I have not much
time to spare you will please to excuse my short letters this term.[111]

➻ Edward Bliss Emerson to Ruth Haskins Emerson, 7 July 1818

I received your letter . . . and should have answered it before unless I
had been considerably pressed for time. I thank you for that money which
you enclosed as I expect to need it before long. In another letter I sent for
that money and gave my reasons for wanting it; but I was disappointed in
not having an opportunity to send it.—

Last Saturday though Independence was not much celebrated here,
the Academy was not dismissed nor was there any particular notice of
the day taken excepting, some of the school met in the afternoon for
a *prayer-meeting,* and some others more pleasantly disposed went down
to Pomp's Pond. Near Pomp's Pond lives an old man named Pomp from
whom the pond is named, and his house is noted for keeping good cake
& beer. He is 96 years old and is still pretty active. You may know from
his name that he is a gentleman of *colour.* Here some of the scholars went

to regale themselves and to give something to this industrious family; and this is the only way Independence was celebrated among the scholars. I passed rather a different day, though I think as happy as if pressed among the Crowds of the Mall. I went in to bathe in the river that day. To prevent all imprudence among the scholars Mr Adams has strictly forbidden any scholar to go in-to water more than twice a week unless they go in the morning; then they are allowed to go in every morning in the week, if they will go before sunrise, and no scholar is allowed to go without some one of eighteen years of age with him, unless he is himself over 14. There is one place where those go in who can swim, and the other for very small boys who cannot. I have learnt considerable about swimming since I came up. I always go in where it is over my head as it is much better and easier then to swim.—

We have plenty of ripe currants in our garden and have free liberty to eat them when we wish. Raspberries are nearly ripe and in a few weeks there will be a great many blackberries and other kinds of fruit. Mr Abbot has very early apples and I think it probable we shall have some before the end of this term. I hope that you will come up to Andover some time this term and see the beauties of the country, as well as the new chapel which is really an elegant building. It is now finished on the outside and mostly inside. Mr. Bartlett who built it expects to come and build a house for himself on the hill.[112] There are new houses constantly building and Andover is growing very fast. It is nearly school time and I must close my letter. Please to give my love to my brothers, and ask them to write letters to me as often as is convenient.[113]

↞ *Edward Bliss Emerson to Ruth Haskins Emerson, 13 October 1819*

[Waltham]

You wish me to be more particular in my account of my health. It has been generally good with the exception of one or two days; but never so good as at Medford. I find that on sundays and especially towards night I am more troubled with coughing and headach than any other days; and as that is the only day that I have the whole care of the boys the inference I think is plain.—

Last Sunday I had as pleasant a sunday as ever I passed in Waltham; Mr. Frothingham preached and I never heard him when I was more pleased. He was not obliged to exert himself so much to speak as in a large meeting house like ours, and consequently appeared much easier and more natural.—. . .

We have had no fire yet, at least none accessible to me, though it has been quite cold and the thermometer has been at 26—6 degrees below freezing point.—. . .

. . . Will Charles have the kindness to get a peice of spanish Liquorice for me at Whites as it is good for my cough.[114]—

➤ *Edward Bliss Emerson to Ruth Haskins Emerson, 2–7 March 1820*

[Alexandria, Virginia]

Yesterday received your kind letter . . . with much pleasure as it was the first which I had received from home after more than 2 months absence. I am very glad to hear of the welfare of the family, of Master [Charles] Emerson's sucess in school, (*I hope he will not be too proud of it*) & all the other good news which your letter contained. I see by your letter that you expected my Journal by the Industry. The reason it was not sent by that vessel, was that I wished to send with it some account of my stay here &c. &c.—It is short & badly written, but I hope you will excuse both of these faults, (if the first is a fault.) I should have copied it, only that I *knew* no one but yourself, brothers & Aunt Mary would see it, & you would easily "pass its imperfections by."—

We have already had some weather here as warm as we ever have at the Northward in April or May, & within a few days we have had some real March weather, yet. I believe it is the general opinion that Winter is blowing her last breath with us now & we shall have no more cold weather this year.—The inhabitants of Alex[a] are busy in their gardens, or rather their negroes are, for nobody else works here.—

There are a great number of Quakers in this place,[115] & they have a meeting house in town, as also the Roman Catholics, & Baptists. Last Sunday attended the Roman Catholic church. Every thing there resembled the church in Boston, tho' on a much smaller scale.—Since I have been here I have seen 3 persons baptized or plunged in the Potowmack, 1 man & 2 Black women; I never before saw this ceremony performed.—

March 7th—

There is nothing going on now but parties, and of these there are enough. There were 5 last night & will be two to night;—I am going to night to one given on account of a couple lately married. It will probably be a very large one, & though the parents of the new married couple are both Quakers, yet they do not seem at all averse to the parade which is making about them.—

I have been here now about 2 months & never yet have I seen more than 3 ladies in the town with work in their hands of any kind; nor do I remember having seen any with a book excepting Cousin Eliza[beth].—

You ask if I have been to Wash[ton]. . . . I have been once & I intend going very soon again, when the walking & weather are suitable.—Hope soon to visit Mount Vernon, Georgetown &c.[116]—

➤ *Edward Bliss Emerson to Ruth Haskins Emerson, 15 May 1822*

[Worcester, Massachusetts]

Yesterday afternoon I *walked* into the street & found . . . the letter & bundle with paper &c for which I am much obliged to you, though I am very happy to be able to say, the kind cautions with regard to my cold come too late, as you will perceive by the letter dated the 13th. They were mostly appreciated; for I despatched Mr. McFarland, immediately upon the attack of the cough, to the street, for 1/2 lb. conserve, & some vit. 4 oranges &c. &c. & the result of my prudence you have already been acquainted with. For the three last days my exercise has been at least equivalent to walking 4 mls. a day & I am confident that I am this day better & stronger than I have been any time since I first trudged into the house 7 weeks since. With respect to the plan of going to Concord, were I convinced that my health would be as much benefited by a residence there as by remaining here I could not hesitate one moment. But on the whole I think it would not: for were I to come to C. I could remain there a fortnight, without giving great trouble, if I should continue as well as at present; but longer I could not well stay without being troublesome or considering myself so; whereas, (with the *funds* now on hand) I can remain *here* 3 weeks or more & I think I need to continue as long as that in the country to be thoroughly recruited. Besides, it is not till within the last 4 days that I have enjoyed my situation at all & now it has become extremely agreeable. I have become so well acquainted at Mrs. F's & so much at home there when I am in town & the weather is so delightful & gunning is such fine *sport* that I *read* not more than 10 or 15 pages in a whole day. Mr Heywood has lent me a beautiful fowling piece & two robins & a yellow-bird have fallen victims to my humanity; before breakfast this morning one of them departed this life. It is a pity to kill them, but they obstruct the prospect, & there are too many of them to enjoy life.— Gunning is excellent exercise when used moderately & I have read just enough since I have been here to know that Lord Bacon mentions it,[117] as an exercise "good for the *lungs & breast*," though I can hardly see why. It is a little singular, but very pleasant, that we had the wind Easterly but two days for the last fortnight, & I imagine that this place is much more free from E. wind than Concord, on account of the greater distance. With regard to my diet, (as I suppose you wish all particulars) I had already adopted broth for dinner, previous to the receipt of yr letter. I take nearly a pint of milk for breakfast & supper with a pretty large piece of brown bread & molasses & generally an egg or a piece of apple pye. Between breakfast & dinner an arrow root custard or bread & molasses, & the same between dinner & supper. Occasionally, when thirsty, a tumbler of milk or a little lemonade. Breakfast at 1/2 past 6 alone. Dine at 12 in the family. Sup at 6 alone. Sit alone in my chamber with a few coals till past 8 & then go to bed. I wish there was some medicine to prevent perspiration for every night I am awake for an hour in a very uncomfortable state from violent perspiration, exactly as when at home (as you will recollect I was troubled in this manner) & *not more violent,* though I call it so because it is so disagreeable.

Perhaps 1/2 past 8 is too early an hour for bedtime.

Please to write to your *own* determination about my coming to C. or staying here though I really think it would be better for me to stay as I am so well situated & am but just settled down & beginning to gain flesh & spirits, &c.[118]

"HARVARD MEN"
The Emerson Brothers Remembered

Among the family traditions on their father's side that had been thoroughly established by the time the four brothers were born was that Emerson men were "born to be educated" (*JMN,* 9:239), and the college Emerson men attended to receive their education was Harvard. With the exception of Edward, who prepared for college at the Phillips Academy and, in the months before his admission to Harvard, at Uncle Samuel Ripley's school in Waltham, William, Waldo, and Charles prepared at the Boston Latin School.[119] The oldest continuously operating public school in America, Boston Latin was founded by the Puritan divine John Cotton in 1635—the year before Harvard was established—to train young men in Latin, Greek, grammar, history, theology, and philosophy, a mission that had not much changed in nearly two centuries. At the time William studied there, William Bigelow, whose leadership style and scholarship were lackluster at best, was headmaster. No reports survive from among the brothers about William's experiences at Boston Latin, undoubtedly because he was still living at home, yet we know that in January 1813 he delivered an "Essay in English Prose" at the school's semi-annual visitation of overseers and local dignitaries, which merited this response from Aunt Mary: "You may well imajane with what emotion I take my pen to write 'a man of your parts and profound erudition.' . . . [W]ithout offense let me say that however lofty the pinicle of fame on which you are mounted, . . . and magnificent your power, if you have not an open ingenuous temper, & humble pious heart, your memory . . . will perish, or your name be mentioned with contempt."[120] When Waldo and Charles were students at Boston Latin, Benjamin Apthorp Gould (1787–1859), himself a Harvard man and a model scholar for these two brothers, was headmaster. One of the first American educators to annotate the works of classical authors, publishing editions of *Adam's Latin Grammar* (1825), Ovid (1827), Horace (1828), and Virgil (1829), Gould took over the school from Bigelow in 1814, and by the time he stepped down in 1828 he had transformed it into one of the foremost preparatory schools in the country. Among Gould's pedagogical innovations were his introduction of declamation into the regular curriculum and his issuance of report cards to the parents of his pupils. Waldo and Charles performed well under Gould's guidance, and as, perhaps, an early indication of the direction these two brothers' careers would eventually take, both enjoyed and excelled in declamation. In August 1814, Waldo and fellow student D. H. Johnson performed "A Latin Dialogue, 'Augustus Caesar and Lucius Junius Brutus,'" and Waldo read his "Poetical Essay—Independence" the following August, and his "Poem on Eloquence" in August 1816 and again in January 1817 at the Boston Latin School's Exhibitions. Charles followed his older brother's lead. At the school's public declamation in June 1822, he recited an "Extract from [the] North American Review on English Universities," and in August, with patriotic pride and fervor, he delivered "An English Essay, 'The Settlement of New-England'" at the school's Exhibition.

Each of the Emerson brothers accepted his place within the family's collegiate tradition after completing his preparatory studies, with William entering Harvard in 1814 and graduating in 1818, Waldo entering in 1817 and graduating in 1821, Edward entering in 1820 and graduating in 1824, and Charles entering in 1824 and graduating in 1828. Their respective records as students at Harvard were mixed and evenly divided, with William and Waldo performing satisfactorily but not spectacularly (Waldo, for instance, was graduated thirtieth in a class of fifty-nine, and though he was chosen class poet, it was only after seven others had turned down the position), and Edward and Charles consistently placing at the top of their classes. With the exception of William, who does not appear to have won many accolades during his years of collegiate study—clearly, a function less of his aptitude than the fact that his education was often interrupted by the necessity to work and teach in order to support his mother, his brothers, and himself—each of the other Emerson brothers took home his share of prizes. As appropriate conclusions to their studies, in 1820 Waldo received the Bowdoin Prize for his "Dissertation on the Character of Socrates" as well as the Boylston Prize for public speaking; in 1824 Edward, who placed first in his class, won the Bowdoin Prize for his essay on "Antiquity, Extent, Cultivation, and Present State of the Empire of China"; and in 1828, Charles, who ultimately placed second in his class and delivered the valedictory oration on Class Day, also won the Bowdoin Prize for his dissertation on the "Moral Influences of Poetry."[121]

After graduating, each of the brothers was a loyal supporter of his alma mater, regularly attended commencement and other celebrations at the college whenever he was in Cambridge, and made public appearances at the college on special occasions. For instance, when Waldo took his master's degree in 1826, Edward delivered the English Oration on "The Importance of Efforts for the Diffusion of Knowledge." Waldo also returned to the college to deliver what became known as his "American Scholar" and Divinity School addresses there on 31 August 1837 and 15 July 1838, respectively; however, after his second address, Harvard's conservative faculty in divinity effectively banned him from returning to the college in any official fashion for over twenty years. When it became obvious that Waldo had achieved success and international respect, though, Harvard officials asked him to participate on standing committees and invited him to deliver two graduate courses in philosophy in the "University Lecturers" series of 1870 and 1871.[122] In 1904, the University dedicated Emerson Hall, now the home of the philosophy department, in his honor.

Writing to Charles on 29 October 1833 from Puerto Rico in response to a series of letters he had received from his brother, including one that described the recent commencement exercises at the college, Edward recalled his own pleasant student days at Harvard. Exiled from his real and his academic homes, Edward seemed fairly well adjusted to his fate, though Charles, who had recently become engaged to Elizabeth Hoar, was apparently at an impasse as to what direction he should next take his career and how he should best capitalize on his scholarship and personal experience to champion reform issues such as abolition. Although Edward has no easy answers to Charles's dilemmas, he assured his brother that he already possessed the answers to his questions within himself.

How shall I answer your unusually liberal favors of the 2^d, 9th & 17th ult^o, three long letters rec^d at once on the 26th cur^t. Nothing but old Doctor Method can avail in a case so urgent; & so I will begin with the oldest state. You tell of Cambridge & of the eloquence of the untiring [Edward] Everett as we may well call him.—To all that relates to literature & its triumphs you will ever find me I trust a ready listener. The milk of Alma Mater has gone into my blood & will course about the heart, till "the wheel is broken at the cistern."[123] But you must not expect no echo from P[uerto]. R[ico]. to such intelligence. We have no returns to make (to use a mercantile phrase) for news of science or letters.—I have attended no Commencement; & the oratory to be heard in the Comptg house, or the street is all to which I have access. This colloquial discourse is indeed at times marked with enough of shrewdness & at others with enough of invective; but it dwells on petty interests, in the one case or in the other expires in vociferation,— "vox et preterea nihil"[124]—But how can you say give us to *act* &c. you who are of the new philosophy, you who know that each visit, each expression in conversation, each thought, I had almost said and may say, is action,—how can you dare on the broad & carpeted stage whereon you stand, to mutter the words of 'obscurity & silence' & prate forsooth of safety & content. I know what you mean though . . . still I who am growing old, look at the forced resignation which you exhibit as somewhat too soon put on.—Were you compelled to *act*, as many are, to the exclusion of opportunity for study & meditation, I am quite sure you would yearn after the hours of leisure, the choice of pursuit, the free air of speculation which you now enjoy. True there is no income from these quiet & sober modes of action; you don't get beforehanded, you don't buy your wedding dress with the acquisitions now made, but you can't be blind (though they say Love is) nor fail to observe that the greatest of obstacles to a young man's peaceful & successful progress is overcome, not when he is married, but when he is well engaged. I leave you to follow out the how & why—They will show themselves to you readily.[125]—

Each of the Emerson brothers had to decide the "how & why" of his future for himself, and Charles was never exempted from the rule. As each brother went off to Harvard, the one constant "how" that he carried with him was to follow his forebears into the pulpit, and the "why," as Aunt Mary explained and re-explained to both Edward and Charles until the day they each died, was because it was their duty. But Edward and Charles, who like William and Waldo were men of a "new philosophy," as Edward called it in his letter, chaffed under the burden of their past, and it would take Waldo and his successful career as a lecturer to show that at Harvard and in their experiences after graduation the brothers had already developed the means to create and answer a new "how & why" for themselves. As in Waldo's case, the Lyceum circuit and the lecture platform could easily have became the sites of Edward and Charles's own itinerant ministries, and although given the circumstances noted in his letter, Edward was beyond experimenting with career possibilities other than those already at his disposal, Edward undoubtedly had such a prospect in mind for Charles when he wrote to him.

Rejecting the traditional pulpit, William took to the law and the courtroom, and Edward and Charles had begun down that path as well. The only one of the brothers who actually occupied a pulpit, Waldo ultimately rejected that call and pursued what appeared to be the secular life of lecturer and writer. However, lifelong friend Elizabeth Palmer Peabody understood Waldo and his decision better than most. Writing after Waldo's death in "Emerson as Preacher," she confirmed that he was

always pre-eminently the preacher to his own generation and future ones, but as much—if not more—out of the pulpit as in it; faithful unto the end to his early chosen profession and the vows of his youth. Whether he spoke in the pulpit or lyceum chair, or to friends in his hospitable parlor, or *tête-à-tête* in his study, or in his favorite walks in the woods with chosen companions, or at the festive gatherings of scholars, or in the conventions of philanthropists, or in the popular assemblies of patriots in times and on occasions that try men's souls,— always and everywhere it was his conscious purpose to utter a "Thus saith the Lord."[126]

Prior to the severe eruption of his illness in 1830 that forced him to leave New England for the Caribbean, Edward had taken the initial steps toward a partial career as a lecturer, when he began to write discourses on "Asia" and delivered one that Waldo thought was "astonishingly good" in March 1829 before Mechanics' Institute in Concord.[127] And by 1830, Charles had also taken his first tentative steps toward a career in the lecture hall that was eventually cut short by his death. On 3 February 1830, he delivered his first lecture in public at the Concord Lyceum in Concord, Massachusetts, where he spoke on "The Constitution of Man as Affected by Outward Circumstances." Three years later, after his own recuperative exile to Puerto Rico, he appeared before the Concord Lyceum again to deliver "One of the West India Islands," a lecture that he composed drawing from his own first-hand experiences in the Caribbean for his text. A month after Waldo gave his first public lecture after returning from Europe on "The Uses of Natural History," which he delivered before the Natural History Society in Boston on 5 November 1833, Charles lectured again in Concord, this time on "The Life, Death, and Character of Socrates" on the evening of 18 December. Charles reappeared before the Concord Lyceum on 29 October 1834 to deliver a lecture on "Civil, Political, and Religious Duties," and then he began to carry his lectures beyond Concord, delivering one on "Modern Society" at Pilgrim Hall in Plymouth, Massachusetts, on 9 January 1835; another on "Socrates" in Lowell, Massachusetts, on 8 April 1835; and another on "Slavery" in Duxbury, Massachusetts, on 29 April 1835. Charles was finally on his way to living his own "how & why."

Edward and Charles had learned their lessons well as Harvard men, and Harvard rewarded them with lifelong friendships that sustained them for the remainder of their tragically brief lives. As happened nearly a half-century later to Waldo, who was remembered after his death as a Harvard graduate who went on to make the English-speaking world his classroom,[128] at the time of their deaths and for years afterward, Edward and Charles were often remembered for the youthful brilliance and promise they both exhibited at Harvard, and whenever a writer spoke of them in comparison to their other brother Waldo, he, rather than they, suffered by the comparison. In the selection of reminiscences that follow, Charles was more often and more elaborately remembered than

Edward, which we attribute to the disposition of the brothers' contemporaries to avoid having to address in detail Edward's mental and physical breakdown in 1828 and his eventual exile to Puerto Rico, and the impression these created for many that Edward ended his life a failure.

➤ Margaret Fuller's Thoughts on Edward Bliss Emerson Written in a Letter to Frederic Henry Hedge after Reading David Hatch Barlow's "Lines to the Memory of Edward Bliss Emerson"[129]

. . . I meant to have mentioned, in speaking of Mr Barlow, his lines on the death of Edward Emerson. I know not whether it was their beauty or the feelings I have always entertained toward Edward E . . . but they drew many tears from my eyes—He was to me, when very young, a living type of noble ambition and refinement. Perhaps this opinion of him was a mistaken one—Fate forbad its being tested—Where such *have* been so I have too often found myself mistaken—But the change which came over his destiny was of a sort which cast a mournful and tender interest round him—We cannot grieve that he was not doomed to linger amid uncongenial scenes and employments far from the scene of his youthful hopes and attachments but I was much affected on seeing his death.[130]

➤ Edward Everett's Recollections of Edward Bliss and Charles Chauncy Emerson as Delivered before the Phi Beta Kappa Society at Harvard in 1837

At the dinner of the Phi Beta Kappa society on the 31st of August 1837,—An oration [on the "American Scholar"] having been pronounced in the morning before the society by Mr Ralph Waldo Emerson,—in reply to a complimentary toast by the President of the society,—Mr Justice Story,[131]—Mr Everett made the following remarks, after some response to the toast:

It was my intention, Sir, if an opportunity of addressing you was afforded me, to express the feelings, which I am sure I share with you, and all our brethren, in reference to the entertainment which we have enjoyed in another place, when we have listened with delight to a train of original remark and ingenious speculation, clothed in language the most exquisite, and uttered with a natural grace beyond the reach of art. You, Sir, how ever, have already done justice to this topic; and I am unfitted for enlarging upon it, which I will not endeavor to repress. You will the rather allow me to indulge this expression, as it has ever been one of the cherished duties of our association, to consecrate our academic gatherings to the recollection of the brethren we have lost, and to strengthen the bond of kindness toward survivors, by common tributes of affection to the departed.

I cannot, Sir, while the music of the orators voice still vibrates in my ears, forget that, in times not long past and within the classic precincts of Harvard, I listened on more than one occasion to the voice of two young men,—connected with him by the closest ties of kindred—but scarcely less dear to such of us as had the happiness to know them well,—each a most valued member of our fraternity; and, young as they both were, already recognized among the rising lights and hopes of our American republic of letters. Our Alma Mater,—considering their age,—never boasted nor deplored two gentler or brighter spirits than Edward Bliss Emerson, and his brother Charles Chauncy Emerson.

My relation with the former was of the largest standing and somewhat more intimate. It was one of the kindliest relations, that can subsist between man and man, that of a pupil grown up to be a friend. He was of a very superior nature intellectually and morally. Although but a young man at the time of his decease he had extended his reading far beyond o[r]dinary professional limits. He had already laid a deep foundation for further eminence. Too soon, alas, the bright prospect was clouded. The fervid action of a spirit touched to the firmest issues proved an overmatch for a sensitive physical organization, and we were compelled to witness

> that noble and most sovereign reason
> Like sweet bells jingled out of tune and harsh;
> That unmatched form & feature of blown youth,
> Blasted with ecstasy.[132]

He left his native land, for a foreign country in search of health; but found a shorter path to that higher and purer sphere, for which he was already mature.

Charles Chauncy, by four years the junior, after an interval of four years followed his brother to the grave. He too was a young man of most distinguished talent, of the most amiable disposition and of a character in all respects as nearly faultless as belongs to the lot of humanity. He had completed his legal education in the Law school and was engaging in the practice of his profession, patient of delay and modestly confident of success. Life was opening upon him, radiant with its brightest promises;—when suddenly and without the melancholy alleviation of a slow decline, he was cut down in the bloom of youth and hope. . . .

It is superfluous to say that I took the deepest and most affectionate interest in these young men, beholding them as I did, in the pure and unsophisticated morning of life, rapidly unfolding every mental quality and every trait of character, which can inspire confidence or win attachment.—But I forbear: I feel that I ought not, on this festive occasion, to pursue farther a subject of this kind. I trust however that I shall not be thought to overstep the limits of delicacy, if I complete this humble tribute to our departed brethren, and fulfill the more immediate purpose for which I rose, by asking you to join me in saying:—The orator of the day;—the beauty of living Excellence recalls to us the memory but alleviates the loss of that which we deplore.[133]

→ *Ralph Waldo, Edward Bliss, and Charles Chauncy Emerson as Remembered by Frederic Henry Hedge in Letters to James Elliot Cabot (1882)*[134]

My acquaintance with [Waldo] Emerson began in 1828. He was then living in Divinity Hall Cambridge, & though not a member of the Divinity School was understood to be a candidate for the ministry preparing himself in his own way for the function of preacher. There was no presage then, as I remember, of his future greatness. His promise seemed faint in comparison with the wondrous brilliancy of his younger brother, Edward Bliss Emerson, whose immense expectation was doomed never to be fulfilled. A still younger brother, Charles Chauncy, had also won admiration from contemporary youth while Waldo as yet had given no proof of what was in him.

He developed slowly. Yet there was notable in him then, at the age of twenty five, a refinement of thought & a selectness in the use of language which gave promise of an interesting preacher to cultivated hearers. He never jested; a certain reserve in his manner restrained the jesting propensity & any license of speech in others. . . .

He was slow in his movements as in his speech. He never through eagerness interrupted any speaker with whom he conversed, however prepossessed with a contrary opinion. And no one, I think, ever saw him run.

He told me that he never went from home on even the shortest journey without leaving his papers & other matters as he would have them found if suddenly overtaken by death.

In ethics he held very positive opinions. And here his native independence of thought was manifest. "Owe no conformity to custom," he said, "against your private judgement." "Have no regard to the influence of your example, but *act always from the simplest motive.*" . . .

I think it not unlikely that Emerson was more rapid in his movements in after life than he was at the time of my first acquaintance with him when he was more of a dreamer. His character gained in decision as the exigencies of life forced him to become more a man of affairs, especially after the death of his brother Charles on whom he had leaned for aid in practical matters. And decision favors rapid motion. But my impression of the slow-moving youth remains.

I was well acquainted with Edward B[liss Emerson]. He was of the class before me in college & we were fellow members of some college clubs. I have never known a more brilliant youth. A beautiful countenance full of force & fire, yet of an almost feminine refinement. He was a favorite in society, especially in feminine society, & a welcome partner in the dance. He was not merely the first scholar in his class but first by a long interval. His orations were epochs in college history; the one he delivered on taking his degree contained an eloquent allusion to Lafayette then present wh. I still recall after the lapse of nearly sixty years.[135] He was looking to political life for his career but the overwrought brain gave out; he fell into conscious & irrecoverable ruin. His death, I fancy, was hastened by grief for his failed ambition.

Charles too I knew very well. He was also a youth of wonderful promise, but more practical than Waldo, with a more ready tongue, a good extempore speaker, somewhat sarcastic, strong in independence & moral courage, a frank confessor of religious faith, speaking freely of sacred things, without a shadow of cant, & without the shyness & shamefacedness with wh. men of the world are apt to approach such topics. "Always do the thing you are afraid to do"—he was a man who would not have shunned to affront the highest dignitary at the bidding of truth. I think he rather dominated Waldo while thoroughly appreciating his genius. It is certain that Waldo was much influenced by him. . . .

I suppose you know about "Aunt Mary" who had such influence over E. in his early days.[136]

↠ Oliver Wendell Holmes Remembers Charles Chauncy Emerson (1885)[137]

I had in my early youth a key furnished me to some of the leading traits which were in due time to develop themselves in [Ralph Waldo] Emerson's character. As on the wall of some great artist's studio one may find unfinished sketches which he recognizes as the first growing conceptions of pictures painted in after years, so we see that Nature often sketches, as it were, a living portrait, which she leaves in its rudimentary condition, perhaps for the reason that earth has no colors which can worthily fill in an outline too perfect for humanity. The sketch is left in its consummate incompleteness because this mortal life is not rich enough to carry out the Divine idea.

Such an unfinished but unmatched outline is that which I find in the long portrait-gallery of memory, recalled by the name of Charles Chauncy Emerson. . . . [T]his youth was the most angelic adolescent my eyes ever beheld. Remembering what well-filtered blood it was that ran in the veins of the race from which he descended, those who knew him in life might well say with Dryden,—

"If by traduction came thy mind
Our wonder is the less to find
A soul so charming from a stock so good."[138]

His image with me in its immortal youth as when, almost fifty years ago,
I spoke of him in these lines, which I may venture to quote from myself,
since others have quoted them before me.

Thou calm, chaste scholar! I can see thee now,
The first young laurels on thy pallid brow,
O'er thy slight figure floating lightly down
In graceful folds the academic gown,
On thy curled lip the classic lines that taught
How nice the mind that sculptured them with thought,
And triumph glistening in the clear blue eye,
Too bright to live,—but O, too fair to die.

. . . [Charles possessed] the dignity which commands reverence,—a
dignity which, with all Ralph Waldo Emerson's sweetness of manner
and expression, rose almost to majesty in his serene presence. There was
something about Charles Emerson which lifted those he was with into a
lofty and pure region of thought and feeling. A vulgar soul stood abashed
in his presence. I could never think of him in the presence of such, listening to a paltry sentiment or witnessing a mean action without recalling
Milton's line,

"Back stepped those . . . fair angels half amazed,"[139]

and thinking how he might well have been taken for a celestial mes-
singer.[140]

➻ Edward Waldo Emerson on His Namesake, Edward Bliss Emerson (1888)

Of Edward . . . [my father] had a romantic admiration, for he saw in
him qualities that he missed in himself. Edward was handsome, graceful,
had a military carriage and had been an officer in the college company;
he had confidence and executive ability, great ambition and an unsleep-
ing, goading conscience that would never let him spare himself. He was
eloquent, but his speech had a lofty and almost scornful tone. My father
said: "Edward and I as boys were thrown much together in our studies,
and he stood always at the top of his . . . class, and I low in mine." He
had, while studying in the office of Daniel Webster with the commenda-
tion of his chief, of whose sons he was the tutor, lost his reason for a time
through years of overwork and privation, and though he recovered it, his

main spring seemed broken, and he went to the West Indies and filled a place as clerk in a commercial house, hoping to regain his power.[141]

➳ George Frisbie Hoar Remembers Charles Chauncy Emerson (1903)[142]

I hope I may be pardoned if I put on record here a slight and imperfect tribute to the memory of Charles Emerson, who was betrothed to my eldest sister [Elizabeth]. It is nearly seventy years ago. Yet the sweet and tender romance is still fresh in my heart. . . . When my father [Samuel Hoar] took his seat in Congress, in 1835, Emerson succeeded to his office, and if he had lived would have succeeded to his practice. Waldo Emerson has left it on record that he [that is, Charles] was led to choose Concord as his dwelling-place to be near his brother. Waldo's house had been enlarged to make room for Charles and his bride under the same roof. . . . He was of a very sociable nature [and] . . . had a very pleasant wit. . . .

He was especially fond of boys, and they of him. When he died, every schoolboy thought he had lost a friend. One had a knife and another a book or a picture which he prized, and another a pair of skates which Charles Emerson had given him. It may be an exaggeration, but I think he was the most brilliant intellect ever born in Massachusetts. . . .

The late Samuel May,[143] who was in the class after Emerson's at Harvard, told me that the impression his character and person made upon the students of his time was so great that when he passed through the college yard, everybody turned to look after him, as in later days men looked after Webster when he passed down State Street.

The Rev. Joseph W. Cross . . . was his classmate.[144] I received this letter from him a few years ago. . . .

> Your first inquiry is "as to his looks." He was about medium height, well proportioned and straight as an arrow, brown hair and clear blue eyes, with fair complexion and handsome features. "His scholarship and talents," both of the highest order. The class regarded him as the first and best scholar, dignified and refined in manners, courteous and amiable in spirit. He had great influence in his own class, and was much esteemed and beloved by all.
>
> I think the impression he made upon all who knew him was that of a classical scholar and a perfect gentleman.
>
> Dr. Channing said when he died that all New England mourned his loss. . . .

Charles Emerson entered with zeal and sympathy into the daily life of the people of Concord. He delivered a few lectures, which were quite celebrated. . . .

Charles Emerson delivered just before his death a very beautiful and impressive lecture on Socrates. It was long remembered by the people of Concord. It is said that they who heard it never forgot his beautiful figure and glowing countenance as he ended a passage of great eloquence at the close of the lecture with the words,

"God for thee has done His part. Do thine."[145]

Chapter 2

William in Germany

*W*hy would William Emerson, the third consecutive Emerson of that name to attend Harvard College, decide to go to Germany for his theological education? The reason why William desired to study theology was obvious: of all the career paths open to someone of his interests and social rank—religion, law, politics—the one that the Emerson family had historically pursued was the ministry, and William, as the eldest son, was clearly the choice to continue the family tradition.

He could have studied theology at Harvard. By 1811 students wishing to pursue that subject were given "a certain amount of systematic guidance," and in 1816 the Society for the Promotion of Theological Education at Harvard University was founded. The theological seminary became a separate department in 1819, and boasted such faculty as Andrews Norton and Henry Ware, Sr.[1] Indeed, as George Ripley (who later co-founded the Brook Farm community) wrote in 1823, no less a figure that the Reverend William Ellery Channing, the most famous of the Unitarian divines, joined others in claiming that the Harvard Divinity School "presents advantages for forming *useful, practical* clergymen not inferior to the foreign universities." Indeed, Ripley continued, Channing specifically advised William Emerson to study at Cambridge rather than at Göttingen, "believing that though Germany affords the greatest advantages as far as mere literature is concerned, yet that the best education for a minister in New England, taking into account the moral influence and religious feeling, can be obtained at Cambridge."[2]

Germany, though, proved of greater interest for a number of reasons. In general, in the words of a modern historian, the "educated and well-read no longer cared or dared confess themselves ignorant of the latest literary intelligence from Germany, the country which it had become the fashion to acknowledge the most advanced intellectually on the surface of the earth."[3] The university at Göttingen was widely recognized as the place where the most exciting work in biblical criticism was being done.[4] Moreover, William had sought and received the counsel of earlier Harvard graduates who had gone there.[5]

From the accounts he had heard, William discovered that Göttingen was an exciting place. The library dwarfed that of Harvard's, having by 1820 obtained 200,000 volumes, compared to the American school's 20,000.[6] The faculty was internationally known, and the theological faculty, particularly Johann Gottfried Eichhorn (1752–1827), was especially famous. Led by Eichhorn and others, the theologians pursued a "higher criticism" of the Bible, one intended as a counterpoint to those who took the words and actions of that book simply based on faith. As described by Elisabeth Hurth, "In Eichhorn's 'higher criticism' the time-honored doctrines of scriptural inspiration and authenticity were questioned by a literary and historical analysis which studied the Bible as a collection of literary documents presenting the same problems as any other ancient writing."[7] There was danger in this approach, as Channing undoubtedly realized, for some of the Harvard students who had earlier gone to Göttingen had suffered qualms about what Eichhorn was teaching. In 1818, George Ticknor had written that as a Unitarian, he felt that he should have "no objection to a serious and thorough examination of the grounds of Christianity," but he complained of Eichhorn's skeptical treatment of "all that I have been taught to consider solemn and important." His fellow-student, Edward Everett, had similar reservations, commenting to another student, George Bancroft, that "I have very little superstition, and I hope still less illiberality, but I did not think the attendance of lectures in this strain likely to be favorable on my mind and heart."[8]

Bancroft, Everett, Ticknor, and another Harvard graduate, Joseph Green Cogswell, had all attended Göttingen between 1815 and 1822. William knew of their journeys, and in fact wrote the first three for information and for letters of introduction. Their accounts of what it was like to study at Göttingen, contemporaneous with William's own stay there, help us understand what it was that William envisioned as he made his plans to travel abroad.

Surprisingly, a reading and speaking knowledge of German was not necessary for attending Göttingen. Although Everett had translated the first two chapters of a book by Eichhorn and Ticknor had reviewed a translation of a book by Wieland, Bancroft studied German for only three months before departing and another student, George Henry Calvert, who was there with William, confessed, "I knew not twenty words of German."[9]

But though German could be learned while at the university, good study habits—and a strong constitution—were a definite precondition to enrollment. Bancroft's descriptions of his daily regimen in 1818 and 1819 are worth quoting at length:

I rise at 5½, of course am ready for study at 6, from 7 to 8 with Prof. Benecke on the German language—from 8 to 9 private study, 9 to 10 with Eichhorn on the Greek of the New Testament merely critical; 10 to 11 with Dr. Köster on Hebrew grammar, and so forth; 11 to 12 the Philological Seminarium (a school where nine Germans interpret in Latin or Greek authors in the Latin language, the Professor superintending; besides these nine who interpret others called adspirantes are allowed to assist from time to time); 12 to 1 dinner and a short walk, 1 to 2 in the library to consult and read in such authors as are never lent; 2 to 3 I shall probably hear Tacitus Annals interpreted by Welcker, a famous man; 3 to 4 Aeschylus and Demosthenes de Corona by Dissen, the best scholar in Göttingen. From 4 till late at night I have several hours to prepare myself for my lectures on the coming day and to pursue my studies . . . [10]

5 am, Hebrew and Syriac; 7–8, Hereen in Ethnography; 8–9, Church history by the elder Plack; 9–10. Exegesis of the New Testament by old Eichhorn; 10–11, Exegesis of the Old testament by old Eichhorn; 11–12 Syriac by old Eichhorn; 12–1 pm, Dinner and walk; 1–2, Library; 2–4, Latin or French; 4–5, Philological Encyclopedie by Dissen: 5–7, Greek; 7–8, Syriac; 8–9, Tea and walk; 9–11, Repetition of the old lectures and preparation for the new.[11]

The others were almost as diligent. In 1815, Ticknor woke up at five, studied Greek until 7:30 or 8:00, studied German for two hours, took a fifteen-minute walk, studied Greek until noon, napped for thirty minutes, rested an hour, read natural history for ninety minutes, attended a lecture on natural history, walked, went to Greek class at five, took fencing lessons three times a week from six to seven, and read German until going to bed at ten.[12] Cogswell was not as detailed in keeping records, but his general comments suggest the daunting schedule he also kept: "I have generally been able to count at night twelve hours of private study and private instruction. This has only sharpened not satisfied my appetite. I have laid out for myself a course of more diligent labors the next semester. I shall then be at least eight hours in the lecture rooms, beginning at six in the morning. I must contrive, besides, to devote eight other hours to private study."[13]

This punishing pace was rooted in the belief that knowledge was obtained by memorization. Because knowledge was bounded, argued contemporary educators, an individual had only to learn a certain corpus of known and received wisdom in order to be considered educated. This knowledge was passed from faculty to students through individual tutorials and lectures, both of which were marked by students taking notes; then the students memorized their notes. This body of shared information then formed the basis for graduation examinations. Faculty had no reason to question this system because they had themselves had been brought up in it. Eichhorn told Ticknor that he had studied fourteen hours a day for forty years, and he stated to Bancroft that "[i]t is a fixed principle that cannot be denied that no man naturally possessed of a good constitution ever died of study."[14] Bancroft saw the virtues in such a system but also discerned the potential problems, for he wrote: "If I were to speak in general of the mode of instruction at this institution, I should say that for practical purposes it was the best that could be invented. It is not the best method to quicken talent, or cultivate taste, but for rapid advancement in knowledge, for thoroughness, and above all, for method most admirable."[15] Others, like Cogswell, were less impressed by the faculty's diligence than they were scared off from pursuing certain subjects. When a Greek professor told him "he had been spending eighteen years, at least sixteen hours a day, exclusively upon Greek, and that he could not now read a page of the tragedians without a dictionary," Cogswell immediately went home and struck Greek from the list of his studies.[16]

The German students did not impress the Americans. Bancroft's description pretty much agrees with the comments of the other three. He found his peers to be a "set of the most rough, uncultivated, uncivilized beings I have ever seen. Most of them wore a sort of coat made out of the coarsest of cloth, & of the original color of wool, the thread so large that it was visible at a great distance. Then many of them wore mustachios, all of them monstrous dirty & large beards. . . . The congregation of vile odours was intolerable."[17]

Even more disappointing was the overall lack of a genuine sense of and feeling for religion. This was surprising, given the emphasis at Göttingen on theological studies, but all four Harvard students saw the way in which "higher criticism" questioned the genuineness of the Bible to be paralleled in the lack of respect for religion demonstrated by both faculty and townspeople. Ticknor discovered that on Sunday the "churches are empty and the streets are full, and the shops are open—in short it is a holiday." As for people going to church, he did not believe that "there is a professor out of the forty in Göttingen who does it habitually or regularly. Planck, being head of the theological faculty and the most orthodox of the body, goes *sometimes* pro forma—Blumenbach never,—and Eichhorn, they say, does not know where the church is."[18] Bancroft was even more damning, writing that

> The theologians form a very peculiar body. They have no idea of the sublimity or sanctity of their science. 'Tis reduced to a mere matter of learning. I never heard anything like moral or religious feeling manifested in their theological lectures. They neither begin with God nor go on with him, and there is a great deal more religion in a few lines of Xenophon, than in a whole course of Eichhorn. Nay, the only classes, in

which I have heard jests so vulgar and indecent, that they would have disgraced a jail-yard or a fishmarket, have been the theological ones. The bible is treated with very little respect, and the narratives are laughed at as an old wife's tale, fit to be believed in the nursery.[19]

When he left Göttingen, Bancroft felt that the university had "assembled the choicest instructors and all good books of all ages and tongues," but his solitary satisfaction from living there resulted "solely from a feeling of gaining knowledge, for of amusements there are none here, and men of polished manners are not to be looked for." He had departed "without much regret," for the "people here are too cold and unsocial, too fond of writing books and too incapable of conversing, having more than enough of courtesy, and almost nothing of hospitality." He admired "their industry" but believed that "they do not love labour; I consider their vast erudition with astonishment; yet it lies as a dead weight on society."[20]

William was determined to go to Göttingen, whatever mixed reviews he had heard of the instructional method or university life. When he wrote George Bancroft for information about expenses, he was told that the ocean voyage would cost between $100 and $120, with another $15 needed to travel to Göttingen. Twenty dollars would supply him with "grammars & dictionaries." Rooms, which were "already furnished, & very conveniently, with chairs, tables, *drawers*" and other things, would cost him between $32 and $40 a year. He would have to buy candlesticks, cups, saucers, plates, knives, and forks, all of which should "most cost you $8." Dinner would cost between $4 and $6 a month, breakfast and tea the same. Servants and washing would run $20 a year and firewood $15. Although the library was free, instruction in German would be "expensive," costing $50 "before you will have learnt a language," and the public lectures were $4 a course, with Bancroft estimating that William "would hear from 4 to 6 courses a half-year, say 10 courses a year" for $40.[21]

The family decided that they could afford William's trip to Germany, but only by economies and by Waldo and Edward teaching school. On 5 December 1823, William embarked on the brig *Ocean* for Ireland, making him the first Emerson to sail the Atlantic since great-great-great-great grandfather Thomas Emerson arrived in the Massachusetts Colony from England in the 1630s.

➻ *William Emerson to Ruth Haskins Emerson, 31 December and [n.d.] 1823*

[Cove of Cork]

About two hours ago we anchored in this harbour, after a very rough passage of 26 days. Our weather was throughout so boisterous, and our accommodations so inferior, that I did not write a word on board. But I am now comfortably seated in an Irish inn, and informed that a sloop is in the harbor, almost to sail for Boston. I am determined that she shall not sail without a letter for you.

Every thing that occurred during the voyage appeared vastly important at the time it took place, but now I am safely on land, I wonder that I could attach so much consequence to the petty inconveniences of close quarters, bad commons, and the like. Some things, however, which were new or striking to me, may be interesting at home.

The day we sailed from Central Wharf, every thing appeared pleasant and promised fair. The wind was favorable, and I amused myself with looking back upon the beautiful city in which I was born and have lived so long, and forward upon the boundless ocean, till my attention was drawn to the faint but delicate colours of a partial rainbow, which was every moment formed by the fall of the spray from the top of the waves. This appearance can only be observed, when from previous bad weather the sea is unusually rough.

We had only reached the lighthouse, when a very troublesome circumstance occurred. The boat, destined to take away our pilot, had run ashore on a little island, and we were therefore obliged to come to an anchor till some other should arrive to take him off. This did not happen till the afternoon; and then, the wind was so strong, that we could not get our anchor—vexatious enough! the very breeze, which, had we been sailing would have carried us forward at the rate of 10 knots (miles) an hour, prevented us from taking in our anchor; nor could we sail till the next morning, when it had almost ceased to be favorable.—(After this, I hardly knew any thing that occurred on deck for more than a week, I was so seasick—(and of all maladies, this must be one of the most uncomfortable) during which time I subsisted upon air and peppermint & water.) Subsequently, the motion of the vessel became less intolerable—but we had many head winds and rough seas, which washed our deck, and even penetrated into the cabin, the floor of which has not been dry since the day we left Boston, as the water would every now and then come in by gallons through the dead lights. On the night of 18th Dec. we had a very heavy gale (our captain called it "tremendous") from the southwest. I could not resist the temptation of going on deck, and the scene was beautiful indeed! The waves were very (not mountain) high, and the small clouds were driven with great rapidity past the full moon. For 12 hours, although heavy laden, we went at the rate of 10 knots an hour—about 4 A.M. of Friday, the wind was so violent, that we could "scud" no longer, and were obliged to 'heave to.' It appeared strange enough to me, that all hands should be on deck and hard at work the whole night, & when in the morning the gale increased, the helm should be deserted, and master and men should 'turn in' (go to bed) very quietly for several hours.—You can judge that things did not go on very smoothly with us, for 3 or 4 times the sea broke over the deck so much, that they were able to cook but one meal in the day, and a third part of the time but 2 meals. But my kind mother had taken too good care of me that I should suffer at all, and your cake lasted till this morning. As for the ham, I have not used more than half.—The worst did not come in the midst of the ocean—As we approached the Irish coast, we had successive squalls of wind and rain for many days together.—To use our captain's expression, "it blowed a gale for 5 days without ceaseation." He is an experienced seaman, and when he came in sight of land this morning, he confessed he never had so rough a passage.—Still there were many things very pleasant—though the weather has been stormy, and we have not had a clear sky since the day we left the lighthouse, yet the captain was kind and careful, the passengers obliging, the sailors obsequious, the brig new and strong, my berth always dry, though the water often washed into my "stateroom," the splendid apartment which Waldo and Charles can recollect. I had a sight of 'Mother Carey's Chickens'[22] & a very pretty kind of duck, which rests on the water. What seemed singular to me, we saw these birds, and seagulls, even in the midst of the ocean. The luminous appearance of the foam in the track of the vessel, that has excited so much speculation, I saw several times. Indeed, you can see it almost every night. Love to all. . . .

Of course I shall write again by the first opportunity, but I know not where I can expect to receive letters from home till I reach Göttingen. I hope the first I receive shall inform me of the health of all at home, particularly of Bulkeley's, who had some bad symptoms just before I sailed. It is not yet decided what port our brig will discharge at—I hope at this.

Should this reach you first, as it is possible it may, it will inform you that after most tedious delays and a wearisome passage through the fogs of St. George's channel, I am at length in France, but so late that I shall be able to stay only a very short time at Paris, whence I shall certainly write again by way of Havre. I am at present in very good health though the inconveniences of the passage made me unwell while in Ireland. I might sincerely hope this letter will find all at home in health and prosperity.

I have drawn on Wells and Greene for what was necessary to defray the expenses of my journey to Göttingen,[23] as well as for what I expended in Ireland, which a little exceeded what I had with me, owing to my being unwell, and being detained so long. Love to all.[24]

↠ *William Emerson to Edward Bliss Emerson, 23 February 1824*

[Paris]

I know not whether it will always be my lot to be so marvellous contented, but when I was at home, I used to think there was no place so pleasant as Boston; when I arrived in Dublin, it seemed to me the grandest city in the world; nothing could equal the splendor of its buildings, the number and munificence of its charities. I have now been 8 days in Paris, and all I have before seen, or heard, or imagined, does not approach to what I here behold. I have hardly recovered from that bewildering sensation, which arose from perceiving how much there was that was beautiful or admirable in this great city. Had I arrived here by the middle of January, I should certainly have remained here a month, which would have been all too little to see and enjoy half that Paris offers, for you might spend a month at the Louvre alone, and think your time well spent.—I have made the most of the week I have had here, and am going to give you some slight sketch of my employment.—Two days I passed at the Louvre, which is a magnificent palace, of vast extent, devoted, as you know, to a collection of all that is beautiful and excellent in the arts. It is impossible to describe it adequately. On the ground floor are many stately halls, appropriated to chefs d'oeuvre of sculpture.—In most of these, the walls are entirely of marble or of polished stone, and the ceiling is covered with paintings and bas-reliefs in bronze and plaster by distinguished French and Italian artists. All around are ranged, in such a manner as to display each to the best advantage, statues, and busts and urns and bas-reliefs in a thousand different forms, all of marble or bronze, many of them claiming the greatest antiquity, and calling up the most lively and pleasing recollection of fabulous history, as well those of later and more certain periods. Before I saw this collection, I was inclined to attribute much of the admiration which is bestowed upon masterpieces of sculpture, to a factitious taste in connoisseurs—but I think far otherwise now. In many of the statues, and in many of the bas-reliefs, there is so much delicacy and so much truth to nature, as fully to justify the highest expressions of enthusiasm. Plaster casts, which you know are all we have, do not, I think, by any means attain to the beauty and delicacy of the marble originals.

My first page is so soon finished, that I must be more concise hereafter.[25] My second day at the Louvre, was passed in the gallery of paintings—This is of great extent, equally admirable in its kind with the halls of sculpture. The same remark might be repeated here, that was forced upon us in regard to the effects produced by the sight of the masterpieces of sculpture. You will laugh at me, and say that I had found out when I had arrived among the works of Raffael, Titian, Corregio &c by their busts, which are placed next to their works—but it is not so. There was no mistaking or overlooking the excellencies of their paintings.[26] They were different from any paintings I had ever before seen. I almost wish I had seen but one of them; for being so much hurried, my attention was distracted by the number and variety of beautiful objects, and I could not look at any one half long enough. There were several and modern paintings of exquisite beauty, in the same style with the Capuchin chapel, which was in Boston.—The works of art contained in this palace do not constitute its sole claim to admiration. It is a splendid edifice, and on one of its fronts, presents a most beautiful colonnade. Every thing is liberal moreover in the exhibition of the Museums. In every part of the palace I saw male and female artists employed in copying pictures and statues,[27] and every stranger is immediately admitted upon presenting his passport.

I should make no end if I undertook to tell you of every thing that is interesting in Paris—It is a noble and beautiful city—the abode of more than 800,000 human beings—traversed by a fine river which forms 3 islands in the heart of the city. Over this river are thrown 15 bridges within the limits of Paris. Several of these are very beautiful. One called Pont des Arts is of iron on stone abutments, and is very elegant in its construction. I believe that all the others are of stone. Magnificent palaces and halls and hospitals are scattered over the city. These are in many instances surrounded with fine and extensive gardens, fitted with statues of marble and bronze, and every fine day, especially Sundays, thronged with hosts of people in gay dresses, and with beautiful children, busying and chatting, laughing and playing in French, and aping those numerous shrugs and gestures which amuse the Yankees so much in grown up Frenchmen.—There are many open 'places,' in various parts of the city, the centre being generally ornamented with some noble column, as the 'Place Vendôme' or with an equestrian statue to some of their kings, or with a fountain of picturesque shape, and elegant architecture, spouting forth water which has been brought to Paris by aqueducts of many leagues in length. The buildings of the greatest antiquity are the churches, many of which would charm Aunt Mary almost into a love of Romish superstition.

In addition to the buildings I have mentioned, there are several triumphal arches, 2 in honour of Louis XIV, and one, a beautiful one indeed, built by Bonaparte, and called 'Arc de Triomphe,' standing immediately in front of the Palace of the 'Tuileries,' besides others.[28] Warned by a horrible pestilence, which took its rise from a crowded cemetery within the city, burials are not permitted within the barriers, but spacious cemeteries are consecrated beyond these limits, perfectly adapted to their purpose.—For the amusement of the living, which is here of infinitely more importance than the repose of the dead, there are more than 20 theatres within the city, besides others in the environs. These are constantly well filled, of which indeed the existence of so great number is a proof. Besides these, there are many minor exhibitions of monkeys and apes accoutred à la militaire, of merry andrews, of fidlers, and singers, and bagpipes, and hand organs, &c &c, which are to be met with every day, but especially on Sundays, chiefly on the Boulevarts. These Boulevarts are in themselves a great embellishment to the city. They are streets as wide or wider than Broad street, entirely encircling the city, although not exactly forming its outmost limit. They are rendered commodious by a raised sidewalk, with which the other streets are not provided, and bordered by a double row of trees. Thus in effect a paved Mall is round the city. Most of the theatres are situated on these Boulevarts. They are almost constantly filled with carriages, and horses, and pedestrians, and here the most splendid 'Cafés' and 'restaurants' are to be found, perhaps with the exception of some in the Palais Royal. The markets are great curiosities to me—such piles of what the French call comestibles and we call eatables, of every kind and price, either cooked or raw, many of which I had never seen, and some which have no name in English, arranged in the neatest order, and generally sold by women. There are other proofs, if other were needed, that you are in the land of good living, for it seems to me as if every other door was either a café or a restaurant, where every visitor is presented with a 'carte' of enormous size, containing a list of the various articles furnished in that establishment. A very large number of these are superb in their furniture—silver bowls and forks, and marble tables are very common.—After passing along the Boulevarts, by the theatres, and through the merry throng in the gardens of the Tuileries, every one I met seeming intent upon pleasure in some form or other, hardly appearing to know such things as pain and care and death, I have found it difficult to realize, in passing over the place of Louis XV, that I stood upon the site of the guillotine, and that large numbers of these very crowds had been partakers in the crimes of that period.

In looking over what I have written, I find I have by no means done what I purposed—but I will try to do that another time. You ought to pardon me indeed, if my letter were still more incoherent than it is, for I have been trying to see a year's sights in 8 days—As for myself, I am very well I thank you, and charmed with this kingly city, where by the way I have actually seen the king, as he passed in his carriage on his return from a ride. He was in a coach drawn by 6 horses, followed by another drawn by an equal number, and escorted by 50 or 60 horsemen.—I should not have dared to stay so long here, but have waited for my surtout,[29] which was off to Rochelle in the Ocean, by a blunder of the officer at Havre. As it is not arrived I must go without it, and Mr. Storrow will send it after me.[30] I set out tomorrow morning in the Diligence for Bruxelles. As soon as I get any time, I mean to write much more particularly, for I have a host of wonders to tell of. Love to any body that takes the trouble to remember me—Tell mother that although I think much of home, she must not imagine I am by any means homesick. Don't forget my love to mother & brothers whether they inquire for me or not.[31]

↠ *William Emerson to Ruth Haskins Emerson, 20 March 1824*

[Göttingen]

In my letter to Edward I told you a little about my visit to Paris. But I should fill a great many sheets before I could tell you all that I saw and felt in that splendid city even during my short stay. The multitudes of people you meet in the streets; the dress, the manners, the conversation of these people; the public buildings of every degree of magnificence, and for every various purpose; the gardens and the cemeteries; the number-less amusements and luxuries of this vast hue of busy mortals; all these things crowded upon my attention, and I felt, and suppose I acted, very much like some New Hampshire farmer boy on his first visit to Boston, staring at every body and every thing and thinking every object a won-der.—Mr Storrows family received me very cordially, and I was there 3 times during the few days I staid in P.; the first time Washington Irving was there and I had the honor of being introduced to him.[32] He is very often there, and they speak of him as extremely amiable and domestic in his feelings. When I saw him, he was engaged in talking stories to a little boy, the youngest of the Storrows.

I reached Paris on Saturday evening, 14 Feb. and left it with the ut-most reluctance on Tuesday morn. the 24th. I felt however that it was very necessary to be in Göttingen as soon as possible. By advice of Mr Willis, on whom I called the day before I left P. I took the road to Brussels. The day was pleasant, and I was of course seated in the 'coupé,' or front part of the diligence, where I made the best use I could of my eyes. The fields were already in their spring attire, and men and *women* were busy in them. Yet there was little variety in the scenes that successively presented themselves, and after a single post, little novelty. I acknowledge I was disappointed, both in what I saw, and in what I did not see. For what I saw—for although it was certainly pleasant to one, who for six months in the year has been accustomed to see the earth of a rigid brown or a frozen white, to pass through fields of a beautiful green in the midst of February, and though our road now and then crossed some pleasant little river with a famous name, yet it also passed through a succession of the dirtiest, most disagreeable looking villages imaginable, in each of which, the houses were all alike, and all alike wretched and filthy. I was disap-pointed in what I did not see—for in the rich and powerful kingdom of France, I expected to have witnessed an appearance of greater comfort and competence in the villages, and moreover occasionally to pass the chateux of the higher order; but of these last I do not recollect but one all the way from Paris to Roye, a town which we reached about twilight, and this was a large irregular pile of brick, that might well enough be called a great house, but not at all a castle. But I suppose in these as well as other aspects, the south and centre of France have much the advantage of Picardy & the Isle of France, in which provinces my route principally lay. Not only were there none of the rich and great on this route, but all the way to Brussels I saw no houses that could belong to a middling class—(always excepting the cities) & my account of the villages, above, is not dictated by peevishness, but truth, & is literally applicable as far as the French frontier.—I had moreover hardly imagined it possible to travel a whole day in the centre of Europe, without passing some highly interesting spot, some field of battle, or some renowned city; but alas! none of these fine things did I see all day; and though we crossed the Oise, and dined on the banks of the Somme, yet Meaux and Soissons and St. Quentin were left far on the right, and Amiens still farther on the left. We dined at Péronne at 9 P.M. and the next morning after crossing the Scheldt, arrived at Cambray; and I know my dear mother loves the name of Fenelon so well, that she will partake the pleasure I felt in passing through this city—nor will she wonder, that as I rode along, I thought much more of this great and good man, than of the two queens with their famous treaty, or any thing else that has given celebrity to this ancient place.[33] I should have liked very well to have made a short stay in this place, but I could not spare 24 hours, and so was hurried on to Valenciennes. There the traveller is not likely to be ignorant, that he is on the frontier of a powerful kingdom, for after passing most formidable gates, very strongly fortified, his passport and baggage must be overhauled, and the seal of the city authorities put upon the former, before he is allowed to proceed. We were again subjected to the like troublesome examination, at a dirty little village called Quévrain, the first place on this route within the kingdom of the Netherlands.

Although French is the prevailing language of *this* country, yet I began now to hear the Flemish spoken; and after leaving Quiévrain,—there was a very striking difference between the French and Flemish villages, altogether in favor of the latter; we were not indeed in the actual province of Holland, yet all the praises so often lavished upon Dutch cleanliness, both as to the exterior and interior of the houses, would certainly apply to the Flemings, all the way to Brussels. The town of Mons, where we dined, (25th Feb.) was quite agreeable in appearance, style of buildings, dress of inhabitants, and its environs were very pleasant, and enlivened by its canal—for I have now entered the land of canals. I was soon aware that

I was likewise in a right populous land; villages, and large and crowded ones too, succeeded each other almost as rapidly as taverns in the old road to Concord. At 8 o'clock P.M. arrived in Brussels. I found the diligence for Germany would leave B. the next evening at the same hour. So I had one night to rest, and the next day to perambulate this beautiful city. Paris was still fresh in my recollection and my regrets, yet I liked it very much, some of its churches are so noble, its buildings in general so elegant and apparently convenient, its walks and gardens and fountains so numerous, with many other objects of interest; but in almost the same proportion I disliked those of its inhabitants whom I came in contact with. You will say that a day could not afford a fair means of judging of the character of a place; but suspicion and roughness are separated by too marked a boundary from politeness and frankness, that even a cursory observer should not be able to distinguish them. I called on Mr. Everett with his brother's letter, and he received me with great politeness, and immediately gave me an invitation to dine with him.[34] The hour I spent with him and his lady was, as you may well suppose, exceedingly pleasant.—But I find my paper is nearly filled, and I must therefore only mention my stages, and reserve till another time the very many subjects of interest I found between Paris and Göttingen.[35]

➻ *William Emerson to Ralph Waldo Emerson, 1 April 1824*

[Göttingen]

You know that I hastened from Paris in the expectation that the semester began here the first of April, (as Prof. T[icknor]. informed me) you may suppose that it was very agreeable on my arrival to learn that it would not commence till the 3d May, and so I had 2 months instead of one to study the language. . . .

I was so fortunate as to find a pleasant room in a retired situation, and in a free air, for it is surrounded by a large garden. I believe too that I have fallen into very good hands, for the people that take care of the room appear to be honest and obliging. Prof. Benecke supplied me with books from the library,[36]—I now set myself to work upon the German. And though as you are aware I had studied it some time previous to leaving home, yet its difficulties are really appalling; its troubles are much more however, as a spoken than a written language. At first, when my attendant spoke to me, I could not understand a word, nor could I express the most simple things intelligibly. I have now been here nearly 4 weeks. During that time I have risen at 6, and devoted the whole day to German in some form or other. Every morning from 8 to 9 was occupied by a lesson from Dr. Bodenburg, and saving this, I was not obliged to leave my room all day; for at 7 in the morning my attendant brings me coffee, at 1 my dinner, at 7 P.M. my coffee again. When I wanted to buy quills and paper, or get a pair of boots made, I studied out my speeches with grammar and dictionary, and then went and practised them on the poor harmless mechanics and shopkeepers. I made it a constant rule to have something ready studied and practised for my attendant, which was duly inflicted every time he came into the room. He is fortunately quite loquacious, and by giving good heed to all he says, I have something of a German lesson every time he comes. The result of all this is, that I can now understand all he says, except when he gets upon a very long story; and when I went the other day to hear a lecture from Heeren on the judiciary of the U. States,[37] I was able to follow him throughout in the ideas, and mostly in the words. Still you will easily conceive that this is one thing, and holding a free and instructive intercourse with the Germans in their own language, or even talking German, is altogether another. But Prof. Benecke has promised to my great joy to begin to give me lessons on Monday next, and I hope much from his instructions. He enjoys a great reputation here as a man of vast learning in languages, and he speaks better English than any foreigner I have seen; and between Havre and Göttingen I have met with not a few who mangled our noble tongue.

I now come to some particulars of which you ought to be informed. During the 32 days I passed in Ireland, I spent 8£19ˢ1ᵈ Irish currency, equal to $36.71 cts. (In this instance, as well as in others, I change the foreign currency into ours according to its nominal value, not allowing for the difference of exchange, with which you know I could not be acquainted, and in the sums I have occasion for, cannot amount to much.) I did not take so much as this from home, and drew on Capt. Wicks for what I wanted. After being in Dublin about a week, I began to fear that the brig would not be immediately discharged, and recollecting George Emerson's offer,[38] I thought of getting to Hamburg or Bremen by way of England, and therefore drew on Capt. W. for 20 guineas, which added to 1£10ˢ10ᵈ which I had before received made my debt to him amount to 24£5ˢ10ᵈ Irish ($99.59). Owing however to my trunk not having been entered in the Captain's manifest, I found the greatest difficulty in getting an order from the Custom House for its discharge, and was thereby prevented from sailing in the steam-packet for Liverpool. Meanwhile I was deluded with promises that the vessel would be cleared without delay, and therefore concluded to give up my English project. (To this other reasons contributed.)

On my arrival at Havre de Grace I paid Capt. W. by an order on Wells and Greene, and as I was thus already supplied for my journey, had no occasion to draw upon them for more. This was the 12th Feb. I was obliged to wait there until the next night for the Paris diligence, and my stay in H. and journey to Paris cost me 55 francs, 2 sous. ($10.33 cts). I arrived in Paris the 14th, and left it the 24th Feb. and my stay cost me 101 fr. 16 s. ($19.09 cts). Reached Göttingen March 5, and this 11 days' journey cost me $44.07 cts.

I will now give you some items of my Göttingen expenses. They reckon here by Rix-dollars and groschen. Finding a difference in the accounts given me, I compared this money as accurately as I could with francs and guineas and dollars, and my statements suppose the Rix-dol. to be 70 cts. I found that I could have my dinner at 5, 6, 7, 8, 10, or 12 Rix-D. per month. I fixed upon 7 ($4.90) because this was nearly the sum allowed in Bancroft's calculation. My breakfast and supper, (coffee and bread) have hitherto cost at the rate of $4.68 cts per month. Add 1 ct. per day for my dinner bread, and my food costs me $2.46 cts. per week. The price of rooms has been higher of late in consequence of the great number of students and was from $30 to $70 per annum exclusive of attendance. I have engaged a small room for the next semester in a very retired, pleasant situation, (in the same garden where I am at present) at the rate of $40.40 cts per year, and $10.88 in addition for attendance (for which my bed is made, and room kept in order, boots brushed, errands done, meals brought, fire made and watched.) This makes board and lodging amount to $3.45 per week.[39] This corresponds exactly with our calculations at home, founded upon Mr. Bancroft's information. I cannot yet exactly estimate what the other items will amount to (viz. Learning German—other instruction—Clothes—Walking—Firewood and Stationery) but as nearly as I can calculate, they will not exceed our estimate; so that I believe without any books a year's expenses would be fully covered by $400.

I have been thus particular in consequence of your express request, and I hope the world yet goes so prosperously with you, that your disbursements for me will not prove a burden. Should there ever be danger of the contrary, I hope you will not hesitate a moment to make use of the papers I left in your charge. For it would make me miserable, to suppose that you suffered privations, that I might be feasted on intellectual luxuries. My luxuries indeed are great. I have the perfect command of my time, and never was in better health, so I have no excuse if I do not employ my time well.

I found that my trunk was both too large and too heavy, and learning that the baggage in Europe is always an additional charge in proportion to its weight, I purchased a much smaller trunk in Dublin, and put into the large one every thing I could possibly spare—among other things my cloak, which I feared would be only a burden, as I meant to ride in my rough great coat, & to carry my surtout in a bag. I know that Charles will not be offended with me for putting his pretty greatcoat likewise into it; it is because I valued it, and because it would be safely preserved at home against my return. I committed the trunk to Capt. W. and he promised to deliver it safely on his return to Boston. At Havre he received information that induced him to sail for La Rochelle—but whether he has yet returned to Boston, or whether the brig ever reached La Rochelle in safety I have not heard.

When I landed in Havre, I had only my greatcoat on, because I expected the vessel would come into the dock the same evening. The Captain sent after my baggage did not receive my surtout through some unaccountable negligence, and I immediately wrote to La Rochelle requesting Capt. W. to forward it to Paris on his arrival when Mr. Storrow had the goodness to promise he would take care and forward it to me. I have needed it much, but have not yet received it—I begin to fear it is lost—and my hope is, that Capt. W. may have put it in my trunk, and thus you will receive it with the other things. If you do, be good enough to mention it.[40]

→► *William Emerson to Charles Chauncy Emerson, 5 May 1824*

[Göttingen]

Don't you want to know what sort of place I live in? I take it for granted that you do, and accordingly have set myself down to gratify your supposed curiosity. To begin thus with all becoming accuracy, Göttingen is situated upon the river Leine, a stream of such magnitude, that I believe a spry Harlequin might with no great difficulty leap over it on either side of the city. It is entirely surrounded by a wall, formerly fortified, but it has for a long time been planted with trees, and forms a fine promenade, half as wide as the Mall. When upon this, you are raised nearly as high as the roofs in the city—of these of course you have a very good view—and they are not the most interesting objects, for they are all covered with red tiles; but below the wall on each side the view is very agreeable, for the ground is laid out in gardens, and beyond on the side towards the country, the eye rests on fertile and extensive fields, with here and there villages scattered over them. The city itself is a dirty one. The houses are ugly—and to tell you how these are built, will suffice for a description of the houses in almost every place I have passed through on the continent. A rough frame of wood is put up, the interstices between the joists are then filled, sometimes with stone, oftener with coarse brick; this is then plastered over, and lastly whitewashed, always taking care to leave the joists unwashed, and to show them off in still worse taste, they are often painted black. You know that Paris is an exception, where the houses are all of stone—as is the case with a few other places where stone is abundant. In Düsseldorf, and the better part of Brussels, the houses are stuccoed, and as stucco takes a fine and permanent colour, these places have an air of much elegance. (In Elberfeld the houses are covered roofs and sides, with slates whose edges are all rounded off.) In the villages the framework is oftener filled up with mortar or mud. Now we have got our house built, suppose we go in. And nobody thinks in G. of standing outside to knock, but you go directly in, and a bell fixed over the door, as in some of our shops, announces your arrival to the servant. The front door moreover serves for the entrance and exit of cow and horse, if any such creatures are attached to the mansion; and it is not a little amusing to see the air of familiarity with which a cow mounts 3 or 4 steps and marches directly through the front entry of a house. The parlours and student rooms have instead of a fireplace a stove with one end built into the wall, so that the attendant takes care of the fire without entering the room. Each student's room has a small sleeping chamber annexed, and their apartments are generally neatly painted and furnished, and above all, very prettily hung with white curtains—though in other respects, they are here no imitators of Dutch neatness.

As to the inhabitants, they seem to be all men, women or children, and in that respect exceedingly to resemble the good people of Boston—but in no other. In the first place, as needs no ghost to tell, they all speak German—and that made it hard for me to imagine, the first month I was here, that they were not all very learned folks, for they were all, even the children, pouring forth with the greatest facility, whole sentences of the very words that I, after hard labour with grammar and dictionary, could hardly put correctly together. Then they did not look as I expected. I was prepared to find two very distinct classes of beings in the students and the townspeople, and walked into the street the first morning after my arrival, to gaze at the scholars of this farfamed university, expecting to see their scholastic bodies enveloped in black gowns, and study marked on all their features. But I saw no such persons. I met a great number of rude, ill-mannered young men, in all sorts of tasteless dresses, many of them with fierce-looking mustachios, and all with notebooks under their arms,—and these were the students of Göttingen. They are always to be seen in great numbers. On Sundays, when there are no lectures, and on Saturdays, when there are but few, this is particularly the case, but instead of a notebook, they then carry a pipe. They are not allowed to smoke in the street, but they visit each other and smoke for hours in company, like the council of the renowned Walter the Doubter.[41] These pipes, which are of most alarming length, (some 4 feet long) they smoke morning, noon, and night. In passing through the streets at any hour, you are sure to see many a student's and many a burgher's head thrust out of the casement, (there are no window sashes) and smoking and staring most imperturbably. From seeing so many idlers, I imagined there could be little study done; but one of the professors has since told me, that out of 1500 students, who were here last semester, 1200 were diligent.—And it is easily conceivable, that 300 idlers might make no small figure in so small a city.—More about these young gentlemen another time.

One or two peculiarities in dress are worth noticing—The professors & the better order of townspeople, who are pitiably few, wear hats; all the rest, students included, wear caps. The cloth of which these are made differs in colour according to their different 'Landsmannschafts,' that is, the different districts of Germany from which they come. The Prussian cap, for instance, is white, and looks very handsomely; the Westphalian is scarlet, and does not suit my taste at all. The students generally appear in a rough frock coat, and in bad weather, they have a great coat, with a cape more than three fourths the length of the garment, reaching almost to the ground. This latter article of dress is very becoming, from the graceful folds of this huge cape.—The school boys dress exactly like the men—and I have often seen boys of 10 or thereabouts, going to school with notebooks, the same with the students', under their arms, and attired in frock coat, high cravat, and boots.—There is one class, however, much too important to be passed over in silence—I mean the young women. (Mädens, as they are called.) These have the burden of all sorts of affairs on their shoulders. They not only take care of the rooms, make fires, bring coffee, but there are always many of them to be seen in the streets, on all kinds of errands. They go to the baker, the butcher—they carry heavy loads on their backs, work in the gardens, and fields. Is a letter to be carried to the post office? The Mäden carries it. Is a book to be taken out of the library? The Mäden goes to get it. And be it wet or dry, they never wear bonnet or great coat. On Sundays and holidays, they put on all their gay apparel, tie their hair with a band, and let the two ends of the ribbon, (often a bright yellow, or scarlet) fly loose, to the length of half a yard.

There is one very good thing about all classes here; they are quite early. Sometime between 6 and 8 they breakfast, the students on coffee, the burghers on something more substantial. The most common dining hour is 12, and then you can see the dinner baskets traversing the streets in all directions. The Mädens carry these to be filled at the taverns; and after what I had heard of the temperate style of living at the German universities, you may judge of my surprise, in seeing large baskets, containing each 5 dishes, for a single student's dinner. But when we are in

Turkey you know how we must do, and so in 3 days time my dinner was going through the street in a basket as big as any of them.—Some dine at one, hardly any one later. At 2 the burghers and some rich students take coffee, & at 8 P.M. the burghers make another dinner—or suffer, as you like.—The professors and students only take coffee or tea (at this hour.) By 10 o'clock every body seems to be abed and asleep—and as that is the hour now, I must go too.[42]

William studied German diligently, taking advantage of the nearly two months that elapsed between his arrival in Göttingen on 5 March and the beginning of classes. On 10 May 1824, he formally enrolled in the university, the fourteenth student from America to do so.[43] If his matriculation followed the same pattern as Bancroft's, he would have given his name, his country, his father's occupation, and the studies to which he intended to devote himself. The Prorector would have then "handed him a paper bestowing upon him the rights of a citizen of Georgia Augusta [the formal name of the university], shook his hand," and he would have been entered into the rolls as "a student, bound by the laws of Göttingen to preserve a good character and pure morals, to appear always neatly dressed, and to avenge an injury by duel."[44] William now began his university career.

➤ *William Emerson to Ruth Haskins Emerson, 2 June 1824*

A little while ago Calvert and I were invited to dine with Prof. Eichhorn.[45] There was a considerably large company, and as it was not exactly like a Boston dinner party, I must tell you about it. The gentlemen took their hats into an uncarpeted room, where the old gentleman and lady received them, and all remained standing till dinner was announced. The company then separated into two lines as if by word of command. Our host after much labour succeeded in shoving two old ministers into the dining room; then Pr. Benecke stept out of the ranks and led Madam E. to her seat, and the ice thus broken, the rest of the company, after bowing at each other for a while, followed in the order of their rank.[46]

➤ *William Emerson to Edward Bliss Emerson, 27 June 1824*

. . . send me one [letter] at least immediately in this way, to tell me you are all alive and well and prosperous, and whether any thing has occurred which makes it wrong for me to stay. I am perplexed whenever I think of these things; for if Waldo be sick, there is but one course for me—the road to Hamburg by the first diligence. Till I hear something, it is plain I should stay where I am.

... Should you choose medicine, you would sooner be distinguished; in law, you would rise higher; in divinity, even you, Edward, might learn to be happy without fame. It may be permitted to a brother's pride to imagine, that in either your career would be splendid.

I live in a solitude Aunt Mary might enjoy. One very pleasant interruption of it is Calvert's dropping in for a few minutes almost every day, to chat about America. At 7 or 8 in the evening I go out to take a walk, and sometimes call on one of the professors. With the students I have no intercourse, and from what I see of them am not desirous of any. There is such a throng of them collected here, (over 1500) that man's depravity breaks out strongly and shamelessly. The students attend as few or as many lectures as they choose, and after they have entered their names with a professor, all that he is concerned about is that he receive his louis, which is paid in advance, and the young gentlemen may then come into lecture every time or not at all, as they think fit. A great many choose the latter, and spend their time in the streets, in the public gardens round the city, where they bowl, and drink incredible quantities of wine and beer, or in the billiard houses. These idlers must necessarily come often in contact with each other, and as jealousies exist between those who come from different sections of Germany, they often clash. These quarrels are invariably settled by duels, which take place in great numbers; for as soon as one individual is involved in a dispute, others of his 'landsmannschaft' make it a point of honour to take his part, and so when one young gentleman has been pushed into the gutter, there are sometimes 20 duels in consequence. The parties usually go to a tavern in some neighboring village on Sunday, as this is an idle day with the students, and then fight with broadswords. This contemptible practice has not even the plea of bravery; for the heads of the combatants are defended by a peculiar kind of hat, and their bodies by a kind of pantaloons stuffed for the purpose, which are drawn up as high as the breast, thus leaving little beside the face exposed. The most serious consequence of these encounters is therefore a cut in this part—and I meet a great many in the street with this telltale mark upon them.

A rebellion is, as you know, not infrequent in the German Universities. I will tell you some circumstances commonly attending one. When it breaks out, the mutineers assemble in the streets and compel all the students to come out of their rooms, and either to take part with them, or quit the city. All these enter into a solemn engagement with each other, never to return to the University. They soon leave the city in a tumultuous manner, singing songs of freedom, and smoking their pipes, which last is not allowed in the streets in quiet times. Last year, about this time, there was an uproar; they did not succeed in making it general, but several hundreds went off in a body to a mill a few miles from here, and there staid some days, eating pancakes, drinking beer, and smoking. They then proceeded toward Cassel. A number of them had avowed the intention of assassinating the Elector. This prince was a little alarmed, and sent a troop of horse to prevent them from entering his territories. (You recollect we had an exaggerated report of this disturbance in Boston via Paris.)—The students are so numerous, that when they unite, they can accomplish almost any thing they choose. One of the 'bourgeoise' had insulted, (I believe, struck) one of the students; a large body was soon assembled, and entirely demolished the house of the offender. They have in a body made repeated exactions of the government, with which the latter have judged it prudent to comply. One of these is a privilege of free hunting for a number of miles round G., a great privilege in Germany. Beside the duelling and rebelling spirit, which seems hardly to have a limit, the indulgence in the lowest excesses is not infrequent. An individual is occasionally challenged to drink ten bottles of beer at a sitting, and actually accomplishes it; the means he learns of Caligula.[47] When this worse than brutal feat has been performed in the manner suggested, the boon companions are ever after sworn friends and testify their mutual affection by thou-ing each other.—The power of the government to restrain vice, is almost nothing. After a regular hearing before the Univ. police court, a student can be imprisoned for debt, and those that the police can catch fighting duels are liable to the same—so that between these two classes the prison is kept tolerably full.[48] There however their punishments stop, without seeming to produce the slightest effect upon the students. Once in a while, too, the protector hears that a student does not go to a single lecture, is dissipated and vicious—and he is forthwith dismissed. But this is very rare. The professors have no more to do with the students conduct than you or I. The only intercourse between them is one of mutual politeness. A few visit the professors occasionally on Sunday noon, the only time when such visits are expected. After all deductions for idlers and revellers, there is unquestionably a large number who are zealously forwarding their education, but I am inclined to think that only a small portion of these pursue their studies judiciously. . . . I do not for a moment question the advantage an American may claim by crossing here, but I thank God we have no German universities among us.[49]

↠ *William Emerson to Charles Chauncy Emerson, 25 July 1824*

My letter will probably reach you during your first college vacation. As Waldo and Edward are at your side, and to a young gentleman of 16 with your previous education the goads of ambition and conscience can by no means be powerless, it might perhaps be superfluous for me to do more than bid you God speed. But I cannot forget that I have spent 4 years at college, and have suffered deeply, irrecoverably for having tread under foot the pearls that were cast before me; and I often think that could you have a history of the past ten years of my life, you would need no other beacon to guide you safely through these perilous waters.

You would see how blindly and childishly my hours were thrown away, how thereby my moral sense became blunted, till I fell into a deep slumber, intellectual and moral, how gradually and painfully I awake from this lethargy by the strings of shame and demured neglect;—awoke, to find those, who a few years before, were my inferiors had now left me far behind, and to feel how low I had sunk in my own esteem, you would see too how slow and toilsome have been my steps towards the point, which it would not have been hard to march unclogged with the burdens of years of folly.—Yet perhaps it might not be necessary for your safety. You are older—your understanding is riper—and your pride & your ambition, though experience and years will verify them may still keep you from low debasement. One thing however, you will allow me to say—I will say—not from myself alone, but from the experience of all history[50]—You will perhaps think all this too serious—perhaps—but I hope not, you will think it common place morality, the advice which an elder brother makes it a matter of course to give to a younger—and will have on your life.

> Do not as some ungracious pastors do
> Show me the steep and thorny way to heaven
> While like a puffed and reckless libertine
> Himself the primrose path of dalliance treads
> And reaks not his own rede.[51]

No—it is because mine has been no primrose path that I earnestly beg you as you love me, and as you love yourself, to copy the lines I have underscored. Amulets we leave to the Orientals; but use the paper as a mark in the book you are reading, think of it often; the experience of every day will verify it.—As for the rank you will hold in your class, you know where my hopes would place you, yet it would be far less for the honour than for the mental development which would necessarily attend it.—I hope.[52]

William also wrote about his doings to friends at home, including John Fessenden, his Harvard College roommate, to whom he reported on 8 August that "my mind seems to have undergone a revolution that surprizes myself," much of which he traced "to the books and lectures of Eichhorn." He continued

I suppose that you are already acquainted with the leading principles of his theology, and therefore I will not attempt to give them here. But his whole manner, and conversation, and mode of life, are interesting and remarkable. He is a venerable old man of 75, with all the vivacity and politeness of youth. He is below the common stature; and when he enters the lecture room in his old-fashioned light-gray coat, and buckled shoes, his white hair combed back from his forehead, there is at once such venerable dignity; and such childlike simplicity in his appearance, you know not whether most to love or to respect him. In his lectures, as in his conversation, one who has heard him, whatever he may think of the justness of his views, cannot fail to believe him perfectly honest and frank. His ideas are almost universally clear and distinct, and he has the faculty of giving them such a simplicity as to be easily intelligible. His delivery is entirely destitute of grace or eloquence, but is animated by his colloquial familiarity both in the tone of his voice and the language he employs, and by the deep personal interest he feels in his subject; as when in his illustration of a chapter he translates a question and answer—he passes instantaneously in manner and tone from his conception of the feelings and ideas of the questioner, to those of him who answers & thus communicates a dramatic interest to what we sober Americans are accustomed to read straight forward with un-changing gravity. He has always been a very hard student, and even at this advanced age he continues to study and to write as unremittingly as ever. Go when I will to see him, I am sure to find him among his books; and he told me the other day that if he should live long enough, he hoped yet to add a volume of a general character to his Introduction to the New Testament. He still reads lectures 3 hours every day. His private life is amiable, and he is popular with professors and students. He has not been sufficiently a timeserver, to be in much honour with the ruling powers; and thence it is thought he has little influence in the administration of the University. I have no desire to conceal my own high admiration of this great man. And I cannot but consider myself as very happy in being permitted to visit Göttingen while he yet lives.[53]

However, most of his letters were sent to family.

⤙ *William Emerson to Ralph Waldo Emerson, 15 August 1824*

You will judge that I am at least in earnest in my endeavour to cor-rect my errours of a literary kind, when I tell you, that I sacredly devote 2 hours every day to writing English. I must confess, that including the hours when I receive lessons or hear lectures, I am hardly ever able to make out more than 12 hours of study in a day. . . . I have an exact ac-

count of the expenditure of every cent. since I left home. Since I have
touched upon this, I will mention one or two circumstances to show you
that I am not wanting in efforts to be economical. An old pair of clothes
which I took to wear on board the vessel, and the boots which were
made a month or two before I left home, I have still in daily wear. Wine
or beer with my dinner would have been expensive—I have therefore
drank water; and finding that rye bread was cheaper than wheat, my constant breakfast is coffee and rye-bread without butter. I should not mention these trifles,—it were contemptible to think them sacrifices—but to
show you I am not forgetful that in the reciprocal circumstances in which
you and I stand, the strictest economy is my sacred duty; and although
my draughts on the banker have been perhaps more frequent than you
expected, they have not been made thoughtlessly or needlessly. I enclose
a summary of my draughts up to this date.[54]

➤ William Emerson to Ruth Haskins Emerson, 13–15 September 1824

. . . And now what shall I tell you about, that you will care to hear? My
fancy and my letters ought in duty to take a professional turn, and so I
shall discourse of churches and ceremonies and priests. Yet if I confine
myself to what I have seen, I shall talk but little of religion, for I have
hardly seen any of it in Europe.—The manner of keeping the Sabbath
has interested me very much. In Ireland it is much better kept than on
the continent. Yet in Dublin, though the churches were full at 12 o'clock
the alehouses were full at 2. On no day were the streets of that fine city
so crowded and so gay. A large portion of the shops, though not those of
the Protestants, were open immediately after noon service. Perhaps you
will be curious to know whether among a quarter of a million people,
in the metropolis of a populous kingdom, and the seat of a celebrated
university, the style of preaching be not something far beyond what we
of the west can have a notion of. It was far—very far below what we are
accustomed to in Boston. I wandered from high to low, from the venerable cathedral of St. Patrick's to the Denmark St Chapel of the miserable
Catholics, and sought out those that were most commended, but I heard
only two tolerable preachers. One was a clergyman of the establishment,
simple, earnest, polished—the other was a Wesleyan Methodist, whose
audience was principally composed of poor sailors, and he poured forth
his piety in so warm and logical an appeal to their understanding and
their conscience, and then setting the tune himself, he so led in their
praises as well as their prayers, that he almost made me a Wesleyan Methodist too. But from the numerous other preachers whom I followed, I
heard tame and vapid performances, words without thought, and form

without religion.—At the ordinary where I dined, was an archdeacon from the neighborhood of Dublin. I felt much interested in one who bore the same title with Paley.[55] But I had not conversed with him 15 minutes, before I found that he swore great oaths, and "had been to the play an hundred times, though he supposed it was not exactly right." So much for his morals—now I must give you a specimen of his intelligence. He related to me one Sunday as one of the most marvellous events of his life, that he had that day heard two sermons from different clergymen, on the same text. Learning that I came from Boston, he wanted to know if I came by way of Cuba—with other questions that betrayed equal sagacity. This was the first European ecclesiastic with whom I became acquainted.—But to return to the public service of religion. In the paltry houses where the wretched Catholics assemble—there was deplorable poverty, both of intellect and filthy lucre. This were worthy of all pity, if it were not accompanied by a ridiculous effort to retain the 'pomp and circumstance' of ancient popery. The painted altars and patched lawn were laughable enough, and yet I could not but grieve over this magnificence in rags. At the doors of one of these chapels were people selling strings of beads, pictures of the Saints and of others on glass, little tin boxes for consecration salt, crosses, &c. One of them offered me a miserable daub, which he called the heart of our Lord Jesus Christ.—A striking contrast to much of this I found in Notre Dame in Paris. Here was a most venerable and ancient cathedral—kings and queens had worshipped here, and the chancel was rich in works of geniuses, bestowed by these great ones of the earth.—There was no lack of gold, and fancy sculptured marble. The choir was filled with friars in appropriate garb, chaunting the offices of the day—and the priests splendidly arrayed stood at the altar. But wherefore was all this? Some 20 or 30 of the laity were there to hear (yet this was Sunday); while the coarsely raftered chapel in Denmark St was every Sabbath thronged by the poor devotees, kneeling on the cold stone, and cheerfully contributing a pittance, wrung from their necessities, for the repairs and tawdry ornaments of their place of worship.—The day which I spent at Aix-la-Chapelle happened to be a high festival of the holy church—and I went to hear mass in a cathedral, the central part of which was built a thousand years ago by the emperor Charlemagne.[56] His ashes still rest below. They showed me the marble chair upon which the body was formerly seated and in which, since it was taken from the tomb, 36 German emperors have been crowned.—I shall annoy you with no moralizing here, my dear mother, but simply tell you what I saw. The service was chaunted by a few monks in black cowl and hood, and the priests were assisted in the ceremonies by young boys dressed in scarlet. Every thing was there which could enhance the splendor of the ceremonial—one only excepted, and this was an audience. A few women and old men were kneeling in the shadow of the vast rich pillars, and crossing themselves and counting their beads.—From this church, called also Notre Dame, I went to another, (I believe, St. Catherine's) and this was sprucely painted, and appeared in much more favour with the devout than that in which emperors have been crowned. There were a great many in the church. The principal object of attention was an image of the Virgin, about as large as a girl of 12 or 15, dressed out completely in gown and hoop, as you have told me the ladies used to dress when you were young—only I believe the headdress was rather more modern. I suppose the doll was of wood, but could not get near enough to examine. It was seated upon the top of the altar, and the prayers and kneebendings seemed all directed towards it.[57]

On 16 September, William began a walking tour of Germany, meeting with Goethe in Weimar on 19 September. The meeting with the grand man of German letters was important for William (as we will see later), and he left this description of it in his journal:

We soon left Erfurt for Weimar, and I must forget all the scenery, to hurry forward to that, which rendered this an ever memorable day to me. . . . We arrived in the pleasant town of Weimar at noon, and I immediately repaired to his house, and sent up my card, on which I had previously added "Boston, N. America" to my name. He sent me word that he was then surrounded with company, but if I would call at 4, he would see me. It may be supposed, that I did not forget the appointment. I was shown into a room, that was filled with works of art. A huge bust of Minerva was placed over one of the doors.[58] A large case with books, which from their great size, must have been drawings, stood in one corner. Göthe, the gentle and venerable poet, entered almost immediately. I was so struck with the difference between him who came into the room, and the formidable portrait that is commonly to be seen of this great man, that I almost expected to see another person behind him. His address and manner were perfectly simple and unconstrained. After finding out my profession, he led the conversation immediately upon the state of religion in the U.S. and afterwards upon the state and hopes of our country in general. His tone became gradually that of an instructor, and yet it ceased not to be unassuming, but all was uttered quietly, as a mere private opinion. He said he thought we had nothing to do with the different systems of philosophy, but that the highest aim of life should be for each one to accommodate himself perfectly as possible to the station in which he was placed. He asked many questions, and talked willingly, yet seemed not loath to be interrupted. The only thing that was American in my possession, a number of the Palladium, I ventured to offer him, as our papers are a great curiosity in Germany. He accepted the trifle very graciously, and said it was 2 years since he had seen one. He shook me kindly by the hand when I took leave. I left Weimar immediately, but I shall not hastily forget this exceedingly interesting visit. He was of the common size, with pleasing and not striking features; his dress was a blue surtout, over a white vest, I should not have judged him to be more than 65, yet he is said to be about 10 years older.[59]

William returned to Göttingen on 9 October, where he again took up his studies.

⤛ William Emerson to Ruth Haskins Emerson, 15 December 1824

As I am here in a strange land, where my eyes are continually met by sights, and my ears by sounds, widely different from those to which I have been accustomed, it is natural enough that I should note some of the most peculiar. But the more I have done this, the more unwilling have I been to rest in insulated facts, and have therefore extended my inquiries to the leading features of German character. So now for No. 1. It may possibly contribute to your amusement; if so, my purpose is attained.—One of the most striking circumstances to a stranger is the mild and quiet disposition of the people. Every man, woman and child seem to have fallen 'just in the niche they were ordained to fill,'[60] and all the operations of society proceed with an evenness and noiselessness which would be inconceivable to the bustles of N. York or Boston. In obedience to a law as uniform and silent as that which governs the motion of the planets, a fixed hour brings the German artisan or trader to his shop, the professor to his study, the student, pipe in mouth, to the window-sill, to look upon vacancy. With the return of a Sabbath, or a festival, a certain change takes place in the dress and place of resort. Political and commercial and literary vicissitudes produce no sensible fluctuation on the surface of character; and when these are powerless, we cannot expect that such ordinary occurances as marriages and deaths should very strongly affect the feelings. Accordingly it is not uncommon to conclude the pathetic newspaper account of the decease of husband or father, (which is here generally inserted as a sort of card, signed by the nearest surviving relatives,) by a notice that business is continued as usual, and a request for further favors from customers.

A man died in Göttingen a few weeks since in the vigour of life. The day after the funeral, I saw the widow with 2 or 3 of her female friends in the garden where I live, hiding her anguish under a calm, and even very cheerful countenance. Indeed they all seem fairly to realize that 'All the world's a stage, and all the men and women merely players';[61] accordingly they sing when at church, and cry bitterly at a funeral or at parting with a friend, because this is the proper scene for singing or weeping; but the next hour finds them in another act of the play, and they are buying or selling or smoking with their usual serenity.—I will relate an anecdote that seems to belong here. A vessel in its passage down the Elbe, ran afoul of one of the floating-mills, that are numerous on that river. The shock was so violent, that the floating-mill instantly parted from her moorings, and drifted rapidly towards the bank. It seemed impossible to prevent her striking the shore, and that must be attended by the total ruin of the machinery. Had the people on board been Americans, or English, it can be imagined what confusion and bellowing and bustle would have taken place. None of this from these noiseless Germans. Not a word was spoken. Each one knew the measures that alone could save their boat. They were immediately taken, and the machinery was saved.

I know not whether it be attributable to this quiet, contented disposition, or to the peculiarity of their climate, but this people is assuredly the least cleanly I ever saw. This is particularly true of the lowest order, but is not inapplicable to the highest. Even in the best houses, the knife and fork are never wiped during dinner, however numerous the dishes, and you must put your fingers into the sugar-bowl. (But these are also French customs.) The worst houses I need not attempt to describe. The inns furnish a pretty just criterion of a neighborhood—and in the villages and small towns, such abodes of filth, and flies, and darkness! It were purgatory enough for an epicure to be obliged to sojourn, only for a short time, among the 'golden lions' &c of Germany.[62] In matter of food, the traveller is safest who calls only for bread and beer; often he could get nothing else if he would. He is fortunate if his sour brown bread have not a fair proportion of sand, and the beer—is different from any liquor known in N. England. And if any luckless traveller be constrained to lodge in a place without city walls and privileges, he must fain content him with Hottentot accommodation.[63]—Out of doors, if there is a puddle to be seen, the children are sure to be paddling in it. This custom is indeed by no means confined to the rustic urchins. I see almost every day the future burghers of Göttingen washing themselves in the gutter, wading in it, spattering one another with it. It appears to be something innate; they take to the gutter as naturally as the ducks.—One walk through the market, where the peasant women sit with their baskets full of the various articles destined to be eaten and drunk, would furnish many particulars that one would be glad to forget. Even as to ordinary features of dress and person,

I could not easily credit all I have heard, nor could you all that I have seen. But these are no inviting topics, and I know you will pardon my entering into further details.

Something much more agreeable is the universal taste for music. Instrumental music in particular is carried to very high perfection. Pianofortes and organs are to be found even in the houses of common mechanics, who can hardly command the comforts of life. Nor do females alone perform on them. One of my first acquaintances was a theological professor, who has a fine instrument in his study. They are also in the rooms of many students.—Though the Germans confessedly are not to be compared with the Italians for vocal music, yet the taste for it is strikingly prevalent. Whether it be a cause or a consequence of this taste I leave others to decide, but it is noticeable, that in every village school, whatever else may be taught or omitted, the teacher must instruct in psalm-singing. So everybody knows how to sing. The students often make the streets ring with their boisterous music. Even the children intermix regular songs with their holiday sports;—and I have often been pleased to hear a joyous concert from a party of mechanics, going home from their day's work in Göttingen, to some of the neighboring villages.—

One who is well and happy has nothing to say of himself; so I will only beg you, my dear mother, to give my love to my brothers, and to any that are kind enough to remember me, and then bid you a very good night.[64]

William did more than send accounts of his education and travels home to his family: he also kept himself involved in the continuing family dialogue over occupations and money. Waldo wrote on 12 September 1824 that, as a result of the plans that he and Edward were making, William had better "be sure when you come back you be licensed to preach since for dear poverty's sake we must be frugal of time," and "Edward smitten to the bowels with ambition," planned to study law. Waldo himself plans to surrender the school he had inherited from William, and he assures William that he has thus far not at all been "incommoded" by his financial demands (L, 1:149). William wrote Waldo and Edward that he considered the plan a "bold" one, wished them "success," and "rejoice[d] that you are rushing to jail in such good spirits." Had he "dreamed of such a revolution when at home," William says, he "should as soon have gone to Greenland as to Göttingen."[65]

On 18 January 1825, Waldo wrote that he had "cast my bread on the waters, locked up my school, and affect the scholar at home" (L, 1:158). Edward sent a letter elaborating on his decision to study law:

For having devoted myself to that profession which is solely occupied in the quest after naked Truth, which is renowned & justly for its down-

right honesty, (you cannot but perceive, I speak of *Law*), it behooves me
to learn early, how to set forth in order an unvarnished tale, & to adhere
to simple *facts*.—But I w^d tell you by the way, that in choosing my path,
I neither allowed myself to think, as you seemed in your letter to expect
that I should, whether in *this*, I should "rise higher," or in "that, *sooner*
attain *distinction*," but I briefly reasoned thus: I am not hardy enough
for a physician, not grave enough for a divine, not lyrical enough for
a lawyer; but diligent enough for either I can be, & diligence is more
competent to supply the want of logic, than it is to make me a grave
or a robust man. Therefore, I will be a lawyer. This I said, months
ago, to myself, & ever since have been more & more confirmed in my
resolution; but I am only *published*, not *married*;[66] and if you have any
thing to offer against the match, why urge it, & if the advice be not
followed, it will be very well received, yes & very gladly if it cometh in
the shape of a letter from you in Europe.[67]

In a similar brotherly fashion, William gave advice to Charles at the same
time as he was sketching student life:

I have to thank you for a very welcome letter, and for something
which cost you more labor than that, a prize poem.[68] And now, Charles
—for new honours,—in themselves they are nothing, but they are the
accompaniments of something real and valuable—desert.

> Keep then the path!
> For emulation hath a thousand sons,[69]

and you know the rest.
If I mistake not, you have been in your day a votary of Hermes as well
as of the Muses,[70] so I am fain to tell you of the overthrow of his altars in
this land of smokers. Eloquence is indeed as completely thrust out of the
German circles, as the free political institutions which elsewhere give it
existence and power. The eloquence of the senate cannot exist, because
there are no free legislative bodies. There can be no eloquence of the bar,
because the processes are all conducted privately and chiefly in writing.
But you will say, one asylum was surely left for it, and when proscribed
in the courts, it might yet have fled to the temple. Alas! even the Altar has
lost its ancient power of sheltering the proscribed. Whether the want of
eloquence in the clergy has thinned the churches, or the fewness of the
worshippers has chilled the enthusiasm of the clergy, I will not decide.
The fact is undeniable, that the house of God is almost deserted, the
preachers without influence or energy.—But do not the professors ex-

hibit models of chaste and harmonious language, adorned by an elegant delivery? Not in a single instance that has come to my knowledge. One is almost led to imagine, from the style in which their lucubrations are communicated to their hearers, that there is a strife among them to see which can make his delivery most unnatural and unpleasing.—The mention of the professors suggests a promise made in a previous letter, to give you some further account of Göttingen university; as the other universities of Germany are on a plan perfectly similar, you may perhaps obtain from what follows some general idea of German views of education.—To begin then with the professors.—There are different ranks among them. They are at first only 'Professores extraordinarii,' with little or no salary from the university. As they become more distinguished, they are advanced to the rank of 'Professores ordinerii'—then they receive successively, as a sort of retaining fee, the honorary titles of Hofrath—Justicrath—Geheimer-rath (There are many other kinds of Raths—and most unluckily for an English ear they are pronounced without the h.—so that I suppose my witty cousin the sophomore will think an 'Universitäts-Rath' a fair mark for a jest.)—in some few cases.—Ritter—which are perfectly untranslateable—and last of all, one or two in a century arrive at the ultimum of a German notion of earthly bliss, in the permission to set 'von' before their name. For the key to all this is what I have told you before, that the Germans are title-mad. With this increase of honour, the salary waxes too; though the larger part of a professor's income arises from the fees he receives of those who attend his lectures.—You are now let completely behind the scenes; and there is hardly a circumstance I can mention, which you will be at a loss to explain. You perceive that the professors act—which means, sit still—and study, under the constant stimulus of ambition of all kinds, and of love of money—which at first is honest hunger, and afterwards often becomes downright avarice.

Their treatment of the students is in general strikingly polite; but you will remember that they are dependant upon the good opinion of the latter individually for the larger part of their salary, and it is hardly to be wondered at, that they neither exert, nor attempt to exert, any useful influence over them.—Their lectures are full of scientific matter, in which all the propositions are arranged with military precision. On the other hand, as I just now suggested, they have no conception of a pleasing and graceful delivery; their voices, probably from their mode of life, are very bad, their manner often disagreeable even to the point of disgust. But this is not the worst. Not a glimpse of the sunlight of genuine eloquence, not a ray of pure, cordial, human feeling or moral sublimity enlivens, even for a moment. Their lectures seem to me like the botanist's flowers—not his withered, colourless stems and stalks,—that were very unjust—but like his most delicately executed coloured engravings, with calyx and corolla to a hair; and the colours most dexterously imitated; but they want the freshness and fragrance and life of the heath and the valley.—*Literary* labor, too, has come to be as minutely divided as *mechanical,* and the advantage in both cases is similar—the more rapid progress of discovery; yet the disadvantage also arises, that subordinate departments of study are elevated to an unmerited degree of importance, and one science is dissected into several, to furnish as many professors with a livelihood.— Most of these literati despise dress—and some of them, decency.—They are rarely seen abroad—still more rarely at church. And to finish with these learned gentlemen, there is an incredible deal of hatred and envy among them, which they often take no pains to conceal; and the greatest of rank, while they keep the professors diligent, produce at the same time a supercilious spirit in the more distinguished, and proportionate jealousy and illwill in the rest. And so they laugh at each other, abuse each other, and emulously throw obstacles in each other's way, to the great edification of their pupils.

The most striking circumstance in the situation of these latter, is their almost unlimited freedom. Their duty consists simply in taking notes of the lectures; but no bills of absences are kept, and as they live in what part of the city they please, and need not, unless they choose, have the slightest intercourse with the professors, it is not surprising that there are many, who do not attend any lectures, and whose liberty becomes licentiousness.—But the large majority are certainly diligent, in their own way; and this is, they attend 6, and even more courses of lectures every semester, (which occupies that number of hours every day,) and all they hear they write off with untiring and undiscriminating zeal. But out of the lecture room their conscience is clear; and I sincerely believe the majority do not read anything worth naming. You perceive this mode of acquiring an education must have this good consequence, that daily listening to the results of the most patient and persevering study of men, who have devoted their whole life, in many instances a very long one, to the particular science they teach—that this can hardly fail of giving them the most correct views of the subject discussed,—and this ill consequence, that the prime end of education, the development of the powers of the human mind, is entirely lost sight of, and the student often becomes a mere copyist; he has no practical exercises—he receives slavishly the dictata of his teachers.

The relation in which the students stand to each other is necessarily wide of that which exists in our colleges, since there are no classes, no literary distinctions; and thus, on the one hand, envy is extinguished, it is true; but on the other, there is no play for a noble and quickening emulation. The chief source of friendly connexion among them is the territorial division of Germany, by which every one appertains to a certain 'Landsmannschaft,' and with this connexion inherits certain friendships and enmities. Thence arise a large portion of those contemptible duels, which are the scandal of the German universities.—Of these I have told you before. Another bond of union is the secret societies, whose objects are political. These have been very quiet for a year or two; but ever since I have been here, such a one was discovered in a Prussian university (Halle), and one third of the students expelled in consequence—report said, 3 were sent as state-prisoners to the fortress at Magdeburg.

Of their manners and dress I have before told you more than you can admire. Of their studies, what I have just said will give you some idea; and now—one word of their amusements.—Smoking is by no means to be reckoned one; that is as much a necessary of life with them as their food. But music of all kinds—a walk on Sunday—or, if rich enough, a ride 6 or 8 together, in a large, open, dirty basket, put on 4 wheels, and drawn by 2 horses, that are harnessed to the vehicle by ropes—playing at nine pins ½ an afternoon, and at billiards of an evening—visits to the gardens just outside the city and to the villages at some distance, where the weary and thirsty refresh themselves with incredible quantities of bad wine and worse beer—these constitute the chief amusements of the future lights of Germany.

Consider this, my dear Charles, as I do, as a very imperfect sketch of the prominent points in these universities. You perceive that like all human institutions, they contain mingled good and evil. To compare them in general with our own—We read, and the Germans write. Among them, the professors must study, & thus great literati are formed; among us, the scholars—and thus useful men are formed. And so we may compare the different modes of education to the different genius of European and American governments. Theirs, elevates the few—ours refines and ennobles the many. Indeed I think we of the new world must appropriate the words of the English poet, and say of European institutions,

> Of old things all are over old,
> Of good things none are good enough;
> We'll show that we can help to frame
> A world of other stuff.[71]

To his mother, he reported on his final days at Göttingen:

I set out tomorrow morning early for the South, and my last moments here I cannot otherwise spend than in writing to you. The time that I have passed here has seemed long, I must confess. I am aware, that in a professional point of view it would be highly advantageous to me could I prolong it. But as far as my heart is concerned, I leave Göttingen without one moment's regret. You will know the hopes I had formed of great intellectual improvement to result from coming here. If I have not fully realized these, it is not the fault of my opportunities nor of my efforts. In the endeavour to be extreme, my diligence has often been injudicious. And though I believe and hope that mind and heart have made some progress, I am forced, without affectation, to lament that it has been so little.—I write this because I desire that you should know how I looked upon the experiment, which I consider myself to have been making for the common good of my brothers and myself, in case any outward accident should befall me in the next few months. In any event, I shall not have so convenient opportunities of communicating with you by letter as from Göttingen. . . .

. . . . Among the papers that I send Waldo will be interested in some of the Notes on Eichhorn's lectures,[72] which he will be good enough to treasure as choice gold for me.[73]

William chose not to get a degree, even though he had completed his course of study, because he did not see it as important. Earlier, on 27 June 1824, he had written to Edward about the possibility of his obtaining a master's degree from Harvard, which then granted the degree a short time after the A.B. was earned by paying a small fee and without taking additional classes: "I leave it entirely to you and Waldo to determine whether you will send me a diploma of A.M. or not, to enable me to become Dr. here. The Germans are so title-mad, that it would much increase their respect for me, but I am personally, I believe, wholly indifferent about it."[74] Waldo wrote in November 1824 that "I shall try to get & send [the degree] immediately" (L, 1:152).[75]

Bancroft, who did receive his doctor of philosophy degree from Göttingen, wrote to a friend at home that "if you wish to be made Doctor of Theology at Göttingen I can present the work [your book] to the faculty, which will be followed on their part by a Doctor's Diploma. It is only to be observed, that these divines are accustomed to receive thirty guineas for the distinction."[76] Cogswell, on the other hand, received the doctor's degree without taking examinations.[77] Calvert declined the honor but spoke frankly of the process, which began when a professor suggested that he take a doctor of philosophy degree: "'Is it so easy to be obtained?' I asked. 'Nothing easier. You have only to choose one of the subjects on which you have heard lectures with me—public law, for instance—and I will prepare you in three weeks to pass the examination. I guarantee your honorable passage through. The most puzzling question that will be asked you will be: 'Have you, sir, in your pocket, thirteen Louis d'ors for the university treasurer?'"[78] William too declined the honor: "I might have had the Doctorate of Philosophy at Göttingen, but it would have cost me 60 Dollars, which I thought too much for the whistle."[79]

William left Göttingen on 30 March and, as was typical of student travelers then as now, took advantage of his trip back home to see some of Europe. He traveled to Milan by way of Frankfurt, Heidelberg, Strasbourg, and Zürich, arriving on 19 April. From Milan he crossed the Apennines, visiting Lodi, Piacenza, Parma, Madonna, Bologna, and Florence, before arriving in Rome in early June. He left Rome on the 15th and on the 22d arrived in Genoa by way of Sienna and Pisa. Then back to Milan, over the Simplon Pass on the way to Geneva, and to Paris, where William arrived on 15 July. From Paris he crossed the English Channel to Dover, arriving there on 2 August. The next day he was in London, where he spent more than two weeks. After visiting Oxford, William sailed from Liverpool in the *Courier* on 29 August, reaching Boston in mid-October.

⤞ *William Emerson to Ruth Haskins Emerson, 18 August 1825*

[London]

'But you are in England, what do you think of our cousins the English? Are they noble or debased, energetic or dissipated, pusillanimous or manly, rude or civil?'[80] They are all these at once. The rest of Europe seems asleep; England is awake in its manhood; and here therefore, the play of all the powers and passions of life is quick and strong. Servility and pride, villainy & virtue, religion and infidelity, benevolence and rapacity, have each their sphere, and each in turn is lord of the ascendant. They exhibit the greatest medley of contradictions; There is no crime that cannot be said to disgrace their character—no virtue that does not adorn it.—London is a city infinitely more moral and more Christian than Paris, yet throughout the French capital you cannot find any thing like the daubs that are daily publicly shown at Carlile's shop-window, in one of the busiest streets of London, in ridicule and gross caricature of the Supreme Being. I could enumerate many more circumstances equally at variance with all probability—but I have no time now.[81]

⤞ *William Emerson to Ruth Haskins Emerson, 28 August [1825]*

[Liverpool]

And now, dear mother, I am bidding farewell to Europe, and hardest of all, to England. Do you think that I am shedding tears at the thought? If I shed any, they will be tears of joy that I am returning to you. But only if it were a continuance of my wanderings, and were I merely about to exchange one foreign country for another, I have now become so accustomed to the traveller's traces, that I have acquired a sort of recklessness of circumstances & change, and pass in cool blood from scenes of pleasure and interest to matters of business, from the market or the courthouse to the theatre or the banker's compting room, and aunt M's. ancient prophecies of my want of sensibility are becoming fearfully realized by the levelling influence of the constant excitement. A traveller's head is too much like that of an intoxicated man. The nerves of both are excited by a stimulus more powerful than the system is able to bear, and the effect upon both is the same—the overwrought spirits must flag, and the poor creature reels along, insensible and indifferent. Now don't for a moment imagine, that I am inventing consolation for myself. I am quite sincere in my complaint against hard travelling. And even while I inveigh against it, I confess that the parallel might be run still further; for the worshipper of Bacchus cannot find the wine more pleasant to behold,[82] or sweeter to his taste, than is travelling to me. But calmly laying aside the love of motion on the one hand, and the love of home on the other, reason and judgment would hasten me home. Travelling is no occupation for a man, who is not scientific enough to benefit the world by his perigrinations, and who hopes there may yet be some niche which he can usefully and honorably fill.[83]

The trip home was a horrifying one, and one that struck William's religious sensibilities to the quick, as he described it upon his return to Mary Moody Emerson:

↠ *William Emerson to Mary Moody Emerson, 27 October* [1825]

[Cambridge, Mass.]

Mother says, and affection whispers, that you will take pleasure in hearing that I am at home. I had a long and tempestuous passage over the great waters. The winds blew so fearfully, and the waves made sometimes such mocking sport of our ship, that I was more than once compelled to sit down in the cabin, and tranquilly to make up what I deemed my last accounts with the world. I was obliged to look nearly at eternity, for death seemed to ride upon the gale that was bending the masts, and to howl in the waves that chased the vessel, as if to devour it—and it was with a strange modification of feelings which I know not well how to define, that at such times I climbed the gangway-stairs, and peered out upon the storm—

> And looked upon the sky and main,
> As things I ne'er might see again.

Even when the rage of the tempest had subsided, & I could stand calmly on deck, and survey the wide field of ocean, I used to think the exulting bouyancy of spirit, and pride in the skill of man in passing these trackless waters not so natural an emotion, as a sense of diminutiveness in the contrast between man's feebleness and the might of the element on which he is tossed, and of desolateness in the cold and dreary solitude of this watery desert.

Yet the sea bestows moments of high-wrought gratification—sometimes, at sunrising, when the clouds are soft and light, and tinged with brilliant and changeful hues, and the sun springs from his briny couch so suddenly, as to recal the poetical pictures of the ancient mythology—while the surface of the deep is here and there agitated by the heavy black-fish protruding themselves awkwardly into the light and air, and shoals of porpoises are snorting and puffing around you—and even at the distance of hundreds of miles from land, the little blackish birds, which the sailors call Mother Cary's chickens, will be seen skimming along, with untired wing in the vessel's wake. And sometimes too, when the mind can divest itself of those personal fears which lower the dignity and poison the happiness of man, it is a proud thing to stand and behold the terrible spirit of storms, gathering up his awful energies, urging on the fierce billows, and cresting them with foam, and careering in his might on the hurricane. I would tell you also of the white foam that eddies about the ship, as she dashes through the water, and of the beautiful phosphoric sparklings in the sea, as you lean over the vessel's side in the darkness of the evening.[84]

When William sat in his cabin to "tranquilly . . . make up what I deemed my last accounts with the world," he was thinking back to his meeting with Goethe. His rather bland notebook account of the meeting (Goethe "said he thought we had nothing to do with the different systems of philosophy, but that the highest aim of life should be for each one to accommodate himself perfectly as possible to the station in which he was placed") did not fully explain the circumstances. William seems to have been disturbed by the questions that had been raised during his theological training in Göttingen, and hoped that Goethe would be able to help him. Goethe's advice was not what William expected—or perhaps wanted—to hear; as Waldo's daughter Ellen later described it: "Goethe unhesitatingly told him . . . that he could preach to the people what they wanted; his personal belief was no business of theirs; he could be a good preacher and a good pastor and no one need ever know what he himself had for his own private views." When William came home to America, he went to Chelmsford, where Waldo was keeping a school, to tell him that "on the voyage home there was a great storm, and in that storm he felt that he could not go to the bottom in peace with the intention in his heart of following the advice that Goethe had given him." When he realized the ship had been spared, William "renounced the ministry" and came home to begin the study of law. In later years, when Waldo told this story to Ellen, he commented that "Your Uncle William never seemed to me so great as he did that day."[85]

William never regretted his decision to leave the ministry, a decision that, ironically, he came to while he was in Göttingen training for the ministry. On 4 April 1830, after having established his law practice in New York, he replied to a theological query from his uncle Ezra Ripley in this fashion:

> Your very kind & much valued letter of the 12th ultimo lies before me, & I take with pleasure this first opportunity of leisure to write in acknowledgment—I say, in acknowledgment—not in reply; for my habits & studies have for several years been so far from theological, that I think it not right to try to answer the grave & powerful argument of your letter, in favour of attendance on the communion, till I shall have time to enter minutely & thoroughly into an investigation of the whole subject. I admire without reserve, that the authority of St. Paul, as stated by you, seems to me to favour the views you cherish of the supper more than I was before aware. Yet altho' I waive all argument at the present moment, both from personal respect to you & regard to the importance of the subject, yet I will not omit to assent most cordially to the following sentiment contained in your letter—"we, at this period, are as much obliged to love & obey Jesus Christ for what he is, & what he has done for us, as were the apostles & primitive disciples." It is by no means *here* that my doubt exists. But my question is, whether the external ceremonies of the communion table are at this day binding & important. To whatever conclusion I may arrive on this topic, I cannot feel otherwise than much obliged to you, Sir, for the kindness which suggested & pervades your letter.[86]

Chapter 3

Edward and Charles

*W*riting to Lidian after his brother Charles's death on 9 May 1836, Waldo lamented the literal and figurative darkness that had descended on his world. One of the greatest joys of his life, he told her, was that he "saw" the world through his brother's eyes, so that now, with Charles gone, he felt his own sight and imagination had grown irreparably "dim." What is more, he thought, "[a] soul is gone so costly & so rare" that no one could ever fix the price of its loss or repair the loneliness that he would now forever feel. With "the immense promise of [Charles's] maturity . . . destroyed," Waldo confessed to his wife, "I feel not only unfastened . . . and adrift," "but a sort of shame at living at all" (12 May 1836, *L*, 2:19–20).

The catastrophe that Charles's death represented for all surviving members of the Emerson family and Waldo's own sense of loss, which was sufficiently profound to shame him at the thought of still being alive, had an extended foreground. The family's catastrophe and Waldo's descent into the darkness—described to Lidian in 1836—have their origin in Edward Bliss Emerson's physical and mental breakdown of 1828, and, before reaching their most intense point in the aftermath of Charles's death, they continued like the rising pitch of a wail through the beginning of Edward's exile to the Caribbean in 1830, Ellen Tucker Emerson's death from tuberculosis in 1831, and Edward's death in 1834. Although he had no way of knowing the terrible precedent his language was setting as a succinct characterization of the way that health would affect her sons' individual and fraternal fortunes over the next eight years, after receiving the first details of Edward's breakdown, William sent a letter to Ruth Haskins Emerson, writing, "We have known something of affliction before, but to your sons, my dear mother, . . . this is the bitterest cup it has been our lot to drink."[1]

Excepting particular details having to do with their respective personalities, the stories of Edward and Charles are in essence a single story, and in terms of Emerson family history, their story anticipates one more exceedingly sad chapter in the family's life—the death of Waldo's five-year old son and namesake in January 1842. As their academic records at Harvard suggest, Edward and Charles were truly "the best and the brightest" of the Emerson brothers, but their intellectual and initial professional achievements did not come without a heavy cost to themselves and their family. In the case of Edward, who had been the most physically frail of all the brothers for most of his life, a maniacal tendency to over study in order to secure academic laurels, combined with his single-minded mature resistance to the darker strains of Calvinist piety as taught by Mary Moody Emerson, foreshadowed his predisposition to read excessively and work outrageously long hours in order to achieve a reputation in that most secular of realms, the practice of the law. Although he eventually fell victim to tuberculosis, there is no doubt that Edward's manic behavior from the moment he entered school contributed to the physical and mental distress that brought about his premature death. In letters that follow, everyone—from William, Waldo, and Charles to mother Ruth and step-grandfather Ezra Ripley—acknowledges the connections among Edward's "careerism" (as we might think of it in today's terms), his weakened constitution, and his inability to withstand the debilitating effects of consumption. In the case of Charles, who would also eventually fall victim to tuberculosis, a predisposition to depression, world-weariness, and self-doubt always suffered alone or in his extensive confessional correspondence with Aunt Mary and Elizabeth Sherman Hoar facilitated the physical decline that led to his own demise. The difference between Charles's death and Edward's, and what made Charles's death virtually impossible not only for Waldo, but for all in the family to bear, is that no one really saw it coming. Still, there is no doubt that just as Edward's academic and professional behavior contributed to his end, so too Charles's tortured psyche contributed to his.

EDWARD, "THE BLISS BOY"

Edward's breakdown in May 1828 completely unnerved the family, which for several months had already been undergoing a series of health-related trials. As sobering reminders of the relatively recent health crises that had forced Edward to take refuge in Europe from October 1825 to October 1826 and Waldo in Charleston, South Carolina, and St. Augustine, Florida, during the winter of 1826–1827, in February 1828, both Edward and Waldo suffered from colds accompanied by headaches. Predictably, Edward ignored his illness and forced himself to continue his readings in the law in Boston "in the erect position," studying at an old red standing desk that Charles had given him in January,[2] whereas Waldo had the sense to spend a few weeks recuperating under his mother's care in Concord, where she was residing at the time. Charles, whose health was fine, remarked to his mother, "So you have persuaded Waldo that he is sick, in order to gratify him with a longer visit & kind attentions. I almost wish I could feel a little cold or head-ache creeping on me, that I might become an inmate of so desirable a Hospital."[3] However, the timing for such a quip could not have been worse, for although Charles continued in good health for the remainder of the winter, the family soon learned that William, who among the brothers had consistently enjoyed the most decent health, was himself ill at this time.

William's illness, which appears to have been a persistent cold and cough brought on and then exacerbated by overwork, created a stir of concern throughout the family, especially since he had not been forthcoming with details of it in any of his letters home. He had written to his mother about the translations of news from French and Spanish papers, reports of the proceedings of the New York City Common Council, and editorials that he had been preparing for the *Journal of Commerce*,[4] and through word of mouth she and his brothers knew that he was lecturing on "English Literature" before the New York Athenaeum at the Chapel of Columbia College—but William had said nothing to them about his health. By late April, when Waldo wrote to him, William was apparently on the mend, but the family was unaware of even this fact. Writing to his brother on 30 April 1828, Waldo told William, "I am very much disturbed, & so is mother, at the idea of your Sickness, and the more, because we have no confidence that you have recovered. Since you did not tell us when you were seriously sick, it may be that you are so now." He continued, unaware, of course, of how prophetic his words would soon turn out to be:

> You naughty boy how dare you work so hard? Have you forgotten that all the Emersons overdo themselves? Dont you die of the leprosy of your race—ill weaved ambition. Pah how it smells, I'll [have] none of it. Why here I am lounging on a system for these many months writing something less than a sermon a month for my main business,—all the rest of the time being devoted to needful recreation after such unparallelled exertions. And the consequence is—I begin to mend, and am said to look less like a monument & more like a man. I cant persuade that wilfull brother Edward of mine to use the same sovereign nostrum. If I have written but five lines & find a silly uneasiness in my chest or in my narvous system to use the genuine anile word . . . I escape from the writing desk as from a snake & go straight to quarter myself on the first person I can think of . . . who can afford to entertain me. . . . Especially

do I court laughing persons; and [when] after a merry or only a gossiping hour . . . I have lost all sense of the mouse in my chest, am at ease, & can take my pen or book." (L, 1:233)

On receiving Waldo's letter, William wrote to him and their mother on 13 May, assuring them that his health had been restored. He never addressed the extent to which he was prepared to take Waldo's advice on maintaining his health seriously, although certainly Ruth knew that none of her sons, including Waldo, who gave advice more readily than he followed it where his own health was concerned, were the sorts of men who would easily "court laughing persons" as a quick cure for their various maladies. In a letter carried to Concord by Ezra Ripley, who had been preaching and visiting relatives in New York, William assured everyone that there was no need for further concern about his health, advised Waldo, who had recently declined overtures and calls by several congregations that although his refusals had "establish[ed his] claim to a right dignified philosophy," additional refusals would cause prospective congregations to suspect him of vanity, and expressed his pleasure at learning firsthand from Dr. Ripley about Waldo's complete recovery from his winter illness.

> As my excellent grandfather intends going in an hour from this, I am unwilling that he should carry no letter to say that all concern about my health is quite unnecessary, & Waldo's good advice quite superfluous, & this for the best of reasons—that I am quite well now, & growing stronger every day. As the anxiety that Waldo's last letter indicated seemed to be a joint stock *concern,* & the letter itself to be the result of a coalition, I shall no doubt be excused for writing to both the kind & worthy members of the firm in one—particularly as I have not time for two letters. . . .
>
> You say something, dear Waldo, about going to Concord, N.H. for 6 weeks—& some thing more about refusing permanent engagements for 2 or 3 years. The former may be wise & agreeable, but I hold the latter to be downright martyrdom. Please to do no such thing—you have already refused enough to establish your claim to a right dignified philosophy, & I trust you will now make equally good your character for true wisdom, by not refusing or avoiding any offer that you like, from any vain notions of the necessity of delay. I rejoice that your health, voice & manner are improved so much as Grandfather assures me they are.[5]

Because he feared that Dr. Ripley's return to Concord by way of Albany, New York, would delay the good news about his health reaching the family, on 13 May William also sent his mother a brief note by post as a follow up to the letter he had written earlier in the day. He begged her, "[B]e persuaded, dear mother . . . that I am very well at present."[6] Yet, literally within days, whatever comfort Ruth or other members of the family may have taken from William's recovery was undone by the horrific events surrounding the onset of Edward's breakdown. For roughly two months, Edward, following his own devices, had chosen to remain outside of any discussion of most of the family's affairs. Indeed, he seemed to have become invisible for some weeks. Sometime in March, Charles wrote to his mother that he had seen Edward in Boston and that he appeared "well & in good spirits."[7] On 5 April, Edward hurriedly wrote a note to his mother, stating that he had "nothing to communicate, which the world calls *news*," and apologizing for the "clumsy, & crooked, & unsightly, & short . . . form & style" of his missive.[8] Because Edward often affected a cavalier and, at times, an almost cynical tone in his letters, Ruth was not alarmed by his tone in this note, nor did she or anyone else report anything amiss in Edward's appearance or behavior when he and Charles came out to Concord for a visit that began in early May. In hindsight, however, Edward's April note to his mother, together with a series of remarks he made in a letter to his brother William, would offer fair proof to everyone that Edward, who as a child referred to himself as Aunt Mary's "Bliss boy," was coming undone. Writing to William from Concord on 19 May, Edward called into question everything he had lived for, everything he had aspired to achieve and had committed himself to resist, for his entire adult life: "I read no law—almost no letters. I have ceased to resist GOD & nature; have consented to humor my body & rest my mind; & the consequence is that from the moment of surrender I have been gaining & tho feeble from the struggle of so many years, yet I am wiser, & *healthier* & happier than ever in my life. My prospect is now very distant but tolerably clear & bright."[9]

Biographers of Waldo, Mary Moody Emerson, and the Emerson family in general have always been able to write at length about Ellen's death, Charles's final illness and death, and little Waldo's death and to assess the impact these events exerted on all those who survived them. However, because the most important and revealing primary documents concerning Edward's and Charles's last years have only recently come to light in the larger body of fraternal correspondence with which we are concerned here, most Emerson family biographers have been forced to produce incomplete portraits of their subjects with respect to how, for instance, Edward and Charles reacted to their own and each other's illnesses or how Waldo, William, Ruth, or Aunt Mary interacted with Edward and Charles during the last years of each brother's life. We are in a position to be specific in our account of Edward's and Charles's last years, fill in a substantial amount of previously inaccessible detail concerning each brother's interactions with others in the larger Emerson familial sphere, and provide future biographers of Emerson family members with a more reliable understanding of how the lives and deaths of these two brothers informed and altered the course of the family's history.

While staying with his mother and step-grandfather Ripley at the Manse in Concord, Edward suffered a complete physical and mental collapse on 25 May. Because in his state of derangement Edward was not only prone to violence toward others but also, the family feared, might be prone to violence toward himself, within two days "watchers" from among the Emersons and Ripleys' local friends were called in to sit with him at the Manse day and night. When his condition was at its worst, two men were required to stay with him through the night. In addition to Ruth, Dr. Ripley, and other family members, Edward's "watchers" included Deacon Reuben Brown, attorney John Keyes (the father of John Shepard Keyes), local businessmen Major Samuel Burr and Colonel Daniel Shattuck, historian Lemuel Shattuck and his wife Clarissa, law students Zwingly Mellen and Bradley Stone, Waldo's Harvard classmate Nathaniel Wood, Edward Jarvis, and Dr. Josiah Bartlett, the local physician and family friend who attended Edward at this time. For most of June, as family and friends watched over him, Edward vacillated between periods of lucidity and calm and periods of unprovoked rage. By the end of June, he appeared so completely out of control that, after advising with Dr. Bartlett and family members, Waldo decided to have Edward institutionalized at the McLean Asylum in Charlestown. This decision was possibly one of the most personally wrenching Waldo ever had to make, for his brother Bulkeley and an elusive collateral relation named Dr. Haskins were themselves inmates of the Asylum at this time.[10] In the early morning hours of 2 July, Waldo and Dr. Bartlett, with Jarvis's assistance, strapped Edward down in the back seat of a hired coach and drove him to Charlestown, where he would remain an inmate until 6 December.

Regrettably, no medical records from either Dr. Bartlett's Concord practice or the McLean Asylum are available to tell us more than what we learn from the letters that follow about Edward's symptoms, treatment, or recovery between 25 May and 6 December, or about the toll his breakdown took on his family. The epistolary accounts by Charles and Waldo included here from late May through early July also include references to their personal affairs, but the information they reveal about Edward is complemented by a series of diary entries made by one of the "watchers," Edward Jarvis (1803–1884). A native Concordian who was Waldo's contemporary, Jarvis graduated from Harvard in 1826, taught for a brief period in Concord, established and then served as the librarian of the Sunday School Ezra Ripley inaugurated in 1827, and after receiving his M.D. from Harvard in 1832, opened a medical practice in his hometown. Although there are gaps in his record, Jarvis provides reliable corroboration of the family's overall impressions of and reports on Edward's condition. After Edward was admitted to the McLean Asylum, he was initially confined to a room in a building still under construction so that he could be kept apart from the other patients, including his brother Bulkeley and his "uncle," and for periods he was not allowed visitors. For most of July, August, and September, Edward's

condition was in constant flux: he seemed to be improving one day, then courting madness the next. But by the fall, when Waldo and Charles began to visit
Edward regularly, his improvement appeared to be sufficient enough for one of
his brothers to secure his release from the Asylum for the day to enjoy walks in
the countryside or a visit to Boston. Together, Waldo's and Charles's accounts
provide the most sustained record of Edward's periodic decline and periodic
recovery from July through early December, when Waldo and the physicians
felt that Edward was sufficiently well—if not actually "cured"—to be entrusted
to his brother Waldo's care. On securing Edward's release, Waldo took his
brother with him to Concord, New Hampshire, where he had been courting
Ellen through all of 1828, including the time of Edward's institutionalization.
Edward was the other Emerson present when Waldo and Ellen announced their
engagement on 17 December.

⊷ *Charles Chauncy Emerson to William Emerson, 29 May* [1828]

Edward is very sick. He was seized last Sunday Eveg. with fainting
fits which left him for a time speechless. Since then he has laid, the
greater part of the time in a very weak, exhausted, almost stupified state,
except that at intervals he is exceedingly delirious. Dr. Bartlett has attended him. He gives us small encouragement to expect his speedy or
total recovery. Dr. [James] Jackson [Sr.] will probably be here to see him
tomorrow.[11] His constitution, body & mind, seems completely spent. I
am afraid that it is Dr. B's opinion that he may continue a good while in
his present condition. Mother is as well as this new affliction, too severe
for any but religious consolation to alleviate, can permit her to be. Of
course all business depending upon Edw. must be stopped or put into
other hands. If I can be of any use in making such transfer command
me. It is late & I am to sit up with him tonight. Goodnight, & may God
preserve your health.[12]

⊷ *Ralph Waldo Emerson to William Emerson, 2 June 1828*

Edward is a great deal better. We were all thoroughly scared, & I was
hastened hither from . . . Concord [New Hampshire]. He had fainting fits,
& delirium, & had been affected strangely in his mind for a fortnight. He
is now restored to his former habits of thinking which I cannot help saying were always perverse enough. Dr Jackson . . . said to me what I think
is true that he will never be cured of a notion that he had that he was
suddenly & totally recovered from his old disease a fortnight before he
came here. Dr J. recommends that he should not touch a book for a year
but as the imperious patient is up & dressed this morning, the doctor's

dominion will shrink back into an advisory council, & come in, I doubt not, for a due share of contempt. . . .

I confess I watch him with painful interest. I fear that any future disorder may again affect his nerves. Still he reasons on business & affairs with force & rapidity & for aught I know his health may be really recovering. (L, 1:235–236)

→ *William Emerson to Ruth Haskins Emerson, 3–5 June 1828*

Charles' very afflicting letter containing an account of Edward's sickness, was received yesterday. I wanted to have come immediately to you— but on reflection, I knew that I could be of less service to you & to him, in all probability, by a visit there, than by remaining here in daily business. But my heart is with you, in deep sympathy with you in this overwhelming sorrow—No—I am wrong, God will not suffer you, nor any of us to be overwhelmed. His judgments are always mingled with mercy. Yet I can hardly trust myself to think of it. We have known something of affliction before, but to your sons, my dear mother, I will not say to you, this is the bitterest cup it has been our lot to drink. I have written as I feel, yet perhaps I ought to tear the paper, lest I may give you unnecessary pain, instead of administering, as I should, some balm of consolation. But I am persuaded, that even while I renew your grief by telling you how sincerely I share it, you will not despond; you will believe that the same kind Providence that has rescued from former evils can avert the present.

You have only to say by letter that you desire me to come, & I will come immediately—meanwhile, I shall depend *on a line, if no more,* with every change of the disease favorable or unfavorable—I commend him, & you & all of us to a merciful God.[13]—

→ *Ralph Waldo Emerson to William Emerson, 30 June 1828*

We are born to trouble. I have just received a letter from Concord to say that Edward is ill again—worse than before—in a state of violent derangement, so as to require great restraint. Mother writes, as you may well suppose, in great affliction. & speaks of the Hospital, as perhaps a dismal necessity. I go [to Concord] tomorrow morning. It will do no manner of good that I know for you to come—so do not think of it.

I do not know but if it continues it will be necessary to send him to *Charlestown.* For besides the state of feeling produced by watching him being unutterably wretched & ruinous to infirm health—it removes me from employment the profits of which are only more necessary to me on account of this calamity.

I have nothing else to say—no spirits to say any thing else. You know Henry Ware is very ill. . . . I have engaged to supply his pulpit but shall probably relinquish it.[14]—

Charles has just been . . . to see me—full of manuscripts and preparation—and all unprovided for my moving tales of wo. He delivers an oration to his class a fortnight from today.[15] Strange how all our prosperous days have been overcast! (L, 1:236–237)

➳ [*Selections dated 29 May–2 July 1828 from Edward Jarvis's Diary that Refer to Edward Bliss Emerson's Breakdown, Care in Concord, and Initial Institutionalization at the McLean Asylum*]

[*29 May 1828*]

I watched with Edward Emerson last monday at Dr Ripleys. Never watched before. he slept soundly. I fell asleep at 2½ or 3 oclock & awoke again before 4. at that time his mother came & I left them.

[*29 June*]

Last Friday eve [27 June] was called to Dr Ripleys [again] to take care of Edward Emerson, deranged. He graduated 1st scholar at Cambridge 1824. His health faild since. he has travelled in England France & Italy & lately been studying law with Mr. Webster. I found him quite cold. Watched with him over night. he slept most of the time. . . . I slept in the morn 9 hours. Dr Ripley was agoing away to change. I staid saturday. . . . E. Emerson was quite troublesome. Col. Shattuck came up & staid in the eve . . . & Dea Brown watched. I came home monday morn. left Col. Shattuck to stay during the day.

[*29 June continued*]

I went to Dr Ripleys; found there Maj Burr & J. Keyes, watchers with Emerson. I slept till 5 next morn & then staid alone with him till breakfast. Dr Ripley staid with us in the forenoon. Emerson was violent & rude. Kicked his grandfather & spat on him. It took all our strength to hold him. The Dr. is irritable & positive. He commended Emerson, who laughed [at] him & got irritated. The Dr was over anxious & watchful. Emerson was jealous, suspicious & obstinate. I read most of the time especially when alone. Emerson seeing me not watching did not trouble me but found other things to amuse himself.

[*30 June*]

This was the worst day we had with Emerson. Stone came up in the afternoon & staid over night. I walked out & came home. . . . Mellen watched with Stone. I got up in the morn [1 July], sat alone with E. as before, reading. He wished me to read to him. I did, he attended & talked about the history as rationally as any man. at 7 his brother R. Waldo came.

After consultation it was concluded to take him to the Insane Hospital. I went to see if he could be admitted. I offered to take our horse & chaise, if at home. Waldo Emerson said I had better hire on his account the fleet-est horse in town. . . . Got to Charlestown. talked [to] Dr Wyman a long time.[16] He objected to taking him for want of proper accommodations, as he had a brother & uncle there already, & to meet them would doubtless make him worse. I had a letter of introduction to 2 of the trustees. . . . [One gave] readily a permission to enter the hospital on the most favour-able terms. . . . Started [home] from Boston at 9½ & had the most gloomy tedious wearisome ride from Boston I ever had. Got home at 11½. went to Dr. R's. told R. W. Emerson of the issue of the negotiations.

[2 July]

Got up at 5. Went to Bartletts. we engaged a coach driver & 2 horses & started from Dr Ripleys at 7. Dr Bartlett, Waldo Emerson & I with Edw. Emerson & the driver. E. E. behaved tolerably well. made no trouble. we bound him with a strap.—Got to the hospital at 9. He was taken in. put in a new room in a building not finished. E. E. was very willing to be there. said he was glad there was a place where he could be taken care of.—We left him quiet, content & whistling.[17]

↦ *Ralph Waldo Emerson to William Emerson, 3 July 1828*

I have just returned from Concord from a desolate house—Yesterday we brought Edward down to Charlestown—Horrible as is the bare idea it was the least of the two evils—for poor mother was almost down, with distress & attendance. He has been now for one week thoroughly de-ranged & a great deal of time violent so as to make it necessary to have two men in the room all the time. Concord people were very kind. . . . His frenzy took all forms; sometimes he was very gay & bantered every body, & then it was only necessary to humour him & walk the room with him. Afterward would come on a peevish or angry state & he would throw every thing in the room & throw his clothes &c out of the window; then perhaps on being restrained wd. follow a paroxysm of perfect frenzy & he wd. roll & twist on the floor with his eyes shut for half an hour.—But whats the need of relating these—there he lay—Edward—the admired learned eloquent thriving boy—a maniac. Poor Charles dismayed at these tidings asks what good it is to be a scholar? . . . Grandfather has been incessant in his kindness & attention. But the calamity is as great as any I ever heard of. For I cannot persuade myself to hope. But God can do all things. I have very little doubt but he will again be restored to reason. But I fear he will now always hold it on the precarious tenure of the state of [the] stomach. And I do not know that it is desireable for him to come to a sense of his tremendous loss.—(L, 7:172–173)

➤ *William Emerson to Ralph Waldo Emerson, 5 July 1828*

I have this moment learned by your letter of the 30th how premature was our joy on Edward's recovery. He is ill again. If frequently meeting with misfortune confers additional power of enduring it, some of our family will have the wretched comfort of becoming heroes in the end. So there is no hope that this attack may last no longer than the former? Did Edward disregard Dr J[ackson]'s advice, & hazard new sufferings by study or reading? What help have you in taking care of him? How is mother's health & how your own, at a time when the strongest nerves & the firmest health are needed?—

It is strange to me that I can write the word *glad* on this sheet—yet I am glad to hear through you of Charles' cheerfulness & success. He has the class oration, which must be as an appointment to him as the commencement valedictory. If his performances come up to his character, they will be such as his friends may be well content to hear.[18]

➤ *Charles Chauncy Emerson to Ruth Haskins Emerson, [8 July 1828]*

I want to come & see you, but I do not think it will be in my power until next Wednesday or Thursday. Meantime I think all the while of your sorrows & our sorrows. I can only hope that God will sustain you & all of us, under his severe dispensations & enable us to see mercy in his judgements. I went to Charlestown on the 4th of July . . . but it was with a heavy heart—Waldo saw Edward on that day, he was pretty much as before & they expressed a desire that he should see as few people as possible, since they wish to break up his old associations. So Waldo has not been since that time.

You perhaps heard, that my Dissertation obtained a first prize—poor consolations are the most brilliant successes, under such afflictions. The parts for Commencement will come out next Saturday. It is extremely doubtful, who will have the first Oration—It is quite immaterial. I know who deserves it, & that is enough for me.

I should be glad to have a line from you saying how you do—I have not wondered to hear of your sickness, but resignation is a balm to every wound, & I hope to learn that you have in some degree recovered. Waldo has written to aunt Mary—I wish she could be with you this summer— There is a sublimity of Christian hope in her views, which bears one up above all earthly sorrows. We however can draw comfort from the same sources, we can cherish the same elevated & pious contemplations.[19]

➤ Charles Chauncy Emerson to William Emerson, 10 July [1828]

Today I received your letter dated July 1. . . . Waldo's has reached you before this time & you will expect nothing very 'cheerful' from me. Still, I feel it a duty, & I assure you, it was at first no easy one, not to suffer all hope & ambition, all relish for life & pleasure, to give way before even this severest calamity. God is good, & whom he chasteneth he loveth. I go [to] the Bible, for no philosophy can meet this affliction with equanimity. He is at present no better. He is (as you know) in the asylum at Charlestown.[20]

➤ William Emerson to Ruth Haskins Emerson, 14 July 1828

I must write to you. . . . But . . . I am tempted to throw aside my pen. We may grieve together, it is true, & there is certainly a consolation in not grieving alone—but grieve we must, & that deeply, too deeply for words to paint. As far as human power can go, it is an affliction past remedy, as it is past comfort—but the end is still with God, & therefore it is not yet past hope. Do not then, I beseech you, my dear mother, do not again wish that he may die. While there is life there is hope. Greater miracles are within the compass of Almighty Power, greater have been performed, even in what man has called the ordinary part of Providence, than the restoration of Edward to health & sanity. Let us not despair, my dear mother; one who surveyed the field of creation with an eye of wonderful comprehension has truly said—Spirits are not finely touched, but to fine issues.[21] And till the body begins to grow corrupt in the strong grasp of death, & the light of the eye as well as the reason is extinguished, I will never believe that the nicely organized frame of Edward's vigorous intellect has answered the purposes of its Divine Contriver. Should he die, it would indeed add another to the inexplicable mysteries of the operations of God. But while he lives, & I pray God to spare his life, I will not—I cannot abandon my hope for his recovery.[22]

~ *Mary Moody Emerson to Ralph Waldo Emerson and*
Charles Chauncy Emerson, 15 July [1828]

I write not to comfort you—this bitter calamity must be lessened only by time. And what that may do for him we mourn—is it vain to hope—to pray? Is it possible—it seems a dreadful dream that the most affection of Sons & brothers lives—but without life—that the sun—the earth—the friend (how dearly he had loved you Waldo from his infancy) are nothing to him—That God is nothing to him! But I meant not this—I write because I have but one thought and that is but Edward—one companion & he is a maniac—And I want either of you to tell me . . . how he is. Does he suffer? Does he eat & sleep like others? Who has the care of him? I am totally ignorant of that place. I have wanted to inquire . . . but hated to name *that* place. But now I beg for distinct knowledge. Suppose the patient alone & reason returning—my God how frightfull the conviction of such a place. Will it not be lost forever? . . . Oh how gladly I would spend the rest of weary wasted life in watching in his cell.[23]

~ *Ralph Waldo Emerson to Charles Chauncy Emerson, 4 August 1828*

Edward is altered again, though hardly for the better. I saw him Saturday & Friday. His present idea is that he is suffering punishment for great offences. It was consoling however that for the first time he exhibits great interest in my visits & great affection for me, & begs me to stay with him all the time. I shall see him tomorrow probably. Right or wrong, I got more hope of him from my last visit than ever before. He stands in need of nothing but God's aid. (*L*, 1:244)

~ *Ralph Waldo Emerson to William Emerson, 7 August 1828*

I take a moment to say I am well & Edward in a somewhat more hopeful state. I have not given you from time to time particulars because I expect [your visit] soon & Edward changes very much & very fast in his moods. (*L*, 1:244–245)

~ *Ralph Waldo Emerson to William Emerson, 17 October 1828*

I begun my letter, as might be expected from the ardour of my fraternal impatience, upside down,[24] & was saying that it is as well if one has brothers now & then just for form's sake to say so that the fact may not be forgotten by ourselves or others which wouldn't be reputable you know, so here's to you. . . .

Edward continues to be & to grow better. He is now better than I dared expect two months ago. His bodily health is much mended & his discourse in general very sane. But he has some word or expression in a conversation which betrays an unsoundness. . . . [A]s he remembers all things you had better send him a few lines about health & weather . . . with the advice not to write much or any—& enclose it to me or Charles. (L, 1:248–249)

↬ *Charles Chauncy Emerson to Mary Moody Emerson, [ca. November 1828]*

I believe that poor Edward's sudden & awful arrest in the high course which he had marked out for himself, with too severe a disregard of human frailty & the weakness of this poor flesh—will have been good for us all—through Eternity; How can I say, in this world, while a shadow of doubt rests upon his case? We feel greatly encouraged now—Waldo who has seen him constantly & whose opinions I value more than the best of Physicians, is full of hope.[25]

↬ *Charles Chauncy Emerson to William Emerson, 23 November [1828]*

Things wear a propitious look—at least they have assumed so much of a smile as it would be safe for us to be favoured withal—Providence that has overruled in mercy the destinies of our family for centuries back, will never I think try us by too rash a prosperity. Through poverty, & labour, through feebleness & scorn, I am content to work my way so it be upward—But I do dread, & I pray God of his goodness to save me from, the hour, when complicated sorrows & sickness & failing efforts & broken hopes, shall oppress the *mind* beneath a load that shall crush its energies & strain beyond recoil, its elasticity. I do believe that man is more intellectual, while he is hungry—& I do not covet a fat & lazy opulence—I only desire, that the winds of human fortune be so tempered to my frailty, that they never do more than summon up the strength within to buffet the ills that are without. There are malignant storms which appal the soul—which make their fatal ravages, unopposed, because the spirit bows beneath their fury—From these I would fain be sheltered.

I dont know how you will relish such a faint-hearted philosophy, which acknowledges events to be dominant over mind—I am half ashamed of it myself.[26]

If one were to generalize on Charles's last letter to William as the Emerson family's summary response to Edward's illness, it suggests the immense toll that Edward's illness took on all members of the family, and it suggests as well

that his brother's breakdown may have exerted its longest lasting negative effect on Charles himself. Although most individuals, including Aunt Mary, came
to terms with their need to deal with the horror of witnessing Edward's utter
collapse within a few months of its occurrence, Charles, who at first remained
calm and appeared strong, seems to register a delayed—and for the most part
mixed—reaction to the events. When he wrote to Aunt Mary in November that
"We feel . . . full of hope," his rhetorical aside that "a shadow of doubt rests
upon [Edward's] case" may have been Charles's inadvertent admission that the
hope around which Waldo and Edward's physicians rallied at the time was not
one that he shared. Indeed, it is only after having come through the darkest period of Edward's decline and institutionalization that Charles dared to expose
his true feelings to his brother William, to admit his fear of those "malignant
storms which appal the soul," and announce his "faint-hearted philosophy,
which acknowledges events to be dominant over mind."

Interestingly, Charles was not the only Emerson brother to restrain his hope
at the prospect of Edward's complete recovery with a degree of caution. Even
though Waldo was glad to be able to have Edward discharged from the McLean
Asylum in his care and to take him on his several week ministerial and personal visit to New Hampshire, in the midst of celebrating his engagement to
Ellen and negotiating a call from Boston's Second Church, he wrote an alarm-
ingly fatalistic letter to Aunt Mary on 6 January 1829. Speaking for himself and
his brothers, but mostly for himself, exaggerating each of his brothers' personal
and professional statuses at the beginning of 1829, and adopting the logic and
archaic form of a Calvinist homily, he told her,

> You know none can know better in what straightened lines we have
> all walked up to manhood. In poverty & many troubles the seeds of
> our prosperity were sown. . . . Now all these troubles appeared a fair
> counterbalance to the flatteries of fortune. I lean always to that ancient
> superstition (if it is such, though drawn from a wise survey of human
> affairs) wh. taught men to beware of unmixed prosperity for Nemesis
> keeps watch to overthrow the high. Well now look at the altered aspect.
> William has begun to live by the law. Edward has recovered his reason
> & his health. Bulkeley was never more comfortable in his life. Charles
> is prospering in all ways. Waldo is comparatively well & comparatively
> successful—far more so than his friends out of his family anticipated.
> Now I add to this, all this felicity, a particular felicity which makes my
> own glass very much larger & fuller.[27] & I straightway say—can this
> hold? will God make me a brilliant exception to ye common order of
> his dealing wh. equalizes destinies? Theres an apprehension of reverse
> always arising from success. But is it my fault that I am happy and
> cannot I trust the Goodness that has uplifted to uphold me? In all these

considerations I believe ye sentiment of ye old hymn is just—"In every joy &c my heart shall find delight in praise or seek relief in prayer."[28] The way to be safe is to be thankful. I cannot find in ye world without or within any antidote any bulwark against this fear like this, the frank acknowledgement of unbounded dependance. Let into ye heart yt is filled with prosperity ye idea of God & it smooths ye giddy precipices of human pride to a substantial level, it harmonizes ye condition of ye individual with ye economy of ye Universe. I shd. be glad dear aunt yt you who are my oldest friend wd give me some of your meditations upon these new leaves of my fortune. You have always promised me success & now when it seems to be coming I chuse to direct to you this letter . . . [so] that if I am called after the way of my race to pay a fatal tax for my good, I may appeal to the sentiment of collected anticipation with which I saw the tide turn. . . . As Bacon said "you may know it was my fate & not my folly yt bro't me to it." (L, 7:176–177)

"I straightway say—can this hold?"—Even while he described the "felicities" surrounding his own and his brothers' lives for his Aunt's and, ultimately, his own edification, Waldo had to be aware that he was constructing a fiction that could not survive a test against reality. He knew full well that he was overstating the status of his brothers' current lives and future prospects. William had definitely not "begun to live by the law." As late as July 1831, William mentioned to Waldo that he was still sorely tempted to move ahead with a career change from lawyer to journal editor because he could barely survive on the earnings from his practice. "I should prefer to get my living as a lawyer rather than as an editor," he wrote, adding, "'tis true, as you say, I have yet waited *only* 3 years, & should be content to wait five; & so I would, if I had wherewithall to subsist on during the remaining two."[29] At the beginning of 1829, the final verdict on Edward's recovery of "his reason and his health" was far from known, and Bulkeley was still an inmate of the McLean Asylum. Although at the level of appearance Charles may have seemed to be "prospering in all ways," the truth is, as his extensive correspondence to Aunt Mary reveals, Charles was hardly prospering in mind and spirit at this time; additionally, he despised his current life as a teacher, a career to which he felt he had been reduced by the circumstance of having to help William and Waldo pay for Bulkeley and Edward's expenses at the McLean Asylum. Writing to Waldo in September 1828, barely three months into Edward's commitment to the Asylum, Charles sent him an unflattering personal impression of his new students and their parents. Playful as it may sound on the surface, Charles was not amused by the lack of serious purpose among those with whom he had to deal when described his situation thus: "As to scholars, they are eels—very eels—I catch 'em in my hand & squeeze hard to hold 'em & they are swimming a second afterward, in the wide ocean—Silly women, not knowing their own minds, & stingy men not willing to educate their own children, are the primary causes of this uncomfortable slipperiness in the young fry."[30] Finally, Waldo's professions to Mary of his own comparative wellness and success are themselves called in to question by the tone and style he adopted throughout the letter; furthermore, as an ironic conclusion to his catalogue of "felicities," his invocation of Baconian philosophy at the end of his letter—"'you may know it was my fate & not my folly yt bro't me [to my end]'"—merely restated the "faint-hearted philosophy" that, unknown to him, his brother Charles had earlier espoused to William, when he "acknowledge[d] events to be dominant over mind."[31]

The two years that follow Waldo's fatalistic letter to his aunt—virtually all of 1829 and 1830—represent a period in which his and Edward's lives each passed through recurrent cycles of personal pleasure followed by personal pain, and contrary to the belief he expressed to Aunt Mary, Waldo discovered that even prayer—at least in the traditional sense—would not be entirely sufficient to prepare either Edward or himself for the "fate" that was steadily engulfing each of them. In Waldo's case, within days of his letter to Mary, Ellen "raised blood," "that dangerous complaint," he wrote to William on 28 January 1829, "which so often attacks the fairest in our stern climate" (L, 1:259). With all in both Ellen's and Waldo's families keeping a watchful eye on her condition, Waldo was ordained as the junior pastor of Boston's Second Church on 11 March, promoted to pastor of the Church on 1 July, and married Ellen on 30 September. Enjoying financial security and a degree of social prominence for the first time in his adult life, relishing the intellectual activity of composing weekly sermons in which he could draw out Unitarianism's humanistic qualities through reference to his studies in biography, philosophy, and history, and delighting in a marriage in which he described himself as possessing "the luxury of an unmeasured affection for an object so deserving of it all & who requites it all" (JMN, 3:149), Waldo comfortably settled into the dual role of pastor and husband. Drawing upon his readings in German Higher Criticism and the works of Samuel Taylor Coleridge and Victor Cousin, among others, he rehearsed in sermons before his congregation many of the themes that would later characterize his teachings for the public in lectures and essays. Emphasizing self-culture and what he would later describe as "the infinitude of the private man" (JMN, 7:342), the moral authority of the individual intellect and conscience over the authority of religious or social institutions and even the Bible, and the liberation from its inherited past that the inventiveness and political freedom of the present offers the human race, Waldo's sermons between 1829 and 1832 anticipated the idealism of Nature (1836), "The American Scholar" (1837), and "The Divinity School Address" (1838).

In spite of their promise, however, these two years delivered several successive blows to Waldo's personal confidence and professional ambition, all of which were invariably associated with Ellen's condition. Waldo and Ellen hoped that rest and winter travel to warm climates would lessen the debilitating effects of her disease and possibly provide an actual cure. But her condition worsened immediately after their marriage; a recuperative journey to Philadelphia in the winter of 1829–1830 and the efforts of several doctors, one of whom, as Waldo told Ezra Ripley, recommended a ten-year relocation to Cuba or a comparable environment (8 October 1830, *L*, 7:194), could not stay the inevitable, and Ellen died on 8 February 1831 at the age of nineteen. As he explained to Mary, Waldo found himself suddenly balancing between relief that her suffering had finally ended and utter dejection at the prospect of his life without her: "My angel is gone to heaven this morning & I am alone in the world. . . . I have never known a person in the world in whose separate existence as a soul I could so readily & fully believe & she is present with me now . . . in her deliverance. . . . [But] I see it plainly that things & duties will look coarse & vulgar enough to me when I find the romance of her presence . . . withdrawn from them all" (*L*, 1:318).

Two months before Ellen's death, Edward, who after his hospitalization at the McLean Asylum seemed to steadily improve, left Boston for St. Croix (Santa Cruz) and, eventually, Puerto Rico, having himself exhibited extreme symptoms of tuberculosis. Although Aunt Mary had her doubts about the wisdom of his decision to return to his readings in the law after his release from the Asylum, everyone else in the family applauded Edward's return to work. From the spring of 1829 until the opening of 1830, Edward worked primarily in Daniel Webster's law office, and then he moved to New York to enjoy what he thought would be a milder winter than in Boston and continue his studies with his brother William. For most of 1830 he moved back and forth between New York and Boston, appearing for all purposes to be enjoying good health but clearly returning to his old ways by overextending himself with his readings and work. For a family that believed woes always visited in multiples, the Emersons must have been alarmed and put on their guard when, in September, Bulkeley, who had been released from Charlestown sometime in the early part of the year, had to be recommitted to Dr. Wyman's care at the McLean Asylum. They did not have to wait long for the proverbial "other shoe" to fall. In November, Edward, who was with William in New York, developed a pulmonary inflammation that persisted for two weeks; after weighing all options available to them, including the possibility of Edward wintering back home, the family reluctantly accepted his own decision to seek relief in the West Indies, but only because he left New York literally minutes before his mother arrived there prepared to insist that he return to Boston with her.[32]

On 12 December, Edward sailed from New York on a ship bound for St. Croix, where he planned to spend the winter. The next several letters exchanged within the familiy describe the events leading up to his departure;

Edward's own and his brothers' hopes for his speedy recovery; his impressions of St. Croix, including his surprise at finding so many other family friends and acquaintances wintering there for their health; and Edward's desire, as he expressed it to William, to return in the spring to practice law again in New York or to secure a comparable position in the Caribbean. These letters also set the tone and establish the contexts for most of the correspondence Edward exchanged with his brothers and other family members prior to his death in Puerto Rico in 1834. Except for repeated requests sent home for cash advances, newspapers and journals, or for tropical-weight clothing, Edward rarely wrote anything that could be construed as a complaint about his physical condition or personal situation; instead, he seemed from the outset of his exile willing to take events as life presented them to him.

⇥ Charles Chauncy Emerson to Ezra Ripley, 4 December 1830

I write now to tell you the bad news we have heard from Edward. William said in a letter we received about a fortnight ago, that Edward had had a very heavy cold for some days—but last Saturday & Monday we had letters saying he had been very sick indeed—passed a very distressed night, with shooting pains in the side & back & was troubled with an ugly cough. Dr. Perkins, their best physician in N.Y. was called in,—he applied a blister immediately—but said that Edward ought to go off directly, to the South.[33] Since then we have had more letters—Edw. remains much the same—his cough is bad—"his strength, weakness"—Dr. Perkins repeats his advice—And Edward is going away, as soon as necessary arrangements be made, to Florida or West Indies. This is at present the whole of our sad story—We knew you would wish to hear it, & sympathise with poor Edw's sorrows.

We are all of us well here. We tried to make Thanksgiving a pleasant day. . . . Waldo & I went to see Bulkeley yesterday—He is quite violent.[34] . . .

⇥ Edward Bliss Emerson to William Emerson, 31 January 1831

Having an idle moment at West End I add to what I have sent to the letter bag of the Eliza Davison as follows.—Mr Geo. Barnard appears to be what you have described him amiable & intelligent—he seems to enjoy his residence at Mrs Boyle's, where he has fixed himself in the room wh. I occupied.—I should be glad to have you mention his well-being when you write north because such collateral tidings may please his friends. It is so probable that I shall remain hereabouts for some time that I would not have you refrain from writing when good opportunity offers, & any news occur to you in your leisure, altho' I shall not hesitate to embrace any very excellent occasion of removal. Well placed at present I seek no change but keep an open ear & shall weigh anchor in the event of a strong breeze of circumstances. I shall not refuse to pull at the law again in N.Y. yoked as aforetime with one of stronger neck—if the health which Providence sends should fit me for the work, but if you hear of other business for me which can keep me in warm latitudes & send me hence to Cuba or where-not—it may be better for the whole of us.[35]

↠ *Charles Chauncy Emerson to Edward Bliss Emerson, 1 February 1831*

We have not yet heard from you, but that is no reason why I should delay longer to write to you. I have a great curiosity to know how you are situated, how occupied, what are your arrangements for the present & your intentions for the future. I wish to know how the state of manners & morals & the various [manuscript torn] of business in a state of society so new to you, appear to your considered mind. If you are well, & go about (as I sincerely hope) you must be much entertained, I should suppose, with violent contrasts to what you left at Home—And these things when endured for a season are more entertainment, than a cross, unless they are violations of the eternal laws of morals.

We hear the Governor & inhabitants of S. Cruz came out & conducted Dr Channing triumphantly into the town[36]—If such respect were paid the minister, a minister's son should be the object of special regard—Do you see Dr. C. & Mrs. Richard Derby? & others. Very likely my questions will be answered before they reach you; what of that,—I ask them now.

Here we are doing & suffering as all the sons of Adam do & suffer—now elate with hope, now depressed with troubles, now choked with business. The Law grows more interesting, but as the recesses open to the inquiring eye, they appal one by their tangled passages & grisly depths. . . . You know I suppose by a letter from him that Ellen is sick—quite sick—& if she should recover sufficiently to live comfortably through the Summer, next fall I think they will fly to a warmer spot than bleak New England. William, I suppose, writes you news of himself. Aunt Mary is still at Concord. We have had an unusually severe & snowy winter thus far & are likely to have sleighing protracted into March or April. So I am glad you are out of the reach of Jack Frost & his great aider & abettor, the N.W. wind.

Last Evening we had a meeting of the Citizens of Cambridge, on the subject of the present situation of the Indians[37]—It was got up by a few of us who felt a strong desire to do the mite which in us lay, to encourage & strengthen the opposition to the measures of Georgia, & the policy of the

Administration. Never was a plainer case of right & wrong. Mr. Ashmun, H. Ware jr, Mr Adams (orthodox minister,) Mr Richd. Dana, Mr. Stowe (Editor of Recorder, now living in Camb.) Mr. Hillard & Mr. Chas. C. Emerson spoke—one or two of the speakers were very eloquent.[38] [manuscript torn]ber of Resolutions was adopted, & a Committee of which Ashmun was Chairman, chosen to prepare a memorial to Congress.

My friend Wm. Swett has gone into your neighborhood, to Cuba, for health, this winter.[39] I name Northern Emigrants to make you feel that you are in a large company of friends. Have you books at command? Do you talk English, or Danish, or French or what? Shall you see anything of this Eclipse of the sun, which at Boston is to be nearly total, a week from next Saturday?

. . . [P]lease rouse my sluggish faculties (home keeping youth have ever homely wits) by the tales & speculations of a traveller.[40]

After spending a few quiet months in St. Croix, Edward decided the time had come to seek employment in order to begin defraying the expenses of what he suspected would be a long exile in the Caribbean. Employment opportunities were not readily available in St. Croix, and in any case, he did not much care for the weather or for the visible effects of what his disease would eventually do to him that he saw every day on the faces and in the withered bodies of so many of the Americans he met on the island. The best chances for securing a position he rightly thought would be found either in Puerto Rico or in Cuba, where plantations supplied a steady stream of fresh produce, liquor, and raw goods to be shipped to processing plants or textile factories in America and American merchants and speculators were still growing rich on the bounty of the West Indian "trade." Passing through St. Thomas on his way to St. John's (San Juan), Puerto Rico, he met Sidney Mason, a New York merchant, who was a commercial agent, plantation owner, and the American consul in Puerto Rico. The two struck up a friendship, which over time would become very close, and arranged for Edward to come work as an accounting clerk and legal copyist in Mason's San Juan office. Mason had a thriving business derived as much from his position as a commercial agent representing the export interests of others as from the successful management of his own large plantation in Santa Barbara, a rural district on the outskirts of San Juan, and he immediately recognized in Edward's law experience and work ethic assets that would be valuable to him. Edward, who formally assumed his position in Mason's office on 1 May 1831, provided details of his new job and the cordial terms under which he and Mason began their personal and business association in a letter to William, which he expected his brother would forward to Boston and Concord for other family members to read.

➺ *Edward Bliss Emerson to William Emerson, 8 May 1831*

. . . I thought you might be glad to hear, that after a weeks experim^t of my new occupations at the comptg house, & residence at Mr Mason's, I am pleased with both. The hours of business—or writing—are from 6. A.M. to 4. A.M. . . . Invoices & a/cs sales have been my substitute for bail-pieces & bills of ex^g—first pecun^y advantage from my new plan was the destruct^n of a bill of exchange which I had on Monday last drawn on you for $100, in expectat^n of going to Havana—& the necessy. for which may be deferred now some time, as my contingent expenses will, I hope, be slow in rising to that amount.—In my first contract with Mr Mason, he said that he had not supposed that any such offer as mere board & lod^g, would tempt me & therefore abstained from making it, till he learned from me that my desire of remain^g in a warm climate & of learn^g Spanish & of getting an acquaint^{ce} with commerce—a sort of foothold from wh. I might afterwards advance if good prospects should appear—would make me content to close with such terms as I should thus cease to be heavily burdensome to those at home who laden enough. Mr M. then readily made the offer, as I mentioned in my last of May 2^d, sent via St Thos, (& Phil^a perhaps). Nothing was then said of my washing, an item of expense in the W[est]. I[ndies]. which is considerable to the neat & enormous to the extravagant in dress. Some days after however, I mentioned it & said that I was prepared to pay for it—as I had neglected to stipulate for it—unless it was convenient for the domestics of the family to take it into their tubs; but Mr M said, that it should be paid from the store & I could employ whom I pleased—which I thought an indication of good disposition on his part, as well as an import^t saving to one who has no income. Thus if health continues improving or even stationary, I shall only be compelled to borrow from the home purses pocket money & for the supply of such waste as time may make in my wardrobe & the little sundries which I may have to buy.—At the end of 6 mos., if all things go on well, my experiment is made & it is understood that then I am free to go to Hav[ana]. or elsewhere, or to make new terms with Mr. Mason. & he intimates that he may find my services to be worth the offer of a small salary. Of course such salary may be very small for the first year—but it will be time enough to talk about that 6 mos. hence—At pres^t I am thinking about my "where withal shall be clothed" so much that I must repeat my request (lest the May 2d letter miscarry) that 2 pair summer panataloons, 2 or 3 pr drawers, 2 or 3 shirts—white vest—cotton jacket, sum. shoes—my black-hat—. . . & socks ad libitum.[41] Another strange article you will think is yet quite desirable here, if all accounts are correct about a rainy season that comes on by & by—to wit my India rubbers. The story goes that when it begins to rain here, the showers fall & the

streets are wet more or less all the time for weeks & even months successively so that in the country that roads are frequently impassable & in the
city a pair of in. rubs might on a special occasion be very valuable. We
have pavements in many streets & sidewalks, so that you need not fear
that the rainy season will disable us from walking or endanger health, not
need you particularly describe its continued humidity to an anxious lady
to the north of New York.—But I have reached the end of my time & so
must seal this to go by way of St Thos.[42]—

Edward quickly found life in Puerto Rico as much to his liking as he imagined in his letter to William that it might be. If he ever felt discouraged or depressed that the high personal and professional goals that his family had set for
him—and that he set even higher than they had for himself—seemed dashed
by his invisibility as a clerk in a foreign land so distant from Concord's storied
past or Boston and New York's vital social and political scenes, he never said
so. For most of his time in Puerto Rico, Edward worked five or six day weeks
in Mason's office, took walking tours of the island with Francis Armstrong, a
physician who, with Mason, became one of his closest friends during his exile,
mastered Spanish and wrote several letters home in his new language, graciously accepted Puerto Rico's slower pace and the pleasures of the island's customs and foods, and even enjoyed observing the religious festivals celebrated
by the Roman Catholics. From December 1831 through April 1832, Charles,
who by then had himself begun to exhibit the signs of tuberculosis, stayed with
Edward in San Juan, but otherwise no one from the Emerson family ventured
to Puerto Rico while Edward was alive.

Between May 1831 and his death on 1 October 1834, Edward returned home
to America only once—for a two-month visit between August and October
1832. The family enjoyed his presence, and his brothers agreed among themselves that he seemed unusually fit and in great spirits. During his visit, he was
able to celebrate William's engagement to Susan Woodward Haven, the daughter of a New Hampshire merchant, which occurred in August, and to toast his
brother Charles's success in being sworn in as an attorney of the Court of Common Pleas and opening his law office in Boston at the beginning of October.
Edward's presence at home was undoubtedly a comfort to Waldo, who, following a protracted disagreement with his congregation over the administration
of the Lord's Supper, submitted his formal letter of resignation to the Second
Church and Society on 11 September. Returning to San Juan after this visit to
New England, and realizing, as the lines of his poem "The Last Farewell" suggest, that he would live in Puerto Rico for the remainder of his life, Edward had
the strength of mind to not wallow in melancholy about the life he had left behind and the strength of character to not rewrite that history to suit his present
condition.[43] Recognizing the reserves of strength that his brother possessed,
Charles wrote to Aunt Mary a few months after Edward's departure: "Edward

has a soul in him—no shadow at all . . . but a large & glowing soul—lighted up by fits with the flame of an irregular genius,—but always odorous with the perfume of a taintless generosity. He is far greater & more admirable than when he was most admired."[44]

The few letters that follow tell the entire story of the last three years of Edward's life. His correspondence with William almost always concentrated on fraternal finances and descriptions of business affairs in the Caribbean, whereas his correspondence with Charles tended to be a bit more personal, as when, in a letter to Charles dated 27 July 1833 and printed in full below, Edward agreed with his brother's assessment of the financial advantages of living in the Caribbean, but acknowledged ever so subtly that another advantage of island life that made it even more valuable to him was the opportunity it provided him to deal with the reality of his physical condition without any familial interference. From the tone of his letter to Waldo on his return from Europe late in 1833 and another that he wrote in June 1834 in which he offered to vacation with his brother at home the following year, it is clear that one relationship Edward truly missed during his exile was that which the two brothers enjoyed, but it is also clear from the few last correspondences he sent home that Edward was comfortable with enduring his illness and approaching his death alone and far away from those sites of his sad and troubled former life which he had successfully consigned to a distant corner of his memory. If we believe Sidney Mason's account of Edward's last days, and there is no reason to suspect that we should not, Edward died a happy young man, surrounded by caring friends in a land he considered home for the last years of his life.

→ *Edward Bliss Emerson to William Emerson, 17 July 1831*

. . . I received your letters of April 10. & June 1. & 5. & the next day the line of 8[th] ulto, wi. Bill Lad[in]g. . . . since which the Sch[oone]r. has arrived here & delivered the Box with its contents. These last agree exactly with your Invoice annexed to your letter, & appear in good condition, saving the salt water that got to some of them (perhaps in the boat) & which the washerwoman will soon remove. Your satisfaction with my present plans affords me no little pleasure, since I had been some what anxious on that score, after noticing the drift of former letters advising a return for the Summer to the North. What I have seen of the climate up to this date, in P. Rico has in my own state of body & according to my own taste—if that faculty have any thing to do with judgments on weather—nearly as much advantage over yours at this season as it has in winter; & that owing to the refreshing breezes which daily & almost certainly are blowing. They threatened me with coming deluges of rain & the rain has come & counting all the showers for a month back, up to that which is now washing the streets, we have had a great deal of water; but "this & much more, yea more than twice all this" as old Will hath it,[45] can be borne with great equanimity & cheerfulness of mind, so kindly does it come & the so does the sun seem ruler of the stormiest sky; now & then he just peers from behind a cloud while the rain drops on; & presumably he 'flatters the mountain top' & the whole wide landscape too 'with sovereign eye'[46] & every body is abroad & no more thought of the rain except in the observation of its effect in deepening the verdure of the surrounding country.—Sometimes I am awaked in the night by these heavy & passing showers, & in the morning rise with as fair a day-break as usual. During one week it is true that the showers fell so frequently, that the tone in which people said 'muchisma aquae,' began to sound like a murmur, especially as it is the consequence of rainy weather, that the loading of vessels & much of the labor of negroes is suspended; but in that very week, were so many hours of fair or 'holding up' weather & throughout the whole such an absence of that cold & chilly dampness which makes, I think, the sting of a storm in U.S. that one who has been bred in Mass. & N.Y. might be severe without needing an Epictetus, or pretending to be one.[47]—To day we have had some heavy thunder, & it is the second or third time that I recollect to have noticed it since coming to the W.I. say 6 months ago.—These rains & above all this thunder are regarded I find by some, & those the men of experience, as a favorable indication in respect to hurricanes which are more to be apprehended after drought & calm heat.—One word more & I have done with the climate; it is said to ameliorate as elsewhere in the progress of cultivation & clearing of the lands; men telling here as with us stories of most dire rainstorms & miry roads & horses perishing in the same & negroes sickening & all work embargoed by the elements, 'in old times' which come down to 4 or 5 or 6 yrs ago—The last great *hurricane*—tormenta ruinosa—noted in the Almanack was in 1825.—Although this is the season for masks and to day the last Sunday but one before its termination, yet there were but few to be found abroad & such as ventured out in spite of sloppy streets must have been I think of the lowest order. If next Sunday shd. be fair, there will doubtless be more & merrier.—You must pardon Dr C[hanning]. for not preaching so soon after his voyage. I remember, months after his arrival at St. Croix that he said he had not thoroughly recovered the tone of his system so much had it been deranged by sea-sickness. . . . As to the lack of information in my letters about the W.I.—. . . You are a lawyer & I retain you to plead my cause.—Jesting apart, I write down almost every thing that I think will escape memory, or will much & agreeably interest my friends; but sometimes I write to Mother sometimes to R. W. &c. &c. & sometimes I note a little incident in my mem[orandum]. book, &

what I thus put on paper in one place I care not to repeat in any other, as, if nothing unforeseen prevent, sooner or later you will sponge up all my little items, in one or other of these forms. . . . And when I come to pass a few summer days amongst those whom I love & whose love is now to me in the stead of company, whose clearly recollected features often cheer & soothe my solitude—then you may put me upon the Stand & examine me at your leisure.—Meantime I thank you for all the information you give, as to politics &c. & friends.—The Whigs were so old that they happened to be behind our information by other arrivals,[48] but let not that discourage you from putting in to any vessel a selected number of any newspapers which you can procure without cost, because we are often visited by Captains who have no interest or forget that we have any, in U.S. news. The latest 2 or 3 Journals may be more acceptable if equally at hand, than a file of any one; and if they come by the way of St. Thos. they should be sealed, as I hear of curious & unscrupulous fingers being sometimes connected with itching ears.—Scandal I hate—but I want what you send should arrive[49]—

⤞ Edward Bliss Emerson to Charles Chauncy Emerson, 27 July 1833

'T'was well said, very well said, . . . that the pecuniary consideration *ought* to be great to induce a man to live in Pto. Rico.—T'was kindly said, that I should do all that was "wise." I wish I might.—I did what I thought best at the given moment. From a given point I drew what I thought a straight line. We are all liable to over rate, perhaps all liable to under rate ourselves as well as others. I used to look on time with an anxious eye lest any hour should fail to bear its portion of the burden of study & labor which I thought was properly to be expected of the aggregate life. From some fundamental defect of the moral physical or intellectual part my well laid calculations failed. I blame no one, not even myself, for the disappointment—being as yet in the dark as to the real cause.—Letting that pass, I found myself sick, in debt, and though assured of the attachment of my brothers & some other friends, yet no less so of the inconvenience & impropriety of deliberately resigning myself into their hands to be nursed with their slender means.—I found a very humble—perhaps in one or two respects a disgusting occupation, promising to afford me a livelihood. Once embraced, all that is learned in any calling, is worth much more to him who stays therein than to him who forsakes it, though to neither lost. So having got into the shop where I would have rather staid in the academy, I have tried very hard to see if aught might be around me to divert me from considering a melancholy change,—or ought that might compensate in time to come for the loss,—which I have felt, though I will not pretend to estimate.—I have tried by assiduity to overcome repugnance and at the same time I have kept up a little corps de reserve of objections and fancies in relation to mercantile life that in case of a happy emergency, I may use their escort and escape to some department of life where figures, and their constituents dollars & cents, are less thought of than they are in commerce.—

. . . To say that I have talents much superior to my station I am not prepared. To say that I feel myself exactly in the niche ordained for me, I am less so. I labor under many disadvantages, at whatever mark I direct my aim. I am far from being a strong, active, healthful adventurer, and so I seek my consolation in adverse circumstances from thoughts like those which you have well expressed in the conclusion of your own letter "What matter it? whether famous or obscure, in wealth or need, the great lessons of this disciplinary world are learned by us & 't'will make little odds presently whether the forms we sat on were of pine or mahogany."—Still if my very feeble thread continues to stretch itself along ones years of earthly existence, as it may, I shall always indulge the hope of weaving or working with it some little sampler with figures & adornments of my own devising,—when God shall send leisure and ability,—and I pray it may be in my native land among my brothers.[50]—

⤙ Edward Bliss Emerson to Ralph Waldo Emerson, 13 November 1833

I welcome you home again; that is to the western hemisphere, to the new world of Columbus,[51] for at least within such limits our straggling fortunes are again united.[52]—I rec^d in Sept. yours of 25 May, dated at Florence. My recollection of that city is but faint—for I stopped but a few days, . . . had to grope my way in a sort of twilight, [and] moreover was dismally ignorant of Italian history & literature & could not approach Santa Croce with the deep veneration due to "its tombs;" moreover had been a month in Rome & predetermined to admire the Apollo more than the Venus—I was not forced to recant; & the eye had so expanded in the contemplation of St Peters & the Coliseum & the marble tenants of the Vatican & the Capitoline Museum that I looked on Florence as a lesser volume, or rather a less striking picture in the series of which a glance was all I enjoyed. I am glad you had so different an opportunity & such troops of pleasant people about you. . . .

. . . You are glad that I am well.—Had I been wholly so I think I should have gone home in the early summer. I have that kind of health that makes me a useful man here: but the trial is such that my resolution is nearly taken to return next year, though the chances of the step, as to its effects on health & prospects are quite dubious. You know I constitutionally *abhor,* yea suffer from continual sympathy & inquiries about ails &c. & therefore avoid mentioning them, as a general rule, & specially to the tenderhearted. . . .

Everybody here pretends to find me less frightfully pale than formerly & I am in better spirits, read & write & work with more satisfaction:—so that if you should not say that the cold will kill, & that every door to employment is shut in the U.S. I hope in the coming year to put all my courage clothes & credit, for I have no other estate, on the way home & try to live . . . in firm continental ground.[53]—

⤴ *Ruth Haskins Emerson to William Emerson, 12 March 1834*

We have at last, letters from Edward, and as I feared, account of his having been sick—Oh how sad! That he should have been so long alone, borne down by such a weight of business, & care. It was even too much for a man, of firmer health, & stronger constitution than his, to have endured, so long a time, through a sickly season—The responsibility he felt, probably, prevented him from riding out of the city, & taking necessary recreation in the fresh air—till Mr Mason returned. It was well, for my dear Edward, that Mr M arrived so soon after he was taken sick, for with his frail frame, he could not long sustain any violent disease, without sinking under it—He must have needed the most kind & interested attention of a friend—I am glad to hear Mr Mason was able to watch himself, with him, & did not leave him with hired persons entirely—But enough of my anxieties—Let us give thanks to God, that his precious life is spared, & for the prospect of restored health—Edward says not a word of coming home—perhaps it was so early in the season that he did not name it—. . .

If you get any news from Porto Rico, you will forward it with speed, for I cannot fail being anxious to hear again. Do write to Edward by the first chance.[54]

⤴ *Charles Chauncy Emerson to Edward Bliss Emerson, 6–17 March [1834]*

And you have been sick, & sick away from home,—neither mother nor brother to amuse the sad hours of pain & languor. But that I trust you are now quite too well to care about sympathy, I should be very very sorry. You do not say what has been the matter, whether fever or more accustomed maladies. . . . But your mother, 'by the love that was in her heart,' knew you must be sick or it would not have been so long since we heard from yourself. Tell us as fast as you grow strong, & if we can help the recovery of health by good wishes & prayers, you know they are yours.

Meanwhile the months stop not for us, whether well or sick, softly cushioned or hardly tossed by outward circumstances. March 'wild Stormy' March is upon us—& going over us, & the winds whisper & the waters murmur of Spring—& the Summer the Summer is it not to fetch you back to us? . . .

I wish I could say that we are all perfectly well here at home. Mother has suffered of late from her old bilious complaints, & a touch of rheumatism. Elizabeth [Hoar] is not well—& I am afraid will have to go home this week instead of staying out her full time in the City, which was to be until April. The beautiful & the good is it not ever the frail? While they 'whose hearts are dry as summer's dust'[55] we know they neither faint nor die.[56]

⇥ *Edward Bliss Emerson to Ralph Waldo Emerson, 3 June 1834*

Your's of 12 April is before me,[57] with its kind invitations and what you call "mouldy speculations" but quite mellow & shining when they reach the West Indies—I have nothing to say to you—& wherefore should they who are already understood say any thing. Shall I take out my tinder box & bit of flint & insult you in your illuminated saloon by pretending to light a farthing candle? I look forward to a good long talk with you. I am curious to hear of some of your European passages. Besides I want to see what you have become & to have an observation, as the seamen & astronomers like to have from time to time of certain conspicuous bodies, thereby forming judgments as to the observer's situation & motion forward or retrograde—I am dis[m]ally ignorant & a few parlour lectures would be invaluable to me as a compensation for a vast deal of instructive reading that hath been & perhaps must be let alone by me. There are many things and many characters I should like well to discuss, as wont to do of old. . . . If you have projects too, how should I rejoice, fling a stone at the ridiculous, and spy out the favorable omens for the success of better schemes.—

Next year let me beg of you keep at home & I will at leas[t] visit you for a time. As to my health which I notice interests you it is such as it has been for years, sufficient to the day—and I do not let myself to imagine the cause extent or probable duration of my infirmities: glad if I am out of pain, and not often called upon to exercise other patience than that which is needful to one who finds himself less fat, less robust, less comely than other men.

But as I began so I end; you know me & having nothing to communicate which would be new, all I can write is but redundancy, tedious & inadequate to express the deep affection of your brother.[58]

↠ *Sidney Mason to William Emerson, 30 September-8 October 1834*

. . . Edward does not write you; he is ill and dangerously so. I have been with him the last night and all this day. I have never seen him suffer so much and fear for his recovery. He has for some time past been in the habit of visiting the country where he staid overnight. I have frequently cautioned him about the dampness of the season this being the rainy part of the year. His avocation as he supposed would call him always punctually at the hour induced thus often to get showered and sometimes wet. The last of these was a drenching rain about three weeks since which brought on a violent cold & little fever. Of this he was ridding himself when on Sunday he confined himself to his bed and took medicine. I called the Doctor on Monday who asked for a consultation immediately and they have so far proved their utmost talents to save the worn out frame. I have told him that the only opp° for the states sails in the morning if he had any thing particular to say to you. he then dictated to me the following: "say to William that I have one of my old fashioned attacks of Rheumatism and the lungs such as I had when Dr Perkins attended me." Something more was articulated when a flow of blood from the lungs took place which nearly suffocated him. he has not spoken and the physician does not wish him to be spoken to. He is ill very ill and but little hopes of his recovery. his strength and constitution is worn out; but little remains. we yet live in hopes of a turn. 5 oclock P.M. I have returned again from Edward and he appears easier and more calm. the pain has been subdued. The change will be great soon and we now hope for the better. I shall have this letter open untill morning that we may possible have the happiness to say he continues better. I enclose you a scroll which he has just made me on paper. he cannot speak for fear of a return of Bleeding. The Doctor has bled him. 9 oclock evening. Edward continues the same, if any thing more easy but very weak and low. I now close this and you must await the decission in another letter probably by the next opp'. The vessel will sail early in the morning. Make our respects to your Lady and to your family also.

[1 October]

I wrote you in detail yesterday of Edward's sickness. It has now become my fate to give you the melancholy tidings. I left my desk at 9 oclock and went to Edward's room, where I remained untill 12. he appeared calm and perfectly aware of his situation but not able to articulate a word. I left him with his nurse untill one when they called me, there appearing a decided change in his form. Soon after I expected to converse with him, but alas my dear Sir the calm change was his last and from that in the short space of a few hours he was with his heavenly friends and died—without a strugle at 3 oclock. I could only obtain from him that he confided in the doing of the all wise God. His loss to you and to us is irreparable and we trust he has gained a heavenly seat. Judge for yourself the feelings of us all have been powerfully moved, beloved and respected as he has been with us all. I shall entomb the body and await your further instructions, remitting you his papers &c the first direct opportunity after this.

[8 October]

Dear Sir I wrote you the foregoing letters on the 30 ult and 1st currt. Since then our establishment has had more the appearance of mourning than of commerce. The inmates of our house and ware houses scarcely can realize the lamentable loss, but the first of Oct at 5 oclock the Body of Edward was removed to the Cathedral and from there accompanied by a large concord of friends to the sacred ground w[h]ere we have entombed the remains. Service was performed and honors to the exequies after. The sudden transit did not permit me to know even his wishes in this respect, and I am happy to say that the leity of Porto Rico never has shown to a stranger the respect that has been shown to my deceasd friend. Dr Armstrong scarcely can be consoled. The loss of Edward to him it has been great.[59]

Sidney Mason's incremental letter to William completed the cycle of what, by 1834, had become Edward's familiar means of communicating with his family in America. Typically, Edward would write a letter to William and enclose it in a packet with additional letters for other family members that he expected his brother to forward to Boston, Cambridge, or Concord, as appropriate. News of Edward's death was received in Mason's New York office and Mason's letter was received by William around 15 October. William must have anticipated the sad tidings for some time, yet he could not have relished the thought of sending them on to Boston, where it would fall to Charles to tell their mother, Aunt Mary, Dr. Ripley, and others about Edward's death.

Waldo, who was then in New York and staying at his brother's house, first heard the news directly from William;[60] on hearing of Edward's death, he made the following entry in his journal and then added two melancholy lines from Schiller's *Death of Wallenstein* to it:

18 Oct. New York. Received the tidings of the death of my dear brother Edward on the first day of this month at St. John's, Porto Rico. So falls one more pile of hope for this life. I see I am bereaved of a part of myself.

> "Whatever fortunes wait my future life
> The beautiful is vanished & returns not."[61]
> (*JMN*, 4:325)

Although his notice of Edward's passing may appear uncharacteristically brief, Waldo had actually composed a partial remembrance of his brother's passing in the days after he had committed Edward to the McLean Asylum six years earlier. Using eulogistic language in a passage he entered in his journal on 10 July 1828, Waldo figured Edward and that portion of himself that his brother complemented and charged with life as already deceased.

> When I consider the constitutional calamity of my family which in its falling upon Edward has buried at once so many towering hopes—with whatever reason I have little apprehension of my own liability to the same evil. I have so much mixture of *silliness* in my intellectual frame that I think Providence has tempered me against this. My brother lived & acted & spoke with preternatural energy. My own manner is sluggish; my speech sometimes flippant, sometimes embarassed & ragged; my actions . . . are of a passive kind. Edward had always great power of face. I have none. I laugh; I blush; I look ill tempered; against my will & against my interest. But all this imperfection as it appears to me is a caput mortuum,[62] is a ballast . . . is a defence.
>
> My practice conforms more to the Epicurean, than to the Stoic rule:[63]
>
> > "I will be flesh & blood;
> > For there was never yet philosopher,
> > That could endure the tooth ache patiently,
> > However they have writ the style of gods
> > And made a p[u]sh at chance & sufferance."[64]
>
> Wo is me my brother for you! (*JMN*, 3:137).

As soon as Charles received two successive letters from William informing him of Edward's final illness and death, he wrote his mother a note and then called on her in Concord the next day. As Charles reported it to William, she had not received his message when he appeared at the Manse for what he had mistakenly thought would be a visit to console her and Aunt Mary in their initial hours of mourning for Edward.

➤➤ *Charles Chauncy Emerson to William Emerson, 20 October* [1834]

> Your two letters containing news of the sickness & death of our dear Edward were received by me on Saturday; the last was handed to me Sat-

urday evening. Sunday morning I went to Concord—Mother had not got the letter which I had sent to her Saturday—& the news came suddenly, & very sadly to her affectionate heart. "Dear Object, said she, is he gone!" She dwelt at first on the wretchedness of that lonely death & stranger's burial—But I reminded her of the mercifully short period of the poor boy's sickness—& when we came to think of *him,* him, the beautiful unblameable ardent Soul, to what he had passed—& all out of which he was escaped, she did not refuse to be comforted—how should she? Aunt Mary was strongly agitated when she first heard the tidings—but the moment the nerves were quieted, she wondered & chided at herself—She felt very glad he was gone.

I am pleased with the sincere tone of Mason's letters—I think we shall bring home the precious dust, & lay it in American soil—Young Francis G. Shaw goes from Boston to Porto Rico in a day or two & will do any thing there we wish[65]—. . .

Mother prays you to send that "pencil scrawl" of Edward's writing—his goodbye word.[66]

With her composure regained, Aunt Mary wrote to Elizabeth Hoar on 19 October, charging her with the responsibility to fill the place of the late "sainted Ellen" by supplying comfort to both Ruth Haskins Emerson and Charles over their loss of a son and brother, respectively. Invoking the ghosts of Elizabeth's own "patriot grandfathers," she said, "You dear Girl will comfort the Mother for a most valued Son—You do—& will help us to regret not always the sainted Ellen. You will shed . . . the constant light of faith & charity round the arduous path of Charles—will always be fitting each other for a union after the tears of love & respect have watered your urns, by family & society. Yes *if* you are worthy of your patriot grandfathers—soci[e]ty will long embalm your memories."[67]

In her message of consolation to Charles written a few days later, Mary extended a theme she introduced in her letter to Elizabeth. Writing as though William and Waldo were only peripherally involved in perpetuating Edward's earthly work or mourning his death, after identifying Charles and Edward as extensions of each other and invoking Edward's spirit, she told Charles that now he had to live for both his brother and himself.

. . . I think of you—now as connected with Edwards life & death. T'was for you more than any in the great web of w'h his meteoric existence made a flash that he lived—aspired—struggled—suffered—failed of all hope and died to gain what virtue not fame could give. Oh yes dear Edward thou are not walking among the haggard forms of eclipsed—dead renown—bending to earth looks of ire & disappointment—No thy sorrows & toils are weaving into thy shekinah unfading flowers—thro his influence I once knew thee to love. And you dear Charles will go forward with new strength to all the labours & weariness of life—labours & duties w'h not the brightest star of love can always gild or always soften. No the magic of nature cannot exorcise them—for depraved man must abide his condition & pass the ordeal of virtue thro the fire & water if he would be a true soldier of the cross. Often may the wasted darkened form of his life & fortunes attend your side to point your brighter way or raise your head above the mists & storms of life.[68]

Perhaps because it was expected, Edward's final illness and death, like Ellen's two and a half years earlier, appears as a subject in the brothers' correspondence for a surprisingly brief period of time. But the fact that Edward was now truly gone became a constant distraction for Charles, which Mary's invocation of Edward's aspirations, struggles, and suffering now haunting his brother in the "wasted darkened form of his life & fortunes" did nothing to ameliorate. Writing to Elizabeth on 24 October 1834, Charles lamented, "Edward, . . . I think of him morning, noon, night—& I say, He the more Fortunate! His life darkly blighted as it was pleases me now. Because it was true to higher principles than a prosperous ambition. It was not he that was blighted, but only his fortunes. It is the earthly-happy to whom earth is all,—the famous to whom fame is life, for whom one mourns when they go away reluctant & hopeless into the eternal world. Not so with thee, my brother."[69] A week after writing to Elizabeth, he confessed to Waldo, "I have had a heart to write to you but not the head." "[H]ow do you do?" he rhetorically asked his brother; invoking the "faint-hearted philosophy" that yields to "the world-ease of circumstances"— the very same philosophy with which Waldo and he had separately responded to Edward's breakdown in 1828—Charles answered the question as much for his brother as for himself:

. . . I know how you do—I know what has been uppermost in your thought. The death of a fully grown man, & that man a brother, & that brother—Edward, is event enough to fill mind & heart, awhile. The letter to mother about him made me glad & yet mournful.[70] To look backward, & earthly forward brings tears into my eyes. But I follow & recognize him amongst the Ardours in heaven. A remarkable life. We see plenty of abuse of genius by the individual, but seldom does the Hand that lighted so overshadow & extinguish the torch. The Providence must be rich that can afford to waste such a rare piece of work—not sacrifice it to the All, but refuse & snatch it back. . . .

Loose enough hangs about one the world-ease of circumstances, even the pleasantest, as he grows a very little old. When he was born into rational thought & affection, he lifted up his eyes, & a bright circle of stars bent their aspect on him & he said in his heart, These will watch over me even to the end—But star after star shoots from its place & sets untimely, & he feels alone, & the new constellations wear not such eyes of love to him.[71]

Even a year after Edward's death—and less than a year before his own—Charles was still preoccupied with thoughts about his late brother. During the commencement celebrations at Harvard in the summer of 1835, Charles's mind constantly returned to the figure that Edward, so easy with his genius and so full of promise, made during his own years at the college. He shared his reminiscences with William.

↠ *Charles Chauncy Emerson to William Emerson, 29 August 1835*

. . . We have just come to the end of Commencement week. You know it by heart, its excitement, pleasures, fatigue, yes & pain, pain in the images it brings out of the Past to follow in the funeral train of our associations with those whom we shall not again find in the places which knew them & were adorned by them on earth. Much thought I of Edward. But he, with his new wing of loftier & bolder flight, casts not one glance of regret at the pomp & festivals of our pinfold here, and sees the cloud that to us is so gaily gilded, to be no more than vapor. We shall join him shortly, & the music of his eloquence, & the electric fire of his eye shall point him out to us afar off as he mixes with the solemn troops & sweet societies of heaven.[72]

After Edward's death, the family had every intention of bringing his body home from Puerto Rico for burial in New England. It is unclear how many of them suspected from Mason's letter that Edward had received the last rites of the Roman Catholic Church on his deathbed, which was required to secure a decent burial for foreigners in Puerto Rico's Catholic culture. During his research in Puerto Rico into Edward's last days and burial, Sylvester Baxter, who spent most of the 1920s and 1930s preparing a study of "The Other Emersons," discovered, through a series of exchanges with officials of the Catholic Chancery in San Juan, that Edward, who was possibly unconscious at the time, was administered the last rites moments before his death, and he also secured from the officials a transcription (in Spanish) of the following entry in the records of the Cathedral of the Holy Catholic Church of San Juan Bautista de Puerto Rico: "On October 1st, 1834, there was buried in the Cemetery of Santa Magdalena de Passis . . . the corpse of Don Eduardo Emerson, a native of Boston, United

States of America. . . . He did not make any will. He received the Holy Sacrament of penance and Extreme Unction."[73] After unsuccessfully searching the grounds of the cemetery, which lies outside the walls of Moro Castle and faces the ocean, for evidence of Edward's grave, Baxter learned that the oven-like structures referred to in the letters that follow were not permanent gravesites in the nineteenth century, but sites rented for periods of up to five years, and then, if the rental was not renewed, the deceased's remains were removed from the graves and deposited in a nearby mass grave.

In February 1835, William, Waldo, and Charles ordered a carved marble slab that they planned to ship to San Juan, where Mason agreed to have it placed on Edward's tomb. Writing to William on 5 February, Charles supplied him with an inscription that he and Waldo had drafted for the slab. Not wanting "to denationalize even his tombstone with Spanish," Charles instructed his brother to send the following inscription to the stone carver:

Edward Bliss Emerson
of Boston
In the United States of America
died Oct. 1. 1834
aged 29—
"Qui in Me fidem habet, ille quamvis
mortuus esset, vivet."[74]

Charles told William that their mother only agreed to have the stone carved on the condition that Edward's remains would be returned to America, "by & by, a few years hence." Speaking for himself, he added, "I agree in this feeling of mother's—& whenever I am able will fulfil her wish. Meanwhile the tomb will guard & discriminate the dust."[75]

On the same day that Charles had written to William, Dr. Francis Armstrong, Edward's friend in Puerto Rico who also attended him during his final illness, finally wrote to the family in care of William. As Armstrong provided the family with several specific details about Edward's illness and death that Mason had omitted in his letter, he also provided them with one piece of shocking news that they never would have suspected.

. . . It was sometime in August that he [Edward] spent one of the holy days with Mr Hoope in Louisa and on his return to the city early the next morning he got a wetting which encreased his cough very much. but he was getting better of that, when on Saturday the 27th Sept: he excuse[d] himself from accompanying me to the country as usual, complaining of much pain in his chest, which he attributed to getting his feet wet the day before—Early on monday morning Mr Mason sent for me. I considered his case hopeless even before I entered his chamber, there being evidently a large collection of pus on the lungs—I immediately asked for a consultation and I remained constantly with him until he expired on the morning of the 1ˢᵗ of October—No foreigner has died here more universally regretted and respected—His body was deposited in an oven (so called here) hired for a certain number of months, and at the expiration of that time his bones will be taken out and thrown to one side of the burying ground indiscriminately with others—I should be very happy if his remains could be removed to the United States and deposited with his relations. I think it could be done without much expense. I will render every assistance should the proposal meet the approbation of his friends in the United States[76]—

Alarmed at the possibility that Edward's remains had already been discarded because the family had not paid any rent on the tomb, William wrote to Sidney Mason for an explanation of where matters stood, and although his letter does not survive, William also must have disclosed his fears that his brother had received last rites from a Catholic priest. Mason responded to William on 4 April, providing him with the following account of the actions he had thus far taken and informing him that Edward had indeed received the sacraments on his deathbed.

. . . I will now for your satisfaction retale to you the actual steps taken by me to secure any . . . villains [from acting] upon the sacred cor[p]se of your brother—after he expired I called upon the principal priest related to him my feelings and requested no impediment might take place in the deposit of your Brother's remains, to secure which I had callᵈ one of the Fathers and he said prayers and put holy water in the presence of Dr A[rmstrong] myself brothers and our families at 3 oclock in the morning of the first day of Octʳ. I by this obtained the safe guard against a no and nothing was said about religion so he was deposited in the church and all of his [friends,] my own [friends,] and a large number of citizens attended his Funeral. . . . I was forceᵈ to hire a tomb of the church and did so for 3 months. they are archᵈ and not unlike the mouth of an oven. they are oval and all shapes. the mouth is closeᵈ with brick & mortar. the body rested there untill I had finishᵈ the one prepared to receive the tablet I had mentionᵈ to you, the moment this place of deposit was finishᵈ and dry which is now distinguishᵈ from most of all the others from its appearance wh being an oblong square. I attended myself in taking the coffin from the first and placing it carefully in that built, where it now remains carefully seal[e]d up and the vacant space mentionᵈ ready to receive his tablet. I trust that when I am called upon the render to your family or another the remains of your deceas[d] brother it will not be inhumanely said of me, it is not him. it can be recogniz[d] and I trust my dear sir it were as safe w[h]ere it now s[t]ays as may possible be in any open tomb.[77]

Comforted by Mason's assurances, William wrote to Waldo on 7 May 1835 to say that he believed Edward's remains would be safe in San Juan until the time came to have them brought to America. He shipped the marble slab on the *Independence* the same week.[78]

Today, many visitors to the Emerson family plot on Authors Ridge in Concord's Sleepy Hollow Cemetery believe that Edward's remains rest beneath the marble slab that bears his name and the inscription drafted by Charles and Waldo. In truth, however, they do not. At some point between Edward's death and the opening of Sleepy Hollow Cemetery in 1855, either the slab came loose from the front of the temporary tomb Sidney Mason had constructed or someone missed a rental payment on the tomb, because the slab was returned to William from San Juan and placed in a cemetery on Staten Island, New York, where William lived at the time. Although no records survive to date this event precisely, in notes provided to Sylvester Baxter by Edward Waldo Forbes of conversations he had been having with his mother, Edith Emerson Forbes, Waldo's daughter, it appears that William sent the slab to Concord after the dedication of Sleepy Hollow Cemetery and Waldo had it set flush to the ground in the family plot he had purchased.[79] No records have been found anywhere, including in the generally complete calendar of interments in Sleepy Hollow Cemetery, to indicate that Edward's remains were returned from Puerto Rico with the slab or were ever interred in the family plot in Concord.

CHARLES, NATURE'S BOY OF "HECTIC BLOOM"

The first serious symptoms of Charles's illness must have occurred early in 1830, when he wrote to Joseph W. Lyman, his close friend and confidant from Harvard days who was also an attorney and eventually practiced in New York, that he was considering a six-month sojourn in Cuba. In the letter that follows, Charles's admission that it is probable he "may have to go" to a warmer climate anticipates the purposely understated manner in which he discussed his health from the time he first admitted having tuberculosis until the time of his death in 1836; at the same time, the depression and sense of moroseness he exhibits in the letter's description of his return to "Canterbury," the home in Roxbury where—with the exception of William who had gone to Germany for his studies—he lived with his mother and brothers in the early 1820s, discloses a side of his character that Charles showed only in his correspondence with Aunt Mary and Elizabeth Hoar and in the pages of a secret spiritual diary he maintained during the 1830s.[80]

> What do you say to my starting next October, for Cuba, to be gone 6 months—It is very probable I may have to go—& this like many other things, you may keep under your own especial padlock.—. . .
>
> I went to ride yesterday, all alone, to the old house in Roxbury where we used to live. It was empty—so I got out, tied my horse to the bars, & roamed about the place in pure & isolateness of spirit. It looked as the Temple did to the Jews, after the rush of the winds was heard, & the voice—'Let us go out hence.' [81] We were new to the country when we lived there, & every stone & bush was a romance to us—We actually waked the poor peasants all about us to a sort of sympathy with our own exhilaration, & I have no doubt that the two years we spent there is still remembered as an epoch in that quiet neighbourhood. But yesterday, it was all dull & still & forlorn—I remembered how many of those whom I used to see there, were dead, or estranged, or scattered to a distance— some now sick & wasted, who were then ambitious, & gay, & stout of heart—I remembered how many things I used to hope & believe when I ran about those fields, which I shall never again hope or believe—And I turned away from these recollections & tried to think about you.[82]

Charles never did venture to Cuba. However, in the summer of 1831, his fears about his health and his need to settle in a more congenial winter environment than either Boston or New York could afford were realized, when after returning from his walking tour with Waldo through Vermont and northern New York, he developed a persistent cold and cough. Although Charles's correspondence with his brothers is silent on the subject, Waldo kept William and Edward informed of their youngest brother's condition. By September, he reported to William that Charles appeared "not half so robust as I wish," and he wrote to Edward, "he is in body like a wilted apple but as fresh of spirit & as disdainful of all of the rest of poor human nature—all except his own platoon—as ever."[83] However, by October, as he confided to Edward, Waldo was beginning to fear for Charles's life. Hoping to send a letter to Puerto Rico on a ship about to leave from Boston, Waldo wrote the following to Edward on 19 October 1831:

> I learn just now that a vessel is sailing for St Johns. I am sorry to have no better news from home to give you than that Charles is quite unwell. He has been laboring for some time under a bad cold & cough which is now continual tho' pretty loose, & attended with a great stupor

& indisposition to any exertion even so much as to speak. He is pale & weak—all sad signs in a frame so slender. Dr [John] Ware attends him & Dr [James] Jackson [Sr.] will come tomorrow.[84] I told Dr Ware he must send him away the first moment he thinks proper to find you in P[uerto]. R[ico]. He thinks it may be highly proper to do so, but not until the inflammation (catarrhal inflam.) subsides. His friend Lyman sits all day with him & reads & cares for him. & [Mother] nurses with faithful love. . . . He desponds of his health but talks as [a] Christian & philosopher, of the future. . . .

I trust in God his life is to be preserved & yet I have some serious apprehensions about him. (L, 1:334–335)

Charles's condition did not improve, nor, it seems, had Edward's, who decided to remain in Puerto Rico rather than return home before the onset of winter. On the same day he had written hurriedly to Edward, Waldo repeated the substance of that letter in one he wrote to William, adding this note of alarm: "[Charles] speaks almost never. . . . Dr Ware thinks his illness shd. give no uneasiness in a person of common constitution, but with his frame & habit is more dangerous, & thinks him a little better . . . tho' not materially." His consciousness of the frailty of human life piqued, Waldo ended his letter to William with this pessimistic remark: "Who would have thot that Edward & Charles on whom we put so much fond pride shd. be the first to fail whilst Ellen, my rose, is gone" (L, 1:335–336).

On 23 October, Waldo wrote to William that Charles seemed to be improved enough to either remain home in his family's care or journey to a southern climate. "Blisters & leeches & bleeding have been the means of relieving his pleurisy & his pleurisy seems to have been the means of relieving his lungs" (L, 1:336). Not yet having this news, William wrote to Ruth and Waldo on 23–24 October, offering whatever assistance they might require in caring for Charles. In the portion of his letter addressed to his mother, William said that he was consoled by the thought that she and Waldo were themselves in good health, and though he admitted that because they were "on the spot" and knew what had to be done to relieve Charles's suffering, he allowed, "to me there seems to be only one thing to be done, & that is, to let him go & spend the winter with Edward." Addressing Waldo, William expressed the fear he had withheld from Ruth: "I know not whether to take comfort or the contrary from your last account as the pleurisie attack may be more alarming than his former complaints."[85]

Charles's condition stabilized sufficiently during November for him to decide to set out for the Caribbean. The choices open to him were the same as Edward and he had each considered earlier: Cuba, St. Croix, or Puerto Rico. Although St. Croix offered a pleasant enough environment in which to recuperate and was the place to which most New Englanders first fled, as Edward's brief experience there had shown, the island at this time seemed like a terminal ward for Americans wintering there and waiting to die of tuberculosis. Charles wisely wanted to avoid so openly depressing an atmosphere; besides, as he suggested to Edward, Puerto Rico's special attraction over any other place available to him in the Caribbean was that his brother was already there. Announcing the news of his "visit" in a letter to Edward dated 1 December 1831, Charles expressed the hope that at least by being together they could repair the fraternal breach caused by Edward's own exile for his health.

> I am coming to pay you a visit. . . . [T]he cold weather feels so uncomfortable to my dainty body, that it was agreed between Waldo & me & winter & Dr. Jackson, that it would be mighty pleasant to eat oranges & wear thin jackets for four months to come, instead of staying here & shoveling snow.
>
> I do not know that you are at this present moment in Porto Rico—since the Catholics may have extirpated such a root of heresy—So I shall *probably* take passage for St Thomas in the Brig Jasper—She will sail about the 10th Decr. When I get there shall write to you in P.R. & ascertain whether to go to you in P.R. or not by the answers I get. Perhaps you will not stay all the winter at P.R. . . . . I shall of course like to be with you.
>
> Do not think I am *sick* because I am coming,—I am only allowing myself to use a most luxurious cordial, in hopes thereby so strong to grow, as to be able thenceforth to abjure all nursing, & be able *unreservedly* to act.
>
> I do not know how or when this letter will go—but write it in hopes it may somehow reach you before I do. I flatter myself my visit will not be any interruption to your extensive mercantile engagements.[86]

As the following selections from his extensive correspondence from Puerto Rico to family and friends reveal, Charles sailed for Puerto Rico aboard the *America* on 7 December and arrived in the port of San Juan on the 22d. Even though Edward had kept the family informed of his life in the islands and written occasional descriptions of the Caribbean's scenery and her people, Charles did not know what to expect on his arrival. Writing home, he affects a light, cavalier tone about his health, but his tone is serious and descriptions detailed when he writes about the people and customs he encountered. One feature of Charles's correspondence that his letters from Puerto Rico highlights is that, like Waldo, Charles was acutely aware of his correspondents' character and what they would most like to hear about in letters from him. For example, though their point of origin has changed, his letters to Aunt Mary from Puerto Rico appear to be modest variations on those he wrote to her from Boston, Cambridge, or Concord. Predictably, a theme he developed for her was his joy at having been born and raised in New England as opposed to the "sensual Paradise" of the Caribbean: "I thank the God who made me to grow up on the rugged soil, & beneath the bleak heavens of New England," he wrote to her in a rambling letter composed between 19 and 26 December; "[t]he purity of her snows is better than the Cyprian atmosphere of this sensual Paradise—& knowledge & truth to be had without money & without price, is a richer plenty than all the gorgeous feast which outward Nature here spreads for a race in whom the animal mounts above the intellectual & crushes the religious principle."[87] Similarly, writing to Ezra Ripley within weeks of his arrival in San Juan, Charles professed that by addressing his step-grandfather he felt that he was finally able to step back from the sensuous distractions that surrounded him and restore equilibrium to his moral sensibility: "My letter has unintentionally taken the same shifting course in which my thoughts perpetually travel—from the delightful climate & luxurious pleasures of the West Indian, to the dreary dearth of all moral resources. What a mystery there is in the Providence which suffers the most lovely spots on the Earth, most frequently to become the nests of iniquity & woe!"[88]

Despite the character of some of his remarks to Aunt Mary and Ezra Ripley, Charles is neither the "ugly American" abroad nor a transplanted Calvinist incapable of changing his inherited opinions or indulging himself in the exoticism of his island paradise. Indeed, there is a charming eclecticism about Charles's letters from the Caribbean that is not apparent in the body of his correspondence to either his brothers or anyone else. Writing to Joseph Lyman on Christmas day of 1831, he offers this idyllic first impression of Puerto Rico: "The island seems to me to have been designed for a little Eyrie where bards & painters & naturalists should be nursed—& the keys put into their hands to unlock all the chambers of science & beauty in our Earth."[89] In the months that he spent on the island, many of Charles's prejudices about Spanish and West Indian culture as well as about Catholicism were worn away by the warmth and geniality of the people he met, and his romantic imagination was piqued to new levels of activity by aspects of the sea and landscape that unexpectedly attracted his eye. Here, as he wrote to Mary, he discovered that the sea is where "Nature has lodged her mystery; here that she images the infinite";[90] and echoing his comments to Lyman, in letters to William and Waldo, Charles confessed that he could not resist for too long the island's "voluptuous" scenery. Finally, although he was comfortable with the distance between his everyday affairs in Puerto Rico and political and reform issues back home, on the island Charles further refined his already keen awareness of horror of slavery by witnessing the institution firsthand, and that awareness informed his views on slavery and Indian rights for the remainder of his life.

➳ *Charles Chauncy Emerson to Mary Moody Emerson,*
19–26 December [1831]

Do not think me weak & recreant because I run away from good New England—and never fear that I shall get acclimated to any change of moral atmosphere. Pygmalion's statue on waking, you remember, says touching itself 'this is I,' touching its pedestal, 'this is not I,' & touching Pygmalion 'this is I indeed'[91]—and even in these same words, do I severally address, myself, my condition, and those principles, that sentiment, wherein I live or have no being,—that orb which embraces me & all I love, yea all souls.

Buonaparte affected to date his imperial decrees from remote capitals of imposing name.[92] I thought in the inland retirement of Elm Vale, it might give a little character to my letter that it was written pretty nearly upon the Tropic line, in the midst of an uneasy sea. Yes, here I sit, ink in hand, in our box of a cabin, from whence I can see nothing but the masts & rigging, but where I can hear the dash of the waves, a music which has become wonted to me ears. This however is by no means my usual observatory or study—The weather is so fine that I am most of the time on deck, & if it were given to man to grow wise by looking instead of thinking, I should be a very Solomon[93]—

A voyage I should esteem quite a nostrum for certain diseases in the manners & opinions. I should think it was nigh as good a purge for conceit as for bile. One feels lonesome, & bubble-like on this broad element which separates him from all the relations in which he found food for self-importance. Here he is "the poor naked forked thing itself"[94]—And if he have nothing to fall back upon, nothing out of which to raise the consciousness of independent thought & spiritual life, he must feel mean in comparison with the great frame of Nature above & about him.

Who shall find fault with me if I make the most of my cockney trip to the West Indias, & moralize the scene with a thousand similies? I am no statesman charged with the interests of a nation—no Cook nor Columbus going out to seek new territory for civilization[95]—no missonary bound on an errand which absorbs his soul—not even a merchant, tributizing wind & wave to my private gains, but I am a simple citizen in search of all the good I can get out of all things.

I am free to say then, though I desire both to live & to die on land, that I think the ocean is the height of matter—it is like to nothing; if you would speak of it, it must be by itself, or you must draw your types from the moral universe—It is here that Nature has lodged her mystery; here that she images the infinite. Mountains are motionless, & noiseless, & we can see their height & breadth. But the Sea is alive with a sound & motion that seem intelligent, & she returns ever into herself unmeasured.

The *terror* of the sea is the feeling that you are left alone with matter. Everywhere on the solid continent you are encircled with the signs of Divine beneficence & human art; these are props & comforts in every peril. But 'when the storm comes on the ocean,' & obscures the order of the heavenly bodies, you have no bow of God, no pledge of human aid, to appeal to: There is no proof even of organized nature, for the moment, in the angry deep on which you are tossed. . . .

Dec. 26. St. Johns Porto Rico. Yesterday was Christmas Day & I heard mass in the churches of the Catholics—gloomy buildings, that seem made to over awe & imprison the soul. The friars in their silken dress go about the streets of this balmy-aired city. Oh that you could have one glance from the ramparts over the 'happy brimmed sea' which lulls & sings itself asleep on these green & sunny shores—Our sky here is laced with clouds of all soft hues—green, golden, & pink—The commonest herbs look fine & rare—You remember the epitaph on Pizarro[96]—which tells of his power, wealth, success, & closes thus "Reader art thou poor, art humble, Dost thou earn thy daily bread by daily labor, Thank the God that made thee, thou art not like Pizarro." Even so say I to this luxurious region.

I thank the God who made me to grow up on the rugged soil, & beneath the bleak heavens of New England—The purity of her snows is better than the Cyprian atmosphere of this sensual Paradise—& knowledge & truth to be had without money & without price, is a richer plenty than all the gorgeous feast which outward Nature here spreads for a race in whom the animal mounts above the intellectual & crushes the religious principle.[97]

➤ *Charles Chauncy Emerson to Ralph Waldo Emerson, 23–24 December 1831*

Yesterday, the Anniversary of the Pilgrim Landing, we anchored in the Harbour of St Johns, & about sundown I came ashore—for the first time planting my foot on a foreign soil. While we coasted along the island, though the features of the country were strange, yet the mere rest of the eye upon solid land & green vegetation, was refreshing, & made me feel a little at home in the scene. When we rounded the Moro, & were hailed by a trumpet-tongued warder in Spanish, a hundred feet or so above our heads,—when we could distinctly see the city, its high walls, & heavy, blank, jail-like rows of dwelling-houses, my feelings of recognition & familiarity died all away—And the dark looks & unintelligible jabber of the Spanish pilot, & the Custom house officers on board ship, prepared me to be very desolate in a community of twenty thousand such. Presently, however, came Mr. John Mason[98]—with honest face, & English speech—Edward was well—I plucked up heart—went ashore with Mr. M. found Edw. in the Café & now began to be amazed & amused by all things I saw & heard—The din almost confounds one—for the people living as it were in the streets, & not being afflicted with complaints of the lungs, do apparently exult & disport themselves in the variety & volume of the sounds they utter.

Certainly it is 'Mundo nuevo' to me in my simplicity, as well as to the Spanish Crown. Yet it is exactly what you should expect to have made out of a delightful climate, & commercial spirit acting on the colony of a decayed empire, on a people who want, the *principle* of civilization.

The streets are regular, but dirty & ill stoned—I cannot call it paved, no use being made of carriages of any sort; & from what I see, I should suppose my intended fellow passengers the mules would here come to a good market. I like the houses—those of the better class are extensive buildings, running (like Mr. S. Mason's for instance) from one street to another, cut into square, lofty, rough finished rooms, & long passages, & a court yard, while servants seem to have lodges here & there in different quarters & everything reminds you of baronial state. All the floors & stairs are of brick or stone. From their balconies, the gentry look out upon a country which looks to me like nothing but W. Allston's landscapes[99]—so warm & softly shadowed—smooth waters & dark browed hills. The air, though from the negligence about dirt you might expect it be foul, is all the time fragrant & cordial. The talk, tho' not understood, & lively action of the people in the streets, chiefly blacks & poor Spaniards, is a continual entertainment—Dec. 24. Last Eveg. I took a walk with Edw. outside of the City—we strolled along a green road, bordered here & there by a few peaked cabins, looking as simple & native as though they had grown out of the spot of earth they covered; on our right hand was the creek of the sea which I have said runs behind the island of St Johns & makes its harbour—beyond it rose the highlands of Porto Rico, in triple ranges, producing the fine effect we noticed in the scenery on Lake Champlain, each chain of hills falling back into a different hue & a fainter haze. On the left was a sloping bank of green on the summit of which run along the fortifications of the City & on whose acclivity the Spanish soldiers were now parading to the music of a full band—This bank we shortly began to ascend—before I reached the top, I could hear the ocean announcing its presence by a long-resounding roar, & a few steps more brought me to a sight as magnificent as ever visited these eyes. Yes, there it lay stretched out beneath me the great Deep, as proud & calm as when the bark of Columbus first ploughed its waters—whitening the shore far as I could see with its breaking waves, & murmuring at the decree, which stayed it even here. I turned as soon as I could to look again on those heights all painted & curtained by Sun & Clouds, whose feet are thus bathed by the ever flowing sea, & I *no* longer wondered at the sanguine dreams & the poetic pomp which filled Columbus's soul, & burned in his descriptions of the world he discovered.

> Wo that the linden & the vine should bloom
> And a brave man be gathered to the tomb.

This glorious region, these wonders of Nature, preach to a servile & insensible race. They need no lessons of eternal beauty & order, no revelation of God, in the heavens which drop fatness, or the earth which teems with fruits & smiles with love.

I have enough to say; but am weary of writing—. . . I am a guest in the house of Sidney Mason—Love to all[100]—

⇝ Charles Chauncy Emerson to Joseph W. Lyman, 25 December 1831

Oh that you were with me to help me see & hear & enjoy! And yet I am glad to have you at home—to make a part of that strong attraction which points all my thoughts & affections northward—so that I turn thither as the plant to the light. Yet you would be very much pleased yourself, I think, with a visit here—where even such a homesick child as I finds a charm in the air, the natural scenery, & the entire freshness & piquancy of the drama of life as enacted by these Islanders, which together with the society of my brother makes the days of the exile glide happily away—

You have such a perverse attachment to *facts* & entertain yourself so often with measuring out to my leaky ear all sorts of *particulars,* that I have a good mind to pay you in your own coin, & stow away for my own future advantage in your nice memory what little details I have collected concerning things & people here, & the place itself.

The City of St Johns stands on a small island about 2 miles long, and of unequal breadth. The island fronts to the North, running parallel with Porto Rico, to which it is united by a bridge at the Eastern extremity, where the creek which divides the two is narrow enough to be crossed by a bridge . . .—we of course, coming from Windward, coasted along its whole length, & to us it seemed only as the base of the lofty cordillera[101] which runs through the heart of P.R. immediately in its rear. We saw cocoa trees & a few scattered houses on shore, but not much of a city till we reached the Moro or Castle which stands on the point of land which projects a little into the sea & where the island makes an elbow, running thence, I shd. say, about S.W—on rounding this majestic fortress, you come in full view of the town which slopes upward from the water which is here shut in between the two islands & makes a safe anchorage for vessels, & a most picturesque bay to the eye. The Moro shoots its white perpendicular rock a hundred feet or more up from the ocean, & we pass so directly under its walls, as to be able to measure their height pretty nearly by seeing the Royal heads of the shop about on a level with the battlements. The city looked gloomy & tomb like from our deck—the houses being low, chiefly of dead wall, stained with dirty yellow & white—When I entered the gate, however, I was astonished at the lively face put upon the whole, merely by the sight of the motley population about their business or amusements all wholly new to your untravelled friend. Here stood the whiskered soldado on guard, with some of his comrads stretched in a lazy group on the ground—a muleteer driving past them his patient animal, with panniers laden with charcoal or grass; there, sat negro women at their stalls laden, with plantains, eggplants, taiotas, & what not—every body in the street & every body chattering—When Mr. Mason led me into his house, had I not known it to be the mansion of a wealthy merchant, & seen it to be like those near it, I might have taken it to be the jail I was visiting—so strange at first appeared to me the heavy gateways, long passages, & spacious brick floored, rough-timbered chambers, which are so well suited to the climate, & wh. soon please the taste.—The City is walled all around & the fortifications are esteemed very complete & are said to have cost many years of labor & immense sums of money, insomuch that a king of Spain once asked if the streets of St Johns were not paved with doubloons; he thought they ought to be to account for the enormous expenditures made upon the place by the crown. 1200 is the no. of garrison. As you walk the ramparts in any quarter, you have continually opening upon you the prospect of the ocean, on one side, of the harbour (an Italian sheet of water) on the other with Porto Rico beyond, died in the hues of its own purple atmosphere. My pen flags as I come to say anything of the scenery either of land or sea—because I cannot describe it—The island seems to me to have been designed for a little Eyrie where bards & painters & naturalists should be nursed—& the keys put into their hands to unlock all the chambers of science & beauty in our Earth.

The Churches of which there are 4 or 5 are dark & ribbed buildings, that look like the Inquisition—They are not handsome within. The Friars walk about town, in black silk dresses, & I touch my hat to the Profession.

We have two meals a day—one at 10 A.M. the other at 4½ P.M. The table is laden with delicious vegetable dishes, & commonly two or more of meats—curiously prepared—your plate is changed several times & both meals are followed by coffee & the dinner by sweetmeats. And now let me rest from telling, & ask how you do . . . & let me pray you to show Waldo this letter, poor as it is, because I keep no journal, & try not to say the same thing in two letters. . . .

I shall probably stay most of my time in Porto Rico—perhaps go nowhere else, except (as I return home) to St Thomas, that is to say, if I find the living in the country at St Barbara (Mr. Mason's estate) as pleasant as I have reason to think it will be. Edward tells me that St. Croix does by no means come up to Porto Rico in the variety & beauty. I will try next time to send you a better letter of its scenery[102]—

→ *Charles Chauncy Emerson to William Emerson, 4 January 1832*

I wish you a happy new year. I am sure I did not think the last time I shook hands with you, that so much land & water would be between us when the year came to its end. But here I am, thankful for the hospitality of a Spanish island—& enjoying great comforts & advantages. I should never have adventured here, unless Edward had been here to receive me—& one must I think have a good deal of courage & a contented spirit who should go from home to dwell among strangers speaking a strange tongue, to seek recreation & the recovery of his health. I suspect too that there are not many places civilized & commercial, where an American feels more 'insolitus,' where the look of things is more entirely new, than in a Spanish West India island. On the continent of Europe, the French language, the general similarity of customs which frequent intercourse has bred, & our familiarity with European names, events, & associations, must make the American traveller somewhat at home on the soil. I do not know but that you must have been rather isolated & homesick (though you contemn the word) at Göttingen, going there immediately on your arrival, as you did, & but little acquainted with that most unmanageable tongue the German. Edward is in his counting room from 6 A.M. till 4 P.M. & in that space I put all my little study, which does not indeed deserve the name. After dinner we stroll in company over the beach or the ramparts, battening (would I might say fattening) on the fresh & fragrant air.

The leap is indeed great out of the land of speaking, preaching, writing publishing, founding, ordering, changing,—out of our busy & inquisitive community—out of the abundance of books & facts & rumors & excitements—into this placid pool of being where the days pass over us as over the summer flies who buzz & buzz but do not act.

There are not many Americans here—almost none except the Masons.

At St. Croix I learn there are a great many invalids—how good the society is there or rather how much to my taste it would be, I do not know, tho' Edw. thinks I should get weary of it—Probably I shall stay here until I move to St. Thomas in the spring, to take passage for N. York or Boston.

What is doing? Tell us of some new thing—of men or of measures, it is all one to us. I went out the other day to Santa Barbara. . . . I enjoyed the voluptuous scenery very much; nor is the condition of the slaves half so bad to see as it is to think of, because they do not suffer themselves—and a man has claims enough in this world on his sympathy without spending it on the merry & fat.[103]

↦ *Charles Chauncy Emerson to Ralph Waldo Emerson, 9–14 January* [1832]

To night we received your packet of the 10th Dec. Thanks my dear brother for your remembering the absent while 'it was early & therefore kind.' And mother's line, her very R. E. is a comfort.—Alas for your obstinate popularity—Why sleep the lightnings of Jaquith?[104] Glad that the hospitality of the old house still finds those who by accepting it, will swell your household to a more respectable & cheerful size. . . .

You say keep one eye a patriot & the other an emigrant. So I try to do, but the West Indian pupil is apt to contract & its brother mean while to dilate, till I look all asquint—& the mind runs backward & enjoys the past, instead of searching, enjoying, & treasuring up the present scene.

I have however in the letters of the last fortnight, (& they are altogether no trifle) meant to say how the green visage of Nature, & the swarthy face of society here struck the newcomer. If the narrative drawls & whines a little, set it down to homesickness, & remember that wiser men than I, have made the malady famous. I began to be afraid I was spinning my yarn too thin—& that my critic brother might turn upon me with the suggestion, that it was above three centuries since a Genoese adventurer discovered the West Indias, & that the islands had been more than once visited by enterprising travellers—But you strengthen me by this demand for first impressions. En avant!

When I first landed with somewhat of a prejudice against Porto Rico, & a dismal idea of the Spaniards—and found myself in a little lively city, which looked so picturesque & smelt like an orange, in the midst of the glorious scenry I have described to you more than once—while the inhabitants instead of knives & pistols wore the most peac[e]able garb in the world, & had a smile & greeting even for the stranger—When I thought of Columbus—that these Islands were in a manner his family seat—that I was conversing with his colony, breathing the air, & regaled by the fruits which intoxicated his mighty imagination—I gave myself up to the genius of the place, & 'my heart was cheered in the sight of mine eyes.' But you must either have Nature *alone* or she must be backed by virtue & intelligence in human society. Columbus came while all was Nature—there was a perfect harmony between the Indian, naked or decked with the feathers he had robbed from the birds in his own woods, & the beautiful country through which he walked—But a garrison of 1200 whiskered soldados, with mortars & twentyfour pounders planted thickly round the ramparts on every side—an irreligious people, in an utter stagnation of all healthy impulses from within or without—is no ways in keeping with the softness but I am sure you are tired of this & so am I—

Today is the 14th of Jany. . . . I have nothing very witty to say—I have been to take my before-breakfast-walk this morning—but it always damps all I enjoy, to think as I cannot help doing, yes, it is fine—fine for them who were born to it—but I, I have no property in the soil—*My* Fathers never shed a drop of precious blood in its defence—their bones do not repose in its bosom—my boot never will tread lightly over the sod that is guarded by the cannon of an imbecile monarch over the sea—No Waldo, we will live, or if God so order, die . . . by our own altars & homes,—& our ashes shall mix with the holy dust of the good & wise who have gone to rest before us.

I feel better—hope to come back well[105]—

→ *Charles Chauncy Emerson to Ezra Ripley, 15–17 January 1832*

After a prosperous voyage of 15 days, in which I got out of the sea, all the wisdom & health I could, we landed ourselves safely at St. Johns, the 22ᵈ of Decr. And now, my dear Grandfather, I am here domesticated in Edward's quarters, with a great deal to entertain me in all I see, albeit there is much to regret, & much that is wanting. It is a place pleasant enough to visit, but not good to live in. The men & women are a growth we could no more raise in New England, than we could oranges or bananas. They are spoiled children grown up—Without any early education, & leading a life whose whole office it is to supply the desires of the body, shut out from all part in the public affairs, with no cultivated society, or circulation of knowledge, they naturally ripen into indolent, ignorant, untrustworthy, irreligious people—good humoured & courteous when not irritated or crossed; but easily enraged, & like most weak persons, prone to be jealous. I ought to say however that they treat a stranger very kindly, & that I find them better than I should have thought their education would make them.—

Jan 17. My letter was begun in the City; but yesterday I came out to

Santa Barbara, Mr. Mason's plantation, about 5 miles from St. Johns.
This morning, before breakfast, I rode to the top of a steep hill which
commands a view of several miles round about,—And oh the beauty
& fatness of the land! I feasted on it as on some delicious fruit. Spread
out beneath my feet, was a valley of thousands of acres—cane-fields &
pasture-lands, a sheet of living green, with lofty cocoas & palmetto trees
standing about like sentinels, & giving an air of stately repose to the
whole. The little village of Bayamon lay full in sight, reflecting the Sun's
rays from the walls of its old Church—& sprinkled over the verdant
map, at intervals, the small clusters of buildings which mark a Plantation—This valley was bounded by ridges of hills, retreating behind each
other to the distant mountains; in some spots they were cleared, in others
they were rough with precipices, & chalky rocks glaring out from under a
tangled & matted vegetation. Flowers of every colour grew in the thicket
through which I made my ascent—the air was loaded with sweet smells,
& trees of oranges, glowing fiery yellow amidst their green leaves, regaled
the sight rather than the taste, being sour as lemons.

The slaves enjoy a good deal, & are humanely treated in this island,
as I am told they are generally through the West Indias—more so than in
the U.S. But I am too lately come from the cheerful abodes of free labour-
ers, to look at them with any satisfaction—I feel grieved, & at the same
time humiliated, as we do when we see the monkey. They do not work
nearly so hard, as does a Yankee farmer—but they work without the consciousness of liberty & property, which makes toil honorable & sweet.
No human society is perfect—In each & all are wrapt up some elements
of evil, which alarm the patriot & ask his constant, watchful care—but
to tolerate slavery is like nothing so much, as sewing up the body politic
(as the ancients did the parricide,) in a sack with a living viper. Slavery
affords a frightful illustration of the infinite mischief which waits on one
false step, a single bad institution.—My letter has unintentionally taken
the same shifting course, in which my thoughts daily move—from the
delightful climate, & outward luxuries of the West Indian, to his dreary
dearth of all moral advantages. The most lovely spots on our Earth, seem
fated to be nests of suffering & wrong.

My Dear Grandfather, the Tropical landscape fades from before me;
& I see in its stead the well-remembered face of your busy village &
pleasant farms—I see the old mansion house, & the image of its honored
inmates. Your religious Sabbath, your Lyceum, your world of good news
& good books, rises to mind. May the God of our Fathers cause the light
of his countenance long to shine on that & every portion of my dear native land!

. . . Edward desires that his message of love & respect may not be omitted—he is well, & likes his situation here—but looks as thin & white as ever.[106]

⤳ Charles Chauncy Emerson to Mary Moody Emerson, 4 February 1832

How often I think of your sister Hannah's critique on you—'There's Mary—Death, Judgment, & Eternity, nothing else will do for her.'[107] I think of it, because when I sit down to write to you, I involuntarily go through a mental process that answers to what Cousin talks about—"finding one's East"—I poise myself on my principles—& undertake simply to tell what is going on in the inner soul, after all the gates of disguise & deceit are passed. What is it to you, how I flutter or creep, through this day's show, or that day's drudgery? And how cold would you feel the style which should affect the Epicurean, & skim over the top of things, as if there were no depths to sound, & no wounds of the spirit to probe.

But the *elements* in Nature are few; truth tho' infinite, is *one;* while the shapes which matter offers to the *eye,* & the forms which ceremony wears, or humour takes, or invention devises, are 'thick as motes that people the sun beam'[108]—Therefore forgive me—So far I wrote, & was interrupted; & methinks the exordium looks dangerous, threatening confessions & metaphysics—I'll none of them—I am as empty-pated here in my West Indian winter quarters, as in my Hermitage at Concord. . . . The mind is evidently meant for a long-lived creature, it is slow in growing—it swallows with so little remorse wide intervals of time, wherein nothing can persuade it to work, it is keeping some great holiday registered in its own gigantic Alamanac, where ages are months or days. And it is for this reason, because of this perverse behaviour on the part of the mind, that it is on the whole wise to put it to the mill of worldly drudgery, & sweat out its lazy & irregular humours. For though the analogy may hold pretty nicely & the mind many times may make no more progress than the horse who goes round & round his track, yet at least we are sure it is busy & turns off a certain amount of work, thus paying its debt to Nature & the social system.

Shakspeare was a proper Pagan—understood the height & depth of humanity in all its tossings on the sea of circumstance—now breasting the waves, mounting even to heaven on their steep sides,—& now drifting before the wrath of the tempest. In himself he embraced this whole sphere—the whole of man struggling with the whole of Fortune. But of Religion as it comes out of the new Dispensation—of Christianity as an element in the soul, controlling all the rest, & exhibiting new phenomena of action & passion, he had no experience, I had almost said no conception. The beauty of holiness, the magnanimity of faith, he never saw—He probably was an unbeliever & looked on the New Testament as a moral code that hampered the freedom of the mind which was a law unto itself & as intruding on the sublime mystery of our fate. Hence he delighted to get out of the way of Christianity & not to have to calculate for any of its influence—

> What's brave, what's noble
> Let's do it after the high Roman fashion[109]—

This was as he felt—& in Cleopatra it is just sentiment; but sometimes in the *English* plays, his men & women talk in just as ante-Christian a fashion as Cæsar or Coriolanus.[110]—Now as they say our very sign posts show that a Titian & a Raphael have been in the world, does not society everywhere attest in some mode or other the effects of Christianity?[111] Certain fundamental truths sink & sow themselves in every soil—& the most irreligious man, unconsciously supposes them in all his life & conversation.—How has the old bard ere now read the universe with other eyes! dramatised, it may be, the sufferings of Martyrs for a spectacle to celestial spirits!

When I last wrote to you I was in the City; I have now been two or three weeks in the country, riding about morning & evening, through sugar plantations, rivers, ponds, dingles & bosky dells. I am very well, & count the weeks of your cold weather impatiently. Yesterday I got two Newspapers from Boston, which I devoured even to the tail, i.e. the advertisements. They told a mixed story of joy & wo, like most mortal documents—science & charity & commerce were thriving at home—but England, our dear mother England was waiting with an aspect of alarm new changes in her old age—& in the East the fire & the plague have been wasting the city & the field—What are our petty griefs? I have received . . . the letter of goodbye you wrote me—It was very kind—& perhaps it is true & I owe my feebleness & disappointments to the want of a faith sufficiently strong, & a devotion to some great object, so entire as the arrest the wheels of disease & death until it be achieved—as the sun stood still in Gibeon,[112] while the battle was won.[113]

↦ *Charles Chauncy Emerson to William Emerson, 5 February 1832*

. . . The day has been an Agape or Love feast—for I had nine letters from home, besides the society & conversation, over them, of my Porto Rico brother, whom since my removal here I see only of a holiday or Sunday. What with this, & with the Newspapers I feel almost brought up with *my* world. Never Jew more firmly turned in his captivity or exile more fondly toward Zion, than I to the bleak shores of New England. I covet health & strength, & knowledge even & goodness, with a reference to home—at least all have a value when I suppose myself there, that makes the rate of exchange, Oh how high, in its favor. *Now,* you seem to me to have hardly stepped over the paternal threshold, in going to settle at New York; though 'stultus ego putavi,'[114] when in Chardon St, that you were no better than a banished man.

What my dear brother is to be done before you & I sleep with our Fathers, with the great question of Slavery? I would jump into any gulf that should yawn, so that the sacrifice might be anyways effectual toward healing this great breach of divine & human law, which gapes unreconciled in our political institutions. The country where slavery is tolerated, has sewed up in one sack with its national being, a living viper. Will not the day arrive, soon, for a public & fearless canvassing, in our books, our Lectures, yes & in Congress, of this subject, from which all our politicians now keep an awful distance—ought not you, & I, & all of us, to be meditating deeply—You I doubt not have done so, but I am all ignorances, on the cure for this deadly evil—whether it admits of salves & palliatives, & dieting, & gradual remedies—or must have the knife at once, & at all costs & all hazards. I love every corner of my native land—that rays of my patriotism, though it be a rush-light, reach its farthest limits & I claim a property in every foot of soil over which the broad wing of the Constitution stretches. . . .

The condition of the slaves here is, physically considered, very tolerable. Self interest prevails with the master to treat them well, when justice or mercy would plead in vain. They are in general neither over-worked, nor ill-fed. They have their patch of ground & sell to their masters on fair terms the products of their land, or of their skill & labour [in] holiday hours. Any one may buy himself free for the price his master bought him with—& the master can demand no more, whatever handicraft he may have taught him. Is this the law of our Slave holding States? Still a slave is a slave, & is made to feel it—If he raise his hand against a white man, it is death by the Law—He is called to his work by the crack of a whip—And the theory is that if he is not soundly flogged now & then, he will grow unmanageable. What the law is in regard to teaching them to read or write, I do not know—& practically, at present, it is of little consequence—for there is but little clerkly lore in the Island, & it is in no danger of finding its way to the Negroes. . . .

I am very well—ride & walk & do nothing else but swing in a hammock & look at a Newspaper & think of my friends.[115]

Returning to America, Charles appeared refreshed in body as well as in spirit. He left San Juan aboard the *Mercator* on 10 April and arrived in New York on 1 May 1832. His recuperative journey had also brought him closer to his brother Edward and, he readily admitted, opened his eyes to a world dramatically larger than the one he was formerly accustomed to see. The generally cheerful and talkative spirit of his letters comforted family and friends who had missed and been worried about him. Only once in all of his letters home did Charles lapse into the language of depression and despair that characterizes much of his correspondence with Aunt Mary and, eventually, with Elizabeth Hoar. Writing to Waldo on 2 February, he bewailed the lack of certainty in his life and the frustration of having prepared himself for great things in this world without any apparent hope of ever accomplishing them. He put the question to his brother, "Who shall riddle me the how & the why?"

. . . If we are not immortals, all of life is wasted; & if we are, how much of it! We should think it a queer preparation for college, if a young man should be put apprentice to a bricklayer or a baker. Yet to our understanding, does this world, seem any fitter school for candidates for the kingdom of Heaven? Here we are with powerful appetites, smelling rank of the flesh, that will & must be gratified; the whole ostensible business of far the larger portion of mankind, is to minister to this gratification; & if intellectual & moral principles happen to be developed meanwhile, it seems to be a matter by the way, aside from the main design. You may say it is mens' own doing—we might live on fruits, drink the crystal well, & pray & think all the time. But it is not so; The luxurious state, we have long ago agreed, is the state of nature. Look then at the panorama of one day in London—at all the sweat of human brows,—at all the work done . . . by its million of inhabitants from Royal William to Jack hostler.[116] This brewing of porter, & filling of writs & passports, this ship-building & trafficking, & ball-dressing, is the discipline ordained under Providence to educate souls for a spiritual state—Where there shall be no marrying nor giving in marriage—where the love of God, the knowledge of Truth, & the society of angels, is to be our employment & bliss. Is it not a Paradox beyond that of the Stoics?— We see very plainly that while we are here below, the present represents, & reaps the fruit of the past. 'The child is father of the man';[117] our Now, sprung from the loins of our Then. There is a retributive economy in our experience thus far. The argument would be for expecting a retribution in a *future* state. But why is *this* so unlike what we are taught *that,* is to be? A few sainted spirits now & then depart out of the world, who might have been changed in the twinkling of an eye, yes caught away like Enoch or Elijah,[118] but they are those who have rather lived against the world, than in it; & have all their life-time been subject to a miserable bondage that checked their souls' free motion & ascent. Nor can I subscribe to Swedenborg, & look to find my apothecary & shoemaker in the streets of the New Jerusalem.[119] Death forbids it. Why such a solemn leavetaking of flesh & sense? Why such an awful break in our existence, except it be the gulf between two worlds essentially distinct?—You shall riddle me the how & the why.

I stick to my old belief that happiness is one thing, & virtue another, & that the virtuous man may be very unhappy. . . .

I stick moreover to my primitive doctrine, that a man should grow like a tree—& that out of certain limits, he cannot be transplanted. "No matter where, so I be still the same." Ay, but I am not still the same, when the air no longer braces, & society no longer understands me. . . . I am an American coin in a Spanish country; the bullion is the same, but the piece will not pass current. . . .

. . . The wing of God's love infold you & my dear mother[120]—

Although Charles said to Waldo, "You shall riddle me the how & the why," in truth he had already begun to riddle out the mystery of his life for himself. Just as William had found his own mission in life clarified by travel and study in Germany and Edward had found peace for himself in the recuperative exile of his last years in the Caribbean, in Puerto Rico Charles discovered that the secret of life was genuine, as opposed to affected, acceptance of whatever life had to offer an individual—any individual, even one as proud and intellectually gifted as he himself was. Acceptance of life, he realized, would never guarantee prosperity, happiness, or love in this world or the next, but as he acknowledged to his mother in one of his last letters from Puerto Rico, he was willing to resign himself to whatever life had to offer him and trust his fate to the "high ends" required of him by the power greater than himself that ordered and unified all existence.

The shells & stones on the sea-beach look more sociable than anything else I see—& last night as I picked up some little fellows whose brethren were already in my bag, their striped faces looked very know-ing & familiar. They are exiles as I am; & their story is one of past joy & present desertion. Yet each particular suffering in the universe, ministers to a good that is greater. The shells & corals are torn from their home under the waves, to strew the barren shore with beautiful wrecks—to preach to the Solitary who comes there to muse on man & Providence—to enrich the stores of Natural History—& bring tidings to the curious student, of fields he is forbidden to explore. And so we, if we are wise, suffer to high ends. We are illustrating great truths, which we ourselves learn thereby & planting graces in an immortal soul.[121]

Charles was undoubtedly struck by the irony of returning home to find Waldo on the brink of severing his ties with Boston's Second Church. For a while, the two brothers seemed to find their former positions reversed, with

Charles feeling better than he had in years, but Waldo uncertain of his calling, concerned about his own future prospects, and anxious to the point of illness over what he ought to do. Edward arrived home from Puerto Rico in August for a two-month visit, and with William also visiting in Boston, all four brothers were once again together for what would be the last time. For himself, Charles debated whether to move from the city to Concord and open a law office there in the fall; after conferring with William, he decided to return to his reading in and practice of the law in Boston, believing that there he could build a reputable and profitable enough future for himself. Writing to Ezra Ripley on 9 August 1832, Charles informed him of his decision and described Waldo's illness, which appears to have been a form of colitis brought on by the stress of his confrontation with his congregation.

When you were so kind as to talk with me about my professional prospects, the last time I was at Concord, I promised to let you know,—whenever I should make up my mind,—on what plans I had fixed. William has been here, & I have advised with him, & I believe it will be best for me to stay in Boston, & try my fortune here. I may have to live on bean-porridge for a season, & find ample leisure for meditation;—yet my native City certainly owes a living to so affectionate a son—I can fill my time up with occupations that will give me bread & salt for the present, & by & by, I may have clients in plenty. My acquaintance here is as numerous as that of most young men—& some of them will probably be able to throw business into my hands—My habits & tastes too are *city*-bred, & I am better calculated I suppose to succeed & be content here than in the country. William, also, will have from time to time occasion to correspond with a Boston lawyer, & we can help each other.—Then if I went to Concord, I should be looking forward to a removal at some future day—whereas now I shall consider myself as settled—or I might be tempted to mix too soon in politics—But it is not worth while for me to weary you with reciting all the reasons which I have so sagely balanced, in making my choice. No; I write chiefly to thank you, Sir, for the paternal interest you have taken in my welfare & prospects. And although I think I see my advantage in remaining in Boston, I see at the same time that the promise you held out for me was fair, & I may have erred in not guiding myself by your counsel. Time will show. Concord will always be dear to me, whether I dwell there or not, & I hope long to be bound to it by the same tie that has hitherto made it a home to me. . . .

Waldo has been sick. . . . He is now we hope recovering health, but very slowly—mother remains very feeble & unwell—I wish, as soon as Waldo is beyond needing her care, that she may be persuaded to go

& stay in the country & recruit her wasted strength. Many people are
sick—scarcely any body retains perfect health. The general indisposition,
& the breaking out of sudden distempers in different quarters of our immediate neighbourhood, seem to indicate that we are breathing the same
infected atmosphere that has carried disease round the globe—I trust we
shall not be visited in severity. . . .

. . . Of course Waldo's sickness & inability to preach has suspended
his affairs ecclesiastical, exactly where they stood when you last saw him.
His opinions will perhaps make a separation from his people, the right
course—but nothing is ascertained & nothing therefore is at present said
about the subject—He will soon preach, & then things will come to an
issue.[122]

During the months that followed, Charles often felt that time was speeding by
at an alarming rate. Waldo submitted his resignation to the Second Church and
Society—as his congregation was formally known—on 11 September; Charles
was sworn in as an attorney at the Court of Common Pleas and opened his law
office in Boston on 2 October; Edward sailed for Puerto Rico on 6 October;
the Second Church and Society voted to dissolve the connection between the
Church and its pastor on 28 October; Waldo presented his farewell letter to the
Second Church on 22 December—three hundred copies of which were printed
in pamphlet form as *Letter from the Rev. R. W. Emerson to the Second Church and
Society* for distribution to the congregation's proprietors and worshippers—and
after settling on a journey to Europe rather than visit to Edward in Puerto Rico,
Waldo set sail for Malta aboard the brig *Jasper* on 25 December.

With William pursuing his law and business affairs in New York and his
engagement to Susan Woodward Haven of New Hampshire (whom he would
marry in December 1833), Edward settled once again in Sidney Mason's counting house in San Juan, and Waldo traveling in Italy, France, and the British
Isles, for most of 1833 Charles found himself completely separated from his
brothers for the first time in his life. Almost all letters exchanged between his
brothers and himself were concerned with financial or legal matters, and he
felt the customary warmth and banter of their correspondence and conversation give way to a preoccupation with detail with which he had little patience.
Nevertheless, this time alone offered him certain advantages. He was able to
devote uninterrupted attention to his new law practice, developing a roster of
clients and arguing his first case in the Court of Common Pleas in April. He
also wrote a lecture on "One of the West India Islands," which he delivered
first in Concord before the Concord Lyceum in January 1833 and for which he
drew liberally from his own close observation of life in Puerto Rico. Although
the pressures of social politeness and meaningless conversation often grated
on his nerves, he threw himself into the Cambridge and Concord social scenes
and, in spite of himself, seemed to enjoy the company of old and new friends.

Writing to William on 14–15 May, he brought his brother up to date on his social life, and in a surprising gesture, he appears to reject a suggestion that William must have made to commit more of his time to securing clients for his practice.

> This morning I returned from Concord leaving Mother to spend the week there. Grfather is disabled with the Gout—& we had on Sabbath day a youngster from Cambridge. Mr Hoar's family I saw & you were particularly inquired after—We i.e. certain young gentlemen & ladies of the village & I, walked through the woods to what is called the Cliff yesterday afternoon—The Country looks like Fairy-land—the fruit trees as yet leafless but covered with pink & white blossoms, like trees of silver & gold. I feel sad now I have got home. How our very pleasures tease us! Whats this dull town to me? . . .
>
> I shall grow rabid for 'business' if it come not presently—nay—I will do no such thing. I despise impatience, & all doubts & distrust—cheerily, modestly faithfully onward—come what come may[123]—

Besides the family ties that always drew him to Concord, a new figure—one of the young ladies of the town—increasingly attracted Charles's time and attention to the rural "Fairy-land." The Emersons and Ripleys had long been close to the Hoar family in Concord, and Judge Samuel Hoar, one of the town's leading citizens, had long been supportive of the Emerson brothers as they made their way in the world. In the spring and summer of 1833, Charles began to walk and talk with Elizabeth Sherman Hoar, the Judge's daughter. The attraction was definitely mutual, and during the first weekend in August, Charles and Elizabeth announced their engagement. Although they had most likely exchanged letters before this time, those letters do not survive; however, within days of their engagement, Charles and Elizabeth initiated one of the most sustained courtship correspondences in the preserved records of New England courtship correspondences (see chapter 5). Although they had not married by the time of Charles's death in 1836, the intensity and character of their relationship is evident in the substantial body of letters Charles wrote to Elizabeth, which she kept and gave to Waldo after Charles's death; regrettably, Elizabeth's letters to Charles do not appear to have survived. One indication of the importance of his engagement to and correspondence with Elizabeth for Charles is that from late 1833 until his death, his correspondence with his brothers and Aunt Mary declines dramatically.

Individual relationships among the Emerson brothers were always the most satisfying when the brothers were together, using evening conversations to exchange thoughts about what they were reading, seeing nature through each other's eyes while on walks in the country, and by their presence, mutually supporting each other's careers. Thus, Charles was pleased to find that Waldo's

return to America in October 1833 restored vitality to the brothers' shared intellectual life, and he heartily endorsed his brother's decision to transform his
former "call" to the ministry into the "call" of a lecturer on the lyceum circuit
that was just being formalized in New England. Charles was also gratified to
see that Waldo and Elizabeth took an immediate liking to each other; it is during this time that the lifelong spiritual relationship between the two—much
like the close relationship between a brother and a sister—commenced, although neither could imagine then how crucial their relationship would be for
each other's comfort during the forty years they shared as friends after Charles's
death.

Charles, invariably in the company of either Waldo, with whom he roomed,
or Elizabeth, spent most of 1834 continuing to build his law practice and im-
pressing colleagues with his ability in the field. His physical health seemed
fine, and if Waldo or Elizabeth ever feared that the dark shadings that occasionally colored Charles's spoken or written thoughts about life and his future
were putting his physical well being in jeopardy, neither mentioned the fact,
nor did Elizabeth allow those shadings to interrupt or otherwise mar their
courtship. The great crisis endured by the Emerson brothers in 1834 was, of
course, Edward's final illness and his death in October. There is little question
that Edward's passing was a terrible stroke for all in the family, but its sting
seemed lessened among the brothers who survived him if only because they
could share their grief together.

Unquestionably, 1835 was outwardly the happiest year of Charles's life.
With his reputation growing and his love for Elizabeth returned by her and
deepening with each passing day, with William's domestic and financial situations increasingly secure, and with Waldo's career as a lecturer off to a good
start, Charles may have appreciated the fact that he and his brothers were at last
reaping the rewards of their perseverance and willingness to resign themselves
to accept and work with whatever life offered them. Publicly, he appears to have
done so. As 1835 opened, he maintained his law practice by day and began
to deliver a new lecture he had written on "Modern Society" in the evening,
whereas Waldo lectured in and around Boston and served as a supply preacher
for several local churches. When Waldo met and became engaged to Lydia Jackson of Plymouth early in the year, the timing seemed perfect for Charles and
his brother to effect a plan they had only been able to dream about: to create
a domestic and intellectual environment in which they and their wives, those
children with whom they might be blessed, mother Ruth, and even, perhaps,
Aunt Mary and a "restored" Bulkeley as well as William and Susan could all live
together as an extended family. It was an ambition that they had long shared,
and they had every confidence that, if it were to be realized, it would serve them
as the means through which to restore the Emerson name to the privileged position it would have otherwise enjoyed had not the death first of their paternal

grandfather William and then of their father William driven the family's fate in another direction.

In February 1835, Waldo began to look for a house or for property on which to build one in Concord. Charles, who had been approached by Elizabeth's father to accept a position in his Concord law office, decided to leave his practice in Boston and return home to "the land of their fathers," as the brothers liked to refer to New England's most historic town. Writing to William on 12 February, he shared the good news with his brother:

> I have written today a letter to Mr. Hoar accepting his proposal to have me remove to Concord. For how long time it will be I do not say— it will not probably last always, & yet it would not be wise & is not by any means necessary at present to fix a limitation. Let it be understood, I am sure I so understand it, to be a 'settling' in Middlesex [County]. . . .
>
> How do you like Waldo's re-engagement? The lady is a sort of Sybil for wisdom—She is not beautiful anywise that I know, so you look at the outside alone. Mother is pleased, & everybody. . . .
>
> I go away from Boston week after next. Until I get married the place will be a poor place for me to live in. . . . But Waldo I trust will hire or build him a house there & by & by we shall have a country—an arcadia of our own, & you & Susan will cry to come & live with us.[124]

Settled in Concord by March, Charles began to draft lectures on "Socrates" and "Slavery," the first of which he would debut in Lowell and the second in Duxbury, Massachusetts, in April. On 3 March, he wrote to William

> I am sitting in my new say rather old office as black as smoke & dirt of twenty years can smutch it, with furniture there unto corresponding. And assuredly when I look out of my window at the still clean field of snow in my rear skirted by the unmoving pines, it does strike the natural man as a little preposterous to quit for this solitude the rattling precincts of Court Street. Yet I am not about to repent a resolution taken & carried into effect with ample light & means of judgment. By & by I shall reap if I faint not. Meanwhile here is opportunity for study, & good influence. Mother & Elizabeth are well. Waldo has a bad cold but is hard at work on the closing lecture of his series, Edmund Burke.[125]

On 13 March Charles wrote again to William and finally confided to him the extent of the Arcadian dream that was then sustaining so much of his own and Waldo's labor. "It would be pleasant," he told his brother, "if we could plant the members of a family in one another's neighborhood. I should be glad to see you & Susan every week, every day. This may be one of these years, when we all retire on our fortunes & build an observatory, & raise apple trees & study geology."[126] By April, perhaps hoping to lure his brother into the Arcadian dream, Charles reported to William that his lecture on "Socrates" was finished and new "country clients" were appearing in his office every day and crossing his palm with "bank notes," that Waldo had settled on becoming a "a citizen in this town," and that he—Charles—was about to publicly announce himself as an abolitionist:

> What are you doing? Making a great fortune? Have you gone to housekeeping? How does Susan like the dignities & cares of the new manner of life? Have you delivered Lectures, & stricken multitudes dumb with admiration? Tomorrow night go I to Lowell, Queen of New England villages manufacturing, to read them a discourse concerning Socrates.
>
> Last week I saw the faces of some country clients, & my palm was crossed with their bank notes. I should think that when I have been here a while, & got a little nest egg or so warm, I may live & be married. . . .
>
> The nineteenth of this month is to be celebrated in Lexington, & the bones of the massacred removed & laid beneath the monument, & E. Everett is to deliver an oration.[127] . . .
>
> Waldo thinks he shall settle himself as a citizen in this town—He went last Thursday to Plymouth & has not got home.[128]
>
> Tomorrow take I my flight into sandy Duxbury, there to speak to the subject of Slavery. I am an abolitionist. And give me an hour & a half of your company, & I'll undertake you shall be one too—do you be not already.[129]

For the next several months, Charles devoted himself to his practice in Concord, to nurturing his relationship with Elizabeth, and to assisting Waldo in his negotiations with John Coolidge of Concord for a house and large parcel of land at the beginning of the Cambridge Turnpike on what was then the outskirts of the town. Relaxed and thoroughly taken with his new life, Charles wrote to William, "Consider, good my brother how I sit here on the banks of the slow Muscatequid & write & seal my epistles,[130] & then commit them, as it were bread to the waters, trusting to a broad & Secular Providence more than to any nicely fitted & adequate means for their arrival in Wall St—So that each which in the end comes safely to its port, is a new & special marvel—a sort of Ulysses,[131] that man driven by winds & tossed on the seas who saw many men & many cities."[132] For most of July and until the closing occurred in August, Charles orchestrated negotiations back and forth between Waldo and John Coolidge, who on 7 July had settled on a purchase price of $3,500, which the brothers took as an incredible bargain for the house and the two acres surrounding it for which Coolidge had paid $8,000 seven years earlier.[133] The proverbial snag in the negotiations occurred when, after making the deal, Waldo had to delay closing until he had secured the settlement owed him from the suit he had brought against his first wife's estate. In mid-July, Charles hurriedly informed to Waldo,

> I went to see Mr. Coolidge—I told him you would like to take the house the 1st Sept[r]; he said you must then pay him interest—no; my brother considers the purchase as made then—but we agreed the other day that it should be 1st August; not as I learn from him,—there was no agreement definitive as to the day,—but I will split the difference & take the house from the 15th Aug. He would not. Then I can not make any agreement with you until I see my brother,—I do not think he contracted to take the house 1st Aug. & I do not think he ought to pay interest simply because your brother to suit his own convenience is going to remove out directly.—I talked a little more, but left him undertaking to learn from you whether or not you considered yourself engaged to take the house 1st Aug. He said that he agreed that paymt. need not be made till 1st Sept. or any day to suit you, but that he objected to 1st Sept. as the day of purchase, & you assented to 1st Aug. named by him—I believed otherwise, & would not give up without your word for it.[134]

Waldo accepted Coolidge's terms, and the deed to "Coolidge House," as the property was known, was transferred to Waldo and recorded in the office of the Middlesex County Clerk on 15 August.

With Waldo's successful purchase of what Charles and William would refer to as the family's Concord "Castle" or "Chateau" and the prospect of an extended Emerson family living under one roof in their ancestral town, the promise of a bright, fresh future displaced the feelings of death, disappointment, and financial frustration that had colored so much of the Emerson brothers' everyday affairs and correspondence since their father's death nearly twenty-five years before. A congratulatory letter from William to Waldo reflected a sense of optimism about the future, if only because the brothers could now feel that after the hardships of their youth and the constant struggle with which they entered their mature years, they were, at last, in control of their respective destinies. Ever the practical one, William applauded his brother on the bargain he had so quickly negotiated—"for the sake of your time & your purse." William knew the house, considered its location prime, and had no doubt that whatever sums Waldo invested in renovations and expansion would be returned many-fold, if not in actual cash, then in household bliss, and he offered him this fraternal blessing: "So long as you inhabit there, may it be the abode of peace, improvement, & happiness, & not to you alone, but to each one of your household! It is not set on a hill, yet I hope its light will shine brightly & far for the benefit of your fellow men. It will be a pleasing occupation for you to decorate your garden & shade your house with beautiful trees & flowers."[135]

If left to her own narrative devices, Aunt Mary would undoubtedly have urged caution against apparent presumption at this point. But she did not. Charles first sounded the caution, which in retrospect sounds eerily prophetic. As the summer of 1835 turned to autumn, he wrote to Joseph Lyman in early October, lamenting, "it is a hard science, this science of human life." In the following letter, which is shockingly at odds with his public happiness, Charles exposes himself to his friend, expressing his fears for the future and sources of renewed depression in the style he usually reserved for introspective letters to Mary or entries he made in the secret diary he kept at this time.

One desires, that his life should be his theory of living, made flesh; and when we feel, as if, through our fault, or the blind force of our fate, the days went & we stood still—the belly was fed but the thoughts were not;—as if we were forgetting 'the dreams of our youth,' which manhood is pledged to remember & make real;—& instead of these, were existing to the dreams of the senses, & to accidents which we have clothed with the strength of laws, how can we help being perplexed & afraid? Great fear comes upon us. And you too have been unable to run away from the scare, you too are waylaid with doubts, you too ask yourself questions. Well: I cannot say I am sorry; hardly that I am surprised. One must be very happy or very busy not to have the Hamlet humor overcome him now & then. . . .

To find the fit sphere of our activity; & then to mix, in just proportions, study & action: & still farther, rightly to divide study between the 'Moi,' & the 'Non Moi,' between listening to the voice within, & acquiring the languages that are from without, here observing the phenomena, & there recognising the law of association—to do this is to know how to live; is to live. Before this knowledge is got we go into our graves. Life is tentative with the best men; & with the common sort, not even that. Yet what is most to be dreaded by us, is, not mistakes, but indifference. While we are awake we may suffer, we may sin, but we learn from both: when we sleep, the calm is not virtue, it is insensibility. Most men do with their business & social engagements—what the poor man does with strong drink,—intoxicate themselves, & drug conscience & reason, as the tippler his stomach & nerves. Pain is quite as often in this world the irritability of returning health, as the symptom of disease. I think a man should thank God especially for all he suffers. I think it is nobler, too, to suffer from one's self, than from any outward fortune—& certainly this 'pain of Thought' gives a man an invincible hardihood against all the thwacks of Fate. If Christianity were no more than a fine drama, how faithful it is to what is in Man: how it symbolizes all our history & constitution of our souls: height out of lowliness, & victory out of sacrifice; here the crown of thorns & the cross, & there the Transfiguration, the Miracles, the Ascension. . . .

What sort of Autumn shows Pennsylvania? . . . I went to New York the other day to carry my mother to make William a visit, & the pomp of the trees, by the side of the rail road in Canton & Dedham, is past telling. Still I never forget it is Autumn; & as my Aunt Mary says—'it is the angel of consumption that dyes the cheek of fading Nature with such hectic bloom.'[136]

Whether or not he actually knew the truth, Charles's letter to Lyman—especially its concluding reference to Aunt Mary's Calvinist-style realism—effectively set the stage for the last six months of his life. Like so much of his life, Charles's end was itself a period of extended but erratic and declining "hectic bloom." On 19 January 1836, he again wrote to Lyman. Charles's voice throughout the letter betrays a curious blend of false bravado, lofty introspection on the challenges to ethical behavior that the law presents to practitioners, and confidence in a promising future that is itself incongruous with the fatalism he expressed at this time in his secret diary, where, imagining himself as a latter-day Socrates,[137] he wrote, "[e]ither the man turns traitor to his principles, or death cuts the experiment short, or accidents confuse & overlay the issue. Socrates was permitted to begin, continue, & finish his work; & now the tools wherewith he wrought are buried or lost, the chips blown away, & the colossal image alone remains."[138] "I have been through the fires of a five weeks' term of the Common Pleas at East Cambridge, & so I breathe still," he told Lyman; he then continued, saying,

Several cases which I expected to have tried did not come on; but I had enough to do to season me to the work. Would you know how I acquitted myself? Why, respectably; I came off without any conspicuous failure or ridiculous mistakes, & bore myself I believe so as to warrant a fair augury of the success of the young advocate. And yet perhaps anybody else would have been disappointed; but I am always tickled when I commit no irretrievable blunder. The practice of the Profession is not without its danger to the character of the man. It hardens the temper, & at the same time makes flexible the moral judgments. Yet the Courthouse has its exhilaration, its heroism, its discipline of the moral powers. If the lawyer can keep the law of truth & right-dealing in spite of the irritations or fear that grows out of his contests, & in spite too of the lures of the love of victory, he is not far from goodness & Wisdom. . . .

> You ask of my whereabouts. I board & lodge at Waldo's. We mean to enlarge the house this spring & I know not what the summer may bring forth. My mother dear is at New York this whole winter.[139]

Charles's tone in this letter to Lyman characterizes the voice and shifts in voice that he employed in his correspondence during the last months of his life. From February through April, he shared epistolary banter with William and kept up an almost daily correspondence with Elizabeth. In his letters to both of them, Charles acknowledged that his law practice had been virtually dormant and that the winter had been weighing on his spirit. He joked to William on 18 February 1836 that he thought New York had an "effeminate calendar" since it "reports only zero cold or four degrees under," whereas in Concord "we make no account of that temperature, & rise morning after morning to five, six, ten & twelve below zero," but in that letter he also complained that the cold and snow made walking difficult, if not impossible, since "the only path, unless I break out my own in snow three feet deep, is to be found in the middle of the highway; & even here I must jump aside into the bank so often as sleigh bells jingle in my rear." For the remainder of the letter, Charles expressed frustration at being confined indoors, and he concluded with an unintended irony as to what this confinement may be preparing him for: "No solitude, no still woodland, no thought-refreshing rambles amongst clean & natural objects. I must dog human footsteps, not trace the Divine. I sit most of the time in my office . . . [where] almost nobody darkens my doors & I am left to . . . silence. . . . If we live & are faithful we are sure to be driven to work sooner or later, & he is wise who appreciates & uses the season of the Preparation."[140] Charles's letters to Elizabeth at this time appear cheerful enough, although in hindsight, the cheerfulness seems more forced than natural as Charles uses it to keep his declining health secret from her and everyone else. He wrote to her in early March,

> Yesterday morning I was glad in the sound of running waters & dropping eaves; I even sat down & bade the gentle Spring, all-hail, in good set terms. The ungrateful hussy! She is as coy as other Beauties & like them will keep aloof & play the Coquette, till her season is past, & we court her no longer. I am on the lookout for the return of my pets, the birds. If ever our dear mother earth shall put her head out from under this sheet of snows, I am sure we shall bless her bonny face, were it only for the seldom sight. Do you see any bare ground in the City? There is a sea of snow yet to melt off our fields.[141]

Charles died in New York City on 9 May 1836 following an afternoon ride with his mother. After descending from the carriage, he climbed the steps to his brother William's house, sat down, and without uttering a word or displaying any awareness that he was about to die, he expired. Everyone claimed to have been surprised by the suddenness of the event; however, Charles's death was no more sudden than Ellen's in 1831 or Edward's breakdown in 1828 and his death in 1834. The signs of Charles's impending end were evident everywhere, but the record is unclear as to whether, like Charles himself, the family chose to ignore the signs or whether—as is more likely—the family, recognizing the signs, simply could not believe that such a terrible stroke was about to visit them yet again.

Charles appears to have caught cold and been sick for almost all of March. In a series of letters to Elizabeth in early April, he provided her with the first concrete information on the course of his illness, although he cut nearly three weeks off of his illness, perhaps in order to not alarm her. "I have not been well this week, but am now getting well," he finally wrote to her from Concord on 2 April;[142] a week later he excused himself from seeing her in Boston, where she was living, claiming that he had not been feeling in a "working mood" and was having doubts about his profession: "I shall not go to Boston tomorrow, & afterward all things are doubtful. I do not feel particularly in the working mood this week. . . . The nearer I draw to my Profession the less comely she looks in my eyes. I think however if I take care she do me no harm, she cannot help but do me much good."[143] On 14 April, he confessed the truth to Elizabeth, although there is no question but that his confession was incomplete:

> I am not quite recovered yet from a tedious indisposition & cold, which I have sought to put out of the doors of my body by all the means in my power. This week with its business inopportunely keeps me here & moving about. I cannot say when the Court will adjourn; the prospect is today less favorable for their early departure. Still I do not know that it is not as well for me to have something to do as nothing—I shall take some time by the forelock (unless as is likely enough I grow well) & go advise with Dr. Jackson. You have such trust in my infinite prudence touching health, that you will not suppose I do foolhardily. I would not have said thus much, as it is more than the matter may deserve, but that you seem anxious about me, & I thought I would tell you the worst.
>
> Now be a good girl & take excellent care of yourself, & wrap up against cold winds. . . .
>
> The Sun is out—the snow melts, time & the hour wear through the roughest day—I think I feel better.[144]

Within a matter of days, the truth was out. On 16 April, Charles rode to Boston to consult with Dr. James Jackson, Sr. about his health, but it is apparent from the events that followed that although Charles had waited too long to seek medical help, Jackson failed to diagnose adequately the severity of Charles's condition. According to Waldo, Jackson did not find anything wrong with Charles other than a cold "& the bad effects of confinement & loss of appetite. His constitution has no power of resistance & therefore shut him up & starve him & he withers like a flower in the frost" (24 April 1836, *L,* 2:14). Following Jackson's advice, the family decided that Charles should travel by train, stagecoach, and boat from Boston, to Worcester, then Springfield, Hartford, and New Haven, and finally to New York, where spring weather had already arrived, rest at William's home, and then continue southward to either Philadelphia or Richmond. On 19 April, Waldo, who was lecturing in Salem, wrote to Lidian, hoping that his brother had already set out for New York and praying "God to make him quickly whole" again (*L,* 2:9). However, two days later Waldo wrote to her again alarmed by the discovery that Charles had not yet left. He told Lidian that because his brother was too debilitated to travel to New York by himself, he had arranged for a break in his lecture schedule and planned to accompany him on the journey (*L,* 2:10–11). The brothers set out on the morning of 22 April and arrived at William's home on the 24th.

Charles initially appeared to regain some of his strength in New York, where William's care of his brother was assisted by their mother, who had been visiting in her son's home for a month. On 28 April, William reported to Waldo, "Charles passed a comfortable night without opium, & with less coughing than the night previous, & seemed about the same this morning as yesterday, tho' mother says he is better. He walked to the Parade Ground yesterday afternoon (between ¼ & ½ a mile) & enjoyed the air without suffering by the exercise. He went to sleep on the sofa directly after breakfast this morning, & I wakened him to propose that he should see a physician today, but he would not consent. . . . I hope he will consent to see a physician tomorrow."[145] Two days later, William wrote again to say that

no material change has taken place. Charles has slept well, but yesterday morning was much exhausted by his cough. In the afternoon Dr Perkins saw him,[146] but will not yet give a very definite opinion. He thought the plan of his travelling . . . was good, but that it would be better to go into the interior, say, to western Pennsylvania, than to Richmond. He ordered some drops to relieve the cough, & a large warm-plaster on the breast, & is to see him again today. Charles slept well last night, & thinks the drops softened the cough. The cough was so bad yesterday morning that Charles said it seemed to him that he could not stand another turn so bad, & he was sore all day in consequence; but the drops had so good an effect, that he is much easier today.—I know of nothing else worth while to mention—about him.[147]

On 3 May, Charles sent Waldo a mixed review of his condition. Although he suggested that his health was slowly returning, Charles's depression and sense of despair over having accomplished so little in his life likely offset any comfort Waldo might otherwise have taken from the letter.

"A valuable life"—ah my dear brother, the words sound like derision, almost, to me, who look back on twenty seven years of such small, such zero accomplishment. Forgive me, Forgive me, my God.

As to my condition, I think it is improved since I came to New York. I raise with ease both by night & by day with scarcely any coughing. Indeed but for those discouraging accounts of how many times their own volume the volcanoes throw out, I should begin to doubt whether this poor mucous membrane of mine could much longer sustain such a prodigality. Mother has nursed me, & brought back to me a little appetite, & in many ways I mend.

But I suffer extremely from shortness of breathing, that makes going up a flight of stairs acute pain. Dr Perkins says it is simply owing to the weakness of the lungs & that riding is the very best remedy; he advises travelling as soon as we are ready—thinks the best course would be to Phil[a] thence to Lancaster &c. & then turn into Va.[148]

Approving of Dr. Perkins's suggestion, Waldo intended to return to New York and accompany Charles to Virginia. However, by 5 May, Charles was experiencing a rapid decline, which he briefly described to Elizabeth and told her, "You must pray for me who am too weak to pray for myself."[149] On the seventh, an alarmed William wrote to Waldo, "Come alone or with Elizabeth, but come soon."[150] Fearing the worst but deciding to wait until Elizabeth could accompany him to New York, Waldo postponed his departure. The decision seemed reasonable enough in light of a brief letter Charles sent to Elizabeth on 8 May. In it, he appears confident that he will ultimately survive this most recent physical assault, but whether he sincerely believed that he would survive or affected confidence as his way of freeing Waldo and Elizabeth from the trauma of witnessing his death is unclear. In any case, the letter has an unquestionable ring of finality about it: "Mother has done what she could to watch my breath, by night, & feed me with jellies & nutricious food by day. And now . . . I expect to move again; it is with pleasure but not without fear that I await the starting. I am still so very weak, helpless, & this shortness of breathing . . . gives me so much pain. . . . But I grow tired. Be a good girl. Love your poor Charles."[151]

Not knowing that Charles had already died, Waldo and Elizabeth set out for New York on the morning of 10 May and reached William's home early the next morning. William had already sent the sad news to Lidian,[152] and on his arrival at William's, Waldo wrote to her as well: "We arrived too late. Charles died Monday afternoon. . . . Elizabeth sits with his body and is soothed by the repose of his face. The funeral is this afternoon. And this is all I have to say with my love to you" (11 May 1836, *L*, 2:18–19). The next day, Waldo sent Lidian this account of Charles's funeral and shared with her his feelings at the loss of "my noble friend who was my ornament my wisdom & my pride":

> Yesterday afternoon we attended Charles's funeral. Mother & Elizabeth heard the prayers but did not go out. The remains are deposited for a time in a tomb of a Mr Griswold a friend & connexion of Susan's.[153]— Mother is very well & bears her sorrow like one made to bear it & to comfort others. Elizabeth is well and the strength & truth of her character appears under this bitter calamity. William & Susan are well & thoroughly kind to us as they have been tenderly faithful to Charles. I have told mother that I think it best, on every account, she should return immediately with me & end her painful visit at New York whither she came to spend a month of happiness in the . . . household of her son . . . [but found instead] sickness anxiety & death. She will return with me & Elizabeth. . . .
>
> And so, Lidian, I can never bring you back my noble friend who was my ornament my wisdom & my pride.—A soul is gone so costly & so rare that few persons were capable of knowing its price and I shall have my sorrow to myself for if I speak of him I shall be thought a fond exaggerator. He had the fourfold perfection of good sense, of genius, of grace, & of virtue, as I have never seen them combined. I determined to live in Concord . . . because he was there, and now that the immense promise of his maturity is destroyed, I feel not only unfastened there and adrift but a sort of shame at living at all.
>
> I am thankful, dear Lidian, that you have seen & known him to that degree you have. . . . And you must be content henceforth with only a piece of your husband; for the best of his strength lay in the soul with which he must no more on earth take counsel. How much I saw through his eyes. I feel as if my own were very dim. (*L*, 2: 19–20)

Because they intended that Charles's remains would eventually be returned to Boston for burial in a plot that they could visit from time to time, Ruth Haskins Emerson and her surviving sons William and Waldo assumed that Charles's burial in the New York Marble Cemetery on Manhattan's East Side would be temporary. In October 1845, during a trip to New York in the company of Elizabeth Palmer Peabody and Christopher Pearse Cranch, Aunt Mary insisted that William take her to visit the tomb in which Charles reposed so that, she hoped, she could gaze once last time on "his well known figure." Writing to Elizabeth Hoar and Waldo on 5 October, she gave the following account of her visit:

> Amidst the revival of old & almost forgotten associations of relative affections & their assiduous attentions the most interesting hour was that of locating the place of dear Charles' mortal repose. I had depended on taking the Sexton & going into the Vault or tomb & discovering his well known figure, to w'h William at length assented, but he found the former forgettfull Intomber gone to another state—worse the Receptacle closed & sealed. But last eve. . . . we [went to the] *Carmine St Ch[urc]h.* It's every stone told a tale of solemn awe—the stars had come out—the opposite lamps threw their light—and I ascended the stairs behind the Chh to view the mansions of the dead—sure that the dust so dear was there. The lessons it read of past hopes—of the obscurity of that grave cannot be forgotten at the last moments of returning to my own so long expected—so connate with the ignorance of a long & useless life. A sadder & more painfull obscurity attended me in a feebler state of health in visiting dear Edwards. Tho I said to William how glad he was there & how delighted to rest my wearied frame behind him. And I should have rejoiced. But why I can't tell—there was a lonliness & burying to society of all that was so bright w'h left a much more gloomy impression than was . . . expected. Charles may mingle with some dust w'h was animated with great & generous principles. And so may Edwards neighbours have been. And his relatives may join him. How would the anti resurrectionists & the transcendentalists scorn my old habits of *feeling.* (*MMEL*, p. 473)

Although Mary's visit to the vault that held Charles's remains ended in frustration, as in her reveries concerning Edward's final resting place—which, in fact, she had never visited in Puerto Rico—she translated her frustration into the pleasant thought that soon enough she would repose with her nephews in a place more accessible than that in which she could find either of them now. In a curious way, Mary's "old habits of *feeling*" saved her a disappointment from which, given the imagination she had previously invested in the opportunity to "see" Charles one last time in this world, she would likely never have recovered. In notes of conversations with his mother that Edward Waldo Forbes gave to Sylvester Baxter, Edith Emerson Forbes is reported to have remembered that, when her Uncle William had the tomb opened in 1855 in order to gather Charles's remains for reburial in Sleepy Hollow Cemetery, he was mortified to discover that name markers had been removed from all of the coffins in the vault. As Edith retold the story to her son, it appears that, because the church sexton— the "former forgettfull Intomber [who had] gone to another state" in Mary's letter—"considered it his perquisite to steal the silver tablets off the coffins" as additional compensation for his labor, there was no way William could identify Charles's remains, and so, of necessity, his body was left in New York.[154]

EDWARD AND CHARLES REMEMBERED

After a visit to Waldo's home in Concord during the summer of 1842, William wrote to Aunt Mary describing his stay in the family's ancestral town. Although he never subscribed to the "Arcadian dream" into which Charles and Waldo had invited him, in part because the dream itself was frustrated by Charles's death, but also in part because he had invented a life for himself and, now, had a family of his own in New York, William appreciated the lure of the dream. Not a poet himself, he nevertheless understood how, as a metaphor for the bond of fraternal unity that he shared with his brothers, the dream was sacred and would endure as long as Waldo, Bulkeley, and he lived.[155] Because she was painfully aware of them herself, in writing to Mary, William did not have to address at length the changes the last year had brought to the family and the town with Ezra Ripley's death the previous September and young Waldo's in January. However, he did tell her about his visit to the Manse, which had been vacant and undergoing renovation since Ripley's death in anticipation of the arrival of its new tenants, the newlyweds Nathaniel and Sophia Peabody Hawthorne. For a moment, William became a poet as he told his Aunt about his experience of taking one last stroll through the house in which so much of his family's and his own history was written. "What a history in those silent walls," he exclaimed. "Ever since my own childhood, how have they echoed to the joyous laugh, the agonies of pain & sorrow, the cries of madness—proceeding from those whom you & I have most prized, most tenderly loved! In the little attic room, my father's, Edward's, & Charles's, handwriting are still plainly to be read on the wall. Some wood & stone seems holier than the rest, is consecrated by our feelings."[156] And if William had talked to his brother about the feelings his visit to the Manse had renewed in him in the way that he described them for Mary, Waldo would surely have known exactly what he meant. He had those feelings too, not only about the Manse and what its structure, with its echoes of the past, represented, but also about the more lasting inscriptions written by persons we love on the hearts and minds of those of us who survive them. In his poem entitled "The House," he wrote that the ideal architect for a house was the "Muse" who

> . . . lays her beams in music,
>   In music every one,

> To the cadence of the whirling world
>   Which dances round the sun—
> That so they shall not be displaced
>   By lapses or by wars,
> But for the love of happy souls
>   Outlive the newest stars.[157]

The family never forgot Edward or Charles. From the moment each died, they began to be immortalized in Mary's correspondence with her nephews William and Waldo, which continued for another twenty years, in William and Waldo's correspondence and conversations with each other, which continued for another thirty years, in the names that William and Waldo's children, grandchildren, and great-grandchildren were given, and in the innumerable remembrances of his brothers that Waldo entered in his journal well into the 1870s. Waldo memorialized Edward as his "brother of the brief but blazing star" in the poem "In Memoriam, E. B. E.," which opens with an allusion to the scene near the Old North Bridge across which American patriots and British regulars exchanged fire at the beginning of the Revolutionary War and beside which still stands the Old Manse built by the Emerson brothers' grandfather William Emerson.[158] He also memorialized Charles in the way that he remembered him best and in the way that Charles would certainly have wished to be remembered in "Notes from the Journal of a Scholar" and "A Leaf from 'A Voyage to Porto Rico,'" which consisted of passages he had drawn from Charles's writings for publication in the *Dial*.[159] However, perhaps the most lasting printed memory of both brothers survives in the lines of Waldo's poem "Dirge," which he composed in 1838, four years after Edward's death and two years after Charles's:

> I reached the middle of the mount
>   Up which the incarnate soul must climb,
> And paused for them, and looked around,
>   With me who walked through space and time.
>
> Five rosy boys with morning light
>   Had leaped from one fair mother's arms,
> Fronted the sun with hope as bright,
>   And greeted God with childhood's psalms.
>
> Knows he who tills this lonely field
>   To reap its scanty corn,
> What mystic fruit his acres yield
>   At midnight and at morn?

In the long sunny afternoon
    The plain was full of ghosts;
I wandered up, I wandered down,
    Beset by pensive hosts.

The winding Concord gleamed below,
    Pouring as wide a flood
As when my brothers, long ago,
    Came with me to the wood.

But they are gone,—the holy ones
    Who trod with me this lonely vale;
The strong, star-bright companions
    Are silent, low and pale.

My good, my noble, in their prime,
    Who made this world the feast it was,
Who learned with me the lore of time,
    Who loved this dwelling place!

They took this valley for their toy,
    They played with it in every mood;
A cell for prayer, a hall for joy,—
    They treated Nature as they would.

They colored the horizon round;
    Stars flamed and faded as they bade,
All echoes hearkened for their sound,—
    They made the woodlands glad or mad.

I touch this flower of silken leaf,
    Which once our childhood knew;
Its soft leaves wound me with a grief
    Whose balsam never grew.

Hearken to yon pine-warbler
    Singing aloft in the tree!
Hearest thou, O traveller,
    What he singeth to me?

Not unless God made sharp thine ear
    With sorrow such as mine,
Out of that delicate lay could'st thou
    Its heavy tale divine.

'Go, lonely man,' it saith;
   'They loved thee from their birth;
Their hands were pure, and pure their faith,—
   There are no such hearts on earth. . . .

'You cannot unlock your heart,
   The key is gone with them;
The silent organ loudest chants
   The master's requiem.'[160]

Silhouette of the Reverend Ezra Ripley, Emerson's step-grandfather
By-Laws of the Corinthian Lodge . . . of Concord, Mass. (1859)

Emerson's aunt Mary Moody Emerson
as a Young Woman

The Journals of Ralph Waldo Emerson,
ed. Edward Waldo Emerson and Waldo
Emerson Forbes (1913), volume 4

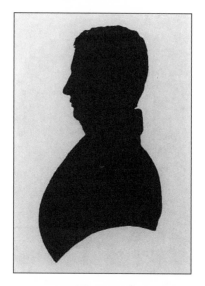

Silhouette of
Edward Bliss Emerson

David Greene Haskins, *Ralph Waldo
Emerson: His Maternal Ancestors* (1886)

Ruth Haskins Emerson
David Greene Haskins, *Ralph Waldo Emerson: His Maternal Ancestors* (1886)

Silhouette of Charles Chauncy Emerson
David Greene Haskins, *Ralph Waldo Emerson:
His Maternal Ancestors* (1886)

Portrait Medallion of
Charles Chauncy Emerson
prepared by Sophia Peabody
Ralph Waldo Emerson
Memorial Association

Watercolor on ivory
brooch of Ellen Louisa
Tucker Emerson by
Caroline Schetky or Sarah
Goodrich, ca. 1829
Concord Museum

Ambrotype of Ralph Waldo Emerson,
copy of drawing by Sarah Goodrich, ca. 1829
Houghton Library, Harvard University
(bMS Am 1280.235 [706.1]), and the
Ralph Waldo Emerson Memorial Association

Drawing of Emerson in
1844 by Caroline Neagus
Hildreth depicting him as
he was in his mid-thirties

*The Journals of Ralph Waldo
Emerson*, ed. Edward Waldo
Emerson and Waldo Emerson
Forbes (1913), volume 1

Miniature oil portrait of William Emerson, ca. 1834
Massachusetts Historical Society

Carte-de-visite of William Emerson
Massachusetts Historical Society

Miniature oil portrait of Susan Haven Emerson, ca. 1834
Massachusetts Historical Society

Carte-de-visite of Susan Haven Emerson
Massachusetts Historical Society

STAATEN-ISLAND
bei New-York.

Staten Island in the
mid-nineteenth century
Joel Myerson Collection
of Nineteenth-Century
American Literature,
University of South Carolina

Lidian Jackson Emerson
in 1853

*The Journals of Ralph Waldo
Emerson,* ed. Edward Waldo
Emerson and Waldo Emerson
Forbes (1913), volume 9

Daguerreotype of
Robert Bulkeley
Emerson by Addison
A. Fish, 1853[?]

Houghton Library,
Harvard University
(bMS Am 1280.235
[706.14]), and the
Ralph Waldo Emerson
Memorial Association

Crayon sketch of Emerson in 1846 by Eastman Johnson
F. B. Sanborn, "Portraits of Emerson" (1896)

Emerson with
his children
Edith and Edward
discussing "A Virgil
Lesson" in 1858
*The Journals of Ralph
Waldo Emerson,*
ed. Edward Waldo
Emerson and Waldo
Emerson Forbes
(1913), volume 10

Emerson's son, Waldo
The Journals of Ralph Waldo Emerson,
ed. Edward Waldo Emerson and
Waldo Emerson Forbes (1913),
volume 6

Carte-de-visite of
Edith Emerson Forbes
Massachusetts Historical Society

Carte-de-visite of Emerson
in the mid-1850s
Joel Myerson Collection of Nineteenth-
Century American Literature,
University of South Carolina

Carte-de-visite of Emerson, ca. 1868
Joel Myerson Collection of Nineteenth-
Century American Literature,
University of South Carolina

Carte-de-visite of
Ellen Tucker Emerson
Massachusetts Historical Society

Chapter 4

Aunt Mary and the Brothers Emerson

[As] I read these yellowing letters of M. M. E. . . . . I doubt if the interior & spiritual history of New England could be truelier told than through the exhibition of family history such as this, the picture of this group of M. M. E. & the boys, mainly Charles. The genius of that woman, the key to her life, is in the conflict of the new & the old ideas in New England. The heir of whatever was rich & profound & efficient in thought & emotion in the old religion which planted & peopled this land, she strangely united to this passionate piety the fatal gift of penetration, a love of philosophy, an impatience of words, and was thus a religious skeptic. She held on with both hands to the faith of the past generation as to the palladium of all that was good & hopeful in the physical & metephysical worlds, and in all companies, & on all occasions, & especially with these darling nephews of her hope & pride, extolled & poetised this beloved Calvinism. Yet all the time she doubted & denied it, & could not tell whether to be more glad or sorry to find that these boys were irremediably born to the adoption & furtherance of the new ideas. . . . Milton & Young were the poets endeared to the generation she represented.[1] Of Milton they were proud, but I fancy their religion has never found so faithful a picture as in "Night Thoughts." These combined traits in M. M. E.'s character gave the new direction to her hope; that these boys should be richly & holily qualified & bred to purify the old faith of what narrowness & error adhered to it & import all its fire into the new age,—such a gift should her Prometheus bring to men. She hated the poor, low, thin, unprofitable, unpoetical Humanitarians as the devastators of the Church & robbers of the soul & never wearies with piling on them new terms of slight & weariness. "Ah!" she said, "what a poet would Byron have been,[2] if he had been born & bred a Calvinist!" (6 May 1841, *JMN*, 7:446–447)

Here . . . is the prayer perpetually repeated in varied language throughout her lifetime.

O forsake me not! All of honor & pleasure & knowledge continually sacrificed to thy will; but not even to that, Oh tremendous Power! Not a conformity to thy commands, communion with thyself, thy presence, will not relinquish the hope, the struggle, the importunity. Thou mayest punish me for the past,—grind my face for the present,—but I will not let go. My importunity *to obey thy will,* to see that it *is thy hand* in secret generating my trials.[3]

$\mathcal{R}$eading through the letters of Mary Moody Emerson, Charles Chauncy Emerson, and Edward Bliss Emerson in the opening months of 1841, Ralph Waldo Emerson momentarily considered once again preparing a memoir of his brother Charles. The idea for a memoir had first been broached formally by Charles's Harvard classmates Francis Caleb Loring and Robert C. Winthrop, and it was reinforced by Henry Ingersoll Bowditch and William Gray within weeks of Charles's death on 9 May 1836. In conveying their idea to his brother William on 8 August 1836, Waldo admitted to being "embarrassed by the proposal," but embarrassment aside, he admitted that his real reservation about attempting a memoir was that he doubted Charles had "left any bulk of papers that are now fit to publish," adding, "nor would he thank me for so doing" (*L*, 2:31). ·

His reservations notwithstanding, Waldo began to collect his memories of Charles, anecdotes from family and friends of his favorite brother's life, and passages drawn from Charles's correspondence, college addresses, lectures, and private journal in a notebook he titled "C. C. E."[4] Within days of returning home from Charles's funeral, he lamented, "I may live long. I may . . . see many cultivated persons, but [Charles's] elegance, his wit, his sense, his worship of principles, I shall not find united—I shall not find them separate. The eye is closed that was to see Nature for me, & give me leave to see." He asked himself, "Who can ever supply his place to me?" He answered, "None," but soon he realized that he had answered too hastily. Reading on in Charles's journal, Waldo was so shocked by what he encountered that he remarked in his own journal, "I read with some surprise the pages of his journal. They show a nocturnal side, which his diurnal aspects never suggested,—they are melancholy, penitential, self accusing; . . . they are the creepings of an eclipsing temperament over his abiding light of character" (*JMN*, 5:152). Some months later he mentioned to William,

I am busy these . . . days in reading over all Charles's MSS particularly his letters to Elizabeth (of which she loaned me a large number) & to Joseph Lyman, & his journal with a view to draw up a memoir. I shall be determined entirely in the use I make of it by the form it shall itself take. Seldom never were such love letters written, characterized as they are by the ambition, that himself & his friend should present in their life, each, an image in every part beautiful. With much truth & beauty they are however all tinged with that melancholy which seems to have haunted his closet whilst it quite disappeared in society. (20 March 1837, *L,* 2:59)

As before, Waldo's thought in 1841 of returning to the memoir ultimately passed. In the opening months of 1837 when he mentioned to William his distress at finding all of Charles's private writings "tinged with that melancholy which . . . haunted his closet," he found it impossible to reconcile the brother he loved and believed he knew so well with the near-stranger who was gradually and painfully revealing to Waldo-the-reader previously unsuspected complexities and contradictions on virtually every page of his personal writing. Charles was himself aware of the potential problem of disclosing too much of himself in his private writings, and his correspondence with his brothers often concentrated on his or their studies, news of the comings and goings of friends he shared in common with them, business and financial affairs, or, as means to avoid having to discuss too much about himself, series of questions about how their own lives were going. Quoting from a now-lost passage once recorded in Charles's journal, Waldo notices that

C[harles]. was very impatient of writing. In conversation all his powers played freely & his success was perfect. One day when his conversation was very picturesque & rich I said to him, if you do not easily compose with pen in hand you ought to go & record your conversations. "It were an impiety," he said, "but when I am old I mean to remember my thoughts."

In his journal he writes . . . "I cannot pinch the genie & shut him into a casket. The life that I live is a various salient widelily life. The spirit of the creature is not to be expressed in sentences of a journal but lives & leaps along the uneven road of human affairs—now wrangling with obstructions now manfully overcoming now sportful now prayerful. It is not the pieces it is the forming whole I study.—If I chose to press flowers of conversation . . . in my book & keep them to entertain me in a winter's day when no such flowers bloom—I might—. . . But I wear them in my heart. They go to perfume & enrich the imagination, a garden where they drop their seed & spring up after snows & dead leaves have covered & deformed the ground." (*JMN,* 6:264)

Although he believed that "every family [had] its own little body of literature, divinity, & personal biography,—a common stock which their education & circumstance have furnished, & from which they all draw allusion & illustration to their conversation," Waldo recognized that in the familial sphere in which he and his brothers grew and out of which they each entered manhood, the "common stock" of knowledge they shared and their Aunt Mary's role in conveying and finally shaping that knowledge made it completely "unintelligible . . . to a stranger" (*JMN,* 7:443). Thus, on one level Waldo could appreciate and accept how Charles preferred to preserve only "the forming whole" of his life and character while keeping secret the "leaps" he made along life's "uneven road," but on another level, as brother but also as author of the marvelous essay on "History" in which he declared "There is no history: There is only Biography,"[5] Waldo felt conflicted over the role he might play as his brother's biographer and what exposure of Charles's life might reveal about his own as well as those of his brothers William and Edward. To open Charles's life for the world to see and to use it as a means to define the Emerson family's history would be, Waldo feared, "to write the annals of sickness & disproportion." No matter how he might try to romanticize or otherwise elevate Charles's life, he recognized that if the dark truth of Charles's secret *ennui* were ever revealed, the brother whose "noble & superior" presence, intellect, and sense of camaraderie made him the object of affection, respect, and even, perhaps, a bit of good natured jealousy among his family, friends, and Harvard classmates would represent a caricature of the Calvinist temperament that he so despised. At the same time, Waldo likely understood that to expose publicly "the real" and often tormented Charles might forever dash his own hope of restoring the Emerson family name and fortunes to their rightful place at the forefront of New England society.[6] Thus, as far as Waldo was concerned, because literally and figuratively they came so impossibly close to home, both the bleakness of Charles's interior, spiritual landscape and what that bleakness disclosed of their fraternal commonality as, he knew, it had been shaped by Aunt Mary, could never be revealed. Indeed, even as he confessed the enormity of his loss to Thomas Carlyle shortly after Charles's death, Waldo's devastation at the loss of this brother, whom he variously described as his intellectual equal, Muse, and truest companion, defied full exposure because, as he wrote, "we made but one man together."[7]

Every family has its secrets—secrets that, though sometimes acknowledged within the family, are kept from the outside world. With "M. M. E." at its center, the family in which William, Waldo, Edward, and Charles Emerson were reared was certainly not exempt from the rule, and as the passage from Waldo's journal quoted above suggests, the Emerson brothers' history as a family was itself a microcosmic rendition of "the interior & spiritual history of New England." Across the two centuries that separate the Pilgrim landing from the nineteenth century, Mary stands as an emblem not only of a form of personal genius that joined those temporal extremes together, but also as an expression of the very genius that was New England Calvinism. The central drama of her life, as in the life of New England since its founding, was "the conflict of the new & the old ideas." In a charmed place where nothing of the promise or the fatalism of the New English Israel was ever lost, Mary was the spectacular heir of what "was rich & profound & efficient in thought & emotion in the old religion," and she was the conduit of the promise and fatalism of that grand past to the young boys placed under her care after her brother William's death in 1811. Waldo captures the essential drama of Mary's life, and through her the drama that informed all of New England's history through the 1820s and 1830s, when he describes her as uniting "passionate piety with the fatal gift of penetration, a love of philosophy, an impatience of words, and . . . religious skeptic[ism]," holding on all the while "with both hands," as he says, "to the faith of the past generation as to the palladium of all that was good & hopeful in the physical & metephysical worlds, and in all companies, & on all occasions, & especially with these darling nephews of her hope & pride, extolled & poetised [her] beloved Calvinism." Though Waldo seems to allow that he cannot decide whether Mary was "more glad or sorry to find that these boys were irremediably born to the adoption & furtherance of the new ideas," the ease with which he rewrites the severe prayer of the New English Israelites falling before their dreadful Lord as Mary's own "repeated in varied language throughout her lifetime" shows that he knew exactly where his aunt stood.

This chapter explores the secret life of the Emerson brothers as that life was primarily shaped by and eventually disclosed to their paternal Aunt Mary in the letters the brothers wrote to her. A large portion of that secret life, the life shared by Waldo and Mary, has been exposed and explored in fair detail for a number of years. Waldo's letters to Mary have long been known through the editorial and biographical work first of Ralph L. Rusk in the 1930s and then of Eleanor M. Tilton in the 1980s and 1990s. However, as most scholars agree, Waldo's letters to Mary tell only part of the story of their remarkable relationship, and the part they tell is not entirely fair to the whole. In recent years, the other—and perhaps greater—part of their relationship has been the focus of groundbreaking studies by, for example, Evelyn Barish and David R. Williams, and the subject of two magisterial works of scholarship in the 1990s: *The Selected Letters of Mary Moody Emerson,* edited by Nancy Craig Simmons, and *Mary Moody Emerson and the Origins of Transcendentalism* by Phyllis Cole. In these works Mary Moody Emerson has joined figures such as Margaret Fuller, Bronson Alcott, Ellery Channing, Elizabeth Palmer Peabody, and the several women of Waldo's immediate household—his wife Lidian Jackson Emerson, his daughter Ellen Tucker Emerson, and his "adopted" sister Elizabeth Sherman Hoar—to nudge Waldo a bit off center stage from considerations of the origins and influence of New England Transcendentalism.[8]

Unlike her famous nephew Waldo, who evidently believed early in his career that he was writing for posterity and, therefore, used even epistolary prose to advantage the canonical figure he wished to become, Mary wrote only for her correspondents, her family, and the social circle that surrounded the Emerson household. Thus, what she has to say in her letters *and* how she says it in them represent acts of extraordinary candor. Sometimes Mary's letters present, as Simmons suggests, "a feminized, spiritualized view of nature and human life" in which "epistolary conversation" is raised to an art form through which she draws out the best in her correspondents and provokes them to new depths of introspection and personal understanding and heights of self-expression; at other times, however, Mary shows herself to be an individual of incredible personal resolve as she preserves her highly independent view of "divine order" while discussing and sometimes openly challenging the merits of Unitarianism or the writings of Thomas Brown, Juvenal, Dryden, various Russian poets and Eastern philosophers, and a host of other sources.[9]

This fraternal biography would be incomplete without the inclusion of and comment on the voluminous correspondence exchanged between Mary and the brothers Emerson; for their part, Mary's letters, which often read like mini-sermons on familial and cultural values, are most valuable for the rare excursions they provide into a world of ideas passed to the brothers through her personal lens of religion, politics, and literature, and by the authority of her being, by birth, temperament, and intellectual disposition, an Emerson.

Even when she has been confined to the periphery of American intellectual history, Mary Moody Emerson has long been a recurrent figure in all tellings of Emerson family biography as well as in most accounts of Concord's Transcendental circle over the past half-century. Born in the Emerson family's ancestral home of Concord to William and Phebe Bliss Emerson on the eve of the American Revolution, by virtue of her longevity Mary took one generational step further than Ezra Ripley personal witness to the amazing range of political, religious, and intellectual upheavals that shaped American culture through the Civil War. Like Ripley, Mary was born into old-style, conservative New England Congregationalism; unlike Ripley, who though praised in the annals of Unitarian church history as one of the prophets of religious liberalism never strayed far from ecclesiastic formalism, Mary was an intellectual and religious eclectic who transcended the limits of traditional Congregationalism by incorporating liberal and Enlightenment thought, and strains of Platonism, New Light pietism, and an affinity for intuition and the Romantic sublime, into her highly personal religious vision. Mary was the guide to her nephews' understanding of the family out of which they had emerged and of the impressive future she believed they were each destined to achieve. Moreover, she served as the brothers' mediator between a mysterious religious world that she had, in fact, outlived and a complex intellectual one that she helped to create during their lives.

Although we might be tempted to think of her as replacing the boys' deceased father by drawing on their father's intellectual and religious views, Mary was her own person and had her own, not borrowed, instructions to convey to her nephews. In fact, the senior William Emerson is virtually invisible in the correspondence Mary exchanged with his sons; when his memory is invoked, it is because Mary uses it to reinforce some particular instruction she had to offer. For example, she invokes him in the following remark to Charles as a reminder to "[c]herish the scenes w'h soften the heart": "When my father left me I was within 6 months of the age you were, at the loss of yours. When you came with your brothers for the last time and stood by age at his bed, his look so tender & anxious rested on your little face (which seemed to me conscious of the scene) with increased regret. Cherish the memory of scenes w'h soften the heart, and show the frailty of prospects the most flattering."[10]

Prior to the editorial and biographical studies of the past twenty years, three portraits dominated our inherited image of Mary Moody Emerson. First and foremost is that found in Waldo's lecture on his aunt that he delivered as "Amita"—"aunt" in Latin—before the Boston Women's Club on 1 March 1869; that lecture was subsequently arranged for posthumous publication as "Mary Moody Emerson" by Waldo's literary executor, James Elliot Cabot. In many respects, the essay that "Amita" became extends and codifies the capsule portraits of Mary scattered throughout Waldo's journals, including the portrait quoted above. Here, despite his aunt's reputed idiosyncrasies—mostly that she wore her burial shroud when she traveled, had her bed constructed in the shape of a coffin, and was highly opinionated—which some in the audience would have heard about at least second-hand, Waldo portrays Mary as an inspiring and complex character who "had a deep sympathy with genius" and "gave high counsels" to the minds of those, like he and his brothers, entrusted to her care. He reports that while reading through her letters and other papers, he is impressed by her acumen and assimilative genius: "Plato, Aristotle, Plotinus,—how venerable and organic as Nature they are in her mind." Remarking on her biblical authority, he writes that her conversation created "paraphrases to signify with more adequateness Christ or Jehovah" than the inspired texts themselves. Her sensibility made her feel at home in "the fiery depths of Calvinism, [with] its high and mysterious elections," but she was also comfortable in the aerial heights of Transcendentalism, "driven" as she was "to find Nature her companion and solace." Consistent with his biographical portraits of most intimates whose character he translated into Greek or Roman terms, here Waldo transforms Mary into an heroic Greek: "Our Delphian"—he calls her—one who could tame and be tamed "by large and sincere conversation"; one who was always attendant to expressions of "thought and eloquence" and whose life and mind "burned . . . [with] the glow of . . . pure and poetic spirit." As preserved in the published version of "Amita," Waldo's Mary is a modern

Cassandra, uttering "to a frivolous, skeptical time, the arcana of the Gods," and in her unification of behavior and belief, representing the great Christian truth, "Faith alone, Faith alone."[11]

In contrast to Waldo's celebratory treatment of his aunt, two other early portraits show Mary in a somewhat more complicated (and negative) light. One comes from Mary's sister-in-law Sarah Alden Bradford Ripley, who, as Mary entered her seventieth year in 1844, wrote that she "still retains all the oddities and enthusiasms of her youth" and has an "insatiable" appetite for metaphysics. Ripley characterized Mary thus: she is "a person at war with society as to all its decorums; she eats and drinks what others do not, and when they do not; dresses in a white robe such days as these; enters into conversation with everybody, and talks on every subject; is sharp as a razor in her satire, and sees you through and through in a moment." Unlike Ripley, who all her life felt herself "enchained . . . entirely to [Mary's] magic circle" of conversation, insight, and wit, Elizabeth Palmer Peabody, writing about the same time, found Mary's "magic" mercurial, irksome, and virtually impossible to take. After staying with Mary in Waterford, Maine, for the summer of 1846, Peabody wrote the following epistolary sketch:

> She is an extraordinary creature. I think I never received a greater impression of . . . genius: the ploughshare of Experience never seems to have broken the wild beauty of her character—which like a wild country of great natural sublimity of feature—retains its untamed rocks & woods & cataracts telling of the creative power of God—but not of the redeeming power of Christ. Now this last would shock her who has such a passionate love of *his name*—& so fine & fresh an idea of the necessity of his redemption. . . .
>
> I enjoyed after all more from her—notwithstanding all—than [one] can imagine. . . . She is so original—& then I like mountains & valleys—cataracts & wild woods—in characters as well as nature. I love her though she does stick hard things into all tender places.[12]

Mary's attractiveness as a highly complex character of deep faith and profound intellect who looked back across multiple generations as well as forward to new ones as she stood at the crossroads of the two-century-long drama of the Emerson family history is precisely what has transformed her from caricature to person in contemporary scholarship. Those who lived in Mary's midst were indeed "enchained" within a unique sphere of influence, and although individuals such as Ripley, Peabody, and the brothers Emerson who found themselves within that sphere sometimes chaffed at the pressures, barbs, pettiness, personal intrusions, and flights of imagination that from time to time Mary imposed on all of them, no one ever asked to be permanently excused from the "magic" of her "circle." Certainly, none of the Emerson brothers ever did. In fact, had they known of it, they would have intuitively understood and approved the insight into her character that Waldo gleaned from this passage out of Mary's writings, which he copied into one of his earliest journals: "Those who paint the primitive state of man's creation are sweet poets; those who represent human nature as sublimed by religion are better adapted to our feelings and situation; but those who point the path to the attainment of moral perfection are the guardian angels. But this is no easy poetic task. The lowly vale of penitence and humility must be passed before the mount of vision, the heights of virtue are gained" (*JMN*, 1:333).

In the letters that follow, William, Edward, and Charles Emerson reveal the extent to which Waldo's insight into his aunt's ultimately poetic character accords with their own sense of Mary's importance to their lives. In his own case, Waldo, with the possible exception only of his brother Charles, knew and understood Mary best, and found the lure of her poetic and prophetic vision impossible to resist. Like his brothers, Waldo could get angry at her, discount her opinion when she demeaned his learning and exercise of personal conscience, discredit her faith when it conflicted with his own, and accuse her as "the Weird-woman of her religion [who] conceives herself always bound to walk in narrow but exalted paths which lead onward to interminable regions of rapturous & sublime glory" (*JMN*, 1:49), but always he came back to her as his teacher—as one of his "guardian angels"—pointing out to him ways to negotiate the invariably rocky "path to the attainment of moral perfection." Waldo understood that just as Mary's life humanized New England's "interior & spiritual history," her presence in his and his brothers' lives served as a cleansing force for dignity, faith, and purpose amidst what he often feared was the frivolousness of their world.

> The new relations we form we are apt to prefer as *our own* ties, to those natural ones which they have supplanted. . . . In reading these letters of M. M. E. I acknowledge (with surprise that I could ever forget it,) the debt of myself & my brothers to that old religion which in those years still dwelt like a Sabbath peace . . . which taught privation, self denial, & sorrow. A man was born not for prosperity, but to suffer for the benefit of others. . . . Not praise, not mans acceptance of our doing, but the [Holy] Spirit's holy errand through us, absorbed [our] thought. How dignified is this! . . . How our friendships & the complaisances we use, shame us now. . . . I feel suddenly that my life is frivolous & public; I am as one turned out of doors, I live in a balcony, or on the street. (1841, *JMN*, 7:444)

AUNT MARY AND WILLIAM

Mary Moody Emerson's first letters to her nephew William are fairly typical of the early letters she later wrote to his brothers. Because William was the oldest of the brothers and thus the first with whom she corresponded as an adult, Mary may have thought of her letters to him as sites in which to test some of the literary postures she would later assume when she wrote to her other nephews. Mary invariably constructed her letters as sites of moral instruction, philosophical inquiry, genealogical history, and literary criticism, viewing them ultimately as "epistles"—in an old-style religious sense—designed to instruct the recipient on a wide range of subjects. In response, the Emerson brothers usually addressed their letters to "Respected and dear aunt" or "Dear Aunt" or, simply, "Aunt Mary," developing them as formal essays in which they answered her inquires about their reading, discussed their studies, and sometimes included informal asides into their everyday lives, news of their friends and pets, and questions about how their favorite aunt was spending her time. In a few instances, the brothers construct Mary in the role of confessor in their early correspondence with her—a role that may have made her uncomfortable, but she seems to have accepted anyway—and their letters read like acts of confession in which the problem they wished to explore with her is usually one of intellectual or religious doubt. With the exception of Charles's extensive lifelong correspondence with Mary in which he routinely bared his soul and revealed the melancholy and self-loathing that so surprised and shocked Waldo after his brother's death, the confessional aspect of the brothers' letters virtually disappears as each enters manhood.

In many respects the Emerson brothers' letters to Mary are epistolary conversations on which we can now eavesdrop. Although she respected her nephews' individuality, one nevertheless senses a stern tone in her letters to them that answers Waldo's query about whether Mary was more glad or sorry to find that these chosen boys were "irremediably born to the adoption & furtherance of the new ideas." Unquestionably, as the boys grew older and became increasingly capable of thinking for themselves, Mary was sorry, not glad. In her early letters to each of the brothers, Mary was never subtle about insisting that the boys had to spend their youth preparing for the grand role they were each to play as the heirs of the Emerson family's ecclesiastic and intellectual dynasty; however, as first William, then Edward, Charles, and finally Waldo rejected her repeated calls on their behalf to the real and imagined pulpits she expected them to occupy in the furtherance of her idealized view of their future, Mary did not hold back from expressing her profound disappointment that, as Waldo characterized it in 1841, "these boys [who had been] richly & holily qualified & bred to purify the old faith of what narrowness & error adhered to it & import all its fire into the new age" found that "the old faith" held little more than sentimental appeal at best or drove them into a spiritual realm that counseled "privation, self denial, & sorrow" at worst (*JMN*, 7:444).

As his letters to Mary that follow indicate, for his part William had conflicting responses to his correspondence with her. Initially, he appears dazzled by her kindness and concern, eager to share news of academic successes that he believes will please her, and, as his letter of 13 June 1813 suggests, easily chastened by her rebuke of his pride and clearly fearful of ever again offending her sensibilities. In that letter, after he makes his apologies, William almost casually fills Mary in on family news, his concern that he is not yet ready to attend college, his disappointment that John L. Abbott—"almost an entire stranger"—had been chosen to fill the pulpit once occupied by the Reverend William Emerson, and his progress in various readings. Although there are periodic gaps in their correspondence, William's letters to Mary are open and generous, extending the character of his early correspondence into that of his mature years. For example, writing to her from Göttingen on 10 April 1824, he describes his four-month journey when he sailed from Boston for Europe. In this letter he describes at length his travels first to Ireland, and then across France, before he finally arrived in Göttingen on 5 March, and as he does so, he writes a true local color sketch for his aunt, including extensive commentary on burial rites in Paris and Dublin, and his sense, which he thinks she would approve, of the democratic arrangements the French make out of death, burying nobles alongside bakers and tailors. A year and a half later, when William wrote to Mary on 27 October 1825 (printed in chapter 2) from Cambridge, Massachusetts, announcing his safe arrival back in America, he did so as much as an expression of his own affection for her as in compliance with his mother's suggestion that he needed to set his aunt's mind at ease. Unquestionably, Mary was gratified not only by William's news of his safe arrival home but also by the style in which he delivered that news. Writing a letter that he knew would appeal to her, William created a full and fine dramatic description of his journey home and drew several edifying lessons from it that could just as easily have come from his aunt's pen as from his own.

Although William may have written to her more often than the record suggests, the Mary-William correspondence after the mid-1820s seems not as full as one might expect. Yet, there is no reason to suspect some sinister motive behind William's relatively scant correspondence with Mary during his early adult life. The character of William's life after his return from Germany resembled that of his life before he left. Unlike his brothers Charles and, to some extent, Waldo, who had the time to engage in extended correspondences with friends and family, from the time he returned home from Germany and eventually moved to New York in September 1826 to begin apprenticing as a lawyer, William's life consisted of continual work, intense reading of the law and studies in real estate and financial management, and administering the Emerson family finances, a task that he shared with Waldo. Mary was regularly apprised by Charles and Waldo of William's life in New York City, his marriage and expanding family, and his occasional financial crises created by inflation, bank panics, and failed land speculations. Thus, there was no need for William to unfold or embellish his personal life to her more than his brothers were already doing. Finally, like Edward after him, whose correspondence with Mary is the most meager of all exchanged between the brothers and her, William had consciously and openly rejected the heroic role of minister and public intellectual that she had drawn from the family past and imagined and then imposed on each of her nephews, so that as a practical matter neither William nor Edward had much to say to her on the subject dearest to her heart.

Although we do not believe that there was any sinister motive behind William's engaging in a relatively small correspondence with Mary, readers may wish to consider a motive that, by implication, emerges from Robert D. Richardson's reading of the value William may have placed on his life in coming to their own conclusions about William's relationship with Mary and what their correspondence (or lack thereof) reveals about that relationship. In his biography of Waldo, *Emerson: The Mind on Fire,* Richardson bluntly—and with uncharacteristic blandness—summarizes William's life this way:

> William Emerson married, had children, and lived to be sixty-seven, remaining on close, warm terms with his New England relatives. He was always the honored older brother. It was never said—but always felt— that the respectable, established figure William cut represented a defeat, a taking refuge in the standing order of things after his personal faith and force had failed. Certainly the law was not what Aunt Mary wanted for any of the boys. She wanted them to go into the ministry, not for respectability or position or fame but from the kind of heroic faith and the personal sense of mission she herself felt.[13]

The extent to which William's life represented a failure; the extent to which he believed his life was a failure; and, if he believed his life was a failure, the extent to which he might have attributed the failure to Mary's influence are all debatable points. As Richardson rightly states, "It was never said—but always felt," and if the "It" is a judgment made by William, his brothers, his Aunt Mary, and his own family a century-and-a-half ago, or if the "It" is a judgment we were to make now, then some of the evidence to support the judgment will have to be found between the lines of the letters that follow. However one decides to speculate on what William intended between the lines of his letters to Mary, one must consider that William's life was never characterized as a failure by any member of his immediate family, and as far as he appears to have been concerned, he had little, if anything, for which to blame his Aunt Mary with respect to the quality of his life. In fact, William's late correspondence with his aunt, and the quality of his remarks about her and concern for her comfort in her last years discloses the otherwise unarticulated degree of tenderness and respect with which he regarded her. This is hardly what one would expect from a nephew who held his aunt responsible for the real or imagined failure of his life.

In addition to their content, the form of Mary's earliest letters to William also resembles those she wrote to her other nephews. Her first letters to her nephews typically opened with her direct response to a letter she had received from one of them, shifted to her description and discussion of her most recent readings as well as comment on what she knew of their recent readings or progress in school, and offered lessons after which the boys could model and measure their conduct in this world against her ideal of their achieving eternal glory in the next. Evidently in anticipation of William's ninth birthday, which was then slightly more than a month away, Mary wrote on 24 June 1810 to reinforce in the boy a sense of filial piety and respect for the care and labor his parents had invested in raising him thus far; at the same time, however, she wanted William to be clear about that fact that all happiness he might enjoy in this world through his practice of "amiable dispositions"—such as modesty and affection—and any happiness he might hope for in the next would come from God's divine labor and his only Son's great sacrifice.

> You, my dear William, are nine years old. In those years how many weary steps and anxious thoughts have you cost your dear parents. And many pleasant ones also. But it is now time for you to reflect on your condition, as a being who has been sent into this world for a short time to prepare for a world which will always exist. If you fear God, and serve Him, He will accept of your services and make you unspeakably happy. You may be sure He will, because you read in the Holy scriptures, how Jesus Christ, Gods only Son, came into this world and died for Sinners. It is for his sake, that God bestows so many and so invaluable blessings upon us.
>
> I often think of you and your brothers, and remember whatever I saw modest and affectionate in you with delight. A man possessed of amiable dispositions is always sure of happiness, and without those, tho' he were a President or Govenor would be despicable. (*MMEL*, p. 57)

Two years later, after the death of William senior in May 1811, Mary wrote young William another pre-birthday letter. It is probably the most significant of any of the early letters that she wrote to her nephews, for after apologizing to William for having mislaid a recent letter from him, she says, "I intend finding it, as it may commence a correspondence which may accompany us thro' life."

Thus, only a year after her brother's death, Mary saw herself as having inherited some portion of his paternal responsibility to prepare his sons as pious and learned members of the rising generation.[14] "Certainly," Mary continued, "I hope, never to see the day when you shall cease to interest your friends [that is, to no longer be of interest to Mary herself], or your letters be a matter of indifference. If you are pious towards God, and of course, benevolent to men, you will not only delight your friends, but find an interest in every worthy heart, so long as you are here in this world, and after death you will find yourself related to all the truly great and venerated who have lived in every age."[15]

William must have accepted Mary's early lessons exactly as she intended. Like Waldo's allusion to "the prayer perpetually repeated in varied language throughout her lifetime," her admonition, repeated in varied language to William and his brothers throughout the days of their youth, emerged from her conviction that "after all is said & felt about publick calamity & prosperity, a large and certain portion of care and ill attend almost every mortal."[16] On 22 February 1813, Mary wrote to express her joy at having received news of William's splendid delivery in January of an "Essay in English Prose" at the Boston Latin School's "Semi-Annual Visitation." Here, as always, her joy and her compliments to her nephew on his "profound erudition" came laden with lessons through which she hoped to improve his knowledge in the ways of the Spirit and his walk on the path of godliness toward true wisdom and understanding.

> You may well imajane with what emotion I take my pen to write to "a man of your parts and profound erudition." But as the gentlest candour and warmest nature are often concomitant with astonishing talent, I make bold to address you. And without offense let me say that however lofty the pinicle of fame on which you are mounted, however vast the m   of your admirers, and magnificent your power, if you have not an open ingenuous temper, & humble, pious heart, your memory, after a few uncertain days, will perish, or your name be mentioned with contempt. Riches are but the dust of the earth; honor, which cometh from the breath of man, empty as air, & learning but the collection of other men's property. Would you be great, throw aside your pomp, descend into the tomb—behold there that *the worm is thy sister, and corruption* thy appointment. Seek not for *honor and glory* on this earth, hastening itself to destruction. Pass the few days in which it carries thee on it's surface in purifying thyself. . . . Fill with faithfullness, the rapid moments, that thy Mother may rejoice in *a wise son*—that the poor and ignorant may be the happier that thou wast born. (*MMEL*, p. 70)

Except for the letter that follows, the body of William's own early correspondence to Mary is scant in relation to the correspondence sent to her by his brothers. Between 1813—the date of the letter that follows—and his journey to Germany to study for the ministry in late 1823, William did not have the time to spend on an extended correspondence with his aunt. During this period, as we know, he entered Harvard at the age of 13 in 1814, assisted his half-uncle Samuel Ripley at his school in Waltham, Massachusetts, in 1815, kept a school at Kennebunk, Maine, in 1817 and 1818, and taught at a girls' school in Boston before leaving for Europe. On the other hand, time may well have been less a factor in William's lack of correspondence with Mary than his resistance to her incessant moralizing and severe, though well-intentioned, advice—a characteristic possibly not only of his response to her but also, in time, of his brother Edward and even, after his resignation from the ministry, his brother Waldo.

↦ *William Emerson to Mary Moody Emerson, 13 June 1813*

I hope you will forgive me for the improper letter I wrote. But I really meant it as a continuation of the jest. However, we will leave this subject.[17]

I was very sorry for Rebecca, who seemed very much affected when she heard of the death of Caspar.[18] But a short time after, she gave me liberty to read a letter she had written to her parents, which was principally concerning the state of her heart. In this she mentioned, that the death of her brother had first called her to reflect that she must die. Last night, which was Saturday, uncle Shepard[19] spent about an hour here, and conversed with Rebecca. Having spoken to her, he asked me, whether the religious impressions, which Rebecca was under, seemed to me rational or not? I answered him in the affirmative, and a short time after he went home.

As to going to college this year, I should like it very much, though I know I shall be a great deal better fitted next year. I do not think myself ready in several of the branches, such as Mathematics, Writing of Latin, Parsing in Greek &c. I went up to Waltham Tuesday night, and was examined by uncle [Samuel] Ripley, and came down Election morning. He said I was not so far advanced as he expected to find me.

I suppose my mother has mentioned to you Mr. Abbot's acceptance of the call of our church.[20] It seems very mournful to me, when I think that that pulpit, which all my life-time I have been accustomed to see filled by my dear father, is to be filled hereafter, by a gentleman, almost an entire stranger to our family. I cannot possibly express what I feel upon this subject.

I am much obliged to you, aunt for that money, you was so kind as to give me an order for. It was very punctually paid. Since you have been gone I have not read much more in Rollin, but have read "Melish's Travels in the United States."[21] From the title, I expected something more than usual. But I was disappointed: for I found nothing as to the history of the country, more than is usually found in the common geography of places. To be sure, he gives you a pretty exact account of his meals, and of his business: but I think, on the whole, it is a very silly thing. I am now reading "Chateaubriand's travels in Syria, Egypt, &c." which I think a more useful and entertaining work.[22] We are all well, as I hope you are. Please to give my duty to my Uncles and Aunts and love to my cousins. I should be much obliged to you to answer this letter as soon as convenient, and excuse my last.[23]

⤳ William Emerson to Mary Moody Emerson, 10 April 1824

If you have not yet entirely blotted my name out of your books, which I don't know but I deserve, perhaps you may yet be willing to turn over a new leaf in my favor.—It is more than a year since I saw you, and during that time I have often visited your retired abode in imagination, and often written you letters in intention. The account would perhaps stand in my favor, were all such epistles counted, yet I fear that in letters which have actually seen the light, I am so ungallant as for a long time been long in your debt—Especially since I left home, have I often thought of my Aunt, and in many instances my interest in what I beheld has been greatly enhanced, by recollection of her sentiments.

I remember in particular, when at Paris and roaming about the cemetery of Pere la Chaise,[24] how forcibly I was reminded of you, for I knew you would take delight in visiting this abode of the dead. It is indeed a beautiful spot. To reach it you must leave all the bustle of the city behind, for it is without the barriers of Paris, and surrounded by fields of the richest fertility. There is a remarkable variety in the monuments. Some are of pure white marble, many of black and even of coloured marble; some in more moderate circumstances have put a slate or other coarse stone over the remains of their friends, those who could not afford this, have thrust into the ground at the head of the grave a small wooden cross painted black. But whether of marble stone or wood, they are all in good taste, and often in the most beautiful forms, such as obelisks, pillars, urns. At the head and foot of the graves, cypresses are planted, but as it is not many years since this place was used as a cemetery none of these have as yet attained a great height, yet they are high enough to import a pleasing solemnity to the place and besides give such an air of seclusion to each separate grave, that mourners may come and weep in perfect solitude over the remains of their kindred, even though many others should be wandering about the cemetery. And here the living *do* visit the tombs; and many are the little wreaths and bouquets of flowers which are strewed upon the ground, or hung upon the small paling that incloses most of the graves. Nor was it only over those very lately interred that these flower garlands were strewn over, but fresh ones were to be seen where the grave had been many months occupied, where the person had been interred more than a year. Sometimes, in lieu of this, or in addition to it,—plants are cultivated on the very sods that cover the dead, and thus the grave becomes a flower garden. Sometimes the piety as well as the affection of the survivors was apparent displayed in placing a miniature chapel at the head of the grave, often in front, in which you might see an image of the Virgin, or of the Saviour, about as big as a doll. Flower wreaths were generally hung [on] these little chapels, [and] before the image, candlesticks corresponding to it in size, in which small lights had been burnt. A lamp was still burning in one of these modest shrines the morning I visited the place. They are only to be seen on the graves of the poor, and very coarsely constructed. In walking through these beautiful alleys, carpeted by turf, and shaded by cypresses thickly bordered on each side by funereal monuments, I was pleased to observe how literally the predictions of the moralist are here verified by the annihilation of the distinctions of society. I noticed a Baron's grave which was closely elbowed by a baker's.—A beautiful marble pillar told at length the virtues and titles of a high born lady, and the next stone commemorated the industry and parental affection of a master tailor. A few ancient monuments have been transformed from their former situations, to this place as more appropriate—among others, that of the poet Moliere.[25] But there was one which particularly arrested my attention. It was in the form of a small open Gothic temple, evidently of great antiquity, the roof of which was supported by four pillars placed at the corners, beneath which lay a full length marble figure in clerical robes, his hands folded on his heart, and on the side of the monument was a long Latin inscription, which recorded the vast learning and genius, and unfortunate love of a celebrated teacher. It was the tomb of Abelard and Eloisa! The tomb is here, but their ashes do not repose beneath it.[26] I have not said a word of the inscriptions. Neither had I time to read half as many of them as I wished. But the national character was as easily distinguishable here as elsewhere. There was an uncommon degree of warmth in their expressions of grief, affection, and piety. And it seemed as if many a pilgrim had wandered here from distant land, to find a resting place in this beautiful spot, for there were many foreign names on the stones, and epitaphs in various languages. Perhaps I might like to be buried there myself; only should that happen, I should have no one there to scatter flowers over my ashes. I was very loath to come away. The objects by which I was surrounded, and the reflections they produced . . . made this the pleasantest morning I passed at Paris and this is saying not little, for the 10 days I spent at P[aris]. filled a large space in my mind's life. In going out, I passed several poor women, who earned their living by the sale of those flower wreaths, that are scattered on the graves—Some natural flowers they had, even at this season (Feb.) but the chief part were artificial.

I had not gone far, when I met a funeral procession going into the cemetery. The coffin was on a modest bier supported by four men, and followed by a dozen carriages, painted black. The persons in the carriages were all males—Every thing was perfectly simple and orderly. It struck me as not a little surprising, that the French, who seem to carry their love of show, and their tastefulness in trifles into every thing, should be out-done in funeral decorations by the Irish. I saw several funerals in Dublin and the body was usually placed on a hearse, surrounded too with black plumes, and drawn by six horses whose heads were likewise adorned with plumes.[27] The drivers & footmen of the carriages that followed, had white bands round their hats, and long white scarfs which were thrown over one shoulder, and tied around the body. When the deceased was unmarried, the plumes and the pall were white, and if poor, the corpse was carried by men instead of being placed in a hearse but still there are plumes and scarfs. I remember well the pain I felt, in seeing the remains of a child carried out to be interred. The house looked very poor, and 4 ill-looking men brought out the coffin, and placed it on a bier, which had six or eight tarnished white plumes upon it, and was hung all round with a dirty white. One or two persons looked anxiously out of the windows after the corpse, but the bearers bore it hastily and rudely away, and laughed and jested as they went.

One Sunday that I passed in Dusseldorf, on my way to Göttingen, I witnessed the funeral of a Catholic, of the middling class. He was fol-lowed to the grave by many of the military (with whom he was in some way connected,) and apparently by all men of his parish—for there came a long line of these after the soldiers, and seemingly to make the more show, in two files some distances apart, singing all the way out the Offico book of the church. They had more than a mile to go, the cemetery being without the city, finely situated directly on the bank of that noble river the Rhine. When they arrived at the cemetery, the singers returned to the city. The coffin was lowered into the grave while the two were alternately mumbling over Latin Prayers with the greatest rapidity. When they were finishing, the priests threw the first shovelsful of earth into the grave, and then went away. The people that remained about the grave then filled it up, each throwing in one or two shovelsful. . . .

I hope my lugubrious epistle will find my dear aunt in a very cheer-ful mood, otherwise I fear it will give you the hypochondria. I did not mean to have talked of graves and tombs and epitaphs alone, but one thing has suggested another till my paper is filled. The circumstances I have mentioned may not much interest you; but it may perhaps afford you pleasure, that they come from so far away, from the hand of your af-fectionate nephew.[28]

➤ *William Emerson to Mary Moody Emerson, 16 September 1840*

Your very kind letter of the 13th June has done me & Susan much good, though I cannot say that we enter with any zeal into the philo-sophical controversies you touch upon.[29] But I must regard them rather as philosophical than religious; & George Ripley & Waldo, notwithstanding their speculations, may be as religious as Luther & Calvin.[30] I look with constantly increasing indifference upon mere theological orthodoxy; his-tory assures me that the theorist Hobbes was to the full as good a man as the world-famed & Unitarian Sir Isaac Newton; nay, a better, if one half of the Flamsteed story be true.[31] The couplet of Pope may have got to be an old saw, & yet it commends itself to my poor judgment.

> For modes of faith let graceless zealots fight;
> His can't be wrong whose life is in the right.[32]

Of course this is not true to the letter; else were poor Dame Holloway's faith preferable to Sir Isaac's; yet I adopt the idea that the mood is com-paratively unimportant. The controversies themselves are useful as whet-stones of the logical powers, & do, perhaps, though very slowly & imper-fectly enlighten the public mind. I presume that there is in New England & the Middle States a greater degree of light on the subjects of religion & theology (which I consider as entirely distinct) than in the days of the Puritan. The dawn glimmered on them, the morning sun is now rising. But why do I, from the low plains of practical life, write to you on such topics,—to you, who dwell ever on the lofty mountains of contemplation? I crave your pardon for such temerity; yet I was led away from my usual reserve by your letter, which seemed to invite me to some discussion. Let me hasten to thank you for your affectionate greetings on the birth of our little Haven boy.[33] On the first day of this month, Susan, the two boys & myself reached Concord. The Patriarch [Ezra Ripley] condescended to come to Waldo's on the 3d and baptize the baby, & seemed gratified at being called upon to perform the ceremony. After spending a few days very pleasantly there, (Elizabeth [Hoar] was at home) we went to Ports-mouth, where I left Susan & the children. Since my return I have been a prisoner at my cottage with a lame foot, & I avail myself of what I trust is the last day of my captivity to write this letter. If Susan were with me, she would send her love to you. She wishes often to see & know you; & if you could think it possible to come hither, I do not think you would find the journey laborious or expensive; & when you arrive here, I think you would be pleased with our island. The children are both promising, & might remind you of those bygone days when you devoted your hours & thought so kindly to the boys that have since become men. I agree with you that the medallion is very unlike to Charles, yet it has enough like him to remind me often of him.[34] It also serves to recall Edward very strongly; & for these things I value it. Your letter to Mrs Dewey (the name Louisa is among bygone things) came some time before they left the city for Sheffield, & I delivered it to Mr D.[35] His connexion with his people is somewhat precarious; not that they cease to admire him, but he says his head will not let him study.—Have you seen Macaulay's Miscellanies?[36] Since Carlyle's books,[37] it is the most vigorous & striking that I have seen. It will not however be new to you, if you have read & recognized him in the Edinburgh Review for the last 15 years beginning with the article on Milton. But is it only I who am deaf, or is it that the lyre of poetry is hushed? Now & then, I hear some wailing from Elliott, the corn-law rhymster; but Wordsworth & Campbell & Rogers are mute.[38] Eloquence seems to have gone mad in party politics, as well as religion in polemic theology. What think you of the Dial? Waldo seems dissatisffied with N° 1 & expects better things from N° 2.[39] It is sufficiently abused by vulgar critics to be entitled to a fair reading from the candid. Lest I tire you, I will say, farewell![40]

➤ *William Emerson to Mary Moody Emerson, 28 July 1842*

I have no events of consequence to tell of, for since the birth of my Charles, & the death of his cousin Waldo, there has been no domestic occurance among us worthy of mention.[41] Waldo came to see us at Staten Island, on occasion of his repeating his last course of lectures here, & his cheerfulness under that severe recent loss was heroic.[42] His lecturing here produced a marked sensation in the best part of our community, & has created for him many lovers & admirers here. A month ago, Susan went to Portsmouth for a few days to visit her Parents, who are feeble, & I went for her, & we spent 3 or 4 days at Concord on our return with mingled pain & pleasure. Waldo is always the same to us, Elizabeth [Hoar], a spectacle worthy of all good angels; mother unfortunately was a little lame; Lidian is always kind & conscientious. But that is a great void which the little boy's death has made. He was the hope of the house, its particular jewel. But why should I talk to you or to any one of the Irrevocable? Let us enjoy with trembling the blessings that are offered to us, & hope ever to the Infinite mercy.

In visiting Concord there were, beyond the circle of home, two subjects of no little interest to me. One was the old Manse, which has undergone some changes, & having lost the old patriarch, was waiting the arrival of new tenants.[43] What a history in those silent walls! Ever since my own childhood, how have they echoed to the joyous laugh, the agonies of pain & sorrow, the cries of madness—proceeding from those whom you & I have most prized, most tenderly loved! In the little attic room, my father's, Edward's, & Charles's, handwriting are still plainly to be read on the wall. Some wood & stone seems holier than the rest, is consecrated by our feelings. I am sorry to see the old house going into stranger's hands.—This is one. The other matter is quite different, but still of strong interest to me. Mr Hoar has been sent some weeks back as commissioner for Massachusetts to an assembly of the Indians in western New York, & he gave me explanations which I had not been able to gather from the papers.[44] The satisfaction was to see Massachusetts standing erect in the person of her upright commissioner, overlooking the treaty makers to see that the red men had fair play, & never stooping an inch from the man's full height to give a smooth opinion.

I attended my cousin's wedding yesterday. The principal parties in the scene will give you all the details, so that I need not spread them on my narrow paper. You will probably join me in congratulating him on having made so good a choice. Literature has within the year poured forth from her abundance many things good & evil. . . . If you think of any[thing] that I can get, send to me . . . for it.[45]

→ *William Emerson to Mary Moody Emerson, [31 April?]–1 May [1845]*

It was with great concern that I heard from Sam[l] Moody Haskins of the death of your last surviving sister.[46] It has been your lot to part with those most nearly allied to you both in blood & in sympathy, many of them your juniors, almost all of them, apparently, far more desirous to remain among mortals than yourself. But though it is not given to us to choose when & how & in what company we shall depart, it is ours to determine with what mind and heart we shall sustain the burden that is laid upon us. The equal mind may have a heaven of its own, not in defiance of Deity, but in harmonious, filial accordance with the Universal Law. As Waldo says in his 'Nature,' we then enjoy the highest triumph, when we can say, 'Father, not my will, but thine, be done.'[47]

It ill becomes me to speak as a teacher to you; yet perhaps you will smile as you remember my ancient calling, & think it not amiss. Truly it does seem preposterous to myself, sitting as I do at this moment, within sound of the clash & the din of Wall Street, that I should presume to speak to you among the mountains & the lakes. Yet the same sky bends over us both, and perhaps even I may be pardoned for speaking to you *ex cathedra,*[48] since a kind regard to those in affliction seems to vest a friend with some new rights.

I fear you may reproach me, & with justice, for my scanty performance of duty as a correspondent. But my daily cases are many, & you will not fail to recollect among your own family certain Marthas, cumbered with much serving, all which takes up the time, better spent in other concerns.[49]

I often wish there were some practicable communication betwen us for other things than letters, for in this publishing age, there is occasionally something dropped from the press, that could not fail to interest you. Carlyle's Past & Present, & Waldo's 2d series you doubtless have.[50] Is there nothing else that you have heard of lately, that I could get more easily than you can? If so, please lay your commands on me.

May 1. Thus far had I written, dear Aunt, when your kind letter of 20 April reached me. The same day I called at Mrs Dewey's & saw her, & Mary, & Mrs Lombard, & her daughter Julia now verging on womanhood. It is rarely that so many reminiscences of childhood & youth are called up at once. Sibyll & her daughter came down to Staten Island with me yesterday P.M. & spent the night here, to return to the city this morning. S. has retained a good many of her early peculiarities, & superadded a strong episcopal bias. Julia is a lovely girl, possessed of good talents.— Your letter suggests several topics of deep interest. I feel so strongly the impolicy & wickedness of annexing Texas, & so extending the area of slavery, that I wonder how any friend of the slave should have hesitated to regard this as the overruling question, & by voting for Clay to have saved the honor of the country, which by the vote of the Birney men has now been sacrificed.[51] But how long, I pray, has your democracy been of the Jefferson school?[52] I thank my early teachers among whom I had always reckoned you, that I never imbibed any more radical democracy than that of Washington & Hamilton & Adams.[53] I grieve that you are surrounded by these new fanaticisms, or rather with the old leaven in a new lump.

My little Charles has no middle name.[54] He is a very pleasing child, bright & affectionate. I prize, as warmly as I can any thing, these fragrant sweets of childhood, too soon, alas! to exhale all their delicate perfume.[55]

→ William Emerson to Mary Moody Emerson, 28 November 1847

I know not in what words to write to you of the sudden departure of your brother.[56] Painful, almost overwhelming as the event is to his family & to us, his friends, yet how desirable to him! I never hear of a transit so speedy, so painless, from this toilsome world, that I do not regard the in-dividual with something like envy. Happy indeed he was, in the cheerful-ness of his temperament, in his frank & manly character, in the rare fe-licity of his domestic relations, wife, sons, daughters, friends; what more could be desired for him, than that he should depart in a moment?—My mother, as perhaps you may have heard, is with us on Staten Island, & we have this afternoon received from Lidian a particular account of the circumstances attending Mr Ripley's decease. The circle of friends who were gathered to celebrate his favorite holiday remained to pay the last tribute of respect to his mortal remains.

I understand that Mr Ripley's family are all in usual health, as indeed all our friends in Concord, & that they are expecting you there to pass the winter. How much you will miss your brother there.

The thread of our life is a mingled yarn, good & ill together. The same packet from Lidian that brought us all these sad details, also conveyed to us Waldo's interesting accounts of his first fortnight in England, with Carlyle, Rogers, Martineau &c.[57] He writes in fine spirits, though in-tensely occupied both in the preparation of his lectures, & the inevitable interruptions of travelling, visits, &c. If he can only command sufficient leisure to satisfy himself in the preparation of his lectures, I think he must enjoy himself highly in England.

Your kind letter, dear Aunt, received in August, ought to have been answered much sooner, but—why say a word more?[58]

→ William Emerson to Mary Moody Emerson, 16 October 1853

I was very much gratified, & so was Susan, at your taking the trouble to write. It seems to bring you quite near to us again, to have actually seen you so lately, & to have ascertained the geographical fact of your being at that end of old Massachusetts that lies nearest to New York. And the region of Ashfield & its neighborhood interested me very much. It is more like pristine Massachusetts, in its simplicity, & some other good qualities, than the vicinity of Boston; which latter region has grown rich, & corrupt, and conservative, & lost all the old enthusiasm. You speak of my interest in political matters; but, dear Aunt, that interest has mostly died out. I have seen so much corruption in politics, that I have ceased to look with any hope to any political party. I hope only in education; and look with more confidence to the young mechanics & farmers than to any political party whatever.

Indeed, if you & I were to converse on those old subjects of interest, the church, the state, the present & the future, inspiration, miracles, & various other topics within the range of your reading, I should be obliged to confess to a gradual estrangement from the free consideration of many of them, and a sort of indifferentism as to some. The whirl of affairs, be they petty or important, in which the inhabitant of a great community gets involved, generates, I think, a kind of callosity to matters of sentiment, and leaves one hardly sensible to any interests out of the sphere of business, except those of family and near kindred. Still, if I should ever be blessed with a period of leisure, which I hardly anticipate, I know not but old enthusiasms might be reawakened, and new ones, still better, kindled, that might possess the soul with a new life and energy. Let me hope for such a consummation.[59] . . .

→ *William Emerson to Mary Moody Emerson, 20 March 1860*

Your valued note of the 14th was received, but headach[e] one day & business the others prevented my answering it sooner. It was quite a pleasure to me to find that if you have ailments which induce you to call in a doctor, you have energy enough to get rid of him very soon. I like your method; after two days attendance "a respectful request for his bill." What would become of Law, Physic & Divinity if all the laity adopt your summary process?

Waldo is at home, & quite well. I have no line from him, but Dr Furness called to see me yesterday,[60] & he was at Concord last week, & saw them all, and rejoiced in Waldo's beautiful health of mind & body, & in Ellen's consideration for her mother, & in Edith's sparkling cheerfulness, & in Alcott's philosophy,[61] & all the other delights of Concord. He had Elizabeth Hoar & her brother Edward for companions in the car to Boston.

This was William's last formal letter to Mary. From December 1858 until her death on 1 May 1863, she lived in Williamsburgh (now Brooklyn), New York, at the home of Hannah Haskins Parsons, her niece. Her health deteriorated dramatically between March 1860 and November 1861. In January 1861, when Waldo and his daughter Ellen came to New York, Ellen, who stayed at her uncle William's home, paid several visits to her great aunt Mary while her father went off lecturing. During the course of Ellen's visits, Mary was drawn closer and closer to Waldo's child, and by the time she was ready to return home to Concord, Ellen had received from Mary's hand all of her manuscript

ʌit, that bright fancy, that stinging satire that have made her so
able.[68]

Mary's death and her burial in the Emerson family plot in Concord's
ʌllow Cemetery, William and Waldo took care of the details of their
ʌte. The brothers thought that Hannah's care of Mary merited every
ʌtion. "If I had not other light," William wrote, "I should subscribe to
ʌine of a special Providence, from the adaptation of Hannah Parsons's'
ʌke devotion to Aunt Mary's infirmities."[69] After seeing Mary's will
probate, William squared accounts with Hannah and paid the out-
costs of Mary's funeral and burial; in a letter to Waldo, he confirmed
ʌment to the final distribution of what remained of their aunt's small

ʌ to what comes from Aunt Mary's assets, I am willing . . . to pass to
ʌredit of our old account what is due you on your old claims against
ʌo, having now paid her doctors, & the board due Mrs Parsons, &
ʌndertaker, I shall now pass to your credit as of Nov. 1, 1863, the
ʌ of $150. This will pay her note in your favor of Feb. 1, 1847, for
ʌ & interest thereon, $27.84, & her note of Apr. 24, 1850, for $83.07,
ʌvhich you were so indiscreet as to stipulate that it should be without
ʌrest.[70]

AUNT MARY, EDWARD, AND CHARLES

ʌ the time of her brother William's death on 12 May 1811, Mary's nephew
ʌrd was barely six years old and her nephew Charles barely two-and-a-half.
ʌdering it her responsibility to fill the intellectual and theological void
ʌd by the boys' "fatherless condition"—as she occasionally and somewhat
ʌdramatically referred to it—Mary committed herself to instruct them in
ʌays of early piety as she believed their father would have had had he lived.
ʌmplement their growth in piety, Mary devised various plans to exercise
ʌhallenge their minds by engaging them in serious discussion of their read-
ʌand what they were learning in school as well as on the street, to nurture
ʌn intellectually by introducing them to a world of ideas with which she had
ʌady grappled through the deft exercise of her own intellect and imagina-
ʌ, and to prepare them for a useful life of service to God and humanity by
ʌng them for the ministerial calls she fervently believed would be coming
ʌr way and that they would accept.
ʌn terms of her overall approach to her nephews' education, and even in

letters, miscellaneous family documents, and
body of Emerson and Haskins family treasu
with her for more than sixty years, and which
to a new generation.[62]

In his letters to Waldo, William now becar
of his aunt's last years. On 24 November 186.
"Aunt Mary's case is a very painful one. Her m
very hard duty for Mrs Parsons to take care of h
It is of no use or satisfaction for me to go and s
stay away. She has written notes to George Rip
suaded him from going to see her."[63] In March 1&
Williamsburgh, and on the 17th he wrote Waldo
tion: "I went to see Aunt Mary yesterday p.m. &
gentle, & extremely forgetful. To use her own ex[
Mrs Parsons showed me the photograph, which I t
at once.[64] Nobody could recognize her."[65] Finally,
William described its approach to Waldo.

➳ *William Emerson to Ralph Waldo Emerson, 26* [*A*

Yesterday I received a note from Sarah Ansley
could not continue with us much longer;[66] that
scious except for a moment at a time since Mon(
for any one; & that there was a perceptible failu
week. Susan & I went to Williamsburgh this morn
but almost wholly unconscious of every thing; quit
between dream & waking; asking for cold water, &
herently.

Hannah Parsons is devoted to her by night and by
mercifully ordained that she should be childless, sc
martyr to Aunt Mary's infirmities, . . . whose path th
been smoothed by her tender care.

It seems probable that Aunt cannot live but a very
event, the funeral service will be read, by her owi
Haskins's friend Mr Clapp, & the remains will then
to Concord for interment.[67] Mrs Parsons will probably
& go at once to your house; but Aunt Mary has repeate
wish that no service of any kind should take place at C
her remains should be deposited there.

She has not taken any food for more than a week; or
& the doctor has administered a little morphine, to c
nerves; so she is much wasted, & her eyes are very dim.

terms of the body of knowledge she felt was necessary to convey to them in order to effect her plan, there was little difference between the ways in which Mary urged Edward and Charles, as well as their brothers William and Waldo, along the path she intended they should walk. In doing so, she respected their individuality and she relied on their kinship with her to smooth over any of the disagreements or hurt feelings that may have occurred as the result of her being a consistently stern and stoic taskmistress. What Mary never anticipated—what she most likely would never have allowed as even the remotest of possibilities—was that as she prized and respected her nephews' individuality, they would, in fact, actually exercise their individuality in, as Waldo observed, refocusing their aunt's contributions to their growth onto the development of their own "new ideas" and, in each case, begin to develop individual minds and ambitions connected to, but increasingly independent of, her own.

We have already seen how William ultimately found his own way in the world by living as an Emerson at a distance; indeed, without having to speculate on the point too much, the extremes to which William went in breaking ties with his New England roots—and with Aunt Mary as the nurturer of them—is a measure of how far he felt he literally needed to go to become his own man. Because he has been gifted with remarkable biographers, and because we have had access to an extraordinary archive of the growth of his mind and reputation, we have long known how Waldo eventually faced and achieved the challenge of becoming his own man. The story that has not been told is of the extent to which Edward and Charles were able to become their own men and how, in order to achieve whatever success they enjoyed in this mission, they each recognized that, first, they had to come to terms with the role Mary had played in their individual development, and, second, they had to be prepared either to resist and finally reject her influence or become the men she wished them to be.

The remainder of this chapter is devoted to that story. Although the basic plot of Edward and Charles's story is easy to tell, the dramatic center of each story is more difficult to describe and explain if only because Edward and Charles—and depending upon one's focus, Waldo along with them—eventually seem to blur into the same person. As Sylvester Baxter observed almost a century ago in his unpublished biography of "The Other Emersons," Waldo, Edward, and Charles assimilated into their own persons "the best qualities that mental and spiritual contact with [each other] could yield and which preëminently entered into the building of [their] character . . . through the most plastic and formative years of . . . life—those of childhood, youth and young manhood." "These influences were reciprocal," Baxter argues, and they continued among the brothers "until physically [Edward then Charles] passed from . . . life." Echoing a view promoted by O. W. Firkins in his early biography *Ralph Waldo Emerson,* Baxter concludes that a spiritual unity—a common spiritual identity—bound the three brothers so closely to each other that, when Edward and Charles were alive and interacting regularly with Waldo, what was best in one was shared by all until, as the sole survivor of the relationship, Waldo channeled into his own life and thought the best qualities of character and mind represented by his two remarkable brothers.[71]

Edward and Charles *were* very much alike, and together they certainly exerted a profound influence on Waldo's life and thought. It is worth remarking that, as the two individuals whose story is being told now, Edward and Charles were individuals of great intellect in their own right. In their early years at least, they were each generally the most cheerful and sociable of the Emerson boys. They were each high strung and a bit arrogant, but with good cause given their distinguished academic achievements. More than their brothers William or Waldo, who of necessity were concerned with the mundane aspects of life— earning a living, supporting their mother, Bulkeley, and Edward and Charles as the latter made their way through Harvard and into the world—they really did imagine that they were destined to emerge as major figures in their world, initially, as their aunt had hoped, by the figure they each would cut in their respective pulpits, but ultimately by the social and public good they would each serve through their practice of the law. Finally, and most important of all, they were, as Waldo stated so clearly, products of Mary's influence, extensions of herself.

As emblems of the spiritual history of New England or as illustrations of the tragic lives that awaited those who assimilated to an extreme the spiritual legacy of New England Calvinism, Edward and Charles, far more than William or Waldo, bore the mark of being Aunt Mary's boys. Edward's story is one of resistance to that mark, a mark that literally reveals itself in the painful blister packs that were applied to his chest to counteract the effects of his tuberculosis, in his increasingly fragile physical and mental constitution, in his bouts of manic depression that led to a madness so severe that his family decided he had to be institutionalized, and then, with the onset of tuberculosis, in his permanent exile from family and friends in Puerto Rico, where he lived for the remainder of his life. Charles's story is a variation on his brother's. Prone to depression, self-doubt, and extremes of loneliness, world-weariness, and despair that conjure up an image of him as a latter-day Michael Wigglesworth meditating on "the necessity of affliction" or Cotton Mather groveling before his God in the dust, Charles never resisted Mary's influence, especially her unmediated Calvinism, but rather strove to become its fullest, most perfect human expression. As Waldo succinctly but painfully recognized, the mark that Charles bore, the mark that disqualified him from serving as an edifying and elevating biographical subject for his own and future generations, was "that melancholy which seems to have haunted his closet" and darkly tinged all the finer aspects of his character and thought.

AUNT MARY AND EDWARD

As boys, Charles was unquestionably Aunt Mary's favorite, and Edward—the "Bliss Boy" as she liked to refer to him in the family and as he liked to call himself because of the connection it made between himself and his illustrious ancestors—came in a close second; by the time they became adults, however, Charles had far outdistanced Edward in his claim on Mary's attention and affection. Beginning with William, then with Waldo, Edward and, finally, Charles, a common denominator in Mary's first epistolary interactions with each of them is a tone of a female Jeremiah urging—if not actually haranguing—the boys in the direction of early piety. That tone is evident in expressions such as those quoted above mingled among Mary's lines of praise to William on his successful delivery of an essay at the Boston Latin School in 1813: "[L]et me say that however lofty the pinicle of fame on which you are mounted, . . . if you have not an open ingenuous temper, & humble, pious heart, your memory . . . will perish, . . . your name be mentioned with contempt. . . . Would you be great, throw aside your pomp, descend into the tomb—behold there that *the worm is thy sister, and corruption* thy appointment." That tone is also evident in the following passages drawn from two letters that Mary wrote to Edward. The first passage, which comes from a letter she wrote to him on 9 November 1816 a month after he took up residence at the Phillips Academy in Andover, Massachusetts, to prepare for his entrance to Harvard, extends the instruction in early piety that Mary had already provided to William. The second passage, which comes from the New Year's letter she wrote to Edward on 1 January 1818, is noteworthy for two reasons: first, it contains the only explicit apology Mary ever made to any of her nephews for the severity of the lessons in which she instructed them on their path toward early piety and the intensity with which she criticized their every youthful enthusiasm, and, second, it reveals a depth of tender feelings for her nephews as when, after addressing Edward in the body of the letter as "My dear Bliss Boy," she assures him, "you were always *loved*."

➻ *Mary Moody Emerson to Edward Bliss Emerson, 9 November 1816*

I rejoice if you love to join your fellow students in the offices of religion. What is man without piety? The most abject and destitute being in the universe. Exposed to all the winds and waves of life's tempestuous ocean, without the pole star of hope to irradiate one of the heavy clouds which threaten to overwhelm his future prospects. Yet it is worthy of the most serious consideration, *in what piety consists!* Prayer is an indispensable requisite. . . . A penitent, humble, charitable heart which prefers the favor of God to the whole universe is indispensable. . . . Private devotion is called by the most eminent Saints, the richest means of improvement and happiness! (*MMEL*, p. 97)

↠ *Mary Moody Emerson to Edward Bliss Emerson, 1 January 1818*

Whether happy or not be the coming year, to My dear Bliss Boy, God grant it may be a pious year. On each of its revolving days may he impress improvement. And while the weary each beginns anew her old course, and we rejoice that she travels the same orbit with invariable order; may his mind begin a new one—rise with yet untasted ardor to the study, the knowledge and practice of his heavenly Father's will. Then will those powers of mind . . . be embued with a celestial complexion, never eradicated. Yes, my loved Edward (tho' I have often wounded your feelings by the severity of my criticisms, yet you were always *loved*) it is *early* piety alone can deeply and with peculiar charms tincture the whole soul—expand and ripen it's good dispositions. . . . [N]othing is little to a soul fired with the love of true glory. It's light never fades in the darkest scenes of outward degradation; but ascends from the lowest grades of human condition to mingle with it's great Original.

When I think of your fatherless situation, I feel stronger hope, that you will have grace to unite your fortune for time and eternity to the Father and Redeemer of your spirit. That He will mercifully conduct your path into the sacred ministry, and that you be a blessing to your poor fellow creatures. *That you live not in vain*—not *ultimately for yourself* in this world. (*MMEL*, pp. 106–107)

Signing himself "The Bliss Boy," Edward wrote one of his more mature early letters to his aunt on 12 December 1817. The letter is pleasant and chatty. He tells Mary about his brother William's new position as a school master in Kennebunk, Maine, reports that he had to delay returning to Andover from vacation because mother Ruth had to help William gather his belongings for the trip to his new post, briefly mentions that Waldo, now at Harvard, seems to like college life and appears to be "a *very good scholar*," comments that Charles and Bulkeley are well, and gossips about the health of his grandmothers; in a touching postscript, Edward adds the following insight and plea with respect to the amount of work his mother has in keeping house and raising her family: "Mother is so much engaged with her work that she is obliged to sit up till about midnight every night and needs you *very very* much indeed." But what is truly noteworthy about this letter is that, like William in his early letters to Mary, here Edward neglects to provide his aunt with any information whatsoever about his spiritual condition—an oversight, perhaps, but more likely a deliberate omission that occasioned Mary's immediate response in the New

Year's letter quoted above that she sent to Edward two weeks later. There, once again, she summoned Edward to "rise with yet untasted ardor to the study, the knowledge and practice of his heavenly Father's will" so that, with "those powers of mind" in place he could be "embued with a celestial complexion, never eradicated."

> I was very much disappointed in not having the pleasure of seeing you, the day that you passed through Andover, and since then I have neither seen you nor received any letter from you. My vacation has expired three days but I could not go back immediately to Andover because Mother had so much work to do for William who has just gone to Kennebunk to keep a school there.[72] We are all hoping he will make a good school master. The idea of being one has caused "his sage face to wear a few smiles." He has recommendations to Dr. M'culloch and to Mr Moody and is to board in a very pleasant family.—
>
> Ralph is in very good health and as good spirits and still appears pleased with College life. He recieved a letter from you about a fortnight ago dated Elm Vale N^{ov} 4.[73]
>
> I believe Ralph is considered a *very good scholar.*—
>
> Charles and Bulkel[e]y are well. The former is a good scholar at Mr Goulds school though not so good as at first because he is now parsing Latin and his not having learned to parse English is a disadvantage to him.[74]—
>
> Our friends at Concord are as well as usual. Grandmother was so well as to dine down stairs thanksgiving day, which she has not done since last thanksgiving. We were all at home on that day, and in the afternoon and evening, our cousins Thomas Haskins and Charles Shepard and William Ladd were here.[75] Grandmother Haskins has had an ill turn lately but is now, in some measure recovered.[76] *Uncle Thomas* and Uncle Ralph are in hopes to be released by a week from tomorrow. Mother wishes me to inform you that the money is ready, which you sent for to Uncle Thomas and that she only waits a safe conveyance to remit it to you.—
>
> Mother sends love to you. I suppose C[harles]. and B[ulkeley]. would do the same, but they are at school. Accept the affectionate respect of your
>
> nephew, The Bliss Boy.[77]

Mary's correspondence with William and Edward is far more limited in the number of letters exchanged and their scope than her correspondence with either Waldo or Charles. Once Edward achieved maturity the fault—if a "fault" it was—for the meagerness of their exchanges was as much Edward's as Mary's. Between 1818 and the mid-1820s, Edward, who was already showing signs of resistance to Mary's lessons, was primarily concerned with completing his preparation at Andover and entering Harvard, which he did in October 1820 and roomed with Waldo, then a senior; with pursuing his studies, which pursuit he threw himself into with such zeal that, as his health began to fail, in 1822 he showed again symptoms of the disease that had forced him in January 1820 to spend part of the winter in the South; with deciding between continuing his studies in America or, as the eminent Harvard physician Dr. John Collins Warren had advised, travelling to Europe for his health and finishing his studies there (L, 1:117); occupying teaching posts in places such as Sudbury (in 1823) and Roxbury (in 1824), Massachusetts, to supplement his finances; finishing his studies at Harvard and ending them on the high note of his taking the Bowdoin Prize as Waldo himself had done in 1820; and, finally, deciding on a career in the law, not, as Mary had hoped, in the ministry. It is fair to say that during this period the activity that consumed Edward's interest and sapped all his energy was his studies; even when, in January 1825, Edward began to read for and practice the law in Daniel Webster's office, the physical and mental exertion that he had applied to his studies at Harvard was transferred to his mastering the knowledge and argumentative art associated with his new profession. The "Bliss Boy" knew no moderation in anything to which he applied his mind and talents, and his lack of moderation would eventually claim his life.

Because the record of Edward's personally informative correspondence with his Aunt Mary—and often with his brothers—is relatively thin during the 1820s, it is sometimes to his brothers' correspondence that one must turn in order to have the fullest picture of Edward's life between 1818 and the close of the 1820s. Here, however, we are able to open this crucial phase of Edward's life with the following letter he wrote to Mary some six months after receiving her New Year's epistle.

➻ *Edward Bliss Emerson to Mary Moody Emerson, 31 May 1818*

Your favour dated January first reached me after a tour of four months *only,* during which tour I heard of it several times and, once it passed through Andover.[78] However I think that my pleasure was increased when I did receive it from that very delay. I am very much obliged to you for your kind letter, for the handsome present which accompanied it and for your benevolent wishes for my welfare. I hope I shall be enabled to follow your good advice, and to walk in the paths of wisdom which have been recommended to me by my friends from my earliest childhood and which have been traced out by the example of my excellent father.—You hope I shall be a Minister but I have some doubts about my ever arriving at that exalted station. Ralph[79] if he lives expects to be a minister and he will doubtless be one as his inclination lends him very much that way. I should like to be one if I thought I should be entirely fitted for the profession.—My prospects respecting entering College this year are not very bright, at present though it is possible that I may go; if not I expect to go to Waltham for some time and assist Uncle in keeping school. Ralph has been there about a fortnight and gives very pleasing accounts of his situation there.[80]

Uncle has a good collection of books, which if I was disposed to react would be of great advantage to me.—If I cannot go to College, I had rather be there, if I can be of any use, than be a burden to Mother.[81]—

Edward entered Harvard almost exactly two years later; in the winter of 1819–1820, with his health in a precarious state, he travelled south to Alexandria, D.C. (now Virginia), to escape the New England cold at the home of the brothers' cousin John Haskins Ladd. In the letter that follows Charles fills Edward and us in on life in and outside of the Emerson household at this time, whereas Mary writes a brief but predictable postscript in which she tells Edward that he is in her thoughts, where she thinks of him as "governing & elevating [his] feelings, by the fear of God which is the highest & only true source of wisdom."

A happy new year to you. I am glad to hear that you have arrived safe at Alexandria, & that you were not at sea in that violent gale. We thought that you had got there by that time. We have fine sleighing here now, as we have had another fall of snow. Last Thursday I learnt how to slide, & now can slide without any jumping. William says that he will give me a pair of skates, and I shall learn to skate this winter. Your skates began to rust, I have greased them and put them away. I should think you would have liked them as you went over so much ice. William has 20 schollars, & 1 or 2 more wish to come.[82] I have had a lame leg so that I did not go to school for 4 days in the week; & I had a fine ride in a booby hack with Miss Stearns in the country on Tuesday. Bulkel[e]y & I had a very good present on new years day, from William; it was a steel pen, one black, one white. I hope you will write me some account of your voyage the first opportunity, & tell me about Washington, Alexandria, and cousin's house. Was M[r] Blagge a pleasant companion?[83] Do you feel any better for your voyage? My Greek and French go finely. M[r] Everett wrote 3 pieces in the North American review, and M[r] Lemuel Shaw one.[84] We are all well. Ralph sends love, Bulkel[e]y sends a letter. My love to Mr and Mrs Lad[d] and yourself, and William Ladd.[85]

P.S. 31st. I expect that very soon I shall go to M[r] Cobs school as William is going to let me go to private there. Bulkel[e]y is next week going to leave M[r] Gs to go to M[r] Lyons.

My dear E^d Bliss,

I rejoice that you are so plesantly situated with friends who are so hospitable. Give them my best love & wishes. I wanted much to see you before your departure, as I think I shall not be here when you return. But to think of you, as constantly improving in some one virtue, in governing & elevating your feelings, by the fear of God which is the highest & only true source of wisdom, will give me more pleasure than even seeing you.[86]

Edward did not forget his aunt or her lessons. However, by January 1825, after years of balancing between Mary's never-gentle nudges in the direction of the ministry and his own inclination to pursue a career in the law, Edward had finally settled on the latter, and he was comfortable with his decision. Waldo seemed a bit bemused by the idea, although, as master of the struggling school for young ladies that William had opened in Boston in 1822 and Waldo had taken over when William left for Germany, he worried about the expense he might have to bear in supporting Edward's decision. Furthermore, because he knew Edward never did anything by halves, Waldo also worried about the toll his brother's readings in the law would take on his already diminished constitution. Finally, having decided to study for the ministry, Waldo was impatient for his future and wondered when his own turn at making something of himself would finally come. On 12 September 1824, he wrote to William, who at the time was still studying at Göttingen. Opening with an unusually direct fraternal demand on his brother—some of whose expenses Waldo was bearing as well—and expressing his concerns for Edward's welfare and his own, he said,

> . . . [B]e sure when you come back you be licensed to preach since for dear poverty's sake we must be frugal of time. Edward smitten to the bowels with ambition will speedily count if he does not already count the tedious hours of his own captivity & others w'd probably be impatient for him if he were not. For his own professional education he is ready to plunge knee-ear-deep nay overhead in debt. Of course I must not be left in the lurch, nor will my delapidated academy let me if I would. So I trust by basket or store by begging or borrowing to be studying in a year at least. Thus far I have not been . . . incommoded by your demands wh have not entrenched unexpectedly on their means. You shall have all the overplus of family expenditure only the less you have the longer it will [have to] last you. (L, 1:149)

As he explains to William in a New Year's letter that he and Edward wrote on 18 January 1825 to their brother in Germany, at the end of 1824, Waldo decided against postponing his studies any longer. "I have cast my bread upon the waters," he wrote from Roxbury in a mood of sudden liberation, "locked up my school, and affect the scholar at home. The truth is [mother, Edward, Charles, and I] think we have got to the Candlemas day of our winter, & that we may be bold to borrow the second half of our wood & hay, assuming that the spring & summer of lucrative exertion is nigh." Commenting that Charles, who has been studying at Harvard and now gone "on a pilgrimage to our lady [Aunt Mary] at Waterford," "is a high scholar," and leaving Edward to speak for himself, Waldo paused to offer a tribute to William's long self-sacrifice in the cause of supporting the family financially and seeing Waldo and Edward through much of their education. Playing Hercules to his brother's Atlas, Waldo wrote, "Fear not but due allowance is made for the sweat & merit of Atlas who bore the burden of all; and a pennyworth of consideration is affected for poor Hercules who stood in the stead of the giant" (L, 1:158–160).

Edward's contribution to the brothers' New Year's letter to William follows. In it, he appears completely at ease with his decision to enter the law, and he gives no indication that he shares any of Waldo's concerns (raised the previous October) about the toll his ambition to succeed in his profession would take on him. However, with Edward what is *not* said in his letters is what their recipients' usually had to worry about the most. Here, for instance, there is little difference between Edward's completely side-stepping Mary's expectation of comment on his spiritual condition years before and, now, his casual neglect of any substantive comment on his work in Daniel Webster's law office. Throughout, Edward applies a cavalier tone to whatever he has to say, particularly when he explains to William how he arrived at the law through a process of elimination.

For having devoted myself to that profession which is solely occupied in the quest after naked Truth, which is renowned & justly for its downright honesty, (you cannot but perceive, I speak of *Law*), it behooves me to learn early, how to set forth in order an unvarnished tale, & to adhere to simple *facts*.—But I w^d tell you by the way, that in choosing my path, I neither allowed myself to think, as you seemed in your letter to expect that I should, whether in *this,* I should "rise higher," or in "that, *sooner* attain *distincton,*" but I briefly reasoned thus: I am not hardy enough for a physician, not grave enough for a divine, not lyrical enough for a lawyer; but diligent enough for either I can be, & diligence is more competent to supply the want of logic, than it is to make me a grave or a robust man. Therefore, I will be a lawyer. This I said, months ago, to myself, & ever since have been more & more confirmed in my resolution; but I am only *published,* not *married;* and if you have any thing to offer against the match, why urge it, & if the advice be not followed, it will be very well received, yes & very gladly if it cometh in the shape of a letter from you in Europe. . . . I have ent^d my name in W[ebster].'s office, thro' Ev[erett].[s] introduction.—I talk of learning Spanish, rather than Germ. Have you any reasons to ye contrary.[87]

As we remarked in the introduction, while reading the voluminous correspondence exchanged among the Emerson brothers, one feels a sense of inevitability about what occurred to Edward between the time that he took up the law in Webster's office in January 1825 and the day six years later when, in December 1830, he sailed out of New York Harbor for St. Croix. Predictably, for most of 1825, Edward threw himself into his work for Webster, and because the toll it took on his physical and mental health must not have been apparent at the time, everyone seemed to miss the progressive decline that resulted in Edward's physical collapse before the end of the year. From October 1825 through October 1826 Edward enjoyed a recuperative sojourn in Europe. Although he appeared outwardly restored in body and mind when he returned home, Edward never revealed to his mother, brothers, or aunt what he was feeling or thinking between late 1826 and mid-1828. Then, against the celebratory backdrop of Waldo's courtship of the young and beautiful Ellen Louisa Tucker and Charles's successes at Harvard, the Emerson family's world came crashing down as Edward fell psychologically and physically apart. In some respects the intensity of William, Waldo, and Charles's sense of loss, impending disaster, and, perhaps, unspoken fatalism parallels the shock their elders must have felt in 1811 at the time of their father William's untimely death.

When the truth about his condition began to emerge, it was because Edward was finally willing to express himself truthfully to his brother William. Writing to his brother on 19 May 1828, as William was still struggling to establish his reputation in New York, Edward said,

> I wish you, disinterestedly, success in your legal as well as editorial labors, & whether their success be one whose fruits are internal or external, in the character, & man, or in his fortunes & situation, must be to you & every true lover & friend, matter of indifference—
>
> I read no law—almost no letters. I have ceased to resist GOD & nature; have consented to humor my body & rest my mind; & the consequence is that from the moment of surrender I have been gaining & tho feeble from the struggle of so many years, yet I am wiser, & *healthier* & happier than ever in my life. My prospect is now very distant but tolerably clear & bright.[88]—

Not having to read very far between the lines this time, William, betraying an initial degree of uncharacteristic panic, responded to Edward's letter on 27 May.

I do not know whether to be more rejoiced or concerned at the contents of your last letter (19 May)—I have heard from various sources that you were thin & pale, & you now tell me you have ceased to study. Alas! alas!—but I am glad at heart that you had the wisdom "to cease resisting God & nature," & that you are beginning, in consequence, to reap a golden harvest of mental calmness & bodily health. Do you remain in Boston? Can you not rusticate yourself? Can't you go & lounge, dream, idle, sleep & laugh away a month or so at Concord? I hate to think that while feeble, you should be within the sweep of those merciless east winds.[89]

But William's response and his proposed remedies to calm, if not to cure, his brother's troubled mind arrived too late. On 25 May, Edward suffered a complete nervous breakdown in Concord. Over the next month the family did its best to help Edward; however, the manic depression that had plagued his mind and the physical disease that would soon enough destroy his body were by this time simply too far along. Seeing no alternatives to the extreme measure that he now had to take, on 2 July 1828, Waldo rode with his brother to the McLean Asylum in Charlestown, where Edward remained a psychiatric patient through December. Writing to William on 3 July, Waldo noted, "Charles, as if in a kind of mockery, has a first prize for dissertation" (L, 1:237).

It is unclear what useful lessons, if any, Edward took from his collapse and institutionalization, because for most of 1829 he was back to his old—and, in terms of his work and study habits—problematic self. One of the first letters he wrote after his release from McLean was to Mary on 24 January 1829. There are several noteworthy aspects to this letter, beginning with the ironic juxtaposition of the claim Edward makes in the opening that, as he wrote to Mary, "before & after my liberation from the Asylum I had entertained some scruples about the propriety of continuing my study of the legal profession, not as being a wicked but a worldly pursuit," with the hope he expresses at the end, "I may be a good lawyer.—I may be a useful man." Also, there is a profound sadness to this letter, a sadness occasioned by dashed hopes and possibilities and expressed in Edward's tone as he tries to explain himself to his aunt. The sadness of frustrated expectations are qualities that Waldo recognized as increasingly characteristic of his brother's later writings. Commenting to William on Edward's epistolary style, Waldo said, "Edward writes always sadly. His faith is not strong & he clings to life. I can readily believe that such debilitating disease shd. have this effect but in health the prospect of death [should be] far less gloomy" (30 March 1831, L, 1:320). Finally, this letter is important for the extent to which Edward's tone in it reinforces our own sense of the fatalism that must have haunted him not only in his last years during the 1830s, but also for most of the 1820s. The source of his fatalism was, he now believed but did not express openly until two years later, Aunt Mary and her tendency always to overrate "the enjoyments of what [she] supposed [his] situation" was "when [he was] weakest—when [he was] nearest to the border line," or when he was overcome by doubt and despair. Fatalism—"so much of earth in me," as Edward wrote to Mary in 1831—is what prevented him from achieving the "celestial buoyancy" that might have enabled him to look past life's "darker passages," "unfinished feast[s]," and "half cultivated field[s]" and "lift the hand & eye of faith."[90]

↠ *Edward Bliss Emerson to Mary Moody Emerson, 24 January 1829*

Your letter of last Sabbath eveg reached me yesterday & Dr Hurds answer I enclose.[91] My communication was held with him through his daughter, on account of his absence from home. I thank you for your reply to my doubt. And now I will tell you that before & after my liberation from the Asylum I had entertained some scruples about the propriety of continuing my study of the legal profession, not as being a wicked but a worldly pursuit. I mentioned my uncertainty to three individuals, my nearest friends, none of whom advised me directly to renounce the law. My mother seemed to wish that I could be a minister, & yet seemed to think that my course had been shaped so long in another direction as to make the *law* expedient. My Grandfather [Ezra Ripley] withheld his opinion until I mentioned my own determination, or strong inclination. & then concurred with me decidedly. Waldo, whom I had requested to give written counsel, refrained, until a similar determination, in favor of the continued pursuit of the Law, had been mentioned by me as nearly adopted, & then immediately stated his entire approbation & pleasure. All this happened before New Year's day & I left Boston on the last day of December for a visit to Concord, with the intention quite fixed of devoting myself while here diligently, but prudently to the calling of a lawyer, & in the expectation of being admitted to practice as such in the course of the year.—I did in a manner thus lay myself open for a season to those influences which I thought most likely to be controlled by Providence; & those influences have operated favorably towards a conclusion prayerfully formed. Ought I not to adhere to it? If the straight & narrow way leadeth through the court I am content to labor there. If not, I am deplorably in error.—

Dr Channing's sermon will procure soon, if possible; but must probably drag it from Boston.[92] Waldo was here on Wednesday & Thursday with Ellen, who pleased our mother & the "Apostle of half a century;" (as Grandfather has been pertinently called in print). Waldo's invitation to become the colleague of Mr Ware is another occasion of gratitude &

joy.[93]—Shall we not hope for the sight of your long-absent countenance soon? Charles does well. Is it proper for me to advise him against the Law? He would ornament our profession. But it is a pity that his fine mind should be chained to it. If you would rescue him from it, you should begin early, before he is too far engaged in its pursuit.—Mrs Lyman of North-Hampton says in a congratulatory letter to Waldo, that Charles is the finest young man she ever knew.—Christ condemns no profession, but he honored one. Is it not possible to argue like a Christian—to defend like a Christian,—to prosecute like a Christian, to inveigh like a Christian? I hope so.—And yet I say, thrice happy Waldo.—And will the grave make us equal? I mean, in innocence: for I say not glory.—I do not ask that you should 'prophesy smooth things,'[94] but I would not willingly consider myself as having run into a fatal error, although I am aware how open to objection is a motive of expediency;—& I am aware also how presumtuous would seem an expressed hope of achieving an elevation of 'the Bar character' as suggested.—I may be a check upon my brothers, whether clerical or laical. I may be a good lawyer.—I may be a useful man.[95]

With Edward seemingly on the mend, the opening months of 1829 brought the Emerson family temporary reprieve from sufferings it had endured during the previous year. The family's celebratory mood that Edward's breakdown interrupted resumed when Waldo and Ellen were engaged on 17 December 1828 and as Charles, who was immensely well-liked by his classmates, continued to accumulate academic awards and recognition at Harvard. Waiting for just the right ministerial call, Waldo finally received one to serve as the junior pastor of Boston's prestigious Second Church. He was ordained at the Church on 11 March in a ceremony that both Charles and Edward attended and describe in their letters that follow, and in a stroke of good fortune that he never anticipated, Waldo was promoted to pastor of the Church on 1 July. He and Ellen married on 30 September, and for a while he believed that he would now be able to enjoy financial security and a degree of social prominence for the first time in his adult life and share them forever with Ellen. In a rare flight of enthusiasm, Waldo privately described himself as possessing "the luxury of an unmeasured affection for an object so deserving of it all & who requites it all" (*JMN*, 3:149), and he comfortably settled into the dual role of husband and pastor.

It is ironic that, after praying all their lives that one of her nephews would enter the ministry and have a pulpit of his own, Mary missed Waldo's ordination and the first sermons he delivered to his new congregation. Nevertheless, Charles and Edward filled her in on all the significant details of the occasion, and Mary wrote to Waldo to congratulate him and offer one piece of counsel. Writing on the evening of 11 March, his ordination day, Mary said, "It is a finer night than even the day—the moon has not filled her horns—good sign my dear Waldo for your inaguration. . . . [M]ay all happy constellations reign over you long after the heart which has prayed for you today ceases to beat. . . . Long may you influence human weal and ever may retain that gift of instructing without ostentation" (*MMEL*, p. 256). As is evident from his letter to Mary, Charles was bursting with pride at his brother's success, and he applauds with gratitude the celebrants' repeated allusions to his father who died too young and to "kind providence which . . . cared for the orphan, & protected the seed of the righteous." Though more casual in his language than Charles was in his letter, Edward informs his aunt that he, too, was proud of his brother, and though voicing his disappointment at her absence, he assured her that even he found much to prize in Waldo's visible and audible expressions of godliness. "Some whom you have so long regarded familiarly as to have divested perhaps of that peculiar & unquestioned sanctity which seems needful to the perfection of an holy ceremonial," he wrote, "peased with a dignity & an unction that overawed & kindled the observer.—The devotion was humble & faithful. The discourse rational & independent & scruptural. The counsel was grave & tender."

⇥ Charles Chauncy Emerson to Mary Moody Emerson, 14–17 March 1829

Last Wednesday was Ordination Day. I should have been glad to have had you here. There were none of our eminent Unitarian preachers, our great guns, who took part in the services; but they had an interest of their own. The sermon was very good; the Charge was in the style of an apostle, simple parental eloquence. The character of the young minister excited a strong interest, of course, as far as it was known—& the repeated allusions to the early death of his father, & the kind providence which had cared for the orphan, & protected the seed of the righteous, started the tears from their fountains.[96] Tomorrow we hear from him—the pastor—his sermons upon the reciprocal duties of minister & people. I shall attend his meeting regularly & hope in the course of a few months to join the church.

Ellen is pretty well—but she is as fragile as she is beautiful. Pity!—. . .

For me, I am vegetating through the year, snatching an occasional excitement & living rather in hope than in fruition. I have the Stoic consolation, that it is good for the *whole* that I should be ordered for a season upon the forlorn station of society—that I should make the head of the pin, & act as a literary mechanic—so I wont repine. . . .

Yesterday Monday [actually, Sunday] we heard Waldo preach his first sermons to his own people. They were excellently good. He reminds you of Everett—but he is warmer, franker & leaves you with a very different impression—He is not I think liable to the charge of preaching himself, instead of Christ Crucified. His morning's text was 'I am not ashamed of the Gospel of Christ for it is the power of God unto the salvation of every one who believeth.' What Paul said to the great & powerful of this world, he said to the wise of this world—I am not ashamed of the gospel of Christ.[97] 18 centuries he thought had justified the avowal & approved the wisdom of the apostle.[98]

➤ *Edward Bliss Emerson to Mary Moody Emerson, 15 March 1829*

Another interesting exciting occasion has gone by;—but the train of the comet is still to come across the eye tomorrow. Waldo was ordained on Wednesday; the youthful herald was consecrated & charged & welcomed;—tomorrow he unfurls his banner & announces his hopes & purposes.—I have heard the first discourse read & remain in city that I may hear it & the second delivered. I should not have been much surprised if your affection had flowed in so full & strong a tide as to have brought hither the romantic canoe of my Aunt Mary's eremite soul. But it came not, visibly, however it might have dwelt with the presbyters or spectators or kindred or pastor elect as I doubt not it did hover over all or some of these, with good wishes & prayers.

You will probably see the performances printed: your imagination will paint, but hardly can flatter the living scene. Some whom you have so long regarded familiarly as to have divested perhaps of that peculiar & unquestioned sanctity which seems needful to the perfection of an holy ceremonial appeased with a dignity & an unction that overawed & kindled the observer.—The devotion was humble & faithful. The discourse rational & independent & scruptural. The counsel was grave & tender. The allusions to the deceased—to your brother in whose stead, Waldo has risen up & to Mr. Ware to whose aid he had been summoned, by a Providence, careful of the church, were affecting to those who were susceptible of emotion, as relatives or Christians.—

Mother is still in town & desires love, saying that Waldo will probably not have time at present to write; wherefore she is glad to see my poor pen inditing something. You must excuse what I lack in quantity or quality of epistolary stuff.[99] . . .

Over the next year and a half the greatest challenges to the serenity of the Emerson brothers' world came from the health crises of Waldo's young wife Ellen and Edward. Both Ellen and Edward knew that the symptoms of their respective tubercular conditions could recur at any time, and so did—or should have—all those around them. Shortly before Ellen's death, Edward's symptoms recurred after a period of remission that had lasted slightly more than two years. Perhaps because it took so long for the symptoms to recur, the family was stunned by the news. Yet, no one ought to have been. As early as his letter to Mary describing Waldo's ordination in March 1829, at least Charles should have guessed that he was only kidding himself if he really thought that Edward had reformed his work and study habits after his recent collapse and institutionalization. In that letter, Charles remarks to Mary almost as an aside that "Edward has been delivering before the Mechanics' Institute at Concord a Lecture on Asia, which Waldo says is astonishingly good—It is Aeschylus bringing his tragedy to prove himself sound in intellect."[100] This behavior was precisely what had compromised Edward's health before. In addition to lecturing, he resumed his study and practice of the law, and with William's support, he eventually moved to New York in the winter of 1829–1830, harboring the illusion that the weather would be easier and the competition for clients less in New York than at home in New England. In New York, while supposedly regaining his strength and seeking clients, Edward also revised the lecture on Asia that he had delivered in Concord the previous year. He expanded the lecture into three lectures and apparently delivered them in April. The first lecture he titled "Siberia, etc., Georgia," the second "China," and the third "Thibet, Bukharia, Baber."[101] By all appearances, Edward was back to the top of his condition, but, in truth, the pace of his life was destroying him. Within six months, he was sick once again. William wrote home to tell the family, and it fell to Charles, who had just mentioned in a letter to his aunt dated 16 November that he himself "was sick—had a little inflammation of the lungs, but tis well long since,"[102] to deliver the news of Edward's relapse to Mary.

> Our dear Edward is sick again. He has a cold (William writes) which hung about him, like his old colds, & would not give way to their joint doctoring—Last Friday night, I think, he had great pain—spasms in the right side & in the back—Saturday morng they called Dr. Perkins, who stands first in N.Y. & he said he had better go immediately away to the South; that he was so feeble that other remedies could not do with him— He also put a blister on. It so happens that Wm. Haskins & his wife, (Mr. John Haskin's son) were going directly to Magnolia in Florida, where he does business, to spend the winter, & Edw. proposes going in the vessel with them.[103] It was to have sailed today—but of course could not in this storm. Mrs. Haskins is a kind careful woman, & has been much a friend to William & Edward. We are glad therefore that he will not be alone nor unattended—But poor fellow! to be once more unmoored & set adrift—disheartened by repeated failure & his constitution broken by many a severe attack—it is melancholy enough—May God keep & support him!
> We are taken by surprise—we know not what to do or forbear doing.

If I were strong enough to nurse him, I would go with him. I know not but that it is wrong in me not to go. Mother looks sad—& prays that his reason may keep its seat—she wants to see & be with him.

We cannot know certainly how he is. But there is every reason to suppose that he cannot long contend with his debility & the diseases to which he is subject. I think, he will be better when he gets into a warmer climate—but it will only be a temporary benefit—and when he comes back, he may be more ill than before.

Oh if man's life were like a flower of the field—If when the frost of sickness came the frail stock were bowed & broken—the hardest trial would be spared us—the gradual waste of life & hope—the slow series of bitter disappointments—a weary track of pain & languor behind & before us & the struggle to keep up the fainting heart to bear the burden of existence—This is the sting of Death. But blessed be God who giveth us the victory, through Jesus Christ our Lord. If Edward's faith be as I believe it is not to be shaken nor disturbed by any press of calamity—If that enduring calm has been breathed over his spirit, which is the Comforter of which Christ spoke to his disciples—then I leave him to himself, without anxiety—for I leave him to his Father in Heaven. I never could see into Edw's mind as into others' so near to me as he—We never could sympatise fully—But we all know that Religion has but one influence on the mind which receives it rationally & imbibes it fully—& this influence is light & joy.[104]

How members of the family responded to Edward's illness, which at some level all knew would lead to his death, is interesting for showing the nature of the relationships among them. Here we offer three of the many responses circulated within the family: one by Ellen and Waldo, another by Charles, and a final one by Mary. Of the three, Mary's response is important to take note of, for it is uncharacteristically bland, reveals that she is more concerned with her own feelings of impending loss than with Edward's physical or mental state of mind, and provides an unflattering portrait of her using Edward's illness against him as she tries to nudge him back into her dream of his taking a place in a pulpit instead of playing the "truant" from his real calling by pursuing the law.

In a letter to Edward composed by Ellen and Waldo around 24 December 1830, Waldo, unquestionably trying to calm his brother's fears that the recurrence of his disease represented some Calvinistic stroke from God, remarked that he had seen Sampson Reed,[105] who, he wrote, "told me that it was now ten years since he had known the fear of death: His new faith teaches him not to regard it as a *punishment,* he says. I trust in Heavens care of you & that we shall yet pass pleasant days of health together but let us rejoice in the New Testament which makes sickness & distance safe to us." He urged Edward to take Ellen's advice, and he made this telling request: "Pray make *written minutes* of places & prices & persons & climate that may be of use to any of us hereafter" (*L*, 1:315). In her portion of the letter (not printed in *L*), Ellen wrote with a degree of calming concern for Edward that could only have been expressed by a person suffering the same curse as he. Her comments are important not only as a measure of the love and affection she had come to feel toward her brother-in-law, but also for an aside she made in them to Mary's unexpected appearance and then just as unexpected departure from their—Ellen's and Waldo's—home.

> Ere this you are breathing beautiful balm and Old Winter has just in good earnest breathed hard upon us—thermometer at 6, snow, wind, long icicles, blue noses and sad looking invalids—you're a king and may hug yourself for your timely retreat—Pray speak kindly to the Santa Cruzians of all your kith and kin and pick out a pretty spot for Waldo and wife to live—for such golden dreams . . . do I indulge. But some day—tut! Inconveniences will meet you like Bishop Bruno or Natty's rats wherever you go[106]—Cold winds and changes here, scorpions and debilities there—The latter I urge are not so soul annoying as the former—One is a slow, uncertain death and an ill spent life, the other a quick and sure remedy or a certain and an not agreeable but more preferable death—You are perhaps so new and transient in the invalid table that you will never understand me when I speak so. . . .
>
> Aunt Mary has appeared in our home an instant but the whole was like a dream—She seems not of the earthly nor altogether of the heavenly—to be wondered at and in some sort admired.[107]

Charles also wrote a comforting, caring letter to his brother, not knowing for sure, but surely suspecting that soon enough he too would be afflicted with the disease he most dreaded. Like Ellen, he approaches Edward's illness calmly, but after expressing his feelings and hopes to his brother, he shifts to just the sort of vigorous discussion about the rise of nationalism in Europe and the slavery and the Indian questions the two would have enjoyed having in front of the wood stove in either's law office.

⇸ Charles Chauncy Emerson to Edward Bliss Emerson, 4 January [1831]

> I wish you a happy new year. I hope the wish does not grate upon the ear as unlikely to be fulfilled. The past is safe & the future is in God's hands. By this time you are in the balm of other minds & please the eye & mind with new landscapes & strange customs. I will not wish myself by your side, for I have no right to wish myself away from my labors, however insignificant to all the world except myself—but I may & do

wish to hear from you, how the body is invigorated, & the imagination entertained, by all you see & hear. If our wishes had a plastic power over nature, if we could by a divine chemistry detect & fetch to our own use, the subtle elements of organic & inorganic matter which restore & strengthen the principles of life & health in the human constitution, how should the medicating & healing atoms, troop to your aid & hasten your convalescence! Tho' we may not bid Nature to do our will, we are sure she will do God's will—You remember those fine lines of Burns—

> Thou Power supreme, whose mighty scheme,
> These woes of mine fulfil
> Here firm I rest, They must be best
> Because they are thy will.[108]

What exciting news we have from Europe! How that quarter of the globe has always been agitated—scarce a moment of repose in its history.[109] Asia sleeps laggard-like from age to age. Africa moves only at the extremities—But Europe like a body animated by a living soul, has a thousand pulses ever beating, & a tide forever flowing & ebbing from the heart to the members & from the members to the heart. I wish we may not in this country sympathise in the diseased condition of our race across the waters. I hope we do not need mar from without, as the nations have been used to need, in order to draw off the bad blood & humours from within. Our own prospect has never I think been darker, since the adoption of the Constitution. The Indian question, & the Slavery question, & the nullifying doctrine,[110] shed an ominous eclipse or threaten to over all our commercial prosperity, our enterprise & intelligence. We want men. . . . Such men as the Lees, the Hamiltons, the Ameses the Washingtons, those pillars of the State on whom the people can safely lay the burden of awful responsibility, to see that the Republic take no harm.[111] But enough of Politics. . . . Aunt Mary is spending the winter at Concord. She is as ever, all alive to the moral world, & scarce alive to any other—She still prays to die—but has lost the hope of dying speedily. I passed a week at Concord with her—we read & talked in your ancient oratory & chapel. They have a most faithful & affectionate remembrance of you in C. Many a kind inquiry was asked & many a good wish expressed about you.[112]

Finally, in late December 1830, Mary, who as Charles says is still "all alive to the moral world, & scarce alive to any other," addressed herself to Edward's plight. Invoking her faith, she tried to bolster Edward's, console him with the positive aspects of his terrible situation, and urge him back to the fold in this letter.

As we still sojourn on the same changing blowing trying planet, it is soothing to meet if only to say how changeable the winds—how bleak the clouds—how weary the sense of mortality! How delightfull to meet (tho' on this pale paper) & say how grand is existence—how inexpressibly rich to exist *in God*—to be surrounded with eternity! To be in that state of health w' places one on the verge of a holier state is far richer. Then the child holds out it's hands & raises it's eyes as tho' its real Parent were present and about to raise it to the embraces of pure reason—active intelligence and real virtue—by w'h we mean wisdom & love. But the *name* of *virtue* answers to our poor ideas of wisdom & benevolence—when we come to see them as they exist in the divine Mind we may be ashamed of our poor copies. Yet there is One who has suffered for us—whose sympathies will extend long long beyond this embryo state—even perhaps—not wholly improbable, after his offices shall close—when God becomes all in all—when we are thro' his ministry restored to absolute communion with the Infinite—even then his intercourse may continue and tho' we shall no longer be ashamed of our poor efforts in the body, we shall love the being who has exalted us to go on—forward & forever with those who have never tasted the bitter woe of sin.

Adieu, dear Edward, I am hasting to solitude—Daily have my prayers accompanied your voyage—I pass the pain I suffered in your illness—and the useless regrets of your removal.

All transient ills are lots in the ocean of events to which we run.

Farewell till better health restore you—if you wandered in your affection from the school of Christ in pursuing earthly subsistence you must play the truant no more.[113]

Writing from St. Croix on 11 March 1831, Edward responded to Mary's remarkable letter. Although he opened by apologizing for having deferred for three months answering her letter because "its nature & topic were such as while they interest & elevate remain also unchanged," his real reason had to have been a conscious act of resistance to the "nature" not of his illness, but to the "nature" of Mary's attempt at a consoling message. No matter how well-intentioned her motives, as opposed to his acceptance of Ellen and Waldo's and then of Charles's expressions of concern and such hope as they could muster, Mary's response to Edward's illness fell wide of what he needed now, and so he had to reject it. If, by urging him back to those "affections from the school of Christ" from which he was truant because he was more interested "in pursuing earthly subsistence" she was really urging him away from the law and back to the religion of his fathers and their pulpits that he had forsaken, her timing could not have been worse. Unquestionably, the conciliatory tone Edward assumes throughout his letter to

her is, as his closing acknowledges, an expression of the respect in which he
held her as a person; however, as the "Bliss Boy" upon whom she had invested so
much hope, Edward, in this cold letter that lacks any display of affection and in
which he signs himself "E. B. Emerson," now all but explicitly rejects Mary and
her ideals as witnessed by the fact that, though he lived for three more years, this
was virtually the last letter he wrote to her.

My dear Aunt,

You will excuse my deferring to answer your kind letter, long ago received, when you consider that its nature & topic were such as while they
interest & elevate remain also unchanged & a reply need not be hurried
"by return mail" as the phrase is. Sentiment—that word which brings up
your image & at which your nephews ignorantly smiled—sentiment is
eternal.—Yes, it is 'delightful' to meet, as you say, on our pilgrimage,—to
speak or hail one another on this great sea & learn the destination of
our several barks & strive to correct now & then a false reckoning of the
moral lattitude & longitude. But you overrated (or perhaps for my advantage preferred to appear so to do) the enjoyments of what you supposed
my situation—I found when weakest—when nearest to the border line—
so much of earth in me & so little of celestial buoyancy that I looked on
this life—acquainted as I am with some of its darker passages—as on
an unfinished feast & a half cultivated field to which I was willing if not
anxious to return. Had I been more what I ought to be, I might perhaps
have been able to lift the hand & eye of faith in the way you intimate. As
it is, I linger content to exist—hoping a little from each tomorrow, pleasing myself with the thought that possibly some corner in this busy system
& noisy world of ours may afford a shelter fit for the tiny improvements
and exercises of an invalid, if I remain one, or the moderate pursuit of a
honest profession if I can engage therein; so that my reprieve may not be
a calamity to my friends or myself.—Your religious views appear to me to
have that feature which has often seemed to me to be the only very desirable & almost unaccountable one in the Calvinistic christians—I mean
a hope that has become an assurance, that has lost all of the dubious &
only stands waiting for the opening of something bright & joyous.—I
wish too that I could attain views of the ministry of Jesus Christ that
should be to me as yours at once consistent & permanently consolatory
& animating.—I thank you again for your letter & wishing you every
good am respectfully & affec^y your nephew

E. B. Emerson.[114]

After a lapse of more than two years, Mary wrote again to Edward on 10
November 1833. In the letter that follows she made every attempt to be con-

ciliatory, but her images, unquestionably drawn from Calvinistic reflection on what she had learned in her own long-imposed solitude in Maine, only drew Edward's attention to her conviction that his illness was a form of divine punishment from which, she believed, he would be restored, if not in this world, then in the next. In the body of this letter, Mary provided Edward with a plan to restore his mind and body by returning to his religious studies. This, she argued, would fortify him for the holy war that she awaited in which the godly will overcome "all hydra headed infidelity."

I want to hear from your own pen of your health—your occupations of mind & heart. You are, like me, alone. Do you have any of the advantages of solitude? Can you sit on the mount of transfiguration, w'h faith casts up, and hear the stirrings & see the whirlings of the puppet show world with tender pity—with wholesome sympathy? And while you look at the pageantry does your eye mount the eagle wing w'h shows you the real & unfading world? The hope that your temporary seclusion from scenes in w'h you had shone with distinguished light—scenes w'h you gave promise to administer to with no common effort & effect will correct your youthfull impetuosity—will discipline you far better than an uninterrupted course of health & prosperity. You will return to society & labour with a soul grown. . . . Read the bible more than ever my dear xian fellow traveller. And tho' it sometimes sojourns in a cloudy pillar—it gives sufficient light to make your path straight to the perfect day. There are true metaphysicks for your intellectual taste—the glorious secret of which lies in finding God in all things—. . . And this ground fact—w'h makes us what we are—agents—free to all purposes of virtue & vice is there found in every history private or publick—in every judgment & mercy dealt immediately or thro' human hands. Yes, dear Edward, read by the light of day & by the stars and by the storm & by the shine and you will find the ultimate *good*. A hallowed sentiment of the Invisible Leader as distinct from the pantheism of the false philosopher as Heaven from earth. . . . That capacity to go on & endure defeat in happiness & perfection & yet go on with hope however chastised. It is the immortal God within. And xtianity reveals the secret. . . . Ah, dear Edward, time is bringing on . . . the fullness of this revelation. All sects—all errors hydra headed infidelity is but hastening the vindication of Providence and the manifestation too of the Messiah. There may be many a severe & bloody contest before. . . . May you be preparing to take part beneathe his banners—to act[n] manfully & soberly the deciple of the cross. (*MMEL*, pp. 347–348)

After a delay of five months, Edward responded to Mary from Puerto Rico by sending her the following letter through William. Even though they often

disagreed—and Mary's last letter had to have struck Edward as disagreeable—
Mary and Edward had known each other for so long and so well that this letter
had to appear to both its author and its recipient for what it was—a farewell.
Whatever resistance Edward felt toward Mary and her lessons he had obviously
let go of by the time he wrote, so that perhaps as the surest sign that she had
raised him well, in Edward's gentle prose and kind remembrances of the times
he had spent with her in Maine, Mary may have recognized her sweet "Bliss
Boy" of old. For his part, William, as he wryly remarks in his postscript (written in New York), recognized that he was serving his brother and his aunt as a
convenient final intermediary; this was a role, he said, that he was glad to play
because he had been accustomed to it for some thirty years.

So you have not yet tired of the solitude of the Vale; nor do I wonder
at it: but you must not think that all solitude is alike sweet & holy. You
may fill your cup with water and I too, but your's is from the mountain
side, and mine is from the city well. Still I am not about denying that
even the degree & sort of seclusion that falls to my lot is valuable & at
times very pleasant. The old saw about seeing a shipwreck from a safe
stand on shore is quite descriptive of the moderated & tranquil (not to
say poetic and romantic) interest with which from this little Island one
contemplates the distant and diminutive nations of either hemisphere.
The sort of government used here exempts the private man from the
trouble of taking any pains about the management of public affairs; he
has only to let the state alone & mind his own business. I mean that no
man here will be drawn away from the studies or the contemplations he
m   love, by any patriotic notion of being compelled to raise his voice or
write his volume about this measure or the other. . . . Even the apathy &
the no less remarkable ignorance of the people aid in rendering the solitude of an educated man more complete. He will not be diverted from
his chosen paths of speculation or inquiry, by any calls upon his time
for literary contributions, labors in this cause & labors in that; hardly
will he be tasked by one inquirer in a twelvemonth to exhibit any of the
stores of information he may have accumulated; and the childish frivol-
ity of the amusements of the place will disgust rather than tempt our
s   recluse. Thus I have often thought that a Dramatist or Novelist
would find here a charming retreat in which to mature the productions
of another 'great unknown.' Sure I am that Scott could not have lived
here 6 months without writing some tale,[115] in which Spanish courtesy
& frankness & selfrespect, blended with Creole indolence and passion
for amusements would be spread out to the eyes of the world in a splendid picture enriched with his favorite decoration I mean descriptions
of fine scenery, droll costumes village merrymakings, and perhaps he

w   have found some among our negroes not unfit to do kitchen work in a novel. Nor less favorable would be the retirement for a religious or moral philosopher if it were not too much for his patience, too much for h   tranquillity to bear the sight of so general laxity and too much for his skill and power to remedy. Happy if he do not find his own stakes loosened, his own anchor dragging: too happy if he should succeed in dropping here & there a virtuous grain in soil that will receive it, or securing one wavered, by the argument of a bright and pure example. After all it will be still true that the highest heavens of contemplation or as you say 'the mount of transfiguration' will be more acceptable from the side of Elm Vale, than from any city; and the Sabbath must be more sublimely holy when the six days have a sober coloring, than when it comes a day of rest to wearisome calculations and plodding industry, and even itself not perfectly secured from what men deem necessary interruptions.

You ask about my health; it is tolerably good. I was so sick in December & Jany as to be in bed many days, and confined to the house 3 weeks, was thought to be in danger, but did not myself despair of recovering nor feel quite resigned to die; not so much from a fear of the future, as from a wish to save mother from unnecessary affliction and a hope that I might yet see some good days and good friends in the land of the living. All this I suppose is natural. Since that attack I have been as well as before.—. . . Please give my love to all our kin about you. I may never realize but still keep the hope to see the 'Vale' and the mountains of Waterford and all that is blooming in nature & society thereabouts. Still remember & pray for one who loves his friends, though [is] sadly unable to serve them. . . .

Dear Aunt,

I have this moment rec'd this letter from Edwd with permission to read before forwarding & I am glad to send you something so refreshing even tho' it cast mine into the shade. You know that I have been used to that for some 30 years, yet am I

Yr aff. nephew Wm E.[116]

This was the last letter Mary received from Edward, and she endorsed it, "E B E / 34 / Last dear letter."

AUNT MARY AND CHARLES

It is unclear exactly how much of Charles's side of his correspondence with Mary Waldo had access to in 1836, 1837, and 1841 as he considered whether to prepare a memoir of his brother. If he had before him the substantial body of letters from Charles to Mary that we have now, he would have known the depths of depression, self-doubt, world-weariness, and despair to which Charles routinely descended but during his life confessed only to his aunt. If he did not have all of Charles's letters to Mary in front of him at this time but, rather, had access to them only after 1861, when she transferred ownership of her papers to Waldo's daughter Ellen, then twice he had to suffer the shock of discovering the enormity of the spiritual darkness in which his brother had languished more than lived. Either way, the first shock of recognition that Waldo experienced and shared with William back in the 1830s was considerable enough; for his own sake, he did not need to know—at the level of detail we do—the anxiety Charles must have faced enduring and suppressing such an inner life, nor, in light of his remark to Carlyle about Charles and him together making one man, did Waldo need to be reminded of their Aunt Mary's complicity in shaping his own life along with that of a brother whom he loved so dearly and mistakenly thought he knew so well.

Although the body of William's personal writings with which we are concerned is substantial, its substance is a function of an epistolary relationship that William and Waldo enjoyed over a period of fifty years. In contrast to the self-revelatory content of Charles's and to a lesser extent of Edward's personal writings, the correspondence he exchanged with William generally concentrated on the practical, which, on the whole, was the defining characteristic of their relationship. Because Waldo's relationship with Edward and Charles was of shorter duration than his relationship with William, and because of the two brothers Charles more than Edward used the process of writing as a principal means of exploring and expressing himself, Waldo's experience of discovering the "real" Charles in his personal writings after his death had to have been incredibly intense. And as intense and, ultimately, disturbing as his discovery of the "real" Charles had to have been for him, Waldo's eventual discovery of Mary's role in molding and reinforcing the darkest characteristics of his brother's hidden character had to be one of the most difficult familial realities with which he had to contend during his life. In his discovery of the "real" Charles, Waldo had revealed for himself all of what it finally meant to be one of the Emerson brothers growing up in a circle of which "M. M. E." served as the center.

In all likelihood, the personal writings by Charles that most unnerved Waldo were not his brother's letters to their aunt, but the entries in Charles's secret spiritual diary that he kept during the last five years of his life. It was in these entries, as Waldo commented in his own journal, that he discovered his brother's "nocturnal side which his diurnal aspects never suggested,—[for] they [were] melancholy, penitential, self accusing; . . . the creepings of an eclipsing temperament over his abiding light of character" (*JMN,* 5:152). But, as Waldo would learn over time, the content of Charles's secret diary and the content of the correspondence he exchanged with Mary were virtually indistinguishable from each other. In fact, more often than not, Charles's diary represented a self-scrutinizing confessional compression of what he had already revealed in his confessional epistles to his aunt.

Nor are we using the word "confession" casually. In the following two letters from Charles to Mary, some form of the word "confession" is explicitly used by both parties to define the discourse these letters and other like them written to Mary represent. Personally lacking the faith that sustained men in the "safer, godlier times . . . of our fathers," in these letter Charles turned to Mary, hoping against hope that by baring his soul to her he might receive a share of her faith and security in return. In the first letter, written in May 1831 (following Ellen's death in February and the beginning of Edward's permanent exile to St. Croix and Puerto Rico), Charles wrote to Mary, "You must be heartily weary of sitting in the confessions chair & listening to so common a story—but you ask to see the inside of my mind, & now you know why I am so loth to show it," and as its recipient sitting in the confessor's chair, Mary endorsed the letter, "Confession C C C '31." In the second letter, written some ten months before his death, Charles, who should have been trying to rein in the overwhelming joy he felt at being in love with, and being loved in return by, Elizabeth Sherman Hoar, at being the darling of his aunt, and at having his brother Waldo as his closest friend, instead feels estranged, lonely, and afraid of life. Writing out of his own painful "crucifixion of self," as he calls it, Charles apologizes to Mary for sending her yet another confessional lamentation. "Forgive me," he writes at the letter's end, "if selfish even in my contrition I seek to add to your burdens that of my miserable confessions."

⤞ Charles Chauncy Emerson to Mary Moody Emerson, 7 May 1831

Yes there is a satirical chamber in my poor brain—or rather that is one of the diseases of my understanding & one which I sometimes am afraid sends up an earthly mist to overcloud the reason. But I am sick to death of talking & thinking of myself. Strange—that all derivative as we are—doubting often the reality of our little peculium of free will—always confessing our low place in the rank of being, we should yet be bound by so strict a necessity to the dismal ever returning contemplation of ourselves—No getting out of the prison house of this individual consciousness, & losing *self* in higher & purer ranges of thought. I believe I do comprehend part of what Fenelon means & what [the Reverend] Channing quibbles about, the crucifixion of self.[117] . . . This wall of individual meanness & sin, must be broken down—this tie which fastens the soul to private ends, clogs it with particular prejudices, pulls it back from mounting upward by the force of appetites & passions which are born & bred in self, & have no existence in the Universal mind, this tie must be severed, before we can be one with Christ & through him one with his Father & our Father. To say that self is not to be crucified, but what is bad in self, what is it but quibbling? The good is not our own so much as it is God's—We mingle with His laws, & are sublimely lost in this agency when we do right. Virtue is an emanation of Divinity. When wrong, depraved, evil, we are separate from God, & it is this evil in us which is self.

This may be poor reasoning—but it has a truth to me. I open my eyes every morning on the spotted creature, part good, part bad which has been before me & which has been *me* for days & months & years. I pray that the new day may pass holy & undefiled by any vice of mine, into the Eternity of the past. The sun goes up in the Heavens & I go out among my fellow-beings & act out the hundredth time the unwritten drama within my breast, & retire at night again to look back on another page of life, of even tenor with all the rest, disfigured with much that is vile, & renewing at its close the unceasing petition for pardon & redemption.

Perhaps you think today has been one of sober reading & thinking. No. Today has been idled in search of physical recreation, & many a pulse of vanity has throbbed in rebellion against philosophy & religion. I seem as I told you t'other evening, to live only to develope a predetermined character. . . .

If I lived in safer, godlier times, like those of our fathers, perhaps I should be better—You must be heartily weary of sitting in the confessions chair & listening to so common a story—but you ask to see the inside of my mind, & now you know why I am so loth to show it[118]—

↠ *Charles Chauncy Emerson to Mary Moody Emerson, 3 July* [1835]

When I said to myself what should I write for, who have so little to say that can either kindle the light of thought, or distil the oil of gladness, Nature answered in me, yet write: "reason not the need,"[119] write, if it be only to divide the blank space between friends with the winged & living message of affection & remembrance. Write too, that in quiet unobstructed page,—over which, the cloud & gust that mar speech, do not come,—you may set down sincere words, & then be sorry in thinking how unlike your better self you often suffer yourself to seem & to be.

What a fragmentary world it is; you & I & each woman & each man, have in us parcels of virtues, but gulfs of Deficiency & Will if there be not mountains of offence. It is not the bird only that lends its own feather to the arrow that drinks its life blood. Which of us that suffers but feels indignantly that his own hand struck the blow, or smeared the weapon with poison?

Yet one would suffer cheerfully & I would almost sin cheerfully, saw I but this, that it was the last time—that the lesson was once for all learned, & this head of the Snake lopped off & the pernicious blood staunched. But we live in a circle, & repeat ourselves perpetually, & because I have done wrong it seems as if it was written that I should do the same wrong hereafter.

Once I believed a better creed. I thought a man was capable of improving. And he is, but how little: it comes to scarcely more than to recognise his weakness & distrust himself, & lay his mouth in the dust, & utter the melancholy 'Unclean,' which is the knell to so many resolutions & hopes.

Forgive me if selfish even in my contrition I seek to add to your burdens that of my miserable confessions. God knows I would gladly, so I were worthy, suffer for you & work out your tax to Evil. Is it not worst of all that a mind studious to learn, & receive truth, should be in the habit of seeing with perverted eye, the coils of a malign fortune in those leading strings of a Good Providence which gird us round. What shall enlighten him whose very eye is darkened?

Tomorrow is the Fourth of July. It is well with the brave dead. What anniversary of noble import shall this generation bequeath to the Future? Does it indeed become those to aspire to public action, whose private is so lean & corrupt?[120]

The shocking, even terrifying, truth Waldo discovered in letters such as these about the hellish abyss into which Charles had descended pales in comparison to the depth of despair and self-loathing he found revealed in his brother's diary. What is most terrifying about Charles's personal revelations in his diary is that here he was writing to, speaking about, and disclosing himself only to himself. Waldo could reason that at least in his letters to Mary, Charles was unburdening himself to a correspondent-confessor who might provide him with absolution for the sin and corruption—real or imagined—to which he routinely confessed. In the exchange of letters, as Charles himself wrote, friends and confidants were able to traverse "the blank space" that separated them and be comforted with giving and receiving "the winged & living message of affection & remembrance." But in his diary, in which he wrote only to and for himself, Charles had no one to whom to send his confessional message but himself, so rather than feeling liberated from the spiritual darkness, and rather than feeling absolved by a force outside of and greater than himself, Charles became the dark, pathetic, self-mocking figure he feared he could become. "I cannot I cannot be at peace," he wrote at one point in the diary excerpts that follow, adding "[t]hat which is within me is too too strong for me." He wonders, "Am I to blame?" "Do other men so wrap inwardly against their own selves?" "Are they like me forced to strangle in the womb of Thought creatures quick with life & keenest sense?" If, as he fears, the answer to questions such as these is affirmative, then, he says, "Ah . . . I pity them. God pity me!"

↠ *Charles Chauncy Emerson, "Diary," 1831–1836 & [n.d.]*

May 19. [1831?][121]

When we look at the world from Self as the centre, nothing can be more perplexed. We are unsafe, standing on our private plot while so many causes are actively at work that may blast & ravage it. 'The race never dying, the individual never spared';[122] this is the chime of all the bells of all human accidents. So long as my own Will is my god, I have a fight to maintain with Fortune. Millions of wills are energetically counteracting mine. All are over-ruled by the Divine Will. I must therefore meet constant rebuffs. And when I study to comprehend the principles of things, & be reconciled by some means to the course which life takes, still if it is only with the design of a partial accomodation of self will to necessity, a topping off a few extravagant branches, while the root is retained & nursed—a cission[123] of a part that is inconsistent with the enjoyment of what is kept;—I do but little mend the matter. It is conflict all. Day by day will see my favorite desires thwarted, my relics of selfish happiness filched. I have got no farther than a Ptolemaic system of the Universe;[124] & the motions are eccentric . . . & these in the end unintelligible & confounding.

With renouncing selfwill & adopting God's will begins true peace of mind. True philosophy is to turn the imperious part of us against ourselves, & the acquiescent part towards God. Commonly men resign themselves to themselves, & their contending is with God & His order of events.

While men are to us merely men—antagonists or rivals or impertinent or offensive persons, there is no way to keep the peace with them. We may devise ever so cunningly to make them our tools,—they will fly out of our hands & wound us. We may brace ourselves with a philosophic indifference or contempt for them, but they will melt us by kindness, or sting us through all our coverings. But accept them as God's creatures, bound in one common relation with ourselves to Him the Cause & Parent of us all, & the crooked paths of our social metaphysics are made plain. . . .

But our compliance, our humility, our long suffering, must be in this spirit, unto God, & not unto men, if we would be pure from all unworthy submission. We have no right to bow to men as men, any farther than as we see them 'greater because more just' than we.

And charity, & graceful behaviour, & talents, whereby we serve, & attach men to us, will beget vanity if these too be not exercised as unto God & not unto men. . . .

Sunday Evening May 24. [1835][125]

The Idea of God—Have I lost it, when I cannot set it out with mites & bounds?[126] I believe in God as Personal, Parental. But it is necessary that my Idea of God should change with the changes in my moral & intellectual character. Hence I ought not to be alarmed because I cannot pray to the God to whom I once prayed—nor because I shall not always pray to the Same God as now. Yet I think it is this very progressive nature of the Idea in our minds, that frequently alarms us with the fear that we are losing our faith in God's being & relation to us. As I know more of myself & other men & the order according to which things exist, I learn so much more of God, & rectify my insect apprehension of his nature & will. At first He is put farther off from me, & I seem to be forsaken. I am as the child who is grown large enough to be sent away from his father's house; he is homesick, & wails like an orphan—but presently can extend his filial thoughts to his distant parents, & feel assured of their love & protection although he sees not their face. So by & by the enlarged understanding, the maturer reason will recognize God equally near as a little while ago he was to our childhood.

. . . Christ's love was patient love. He was the Son of God. The cup that the Father gave, should he not drink it? The sparrow is remembered before the Divine Mind[127]—we are not alone, we are not neglected—My Saviour,—My Maker,—draw us unto Thyself. Satisfy us from Thyself. Smite thou the rocky heart that the living water may spring, & we never thirst more, nor go any more to broken cisterns, & wells of which when we have drunk, straitway we again thirst.

July 31

But this afternoon I have been aired—Above me was the blue firmament & beneath my feet mother earth in her weeds of green—& although the lazy birds had all gone to bed, the wind made music in the leafy trees. Why do I live in the City? Why have I not the taste & courage to seek some modest fortune in the innocent country.

The countryman said Cato has the fewest evil thoughts.[128] This is scant eulogy. The thoughts of the countryman, like those of children, have much Divinity in them. He lives in God's house; furnished & decorated by the Author of Art & Beauty.

> "My garden is the immeasurable earth
> The Heaven's blue pillars are Medea's home."[129]

His thoughts take hue & moulding from the great frame of Nature. The inhabitant of cities sees little else about him than the work of man like himself—The artificial is everywhere suggested, taught & learned. . . . The erect mountains, the solitary woods, are images of self dependence & liberty. . . .

Sunday Evening Aug 22.[130]

Almost autumn the sunsets say & goldenly publish along half the horizon. And I am glad—If oaks have spiritual creatures whose being is linked with the life of the tree, I do not know but there is a like sympathy between my nature & the seasons: in Spring there leaps up a fount of love & hope & animal exhiliration—in Summer I suffer a Hindoo repose—in Autumn a proud clear spirit is mine—which if it partake of a Stoical Scorn is perhaps armed the stronger to endure the labors & pain of living. . . .

Respect the old—Honor the King—speak not evil of dignities; these are canons of old morality & they approve themselves to a sober taste. Yet I break these commandments & erect the standard of mine individual will in opposition. Father & Mother & kindred & acquaintance are ties that hang loosely on me & not infrequently are slipped—. . .

Nov. 29th 1835

. . . I am never at rest in the speculations of the philosophical—I seldom find God in them; they seem to me like card-houses, built with a world of pains, & demolished, (i.e. potentially) by a breath. I am thinking of speculations that propose to answer the questions, "How comes the Spirit to have a body," "how happens it that a man dies," "what condition will the spirit find itself in immediately after death," & others like to these. So long as philosophy applies itself to interpret human history, & human biography,—so long as it contents itself with circumscribing (I use the term in its mathematical sense) human nature, that is, exclusively determining all the parts of humanity; & then taking its station within this boundary line discriminated between part & part, ascertains their relations, suggests their final cause, & furthermore & chiefest returns from this deep study, this descent into Hades, with lights & revelations which Instruct the Spirit how to live in harmony with the laws of its own being—so long I respect philosophy, because I need it. I cannot fight against Evil without this ally; it is my Harmony, my herb of grace—it is part of my religion, its buttress, its line of defence. . . . Do not tell me I am God, or that God is in me & I know it not—that when I seek often Him I shall not find Him save in that Reason whereof I partake, & which itself hastes to worship the *unknown* God, attesting the existence & Personality of its Author. This can I not receive and be happy. . . .

It is night—a sighing fitful wind moans about my chamber. The lights one by one in the houses near me are put out. It comes strongly across the mind, the idea that when the human race sinks asleep, other beings people the untenanted fields, & other scenes of wild & chequered action are presented to the silent Night. But the gentle Night is no tell tale—& whatever be the character of these that play this noiseless interlude to our loud & busy days,—or doomed Spirits dedicate the hours to penance & hover about the place of their sin,—not a trace of these visitants does morning find, tho' she steal ever so softly over the Eastern hills. . . . I cannot understand how those who have the same experience & intellectual culture that I have had, can take the world so imperturbably—never speculate, never exult, never tremble. Their minds, I always say to myself, must be differently constituted from mine—perhaps it is a better constitution—they certainly seem to enjoy more, for they are not pestered with this sentiment of insecurity which with me is inseparable from every action & event. . . .

. . . If we are not immortals, all of life is wasted; & if we are, how much of it! We should think it a queer preparation for college, if a young man should be put apprentice to a bricklayer or a baker. Yet to our understanding, does this world seem any fitter school for candidates for the kingdom of heaven? Here we are with powerful appetites, smelling rank of the flesh, that will & must be gratified; the whole ostensible business of far the larger portion of mankind, is to minister to this gratification; & if intellectual & moral principles happen to be developed meanwhile, it seems to be a matter by the way, aside from the main design. You may say it is mens' own doing—we might live on fruits, drink the crystal well, & pray & think all the time; But it is not so; & the luxurious state, we long ago agreed, is the state of Nature. . . .

Oh God, Bless thy child. Help me to read aright the book which is fairly opened before me in the morning of my being, in the various drama of this busy world. I look within, but not there do I find the Peace—the serene rejoicing temper of soul, which belongs to the Spirits of the Just. I would live on a fair hill-top, with cloudless skies, & boundless prospect,—& lo I dwell in a hollow, where rush together gusts from the four quarters of an uncertain heaven, where I see but a little ways, & now faint with heat, & now smart with the contrary vicissitude of cold I speak. . . .

Monday Night Nov. 9. [1835][131]

Life wears away. Day follows day, night night. A few more mornings & evenings & it will little matter to us which carries the election, Whig or Tory—Blessed emancipation from flesh, & all the ills that flesh is heir to—may I desire it unblamed? It shall be nothing then to me that the cold rains of November drench the bare fields, or numb winter sits on the hills whence he has chased far away the beautiful leafy Summer.—What care I? The lover shall still, as now, feed on his rich expectancy—the poet mould & carve his immaterial sculpture—the fool & the wise man play at cross purposes & the world altogether repeat & perpetuate itself, but I, the some time tenant of this wooden house, I shall not be touched with its changes nor deceived by its show. . . .

Saturday Feby. 13. 1836.

I am reading Plato's dialogue, 'the Phaedo.' The charm of the thing is not a little owing to the style, so seeming artless yet so beautiful. It is like hearing talk twixt those 'rare creatures that in the elements live, & play in the plighted clouds.'[132] The philosophical speculations are patient & sustained & infinitely easy & good humored. We who read breathe a high & pure air, but not thin or medicated. The Friendliness of God Socrates is confident of. Did he ever doubt & despair of himself? Did he ever sink down under the repeated buffets of a Force of Evil to overcome which his own force was ineffectual? Had he passed through the Valley of the Shadow of Death?[133] Love & faith & heaven are with him as flowing & unconstrained as the verses of Homer. Yet we cannot doubt that Socrates had known sin & pain & shame & fear. He had come out of the cold before we are introduced to him. Virtue & age had laid his passions, & refined his mind. The truth had made him free.[134] It is seldom that an Idea is lived faithfully out in a single life. Either the man turns traitor to his principles, or death cuts the experiment short, or accidents confuse & overlay the issue. Socrates was permitted to begin, continue, & finish his work; & now the tools wherewith he wrought are buried or lost, the chips blown away, & the colossal image alone remains, 'in every part beautiful.' . . .

March 5. 1836

Now cracks the ice in many a broad bay where the green sea was snared & held fast; now melt & disappear the snows, silently wasting, quite crest-fallen from hill & field, from travelled way & from the untrod forest-glade; now darts the sap in its warm canals, now shoots fibrous root, & green germ, now, moves again the orderly Procession of the Plants, each knowing his place, & making ready against his time, flower-cup & fruit. . . .

March 9.

. . . In Oriental philosophy, the globe is not sustained on the great shoulders of a struggling Atlas,[135] nor do Dawn or Day last up the steep heaven their laboring steeds. All is repose. The earth is poised on the back of a tortoise, & the tortoise again stands still & firm on some other monstrous living pedestal.—

June 10. [1835] Wednesday Night.[136]

Oh my God, author of every pang that shoots through the heart, bend my will to Thine—make thyself known as Healer, Comforter! I cannot I cannot be at peace. That which is within me is too too strong for me. Am I to blame? There is a deep of passion underneath the ceremonial life, & the orderly play of the understanding, & God save my *reason* when that deep is upheaved by the storm. Do other men so wrap inwardly against their own selves?

Are they like me forced to strangle in the womb of Thought creatures quick with life & keenest sense? Ah then I pity them. God pity me! . . .

. . . The moon shines tranquilly down on the still waters. Plant & animal are sleeping while the curtain of darkness is drawn around them—all is calm, but thou my soul art not calm. Within thee is tumult & strife. Thou throbbing breast, thou throbbing breast, canst thou not seek out God & find peace & love with Him? Tho' in the multitudes of men thou canst find no sympathy—tho' thou hearest voices, & seest visions, which they neither hear nor see, tho morning & evening come & go & no friend saluted thee, & thy prayers ascend alone to thy Father—yet He will fill & satisfy thee with himself—In his air & light & vernal influence thou shalt recognise His presence & blessing—The trees & the high hills & the waters shall talk to thee of Him. Oh repose thyself in this boundless goodness—thou art a finite mind embosomed in an infinite mind—go out then of thy separate & disturbed self & enter into more intimate union with the eternal source of being & happiness.

One of strong affections & sensitive temperament languishes without sympathy—He can no more be deni[e]d this communication of himself to other minds, than the teeming Earth can suspend its evaporation. There are men who cannot be satisfied with the ordinary interchange of courtesy & expression of opinion. They are conscious of having thoughts & feelings which wait day after day for utterance, & which cannot be thrown on the hard ground of common conversation. . . .

It is just as necessary to each an one to impart this finer portion of himself to a kindred intelligence, as for the man of common constitution to have his associate. Every body naturally insists on being comprehended, there is no greater pain than that of being misunderstood. But the fine mind amid gross minds, dwells in a cloud of mis-construction & concealment. There is no good sentiment that was ever in the breast of man, which did not naturally seek an expression of itself to the mind that will understand it.[137] . . .

Because the Emerson brothers began their lives as individuals of great promise and in whom the hopes and dreams that motivated two centuries' worth of
Emerson, Bliss, and Moody family labor in the New World had been invested,
it is reasonable to ask, "How did Charles, who after Waldo has often been credited as the other great Emerson intellectual, evolve to this point?" "How," to
put it another way, "were the hopes and dreams of three of America's most élite
ecclesiastic and intellectual families so frustrated and so displaced?"

It is unlikely that everyone reading the family archive that we have assembled would arrive at the same answer; however, no matter how one were to
answer these questions, he or she would have to agree that of all the Emerson
brothers, in his youth and early adulthood Charles's privileged life eclipsed
the lives of his brothers. A unique aspect of the privileged life Charles enjoyed
was learning about his past and imagining his future under the tutelage of
Aunt Mary Moody Emerson. Living with Mary in 1813 and 1814 in Waterford,
Maine, the site of the farm she called "Elm Vale," Charles received first hand in
conversation with his aunt, in walks with her through Maine's rural landscape
during which he encountered nature first through her eyes and then through
his own, and in readings and studies that he pursued under her direct super-
vision the lessons that Mary delivered mostly in epistolary prose to nephews
William, Waldo, and Edward. The difference is significant; indeed, as virtually all biographers of Waldo Emerson have remarked, the bond they believe
existed between Waldo and Charles had its closest parallel in the bond that
existed between Charles and Mary. The character of that bond is evident from
the ease and sense of trust with which they express themselves in the correspondence they exchanged, in the freedom with which Charles felt he could
open himself—expose his own hopes, dreams, fears, and frustrations—fully
to his aunt's scrutiny and counsel and with which she felt she could respond by
speaking her mind and even by exposing herself and her own vulnerability to
her nephew, and, finally, by the degree of closeness, of familiarity, with which
they addressed each other in their letters. In other times, and in other places,
they may have referred to themselves as soul-mates; no matter that they did not
use that exact expression in their correspondence, because they did use about
every imaginable approximation of the expression.

It has been more than once remarked by Emersonians that a splendid scholarly project would be a complete edition of the Waldo and Mary correspondence; the same is certainly true for the correspondence exchanged between
Charles and Mary. It is a unique correspondence—unique even in comparison
to that between Waldo and Mary—for the way it unselfconsciously incorporates
and then reflects upon elements of genealogy, family life and gossip, observation on national and international affairs, intellectual and theological speculation of the highest order, and personal responses to a body of readings across
all the disciplines as they were arranged in the early nineteenth century. Mary
and Charles not only quote the classical writers, Shakespeare, Milton, Pope,

Bacon, Montaigne, Wordsworth, Coleridge, Byron, and Swedenborg—indeed, the whole company of writers and thinkers associated with the rise of Romanticism and Transcendentalism in America—but they also express themselves to each other with a facility that, at times, equals theirs.

A difference between the Charles and Mary correspondence and that exchanged between Mary and her other nephews or correspondents is the extent to which the writers remove all barriers to candid, to even emotional, exposure of themselves, a point admirably proved by the publication of Mary's correspondence. On Charles's side, the exposure is similarly open and complete. In his early letters to Mary expressions such as "You, & I, forever" are commonplace as are his repeated assertions to the effect that he believes himself to be Mary's "affectionate & only son" and that she is the muse otherwise lacking in his life.

After reporting the latest family news and delivering multiple messages from his mother, brothers, and others to his aunt, Charles, then almost 14, wrote this to Mary on 14 April 1822:

> . . . And now aunt as Ive said all they told me to, I am going . . . to talk about our private affairs; You, & I, forever—I wish your letters would not be so long coming—this is the third letter Ive written to your one—Remember you owe me two—To be sure in one of your letters is more thought & wit than I can get into a round dozen of mine; but for that very reason, I anticipate & welcome their arrival—& now I wish to know aunt what right you had to pay for that letter which you sent me—I really do not think it is fair.—I depended on your honour to let me pay for my own letters—I hope next time you'll do as you'd be done by—You know I promised you in my last letter, to send you a piece from my Receptacle—but supposing that you dont care much about ever seeing it, & having beside not room enough to insert it, I have deferred sending it till some time when Ive nothing else to tell you. Though Mercury does not much favour my chyrography[138] yet the mania for letter writing has so seized me that if the *folks* here, were not so cautious I should deluge you with my letters—Though you often proved to me that I have no heart, yet I [have][139] some few of the feelings of humanity—As for [now][140] when my friends are absent I think much of them—but when *you* are absent—there seems a kind of void which I cannot fill up—& which I do not wish to fill up—

> > Whenever you go whatever realms to see
> > My heart untravelled, fondly turns to thee
> > And drags at each remove a lengthening chain.[141]

And now aunt as Ive said my say out, I end in the old manner, by sending the love of all—wishing you well &c. &c. And thus I remain in sum & substance (perhaps I had better say bone) your affectionate & only son[142]—

In the mid-1820s—when William was returning home from Germany after having decided against a career in the ministry, and Waldo was operating schools in Chelmsford and Roxbury while irregularly attending the Harvard Divinity School, and Edward's health was worsening to the point that he needed to leave New England for the warmth of southern Europe—several themes begin to recur in Charles's letters to Mary that introduce and characterize the themes that, with little variation other than the intensity with which he expresses them, dominate his side of their correspondence until his death. In most of his letters, Charles is concerned about what he should make of himself—with, as he writes, "what . . . character I am to sustain, the part I am to act, in my future life." Fretful that Mary will be disturbed by his preoccupation with himself as an example of unmanly self-indulgence and egotism, Charles apologizes to her. Her response, typically, is that with which she opens the letter quoted below—"Your letter dear Charles was what it should be in point of friendship—none genuine without egotism."—but then she turns the tables on Charles and counsels him—as earlier she had counseled William, Waldo, and Edward—to pursue a life of piety that will, she expects, eventually lead him to pursue a career in the pulpit. In response to her gracious allowance of his momentary pride and her subsequent counsel, Charles writes, "I know very well, that there is great danger of self-delusion, in an age wh. like this, is continually striving to write the cause of religion & the world. But the solemn declaration, 'thou canst not serve God & Mammon,' will forever be true—And I think that being constantly on my guard against error on this point, I may by the blessing of Heaven escape the snare." He then concludes by saying, "[W]hether I be successful or unsuccessful, whether I walk seen or unseen by the eyes of men, I hope, I resolve, to keep constantly before me the source & the aim of my existence—I believe the same actions wh. are great & good in one, to be weak & evil in another—& I think my character, my self, will be the same whether the sum of human prosperity shall gild or the clouds of adversity darken my path."

➤ *Charles Chauncy Emerson to Mary Moody Emerson, 12 September* [1825]

My dear Aunt [nobody must read this to you][143]
    I have been busy, & I have been sick since you heard from me last, but neither my sickness nor my business has excused me to myself, for

not writing to you—Letter after letter, has been begun or written, & then committed in disgust to the fire. . . .

The principal subject, exclusive of family troubles, wh. has occupied my thoughts, is 'what is the character I am to sustain, the part I am to act, in my future life'; were I to choose for myself, I confess it would be a distinguished one; & sometimes I indulge the fancy that it will be—then again I am checked by the reflection, that I may be storing up misery for future years, by giving heed to illusions, wh. will forever mock my grasp—These thoughts naturally induce the question, am I possessed of superior abilities—I dont mean powers equal to those of a Buckminster or Webster,[144] but am I at all above the common level—There are moments of enthusiasm, when I feel a nascent greatness within me, & then anon comes the hour of dejection & melancholy, when I mourn over my humble capacity; at college among my classmates, I see none whom my vanity acknowledges as more intelligent than myself—but at home where they surely ought to know best, why they think but little of me. Balancing these contradictory results, I have come to the sage conclusion that I shall never blind the world with excess of light, & it is also my firm resolve to strive never to disgrace my name or my country.

You will pardon all this egotism, & if it is foolish, I ask you to forget it; but if such thoughts occupy the mind, they may as well be written down, & years hence, when I am known or forgotten, it may be pleasant to review the anticipation of youth.

I wish that our journey lay toward Waterford, I want to see you, & the more because you do not now write to me as you were wont—as soon as you can I hope you will—I have been reading, I hope improving this last year—My mind it seems to me is constantly enlarging, but that only serves to show still plainer its emptiness[145]—

⤙ Mary Moody Emerson to Charles Chauncy Emerson, 2 October 1825

Your letter dear Charles was what it should be in point of friendship—none genuine without egotism—[none] could not have interested me so much as to hear your queries of future character. Why think misery attends illusion about *distinction?* Is it not because you are on the contrary way to real greatness? That glory w'h attends true greatness is very far out of sight of mortal distinction. . . . And, it may be an erroneous notion, that the love of distinction is incompatible with fame in a world of durability—of high event—of tremendous worth of internal character. . . . You speak with good sense & modesty of your talents—less than your family & the world think perhaps—

But that you will arrive at greatness—at even worldly greatness is doubtfull—there have been so many ship wrecks—there is a charm—an underpinning . . . a postponing—a universality of soul—of sympathy—an habitual—as well as constitutive superiority to trifles in fame & self love—what the stoics called a generous surrender of ones self to the order of events—which seem the requisites to greatness & success even in this unweeded garden. You have at these times—this nascent greatness—. . . To be serious, you, my beloved friend, who still bind me to earth, are defective in those parts w'h religion can only remydy. Not its holiest faith—its praying forms & modes—& its burning verities—but its indwelling love of the Author—its transforming power—w'h nothing but God can give to the efforts of your soul—to the obedience he demands. He has constituted man never to be good & grand, but as he is in communion with Himself. Glorious nature—tho' sadly fallen. This principle will like the ethereal fire w'h penetrates the world of matter diffuse light over your *habitual* character & you may leave a track w'h after times may point out. I write with trembling—for *at twenty the character is said to be formed.* How rapidly you approach it.[146] Amidst those too, who call in question, by their non existence only in the present, our very faith in the immortality of souls—It is, it is an enervating thing to live in a croud . . . but there is a magnet true & omnipotent in piety w'h will give you to enjoy talents learning & fame in their proper place Alas alas, you will not listen to its stern requirement; its sacrifices are great—for its prize is immortal. (*MMEL*, pp. 200–201)

↠ *Charles Chauncy Emerson to Mary Moody Emerson, 11 October* [1825]

. . . It is indeed '*an enervating thing to live in a crowd.*' The manly resolution, wh. in the closet, is breathed from the soul with the spirit of virtuous independence, is trimmed & modified & shaped to suit the laws of fashion & society, & the wishes of friends & relations, till it loses its influence & even its memory—I was affraid that you wd. think me too worldly & timeserving—For I spoke only of *present* prospects;—But I have always considered piety not as a separate, individual, quality, but as a pervading & operative principle—an atmosphere wh. we inhale at every breath, & in wh. & by wh. we live—And whether I be successful or unsuccessful, whether I walk seen or unseen by the eyes of men, I hope, I resolve, to keep constantly before me the source & the aim of my existence—I believe the same actions wh. are great & good in one, to be weak & evil in another—& I think my character, my self, will be the same whether the sum of human prosperity shall gild or the clouds of adversity darken my path.

I know very well, that there is great danger of self-delusion, in an

age wh. like this, is continually striving to write the cause of religion
& the world. But the solemn declaration, "thou canst not serve God &
Mammon,"[147] will forever be true—And I think that being constantly on
my guard against error on this point, I may by the blessing of Heaven
escape the snare. I shall commit myself cheerfully into the hands of
Providence—I shall labour to do all that I can for my own eternal improvement, & the welfare of my country & mankind—If Honour cross
my way I shall remember that to whom much is given, of him will much
be required—& if I shall be unnoticed & unadmired, I will not be *unloved*. . . .

. . . Goodbye my dear aunt—you say 'you have no claims on me,'—
What you mean I will not pretend to say—But if love & kindness, disinterested & unmerited acts of benevolence, prayers & blessings (wh. I
rejoice to believe avail much in heaven) are not the holiest & most lasting
claims—then indeed the firmest ties of society are loosed—& we live
isolated—alone.

These claims, though you may renounce them, will still exist—
nor will I ever disavow them—I am glad that the debt of gratitude
can never be paid—For says Cicero tis the mark of a noble nature to
choose to be under obligation to those from whom it has recieved great
favours[148]—

Although Mary was the principal recipient of Charles's repeated confessions
of depression, self-doubt, world-weariness, and the like from this point on in
his life, in fairness to her, it has to be said that she was not the only recipient of Charles's expressions of spiritual turmoil. His brothers received those
expressions as well, and whether—as when they neglected to notice or simply
failed to comprehend that Edward's work and study habits were literally kill-
ing him—they simply missed seeing the severity of Charles's situation or they
purposely avoided having to confront the obvious is a question open to debate.
What is not debatable is that in ways sometimes subtle and other times not,
Charles did reveal himself to them.

For instance, writing to William on 4 January 1828, Charles complained
about the lack of heroes in their world. Complaining to William that people of
distinction and talent such as Dr. Channing as well as people of larger-than-life
proportion such as Napoleon all failed to satisfy him personally, he exclaimed
in frustration that inevitably all such figures were destined to "disappoint the
excited expectations of the world!" He concluded, arguing, "[w]e little folks,
that peep from under the legs of the Colossuses, are grieved to find them as frail
as ourselves—we are not pleased to see them descending to our own level, we
are sorry that they are not as noble creatures as our imagination had painted
them."[149] Later that year, while Edward was still committed to the McLean Asy-

lum, Charles again opened himself to William, this time complaining that he thought he was not suffering enough. "I don't think much of this world," he wrote on 9 November, and then he continued

> I like man . . . but I dont think much of myself, nor do I imagine I shall ever be very useful or very happy. You would laugh hard enough if you should see the person who writes thus, in his every day looks & behaviour. Why I am the merriest dog alive. But it is precisely this that I am ashamed of—that I am pleased & tickled with straws & rattles, careless of those solemn interests & purposes to which I was born, & which ought if I gave myself rightly to them, to imbue my character with a sober dignity.[150]

William never replied directly to Charles's letters. It may be that "practical" William either chose not to take Charles's complaint seriously or he missed it altogether, but since he left no written record of his sense of what Charles was saying, we will never know how much of his brother's lament he understood. However, when Charles repeated his complaint to Waldo a few weeks later, the language he used to express his disgust with himself and the world was so explicit that it defied being misunderstood or missed by anyone. At the time, Waldo never recorded in his journal or in his letters to anyone in the family his feelings when Charles wrote the following:

> As to my dis-cretion, I have not hitherto pretended to exercise of any such quality in respect to going into company—I have made no distinctions—I have been to every party, to which I was invited. And in so doing, I have consulted not inclination, but injunction—Here for four long years I have withstood the counsels of my wise friends who 'wanted a young man to go into society & grow refined'—And now that society happens to fall into my way, so that I can't well avoid it, I am beset with cautions, 'lest the mind be dissipated,' or 'the manners become foppish.' As if a man of sense were a very moth to burn his hair in every room that has a candle in it—As if he did not feel ashamed of himself whenever he comes out of a ball-room (especially if he has a long walk home in the dark) to think how he has been entertained, & how he has entertained his fellow-creatures; as if one who had been in any measure acquainted with the enjoyments of seclusion & study, 'that sober certainty of waking bliss,' was to be cheated out of his admiration by these parties which are an ingenious device of mankind & womankind to preserve somewhere an universal level—to keep one retreat sacred, where the coxcomb & the simpleton may parade his advantages before the man, & the scholar.[151]

No matter how or even whether his brothers replied to his concerns, Charles always could depend on Aunt Mary to receive and respond to his confessions or complaints in as serious a manner as he expressed them. However, the only tangible measure we have of the effectiveness of Mary's responses to Charles's confessions is, unfortunately, the lack of any visible alteration in his point of view occasioned by them. In the winter of 1828–1829, he complained to her as he had to his brothers about his feeling that his ambitions would never be fulfilled. Writing over a period of weeks, his message to Mary was consistently this: "I am young, anxious to do good to my country & mankind. I am anxious therefore that great thoughts should be stirring in my mind . . . I want the light of a gifted intellect fed by the oil of knowledge, to illuminate for me the dark passages of human nature, history, & philosophy."[152] Her response back to him came in installments, the last of which, arriving in April 1829 and summarizing those that had come before, was as insufficient as it was predictable: "Ah dear Charles give your bright gifts & days to the study of theology" (*MMEL*, p. 260).

Charles's despair over his lack of self-confidence, sense of personal failure, and terrifying spiritual condition never left him. Instead, until his own death in 1836, as Charles watched first Ellen and then his brother Edward languish and die from tuberculosis, a sense of gloom expressible only in the pages of his secret diary gathered around him. He grasped for remedies to his situation, and he found moments of reprieve in his relationship with Elizabeth Hoar, but as his correspondence with Elizabeth and other private writings show, even that relationship—which all called love—never displaced the demons slowly devouring Charles's soul. In fact, it is fair to say that the depression and relentless soul-searching he had disclosed in his long correspondence with Aunt Mary, he now merely transferred to his courtship correspondence with Elizabeth.

Among the remedies that appealed to Charles, three struck him as offering viable cures for his situation. One that he initially pursued drew its authority from Mary's own sublime confidence in the moral and emotional efficacy of Calvinism. Writing to her in November 1829, he rhetorically asked the question to which Mary's own life had offered him an answer: "Is not the old fashioned Providence in which our fathers believed, a safer guide to the interpretation of this 'various scene below' & is it not as noble a guide?" Beginning with a consideration of the relative merits of the Germans' romantic distinction between the idealism of "the literary man" and the realism of "the mere practical man," in a letter to Mary, Charles attempted to find room for himself in a variety of Calvinism through which he could negotiate between these two extremes.

> That is a fine division of men into two classes, which the Germans make—The literary man, who has caught glimpses of the Divine idea which pervades the world, who sees beneath all the trades & arts &

learning, the policy, the amusements, & every circumstance of human life . . . about which the affairs of men arrange themselves as the steel dust about the magnet, loosely, yet with enough of form to betray the influence which orders & disposes them; & having once caught these glimpses, he spends his whole soul in following them up—pursuing the Divinity through his works—& looking on all about him not as a world of men & women, of barter & sale, of wealth & poverty, power obscurity or sickness—but as a system of deep & meaning emblems, which rightly interpreted will speak to his spirit of God. The other, is the mere practical man, who takes the external coating of the world to be the whole—& builds his fortunes, speculations, hopes, upon those courses of events, & uses of society, which appear to him to be final facts— to be the machinery of the clock, & not, as they are, the hands which obey the machinery.—Now this is fine—They cant mean by their Divine idea, the apotheosis of their own feeble intelligence. But is there no danger of delusion & error in assenting to such a theory of life? Are we s   it is not immodest in us, to attempt with premature hand to remove the veil of matter between us & the brightness of that Truth on which we are not yet prepared to look? Shall we not go wide of the mark in seeking to trace these big & mysterious shadows of things, while these things themselves, the proper implements of our action are neglected? Is not the old fashioned Providence in which our fathers believed, a safer guide to the interpretation of this 'various scene below' & is it not as noble a guide? If I believe every event which befals me & my race, to proceed from the will of God, & to declare more or less plainly his will to us, is not such a belief as sublime in its practical effect, & more easy to be understood & adopted by every mind, as the endeavour, out of the whole motley assemblage of human institutions & histories to evolve a great & Divine truth?[153]

Mary heartily approved of Charles's view, believing that he would eventually find answers to all the questions he had posed in the lessons she had so patiently taught him. Endorsing his epistle of late November "A priceless letter," she responded to it on 27 December 1829:

As your time, dear Charles, is so full I dont hasten to answer one of the best letters written (I believe) in any age. Yet it is shaded with "doubts." But of what kind I pray? . . .

. . . Of what do you doubt? Of the conscious presence of God? Your intellectual—& moral nature—(conscience) prove it—and as they are enlightened, prove the adaptations of our old out of fashion, Bible to be divine. "Why then not universal & coeval with man?" Who has ever been left without wittnesses of God & conscience? And a few ages of darkness & barbarism will only serve to inhance the worth of the hidden treasure—as its propagation by human hands will tend to increase virtue. It's sometimes trackless existence—its often calumniated state, is but like the infancy of youth & earthly career of it's Messiah—and alike before their mission is ended, will be owned and honored by the universe. It has been a wonderfull source of virtue & opinion & knowledge to ages & sects—each of which is laden with some tribute to it's worth. The ethereal & often noble Idealist, who seems in his excentric orbit to lose sight of it's light, is bringing new plumage to the wings of a spiritual faith. And even the *grub* existing materialist has his weights to throw into the scale of truth—and the bibleist often looks to the revolution in our little world when it's fires will master all other elements &, perhaps, by a natural process restore the purified body to it's spiritual inmate.

But Klopstock has that w'h no other man has—w'h every good theist will love on every belief.

> "Joy thee of thy death, oh body;
> Where thou dost corrupt beneath
> There will he
> The eternal be
> Joy of thy death, oh body; in the deeps,
> In the hieghts of creation, will thy wrack blow away;
> There also where thou wilt anew decay,
> There where it's dust in sightless ruin sweeps,
> There will he
> The eternal be."[154]

Farewell dear Charles. May your spirit beginn to look out with a somewhat more earnest manner, not on the gew gause of events, but on existence, that the very "outward shape may imbibe its east" and throw off the non chalance which is sometimes taken for better than it is. (*MMEL*, pp. 268–270)

Mary's response to Charles's questions discloses precisely the type of certainty Calvinism represented and which Waldo found and approved of in his review of her letters a decade later. At that time, he wrote, "How dignified is this! . . . How our friendships & the complaisances we use, shame us now. . . . I feel suddenly that my life is frivolous & public; I am as one turned out of doors, I live in a balcony, or on the street."[155] But, try as he might, Charles never could find comfort in Calvinism's message. However, on one occasion, after hearing Edward Thompson Taylor—"Fr. Taylor"—preach at the Seaman's Bethel in Boston, Charles thought he had discovered a model of one whose confident acceptance of Calvinism might inform his own. Feeling a rush of admiration for Taylor as the type of man he wished he could become, Charles wrote the news to his aunt.

↠ *Charles Chauncy Emerson to Mary Moody Emerson, 16 November 1830*

Last Sunday night I went, (Waldo & I) to the Seaman's meeting, Bethel as it is called, down in Hanover St. It is a little chapel, & was thronged & overthronged with common sailors, & one gallery with females. By & by came the minister—Mr. Taylor.[156] In the Pulpit he found a note, saying that such a brig was to set sail next morning, & the crew desired prayers for themselves & their families—He chose for his text the last verse of the XVI chap. John[157]—as applicable both to the case of the outward bound vessel & to all—for he himself was going away from his people for several months, to obtain subscriptions to aid the cause & build Bethels. His sermon was wholly Extempore—He applied with wonderful propriety the parting words of Jesus throughout his last conversation with his disciples, to his own & his people's case—but when he came to the main doctrines of his sermon—the tribulation that is in the world & the peace that comes from Christ who has overcome the world—he seemed inspired—His weatherbeaten, muscular frame, his strongly marked face, he heaved & swollen with emotion. He made the tears start from our eyes. The rough seamen about us, grew beautiful & angelic in the common relation of sons of God & disciples of Christ. I felt as if I could have embraced them all. Not only was he eloquent like Demosthenes,[158]—but the lofty religious sentiment, that spoke in every word, made him dear to us. He is a glorious instance—of one educated to great height & power of intellect, by the Religious principle. Twelve years ago he was a common sailor. He has, I am told, the same absolute control over his flock that Cheverus had.[159] We stopped & spoke with him. We staid to the Seamen's Prayer-meeting, & saw how religion could soften those old flints into human souls—so that we sympathised one with another. I never passed so delightful an evening. It seemed to me a particular Providence—a sort of Revelation in Patmos[160] not a real scene in Hanover St. Boston.[161]

In spite of his inability to find a remedy for his spiritual ills in Calvinism or to emulate Father Taylor's "glorious" illustration of how one could develop "great height & power of intellect, by the Religious principle," Charles had one more remedy at his disposal, which he tried to pursue on more than one occasion. "Restoration in nature" Mary herself had preached to Charles from the earliest days of their association, and personally experiencing it in Elm Vale's setting or calling it up in memory years later, Charles appreciated nature's restorative powers. For example, in late 1823, after exchanging news of William's departure to Germany and Edward's taking on the instruction of some one hundred pupils, Charles asked his aunt,

[H]ow look the rocks & mountains of Waterford—have they robed themselves with the white garments of winter, or do they stretch on in cold & barren grandeur?—You must not find fault with me for not writing a better letter. I have told you, & I tell you again, that I cannot send themes for letters, nor do I think you wish me to yourself—Tell me what kind of letters to write & I will follow the path of your point out. And beside, it is not common, every-day, intellects, that can "robe themselves with imagination as a garment" & it is no ordinary pen that leaves behind it a track of light, blazing with the fires of genius—You must look far & wide for him who is to write a line which you could wish to blot—You must be content to bear with much that is uninteresting, much perhaps that is foolish, though something I hope affectionate from your dutiful boy.[162]

Two years later, after visiting her in Maine, Charles's first act on arriving home was to draft his own sermon on how in his mind and imagination Waterford had become synonymous with nature and the sublime.

For sometime after I left Waterford the White Hills were in view; I know no sight wh. so raises yr. thoughts above the trifles around you as this— when you look upon those venerable mountains white with perpetual snow, & reflect that they looked down with the same immoveable grandeur, upon the naked savage, long centuries ago, & that though many generations have succeeded, & many revolutions happened, in all this time, yet there they stand—the same beautiful monarchs of the surrounding scenery—you can hardly help rising above petty concerns & feelings—I know not how it is with others, but for my own part, "I felt myself ennobled"—and when at sunset a golden cloud rested on the top of one of the highest peaks, I almost imagined an angel had de-scended, wrapped in this gorgeous veil to look out upon our fair world & perhaps to execute some mighty errand.[163]

Finally, on 4 August 1827, while visiting Concord, Charles wrote a description of discoveries he had made in his ancestral home's rural setting. What follows is one of Charles's purest expressions of his own nascent romantic impulse; it rivals in stylistic grace any of the naturalistic writings that either Mary or Waldo ever composed, and discloses a wonderfully bright but wholly unexpected side to that depth of feeling that Charles found he could reveal only to his aunt.

This is the season of maturity in nature. The energies of spring are exhausted, & the vegetable world seems to delight itself in basking quietly beneath the sunbeam of subsiding summer. A great part of the literary & fashionable world improve in like manner this sultry season as a season of rest. And during the interval of academic pursuits, our college-scholars are scattered over the country, to learn, I hope, the providence of God & the beauty of his creation, & to unlearn somewhat of the pride of imaginary acquirements. Here by the banks of our tranquil river, I hang my thoughts on the willows, that the breezes may freshen & the shifting scenery of nature enrich them. Here I write to you, because in this calm of body & mind, I shall be less likely to be betrayed into any of that worldly cant, which one can scarcely avoid infusing into letters written in the midst of turbulence & gay excitement—a cant so quickly detected, & so severely rebuked. But in truth I know not that I need take these precautions; for I cannot find myself guilty of any undue attachment to society, its spirit, or its forms. I oftener feel & subdue a little rebellion against all its modes & manners & morals—sometimes I find a response in my own heart to the saying about the poor man's son whom Heaven in its *anger* has visited with ambition. But when the dark hour is over—when kindness or religion or hope have recovered m from the sickness of the soul, that was caught in the infectious atmosphere of jealousy & impertinence, meanness & malice; When I remember that no man ever yet fled from that fleet enemy Care,—that thorns lurk beneath the dewy rose buds of the rural glen, as well as strew the couch of the statesman, & the floor of the palace; when I am warmed by the love of virtuous action, cheered by the sight of its success, & strengthened by prayer to God that he would bless my feeble efforts with an *affectual* blessing, then I no longer wish for the hills & the rocks to cover my secluded life, but acknowledge that the lines have fallen to me in pleasant places.[164]

Much as his spirits were buoyed by his familiarity with nature and his discovery in her of many valuable lessons by which to calm his soul, Charles was never able to find peace within or outside of himself. Just as his own self-loathing prevented him from finding in Calvinism that sense of the dignity of life that even Waldo recognized in its fiery message, and just as his perception of his own incurable spiritual weakness undermined the authority of Father Taylor's valuable lessons on how to live while acknowledging forces in the world larger and more powerful than oneself, Charles could not sustain the hope that nature and her beauties seemed to offer him. Betrayed even by his imagination, in 1830 Charles invoked nature as he began preaching to himself an extended sermon against hope. Depressed and now reckoning his own mortality according to the pace and changes of the seasons, he wrote to Mary, lamenting that "A few more summers & winters, & I too shall be changed & sent away," and wondering, "Why multiply attachments that will soon be all broken? Why strike the root deeper & so make it harder to tear the tree up?" Both she and he knew that whatever answers either might give to such questions would never prove sufficient enough to calm Charles's spirit.

➳ *Charles Chauncy Emerson to Mary Moody Emerson, 12 September 1830*

Another year of study is begun. 'Thus build we up the being that we are'[165]—thus slowly, anxiously, painfully. Were it not for the solemn lesson which religion teaches—that having received all we owe all—& that God will accept the sacrifice of our *whole* life, however small its fruits—one would choose to sit down contented with little efforts & little success, rather than surrender himself up to great motives, & continually grieve over the huge contrast between what he seeks & what he reaches, what he does & what he wants to do. When we are in the active world, the press of business is itself a relief. We are kept too hard at work to have leisure to muse on our inefficiency. But in the closet, the mind upbraids its own failures, is alive to its own weakness, & so preys on its own spirits.

Autumn . . . is a monitory season. It shows us the yellow & faded remains of the plant which a few weeks since thust out its green & vigorous bud. The woods which rung with the cheerful song of birds, chant their own death song as the wind shakes their branches. The falling leaves, too, are eloquent types. A few more summers & winters, & I too shall be changed & sent away. Why multiply attachments that will soon be all broken? Why strike the root deeper & so make it harder to tear the tree up? Because the ties that bind me to my brother man, bind me to my Father God. Because the root that penetrates the lighter soil at the surface, will by & by as it goes deeper suck life from the everlasting fountains. Because the more thoroughly this life is understood, the more diligently it is improved, the more does it speak to us of Heaven & the better does it prepare us for death.

To you, my dear aunt, this is needless talk. But I have need of every consideration that shall give value to those exercises of duty to which I am called. So suffer me to preach to myself while I write to you.

What is the object of study? Is it not to provide that necessary store of learning & facts that shall enable us to give to our fellowmen, our own convictions—the pittance of Truth we have been permitted to gather,—in a form intelligible & respectable. Is it not simply acquiring the language current among those with whom we live, so as to be able to express our own nature—& so that portion of the divine nature which it contains.

We can develope ourselves without the aid of what is technically called study—scholarship. We can think & pray & love. And the fruit of these exercises will be knowledge. But we shall not be furnished with the usual sceptre to which human reason has been wont to bow—nor with the weapons of defence which have commonly been wielded against the assaults of error.

I live in a solitude nearly as entire, as if I were in the woods. I do not visit—& except at recitations in Law, & at the Library, I meet no companions. The reward I look forward to all the week, is my talk with Waldo on Saturday. I love him; altho' his own affections except a universal benevolence seem all called in & centered on Ellen. Now I pray you illumine my long dark evenings, now & then, with a letter.[166]

Neither Charles nor Aunt Mary was able to provide satisfactory answers to the questions he raised in this letter. Charles's own failure to arrive at any lasting resolution to the internal tensions and spiritual chaos that defined his life made it impossible for Waldo—and perhaps makes it impossible for us as well—to reconcile this promising and brilliant brother with the tortured figure he finally became. Yet the record is unarguable. Charles's lifelong search for a way to identify and solidify a truly Christian character in himself ended in a failure the extent of which only Mary understood. Reading fragments such as these found among Charles's papers after his death, Waldo also came to understand, if not necessarily to accept, the darkness in which his brother lived and died.

➤ *Extract from a letter to M. M. E.*

Tis a good thing sickness to teach humility. One is apt in health to lean towards a philosophy too stoical for our constitution, & to require of all mankind an impassivity & self-dependance, which the sound mind in the sound body is conscious of.—But loosen the joints, dry up the oils which make part move easily upon part, send a sickness into the vitals, or bring a stifling cloud over the brain—disable this would be Godling from the power of attention, of imagination, of clear intellection—tease him with the pains which invade irritable nerves.—let him grope for light in the darkness which overcasts his spirits—and he comes to understand his own & so, other mens' capacity of suffering & need of sympathy.—The trouble is to teach them that they are strong to bear the infirmities of the weak. We so fast outgrow the remembrance of that which has gone out from us, that we have to act rather by rule, than by feeling or conviction.

This world was made for the well. The moment hand or foot is lame, stomach or head disordered, the sky ceases to be blue, & the grass to be green, & the light to be sweet. And as soon as you quit your work bench in the manufactory, & no longer help govern the machinery & add to the amount of production, you are stunned with the noise of the wheels, & well if you be not drawn between them & crushed. Tis a workaday world altogether. Might there not be some nice arrangement by which the invalid should removed from the sight of activity that appals or disgusts him? Might not pleasant tracts of country be set apart in every civilized nation, into which all the feeble should be straitway transported & there bolstered up with easy circumstances, be never insulted by the contrast between their own inefficiency & the labor of the strong?[167]—

↠ *Extract from a letter to M. M. E.*

We are lonely beings in much of our history, multiply as we will our communication of self outward—man's life is a voyage of discovery on which each one sails alone. For much as we are all formed alike, & bound together as we all are in societies, yet in every case that which makes the individual separates him from the rest of his kindred, & renders it more or less hard for him to explain himself to their comprehension & rest in their sympathy. We publish our memoirs to one another, but how loosely! & we are always leaving the past behind, & changing as we move forward. . . .

I learn now to respect all those who act to good ends, however imperfectly that may understand their own principles—however shallow may be their intellectual philosophy, & uninteresting the history of their thoughts. Their energy strikes outward instead of inward—& it will not do for the thinking man to look down upon those who build the house of which he studies the place.[168]

Chapter 5

Charles and Elizabeth

*C*harles Chauncy Emerson's relationship with Elizabeth Hoar can only be understood by recognizing the influences that the earlier loves of William, and especially Waldo, had upon him. In some ways this chapter is as much about "the brothers in love" as it is about Charles and "Lizzie," as Charles called her. The brothers themselves shared a love for each other, and whenever a woman entered their world, she was immediately adopted as a sister, and responded in kind. As a result, each of the brothers perceived themself as being part of an extended family; and to understand how Charles perceived his own role in this grouping, it is first necessary to examine Waldo and his wives and William and his wife.

As shown earlier, the image and person of Ellen Louisa Tucker Emerson informed all of Waldo's life, from his conception of immortality to the monies received from the settlement of her estate (an extended discussion of which is in the next chapter). Waldo had first met her on 25 December 1827, while he was supply preaching in Concord, New Hampshire.[1] After a number of return visits, Waldo became engaged to Ellen on 17 December 1828.[2] Because he had spent about a month and half in Ellen's hometown during his trips there, Waldo was clearly aware of Ellen's propensity towards tuberculosis: her brother had died from the disease; her mother and sister had the disease; and she herself was suffering from it, as Waldo knew from the two extended trips in August and September 1829 that he went on with Ellen and her mother as a means of improving her health. Indeed, Ellen, after once seeing how her mother had "raised blood," declared that a drop of blood "should be the family coat of arms."[3]

Charles was the best man at his brother's wedding on 30 September 1829, and often visited the couple while they lived in Boston. He was charmed by Ellen from the beginning and, like Waldo, recognized both her spiritual and material assets, as when he wrote Mary Moody Emerson on 1 January 1829: "Well Waldo's prosperity comes as you always predicted, *late;* Ellen, is, we understand, for we do not see her till next week, a beautiful, sensible, religious, girl. She is rich too. Though this seems forgotten in her loveliness & excellence."[4] He was aware of her ethereal quality, as when he noted that "Waldo says she is too lovely to live long. He thinks, that should she be struck out of existence tomorrow, it would still have been a rich blessing to have been permitted to have loved her."[5] Charles was also present for the deathwatch preceding Ellen's passing on 8 February 1831, as these three letters show:

Ellen is still with us—tho' her spirit seems winged for its flight. She suffered a great deal of distress last night, but to day (with the exception of perhaps two or three times a halfhour) she has been in less pain—sometimes torpid under the influence of her opiates, but at others serene & fully conscious—She spoke this afternoon very sweetly of her readiness to die—that she told you she should not probably live through the winter—tho' she did not know that she would have been called so soon—She saw no reason why her friends should be distressed—it was better she should go first, & prepare the way—She asked Waldo, if he had strength, to read her a few verses of Scripture—and he read a portion of the XIVth chapter of John.[6]—Waldo is bowed down under the affliction, yet he says t'is like seeing an angel go to heaven.[7]

Our dear Ellen is on the brink of the grave—Every breath is distress—She may not live the day through. She has failed very rapidly the past week—& when I saw her yesterday, I was convinced I as well as her poor husband must soon take leave of her forever. Waldo is as you may believe a man over whom the waters have gone—Mother is well—When you hear from Edward, you will let us immediately know—If you have opportunity write him these sad sad tidings.[8]

. . . We have none of us, I believe, been aware until within two or three days of Ellen's immediate danger. I saw her last Wednesday. She was able to ride twice that day & Waldo felt encouraged. Saturday morng. I came into town & found her sadly altered & her husband & mother without any hope of her recovery—You can think, my dear brother, how sad a house we are—Last night was a tedious & distressed one—today has been a little easier.—She speaks of her situation, of her death with serenity & sweetness. This is a comfort to Waldo—He is bowed down under his affliction, but he says 'it is like nothing, but an angel taking her flight to Heaven.' . . .

Monday A.M. Ellen passes a more comfortable night than the one before it. She grows gradually weaker, but whenever she is free from pain, she talks cheerfully & expresses her thanks for all the kindness of those about her, her anxiety for her mother & for Waldo, lest they should take cold or be sick—. . . .

She may live a day or two—I think she will not. . . .

Tuesday 10 A.M.

She is gone—She died about an hour ago—Waldo is well & bears well his incalculable loss—[9]

Charles's response to Ellen's last days was natural because, according to one biographer of Waldo, Ellen was a "beautiful girl, dying at nineteen, her face aglow with the hectic bloom induced by the illness that ravaged her and the good will her faith engendered," all contributing to a "radiance."[10] Later, while courting Elizabeth Hoar, Charles recalled Ellen as "an Ideal that, if I were a Platonist, I should believe to have been one of the Forms of Beauty in the Universal Mind. She moved ever in an atmosphere of her own, a crystal sphere, & nothing vulgar in neighboring persons & circumstances touched her."[11]

Edward, Charles, Waldo, and Ellen all suffered from tuberculosis and this fact naturally affected their outlook on life. John McAleer has noted that when Edward's health "gave way" in mid-1828, Waldo had "new cause to be aware of the transitory nature of human existence and of the need to seize on those moments of happiness that were offered, without insisting on perfection of conditions."[12] Robert D. Richardson, Jr., writing of Waldo's state of mind in the months following Ellen's death, has noted "a sort of romantic longing for death" in his writings of the time.[13] Charles, though, seems to have been more affected by the attraction of death than by the potential affirmation and enjoyment of one's transitory life, positions no doubt reinforced by his correspondence with Mary that examined the Calvinist meaning of life.

Certainly, in the years after Ellen's death, there were many memories of her to remind both Waldo and Charles of her presence. Not only were there the tangible monies from her estate, but Waldo kept a miniature of her as well as her rocking chair, both of which stayed in his house until his death.[14] He would not let go of Ellen's memory—as late as 1879, in his late seventies, he entered the dates of their marriage and her death into his pocket diary (*JMN*, 16:525). And he unabashedly brought these memories to his new marriage.

Lydia Jackson had heard Waldo lecture and preach in 1833 and 1834, and was struck by his appearance and ideas. Indeed, her friends commented to her that her ideas and Waldo's were remarkably alike. Lydia was something of a spiritualist, and one day, when she was going up the stairs in her house, "she saw a clear image of herself dressed as a bride walking down those stairs . . . to be married." (Later, when she was late coming down the stairs for the marriage ceremony, Waldo went up to get her and "met her on the landing, and behold! exactly as that vision had presented itself to her, months ago, they were going down stairs together to be married!") In January 1835 she had another vision, of Waldo's face, "very beautiful, close to her gazing at her, just for a moment." The next day, his letter proposing marriage arrived.[15] They were married on 14 September 1835, after which they moved to Concord, and Waldo began calling her Lidian, possibly because the New England pronunciation of her name would have resulted in the awkward "Lydiar Emerson."

Waldo in 1835 was very different from the Waldo of 1827. He had met Ellen when he was 24, and was 26 when he married his 18-year-old bride. Now, at age 32, he was marrying someone who was 33, making him eight months younger than his wife, not eight years older. As Richardson describes the two marriages, whereas "Ellen meant delicious memories of youth, brief moments and meetings 'when affection contrived to give a witchcraft surpassing the deep attraction of its own truth to a parcel of accidental and insignificant circumstances,'" Lidian "meant a meeting of minds"; and, while "this sounds less romantic, we should recall that mind—that is consciousness—was everything to Emerson; no higher compliment was possible."[16] Emerson's proposal in a letter of 24 January 1835 is no young swain's romantic pleadings: he noted "the feeling of deep and tender respect with which you have inspired me," and that he loved her "after a new and higher way" (L, 7:232). And in announcing his engagement to William, Waldo called it "a very sober joy," for this is "a very different feeling from that with which I entered my first connexion" (L, 1:436).

Waldo's somberness may be seen in the events leading up to his wedding: as Charles explains in a letter to William, on the 12th Waldo gave his discourse upon the bicentennial of the founding of Concord; and the next day he left for his wedding, which took place on the following day, when he returned to Concord with his bride without benefit of traveling on a honeymoon:

> Last Saturday we celebrated our two hundredth municipal birthday. It was a bright day & men & women wore pleased & excited faces. At about ½ past 10 o'clock we found ourselves in the Church. There we had music enough—voluntary, & ode, & psalm, & ode again, & original hymn. The psalm was the from the old New England version, written chiefly by John Eliot,[17] & used in the Churches from 1640. It was a noble ancient strain, & had the more effect from being "deaconed" out, a line at a time, after the fashion of our grandfathers, & sung by the whole congregation. The orator occupied about an hour & forty five minutes with a discourse which none but the children I think found too long. It was a faithful historical sketch of this Town—honor due was done unto the brave company of First Settlers, Peter Bulkeley, Simon Willard, & their faithful associates;[18] the harmony with which the negotiation was

conducted with the Indians suggested the name of the town which it received from Peter Bulkeley. There was much said of the red men the original lords of the soil—of their astonishing physical powers, before the blight of English civilization came nigh them, of their manly friendship toward the whites, & by & by of the prophetic fears of the best among them of the decay & extinction of their race; and these prophetic fears were accomplished to the uttermost.

> "Their fires are out by wood & shore,
> Their pleasant springs are dry—"[19]

Then came the record of the doings & counsellings of the good town of Concord down to the epoch of the Revolution;—here the quiet river of its fortunes again opened into a capacious sea, or rather, swollen by tributary waters, rushed over the rocky barriers that would have choked its course, & this triumph achieved, held on its modest noiseless way.

The wise invention of 'a Town,' an invention which was the daughter of that prolific old mother Necessity, was commended to notice. It is a school wherein men learn how to be sovereigns & legislators. . . .

Waldo went away last night & is to be married tonight, & tomorrow night is to be at home—[20]

Lidian was quite different than the younger Ellen Tucker. Lidian had had time to form her ideas and opinions; she was well-read and intellectual. In her Emerson found a soul mate, not someone with whom he could grow and discover likes and dislikes, ideas and beliefs. Also, unlike Ellen, Lidian brought but a small dowry (later to be decided upon at six hundred dollars). Lidian shared with Ellen a sense of religiousness, though hers was far more serious and developed; and whereas both Ellen and Waldo had been moving towards religious knowledge within the established church, Lidian, according to Ralph Rusk, although "still nominally a Unitarian," had "in reality become a seeker, as [Waldo] himself was."[21] And although Waldo had rechristened Lidian with his own name for her, she continued, throughout their lives—in public and in private—to call him "Mr. Emerson."[22] This belied her love and genuine affection for Waldo; their daughter remembered that the "tremendous manner in which she loved Father was always as astonishing to me as the coolness with which she treated him."[23]

Waldo made it clear from the start that Ellen's memory would be a presence in his new marriage. In his proposal he alludes to "second considerations" to which he is not "blind," including "the past" and "the Departed" (L, 7:232). Lidian often asked Waldo about Ellen, and their daughter recalled her father's journal entry in which "he says 'I had a long, long remembering talk with Lidian about Ellen, which brought back that delicious relation.'" He gave Lidian a diamond that had belonged to Ellen for her to wear in a new setting. Lidian recalled that Waldo gave her Ellen's letters to read, and in them she found "a holy creature, truly religious." One night Lidian dreamed that she and Waldo were "together in heaven and they met with Ellen and she went away and left him with her," and when she told Waldo the next morning of her dream, he replied "None but the noble dream such dreams."[24]

When a daughter was born in 1839, Waldo wrote in his journal, "Lidian, who magnanimously makes my gods her gods, calls the babe Ellen," and he added, "I can hardly ask more for thee, my babe, than that name implies. Be that vision & remain with us, & after us" (*JMN*, 7:170). Ellen remembered Lidian telling her that "I was happy in my name, that she hoped Ellen was my guardian angel." And when she was 10, Lidian gave Ellen her namesake's bible.[25]

Family tradition has it that not everyone took an immediate liking to Lidian. She was, after all, rather old for a bride, and her husband was an established and well-to-do figure. She was opinionated and did not hide it, which made Ruth Haskins Emerson look on their marriage "as a Petruchio sort of affair," suggesting that Waldo would, like Shakespeare's hero, need to tame a shrew.[26] All agreed that she lacked physical beauty, including Charles, who wrote that Lidian is "a sort of Sybil for wisdom—She is not beautiful any-wise that I know, so you look at the outside alone." Still, he added, "Mother is pleased, & everybody."[27] But within a month, Charles declared that "I like her transparent character very much."[28] For her part, by May 1835 Lidian was declaring Elizabeth Hoar a "Dear soul" and that "we love each other truly," and Charles was "very pleasant towards me and we have had some grand talk."[29] William offered felicitations: "I congratulate you on an event which my confidence in your correct judgment makes me sure must be a fit subject of congratulation." His wife was "as much interested in it as I am, & loudly demands a minute description of our future Sister, & tells me to add her greetings to my own on the occasion."[30]

Charles was not completely accurate about everyone being pleased; and one example of displeasure foreshadowed his own situation with Elizabeth. When Mary Moody Emerson interviewed Lidian and then complained about her to Waldo, he warned Lidian that she was "guilty of valuing herself too highly and imagining that she was able to judge others." Lidian explained that an "innocent remark of hers had been twisted out of its meaning." Years later, Mary confessed to Lidian that "I spent the whole time . . . trying to make Waldo give you up, and ran you down in every way I could. I cannot bear to lose my nephews and I did the same when Charles was engaged to Elizabeth."[31]

In August 1832 William became engaged to Susan Woodward Haven, who came from an upper-class family in Portsmouth, New Hampshire. Her distance from Boston meant it was hard for the brothers to see her; indeed, Waldo was kept busy in September and October with his dealings with the Second Church over the Lord's Supper, and he was overseas from December 1832 through October 1833. The couple married on 3 December 1833, when William was

32 and Susan 26. Waldo was unable to attend the ceremony because he was preaching in New Bedford; Ruth Haskins Emerson declined to make the long and uncomfortable trip; Edward was busy with his law practice (*L*, 1:398). Still, as he did for Waldo, Charles attended as best man.[32] Susan eventually bore three children who lived to adulthood. Over the years, both Emerson families vacationed at their respective residences, and Elizabeth Hoar, Ruth Haskins Emerson, and Mary Moody Emerson often stayed with William's family in New York and on Staten Island.[33] (Also, because both Lidian and Susan were sickly, the families possessed a common thread of conversation.)

Charles was able to watch his brothers and their wives in their marriages: Waldo and Ellen represented a type of sentimental early love, one touched by a spirituality heightened by Ellen's illness; Waldo and Lidian stood for solidness and a love that promised to mature and deepen; William and Susan represented a type of middle-class, materialistic marriage that reflected the seeming failure of William to achieve the lofty spiritual goals set for him earlier. These views of the relations between the sexes helped to form Charles's character, as did other events, before he met Elizabeth Hoar.

Mary Moody Emerson's influence on Charles and how she was a pivotal player in his development was discussed in chapter 4. A series of early letters to her suggests the main problems that Charles would face as he went about his worldly business: he was obsessed with questions of religious salvation; he felt himself both a casual scholar, without promise, and one unworthy of the world's praise; he was caught up in a struggle between the spiritual and the material; and he welcomed release from his struggles, be it spiritual enlightenment or death. On the latter point, Ellen's example was a telling one:

↠ *Charles Chauncy Emerson to Mary Moody Emerson, 30 April 1834*

I pray, & for the moment breathe freer. But when the hands fall Amalek prevails.[34] Do you remember Ellen's verses—

> My restless spirit, rocking ever,
> Is not seeking sordid wealth;
> Nor is every fresh endeavour
> Made to gain high roseate health—
> Some thing which I have not tasted,
> But which longing still I seek—
> T'is for this my hours are wasted,
> This that keeps my Reason weak.
> Light in Prayer seems but a ray
> Breaking from a world of Day;
> Cares & troubles soon come oer
> All is darker than before.[35]

They utter my feeling very faithfully. Sweet spirit, She has ceased from disquiet & doubt, & the Eternal Day has shone on her. When shall we too deserve to die?—I do not mean to affect a passion for death—I do not feel any—I merely say it is with me an idea of unbinding—Loose him & let him go seem to me words more appropriate to the parting than the recovered ghost.[36]

Though Charles seems to deny he means "to affect a passion for death," the family's history of illness and his own tuberculosis argue for his recognition of this as one way of "unbinding" his problems.

Perhaps Charles's major problem, as he wrote Waldo, was that "I love everything better than myself."[37] This lack of self-worth informed Charles's life, from his compensatory desire to succeed in college and the law (balanced, of course, by his shaky confidence in his abilities and lack of belief in the pursuits themselves), to his approach to theological issues, to his relations with women. Early on, he had shown, in a letter to Mary, why she saw in him one of her prized Calvinist students:

. . . To day aunt we had two *very fine* sermons from M[r] [James] Walker of Charlestown[38] . . . the *native* depravity of men, all their faults & transgressions, he says "Many may preach to you these flatterys & you may believe them, but this will not anul, the fixed, immutable, law of God—according to your works, ye shall be judged—whether they be good or whether they be evil—they may tell you, if they please, that if you are one of the elect you will be *saved* & if you are not you will be *damned,* & that nothing, which you can say, or do, will weigh one feather in the balance; & you may believe them if you please, yet all this will not alter the Law of God—For heaven & earth may pass away—but one jot or one tithe of this law shall in nowise pass away, until all be fulfilled—They may cry peace, peace, when there is no peace—But would ye have the ambassador of God come to you with a lie in his right hand? with a dream to amuse, or a drug to stupify you?" And he went on in the same style; & it corresponded so well with his earnest & impressive manner, & his forcible & powerfull gestures, that nothing, for this long time has so interested & struck me.[39]

Not only did Charles worry about the issues Mary and society at large laid before him, he felt himself unable to deal with them:

I read so very little, & think so very little, (that is, continuously,) that I am most unfit for metaphysical & moral speculations—I am like a ship dismasted—& if launched on the waters in such plight, she must quickly be ingulphed in the billows over which she was wont to bound. . . . Indeed I now continually feel conscious of something in me which may not ever burst its buds & sheaths in this murky mundane atmosphere, but wait the sun & dew of a celestial climate.[40]

His brothers unwittingly played into these fears. Like many people suffering from self-doubt, Charles covered this by being outwardly pleasant and confident. Unlike Edward, who was beset by physical and mental illness as he strived to meet the family's expectations, Charles seemed not to pay any price for his attempts, as Waldo wrote to William on 8 February 1828: "Charles comes down to see me occasionally; he is still the same honey catcher of pleasure, favor, & honour that he hath been & without paying for it like Edward with life & limb" (L, 1:227). Letters of encouragement from the family seem to have shaken his confidence more than built it up:

➤ *William to Charles*

. . . my letter will probably reach you during your first college vacation. . . . But I cannot forget that I have spent 4 years at college, and have suffered deeply, irrecoverably for having tread under foot the pearls that were cast before me. . . .

You would see how blindly and childishly my hours were thrown away, how thereby my moral sense became blunted, till I fell into a deep slumber, intellectual and moral, how gradually and painfully I awake from this lethargy by the stings of shame and demured neglect;—awoke, to find those, who a few years before, were my inferiors had now left me far behind, and to feel how low I had sunk in my own esteem.[41] . . .

➤ *Waldo to Charles*

Give yourself to study with boundless ambition. despising as much as you please the primary & vulgar landmarks of success in the consciousness yᵗ [that] you aim to raise your rank not among your compeers alone but in that great scale of moral beings which embraces the invisible & the visible. There is one drop in the number of its drops wh makes the ocean greater than any sea. & by every discovery of a thot or a relation wh. your diligence accumulates perchance you overtop another & another individual in those enormous congregations of aspirants which in the body & out of the body environ you. (L, 1:200)

There is no doubt that Charles felt this pressure. In a letter to his mother, written in March 1828, he asks her to thank Ezra Ripley "for the interest he has expressed in my little distinctions, & remind him of the text, 'Let not him who putteth on the armour, boast himself as he shall taketh it off'—a life of temptation, trial, action, is before me,—God grant I may not degenerate from the purity or fall behind the example of my fathers!"[42]

Mary had catechized Charles from an early age, as she had tried to do with all the brothers, about his role in the family's great destiny. Charles was continually pulled between Mary's lofty goals and what he saw as his own meager abilities. Once he wrote her that the "principal subject, exclusive of family troubles, wh. has occupied my thoughts, is 'what is the character I am to sustain, the part I am to act, in my future life.'" He has, unfortunately, "come to the sage conclusion that I shall never blind the world with excess of light."[43] To Charles, "scholarship" had come to him "unsought—that is, I never studied more than it was my duty to do; it is the desire, the expectation, of the friends on whom I depend, that I should be first"; and, were "I possessed of an independent fortune, probably I shd. not wish to be the first scholar—As I am now situated I feel it *my duty to endeavour to be so.*"[44] He felt that he was "young, anxious to do good to my country & mankind," and for this reason "I am anxious therefore that great thoughts should be stirring in my mind—that undying fires of benevolence should there be kindled—that noble designs should be uncovered before the eyes of my understanding, till I grow familiar with the mighty visions & learn to summon & be instructed by them, myself." What he wanted was "the light of a gifted intellect fed by the oil of knowledge, to illuminate for me the dark passages of human nature, history, & philosophy."[45]

For much of his life Charles was skeptical of the world and his place in it; and as early as 1826 he wrote Waldo "All this scepticism I want you to write out of me."[46] Charles spent his entire life caught between twin dilemmas rooted in the material world: on the one hand, we can never achieve the goals to which we set ourselves (a condition Waldo thought positive and a basis for his process philosophy in such essays as "Circles"), and on the other, to become mired in worldly things is to lose sight of God (as some thought William had done in going from divinity student to lawyer and land speculator). In a series of undated manuscript notes, Charles addresses the first problem by stating that it was "meant we should be disappointed & dissatisfied with what we do & what we reach; that there should always be a comparison made in the mind between our present condition, & the plan according to which we would have circumstances laid out."[47] As to the temporal/spiritual split, he commented to Mary that "I have still the same appetite to crawl out of *self* & mix with some new, some better consciousness."[48] He also complained to her in a similar vein that "I am afraid of almost everything good on Earth, when I find how fond I am of relying on it, & clinging to it, & lessening my conviction of dependance upon God—lessening, I may use the word, my intimacy with the Divinity."[49]

Charles found himself in a bind: his family wished him to pursue worldly goals—scholarly distinction at college, worldly success as a lawyer—but as he attained these goals he believed himself more and more withdrawn from God. In a defensive gesture, he refused to let himself fully participate in worldly events in the hope that he would not lose sight of divinity. This, of course, brought complaints from those not aware of his dilemma, as is clear in his response to earlier comments from Edward and William, as well as his use of a different litany of explanations:

> You spoke, or Edward did, about my lazy, epicurean system of life— some time since it was. Now I plead guilty only to a certain extent. I have found my constitution a feeble one; & now & then, when I have set vigorously out to study severely hard & accomplished a good deal, I have been reined in short in my course by little inconvenient physical weaknesses which insisted on an easier way of living. . . . If I had confidence in myself—If I believed I was capable of a stoic abstinence from luxuries & sensual pleasures—if I supposed the body would bear what the spirit should address itself to achieve—believe me I would be found no laggard—. . .
>
> I have thought, well, since I am forbid to rise much above mediocrity in my powers & attainments, let me at least be too wise to be pestered with an ineffectual ambition—Let me take the world philosophically; learn all that can be learned without great effort, & husband what strength I may have for the most interesting subjects & the most important occasions.[50]

His "lazy, epicurean system of life" was employed by Charles as a defensive shield. He confessed to William that "I don't think much of myself, nor do I imagine I shall ever be very useful or very happy," and that William "would laugh hard enough if you should see the person who writes thus, in his every day looks & behaviour"; and he called himself "the merriest dog alive." Nevertheless, to Charles it was "precisely this that I am ashamed of—that I am pleased & tickled with straws & rattles, careless of those solemn interests & purposes to which I was born, & which ought if I gave myself rightly to them, to imbue my character with a sober dignity. I study & read *not at all*."[51] Charles's counterproposal was to recognize his limitations and live within them: "I stick moreover to my primitive doctrine, that a man should grow like a tree—& that out of certain limits, he cannot be transplanted."[52]

Charles's world view also brought about a sense of loneliness: because his positions were at odds with his mother's and brothers', he tended to keep them to himself or share them with Mary, to whom, for example, he voiced his concerns in 1831 about the family's history of illness: "For a week or two I thought myself in a consumption—I looked on on through a long narrow passage, & at the end I saw a white couch & a peaceful sleeper."[53] In an extraordinary letter

to Mary, he defines not only humankind's split nature but also its propensity
for self-destruction: "What a fragmentary world it is; you & I & each woman
& each man, have in us parcels of virtues, but gulfs of Deficiency & Will if
there be not mountains of offence. It is not the bird only that lends its own
feather to the arrow that drinks its life blood. Which of us that suffers but feels
indignantly that his own hand struck the blow, or smeared the weapon with
poison?"[54]

This sense of isolation increased as he grew older and the Emerson brothers began to go in different directions: Waldo and William into marriage and
Edward and Bulkeley into mental illness. Because of all the brothers he spent
the most time with Waldo, it was Waldo's seeming loss that concerned him
the most. Charles had earlier written a friend about "the incalculable influence
that an older brother may exert, & does always exert, for good or ill," over the
younger ones.[55] Thus, when Waldo found Ellen, Charles was jealous, though
he covered his feelings with humor, as when he wrote of visiting Concord,
New Hampshire, with Waldo and spent "3 whole days in that big house full of
women . . . while Waldo & the fair Ellen were whispering honied words above
stairs." He thought the lovers "blind" but "I forgive them freely."[56] To Mary he
confessed that the "reward I look forward to all the week, is my talk with Waldo
on Saturday. I love him; altho' his own affections except a universal benevolence seem all called in & centered on Ellen."[57] And in another letter he complained to his brothers about Waldo in a way that raises serious questions about
his own ability to freely give himself to a woman later on: "Waldo is so busy
that I see little of him. I wonder if every body is lost to their brothers & all ties
of blood & sympathy, the moment they are settled & married? I mean not to
murmur at any neglect—not a bit—I mean just what I say—to wonder whether
t'is the invariable effect of business & marriage, to make one independent of, &
therefore indifferent to old relationships & intimacies."[58]

Love itself was a puzzle to Charles. As he confessed to Mary, "Great need
have I of instruction; Love is a teacher but it prompts more questions than it
knows how to answer; fears are in the way, & weakness."[59] Even the communication between lovers concerned him: "It is difficult for two separate intel-
ligences, to commingle thoughts & feelings so as to make their experience
& knowledge & speculation, common stock," he wrote a friend; there are "a
hundred prejudices & a hundred fears to be overcome—a hundred awkward
efforts to be made. And when the work is all done & you have brought your
two minds together & thrown open the folding doors between, what folly
would it be to reduce yourself again to the smaller dimensions of your own
single capacity."[60] Love, then, both prompts questions whose answers might
be uncomfortable as well as leads to the possibility of becoming intellectually
joined with the loved one only to risk separation at some future date. Elizabeth

Hoar was going to be faced with these challenges in the person of Charles Chauncy Emerson.

Elizabeth Sherman Hoar was ten years younger than Charles, having been born on 14 July 1814.[61] Of all the women wooed by the Emerson brothers, she came from the most distinguished stock: her grandfather on her mother's side, Roger Sherman, had signed the Declaration of Independence, and her great-grand-uncle on her father's side had been a president of Harvard College. The Hoar family had settled in Concord by the mid-seventeenth century, and her father, Squire Samuel Hoar, was the leading citizen of the town, a lawyer, judge, and active politician. She was part of a large family, with a sister, Sarah Sherman (1817–1907), and three brothers who lived to maturity, Ebenezer Rockwood (1816–1895), Edward Sherman (1823–1893), and George Frisbie (1826–1904). As a young woman, Elizabeth had been well-educated, and she was fluent in Greek and often tutored others in the language. Indeed, it was through Greek that she first met Waldo: he was a substitute teacher on the subject for her one day in 1821, and she recalled his voice being "as if an angel spoke."[62]

Elizabeth may have first seen Charles in 1830, when he lectured on "The Constitution of Man as Affected by Outward Circumstances" at the Concord Lyceum, followed by a discussion about whether the corpses of convicts and indigents be given to surgeons for "the study of Anatomy," in which Squire Hoar spoke in the affirmative.[63] In addition to the chance to watch her father, Elizabeth may have been present because she served on the social committee. Charles was certainly present when Elizabeth was graduated from the Concord Academy in August.

By the summer of 1832 Charles was in and out of Concord visiting Elizabeth. She represented a bright light in what was often a trying time for Charles, as this letter to a friend shows:

> When a man has been forced to quit his home, & all he was doing or studying to do, & wait, & watch the issue of sickness & debility—when the recovery of health comes to be his business in the world,—he cannot feel careless while the scales are turning. He may be ready for either event, life or death. But either event is interesting, & suspense is painful. Moreover when he has begun to grow well & gain strength,—when earthly hopes rekindle their almost extinguished fires,—he cannot help dreading to slip backwards & wander again in the dark valley whence God seems to have rescued him. I hope I am not afraid to die, but I acknowledge I am afraid to be sick. Yet against this fear, I pray & struggle, & think what a trifle t'is whether the scene be within doors or without.[64]

That August Charles was graduated from Harvard with a Bachelor of Laws degree and began to think about his future employment. Concord, where Squire Hoar had an established law practice, was an obvious choice, especially because Hoar had offered him a position, but Charles demurred.[65] To Ezra Ripley he wrote

> My habits & tastes too are *city*-bred, & I am better calculated I suppose to succeed & be content here than in the country. William, also, will have from time to time occasion to correspond with a Boston lawyer, & we can help each other.—Then if I went to Concord, I should be looking forward to a removal at some future day—whereas now I shall consider myself as settled—or I might be tempted to mix too soon in politics—[66]

But it was also Waldo's future that made it hard for him to commit because Charles wanted to be where Waldo resided: as he wrote Mary, "I wait a little on Waldo's determinations before I decide where to practise law—If he stays in Boston, t'were a pity to dissolve so brave a partnership."[67]

Charles and Elizabeth attended Waldo's final sermon to the Second Church and Society in October; and he later described her, while they attended another sermon of Waldo's, as "fairer than Spring flowers, & droops not with leaves of the Autumn."[68] In the winter, Elizabeth moved to New Haven, Connecticut, for schooling. By January, Charles was jokingly writing a friend that "I shall turn basket-maker or leach gatherer or some such rustic laborer, & live in a shealing[69] on the hills, & look at the heavens by day, & read holy love by night & forswear feverish ambition (which is indeed well nigh purged out of me already) & marry some violet flower amongst village maidens."[70] Maxfield-Miller believes the "violet flower" is Elizabeth, but Charles called Ellen by that name and may have been familiar with her poem "The Violet," which Waldo had copied into one of his notebooks.[71] The confusion of Elizabeth with Ellen was not a good sign.

Charles made numerous trips to Concord in May, June, and July, culminating in the announcement of his engagement to Elizabeth on the weekend of 2–3 August 1833. It is with their engagement, and Squire Hoar's approval of it, that their correspondence begins. Unfortunately, Elizabeth later destroyed her letters to Charles,[72] so we can only see his part of the correspondence, but many of her letters are described in his. Charles spent enough time in Boston over the next few years practicing law and writing to Elizabeth in Concord (or in Boston, when she was attending school there) that we have a satisfactory documentary record of his side of the correspondence. We should expect in Charles's letters confusion and doubt, but Elizabeth seems to have shared these feelings as well. In a rare moment of frankness, Lidian Emerson, who got along famously with Elizabeth, acknowledged that "Her experience of a state of engagement though with no such real cause of suffering—(being quite worthy of Charles) was for the first few months as bitter as mine. And she occasionally suffers still." Lidian continues about herself, but with a depiction that might be applied to Charles and Elizabeth: "If I observe in Mr E. the variations of feeling I constantly observe in myself, I fear I shall be so foolish as to suffer. But I mean to be fore-armed and to set it down in my mind as I do on paper, that to allow myself to turn a speck into a cloud is both folly and ingratitude."[73] The older and more secure Lidian had a good game plan, but, as these letters show, Charles and Elizabeth continually "suffer[ed]" and grappled with "folly"; indeed, one reader of this correspondence has concluded that Charles's letters demonstrate "his own bipolar, manic-depressive swings."[74]

[6–8 *August 1833*]

No, Elizabeth, we cannot repent what we have done.[75] A familiar acquaintance, finished at all points, might have made it seem more easy & natural, but where then had been the beautiful *trust* we now repose in one another? Love is confiding; & doth not make a trade, & ask security beforehand.

You & I will study one another like books in which our fates are writ, & not a syllable of evil import but shall be efaced before t'is is read.

When in College, I had a friend to whom I was wont to boast that he knew more ill of me than any body else in the world—for with him I had used no disguise—. But in this there was more of pride than love. And you shall know no ill of me, if I can help,—your spirit shall prevail against it, as 'the Light dispels the Dark.'[76]

Oh what have you been thinking about me since that sudden goodbye? That I made rude haste to be gone? I could not bear to stay & feel a barrier between us, & look & talk commonplaces, while my thoughts were tossing like a sea.

The kiss I took at parting, Dearest, was it cold? It was the first my lips ever printed on youthful maiden's cheek. Nay you shall suffer no naughty doubt to spin a cobweb in any corner of your heart; I will have it all sunny & brave.

—And now t'is night. I will go court the dewey-feathered sleep, & we may meet in Dreamy-land. What thinkest of those pale counterfeiters, the Dreams? They are an elfin brood, & there's a spice of malice in their very favors. Yet are they sometimes kind. When you are far over the sea, or when you are on the sea, & you lie down in a cribbed berth, & the waves plashing against the ship's side rock you asleep; then is their kingdom. Oh I have had saucy dreams in my lone house at Santa Barbara, Porto Rico;[77] you shall guess about whom.

Wednesday—

The moon is up again, the dewy morn with breath all incense & with cheek all bloom and I bid you good morrow, love. Fair Day is shaking the clouds like wet tresses from her forehead. I will try go patiently to work, & leave wildering myself with hopes & fears of what your father shall decree.[78] 'Be thou my speaker, taintless pleader.'[79]

Evening again—& I can dedicate me to your 'dear idea'—Will you believe, that I insisted both yesterday & today, upon faithfully accomplishing my 20 pages of Reports, besides other Law, & a morceau of Ancient History—Was it not heroic? I should like to know if you have been demurely studying German, & whether you or Rockwood got the lesson best.

But you were spared such a trial of your self possession as beset me in my ride to Boston.[80]

Monday afternoon, I was to have come in the stage, & then could have flung into a corner & wrapt the drapery of my Thoughts about me—but as I left your door I met a sort of cousin of mine, who was in Concord with horse & chaise, & offered me a seat to town—& with him I went, & all the way I was like one with a twofold consciousness—I sustained an interminable conversation about horses, keeping a small detachment of my faculties on the alert to answer when answer I must, while all the rest of me was far enough away from my worthy companion, roaming through bowers of sweet recollections & sweeter hopes.

I feel anxious. I was afraid you would be displeased with the suddenness with which I urged my suit. And now, I fear you think it had been more delicate if I had waited until you knew me better, & if I had sought to engage affection before I claimed it. I acknowledge I was venturously bold—that I had no right to expect to be listened to—I will acknowledge all save that my offence meant disrespect to the woman whom I addressed. No—I saw in you one of too simple & noble a character to desire the adulation of a lingering courtship—Nor was I sure that your affections were not already fixed on another; but even had that been so, I chose to make the proffer & the avowal of mine own; because it was the most sincere & costly compliment I could pay. And you did understand me, & you do understand me, & I wont be anxious a minute more.

Thursday Night—

Now blessings on the head of your dear father—& Oh our Father who didst form these beating hearts,—author of all the happiness that comes to us from out these infinite affections—Thou whose very self art Love, Oh bless thy children—In all our undying Being, let thy favor follow the vows we have plighted![81]

Mary Moody Emerson's response to the engagement was both earthly and spiritual in its tone:

> Her family! Roger Sherman a signer! Her father so good & influential—
> Her mother excellent pious & charitable & sincere. Herself beautifull
> & what is incomparably better *ardent.* I estimate this beyond price of all
> kinds as it's agency on your tendency to nonchalance apathy stupidity or
> whatever name—no matter—I could beat you for not telling me before.
> . . . Yet I would have known of your doubts fears & hopes—ah is there
> more pleasure in the chase than—? (*MMEL,* p. 346)

A few weeks later, Charles's letters to Elizabeth resume:

[*23 August 1833*]

What a shame it is we have to bid good bye almost before we have met—for it takes the thoughts some little time to harness their chariot & get into the high way of communication—& even then we have to turn rein, & ride away. Love gives us property in each other, & we cannot help feeling that—but never mind—I will not fall foolishly to fretting.

If we be molested with little vexations—if the spirit is galled by interference, kindly meant but ill-timed—by words & looks cruelly ajar with what, at the instant is passing in our own mind—the only way is to be still, to forgive,—(for I do not think forgive too bold a word even were it a parent who thus crossed us,) but above all to be careful that we be altered as little as possible from the even tenor of our own thoughts, the tone of our own manners—that we do not suffer ourselves to become slaves to trifles. And in time we shall acquire a quiet dignity which will rebuke & put an end to these encroachments on our individual domestic liberty. The period of transition from pupilage to man—& woman-hood, is for this very reason beset with various small trials. If you do not guess what I am thinking of while I write this, I will tell you one day.

You & I dear Elizabeth are of one mind on this point, that the friends & circumstances amidst which Providence has placed us, ought not,—cannot—educate us, but only enable & assist us to educate ourselves. No thinking being has a right to allow himself to *be educated;* passively that is—"Keep thine own hand upon the helm." Now prithee don't mistrust me for a naughty & irreverent talker. I am not. But there is a higher reverence due to the Teacher within, God in our souls, than to the Father that has brought us up, ay or the mother that bore us.

And you know that I say these things to you as into the ear of mine own Spirit & all they have of presumption will be chastened by your own holy & duteous temper. I am not afraid to trust myself with you without a word more of qualification. Still you shall chide me if I have written amiss—[82]

[25–26? August 1833]

Dearest, has the Sabbath been a peaceful day—or would the thoughts wander, & moods of feeling have their wilful way? Aunt Mary & I have written a deal in times past on the ancient questions of liberty & necessity. T'is a reel in a bottle to exercise the ingenuity of all mankind forever. Did you ever puzzle yourself with doubts how far you were free to have a will of your own—rather did it ever occur to you that what *seemed* your Will was manufactured for you, foisted on you, by trains of agency & events which contain & form the individual, ay, generations & worlds? No good man doubts his own moral responsibility. The Eternal testimony of Conscience is enough on this head and of other liberty, we have as much, yea more than we make safe use of. Who does not feel comforted, whenever he is called to act in things important, by the philosophical,— the Bible-truth, that even if he err there is a Power in the universe counteracting error, & still fetching good out of ill.

> There's a Divinity that *shapes* our ends
> Rough-hew them how we will;[83]

For my part the doctrine of Necessity, so far as I believe in it, is consoling to me—& I am not at all ambitious to have my string of liberty one inch lengthened.

It is a benignant Evening—& wears such a face as if a poor wretch felt desolate, might assure him of an Eye of infinite love bent on him from above.

Are you writing to me now, I wonder. How the castles we build in the air tumble over our heads as we live on. I used to think I would never fall in love till I was a great man & was worth the loving. Like the Knights in the Journeys I would first be victor, & then lay my wreath at the feet of the fairest, the best; & lo you now, here have I knelt to you in my poorness & obscurity, and you have taken me in my russet weeds! Perhaps I may never doff them. Still (as Waldo says) we can somewhere be sure of our bread & shows, & for the rest, like Medea,[84] 'we have *ourselves.*'—I will go dream of you as I did last night.

[29 August 1833]

This very evening I can do nothing but write to you. In the first place, Geo. Emerson has returned—& I have been an hour with him . . . The thought of you Lily, (I have said before, no matter) has made me keenly alive to my own poverty of means, of faculties, of virtues—Tranquil! God knows my mind has been a stranger to calm, however the face & manners may have been smooth. It is natural we should be indifferent to trifles, when a great fear & a great hope is in the Soul. . . .

In the second place—that same letter you have read of Aunt Mary's—Be not offended at it—any of it. If I had time & room here I could paint you out as on canvass her entire state of feeling as she wrote, looking backward, looking forwards, & you would allow & forgive the whole. I don't do it here, because we shall meet so soon.

Again your father & I walked together to the Town. And as we walked we discoursed, and I was put on my good behaviour, as you forewarned me. Yes & I promised him to be very proper & discreet. And I may not wait on my Lily Sabba-days to meeting—aweel.[85] We shall worship together, though the sea were between us. Nothing keeps Prayers apart which they who pray have joined together.

But I covenanted for walks (daily?) together; and agreed the visiting should be chiefly so done. Doth it not please you? So shall we be *free*. . . .

Shall I fill up the little blank here with 'sententious precepts,' with proverbs & preaching? I say then as before—Be sometimes, nay, frequently, alone. Seek always (that is in *the world*) to be serene. With common people talk of *things*—with the wise, of *truths*, seldom very seldom of *Persons*. I will read you what Aunt Mary wrote me when younger, on this head, out of a letter when you come—Write[86]

[1–2 September 1833]

'And all the air a solemn stillness holds': & I sit this blessed morning thoughtful of you, of the Future, of Duty, of God, yet I hardly know how to tell what I think—So weak am I in goodness, so little have I learned Christ—that the Sabbath is necessary to me as a spiritual medicine. Contemplation's wing is 'all too ruffled & sometimes impaired' by the low earth-skimming flight of six days out of the seven. Too often I forget what is real & come to believe in shadows. I am false to my own principles, & am sad and pleased with things that are unworthy that for them I should be sad or pleased. Sunday, if well used, gives me back again, myself. Religion, Devotion put the Soul in tune. Life, everybody finds out, is a contest—not only with all sorts of difficulties, but between the different parts of our nature, & the opposite forces of the Will. And many times we become wholly perplexed, & know not how to adjust the scale of Conduct, one duty seems to clash with another. Then 'if we put ourselves in the attitude of Devotion' (the words as well as thought are Waldo's) if we refer ourselves simply to God, we shall see Truth, & recover peace & balance of mind. . . .

Certainly we shall help & comfort each other, when you come, however brief & broken our intercourse. I look to learn a great deal from you; for the affections are our best teachers. Our very self-constraints & selfdenials, if sweetly taken, will have their charm. It is happiness enough to love, did we want all other. So come, come, & I will try to be very prudent & very good.[87]

20 November [1833]

Sometimes it seems to me as if I had done very wrong ever to ask you to tie your fortunes to those of one who has so little to offer or promise as I. Few people sympathize with me. Almost none love me. Some Sprite blew cold on my cradle, & I carry the atmosphere through my life.

You might have wedded with some favorite of Society, rich with gifts & graces that would have reflected their lustre upon his beautiful wife. He would have loved you, & the dance of life would have been led pleasantly down.

Now to what have I diverted you? To the affection of a poor boy who can only pray for the blessing upon you which he feels himself too poor to bestow—to share the thoughts of a restless mind, the hopes of an unsatisfied heart—to go with him on a sober voyage of discovery on an unfrequented sea, where the storm may overtake our little bark, instead of riding in a convoy of brave ships over smooth waters & with prosperous gales.

You do not know how fearful I sometimes am that there is not in me that which can make you happy. Am I not of too frigid & insulated a temper? You do not tell me so, but it may be you have felt it. Can you love me as I am, trust me for what is to come? Ah if you can, you may set a new light in my firmament, & call up new faculties within my soul.

Goodnight—& I will repeat my constant prayer; May God keep you & cause me to bring you only good![88]

[30 November 1833]

And how does my Beauty, my flower, my queen? Call you me a philosopher, & say you I need no pity because I can bear what befals? Aweel: I know I should think I was wickedly selfish if I desired for you one half the pain it costs me to live without seeing you. What thing is that which is at once the strongest & the weakest of all others? Read me my riddle Lizzie. Why Love it is; which can brave the whole world, yes & conquer, but cannot bear a short absence, & turns pale at its own imaginations. All the way down in stage-coach dull I shut mine eyes—I thought they were mighty useless afairs, for when they were fast closed, still bright before me sat the picture I cared to look at. And that dear music of Thursday eveg was all sung to me again by some dainty Ariel who caught it in the air.[89] Now do not say I am a silly boy; yes, say so and if you will, only let me have the comfort of telling you everything I have a mind to. . . .

I am well satisfied tis a poor plan this living in a world half matter half spirit. They don't mix—they are oil & water—or anything else that is contrarious. I am ashamed that it should be in the power of a few miles of distance, & a few days or hours of time, to come between you & me, heart & heart, that would spring to one another forever, & beyond the touch of this impertinent law of divorce. But I will be patient.[90]

9 December [1833]

I have been so used to disappointment & have lived so much in neighborhood to affliction, that I have almost learned to think prosperity—'honor, love, obedience, troops of friends'[91]—an unnatural & unsafe state, something that was not meant & cannot last. I hold every good tremblingly. I do not doubt God, but distrust myself. I am afraid I do not deserve to be so happy as I feel. The very possession of a jewel it would break our hearts to part with, suggests the thought that it may be required of us, & we can scarce bring ourselves to say Thy Will be done,—without making one condition, keeping one thing back. Yet this is mean & ungrateful & presently comes the faith 'which the clear mind doth raise,' & we know we shall not be left of our Father.

There *is* a Pity sitting in the clouds,
That sees into the bottom of our grief.[92]

Perhaps this sounds cold to you—but it is not coldly written. Never were you more really present to me; I have seen Waldo since I bade you goodnight, but while he sat here, I was thinking of you & of her that is dead.[93]

19 December [1833]

You bid me write you a sermon. Very sleepy & incapable do I feel tonight because of my vigils yesternight in that windy Ilium where we lay.[94] But asleep or awake I am yours, & what you will shall be done, with whatever strength is in me.

And since writing the last line I have been leaning back in my chair, I cannot tell how long: & I shut my eyes, & went down into myself, & thought, thought about you. I could not I suppose if I were to try say it all faithfully & transparently in words. But neither am I sure that I desire to do this. I know my fault; I am too impatient that we should think alike in all things, when it is not possible quite yet. True love will trust even in itself & wait. Who would pick open a bud which he knew would presently be blown?

Ah Me! Why are we not always together? When will God suffer me to be so happy? Then might we live in the light of one another's smile, & by it as by a glass we would dress our daily lives. I cannot dare not at this moment paint all I hope from the future.

The Present, is it not sufficient to us? No—not for enjoyment—but perhaps for improvement. What tho' we meet for a few minutes only of each day & many times then in company. Have we not the consciousness that one heart beats in us two; that every grace which ripens in us is an ornament added to the Friend who is dearer than ourself? Have we not that intelligence quick & sensitive of each other's thoughts & tastes, which tinges with the like hue even our divided hours? Do we not feel each others Presence, while apart, & does it not infuse new sweetness & dignity into every motion, & give a deeper significance to all we learn & do & are? You remember Halbert Glendinning's story—& how the passion of love changed Churl into Gentle, & he scarce comprehended his own metamorphosis, till the White Spirit read him the riddle, "T'is for Mary Avenel."⁹⁵ This influence is on us, Lizzie; let us surrender ourselves to it, & thank God for these Affections that have in them such sweet uses.

When Crito asked Socrates before he died what they his friends should do to please him after his death, he answered, 'Only take care of your own selves, so will you best please me."⁹⁶ And if you, Beauty, would have a sermon from me, it is simply this, Be Mistress of Yourself. With yourself I never will be afraid to trust you: be your own oracle . . . I shall be incredulous & fidget & murmur. The soul that is in you must traverse freely like the magnetic needle, & obey the laws of its own attraction. Whatsoever in manners in study in the conduct of life approves itself to the Judge who sits ever in your dear breast, I joyfully will abide by. But that Judge & none other shall try my cause. To Cæsar I have appealed & before Cæsar I will go.

Now if this is a hard & dark saying, why count it my cloudiness of brain just now that makes me talk *un*sense. But oh love me love me if it were only to see how much worthier a creature you can educate me to become—⁹⁷

12–[13] January [1834]

A long while it is since I talked to thee with my pen: & yet not a long while, for more than once my heart has failed me to furnish & give you what I had begun to write. I do not wonder Lizzie that lads & lasses after they are in love want to be married. I used to think that being engaged was being married; but now I see the difference—There is something unnatural in our being so much separated who desire in all things to live for one another. It is as if the artist were not suffered to look the person in the face, whose portrait he was to paint. I suppose I feel the constraint more than others because so often when I go away from you it is with a painful consciousness of having been thought-bound & tongue-tied, of having misrepresented myself by my own manners all the while I stayed. And I say if I could always be with Lizzie she should not think me frivolous, & formal & frigid.

Sometimes I have been afraid you were bitterly disappointed & believed that I had no soul at all. And then I have trembled at the ache that must have gone through your heart.

And sometimes I have worse fears than this. I doubt whether it is possible for anybody to love very warmly such an one as I—I seem to myself to have done wrong to engage your affections upon an object so unamiable—a spirit so moody & fastidious. But then I pray to God (as I do now) to render me capable of making you happy; & I think it is a prayer which seconded as it ever shall be by the endeavour of my whole life, He will not deny.

If I saw you more continually & freely there would be no need to write these things soberly out. Perhaps you have read me so truly that I can tell you nothing which you have not become acquainted with. Still I am pleased you should know there is nothing I am not ready to confess, that I desire to make a clean shrift.

Monday PM

I do not know that I do right to trouble you with fantastic fears which perhaps are the coinage of a sick brain—nor would I say a syllable about them, except I thought they might serve you as a key to something in me which might else give you pain. What I suffer is really a matter of little interest to me, so it do not touch her whom I love. If the 'wants of your heart' are satisfied, I am happy. If not, oh deal frankly with me, & as I live, you shall not be sorry in the end. I need to be trusted. I need to be loved with a confident, yes a playful & imaginative affection,—& I believe that like Hamlet's lute,[98] if my stops be rightly governed there is much music in me. But t'is almost time for me to see you, so away with the interloping pen.[99]

13 March [1834]

Ah Lizzie I said it was my nature to talk fearlessly & to feel my advantages with common folk but alone,—what am I? Do I not make amends here, for whatever airs I may take on me in Society? And the nearer we come to being alone, the modester we grow; the plainer we see what a little heap of fine wheat is left us, how little pure truth, virtue, love, after all the bran of 'seeming' is sifted out. When I sit by your side, again &

again, springs that wish of Portia's to mind, & I would be a hundred-fold richer "in virtues, beauties, livings, friends;" yes, for you,

'I would be trebled twenty times myself.'[100]

But perhaps you have thought—no you have not thought about it,—but I am aware, I have not used towards you the passionate language natural to lovers. I have not dared to exaggerate any feeling even to myself, much less to you. Surely all that is simple, is sufficient for all that is good. If I should worship you as perfect, I should do us both wrong; you in thus cramping your Idea; & me as not judging myself capable of an affection worthy a progressive creature. It seems to me to make Love poor, to put it in opposition to Religion. It is as a daughter of God that you are dearest to me. I cannot give my whole heart to any sentiment that does not unite itself in the infinite Future. So related, our Friendship is made immortal—this Undine receives a soul[101]—it becomes part of the Divine plan of our being. Oh for this reason I suffer when I see you in a silly company, as tonight; heaven fades away & we are dragged down, being mixed with what is around us. Your very smiles Lizzie lose their charms for me; for I would have them lighted by a glow caught from above; they should be thoughtful & superiour—in sympathy with what is finest in creation.

Since however the world is not all made of porcelain clay, since we must fulfil the offices of neighborhood to little & disagreeable people, it would be queer, a casus omissus[102] in the laws of Providence, if we could not do our duty to others without sacrificing what we owe to ourselves. But we can. We can be reserved & yet not proud, & kind without encouraging too near an approach. We can satisfy to the last every claim whether of blood, or affection, or courtesy, yet still retreat upon ourselves, & measure (we *ought* to do it) with regal scrupulousness the degrees of our familiarity. Nor is this a mere point of fine manners. It is a trait of character. It serves as the glass with which we cover a delicate piece of workmanship to save it from being fingered & soiled by all who pass that way. It is a part of religion—Thus watching over our conversation we may preserve even in the midst of society, that holy composure which is the best offering of Solitude.

But I need not heat myself with writing any longer about this matter since you & I are of the same mind.

Perhaps it was truly told you that I was *ambitious*. I believe I am. For Thee & me, for what is really *us* (à la mode Carlyle) I am so ambitious that I will not promise to be content with anything short of perfect proportion & beauty of life. God forbid I should say this presumptuously: no—to claim to have attained is widely different from claiming the right to seek & to choose.[103]

[6–7 April 1834]

I have great comfort in thinking of you. I look at myself & see much that is weak & wrong, & what is best very imperfect—I see my present ability, how mean it is—my immediate prospects uncertain & uninviting—moreover I see that from my nature it is impossible I should find in me that idolatrous passion which women commonly expect to have *avowed,* & some,—that it should be felt; and I think if you were other than you are, you could neither love me nor be patient with my fortunes. But 'all that is simple is sufficient for all that is good.'[104] There has been nothing strained & nothing disguised (I mean intentionally) in our intercourse, & yet you are not dissatisfied, at least, nor disappointed, in me; & this makes me happy. You have made me not to be afraid to speak the Truth to you; and what more could I say? For I told Waldo yesterday that friendship was then perfect when it permitted us to say all that was true, at all times—and to this he assented. If it seems to me not only safe but pleasant, & I am urged by desire, to impart myself precisely as I am,—& this in each variety of intellectual mood,—to the Soul of my friend, is this not the wedlock of spirit with spirit?

I am well aware that my views of life, & action, & affection, are not in tune with those generally entertained—& so I am likely neither to live, nor act, nor love, after the same plan as my neighbors. Now if I had perceived that this diversity in me made you uncomfortable,—that you would have me wear motley because "motley's the only wear."[105]—that you chose to have your Charles like other Charleses a very proper & pretty & praised person—I should have been sad. But you have chosen for yourself & me the better part. And I understand that I have your consent that I should still postpone present advantage to future good, even tho' I thereby embrace poverty & worldly insignificance & turn my back upon the gold & the advertisement that may be had for the asking. You are willing that to *you* I should speak plain & manly truth—& will not doubt me because, like Cordelia, 'I cannot heave my heart into my mouth,' but love you 'according to my bond.'[106] Deal you openly with me & say if any word I use offends your finest ear.[107]

8–[9] April [1834]

Lizzie if I live to Self, it is not with mine own good will. If you have not the whole property & use of all that which I am, it is not because I hold back any part of me from your disposal. Every form of Deed Spiritual, all conveyances of right, title, interest in all my faculties & affections, I hold myself constantly ready to sign & execute. Nay have I not already signed & executed? But nothing can be given away which is not rightfully owned—and that only is rightfully owned which is derived from God—

goodness & truth: what is weak and mean & vicious, is not mine—it fills the place of other qualities that should be mine, & to its whole extent makes me a stranger in my own house & lessens my property in myself. Who then can wholly give himself to another but he who is wholly his own, that is wholly God's? So I will try day by day to purge out of my present Self whatsoever is evil & comes of evil, & then I can entirely & effectually give myself to you.[108]

11–[13] April [1834]

I am glad Lizzie to see by the letters that you confirm what I said of you & me. Sometimes I wish I was other than I am for your sake; that you had known me younger when the sun of your affection might have wrought upon more plastic clay. Even now, if you will love on,—& not grow impatient of all the demands I make upon myself & you, you may give me a new soul, unseal for me depths of Hope & Joy & Power that lie still unexplored in my nature. Oh sometimes I play teacher—but it is merely in the *forms* of things, the dress of life, words motions manners. Afterward I am sorry that such outward things dwell in my Thought. 'I am out of love, as Prince Hal says, with my greatness'—as a child of God, that is,—for entertaining 'these humble considerations.'[109] Truly, really you must be Teacher, & I, how blest shall I account myself in sitting at your feet to learn—Or if teacher & scholar imply a relation too distant & unequal, heart to heart we will reflect each to the other the sublime laws, the infinite beauty & pathos of Being, & dwell together on the 'bosom of the All'[110]. . . .

My letters I suppose say the same thing each one over & over. Well— how can I help it—Are *we* not from day to day the same thing over & over?[111]

Occasionally Charles dealt with issues other than those concerned with Elizabeth, as in this letter about Waldo:

[28–29 April 1834]

A better day this than its predecessor. I have a better right to think of you & be by you thought of. The Φ. B. K. have asked Waldo to deliver their poem next Anniversary—I have not seen him to know what he says.[112] I forgot to tell you in that brief Sunday (tho' I boasted I had said all) of an explanatory passage of fraternal talk twixt the minister & me. Strange. He thought I 'tolerated' him—no more; my manners said as much; I re-pelled sympathy as if t'was something I did not care for or at least choose to acknowledge—& *he* felt afraid half the time to speak brotherly-wise to me. Strange. I, his pupil, his 'lover this side idolatry as much as any,'[113] who slights other society because it is beggarly in comparison with his: I who have always been afraid to trust him with confessing in word or deed the sum of affection I bore him lest to his unexciteable & retreating temperament it should be an undesirable & awkward consciousness—I 'tolerate' him! I very simply answered that I might often have been un-courteous for that I felt so sure we understood each other that 'manners' seemed superfluous—assured him his company was not 'tolerable' merely but a chief comfort & satisfaction—more, I remember, we said, but it was general criticism of manners & what was pleasant in the fraternal relation & so we bade goodnight & slept on the eclaircissement.[114] But I have behaved better since then, & we are not like to find another snarl in intertwisted threads.[115]

But mostly the correspondence was about their own lives and concerns:

14–[16] May [1834]

I cant think what you mean by 'dark' thoughts about [Elizabeth's friend] Martha Day's dying—Why it is living that is the puzzle—hic labor[116]—It is this state that is *dark*. Once put us out of the gaol limits of the body, & we souls are in our own element, 'we can fly or we can run.' It is all body the very shrinking from death we feel; the old carcase shudders & twitches in the prospect of worms & dissolution. But mind, she laughs, as the duck who takes to water at the chicken who drowns. Sometimes I have difficulty in keeping from a hearty expression of satisfaction at the tidings of the death of persons of no particular merit or close connexion with the go-cart of society. Death is hung with black to scare us away—just as old rags flutter in the cherry trees to keep off the birds. All the real sadness of it is on this side—the goodbyes—these are to untwine the roots of man from what earthly they have clung to—these over, his sail-broad van he spreads & earth is a speck & Eternity his field, hark away.—Goodnight. You don't come see me as you were wont in dreamy-land. Why not?[117]

1 July [1834]

It is rather sad as one grows up to find himself always at a distance from society. The studious ambitious boy is shy of people, & would wait till he could choose his company & his place amongst them. He is sure the time is coming when he shall be fast bound in with his fellow creatures, necessary to them & they likewise to him,—a firm compacted arch—But while he is getting ready to serve society, he is losing the relish for it, & there are ten chances to one against the solitary limb that it will never be well knit to the trunk like those that have always clung &

grown there. I am not sure but the branches that abide in the tree receive more nourishing sap & shoot higher & stronger than they who are impatient to be off set & take root in the ground for themselves. We must dree our weird[118]—Another thing: I believe the Social state, rightly used, is the cure for the over conscious, it reduces the unnaturally high pulse of Egoism.[119]

[*12?–13 July 1834*]

Is it always what is frivolous that is satisfied & gay? Are there always clouds of doubt & melancholy in the heaven of love? Shall we forever distrust ourselves? Sometimes I am afraid to 'consider too curiously' my own state of mind.[120] Are you ever afraid to put certain questions to yourself because you cannot bear to hear the answers & are sure that if the examination can be put off a day, an hour, the pain will be saved, & the questions well & cheerfully answered? A week & I shall see you Lizzie. God keep us both, meanwhile, & always!

> Then on Then on where Duty leads
> Our course be onward still—[121]

[*21 July 1834*]

This afternoon, or by & by I will read law; now I will write to you. Still it is more because I am 'drawn to you' & must think about you, than that I know what I would say to you. Enough there is to say, never doubt that; but it is in the cloud state, & will not rain down in words. Yes I am impatient at finding myself in servitude to any force without or within me that separates my life & thought from yours. When will the cords snap? When I went to bed last night, & thought how it was all to be gone through again & again for an indefinite future, I was weak enough to indulge for an instant a half prayer that the great God would end the strife & take back our spirits unto Himself. Whatever may be beyond death, I seldom rid of the idea that all there is calm, no winds blow, nor storms beat. What think you Lizzie? that I am a pusillanimous soul, too feebly framed for anything manful? That is not true. I am valiant many times where others shake. But there are certain pains that incamp so within the citadel, dividing a man's soul from itself, he does not know how to make head against them, nor from what quarter his help shall come.

Now you will quote Ellen's verses

> Oh woman wise, who saw in us,
> The *appetite* for Pain![122]

Perhaps it is being 'sad for very wantonness,' & I ought to be ashamed of it, & you must tell me if it is, but I owed you the confession as some sort of apology for the fretful things I blurted out last evening. If I could have used my Sunday better, oh if I could have knelt down by your side & prayed for the blessing which we needed,—'Bless us even us oh our Father,' I might have found the peace & strength which would have saved me from my fault, & you from being grieved by it. . . .

Lizzie I would not be selfish. When I think of you as mine, & would see you 'in every part beautiful,' according to my standard of Beauty, & quarrel with the relationship in which you stand towards others, & whatever interferes with my absolute desire, I am checked by more lowly & pious thoughts. God in bringing us together did not dissolve the ties that bind us to others. We entered upon new duties, we were not released from the old. What am I that I should monopolize & absorb your sweet soul from any ministry to which its maker appointed it? No. I will not be selfish—Live you for all those with whom the Divine Providence has connected your lot. But in that Self which must take its form & energy from your own will—where God himself respects the freedom which is his highest gift; in those fine affections to which in the wide universe no right can be asserted save that which you yourself confer,—there, there be my place kept for me![123]

8 August 1834

Dear Lizzie, the harp of Joy is ringing in the morning wind; God has strung it for us, & His breath moves over the chords. You ask if I have been writing to you—yes, a long letter & you might have had it this morning, but it was a sort of experiment, a feeling of my way amongst mine own thoughts, & the mists were there, & I said Lizzie shall thread the tangled grounds when the mists have overblown.—You would know how the Lizzie I love is different from the Idea of which I was enamoured. If I don't tell you, what then? Do you think it will be because I have been disappointed? no, but because the two cannot stand side by side, & challenge judgment, as the goddesses before the young shepherd on Ida.[124] Before you promised to be mine, Love with me was a Blessed Araby, a spice-country, lying away like a white cloud in my horizon.[125] I eyed it, "wishing my foot were even with my eye."[126] Friends I had had, & my friendship for [Joseph] Lyman had been a passion. But that was all unease & effort, 'the embrace of a cloud,' & contained in itself the worm which ate out its heart. It had revealed me, however, to myself; & I said, if the pseudo-Psyche was so fair,[127] who can paint the true or how can I be happy while I have not found her?

Thenceforward all things prophesied to me concerning my future

Bride. Whatever was beautiful in form & motion, whatever was fine in manners, whatever was boundless in affection, pointed at her. Ellen was the Spirit of Annunciation, & brought distincter tidings of the sky-born for whom my soul waited—Still I had no finished idea, no model-wife. It would have been unpleasing to me to have laid line & compass to my imaginations, & produced one of those pictures, which should always be portraits & not fancy pieces.

I saw you Lizzie, & there was that in your eye & voice & maiden wit, which printed your fair image on my heart. Away I went, & came & went again, & yet the image was there. It was in my dreams by night & my dreams by day. I scarcely knew you—but I grew familiar with 'Portia's counterfeit'[128] & would not acknowledge to myself how slight the acquaintance was between us, nor the thousand chances there were that I was hugging a delusion. I could bear it no longer, I chose to trust myself to you.—

This then was my first homage to woman. It was an unexplored world, this intimate relation of lover to lover. I had been bold, & now came the reaction, & I was a coward. I cannot tell you what I felt & feared for awhile—It seemed as if this was a crisis in the fortunes of my life, & not only so, but it changed the very nature in me. I thought I owed more than my whole self could pay. Fear almost overcame love.

Your simple & noble character restored my faith in my own affections, & brought back the sweet hopes which should ever give tone to the intercourse of the betrothed.

Ah the real is better than the ideal. I believe you have made me better & wiser than I was—If not the fault is mine. You have shown me a sincerer truth, & a higher beauty than I had foreseen. You have enlarged my idea, chastened it; oh then complete it. I am sure you can.[129]

16 August [1834]

Dying, you fear dying. I say with Socrates, I know nothing about it, how can I fear it? When I am well, it seldom occurs to me, & then merely as a phenomenon in the course of nature, a sun set. When I am sick, nothing can be frightful which promises to deliver me from the mean estate in which I am. But, to speak more generously, the necessity of the event reconciles one to it. And·then a brave spirit quarrels so often with life, that death by way of contrast, comes to have beauty in our eyes. Most persons, when they die, seem to me to be kindly removed. I have no more disposition to be sad than at the falling of the rain, or the melting of snow. Sometimes, indeed a darker Providence appals us. The young & the strong, the pillars of hope, & centres of affection, are snatched away. Sometimes we lay in the tomb the Ellens. What then? Is death more terrible? Not to me. We ever hold a sort of balance between Life & Death, & as a jewel is thrown into one scale, the other swings lighter. But I remember when I felt as you say you feel I found it in my thoughts, & prayed against the fear of it. Now I let it alone.[130]

[3–4 September 1834]

Lizzie, the thought of living to be ever negligent of your happiness;—to grieve you,—years hence, after we shall long have lain in one another's bosom,—with the selfishness or ill-temper that have sinned against those around me since consciousness began, this thought, has real terror in it. Better, oh a thousand fold better to die,—& say the last farewell in the unstained morning of love & honor; to part before unkindness has ever, for a moment, come between thee & me. Is it not sad to have to anticipate, that with the lot of human imperfection on our heads, we shall sometimes offend, one against the other? But if sin abounds (I thank my Bible for the word) love shall much more abound; & high above the weeds that cling to the slimy bottom of our life, shall flow the great sea, heaven-fed, of faith & affection. Goodnight. Will you not come to me in my dreams?[131]

14 September [1834]

Waldo urges the doctrine heretofore broached of '*having no choice*'; of standing by & letting God decide for you. I doubted at first whether the rule would bear the weight of the whole that is in man & carry him cleanly & swiftly (for this too is to be cared for) through the great & little questions of duty which each busy day accumulates. Yet why not? It is the simplest of principles—It is no more than acting ever from the impression which *all* the *facts* make on us—It is studying to live unconsciously as far as possible. We are to go forward with freedom until we feel ourselves checked. This check we are never to contend with, when it is right for us to act it will be removed. Is the rule liable to abuse, what rule is not? We suppose the mind to keep faith with its oracle, & always to distinguish (as the sincere mind *can* always?) between the voice of self & God. The beauty of the principle is the courage it will inspire, the harmony & cheerfulness to which it will compose this bustling life of ours. We shall all wear La Fayette's smile. Good men & women are now tormented with the contrariness of what they believe they ought to do with what is natural for them to do—They are living to other peoples' consciences, as Dr. [Benjamin] Franklin said about the Eyes.[132] The grave injunctions of the New Testament, 'Deny yourself'—'Bear thy yoke' 'Take my cross upon you'[133]—will still & eternally apply to the strife between the lower nature & the higher, flesh & the Soul—They have been obeyed, when we have come to have *no choice*.

I write these things to you Lizzie, the rather because you could not be persuaded to hear to my phenomenal philosophy, & this may yield the like fruits of calm independence, without the trail of the selfish worm indifferency. Act from yourself then, not because it is more dignified, but because it is a necessity. Yea, wo unto me if I do not so act. There is no other law by which my whole being can be governed—and if I suffer myself to be haled before lesser tribunals, to whose jurisdiction I am not subject, I have compromised along with my dear freedom, the perfect service I owe to God.[134]

21–[22] September [1834]

Another 'warm calm day'—& what a show blue & golden make the fields! I have been out under the cope of heaven, thinking, praying. And now I sit writing until Aunt Mary comes from her chamber to hear me read. Lizzie I do not like to think of you as another person, but as part of myself. Sometimes it is not pleasant to write for this reason—It breaks the charm, & you & I become straitway two creatures, & not one. For this reason too I don't like the long separations; they reduce us to say things, instead of having them *understood* between us, by mere influence.

Aunt Mary & Waldo & I have been measuring over again the old grounds of religious speculation. Why could not you be at our Symposium. The lady in the beginning mourns at the latitude we allow to our faith—& will have it that the faith is naught. But presently as she or we persist & from words pierce to things, we have shot the gulf that divided us, & are guiding our course by the same pole-star, or are moored by the same rock. Carlyle she finds fault with for his storm-garment of words, the which is woven by his Thought not enough simple. And you & I are agreed that the more 'inspiration' the less of the 'individual'—The greatest man, says S. Reed, reveals the simplest truths. Shakspeare has no 'manner'—& we love the New Testament & go home to it for its sincereness 'merum vinum,'[135] at times when all human styles offend us. The inspired is God speaking through man's lips—The witty, the philosophical, is man asking questions of God & with more or less faithfulness conducting the examination & reciting the answers. All true & good is revelation—But ordinarily we look through a prism, which varies the proportions of things & their colours—It helps us to an achromatic telescope.

It is now 10 o clock. We have been sitting talking these two hours—& I have laughed more than for a long long time, & more than you would have chosen to see me,—because more than I think became me at the close of a day that should be given to "calm thoughts regular as infants' breath."[136] No I do not feel satisfied with myself tonight. The day has been selfindulgent. But if I were to enter on my shrift, t'would be a heavy story, & I should but grieve you with a burden that is mine alone. You shall have part in all but my sins:—I am afraid you think I give you little encouragement even to rebuke these—because the only fault you ever spoke to me about is scarcely at all amended. Yet I will try, Lizzie; & sometimes I accuse myself of miserable vanity & weakness that I suffer you to acknowledge defects of character, & I dare not be as honest & tell all the evil I know of myself. But trust me, Lizzie, I shall count it the dearest instance of true love when you shall be my 'other conscience' & put your finger bravely on the faults you see, ah how many![137]

1–[2] October [1834]

I fear I grow imbecile, so long have I been musing over those two first words, (no, not them, but the thought for which they stand) & no progress made. I begin to feel as if I were anticipated in everything I would say, because you know me altogether. And yet to look about & lay hold on the 'not me' for matter, I am sure you would think naughty. I do not remember that in any loves that ever I read of in Poetry or romances or the lives of true men & women, it was related that the passion wrought a weariness of self—a sense so keen of deficiency as to drive one to sad doubts whether his happiness must not fall away from him, nay, whether even now it were his, for the want of a nature large enough to contain it. Ah how does love, even this human, open the door into the infinite! How fast we learn of one another. I cannot easily distinguish the idea that is born in me from that which I received of you. So we repeat one another & think it is ourself. All things tend to oneness said the philosopher. You & I are one sayeth the lover. There are not three parties—you, I, & the Universe—but we twain one party, & the universe the other—Do you think this is a mere night-fame; no for you are of the same faith when the fit is on you.

Thursday.

I went to bed last night by the time I had written myself gloriously awake & now it is vain to seek for the visions that have withdrawn into the "interlunar cave"[138]—

What I think most about & desire chiefly to say is, that you must study to keep well. You will not let me talk about headaches & ills physical when I see you, & when I come away I feel sorry that I did not learn more, & afraid lest you may lay up some evil in your constitution. Sweet, do not so. I cannot see it to be wise to let a great malady or a small go untended—& so suffer the beautiful & knowledge-hiving days of youth to be defrauded of their right. I know I would not. Better tell your father you would like to see Dr. [James] Jackson for ten minutes, & the reason why.

You read very little you say; is that because it is your will to read little—then it is well, because the mind is its own best measure, as to the excitement it needs. But if you feel a hunger to read & study which you fail to satisfy, it is not well. Do not cease to stipulate for yourself, if possible, that you shall have some hours that shall be your own—wholly,—despotically. And now forgive me for touching at these points along the low shore of Circumstances, & consider we have a mixed being, & must be faithful in small things, if we would be masters of the wide diverging consequence. . . .

For me Lizzie, how am I a-weary of philosophy, & find a world of odds between that & religion. The one is a laborious effort against the senses—a raised & refined view of life which we are capable of so long as we are calm & strong, but from which we fall down so soon as the mind is distracted or tired out & the grasp of its faculties is relaxed. Religion is itself a life—it is the regenerate soul, not estranging itself from what is about it, but welcoming it all, the very meanest relations to the material, its bondage to pains & weakness,—& piercing through the dusky rind of things into the divine love that is their centre & cause; and this too as naturally & easily as if it were its genius & native to it. Ah pray for us that we may give ourselves to God with the confiding affection of children—that the strife in us may be stilled forever. . . .

The perfect philosophy is one with Religion, no doubt. But we need a revealed will of God to bring us to this perfect philosophy—I mean that the frame of our philosophy must be religious, & reared reverently on the basis of revelation, because if we start aside, & construct a human philosophy & seek to approach by that way to religion, it is a work too high for us—thence comes confusion, inward dissension, often despair or else a downward course to sensualism, scepticism.[139]

10 November [1834]

I can do & think of nothing with peace of mind until I shall hear from you that you have wholly forgiven me for suffering those frightful doubts to make head in your affectionate Soul. My brain swum, & my faculties were afaint, last night. I knew not what to say; know not, what I said. It stunned me—to hear that thrown into question what I believed was long ago forever determined between us two. It seemed to 'ravel out my weaved up' being—.[140] Have we not thought, wished, enjoyed, sorrowed, loved, prayed for & with each other? Have I not waked every morning to the consciousness of our mutual vows, & day by day lived to the hope of making you worthily happy? Ah, if I have too ambitiously aspired, if I have quarelled with low fortunes, unfinished character & manners—if I have too impatiently pushed aside any compromise with inferior degrees of virtue & beauty—pardon me,—it was not a selfish dream,—you were in all my thoughts. It was your bower I sought to dress with laurels & myrtles.

But I have done wrong. I have been too proud & fretful. Yes, it was selfish for me to postpone & sacrifice to my ideal, a loving contentment with the actual, the present. I am punished, I am ashamed. I have vexed your heart with needless fears, & strewed thorns in your quiet path. My fastidious tastes, & 'too curious' speculations, & unsatisfied temper, have made you sad & afraid. God forgive me, if I have been wanting to your true affection. Before Him, I love, & give myself to you. I will be more humble, more faithful henceforward. You shall never terrify me again with the question you asked last night.

Lizzie, there is much more in my heart to say, but I forbear now—I do not wish you should seek to justify me or blame yourself. Let me, let me charge myself with having offended—only do you restore to me your confidence; and consider my infirmity of temperament,—how that by nature I am slow jealous in the expression of deep passion,—cannot suddenly utter or measure my own emotion. And I dare not promise I shall never forget to be patient & manly in bearing. My eye unhappily quick to discern the wrong, & over excited consciousness may betray me into irritability. You must wait for me to grow wise.

And now if you truly forgive & love me, accuse not yourself, but kneel down & pray to God that He will keep us both encompassed by the arms of His love, & that by the influence of this infinite Spirit, our human affections may be raised & tranquillized.—. . .

I think you have hardly been to see Aunt Mary. Well, you are right; she certainly behaved herself not very prettily Sunday night. But she is one of the persons to whom I can forgive almost everything, a sort of Cassandra-Pythoness.[141] The God rushes, & She speaks.[142]

21 November [1834]

Lizzie, do you care to hear from me when the tides of life run so sluggish in me? I think when I am 'Heart up,' I should like to be at your side that you might joy of the bright beams that are shot through my soul—and again when I fall asleep,—& the earth beneath is iron, & the heavens above are brass, I would be near you, that the nightmare might be chased away at your touch. Yet think not I am sad. I am too coarsely moulded for that delicate sadness which consumes & yet is beautiful. No; mine is pure dulness, dyspepsia materialism—a primrose is to me a primrose & 'it is nothing more' in these moods.[143] But I still urge the plough along the furrow—read, talk, believe, if possible, & pray,—& hope hope on. I have got deep in Hubbard, Morton, & the early history of Plymouth & New England.[144] History from Charles I downward is true modern history & may have uses in the way of parallelism, precedents, & analogous reasoning.[145] Before that time, it is like all study, liberalizing—making wise the mind, & giving a general clearness, justness & force to one's perceptions & opinions—excellent as light & air, elements of growth intellectual—but not to be served up to practic. application in its organized body. The Puritans, what an Orion in the world's sky they were & are evermore.[146] That they should have reproduced at that distant time an age & a race so apostolic—simple as the babes whom Jesus blessed, & sublime as John & Paul in their pious magnanimity, does it not cheer us—affirming the inextinguishable principle of Faith in man & how God waits for us in our long cold aphelion, & draws us at last to Himself—You must read one of these days, yes I will read to you, about Roger Williams;[147] & how many more.[148]

21 December 1834

In this world, mundus sensibilis,[149] is not the trouble, the divorce twixt the Thought & the Act? So that our Thought pines because of obstruction, & our act becomes ridiculous wanting life? For power we have prayer; & for action we have forms.—I look at the curled moon when her maiden cresset is newhung in heaven, & I 'bless the firmament unawares' & I would call all the stars by name, & the lore of the astronomers is precious in my eyes, & nothing stands between me & the science, (the mind being thus in the very blossom of this fruit) but mechanical means of sight or instruction. These are not at hand, or if they were, the vision & the beauty & the desire pass away or ever the cold material laws be in any part learned.

While I study I forget that to which I study. Yet all things good are placed just beyond the reach of our hands. Affection prompts us to effort, & effort absorbs the soul & we forget on the road the question we undertook the journey to get answered.

Performance is wide of wish. But performance, in the true world, should be one & simultaneous with wish. The shadow should keep company with the object—but here the things exist independently & unimaged, & by & by walk forth the shadows, Phantasmagoria, ghostlike.—

Thus I consider that most of what is publicly done by men,—their social festivities, their scientific & commercial enterprises, their political enactments, their religious worship, their written books, yea their speech, their very courtesies & salutations,—is the representative of opinion & emotion which truly is ours, but which may chance to have given place to a mood of mind very different, at the time we have chosen for its Epiphany.

All is true, absolutely, while it may happen to be false relatively. A man grieves & rejoices, doth alms & denieth them, loves his neighbor, & says 'Thou Fool,' celebrates weddings & funerals,—all, by turns, in the bottom of his soul. But when he draws on his white gloves or waits on the bridal party, he may be in tune to talk of graves & epitaphs or to go alone on the sad sea beach. And so the life & hope in him may mount highest in a season of sables. Church-time may be his play-going hour; & in the interlude of the Merry Wives of Windsor he may lift up his most earnest prayer.[150]

Still the Balance Wheel of Association helps to steady & compensate the irregularities. And through the influence of this, & the exertion of our own *will*, we shall find the Act to average tolerably near to Thought. The present life is not an optimism. It is a dissected map. All the pieces of the picture are here, but not in right place. Nor is it allowed us to alter at will their position—but we are to educate our eyes to put them on their feet even where they stand on their heads—We are to be content to fight against the false,—but the true misplaced, we are to bear with, to conform unto. Doth not manhood begin with Renunciation? Is there not a sacrifice here to be offered in & of every being which hath life—Well, if it be a self sacrifice!

Sometimes, oftener as we grow up into the nearer light & society of God, a blessed correspondence will reign between thought & act. Duty will be one with love. Marriage is the most expressive type of perfectness & joy.

Now be an honest girl & tell me whether you are not tired of this dwarf metaphysics, & would not much rather have me write in a kindlier strain. I don't know that I should send it but that it seems to me there are corollaries of quite every-day value to be drawn from this doctrine of the divorce between Things & their exponents, Thought & the correlative act. You will say it is like those valuable inferences which we have before now known 'the reader to be advised to draw'—But I assure thee, Beauty, I have myself found benefit in the waters I commend to your drinking. Besides you rather invited a didactic & homiletic letter.

I shall hear from you Tuesday—There were living words darling in the midst of your confession of "so sluggish a soul"—and you "can't guess what it was made for"? Did not the wise Virgins slumber until the Bridegroom came? It was for Him their lamps were filled. Fear you not but in the Universe your portion of activity shall be allotted you. They also serve who only stand & wait.

What if here our sole office be to love & be loved? Is it not enough for which to live & thank God?[151]

29 January [1835]

A beautiful day & so it must sympathise with you—"For Beauty is Beauty in every degree."[152] I have been in a dream since Sunday. I do not know the reason. The whole universe, yes I myself, have been to me phenomenal. Underneath & within there must act the centripetal force of love & faith, else sure I were dissolved & floated over the backside of the world to the Limbo where whatsoever loses itself is found.

Your father proposed to me to come to Concord & go into his Office & succeed to such business as might be left with me or accrue to me in right of the place. He simply proposed, would not advise, not being able to pronounce on the expediency of my so doing. He thought I might at the first make no more than a livelihood for my single self. I suppose he was careful to speak in terms the least flattering.

To go implies the being married & sitting down in Concord at least a few years. To me not the most agreeable plan of life because not what I desire for you.—It moreover in some sort hurts one's pride of independence,—but this may be put out of the question as silly, since the place would be to be occupied by somebody, & whoever takes it will be mainly indebted for his success to his own industry & ability.

Until I shall be married the sacrifice of personal comfort & social intercourse will be great. Because we shall be hindered from each other in a way more irksome than that of absolute separation. If I believed otherwise, & that our rights in one another would be respected—that we could study together—& have the order of our lives intimately associated—then Concord were all a Temptation.

But on the other hand, Professionally, it may & is likely to be of much service to me—giving me that which most I want, Practice—And if I have enough to do, & can dispose of the time left from my business in serene study, why the sacrifices will be compensated, & we shall be living to the future.

To go to New York would be to bid a long goodbye to New England & that neither you nor I should like to do. To stay waiting in Boston is easiest, but may prove mighty wearisome—there are always chances of change & good establishment here, but it is *only* chance, immediately— & to be ground for calculation one must embrace several years.

I hate to annoy you with spreading out these paltry temporal considerations which I am balancing in my mind. They always disgust me. I wonder God made them necessary to his creatures. Ought I to be ashamed of them?

Nay I do but tell the thing over to you because I would have you know exactly on what data I decide, however the decision go.

I think my phenomenal condition of mind is owing to a disordered body for today I've a headache quite rare for me—But don't be afraid—I'm strong & well—it is simply some 'eccentricity' in the system.

I wont write anything better at the end of this cold debate. Only I will ask God to bless you & promise to love you.[153]

16 February [1835]

All yesterday was full of you, but I resisted & would not write till today. Sometimes I like to coquette with my own will & impulses.—I seek continually the unchangeable; The living from hand to mouth, the getting up in the morning without any knowledge where one shall sup or sleep in the evening, might I should think have charms for a venturous nature—But the shifting & trimming the sails of our bark to the breeze as it blows now from the quarter of one principle, & now of another—the uncertainty of motives & springs of action—this is undesirable enough, & scarcely better than polytheism. I call myself Christian, & acknowledge one God. Yet Christianity is only my faith by eminence—that which in my best moments I hold to—for were the religion to be gathered from the plurality of the thoughts, I am afraid the altar would be found inscribed "to an unknown God." Power is rival with Patience. I am caught by the low ambition to accomplish my own ends, yea to have ends of my own, instead of dedicating myself, unreservedly, to filial submission. The world as it is constituted lays snares for our virtue. We would be content that Divine Law should be our Master, Disposer; but we do not choose to be puppets wire-twitched by the showmen official & unofficial in Society. And our choice seems to lie betwixt governing & being governed. So like Artevelde I choose to be of that small class Self-moved.[154] But I would erect no rebel Principality, & uncrown my God, my King. Nay more; & feel sad & ashamed all the time I am separate, in spirit, from the Infinite Spirit. I come back after my little successes, & selfassertion, & the thought of it is mortification, & the prospect of other such, disgustful. While I am alone the feeling remains: and when I am again in contact with men & women, the temptation to overtop them on their own ground,—the vanity that runs after others' opinions, & comes from a higher standard to a lower for want of support round-about,—these for a season prevail, until Indignation again chafes & contrition weeps at the backsliding.

I therefore am penetrated with the truth that we need to have Strength ministered in aid of ours which is weakness. I am sick of false independence; pretension abroad must be made up for by confession at home: of this too I am sick. Will God help me to work in the right spirit—claiming nothing, because having received all—& yielding nothing, where principles are involved, because nothing is mine to concede. There is an Art of life, Lizzie,—I said it was a simple thing to live well, yes, it is living ill that is so double faced & perplexing.

I desire in that I do to respect the Higher Will. I desire to stand by & let truth & justice & love act for me, in me. Ah if the soul were competent to keep the height!

Washington St. [Boston] Evening.

Thus you see how poor a possession I am like to be to you. I should be dishonest not to hold the light so that you may see the imagery on the walls of the house into which I have besought you to enter. Yet I have no perverse satisfaction in exhibiting defects & vices. As I am ambitious for you on my account, so am I for myself on yours. As I would have the woman I love, matchless, so would I go to her a complete man. That one should think of himself, at all, is a sign of wrong either within or without. Let us hope we may sometime deserve of God to be so fitly employed that there shall be left in the soul no faculty to prowl in these desart places of reflection.

I ought to say that to you & to me, at this time different duties are assigned. I need to beware that I do not set my will in opposition to God's will; you, that you do not decline accomplishing God's will concerning yourself, out of compliance with any human will.

Dear Lizzie are you wondering, quousque tandem?[155] Well my metaphysics are spent, I trust. Your letter did me good many ways & many times. You chose to read me backwards, for I mourned that I should not have any art to draw letters from you after we lived within seeing distance. As to inhibiting the pen, God forbid. Writing is a purgation of our thoughts that we need. I hope you will find in yourself the motion towards it. . . .

Will you pray for me tonight, Love, & hope well of me notwithstanding all the evil I am constrained to testify of myself?[156]

21 March [1835]

Here are the Sybilline leaves,[157] I think they may as well follow the great company of their brothers & sisters & die gloriously by fire—I only spared them out of the feeling which leads one to save an old almanack, supposing he may possibly like to refer back to some memoranda that now are indifferent to him. You may come to the conclusion that it would have been wiser for me to have executed my own sentence on the MSS. & not have wasted your time.[158]

If you please however you may keep from the flames the Porto Rico fragments, since they are my sole record of that piece of my biography. I will not make more words about the withered leaves, except to say they are of all dates back to the Spring of 1829.[159]

Let us come to the living Now. Yesterday is naught but as it fashions To Day; & today (to you & me at least whose estate is still in reversion) today is great only from its power over the future. If we were perfect creatures, liable to no mildew nor blight from the bad influence of what is without us, we could laugh at Time, yea set our foot on his bald pate. Were the All Fair constantly present to the mind—Did this Idea wholly possess & encompass us—circumstances would be indifferent. And even while we are far short of such excellency of nature, or triumph of principle; even while we walk in the valley of the shadow of human troubles & excitements, we may yet defy circumstances to bend & deform us to their crooked will—We may say to them as Hamlet to his persecuting companions—"S'death you may anger me, but you shall not play upon me."[160]—When this is attained, if not happy, we are safe; we have passed out of childhood into manhood—But until this, our portion is insecurity, anxiety. And therefore I exhort you & myself to make fast the doors of the Soul against the entry of these robber circumstances—that we guard our tempers, judgments, & manners from assimilating to what is in our neighborhood but which does not approve itself to the clear eye of our mind.

You like to have me write my homilies, but I cannot help being afraid you will think I am like an old woman in her dotage who repeats over & over & over the same story, till the very walls of the room are weary. Forgive me, Lizzie, my monotonous fears & preaching.[161]

[23 August 1835]

"Do you love me Charles?"—What shall satisfy you?—For though you say that you do not ask because you doubt, yet I know you could not ask if you were sure without a cloud in the heaven of your assurance. It always frightens me to have the question put; it grieves me, as if I wanted that which should inspire trust, & there where I have given my all, were still a stranger. God forgive me,—it is my sins that stand between me & the happiness of them who are more humble & kind. When I shall be good you will cease to question of my love for you.

Is it because I confessed aforetime that Love in me was anxious & stayed not at the 'is' but looked to the 'shall be' the perfect accomplishments & beauty? I beseech you to believe that I have not postponed love to some indefinite future—I am not like the miser that lives in poverty while he hoards gold which by & by he will enjoy—You are at this hour more to me than all the world beside—I did not think it needed that I should say it.

Lizzie I know I am capable of love & God helping me you shall not be disappointed in the Affection to which you trust. My chief wish to live is that I may make good my vows to you. If the duties of every day are suffered to estrange me in a manner from your side, it is that I may the sooner be able to claim you wholly for mine—If the interference with your freedom, & needless & ignorant offences against your happiness move me to speech too hasty & sharp—if the constant sense of hindrance & bonds cast its shade over my thoughts to you ward,—it is my infirmity, but do not therefore doubt my truth. I struggle to use a philosophy that I have not yet fully acquired. Do not mistake my ill-worn disguise of indifferency to trifles, for coldness & hollowness at heart.

I have two lives—outward & inward—The Thought & Love of you belongs to the inward, & it is not yet permitted me to make the outward correspond to it & fully express it—If I am worthy ever to do this, God will bring it to pass. Until then have patience with me knowing that I also suffer.[162]

[21–23 December 1835]

I remember your farewell, that was looked, not spoken, as I turned to shut the parlor door last night;—it was half reproachful; it was before my eyes all the way as I plodded home through the dark, & was sadder to me than sad face of the heavens or the earth. There was a cloud over our evening which I wanted energy & heart to scatter. You must never let me stagnate in such humors, but walk strait up to the foul fiend & say 'Aroint ye.'[163] Who does not love to have his moodiness charmed away,—& yet if we are not sick we ought to be sunshiny, or in the softest summer shadow, ever. Perfect love casteth out fear, & the least as well as greater suppressions & concealments; But do we not sometimes keep back a question, or a confession, that is pressing to the lips, & which when it is sent down again into the breast, lies like a lump, or pricks like a thorn? I despise myself for being afraid; you must cure me of fear, & tread it under foot yourself. . . .

The days run by with their large or small account into the eternal irrevocable past. Tell me what they have chronicled of you, Love, since we parted.—How little we learn in the world: how our opportunities seeming-great melt & dwindle & shrink when they come to be expressed in the advantage realized. Is it not a sponge from which we wring a drop of water? Because we are so seldom free to make the best use of what is in our hands or under our eyes. We have a wheel to tend, a thread to spin, a trust, albeit minute, to discharge—& sufficient to each day is its own evil & its own burden, & the grand panorama revolves scarce noticed.[164] Each of us bends over his task—the making or fitting of a pin's head, it may be, & that is all we have faculties to attend to. I was thinking last night how many people I daily saw—how much they knew which I should like to know—yet how almost certain I was to learn nothing from them because of adhering to my track in the conversation, instead of seasonably crossing over into theirs. I am apt to deliver my message, & occupy so the time in which I ought to be listening to another of Truth's servitors. It is a vice, yet I am so fixed in it by nature, I hardly hope to over come it. Then Society, when I think of the gems that ever & anon sparkle from underneath the disguises men & women wear—when I retreat on myself, & compare what is in the breast with what my neighbors exhibit in their shop windows, I feel as if the fault was terrible some where, that our social relations are no better tilled & yield no more wealthy returns of knowledge & love. What think you?

Yet t'is better, of this I am sure, to adhere too closely to one's self, than to depend servilely or weakly on others. T'is the manlier though it be the less pleasant & seeming amiable part.[165]

When Charles moved into Bush, Waldo and Lidian's Concord home, in September 1835, he was "made part of the family" until his death eight months later. His high opinion of Lidian soon increased; for example, he discovered that he "rejoiced" in her sense of taste, especially interior design, because it "agreed with his own."[166] Lidian found in Elizabeth a "darling" whom "I can hardly keep from starting up and kissing as she talks." She considered them "born sisters," and her answer to Elizabeth's "communication of her thoughts feelings—experiences—is;—'You speak as from my own heart. How true that is. I have passed through all that.'" She, too, found in Charles "both head and right hand" in "all matters of taste," and declared him "as full of wit as sense."[167]

By January, Charles could write a friend that "We mean to enlarge the house this spring & I know not what the summer may bring forth."[168] In her life of her mother, Ellen Emerson reports that wedding plans were set for September and by April carpenters began to build "a room & dressing-room over a new parlour" for the bridle couple. Elizabeth's piano was to be placed there, but as she was measuring the room for it, she suddenly cried "It is of no use. It *never* will be!" Lidian, who herself had had visions of Waldo prior to their marriage, was later "impressed" by this as "real prophecy."[169]

4 March 1836

If you had gone away while your mother was in Boston, I might honestly have written that I was lonesome without you; that my day wanted its finish, & my draught of life its sweetness & its sparkle. But I confess to you that I am so unlover like a lover, that it is pleasanter to me to think of you where you are, than to see and talk to you, under the cold atmosphere of observation. I have said so much before; I repeat it because I love to have the truth spoken out, & in all intercourse with my Friend I breathe freer when I feel that we are dislodged from all false grounds. I begin to believe that the love of Truth is the realest & best part of me. The moment that the suppression of the thoughts & formal behaviour take the place of openness & genuineness, love goes away, & ice makes round my heart. If we can dare always to speak the truth to one another, then we shall always continue to be lovers. Love is a flower that never fades while it is breathed on by Truth.

I sometimes am fearful that you are impatient of my perpetual criticism, & count it unloving. No Lizzie, it is born of love. We have our Ideal,—that style of 'perfection' to which our individual self may be conformed.[170]

6–[7] March [1836]

Mrs Farrar whom Waldo saw yesterday at Cambridge is going to Europe in August[171] & wants to have Miss M[argaret]. Fuller cared for spiritually & wants I believe that you should give Miss F. an invitation to come & make you a visit in Concord so as to draw that lady within the potent circle of the enchantments of Criticism & the First Philosophy.[172]

14 March 1836

Your letter which I had yesterday told of the external world simply; now I do not hold it in such high respect as to be contented to have you fill three pages in the style of a faithful Reporter, without you season your account of what is done & said, very highly, with the aromaticks of your own infusions. It is not what this & that man say in public or private that I would know from you—except as they are fingers that play on the keys of that sweet instrument to whose least sound I am all ear. It makes me feel dull & unloved if you merely hold the pen as Scribe. I gave you leave to be the Æsthetic, but that is quite another thing from annalist or secretary. See with your own eyes, hear with your own ears, let loose your own winged fancy—'draw the world up into yourself'—was not this the charge? Enter into what is Beautiful, & possess it; into what is grand & over top it. Do not look at men & women to advise me of their estate, but of the influence they rain upon you.[173]

29 March [1836]

I am more & more of the mind that it is high time you & I were joined together not again to be put asunder. I think it frets me to live without you. My theory or rather theories of life are floating & changeful. The Gods however who filled the box of my brain with all sorts of tastes & caprices loaded it at the bottom with cold leaden prudence that has prevailed, & may yet, to steady the creature & make him a thriving earth-worm in spite of the sallies of transcendentalism. Once in a while I think I shall presently throw up the Law, & step aside into some unambitious occupation that may just furnish bread, & leave one his leisure vacant of claims & so capable of improvement to chosen ends. But I am not disposed to act very energetically in the matter, certainly not wilfully, for I should count it a weakness. Trust God; yes trust the Spirit who unasked awoke you into being, from whom you cannot separate, who has bound up your particular in his own infinite existence, & through whose influence your every thought & affection is prompted & determined,—poor nursling. Trust Him. Every man walks in a vain show, & the wise man will not be nice as to the figure he makes. So we can but trust God & thank God, we may feel that we are approved of God, & thus in harmony with the divine & majestic universe whereinto we have been invited, every day, will it not be to us a Festival?

Is it not a sunny thought that we live necessarily in God? Does it not often chill & deject us, that loving one another we cannot mix with one another, be no more two, but one,—Soul passing into Soul? This union we have with God; all of Him that we know & love, is already, even with the wish, part of ourself. And all spirits partake of one another as they partake of God. Lizzie, does not this thought help us to love God & to love each other?[174]

By mid-April it was clear that Charles's health had taken a turn for the worse. Waldo postponed a lecture series at Salem in order to help Charles travel to New York because he was too "feeble" to make the journey by himself (*L*, 2:10–11). Three days into their trip, when they arrived at Springfield, Massachusetts, Charles wrote Elizabeth on the 24th about how he was:

How have we borne our journey unto this point, is written, when I say that with manifold aches & exhaustion that seemed almost intolerable both yesterday & the day before, still, here we are, & quite visibly improved. It was a rough medicine, but by far the best. I mend every way. I drink none of the opiate, & yet sleep pretty quietly through the night; there is a dawning red in the cheek, & some motions towards an appetite where an appetite should be. But I am as weak as an infant, & some days more travelling & a heartier diet must furnish strength.[175]

At the same time, when Waldo wrote William to bring him up to date, he confessed that he had "never told" him about the present journey, and that "Charles has been withered by a four or five weeks cold & racked by a cough." Waldo was "uneasy" and decided that they should visit William. Although a Boston doctor had failed to find anything "the matter with Charles but a catarrh[176] & the bad effects of confinement & loss of appetite," Waldo is concerned that his "constitution has no power of resistance & therefore shut him up & starve him & he withers like a flower in the frost" (L, 2:13–14).

The brothers arrived in New York (where Ruth Haskins Emerson was also staying) on the evening of the 26th, and Waldo returned to Salem the next day to continue lecturing. That day, Charles wrote Elizabeth "I have been very much tired by the journey, but I am, I think, a great deal better, than when it was begun." He intended "to enjoy the luxury of rest for a few days before I travel farther South," probably intending to visit Phildelphia or Richmond, Virginia. He found the air "much milder than Boston air," but, ominously, added: "I am sitting writing to you in a room where there has been no fire for (I know not how many days,) & yet I am very comfortably warm."[177]

On the 28th, William reported to Waldo that "Charles passed a comfortable night without opium, & with less coughing than the night previous. . . . He walked to the Parade Ground yesterday afternoon (between ¼ & ½ a mile) & enjoyed the air without suffering by the exercise." But despite William's entreaties, Charles would not "consent to see a physician."[178] On the 30th, William told Waldo that the "cough was so bad yesterday morning that Charles said it seemed to him that he could not stand another turn so bad, & he was sore all day in consequence; but the drops [prescribed by a local doctor] had so good an effect, that he is much easier today."[179]

To Elizabeth, Charles wrote on 2 May that by "night I do not cough, but raise without coughing, & easily." Harkening back to his earlier concerns, he added "I have often said I have believed I could die courageously, but to be sick I have no strength."[180] But by the 5th, he was much worse, as he warned Elizabeth:

> I have almost lost the use of my hands & feet it seems to me, so feeble am I—& what is strange that when I am confessedly growing better I should be only more & more conscious how weak I am.[181] If this be health I'll none of it. Instruct Waldo to come armed with the tenderness of them who deal with infants. . . .
>
> I cannot think—I am all the time in condition of mind of one just falling asleep—Even so dimly & & by fragments, things swim thro' my brain.
>
> You must pray for me who am too weak to pray for myself—God will hear you I am sure—for you cannot pray for that which is not agreeable to eternal Good.[182]

On 7 May, William alerted Waldo that "Charles grows rapidly more feeble. Mother & Susan & I have now given up all hope." He had written to Elizabeth's mother, "but I distrust myself, & want you to judge whether to send the letter or not, & therefore inclose it unsealed." And he concluded: "Come alone or with Elizabeth, but come soon."[183] The next day, Charles wrote his last letter to Elizabeth:

William says he has furbished up this pen for me—& I have all day been wishing to write a word to you if it were no more. Mother has done what she could to watch my breath, by night, & feed me with jellies & nutricious food by day. And now on Tuesday I expect to move again; it is with pleasure but not without fear that I await the starting. I am still so very weak, helpless, & this shortness of breathing (which however is to disappear with journeying) gives me so much pain.

I went to ride this A.M. on what is called the Bloomendale Road—saw the Houstonia, Saxifrage, & I think Gnaphalium in full bloom. Forest trees are clothed with leaves. Are these things so with you?

As to where I am going I hardly know—Dr Perkins [of New York] said better go to Philadelphia, & thence into the interior of the State & after come back through Virginia. In such case I might go see Rockwood.

But I grow tired. Be a good girl. Love your poor Charles.

I have gained a scruple of flesh since leaving Concord.

A kind lady sends me beautiful flowers—a leaf of spikenard I will inclose to you which crushed will breathe its perfume—[184]

Waldo was prepared to set out for New York on the 9th, but postponed his departure until the next day so that Elizabeth could join him. Also on the 9th, William wrote Lidian that "Charles is no worse than he was several days ago, & there is a seeming, possibly a real improvement yesterday & today upon his condition the two days before; his feet are not so much swollen, his spirits & his voice are a little better, & perhaps, he has strength enough to journey by easy stages." He suggested that if this optimistic prognosis held true, then Waldo set out with him for the south immediately.[185] The next day, though, he described the worst possible news to Lidian:

New York, 10 May, 1836.

My dear Sister,

Our worst forbodings are realized and sooner, much sooner than any of us expected. Charles is no more with us. He went out to ride yesterday afternoon with mother, as usual since he has been here, enjoyed the ride, & ascended the door steps on his return without assistance; then sat down on the entry stair, & never rose again. His departure was probably free from pain. Farewell, my brother!

Mother is much distressed, but calm & self-possessed. We have been expecting Waldo all the morning, & now that he does not come, we are dreading that Elizabeth will come with him tomorrow.

I wrote you yesterday, from my office & within two hours after my letter was sent, I returned home, too late.

Affectionately Your brother
Wᵐ Emerson.

Mother sends her love to you.—You will tell Mrs Hoar & Grand-father.[186]

Elizabeth and Waldo arrived to find Charles already dead. Elizabeth stayed with his body and, as Waldo wrote Lidian, "is soothed by the repose of his face" (*L*, 2:19). The funeral was held on the 11th and Charles's remains were held in a New York church. Waldo announced to Lidian that Ruth Haskins Emerson would return with him and Elizabeth (who "is well and the strength & truth of her character appears under this bitter calamity"); as for himself, Waldo wrote "I can never bring you back my noble friend who was my ornament my wisdom & my pride" (*L*, 2:19–20). Elizabeth Palmer Peabody, a friend of the Emersons, was in Concord when Lidian received this letter, and when Lidian showed it to her, she exclaimed "It was a wonderful letter for the idea it gave of a friendship—[Waldo] feels his life *wrecked* completely. . . . He seemed to think he was annihilated now. . . . It [the letter] was a wild heap of beautiful ruins. . . . Broken melodies—beautiful even in ruins seemed his shattered soul." Of even greater concern were reports Peabody had from friends who had attended the funeral with Waldo. Lidian's brother reported that Waldo "bears his grief . . . like a philosopher—calm, even smiling" (a description at which Peabody "ab-solutely *shuddered*"). A ministerial friend "stood at the grave with Waldo" and when the latter "turned away from it—compressed nature found its way *in a laugh*—and an ejaculation 'dear boy.'" Waldo's comment to her friend was "When one has never had but little society—and *all that society* is taken away—what is there worth living for?"[187] Waldo himself entered into his journal: "My brother, my friend, my ornament, my joy & pride has fallen by the wayside, or rather has risen out of this dust. . . . Miserable is my own prospect from whom my friend is taken." Waldo forecasted that "Now commences a new & gloomy epoch of my life." "Who can ever supply his place to me?" he asked, and then responded with this sad reply: "None" (*JMN*, 5:150–152). Writing to Thomas Carlyle a few months later, Waldo confessed the source and the depth of his gloom: "we made but one man together."[188]

Waldo was approached by Charles's friends to collect his writings and pub-lish them with a memoir, but as he continued to research the book, he dis-covered that Charles's journal showed "a nocturnal side which his diurnal as-pects never suggested,—they are melancholy, penitential, self accusing; I read them with no pleasure" (*JMN*, 5:152). Even Mary Moody Emerson, who was re-reading Charles's letters to her, commented "Singular how often he recurs to his death—& welcoming it—yet I never looked to it" (*MMEL*, p. 381). These thoughts, written a few days after Charles's death, remained with Waldo as he continued to read in Charles's manuscripts. His early belief that he did not think his brother "left any bulk of papers . . . fit to publish" was not shaken over the next year as he continued to mull over this project (*L*, 2:31). When Elizabeth allowed him to read Charles's letters to her, Waldo found them to contain "much truth & beauty," but they were "all tinged with that melancholy which seems to have haunted his closet whilst it quite disappeared in society" (*L*, 2:59). The project was abandoned.[189]

Upon returning to Concord after Charles's funeral, Elizabeth moved into Bush for week. Her mother wrote Mary Moody Emerson that "Elis. was 'composed & thinks every thing has happened in mercy & love to him'" (*MMEL*, p. 370). Lidian commented that her "demeanour in the endurance of this unspeakable affliction—is touchingly beautiful—I regard her spirit and conduct with nothing less than reverence"; nevertheless, Lidian saw that there were "times when her heart dies within her and she is overwhelmed with the sense of her desolation." And Lidian described Elizabeth's sense of being with Charles—in the past, present, and future—that would, over the years allow her to become a member of the Emerson family: "She loves to hear and to talk of Charles—feels that she is still highly privileged in having had—in still having—the precious gift of his love—sets before herself the aim of becoming all that would make her most worthy of that love—as distinctly as though he was yet on earth to watch her progress."[190] The family invited her to stay on at Bush: "We try to persuade her that she had better come & live with us the alternate months," Waldo wrote Mary, "for at home with all their virtues, they do not understand her or leave her Peace" (*L*, 2:154). And although Elizabeth did live at the Hoar residence, she continued to be a frequent visitor to Bush.

Elizabeth evolved into a devoted sister to Waldo and Lidian, and the beloved "Aunt Lizzie" to their children; even the erratic Aunt Mary wrote her that "I hope you will always think 'Charles left me to you.'"[191] Ruth Haskins Emerson cherished her, and after her death (at which Elizabeth held her in her arms as she passed away) she left Susan Emerson, Lidian, and Elizabeth "whom I look upon as my daughters ten dollars each to buy a ring or other ornaments."[192] Elizabeth never married and wore black for Charles for most of her life. Nathaniel Hawthorne, who was an occasional neighbor, commented that she seemed "more at home among spirits than among fleshly bodies."[193] In some ways, she was dutifully living the role of the devoted eldest daughter, the one who did not marry and stayed home to take care of the family. In her case, there were two families: the Hoars and the Emersons. Elizabeth continued in the role of the grieving widow, and in the words of at least one visitor to the Emerson household, who called Elizabeth a "sister-in-law" wearing "widow's weeds, living upon the sweet memory of Charles," she "was treated with something like worship in the family," and Waldo said of her "'Angels must do as they will,' and she certainly carried with her a heavenly presence."[194] Margaret Fuller keenly appraised the situation: writing in her journal during a visit at Bush, she described how Elizabeth was "happy because her love was snatched away for a life long separation, & thus she can know none but ideal love."[195] Even on her deathbed in 1868, she was able to describe the now-sainted Charles in this fashion to Ellen Emerson: "I have never seen anyone like him—never have seen any elegance, any form of grace, that could approach his, so that I could once say, 'That is like your Uncle Charles.'" Ellen reported how Elizabeth "said more of the same kind," leaving Ellen with the impression that "his beauty and manners were a creation allowed to dazzle mortal eyes just once, and never would be repeated."[196]

All the family gained from Elizabeth's presence. Lidian found a confidante and her children a fond aunt. But Waldo gained not only a friend who was sympathetic with him philosophically and emotionally but someone who was useful as well as an amanuensis for his publications. By 1841 he would write "I have no friend whom I would more wish to be immortal than she" (*JMN*, 8:105). He wrote a poem about her ("So perfect in her action one would say, / She condescended if she added speech").[197] At her death in 1868, Elizabeth left equal amounts to her family members as well as to Waldo, his three children, and William's children. Later, in about 1880, Waldo gave Rockwood Hoar a manuscript notebook in which he had copied out the best of his comments about Elizabeth from his own journals.[198] The poet Ellery Channing, who had lived in Concord for many years, commented that Elizabeth had "got more from [Waldo] than anybody" else had.[199] And Maxfield-Miller makes this final, interesting speculation: "Yet who is to say that a marriage between Elizabeth and Charles would have been a happy one, with such dark psychic shadows hanging over it?" She continues: "Who is to say that the abiding love and brother-sister companionship between Elizabeth and Waldo for forty-two years after the death of Charles was not the real love story and a more rewarding relationship?"[200]

Chapter 6

William and Waldo
Finances and Family

$\mathcal{A}$fter Charles Chauncy Emerson's death, Waldo and William Emerson settled into an easy and familiar relationship, the type that is typical of brothers who care for each other and who have gone through rough times together. There were other family members who needed care and assistance: Bulkeley was boarded out for the rest of his life and there were expenses associated with that; Ruth Haskins Emerson stayed with Waldo's family from the mid-1830s onwards, visiting with William's family in New York at regular intervals; and Mary Moody Emerson needed a great deal of help to extricate herself from a bad real estate deal. On a more positive note, there were visits the two families exchanged, and the road from Concord to New York was well traveled. But, as the years progressed, money became a major theme of the brothers' correspondence, both in terms of William's helping Waldo to arrange for lectures in New York and Waldo's assisting (actually, bailing out) William with his real estate speculations on Staten Island.

The correspondence between Waldo and William, which spans nearly fifty years, discusses their professions, their families, where they lived and their houses there, and, most of all, their finances.[1] To be sure, most of the correspondence has a chatty demeanor to it, similar to that between any two brothers, but a significant portion of the letters deal with their respective finances,[2] mainly because Waldo had become the family banker as early as the 1820s.

To many people, used to associating Waldo with philosophical speculation and an idealist's lack of concern for the problems of daily existence, the portrait of a man who was not only competent but also genuinely proficient with money comes as a surprise. This should not be so: Waldo, from an early age, was keenly aware of the importance of money and the need to manage it.

When Waldo's father died in 1811, the family was left in poor financial straits, as they went from the comfortable existence associated with a prominent and sociable Boston Unitarian minister to running a boarding house to make ends meet. For a period after William Emerson's death the family was kept on at the parsonage through the good will of the congregation. Waldo and his brothers went to Harvard as a beneficiary of the Pen (or Peen) Legacy, a charity administered by the First Church, where their father had preached.[3] All four brothers taught schools in order to secure needed income for the family. They were not rich people. To be sure, the Emersons managed their finances well enough to send four children to Harvard, and three of the four brothers went to Europe (Charles traveled only as far as the Caribbean). But these early hard times instilled in Waldo a type of "depression mentality," a memory of the bad times when money was scarce, that followed him through life, so that even in the best of financial times, he remembered the past and promised himself never to be in such a precarious fiscal position again. But these concerns over his own money never stopped him from assisting others with their expenses.

Waldo initially became the family banker for the same reason that he assumed the role of the family breadwinner: he fell into it. His father was dead and his mother, even if she were so inclined, was subject to her own lack of financial skills and the gender restrictions of the time. When the eldest son of the family abdicated the traditional role of being the first to attain gainful employment, it fell upon Waldo to take up the slack. Unlike William, who needed to read for the law before practicing and earning money from it, Waldo was guaranteed a good income from, first, supply preaching, and then a regular salary from the Second Church, which helped provide for all the Emersons, including Waldo's bride, Ellen Louisa Tucker.

Waldo formally assumed the role of family banker when William went to Europe, being the eldest of the three brothers left at home. William's desire to account for the expenses of his travels is evident in many letters, especially the one of 1 April 1824 from Göttingen quoted earlier.[4] When Waldo discovered that his mother's inheritance could be invested in the Lafayette Hotel with a good annual dividend, he decided to quit school teaching and pursue a ministerial career, which meant a potentially significant decrease in the family's income. As Edward wrote William on 1 November 1824, "Waldo shuts the shop of education in Jan. next . . . & enter[s] a year or more forward if possible at Cambridge"; still, Edward's own school "brings about 700. & we shall get along by hook & crook & by taking up $1,000 on [Ruth Emerson's] estate wh. Uncle R[alph]. H[askins]. will do for us."[5] William responded to Edward and Waldo on 10 January, exclaiming about the

bold plan which looks forward 2 or 3 years without any certain means of bread. But I am sure I wish it success. And I rejoice that you are rushing to jail in such good spirits. . . . Had I dreamed of such a revolution when at home, I should as soon have gone to Greenland as to Göttingen. But as it is, I am ever inclined to fall into the same humour myself, and though I can conceive of nothing but future deprivation to pay for it, to run myself in debt for a look at the Coliseum.[6]

William's letter of the 18th crossed Waldo's, which gave further explanation of their financial state:

You are I doubt not suitably shocked at the innovations & rumors of innovations which by this time have thunderstruck you. . . . I have cast my bread on the waters, locked up my school, and affect the scholar at home. . . . But ambitious hopes have been engendered by the real or supposed increase of value of the old property on Maine Street. A great hotel has been builded thereon whose cost it is hoped the Carver St land will pay—and thereafter $200 pr. annum shd. come to every thirteenth, with a reasonable prospect of more.[7] In hour of need this can be easily mortgaged for $1000. Moreover if I go to Cambridge at the end of the present vacation, as I shall, the learned & reverend have consented to admit me to the Middle Class of which measure whatever may be the moral & general expediency, the pecuniary is apparent. Next I possess in fee simple $518 at interest. Lastly Edward retains his private school of 7, or $800, though the uneasy child whispers pretty loudly of slipping his neck from the ancient noose in August. When I have added that in April we shall probably migrate in a flock to Cambridge & occupy Mr Mellen's old house for $100 or 200, you will have all the data whereon our calculations proceed. (L, 1:158–159)

Ellen's death on 8 February 1831 ushered in a new personal and financial era for Waldo. His grief at losing her was real, but he frankly acknowledged the compensatory nature of the aftermath of her death, "as it seems that Ellen is to continue to benefit her husband whenever hereafter the estate shall be settled," adding, "I please myself that Ellen's work of mercy is not done on earth, but she shall continue to help Edward & B[ulkeley]. & Charles" (L, 1:232).[8] Soon after Ellen's death, when William informed his brother of incurring some debts, Waldo replied "I do not know what I am worth." He noted, "Ellen's estate remains wholly unsettled," but ventured that Pliny Cutler, the executor of Ellen's father's estate, "was favorable to my claims" (L, 1:327).[9] This led to a long period of litigation involved in the settling of Ellen's estate after which Waldo was finally installed as the family's banker: he had the ability to keep up with everyone's finances and—most important—he had the money, even though for many years he was unsure of what he would receive when the suit was finally resolved.

Waldo was initially optimistic about a quick settlement of Ellen's estate because he was on good terms with most of her relatives. Ellen's half-brother, Edward Kent, had been a classmate at Harvard, and he got along with her mother, Margaret Tucker Kent, and Margaret's husband, William Austin Kent. Although Ellen's sister Margaret Tucker was also a friend, the other sister, Pauline Tucker Nash, and her husband fought for a larger share of the estate, which was primarily derived from the estate of their father, Bezaleel Tucker.

By 26 March 1832, Waldo was "sadly" reporting overhearing rumors that "Mr E. had refused all compromise with his wifes friends & was gone to law with them." At the time, he was trying to get the Massachusetts Supreme Court to distribute the estate, using John Ashmun as his lawyer, and he had kept the Kents and Margaret Tucker aware of all developments (*L*, 1:349). Margaret Tucker died 24 November 1832 and Margaret Tucker Kent died 28 February 1833, further complicating matters, but both had apparently willed any claims they had to the estate to Waldo.

In April 1833, Ashmun argued the case before the Massachusetts Supreme Court. Waldo was in Europe at this time, but he received a report in Italy from Charles:

> A week ago last Friday Mr. Ashmun argued your case. . . . He was very ill, & very brief [in fact, he died a few days later[10]]—Still, I think (as he thought) the case was one which on our side could be little helped by argument—part of it was too plain & part too minute & unconnected in its points to allow of much more than a simple & forcible statement. Washburn was tediously long[11]—I should judge that there was not the least doubt as to the principal claim being decided in your favor—i.e. the claim on the share of Personal Estate bequeathed to Ellen in "the rest & residue" after the 1/3 had been given to Mrs Kent. As to the direction which will be given to the 1/3 in which Mrs K. had her life-interest I think there is considerable uncertainty. There were six different points presented for the decision of the court, & this makes it possible that they may reserve the case & postpone delivering an opinion until next Law Term—or in plain language, till next March. But we hope not. Saturday next, several opinions are to be pronounced, & we trust our case will be amongst those then decided.—[12]

Unfortunately, Waldo's case was not one that the Court decided upon, and it was not until the following June that partial closure was reached, when the Court decided in Waldo's favor, granting him Ellen's two-thirds of the estate willed by her father to his three daughters. Charles again described the proceedings, writing to Waldo in Paris:

I have just come out of the Court House, where Judge Shaw gave the opinion in the case of Emerson vs. Cutler & al. All the points raised in the argument were decided in your favor, excepting that which related to the claim upon the 1/3 given to the children after Mrs [Margaret Tucker] K[ent].'s decease. This at least the pres. estate was held to be given only to the children surviving at the time of Mrs K.'s death, & therefore you have no claim to it. I don't know how many thousand dollars the award will finally be worth. Perhaps you know better than I; probably somewhere between twenty & thirty thousand. So you may travel as long as you will.[13]

By the end of January 1834 he was allowed to draw against the estate to pay some of his more troublesome debts. As Charles reported to William,

Mr Cutler—on Waldo's applying to him, representing the inconvenient & unreasonable delay of the settlement of his claim on the Tucker Estate, & the fact that he was indebted to considerable amount—that Mr. C. probably could feel no insecurity in furnishing him with what funds he required from time to time & taking his acquittance for the same to be deducted from the amount finally to be pd. over—paid Waldo yesterday $200, & agreed (so at least W. understands) to pay his debt to Barnard Adams & Co. unless the whole business shall *very speedily* be settled & also to advance to him what monies he stand in need of. If this be so Waldo will be able to pay whatever expense mother shall incur above her income, & so thanking you for your assumpsit in this behalf, he thinks it unlikely you will be held to it.[14]

The Court made its final decree in March 1834 and the stocks and monies valued at $11,600 were given to Waldo in May, with a second installment to be made later. Charles's description to William of the final disbursement is detailed:

Waldo has received from Pliny Cutler Esq. under an order of Court 67 shares in the stock of the City Bank; 19 shares in Atlantick Bank—31 shares in Bost. & Rox[bury]. Mill Dam (these last worth say the assessments)—& a balance of cash of between 3 & 4 000.—I hope he will be able to pay his debts & invest $3000. Well $11 600.—on this he is to subsist on the interest of it—for he gets but little income now from any other quarter. The other ½ of Ellen's property (for reasons too long here to be fully set out) remains at present undivided & in Mr. Cutler's hand. Now the interest of this 11 600., will scarce support both

Mother & Waldo at the rate they live at—Therefore for the present we seem pretty nearly as poor as ever only Waldo does without a Profession. They board for $12. per week at Newton & have the right to make their number 3 when they choose. I tell you these facts that you may judge for yourself as to bearing part of Mother's expenses. Waldo has paid for R. B[ulkeley]. E[merson] this year wholly.[15]

Waldo hoped his share of the estate would bring him $1,200 annually in interest (*L*, 1:413), and, until the final settlement, he also received up to $500 a year from Cutler from the part of the estate still in his hands. As Charles suggested, Waldo was bringing in little money on his own, William was not on a sound financial footing, Bulkeley's expenses needed to be paid, and the difference between their mother's income from the Lafayette Hotel and expenses was $225 annually.[16] When the estate was finally settled in July 1837, Waldo received $11,674.49 (*L*, 2:87), all in stocks. The total value of Ellen's estate, then, was $23,274.49.

Waldo, William, and Charles together were involved in the brothers' attempt to save Mary Moody Emerson from a long-term imbroglio involving a real estate transaction of hers.[17] In 1805, Robert Haskins, Ruth Haskins Emerson's brother, had bought a farm of 165 acres in South Waterford, Maine. After he went into debt, his brother bought the mortgage and allowed him to remain as a tenant. In 1811, Mary purchased the mortgage and continued the practice, hoping for a return on her income, desiring a place to live (although she traveled elsewhere more than she resided there), and wishing to do a good deed for Haskins (whom she also helped by keeping their arrangement secret, leaving the locals to believe *she* was the tenant on *his* farm).

During a visit in 1832, when Charles researched the deed to her property, he discovered she in fact owned it and he turned down a generous offer to purchase the land because Haskins had overstated his investment in the place. As he did all this without Mary's knowledge, she was understandably upset. Two years later Charles participated with William in a gesture that was more favorably received: they established an annuity for her that paid ninety dollars a year.

Waldo and William were also involved—albeit at a distance—in the sale of her farm in 1848 for $1,450 (which included paying off a mortgage to Waldo of $325). The work frustrated them: the editor of her letters commented that Mary's "admitted ignorance about legal questions results in confused syntax and an impatience with details concerning mortgages and rents, leases, bonds, claims, deeds, quitclaims, interest, and notes"; moreover, in "her blithe inattention to details, she made casual purchases of additional parcels of land over the years which she gave away, with equal insouciance, while signing documents she did not read or understand or bother to record."[18] Equally frustrating were the many versions of a will she left at her death on 1 May 1863 at the age of 88.[19]

Despite these frustrations, all the family helped her: she stayed in Concord until a dispute there in 1836 with Charles and with Waldo's family drove her to resolve never again to stay with them (though she did board with others in town), and she often visited William's family. Her influence on Charles was profound and Waldo utilized her private writings in his own published works; but William, after leaving the ministry, responded to her letters that were fraught with religious inquiry only on secular terms, as can be seen from this example in 1853:

> Indeed, if you & I were to converse on those old subjects of interest, the church, the state, the present & the future, inspiration, miracles, & various other topics within the range of your reading, I should be obliged to confess to a gradual estrangement from the free consideration of many of them, and a sort of indifferentism as to some. The whirl of affairs, be they petty or important, in which the inhabitant of a great community gets involved, generates, I think, a kind of callosity to matters of sentiment, and leaves one hardly sensible to any interests out of the sphere of business, except those of family and near kindred. Still, if I should ever be blessed with a period of leisure, which I hardly anticipate, I know not but old enthusiasms might be reawakened, and new ones, still better, kindled, that might possess the soul with a new life and energy. Let me hope for such a consummation.[20]

For her part, in looking forward to a visit to him, she wrote that she never recalled William's "kindness without recalling your patience with my partial attentions to the younger brothers and the impatience with w'h I became engrossed by the share I took in family concerns & education. A recluse needs the candor of those for whom she is heartily concerned as the cares & sympathies are new in that form. But if we meet, as I hope, every affection will be purified and every enigma solved."[21] And it was William who visited her when she moved to New York (on one trip he "found her very quiet & even gentle, & extremely forgetful. To use her own expression 'My capacity is gone.'"[22]) and he assisted in sending Mary's body back to Concord for burial.[23]

The brothers' correspondence gained intensity after Edward's death in 1834, when he was found to have accumulated debts. William complained to Waldo on 4 January 1835: "I feel the claim of Edw's creditors to be next to my own—but not on a level with them. Therefore, thanking you for the information you give me concerning them, & pleased to find they do not exceed $500, I shall not now offer to aid you in paying them. My own exceed $1500, & if I can shake them off, I will then see what is the next best thing I can do."[24]

Similarly, after Charles's death in 1836, financial matters again play a significant role in the brothers' correspondence, especially because Waldo was the executor of the estate (Charles died intestate). At first, as Waldo wrote William on 15–17 May, the news was good: "He owes mother nearly $100. Aunt Mary [Moody Emerson], $100. In our current account I am his debtor—Barnard, Adams, & Co owe him I suppose $308.71 with interest. Weston, he said owed him say $25. He has a good many books, some valuable ones, and the organ"; in addition, Waldo believed Charles had "very few debts of any amount" (*L*, 2:22). The brothers split the $28.29 in legal costs to probate the will (with Waldo absorbing the odd cent). When Waldo recorded the estate with the court in August, he listed $1,187.58 in assets and $950.75 owed to creditors.[25] Two more letters from Waldo continue the discussion of finances:

> As to the subject whereof I promised to write the removal of the remains of C. I find Mother desires not that they should come here, but to Boston, to the Haskins' tomb. If they were to be bro't, I should wish them here, but I have now no tomb, nor can I at present have one. None is to buy; I must build; and that I cannot do, now, for the expense—$80.00. I think therefore that it will be best that you should procure some safe interment in such place that, in another year, I can if we are so minded, carry mother's wishes into effect. How is it? Can a place of safe deposit be procured in which there will be no mixture or confusion? Whatever you do, will be done of course at the expense of his estate.[26] (*L*, 2:39)

➺ *Ralph Waldo Emerson to William Emerson, 23 October 1836*

We are sorry to hear that Susan is again a sufferer or threatened to be so—glad of Willie's [William's son, born 18 June 1835] health & that the worst omen you have is his perfect temperament. I wish you may always have the same affliction. Lidian is still a prisoner to her chamber & to hope, and is better than when you heard from us last. Mother is very well. Bulkeley is still at Charlestown: he had become so well that he was promised he should go home soon, & the expectation excited him too much. . . .

   . . . I sent a letter to Rev Dr Palfrey containing $80.00;[27] i. e. $50. loaned to Edward in 1826 & $30.00 interest for ten years, accompanied with thankful & affectionate acknowledgments of the family for this kindness, & stating the reason, in general, why it had been so long delayed. Dr Palfrey has returned the money in a kind letter saying that it would not be honest in him to receive it as not being agreeable to the contract made with Edward. It was to be paid after he should be successful at the bar, &c. I will keep his letter for your inspection.

The secretary of the Φ B. K. has written me to demand payment of Edwards note to the Soc. & interest; the amount $136. to be paid 1 January. The appraisers of Charles's property have returned their inventory. Its amount is $886.00 reckoning the organ $300. & including his deposit with B. A. & Co $357. of which $100. is Aunt Mary's & $75.00 is Mothers. I shall keep an account of all for your examination. The organ is not sold & thus far my best agent in dealing with it is Mr T. W. Haskins. . . .

Do you wish to know how my account stands. I am sorry to find that the charge on account of R B[ulkeley] E[merson] is so large.

> Aug 4 pd R. B. E's bill at M'Lean Asylum to 1 July $28.29—½ the same 14.14
> Sept 20 pd Balance of R B E's debt to Mr [Joseph] Putnam 9.50—½—4.75
> Oct 11 Pd R. B. E.'s bill at M Lean Asylum to 1, Oct. 41.40—½——20.70
> Oct 1   Int. due on Note of $800. 24.

For time use your own convenience. I am ashamed to present so large a bill. (L, 2:41–43)

Waldo received the balance of Ellen's estate, $11,674.49, in July 1837, comprised of shares in the City, Atlantic, and Massachusetts Banks in Boston. He had lent over two thousand dollars to William, and the interest on this also augmented his income (L, 2:87). Although William was Waldo's debtor, the two combined their resources to take care of their mother and Bulkeley, who was variously institutionalized and boarded out for his entire adult life, and these expenses too were shared by both brothers, even though they were miles apart.[28]

When William had moved to New York in the fall of 1826 it was an act of starting his life over. He stayed in a small room above the office in which he was reading law; he also seemed to still be suffering from the physical and mental effects of his choice, for his roommate then remembers him as being "feeble" and "quite reticent."[29] He began renting rooms when he married Susan Woodward Haven in 1833, and probably began looking for a house soon after the birth of William ("Willie") Emerson, Jr., in 1835. By 1838 he was warning that the family would rent their New York residence at 130 Fourth Street "with the view of taking up our abode in a cottage to be built at Staten Island."[30]

Given his love of the country, it was natural that William would turn to Staten Island, about five miles southwest of Manhattan and described by a mid-century guidebook as "one of the most beautiful spots in the environs of New York, and a favourite suburban retreat."[31] Staten Island—which is 13.9 miles long and 7.3 miles wide, and comprises some sixty square miles—had been settled by the Dutch in the seventeenth century; by the eighteenth century it was supporting an agricultural economy that included farming, fishing, shipping, piloting and other maritime trades, and flour and lumber mills.[32] Following the War of 1812, it became a popular retreat for New Yorkers and a fertile area for real estate speculators catering to them. The population jumped from 4,564 in 1800 to 10,960 in 1830 and 25,492 by the 1850s. Besides its rustic setting, Staten Island was appealing to New Yorkers because there was a steamboat ferry service that made the journey in about half an hour, and which was described by contemporaries as sumptuous, with "bars and lunch counters stocked with biscuits, sausages, dried beef and citrus fruits."[33] It was, in other words, a fitting setting for William Emerson, who had grown up knowing such similar rural places as Kennebunk, Maine, and Concord.

William was serious about country living, as demonstrated by his being a member and vice president of the Horticultural Association of the Valley of the Hudson, where he met one of its founders, the rural landscape architect Andrew Jackson Downing.[34] He bought land on Staten Island in 1837 or 1838 on which was situated a pre-Revolutionary cottage christened by Waldo the "Snuggery."[35] While William was practicing law in New York, he was named a Judge of Richmond County on Staten Island in 1841. When the family outgrew this "cottage" (John Haven had been born in 1840, Charles in 1841), they built a new home, "Helvellyn," in 1852–1853, about which William said: "Is not the old Scotch mountain strong enough to thrust out a Transatlantic spur?"[36] (William seems to have kept the Snuggery while living in Helvellyn, for when the former burned down in 1855 it was said to have contained a number of William's and Waldo's belongings.) But by 1854 they are back in the City, renting rooms from a cousin at 33 East 14th Street. Although, as William bemoaned, "we have bidden farewell to the golden sunrise & the blue ocean, and to all the changeful beauty of hill & meadow, tree & flower," Susan was closer to friends and the boys closer to their schools.[37] For much the same reasons, William put Helvellyn on the market and returned to the Fourth Street residence later in the year, though he admitted it was with "great reluctance that Susan & I give up our dwelling in the country, but we feel obliged to relinquish both Staten Island & Concord for the present.[38] The boys must go to school, & you perceive how solitary that must leave Susan."[39] Fortunately, no one came forward to purchase Helvellyn, and in 1856 he and Susan returned to Staten Island, where "our talk is of chickens & cows & garden seeds & peach trees." But the stay at Helvellyn was short lived, and in 1860 the Emersons leased it for three years and William, Susan, and Haven moved to board in the City, moving again in 1863 to "a hired house in 22d Street, bringing there our feeble bodies, & the accumulated household lumber of 30 years."[40]

William's land dealings helped to provide the correspondence with Waldo with a financial tone that it would hold for almost thirty years, as in this exchange between the two during April 1837:

↠ [*William*] As to my Staten Island property, the present state of things will make it a matter of common prudence to avoid selling now, if any way possible. So I hope for the indulgence of the Globe Bank. Then you ask me my further liabilities—they are a note for $1248. falling due the 14th May, & another for $1100. on the 23^d June. If these, & particularly the first, can in any way be paid, I think the amount due on mortgage prior to yours, tho' nominally payable on the 15th of August, could be easily postponed on payment of interest. If I do not come to see you on Tuesday, I wish you would write me if you can do any thing for me without embarrassing yourself. It is with a reluctance I cannot tell you how painful, that I make this request. But it is still my opinion notwithstanding the change in the nominal value of property, that the land in question will be a sufficient security for all my liabilities concerning it.[41]

↠ [*Waldo*] Were you here, it is possible you could make me helpful to you, as I cannot myself. I would put myself in your hands with all the facts & you should decide whether to use my means or not.—I have no large sums of money at command. I have, say, 300. on hand, to pay my bills 1 July. I hold 10 shares Commercial Bk stock & 67 City Bk. Of these last, [blank space] are transferred at present as security to the Savings Bk. for 3500. borrowed there to pay for my house. And I receive the dividend on these thro' the hands of the Cashr. Sav. Bk. I have 1100. invested in the Haskins Estate of which Uncle Ralph pays the interest semiannually. This with your debt, (which is partly mine, partly Mrs Browns, &: partly still anothers,) is all my fund that is under my control. I own moreover say 11,000. in the hands of Pliny Cutler, from which I receive an annual income of $500. by an understanding that I should always draw a sum *within* the income, as it is subject to some incumbrances.

I omitted 19 shares Atlantic Bk lodged as you know as security I receiving the dividend & $150.00 loaned on note—& some unprofitable Mill dam shares. Now you have my entire inventory.

Now as to the availableness of these. The City Bk stock is my best property. It is in common times worth 5, 6, 7, 8 per cent above par & yields for the last year 7 per cent. Of course Abel Adams would mightily resist any sale of it,[42] as it would not now bring more than par & perhaps not so much. The Commercial stock is not worth more than from 90 to 95 cents to sell, though it always yields me 6 per cent. For the Cutler part—Could you be here I should think you might help yourself therefrom. For years a settlement is delayed though always promised. I am but one of several parties & my interest too small to bear the labor of overcoming their ponderous inertia. I agreed three years ago verbally &:

possibly *on paper,* to draw *within* the income, in the expectation that in a few months a final settlement would be made. Wm Sohier is my attorney in the matter. I do not know but some hundreds might possibly be drawn thence, though I have hitherto found my whole force not equal to more than two or three questions. . . .

I suppose there is no doubt that the sums you want might be raised on the stock above named by sale, but at much loss. You are to consider on the other hand, whether it be expedient in the view of all the facts to expose this property to risk. I, not being in business, can of course offer a secure home to Mother & resources to Bulkeley & these ought not to be jeopardized. When you have considered that, you need not consider more, because I am quite willing to put my own living at any stake which you shall think prudent.

I do not think of anything else that belongs to the matter. I will cheerfully assume the expenses of Bulkeley for the present; & Mother shall stay with me next winter & we will thank you therefor.—It occurs to me that I can borrow $100. for you at 6 per cent. for several months. Shall I do so? (*L,* 2:65–67).

➤ [*Waldo*] You want 2100 dollars. If you see no way but I must pay them why do you not inform yourself & me of the very best way in which that can be done. I have possessed you to that end with my entire inventory as far as it is known to me. If 20 shares of Bank stock shall be worth next year to me $2000, it would seem unwise to sell them for $1800, or perhaps much less; yet all that I know how to do, is, when I get my stock, to carry it to a broker & say, Sell it for what you can get. This looks like doing things, as the seamen say, "by main strength & ignorance." Is this the only way or can you show me any more? I want advice the more because this matter not being agreeable to Abel Adams, I cannot so well, perhaps cannot at all use his skilful hand. But can you not show the whole fact to some Mr Dodd or other & learn if there be not any better way than to sell stock outright, at any loss. Thus will not an individual or a bank lend the money in New York on the security of so much scrip as is security; just as the Savings Bank lent me $3500?

Then again you do not tell me when the first note of $1095 is to be paid. the second you say, 10 August. The time is so short it needs, I should think, prompt attention and I should gladly do whatever is for me to do before August begins for I have found that a little business spoils a great deal of time for the Muses.

Mr Sohier has yet made me no communication such as I expected in the beginning of last week announcing a final distribution of property. I have nothing still but the fact of their intention to pay me out of those three classes of stock I named to you. I must, I suppose, go to Boston on Monday or Tuesday and see him.

I have borrowed of Mrs Brown on my note bearing interest from 20 July 1837 one hundred & fifty dollars.[43] It is possible that I may get together $200. more; You have—have you not?, 250 ready to pay me 1 August. These sums added will make $600. and therefore if, early next week, I inclose to you a draft for $350. you must add the 250. & credit me with 600. against that $1095.05. And please write immediately acknowledging the receipt, & say the latest day on which the remainder must be raised. I can raise no dollar more in any way that I know of, except selling stock. I do not know but you will have to come here & be your own broker before the whole sum can be paid.

I will not try to elevate this letter so base & mercantile by a single word of better matters. . . . (L, 2:89–90)

The monies that the 34-year-old Waldo is dealing with are not insignificant. To put all this in perspective, when Waldo had been appointed senior pastor at the Second Church in 1829 his salary was set at $1,800 (L, 1:267). By 1838, the Concord assessor's books recorded the value of Waldo's stocks and money lent at interest at $19,400, and that of his house, barn, and land at $3,450.[44] (Lidian also had a small inheritance, but it was not a dependable source of income.[45]) And in 1851, Waldo was listed as one of the Rich Men of Massachusetts with a net value of some $50,000.[46]

Translating Waldo's monetary worth into 2002 dollars results in startling figures.[47] His 1829 Second Church salary of $1,800 becomes a comfortable $34,450. The first half of Ellen's estate would be worth $242,000 and the second half, $296,000. The $1,200 in interest Waldo hoped to obtain would be $25,050. His 1838 Concord assessment evaluation would come out to $411,000. And if his estimated worth as a rich man of Massachusetts is correct, then in 2002 dollars he had a comfortable nest egg of at least $1,085,000.

Having this much money would have made most people relax their fiscal vigilance (as it did, vicariously, with William), but Waldo remained wary. It did not help that Ellen's estate was fully settled just in time for the Financial Panic of 1837, when interest from the stocks dried up. As a result, Waldo relied more and more on his increasingly successful career as a lecturer to keep him from reaching into his reserves and to provide a needed cushion on the many occasions when the bank stock paid few or no dividends. Nevertheless, Waldo did not turn into a hoarder: he used his money to help not only family, but friends as well.

After the final settlement of Ellen's estate in 1837, Waldo wrote, on 10 July, in reply to William's request to invest a portion of the monies from the settlement in his real estate ventures, that the lawyer who handled the legal issues had a great deal to say about your project of investing a portion of the principal. He took a deal of pains to impress me with the prudence (since I do not hope to increase my estate, and it is as he said only enough to live upon,) of not diminishing or risking the capital. Lend or give, he said, all your income, & live like an anchorite that you may, but do not touch the stock. He said you & he would probably differ entirely in opinion as to the judiciousness of the N.Y. investment. He apologised for volunteering his advice so strenuously but seemed to feel that what he had so kindly & laboriously gained for me he should be sorry to see slip away. (L, 2:86)

This was not good news for William, who needed to raise a large amount of money. Waldo knew this, and he closed his letter by asking "Are the $2348. yet to be paid? When? & have you any means? Tell me what is the utmost you wish from me? What is the least? and then I will try the farthest that quiddling will do" (L, 2:87). Waldo followed this up with a letter on the 29th, quoting his friend and banker in Concord: "Mr [Abel] Adams is quite sure that every dollar you spend on this matter is wholly lost and will be satisfied if you act with your eyes open to that fact. Moreover he says what I had said, that I have not all the facts. I wish to know the whole of the Staten Island contract. For what sums are you further bound, to the original proprietors?" (L, 2:91). Fortunately, after Waldo received the disbursement from Ellen's estate, he was able to assist William.

In 1838, William confirms a mortgage of his home and lands at Staten Island to Waldo, and seeks more for purchasing additional land:

Inclosed is the mortgage of the Staten Island property to you for $2000. which I have had recorded. I am continually encouraged the more as to the ultimate value of the property. I find that every acre of that ridge, beginning at the N.E. extremity, nearest the landing (the old Pavilion) southwards down to me, is in few hands, & not an acre of it can be got for $200 per acre, a price which would reimburse me for principal, interest & expenses. On that ridge, half a mile nearer to the City, Mrs Grimes lately offered Tyson, another proprietor $500 per acre for some few acres to enlarge her grounds, & was refused.[48]

But soon William is reporting on the full extent of his finances, which garnered a detailed reply from Waldo:

➤ *William Emerson to Ralph Waldo Emerson, 31 May–1 June 1838*

Now as to my troublesome money matters. Of course I desire that the $200. you obtain from John Milton Cheney[49] on the 1st June should be retained by you to offset the loan of your *peculium*[50] at the Atlantic Bank; then the remaining sum w'h you should have taken from me April 13, say $65.61 I will send you whenever you please. Next as to the $100. rec'd from T[homas]. W. H[askins]. & the $300 from Concord Bk, may I understand them to be loans which will be as permanent as my necessities shall require? Again, on finding that you could obtain the $200 from Mr Cheney, why therefore lessen the demand on the Savings' Bank? If that demand is yet to be made, as I suppose, why should it not be for $500. as you at first intended. I grow as craving as Regan or Goneril in the play.[51] The Savings' Bank must needs lend all it has; why leave them a dollar till they have lent me all I want?

Don't let Mr Cheney with his fine name & friendly deeds delude you a third time with the idea that his checks are at a premium here. The $300. cost me $2.25 to get it into N.Y. money.

June 1st

I went down to the Island last night, & found the house in a state of progress, if that be not a rank solicism, but I cannot judge when it will be done, except from the fact that Egbert is building no other, & that he still says that mine shall be done on the 1st of July. It has turned out on examination of the roof of the old part, to be necessary to put an entire new roof on, and as that must be done, it would be but little more expense to raise that part to the same height as the other, & both items will make an addition of $160. to the before estimated expense of $1100. The matter stands t[hus] then; when the house is inclosed, which Egbert says will be next Tuesday,

I am to pay	$550.
when it is done (1st July)	280.
& the balance 90 days after (say) 1st Oct^r	430.
	$1260

Even then I shall be without a woodshed & gate & fence must cost something more. To provide for this I have from you

per T. W. H.	$100.
Check on Atl. Bk	200.
Concord Check	300.
& bal. left Apr. 13 (say)	65.61
	665.61

Now because you have been so good as to financier for me, I have not done any thing as yet, save to provide you security in case of my death, which I think is the chief mischief to be apprehended in this matter. I have this day taken out a policy on my life for $2000. & assigned the same to you, & I shall this eveg send it with a small packet for you to the care of Mr Abel Adams. So that if you can easily get the rest of the money I want, please to do so. If you cannot, or it is troublesome to you, tell me so, & I can get it on the pledge of some of your stock, & in either case you will be secured by the policy, or by my continuing in life.[52]

⤙ *Ralph Waldo Emerson to William Emerson, 10 June 1838*

On 1 June I received of J. M. Cheney on your account $200. & gave my note therefore on demand with interest—with the understanding that it should be paid when he wants it. He will probably be glad to keep it where it is, a good while. This sum I retain & credit you with the $200. of Atlantic Bk. as returned. For this 200. & the 300. sent from Concord Bk in May, you must send me your note, bearing 6 percent interest. You ask, if these sums can be retained ad libitum[53]—I gave you, before, a statement as to the 300 borrowed of Concord Bk., that it was to September, & then is to be paid by a new borrowing of Savings Bk., say for two years. It is usual to specify a period, & *two* years was named. I suppose it could *then* be renewed, if occasion be, as I have done in my own case at Boston Savings Bk. The $100. of C. C. E's estate, I suppose you can have in perpetuity. You can tell best when you see his accounts.

I have told Mr Cheney that you want 500 still & not 300 of the Concd. Savings Bk. & bid him write his minutes so. He made no objection to so stating the demand. Whether the Directors will give so much, I know not.

I can raise no more money here, having quite exhausted my finance faculty. But if it is necessary, I have still stock which you can pledge to raise money in N.Y. But Heaven send the good times that shall sell this land for just its price to you, then will you not hesitate, I judge, to jump out, outright. For I ought not to let the Globe Bk. debt run indefinitely. (*L*, 2:136–137)

By the next year, William is able to report a decided upturn in his condition, even though, as the second letter makes clear, he still is in considerable debt to Waldo:

The office continues to reward my attention. My share of the net profits of 1838 was somewhat over $3000.—The excess of expense over income

on the Staten Island property for that year, including building, interest &
every thing else was

	$2251.53
of which sum I borrowed from you & Mr Townsend	1088.10
& paid the balance myself, being—	1163.43

without depriving ourselves of accustomed comforts. We now have a
pleasant & commodious house; we have made the experiment of seven
months residence here including the worst season, & Susan would not
willingly go back to the city. The health of all the family has been better
than ever before for the same period of time. The distance from my office is certainly an inconvenience to me, but it is over-balanced by other
advantages. I design gradually to improve the condition of this property,
without undertaking any thing that would oblige me to borrow, & of
course appropriate all that I can spare from current expenses to reduce
the principal of my debt. Meanwhile, the change I have all along been
anticipating is taking place; real estate is rapidly rising as our own city
has again become prosperous, & Staten Island already feels the effects of
the change. Whenever a favorable opportunity offers, I shall be ready to
sell, but feel that I now stand on such vantage ground, that there is no
need to sell at a sacrifice.[54]

   I don't know how it happens, in spite of my wishes & best intentions
to the contrary, that I write to you so seldom. To begin with a part at
least of what you have been expecting since March, I send annexed a
complete memorandum of the loan a/c between us. It is unnecessary to
send you any other at present, as all the details of our a/c current have
been furnished to you from time to time, & shall be again, if I live, by
the 1st Oct[r] next, when interest again becomes due. By the subjoined a/c
it appears, that the total am[t] of my debt to you is $6400. But as you have
all along received, & still receive the dividends on the Bank shares, I pay
you interest only on $5100. Of this only $4300. is cash advanced by you
on the Staten Island property, yet the whole is rightfully covered by the
mortgages, because I have paid $800 (& much more) toward that prop-
erty, & so have charged you with that sum in private a/c & credited you
with it as advanced on S. Isl[d] a/c. Still, your mortgages amount to only
$5500. while my debt is $6400. I shall therefore take care to keep more
than the difference covered by a life policy. I have ordered a new policy
for $3000. & will send it by an early opportunity.
   Mr Townsend, I am sorry to say, has spoken to me about paying up his
loan. I had hoped before this to have made him a payment of $300. but I
have not done any thing yet. I reminded him that it was in his power to

sell the stock, tho' I wished he would not do so. He desired me to write to you; probably, because he thinks you will know the present value of the stock, & whether it is now a favorable time to sell, or not. Please to write me on this subject as soon as you can, by mail. If Mr T. would be patient until August, I think I could pay him $200. . . .

R. W. E. in Loan a/c with W. E.

Cr	1836	By am't due before this date		$800.
	"	Decʳ 29	" cash———	2900.
	1837	Apr. 25	" "———	250.
		July 31	" "———	350.
		Aug. 10	" "———	100.
	1838	May 2	" "———	200.
		16	" "———	300.
		Sept. 12	" "———	200.
Also	1837	Aug. 18	" 13 shares Atlantic Bk	
			pledged to E. Townsend—say—	1300.⁵⁵
				6400.
Dt				
1837	Jany 2	To joint bond & mortgage of G. Folsom		
		& W. Emerson for		$3500.
	Aug. 18	" do for		2000.
1838	May 31	" life policy (expired) for $2000.		
1839	July 1	" " " " 1 year		3000.⁵⁶
				8500.⁵⁷

One thing that plagued both brothers was the occasional failure of the banks to pay dividends on Waldo's stock. One such occurrence in 1840 led to a typical exchange of letters, in which the bank stock, each brother's finances, William's assistance in arranging Waldo's lectures and the payment for them (see below), and family matters are all intertwined:

➤➤ *William Emerson to Ralph Waldo Emerson, 6–8 April [1840]*

8th. This morning I have yours of the 4th, & am very sorry to hear that the great Atlantic ceases to dispense its fertilizing showers. Tell me if you are likely to be embarrassed for want of funds, & if $100. or so from me in May would be of any service, not as loan, but payment in small part. Otis called on me yesterday with the accompanying letter; he said that the two courses had left a deficiency of about $100. & if it had not been for your lectures in the second course the deficit would have been $500.; that more single tickets were sold to your lectures than to all the rest.[58] And he added with the self-complacency of his tribe, that the Board were now deliberating about asking you to give another course next season.— Mr Anthon said he liked your first two amazingly, & should have liked the last also, but that you ran athwart one of his cherished fancies, his fondness for books.[59]

⤞ William Emerson to Ralph Waldo Emerson, 13 April 1840

Since you wrote me about the sad turn which the Atlantic Bank has served you, it has occurred to me that it might be advantageous to both of us that you should sell me your Atlantic stock, & take a further bond & mortgage from me for the surplus not covered by your present securities. I do not know at what price the stock sells; but if it sells for $94. per share, I will take it at $100., sell it, & pay Mr Townsend with the proceeds. The benefit to you will be that you will (as I think) be more sure of having your six per cent. per annum for these 1300 dollars, besides getting full price for the stock, which, I think I understood you, could not be obtained for it several years past. The benefit to me will be that I shall pay off Mr Townsend in full & at once. The benefit to both of us will be that I shall then be left free to work at paying off the Globe Bank note, instead of dividing any surplus, as I must as things stand, between Mr Townsend & the Globe Bank. Please to let me hear from you as soon as you have weighed the matter.

. . . The little Southfield house is occupied, & by civilized & agreeable neighbors. Mother said last evening, when I asked her what message she would send you, that I must give her love to you, & tell you, that since the Boston people don't pay you dividends, & the Concord people tax you so heavily, you had better come here & live on Staten Island. Which excellent advice Susan instantly echoed, & I now do the same; so again please reflect upon it.[60]

⤞ William Emerson to Ralph Waldo Emerson, 15–[16] April 1840

You will be glad to hear that Susan has this afternoon given birth to a son. All things were favorable, the nurse present, the doctor arrived seasonably, & mother & child are both in very promising condition. Our good mother says the child is a pretty one, but of beauties so very infantile I am not a particularly good judge. Willie is beside himself with joy at having a little brother, & when Susan told him she must now divide her love between him & the new comer, Willie proposed that she should give the little one three quarters, & himself the other quarter. So you perceive that John Haven (as his mother calls him) is very cordially received. Susan sends her love to you all, & says that Elizabeth must keep a corner of her heart even for this young stranger.[61]

➤ *Ralph Waldo Emerson to William Emerson, 20 April 1840*

Waldo shows me this morning a paper on which he told me he had written with pencil John Haven Emerson; but it was in that archaic arrow-headed character which I have never yet mastered.

I received your letter containing the Account which I find true & transparent as usual—I heartily thank you for your kind proposition to buy my Atlantic stock, but cannot understand how you shall be benefitted by buying 95 cents for 100. The fact however is still more unfavorable as I read the last quotation at 85 cents, so that we must wait for their better prices.

If it should be in your power to pay me a hundred dollars as you suggest in May or June, I suppose I shall be too glad to accept it. I suppose that now I am at the bottom of my wheel of debt & shall not hastily venture lower. (*L*, 2:283–284)

A more personal type of correspondence occurred when Waldo's son was born on 30 October 1836:

➤ *Ralph Waldo Emerson to William Emerson, 31 October 1836*

I have a son born last night at eleven o'clock, a large healthy looking boy. All the circumstances are favorable. Lidian is very comfortable, and we are all rejoiced & thankful. Mother & the bystanders all, pronounce favorable opinions upon the aspect form & demeanor of the bantling. He sucks his thumbs immediately as his grandmother says his father did, at his age. His eyes are of a color not ascertained, as he keeps them shut this morning, but it is thought they are dark blue. You shall have more particulars, shortly. Meantime with much love to Susan & Willie (to whom present greetings from his cousin) I am your affectionate brother (*L*, 2:44–45)

➤ *William Emerson to Ralph Waldo Emerson, 2 November 1836*

Your brother & sister send many cordial greetings on the birth of your son. You did not mention his name, but that will be of little moment, so he imbibes a good spirit from the kindly influences that attend his coming among mortals. I suppose there is no period in the domestic history so full fraught with happiness, as the day when it is said, 'there is a man-child born.'[62] And where this light of the eyes, & hope of hearts enters the world with so many chances of good nature & kind usage in his favor as your little boy has, I can see no ground for any feelings but those of joy & gratitude. These I am sure you indulge, & in these Sue & I most heartily share with mother, & Lidian & yourself. Let us know all about the little stranger, his physical & moral constitution, as fast as either is developed. There is another Emerson under the roof where Charles dwelt, &—the best wish I can give the newcomer is that he may succeed to Charles's independence of spirit, justness of thought & eloquences in speech.[63]

➤➤ *Ralph Waldo Emerson to William Emerson, 29 November 1836*

Tell Susan that I count upon the two boys being the best friends, & having both the manliest education, and they must be gentlemen, but not fashionists. And I will instruct my boy to love & serve his cousin. They must speak the truth, be just, & reverent. I believe I violate the wishes of almost all his friends in calling mine Waldo & not Charles. I call him so because it is his natural name; then because it is an old family name; & lastly because it is a convenient & somewhat rare name. On some accounts I should like well to call him Charles, but C. C. did not like his name because it was not patronymic; and I should still have to choose between C & Edward. (*L*, 2:48)

News of births and deaths went back and forth between Waldo and William with regularity, as the death of their step-grandfather Ezra Ripley was followed a few months later by the birth of Waldo's daughter Ellen, and a few months after that by the death of little Waldo, and then after a couple of years, the birth of Waldo's son Edward Waldo Emerson:

➤➤ *William Emerson to Ralph Waldo Emerson, 26–[27] September 1841*

Your kind letter of the 21st reached me on Thursday morning, & brought me the first intelligence of the death of Dr Ripley. We were thankful for the particulars you gave in regard to this interesting occurrence, & we heartily subscribe to your eulogy on the departed. He has indeed been a good friend to all of us. With what hospitality he always welcomed & entertained us! With what pleasure he heard of any progress, good fortune, compliment, or honor, that touched any one of us! Yet this feeling in him was entirely disinterested. He arrogated no merit to those he called his grandchildren, to himself. And what a catholic and humane spirit he had, that would make all who needed his kindness or advice, his neighbors & parishioners; a Massachusetts Oberlin.[64]—I am glad that his brother, his son, & his niece, were around his dying bed. Remember us affectionately to them, if you have opportunity.[65]

↣ *Ralph Waldo Emerson to Susan Haven and William Emerson,*
22 November 1841

Dear William & Susan, Be it known unto you that a little maiden child is born unto this house this day at 5 o clock this afternoon; it is a meek little girl which I have just seen, & in this short dark winter afternoon I cannot tell what color her eyes are, and the less, because she keeps them pretty closely shut: But there is nothing in her aspect to contradict the hope we feel that she has come for a blessing to our little company. Lidian is very well and finds herself suddenly recovered from a host of ails which she suffered from this morning. Waldo is quite deeply happy with this fair unexpected apparition & cannot peep & see it enough. Ellen has retired to bed unconscious of the fact & of all her rich gain in this companion. Shall I be discontented who had dreamed of a young poet that should come? I am quite too much affected with wonder & peace at what I have & behold and understand nothing of, to quarrel with it that it is not different. (*L,* 2:465–466)

↣ *Ralph Waldo Emerson to William Emerson, 4 December 1841*

I was in Boston when your letter arrived as it did in safety with its enclosure of $84.20 the day before yesterday. The letter is very grateful to us all. The little Lidian [that is, Ellen] after whose titles you so kindly inquire, shall not be anonymous. I call her Lidian. Lidian does not seem very well content with that name & hunts for graceful combinations; likes, for instance, Mary Lidian, which I do not; then offers other names as Agnes, Grace, & Eva, even Theodora I have heard; she can be Lidian meantime, until a name that will fit her like a skin, can be found. (*L,* 2:469)

↣ *Ralph Waldo Emerson to William Emerson, 7 January 1842*

My dear brother,
    My little Waldo died this evening. He was attacked by the *scarletina* on Monday night. Little Ellen has the eruption today but is not yet seriously sick. But what shall I say of my Boy? Farewell & Farewell! Lidian is very well, & Mother. Your affectionate brother

Waldo—(*L,* 3:6)[66]

↣ *William Emerson to Ralph Waldo Emerson, 30 January 1842*

I cannot tell you with how much sorrow we received the sad tidings of Waldo's departure. We can hardly bring ourselves to the belief that he has so suddenly, irrevocably gone. Yet for him we cannot grieve; 'wo

unto us, not him, for he sleeps well.' It is we who are left to the cares, &
doubts, & sins, that darken & embitter life; but for him the Gods have
shown their love.—Susan wants to write, but knows no more than I what
to say; we feel your loss as our own; but why or how should we attempt
to comfort you? All the sources of consolation are known to you. We can
only commend you to the love of our Heavenly Father.[67]

↣ William Emerson to Ralph Waldo Emerson, 16 October 1843

I send you a sketch of my loan a/c with you, omitting therefrom all charges
& payments of interest.[68] From the balance it appears that I owe you Five
Thousand Eight Hundred Dollars. The meaning of the credits put down
as "Charged to his private a/c with W. E." is this, (as perchance you may
have forgotten) that before this unlucky land business of mine I owed
you $800. & being sanguine of a happy issue from these Staten Island
embarrassments, was minded to give you such security as mortgages on
the farm afforded for all my debt to you, including the $800; accordingly,
when I had payments to make on the Staten Island a/c & had money of
my own to make them, I did so, & credited you therewith on the Staten
Island loan a/c to the extent of my individual debt to you, viz. $800. to
which sum you will find those credits to amount.

I now inclose a check on Boston for Thirty Five 84/100 Dollars being
the balance due from me on current a/c so far as I know it. . . . .

The other side is for dollars & cents. Let me tell you on this about
Susan. I was beginning to feel very anxious lest her lungs were diseased,
& on Thursday last she expressed a wish to see Dr [William] Swett,
Charles's classmate, who is distinguished for his skill in diseases of the
chest. Dr Smith assented, & on Friday Dr Swett went down, & after careful examination & consultation with Dr Smith, gave it as his opinion that
she had no disease either of the lungs or the heart—that her disorder was
mere fever. This greatly relieved her own apprehensions, & mine. She
continues however very feeble, & the fever subsides so slowly that we
can hardly say it does subside. She takes a little nourishment, & sits up
about an hour a day. I think she has visibly improved since Saturday. Mrs
Cheever went home on Monday last; Caroline Haven arrived before Mrs
C. went, & will I trust remain till Susan gets well.[69]

↣ William Emerson to Ralph Waldo Emerson, 15 July 1844

Mother's diligent kindness has possessed us of very interesting tidings—the birth of a son to you [Edward, born on 10 July 1844]. Susan &
I do heartily congratulate you & Lidian on this event. Fortunately for all

of mortal birth, it is not given to us to read his horoscope, to know beforehand whether he will be gifted or deficient, happy or hypochondriac, agile or cripple, learned or mechanical; and in this utter uncertainty of all that Providence or fate may have in store for him, sure we are that hope remains at the bottom of the heap. And we will hope, therefore, that he may have a healthful body and a sound & solid mind; that if he be not noted for wit, he may ever abound in cheerfulness, that whether his profession be liberal or mechanical, he may always be contented with his lot; that he may never know the gripings of penury, nor the corruption of excessive wealth; & that his distinguishing characteristics may be kindness, industry & usefulness. We feel, I assure you, no little curiosity as to his name, & if it is not too late for a recommendation on this head, I would suggest the name of the Pretender.[70]

Other discussions dealt with more weighty subjects. When, in 1840, George Ripley invited Waldo to become part of his new communitarian venture, the Brook Farm community, Waldo discussed the matter with William:

➤ *Ralph Waldo Emerson to William Emerson, 2 December 1840*

We are absorbed here at home in discussions of George Ripley's community. I forget if I have mentioned it to you. He is very anxious to enrol me in his company, & that I should subscribe money to its funds. I am very discontented with many of my present ways & bent on mending them; but not as favorably disposed to his Community of 10 or 12 families as to a more private reform. G. R. wishes to raise $30,000.; to buy a farm of 200 acres in Spring St, Roxbury for 12000—build $12000. worth of cottages thereon & remove himself with pioneers to the premises on 1 April next. The families who shall come are to do their own work which a studied cooperation is to make easier & simpler. The farm & such mechanical operations as are practised is to give subsistence to the company. A school or college in which the learneder clerks are to teach, it is presumed, will pay a profit—and out of many means the interest at 5 per cent of the capital is to be paid. If I should go there I get rid of menial labor: I learn to work on a farm under skilful direction: I am provided with many means & opportunities of such literary labor as I may wish. Can I not get the same advantages at home, without pulling down my house? Ah my dear brother that is the very question we now consider. Lidian is gone today (as she goes every Wednesday) to Boston to attend Margaret Fuller's "Conversations."[71] Elizabeth H[oar]. is very well. I suppose Mother has written you of Bulkeley's visit here & that he is gone to Charlestown—I hope for no long time. (*L*, 2:365)

✦ *William Emerson to Ralph Waldo Emerson, 13 December 1840*

But our pleasure was not a little dashed, in this instance, by these schemes of Utopian communities which you mention. We are such plain matter of fact people that we look with distrust & suspicion upon the Lebanons & New Harmonys which Fanaticism or Philosophy builds up from time to time.[72] We are so old fashioned as to think, that, however human & republican it might be to do away with all menial labor & to perform ourselves all that is needful, habit still is second nature, & when Lidian is unwell, you would find it quite irksome to do the cooking & the washing of your family, & when you chance to be rheumatic, she might find it beyond her strength to split all the wood, milk the cow, make paths in the snow, & the thousand etceteras which would of course fall within your province when well. But then you would be nearer to Boston; & this, so far as you have opened the plan to me, seems to be almost the only advantage you are to gain. You are to have, possibly, 5% for the money you invest, instead of 6 which it yields you now, if indeed the principal is not lost altogether. You lose a certain rent for so much is invested in your Concord house, & there remains only the chance that it may sell for what it has cost you. I freely admit, that all this croaking is quite at random, as you have not communicated the details of the plan, & every thing may be so judiciously arranged, that even Aunt Mary herself should have nothing to carp at. But if possessed with the desire of change, why not come to Staten Island? There would be no uncertainty, in that remove, on the point of the good you are to do, & the happiness you will communicate, to us at least, who fancy that we have a sort of natural claim on your society; & your spleen of usefulness may be as wide as Spring Street, or Newton Corner, without having our island; & when you come to know New York more intimately, perchance you may conclude that there are souls, & imaginations, & friendships, & progress, & moral influences, even among her trade-benighted legions. I know very well which way mother's opinion will tend in the matter of this Utopia, & Susan had the pleasure of receiving a letter from Elizabeth the other day, showing plainly enough that she sides with mother.—To all these good influences, & your own calm reflection, I confidently commend you.[73]

✦ *Ralph Waldo Emerson to William Emerson, 21 December 1840*

I shall not go to Mr Ripley's Community having sent him my final negative a week ago.[74] Whatever inducements the design offers for others it is not good for me. I have or easily can have the same facilities where I am that his plan would laboriously procure me. But I am quite intent on trying the experiment of manual labor to some considerable extent & of abolishing or ameliorating the domestic service in my household. Then I am grown a little impatient of seeing the inequalities all around me, am a little of an agrarian at heart and wish sometimes that I had a smaller house or else that it sheltered more persons. So I think that next April we shall make an attempt to find house room for Mr Alcott & his family under our roof; for the wants of the man are extreme as his merits are extraordinary. But these last very few persons perceive, and it becomes the more imperative on those few—of whom I am in some respects near-est—to relieve them. He is a man who should be maintained at the public cost in the Prytaneum,[75]—perhaps one of these days he will be—though of late it has rather seemed probable it would be in the county jail or poorhouse. At all events Lidian & I have given him an invitation to estab-lish his household with us for one year, and explained to him & Mrs A. our views or dreams respecting labor & plain living; and they have our proposal under consideration. (*L,* 2:371–372)

Although Waldo spurned Ripley's offer to join him in one sort of social re-form, he did institute his own version, on which he reported to William on 30 March 1841. Writing "Lidian & I had dreamed that we would adopt the country practice of having but one table in the house," he tells of how "Lidian went out the other evening & had an explanation on the subject with the two girls. Louisa accepted the plan with great kindness & readiness, but Lydia, the cook, firmly refused—A cook was never fit to come to table, &c." The result was that on the next morning his son Waldo was "sent to announce to Louisa that breakfast was ready but she had eaten already with Lydia & refuses to leave her alone" (*L,* 2:389).

Much of the correspondence between Concord and New York or Staten Is-land discussed common friends and books, including Waldo's, as when Wil-liam commented on *English Traits* (1856) that he was surprised "at your suffer-ing the printers to use so poor a type," and made these complaints: "On page 113, I am posed for the sequitur in W.'s not being able to stir abroad, &c. On page 212, the sentence beginning 'English wealth' is not a little embarrassing to me. As to 'responsibleness' on page 103, I suppose it is only a misprint for 'responsiveness,' & 'surloin' for 'sirloin,' page forgotten."[76] Of the first number of the Transcendentalists' periodical, the *Dial,* William wrote "Much of The Dial I like well; its sincerity, its freedom from cant & humbug & party, always excepting [Bronson] Alcott's unintelligibles, & not all his Orphics are such."[77] In one letter, William tells how he had promised to keep his son's engagement and the addition of a new daughter to his family secret from a surprised Waldo ("For I was taken by surprise the other day with the intelligence that William [Jr.] was betrothed, and now I am told that you & Susan have a new daughter who has leaped into life looking thirteen years old,—and all this without the leave of me" [*L,* 5:103]):

I did not mean to leave you uninformed of any thing which interested us; and as to my little Emily, I have been on the point of writing you all about the matter. But as to Sally, William had special reasons for trying to keep the affair secret for a time; he is not yet admitted to practise his profession, & very justly felt that it was indiscreet to get betrothed before he was prepared to get a living.[78] So the secret was guardedly intrusted to the selected circle of those friends who could not help seeing how matters stood, & as a necessary consequence, every body knows about it; & Susan & I find we have been padlocking our lips to no purpose. Sally is a very good, practical, kindhearted, straightforward girl, whom every body loves who knows her, & we old folks are well satisfied with William's choice.

Now for Emily; Horace Jenks was a brother of Mrs W[m] H. Furness who married Prudence Haven, a cousin of Susan's, & settled in Missouri, where he died 8 years ago. Prudence brought her children to Phil[a], and lived there till about three weeks since, when she died of consumption. She appointed me the executor of her will, & guardian of her only daughter, making James T. Furness the guardian of her two sons.[79]

William no doubt enjoyed having Emily Jenks as his "new daughter": earlier, the daughterless father had written his brother "What locomotive volumes of correspondence are those two daughters of yours! When they get into the Assembly's Shorter Catechism, & are asked 'What is the chief end of Woman?' they will assuredly, nor with one voice, but with two pens, answer, 'Letter Writing.' I never formed a conception before of what a blessing is a daughter. Why, when you go away, & leave one of them at home, you leave every thing that happens there photographed to your hand. Commend me to one daughter, over half a score of sons."[80] And when Waldo's daughter Edith became engaged to William Hathaway Forbes, William told of his meeting the couple, "It was a sight for our old eyes. Such a noble youth! Modest & sensible he surely is. How many other fine qualities lie hidden under that soldierly exterior you know much better than I. Then such a maiden as our Edith! But I shall not enumerate her good qualities; it would be needless either for your information or mine. Suffice it to say, that the old uncle & aunt were perfectly delighted with both the lovers, & heartily rejoice that they have found one another out."[81]

Henry David Thoreau stayed with the William Emersons from early May through mid-December 1843. William's original proposition to Thoreau—that he board with the family and tutor Willie Emerson—is now lost, but Waldo's letter of 12–13 March 1843 describes the agreement:

I have to say that Henry Thoreau listens very willingly to your proposition he thinks it exactly fit for him & he very rarely finds offers that do fit him. He says that it is such a relation as he wishes to sustain, to be the friend & educator of a boy, & one not yet subdued by schoolmasters. I have told him that you wish to put the boy & not his grammar & geography under good & active influence that you wish him to go to the woods & to go to the city with him & do all he can for him—This he understands & likes well & proposes to accept

I have told him that you will give him board, lodging (washing?) a room by himself to study in, when not engaged with Willie, with fire when the season requires, and a hundred dollars a year. He says, it is an object with him to earn some money beyond his expenses, which he supposes the above named terms will about cover, and that his health now will not allow him to stipulate for any manual labor: he therefore wishes to know if there is any clerical labor from your office or from any other office, known to you—which he can add to his means of support. He is sure that his handwriting is not so careless, but that he can make it legible for such work. He would like to know if there be such employment attainable, pending the time when he shall procure for himself literary labor from some quarter in New York. He further says he shall be ready to come as soon as 1 April, if you wish, & he asks whether it will be convenient to you to advance to him $20. before he comes, in case it is agreed between you that he shall come.—I recite this last proposition as he made it, but I can easily do it myself, if you prefer. You shall write in reply either to H. D. Thoreau or to me. Lidian & Elizabeth are charmed with the project, & think it auspicious on both sides only Lidian cannot spare Henry. (L, 3:158–159)

William wrote Thoreau on 29 March, asking him to arrive at Staten Island on 1 May,[82] and on 3 April, Waldo, acting as Thoreau's agent, replied:

Mr Thoreau was about to write you today that he would hold himself ready to come with Mrs E. on the 1st May. I told him I would say so. One thing Henry remarks in your letter that you promise a room with fire to himself for most of the day—He says that if he remains until the winter he shall wish to make a special arrangement. This is in winter when the evening is the best part of the day for the study, a matter of vital importance to all book reading & book writing men, to be at night the autocrat of a chamber be it never so small—6 feet by 6,—wherein to dream, write, & declaim alone. Henry has always had it, & always must. He can very well sleep all the year without fire in his apartment. I do not see that this will be inconvenient to you. You can take the library in the evening, & give him the basement, or give him the library when you wish the basement. (L, 3:162–163)

Thoreau impressed William, who wrote Waldo on 4 August, that Thoreau "makes us all like & respect him, & he is doing William much good."[83] On the 29th, William gave Waldo a more detailed picture of Thoreau's activities: "Mr Thoreau tried last week a scheme for making money, which not succeeding, he came back to us after one night's absence. He undertook to read books for a commission. I grieve that he cannot make as much money as he would; but the same is true of many besides philosophers. Something will offer in due time."[84] Thoreau found his excursion to be neither pleasurable nor profitable. He did not like the city and did not "feel myself especially serviceable to the good people with whom I live, except as inflictions are sanctified to the righteous." He was homesick, had trouble sleeping, was depressed by the news of his former college roommate's death, had little success in getting his writings published in magazines, and was bothered by his tuberculosis flaring up. Thoreau also did not like Willie, and felt that he could not be "in his neighborhood hereafter as his Educator. . . . I am not attracted toward him but as to youth generally. He shall frequent me, however, as much as he can, and I'll be I."[85] On 21 October 1843 Thoreau made this entry in his journal, possibly in reference to William and his family:

> O I have seen such a hollow glazed life as on a painted floor which some couples lead—with their basement parlor with folding doors—a few visitors cards and the latest annual. Such life only as is in the shell on the mantel piece—The very children cry with less inwardness and depth than in the cottage. There they do not live. It is there they reside.
>
> There is no hearth in the center of the house—The atmosphere of the apartments is not yet peopled with the spirits of its inhabitants, but the voices sound hollow and echo and he sees only the paint and the paper.[86]

There was no formal break between William and Thoreau, but clearly the two did not get along. F. B. Sanborn, who knew all the participants, thought William "a faithful, courteous, but slightly formal gentleman, well read and affectionate, but rather antipathetic to Thoreau and the more eccentric Transcendentalists."[87] He also recorded in his journal in 1878 that Waldo told him that William and Thoreau were "not men that could get along together.—Each would think whatever the other did was out of place."[88] Margaret Fuller, who had tried to get into William's school as a girl, still found him "as unlike his brother as possible: he is very gentlemanly, very amiable very clear headed, but a mere business man."[89] Still, Thoreau and William seemed to have parted on good terms, and Thoreau visited the family when he traveled to New York in 1858.[90]

William also kept Waldo informed about some of Walt Whitman's publications. On 15 September 1855 he sent a "notice of Walt Whitman" (possibly a review of *Leaves of Grass*[91]) to Waldo, and a decade later he enclosed with a letter "the [New York] Times of the 12th, containing a fine letter from your old protégé, Walt Whitman."[92]

The correspondence dealing with friends also shows how Waldo learned enough about publishing his own books to act as their unofficial agent. He helped negotiate publishing contracts for Ellery Channing, Margaret Fuller, Thoreau, Jones Very, and others. He was a shrewd businessman who paid for the production costs of his own books (composition, stereotyping, printing, and binding) and gave the publisher and booksellers a percentage of sales on the copies they distributed. He describes his reasoning in a letter to William of 21 September 1846:

> . . . I am settling into the belief that the best offers of the booksellers are not good and that it is best for me to keep the property of my own book as I have usually done and only employ them as publishers. I have usually found that in that way, received at last only a little less than 33 per cent on the retail price of the book or if I cheapen the book to the trade say 30 or 25 per cent. there is no risk in so doing, for my books uniformly pay for themselves, and this book of poems is much more sure of an easy sale than its foregoers. The objection to this course is, that the bookseller will not press the sale of the book at a distance which he prefers to sell at his own counter and monopolize the retail commission, which is larger.[93] But if the book is good, the distant trader will have to send for it, & then it will go to him at trade prices. If I publish it myself, as I incline to, I shall have to employ, I suppose, my old agents here; as I can more easily work with them, & can know if they do me any wrong; but at a distance I cannot work so well, nor know if I am fairly treated. (L, 3:350–351)

By 1850, when he began to accept straight royalties of 20%, he required the publisher to advance him the full amount of his profit for each book immediately upon publication, thus limiting his own financial risk. In all instances, Emerson kept copyright to his books and, after stereotyping was introduced, he owned the plates used to print his books, so that any future reprintings generated revenue for him, not the publisher.[94]

His business acumen allowed him to edit Very's *Essays and Poems* (1839) and front the monies for its publication, which he eventually recouped, netting Very—who had risked nothing—a "royalty" of $7.54 (L, 7:452). But it was with the American editions of Thomas Carlyle's works that Waldo played the largest part—and involved William.

Waldo had met Carlyle in August 1833 during his European tour. He received three of the fifty-eight copies of *Sartor Resartus* (1836) Carlyle had printed from the plates of *Fraser's Magazine* for distribution to friends; and one of them was used in the publication of an American edition, to which Emerson contributed an unsigned preface.[95] Although Carlyle received no royalties from this publication, he received payments of $242.22 (in a £50 draft) and £100 for *The French Revolution* (1838), for which Waldo wrote a prospectus for signing up advance sales,[96] wrote an unsigned review for the *Christian Examiner*, and completely assumed the financial risk whereas all the profits went to Carlyle. Waldo even sent ten copies to William in New York, some for sale (ensuring monies for Carlyle that otherwise would have gone to a bookseller) and others to be distributed as review copies.[97] For *Critical and Miscellaneous Essays* (1838), Waldo helped with the selection, prepared another prospectus for advance sales,[98] and wrote a brief introduction. More important, he paid the printing and paper costs of some five hundred dollars in advance; sales fortunately exceeded expenses. Also, Waldo brokered a second edition that netted Carlyle a flat fee of £50. He also obtained $150 for the publication of *Chartism* (1840) and $200 for *Past and Present* (1843), for which he again wrote a preface and fronted production costs.

William was caught up in this bibliopoly in 1845–1846. Not only did he attempt to find a New York publisher for Waldo's forthcoming edition of *Poems*,[99] but he was called upon during a crisis involving *Oliver Cromwell's Letters and Speeches* (1846).[100] Carlyle had mailed an advance copy to Waldo through the New York firm of Wiley and Putnam. Meanwhile, Waldo had made an agreement with Horace Greeley for a New York edition with the profits going to Carlyle. However, Wiley & Putnam refused to surrender their copy until they had produced their own edition, one that they said had been authorized by Carlyle's British publisher. Waldo asked William to look into the matter and "if you see fit, to commence usual [legal] proceedings" against them (*L*, 3:316). William replied on 16 December 1845 that he had gone to see John Wiley

> & told him I came to ask an explanation of his position with you. He told me he had written to you, & furnished you with extracts from his partner ([George Palmer] Putnam's) letter to him, stating that he was authorized to instruct him (Wiley) to withold the parcel addressed to you until their (W. & P's) edition should be well under way. Wiley further said in answer to my questions, that he had not opened the parcel addressed to you; that it had been opened at the Boston Custom House, & that he had placed & kept it in his desk, without using your copy at all, & that he had sent it to Boston to the care of [James] Munroe & Co on Saturday last, addressed to you. He further admitted that he did not intend that Mr Carlyle should have any part of the profits of his (Wiley's) editions; that he had bought

the copy he had used in printing fairly from Carlyle's publishers, & with their knowledge & approbation had published; that he did not intend to publish until next Saturday but being informed that Burgess & Stringer were printing a cheap edition he hurried matters, & published half the work, the two first N^{os}, yesterday. He also showed me the English copy from which he had printed, & which certainly attested the use to w'h it had been put.

Under these circumstances I did not think it suitable, at present at least, to take any legal measures against these people. If it shall appear that the partner has surreptitiously obtained the copy from w'h they have printed, & given false instructions to Wiley, you may have a claim on the firm for the profits of the publication, for C's benefit.[101]

Unfortunately for Carlyle, he indeed had given misleading instructions to his London publisher, who had assumed Waldo's copy was a gift from the author and, as a result, sent another copy to Wiley & Putnam for their edition. Although Carlyle did obtain the £10 that his publisher had received from Wiley & Putnam, that was about all he gained from the book's sale in America.

Still, between 1836 and 1847, Waldo (with some help from William) was directly responsible for Carlyle receiving some £655 from the sale of his books in America (approximately $60,000 in 2002 dollars). In the days before international copyright, when American publishers were free to do new editions of British books without payment to their authors, this was quite an accomplishment.

William's major financial assistance to Waldo was in helping him with his lectures in New York, as selections from their extended correspondence on this subject show:

↦ *Ralph Waldo Emerson to William Emerson, 19 February 1842*

Be it known to you therefore that I purpose to come & advertise in your city, say to begin a week from next Monday, a course of Lectures *On the Times six lectures,*[102] I think, and to invite all New York to come & pay for hearing my wisdom. If you see any impossibility in my plan, write me word instantly; if I do not hear from you immediately, I think I shall appear there so soon as I say. Perhaps you may see that no steps can be taken to such an end until I come.: If otherwise there be any good hall you can engage for me, I should like to promise the six in two weeks, three in each week, if that is admissible. If you see fit you may advertise for me thus "R. W. E. proposes to deliver a course of Six lectures ON THE TIMES in [blank space] Hall, on Monday Wednesday & Friday Evenings to begin on Monday Eve Feb [blank space] at 7 ½ o'clock Tickets &c."— Possibly Mr Eames might know how to fill up these important blanks,[103] the proper price of tickets &c. I incline to make low prices. In Boston to a course of Eight Lectures the ticket admitting one person is 2.00 & the single evening ticket 50 cents. (*L*, 3:14)

↠ *William Emerson to Ralph Waldo Emerson, 23 February* [1842]

. . . I am rejoiced at your determination to try your fortune as a lecturer in New York. I have this morning called to see Mr Bellows about it, & he is glad you are coming, & at his request I have not taken any steps towards engaging a hall, &c. to enable him to consult Horace Greeley & Chas. Eames & 2 or 3 others in relation to these matters,[104] & then to see me tomorrow. We shall have the matter duly advertized in tomorrow afternoon's papers. You must not think of giving more than two lectures in a week. And will you not have the goodness to put into your trunk one lecture which may answer as an Introductory to a course expected to be delivered before a nascent Institution on Staten Island? As to your residence, our cottage must of course be your headquarters, & (your suggestion in yesterday's letter not withstanding) we shall probably be able to reconcile that arrangement generally with your convenience. Will not mother come on with you? We fear that it is only in that way with an opp[y] to go & return marked out, that we shall ever see her here.[105]

↠ *Ralph Waldo Emerson to William Emerson, 25 January 1843*

I have this day received a letter from the Committee of the N. Y. Berean Institute inviting me to read my course on N. England before their society[106] & they write the "Terms" thus.

"The Committee promise you an average audience of 1000 persons, per evening, more or less; & after the net cost of advertising, church hire, &c which will amount at most to but $15. per night, they propose to give you one half of the clear proceeds of each lecture,—x x x x"

(There are two words at the close, which I
do not make out.)

Mr [Horace] Greeley, to whom they refer me for an account of the Society, kindly writes me that "they ought to advertise in 8 principal papers, pay all expenses, & divide the gross receipts (& not the expenses) equally with you."

I should like better to have the details of the matter taken out of my hands than to do them myself or put them on personal friends. But I do not even understand the value of this offer or what the attendance of

1000 persons promises me. Will you not then let me refer them to you for an answer. They can explain to you what amount their arrangement will probably pay for each lecture, and you shall answer for me Yea or Nay as you think it expedient. I think I ought to receive not less than 50.00 for each lecture and I make five in the course. But if the times say I shall not have so much, I submit. If they say I shall have more, I accept.

If you think it best that I should not read to the B. I.; then can you not put me into the hands of Delf or some other bookseller whom Greeley would name,[107] who will take the trouble off your hands that I gave you last year. The facts then are these. I shall come to N. Y on Thursday 2 Feby., and should like forthwith to read my course, calling them, Lectures on New England: on the Descent, Religion, Trade, Manners, Genius, & recent Spiritual features of the Inhabitants of N . England. Five Lectures. (to be read in ten days)

3 evenings in one week 2 in the next

These are all my facts. If on any account you cannot answer for me, throw it back again on me. . . . (L, 3:134–135)

Sometimes the communications about the lectures could be brief. When Waldo was invited in 1847 to speak by an institution of which he had not heard, he asked William for advice: "This morning I received a letter from a committee of students in the 'University of the city of New York,' inviting me to deliver their annual Oration in June before the Literary Societies. Before I reply to them, will you be good enough to tell me what you know of the College,—particularly whether it be a college, & not a school; whether the students are of the usual age & acquirements of our New England Colleges?" (L, 3:369). William's reply indicates not only how fluid were college titles at this period, but also how comparative rankings were already well in place: "The university of the city of N.Y. is a college, & not a high school, as these things go in the U.S. . . . I do not believe that said University is on a footing with Harvard & Yale, but it probably is with Columbia College & the 2ᵈ class colleges."[108]

William's detailed statement for Emerson's lectures in the "Conduct of Life" series in February 1852 indicates just how much accounting was involved (both for him and for Waldo, who made these types of arrangements for most of his own lectures):

➤ *William Emerson to Ralph Waldo Emerson, 30–31 March [1852]*

This morning Evans called & settled with me, & I am sorry to say diminished even the slender result he led us to believe certain on Saturday night. His credits are as follows:

1st	$66.50		
2d	42.75		
3d	49.50		
4th	51.		
C. S. Francis	2.75		
	212.50	212.50	

From which I deduct

Room	64.00	
Advertising	25.75	
Printing	7.75	
Discount	.25	
E. & B.'s comm^{ns} 7 ½%	15.57	
		113.32

The result to you is only—	99.18
So that I had to pay Evans—	25.82
to make up his am't paid me	125.00

Evans brought me the printers' bills, so that the only question that can remain is whether he has given an honest account of the receipts, & that must remain between him & his conscience.

Then as between you & me the account stands thus. I credit you with

$99.18

against which I charge

Mar. 26.	Cash p'd you		$10.
	" " Garnet	18.	
28	" " you	10.	
30 Balance due you	61.18	99.18	

This balance of $61.18 I will try to send you tomorrow in a bank check. I wish I had a better story to tell. . . .

31st I have obtained & inclose a bank check for $61.18.[109]

On one occasion, William unintentionally contributed to the text of one of Waldo's lectures. Writing on 15–16 January 1853, William mentioned an anecdote told him by a friend: "A Frenchman having lost his wife, appeared so much overcome with grief at the funeral, that one of his friends, who was present, on the first occasion of greeting him afterwards, offered his condolence, & said that he had perceived how keenly he felt his loss. When or where did you observe my sorrow? asked the widower. It was at the funeral service, said his friend. Ah! mon ami, said the disconsolate, you should have seen me at the grave!"[110] This later appeared, slightly changed, in Waldo's lecture on "France."[111]

As Waldo's career as a lecturer became more and more successful, he often gave a series of lectures arranged for him by friends in private rooms (rather than public auditoriums or lecture halls) attended by a small but well-paying group of people. The publisher James T. Fields and his wife—the author Annie Fields—did this for Waldo in Boston; and, as the following letter shows, William did it for Waldo in New York:

> Mr Ashley came to see me this morning, & desired me to mention to you that the arrangement of the Atheaeum Com[ee] is, to have your lecture read on Thursday, the 10th, at the Athenaeum itself, & not at any hired hall.[112] The place is not so convenient for a lecture, but it is the most suitable for the occasion; for you are invited, not to address a promiscuous audience, but only the members of the club and the ladies invited by them. Thus you see it is quite a private affair, & tho' the rooms are only those of a large private house, the numbers admitted are proportionally small, not to exceed 300. Then there will be no awkwardness in going from one place to another, which would be no trifle if it should be rainy & muddy. So you perceive, as you will please to perceive, that this is the best possible arrangement.[113]

The brothers' accounts show attention to small details as well as large ones. Waldo often had William subscribe to New York newspapers for him.[114] When the families visited each other, both brothers were scrupulous about the expenses involved.[115] Nor was the borrowing a one-way street from Waldo to William: there were occasions when William was able to return the favor during periods when Waldo was short of cash, as when he told William "I have some besetting temptations, for instance a cow pasture right across the brook, instead of hiring, as now, pasture a mile off, to & from which my cows are driven. Then a horse,—horse, or no horse? that is a question that comes nearer every month" (L, 4:260).[116] Nevertheless, over the years the correspondence is filled with letters like these:

⤬ *William Emerson to Ralph Waldo Emerson, 25 May 1857*

I wrote you yesterday stating our account, & though I received your letter of the 22[d] this morning, I thought I would send my letter just as it was. I have now come home, & looked back a few years in my Leger, & I think your own entries & your files of my letters will verify the results I arrive at. I find there that the joint account of G. Folsom & W. E. with you was closed on the 13th of April, 1853; previous to which time we owed you $3375. On that day G. Folsom paid his share, $2000. in cash, which after some correspondence between us I remitted to you on the

23ᵈ April in a check on the City Bank of Boston. As a memorandum of my own indebtedness I sent you my promissory note dated 1 April, 1853, for $1375.

This amount I paid by the cash remittance you mention, June 29, 1853

$375.

And the balance by assigning to you John A. Eaton's Bond Mortgage for

1000.

1375.

Thus you perceive our old account which had threatened to be immortal, was finally balanced.

From the 1st July, 1853, to which time I credited you with interest on $1375. I received from Eaton the interest on his bond & credited you with it until Apr. 1, 1855. Your executor's a/c then showing that you would owe me about $1700. I suggested to you that your most convenient way of paying me $1000. would be by assigning Eaton's bond, which was accordingly done. That left the $700. due, which, by your payᵗ of $100 in Decʳ & R. B[ulkeley]. E[merson].'s expenses of w'h you bro't me a memorandum, has shrunk to $574.

If further particulars would be more satisfactory to you, I can give you a copy of my account, beginning at any period you will fix upon. But as it exactly balances itself from July 1, 1853 to Augᵗ 1, 1854, I began my copy for you at the latter date.[117]

⤚ Ralph Waldo Emerson to William Emerson, 21 January 1862

You must give me a little longer day than 1 February, but I will instantly bestir myself & see what can be done to begin to pay my debts. The 1 January has found me in quite as poor plight as the rest of the Americans. Not a penny from my books since last June,—which usually yield 5, or $600.00 a year: The Atlantic Bank omitting its dividend: My Mad River & Lake Erie Bonds (Sandusky) which ought to pay $140. *per ann.* now for several years making no sign. Lidian's Plymouth House now for 3 years has paid nothing & still refuses. Her Court Street rents, which have grown important, are now withdrawn for the last year & a half & will not come to us again for a year & a half more, as they are paying a mortgage. Then lastly, almost all income from lectures has quite ceased: so that your letter found me in a study how to pay 3, or 400.00 with $50. My purpose now is to go to the Atlantic Bank & see if they will lend me what I want on the security of their own stock. For their shares are so reduced in the market, at present, that it would be unwise to sell them. This is my present dependence. For I have no stock which I should like to sell at present prices. I have been trying to sell a woodlot (the Saw-mill lot) at or near its appraisal, which would give me something more than $300. but the purchaser does not appear. Vt. & Canada [railroad] pays its dividend, but not yet any back rent, so it sells for 100., tho' Abel Adams thinks it worth 150.

My fortunes must repair themselves by a new book, whenever books again sell; &, if things come right again, by the return to payment of the unpaying properties. Meantime, we are all trying to be as unconsuming as candles under an extinguisher, and tis frightful to think how many rivals we have in distress & in economy. But far better that this grinding should go on bad & worse, than that we be driven by any impatience into a hasty peace, or any peace restoring the old rottenness. (L, 5:263–264)

To a great extent, Concord served as a beacon light for William as it did for Waldo. Walden Pond, for example, served as a topic of conversation. In 1844, Waldo announced his plans to buy land there:

I have lately added an absurdity or two to my usual ones, which I am impatient to tell you of. In one of my solitary wood-walks by Walden Pond, I met two or three men who told me they had come thither to sell & to buy a field, on which they wished me to to [sic] bid as pur-chaser. As it was on the shore of the pond, & now for years I had a sort of daily occupancy in it, I bid on it, & bought it, eleven acres for $8.10 per acre. The next day I carried some of my well beloved gossips to the same place & they deciding that the field was not good for anything, if Heartwell Bigelow should cut down his pine-grove, I bought, for 125 dollars more, his pretty wood lot of 3 or 4 acres. and so am landlord & waterlord of 14 acres, more or less, on the shore of Walden, & can raise my own blackberries. I am now, like other men who have hazarded a small stake, mad for more. Since Mrs [Lucy Jackson] Brown wishes me to build her a cottage on some land near my house; & the dreaming [Bronson] Alcott is here with Indian dreams that I helped him to some house & farm in the Spirit Land! These are the light headed frolics of a hack of a scribe when released at last from months of weary tending on the printers devil! I expect to grow fat & plump now for weeks to come. (L, 3:262–263)

William's reply shows that he had not forgotten Alcott's "Orphic Sayings" from the *Dial:* "If you had bought the shores of Walden pond before they were thrown open to the garish eye of rail road travellers, I should not have marvelled. But I confess I shall hardly think those years bring you wisdom, if you throw away even these cheap acres upon such a sieve (pardon the confusion of metaphor) as the Orphic philosopher." He added, that if Waldo "want any money to complete your purchase, I will furnish whatever you call for."[118] Within a few years, Waldo was to boast that "I am not without a prospect that my woodlot by Walden Pond will get an increased value soon; as Mr Tudor has invaded us with a gang of Irishmen & taken 10,000 tons of ice from the Pond in the last weeks."[119] However, Waldo added, "If this continues, he will spoil my lot for purposes for which I chiefly value it, & I shall be glad to sell it," resulting in this reply from William: "I am sorry, if you regret it, that the ice-cutters have invaded the silence of Walden Pond."[120]

The subject of Concord also entered into a practical discussion about death. Waldo had given the address when Sleepy Hollow Cemetery was dedicated in September 1855, and soon after there was correspondence about locating the Emersons—past and present—there:

⤖ Ralph Waldo Emerson to William Emerson, 24 September 1855

We are laying out Sleepy Hollow it is to be Consecrated on Saturday next. I am to make an address to those interested. Mr Sanborn has written an ode which will be sung.[121] Then follows an auction of lots. We have staked out a hundred, & settled that the average price shall be $15. Then a committee are to appraise these lots at prices not exceeding $25.00. One may sell for that sum, & another be rated at $5. or $3. It is also proposed to sell the privilege of first choice, & so on. These are all the facts. William, in talking with me, thought you would perhaps like to purchase a lot. I don't know whether he spoke from any hint you had dropt. If you have any such wish, it is quite easy to do, if you will send me word. I can buy two adjacent lots. Or it can be arranged at more leisure hereafter. I shall probably buy something now. The ground is wonderfully improved by all the little that has been done to it in two months. (*L,* 4:530)

⤖ William Emerson to Ralph Waldo Emerson, 27 September 1855

I was glad yesterday to receive your letter of the 24th. 'Let the dead bury their dead' is a text,[122] which has always preached its own sermon to me. But Susan & William desire to have a plot in the Sleepy Hollow Cemetery, and if you will take two adjacent lots that please you, you can have one of them registered in my name, & charge me accordingly. You can then inclose or otherwise arrange the lots on one plan.[123]

The exchange over Sleepy Hollow indicated how the health of the families was a prime matter of conversation—not surprising given the strain of tuberculosis and other illnesses that ran through the Emerson line.[124] At one point in

1852, William alarmed Waldo by his report of a sudden illness of the visiting Ellen Emerson:

> I am grieved to tell you that Ellen is quite unwell. She went to the city yesterday (Monday) morning with Edith and Haven, on an excursion of pleasure, to see Barnum's Museum & the Dusseldorf Gallery, & returned home by the 1 o'clock boat. The day was beautiful & the air temperate, & they enjoyed themselves much; but Ellen looked pale on her return, & had no appetite for dinner, & soon complained of her throat. During the night she was quite feverish, & craved ice-water. This morning I sent for Dr Anderson who told us that her throat was ulcerated, & advised flax seed poultices, & gave some drops. She was soon greatly relieved of her fever; but she continues quite sick, and as we think it best that the Dr should see her again tonight, William has now gone for him (10 P.M.)
>
> Wednesday morn^g.
>
> Dr Anderson thought Ellen better, when he came at night; and she passed a very good night, slept well, & was comfortable & nearly or quite free from fever this morn^g.
>
> It seems probable that the throat will not get rid of the inflammation, entirely, for several days. But the Dr has no apprehension but that the disorder will be soon removed. I shall send you bulletins daily. Ellen bears her illness with great equanimity, & Edith is earning perennial laurels as a tender nurse.[125]

William apologized the next day for giving Waldo "anxious thoughts about Ellen." He was now delighted to report that she was "much better yesterday afternoon on my return home; she had a quiet night, & this morning is cheerful & comfortable, & took some breakfast with good appetite. The inflammation in her throat appears to have subsided almost as rapidly as it came on."[126] Susan Haven Emerson was continually ill and her movements restricted; she once came down with erysipelas—a disease that inflames the skin—and, ironically, the same problem that had plagued Mary Moody Emerson.[127] When Edward Waldo Emerson became too ill to attend Harvard, William suggested that he join Willie in Curaçao, where he was recuperating for his health.[128] Edward recovered without making the trip but Willie did not; and William wrote with sadness to Waldo on 29 February 1864: "You will know by Edward, who left us this morning, that William died at 3 A.M. You know he was our chiefest jewel. His mother had long since made up her mind that he could not stay in this world, & bears the bereavement as well as possible for a mother to do."[129] William suffered from headaches, what he called "that troublesome customer, my dark shadow," sometimes as many as three debilitating ones in a week.[130] Indeed, one of William's last letters to Waldo deals with health, as he writes that the "doctors have given me a variety of drugs, but not much encouragement that they ever expect to cure me. I can't walk but a little. Sometimes I get a good night's rest, often not."[131]

For many years a recurring subject in the correspondence between Concord and New York or Staten Island was the ongoing dialogue in which William tried to convince Waldo to come south and Waldo attempted to get William to relocate to Concord. One early letter from William shows how the arguments generally went:

> Susan & I think you had better at once make arrangements to sell out at Concord, & come to Staten Island, where the mercury never goes below zero, & east winds are not so keen as in the Bay State. We are glad that you took such decisive measures to expel the enemy, & think from the pleasant tone of your letter, that you must have met with some success. But what use is there in staying on the very top of Olympus, aye, surrounded by celestials, if the airs of that pure region are fatal to life? Better come down & dwell with us mortals, where the summer winds do blow. Even if your accustomed associates are wanting, all past worthies will sooth & enlighten here as well as in Middlesex. Life & thought & action brood & ferment in our great city as intensely as elsewhere, & you might at pleasure mingle in its turmoil, or watch its processes from our quiet cottage. And if you would roam through our woods, you could from them see sky & ocean as glorious as from the Apennine. I know that you have all things comfortable round you, & that you will use all due prudence, & Lidian all possible care & kindness; but I don't believe that Emerson lungs are suited to the climate of Boston, & seriously think you ought to turn your face away from it.[132]

By the 1860s, when William's children were grown, the argument gained steam in the other direction:

➵ Ralph Waldo Emerson to William Emerson, 11 March 1863

> Mr [Moncure Daniel] Conway came to me this morning to say that he wished to sell his house in Concord.[133] He is, you know, the editor of the "Commonwealth" newspaper in Boston, & begins to find it very inconvenient to live here. Then he is now proposing to go in April to England, & there stay till October. And he added, that he had promised (I so understood him,) Mrs Wm Emerson, that he would let her know if he should at any time wish to sell the house. I asked him, on what terms would he sell it? He said, he wished to sell the house *and the furniture* together, and the real price for both,—for he had no "asking price,"—is $5000. I

asked, if he had made any repairs, since he took the place? "No, none; but the garden, vines, &c were now in perfect order." He gave $4000. for the house; a very low price, as we all thought: but, in the depreciation of the currency, I suppose, might well ask 4500. now, for the same value.

I also remember that he had it on very easy terms of payment, & I suppose might transfer to the purchaser whatever of the debt is unpaid, on the same terms. If there be any such good will in you as has sometimes been to buy a house here, write me at once what your wishes are on the matter. (L, 5:319–320)

⇥ William Emerson to Ralph Waldo Emerson, 14 March 1863

I have a strong wish to sit down in Concord & pass the rest of my life there, & Susan's desire to do so is even stronger than mine. But there are lions in the way. I cannot see how it is possible for us to buy the Conway house at present. And Susan thinks she never could have said to Mr Conway what he attributes to her; or, more properly, she has no recollection of having ever received such a promise from him as you allude to.[134]

This time, the pleas for a change in residence had an effect, and, in January 1864, Susan and William leased the house in central Concord of Colonel William Whiting.[135] Willie's death in February complicated their plans, but by April the move from New York to Concord was underway, with Susan coming first, followed by William in July.[136] Although Susan and William returned to New York for periods of time, during the next two years they enjoyed being treated as part of Waldo's family by Concordians and visitors alike.

In 1868, Susan's health—never good to begin with—became worse, and it was clear by January that she was terminally ill. Ellen nursed her and was distraught, for Susan was "loved and needed by her husband and children," and she had been to Ellen and Edith "a second Mother, every visit to her [in Staten Island] was a new pleasure and her counsels and instructions had been of value to us from early days." She died on 6 February and was buried in the family plot in Sleepy Hollow on the tenth. Soon after, William had "a difficulty of breathing" and was nursed by Lidian.[137] In May he returned to New York and established a residence at 33 East 19th Street to be with Haven and his new wife.[138] He continued to decline, and his last letter to Waldo, written 4 September 1868, ominously told of his condition: "Ellen & Edward have both written me very kind letters which I have not had the energy to answer. Indeed, I am but poorly. The last two days I was not able to get down stairs."[139] Waldo went to New York, arriving on the morning of the 13th. He talked with William for half an hour (he was "much altered in face & in speech, but entirely intelligent . . . though speaking with difficulty"), had lunch with his nephew Charles, and saw William once more before he died at one o'clock (L, 6:33).

The next day Waldo, Charles, and Haven accompanied William's casket on the train to Concord. William was buried on the 15th next to Susan and their two boys in the family plot in Sleepy Hollow. Elizabeth Hoar spent the afternoon with Waldo's family mourning the loss of yet another Emerson brother. When he returned to New York, Haven sent a trunk of books to Waldo that William had wanted him to have. And, in a fitting coda to lives of thrift and utility, Ellen later gave Haven the news that William's clothes either fit Waldo or could be altered for his wardrobe by a Boston tailor. The brothers were still helping each other, even in death.[140]

Notes

PREFACE

1. Waldo's letters are in *The Letters of Ralph Waldo Emerson,* ed. Ralph L. Rusk (vols. 1–6) & Eleanor M. Tilton (vols. 7–10) (New York: Columbia University Press, 1939, 1990–1995); hereafter cited as *L.*

2. In addition, there are letters written by Charles, Edward, and William to their mother Ruth Haskins Emerson and step-grandfather Ezra Ripley, as well as Charles's 181 letters to his fiancée Elizabeth Hoar and 86 letters from the three brothers to their paternal aunt Mary Moody Emerson, in which they discuss their moral and theological upbringing and views.

3. Because all but one of the major characters in this biography share the same last name, we adopt the practice of referring to everyone—male or female—by their first names as a matter of convenience.

4. See, in particular, Ralph L. Rusk, *The Life of Ralph Waldo Emerson* (New York: Scribner's, 1949); Gay Wilson Allen, *Waldo Emerson: A Biography* (New York: Viking, 1981); John McAleer, *Ralph Waldo Emerson: Days of Encounter* (Boston: Little, Brown, 1984); and Robert D. Richardson, Jr., *Emerson: The Mind on Fire* (Berkeley: University of California Press, 1995).

5. At the time of his death, the Reverend William Emerson (1769–1811) was the pastor of Boston's prestigious First Church. Among his accomplishments outside of the pulpit were his editing of the *Monthly Anthology,* a journal that ran from 1803 to 1811 and featured articles and reviews on literature, science, and history, and his work in establishing the Boston Athenaeum. Writing to his brother William in 1850, Waldo remembered his father's manner as severe and his theology as docile, but he praised his fostering of "the Anthology & the Athenaeum" as "things [that] ripened into [Joseph Stevens] Buckminster [William Ellery] Channing & [Edward] Everett" (Waldo to William, 10 February 1850, *L,* 5:178–179).

6. See Phyllis Cole, *Mary Moody Emerson and the Origins of Transcendentalism: A Family History* (New York: Oxford University Press, 1998), and *The Selected Letters of Mary Moody Emerson,* ed. Nancy Craig Simmons (Athens: University of Georgia Press, 1993).

7. Robert Bulkeley Emerson (1807–1859), a fifth Emerson brother to survive to maturity, is a shadowy figure who exists only in the brothers' correspondence and, occasionally, in Ruth Haskins Emerson's or Mary Moody Emerson's. Although he was mentally disabled, he was physically fit and for many of his adult years worked on local farms in exchange for room and board. Prone to occasional outbursts of violence, Bulkeley, as he was called within the family, was periodically institutionalized at the McLean Asylum in Charlestown. Waldo and his brother William paid Bulkeley's medical expenses and, with occasional help from Charles before his death in 1836, routinely made up the difference between the value of Bulkeley's labor and the costs associated with his room and board at farms near Concord, Massachusetts.

8. In our form of presentation, we acknowledge the success of two such earlier works, both of which are still routinely cited by Emerson scholars today: James Elliot Cabot, *A Memoir of Ralph Waldo Emerson,* 2 vols. (Boston: Houghton Mifflin, 1887), and Edward Waldo Emerson, *Emerson in Concord: A Memoir* (Boston: Houghton Mifflin, 1889).

9. Available at http://www.emersonsociety.org. We have regularized the texts in our edition by silently emending punctuation where it was lacking or caused confusion; also, we have inserted words within brackets when clarity requires it. The electronic texts follow the rules of transcription traditionally employed by Emerson editors, including surrounding cancelled material with angle brackets (<word>) and insertions with up and down arrows (↑word↓); see *The Journals and Miscellaneous Notebooks of Ralph Waldo Emerson,* ed. William H. Gilman & Ralph H. Orth et al., 16 vols. (Cambridge, Mass.: Harvard University Press, 1960–1982), 1:xlix–l.

10. We have included a detailed chronology for ease in following the outward events in the brothers' lives during the years we examine in this book.

11. "Nominalist and Realist," in *The Collected Works of Ralph Waldo Emerson,* ed. Alfred R. Ferguson, Joseph Slater, & Douglas Emory Wilson, 6 vols. to date. (Cambridge, Mass.: Harvard University Press, 1971–), 3:137.

12. "Experience," in *Collected Works,* 3:30.

13. It is a testament to the quality of the manuscript materials with which are dealing that we have, on occasion, felt the need to repeat some letter texts because the material bears so strongly upon multiple threads of our narrative.

14. The various typescripts of this are at the Houghton Library, bMS Am 1280.235 (709–710). We acknowledge the pioneering work Baxter performed in discovering information about the death and internment of Edward Emerson in Puerto Rico.

15. See Ronald A. Bosco & Joel Myerson, "Resources for the Study of Ralph Waldo Emerson at Harvard," *Harvard Library Bulletin,* 13, nos. 3–4 (Fall–Winter 2003): 93–102.

16. The galleys for Haven's talk, "William Emerson Travels Abroad," as well as the typescript of his abortive biography, are in the Joel Myerson Collection of Nineteenth-Century American Literature, Thomas Cooper Library, University of South Carolina.

17. Karen Kalinevitch, "Ralph Waldo Emerson's Older Brother: The Letters and Journal of William Emerson" (Ph.D. diss., University of Tennessee, 1982), and Henry F. Pommer, *Emerson's First Marriage* (Carbondale: Southern Illinois University Press, 1967).

18. A complete catalogue of this collection (Ms N-251) is available at the Massachusetts Historical Society: Sarah E. Burley, *Emerson Family Papers 1786–1959* (1993); it is also available on-line at http://masshist.org/findingaids/doc.cfm?fa=fa0012&hi=on&t ag=archdesc&query=emerson.

19. See also the shorter version: Albert J. von Frank, *An Emerson Chronology* (New York: G. K. Hall, 1994).

CHAPTER 1

1. Daniel Webster (1782–1852), politician and orator; William Ellery Channing (1780–1842), the most famous Unitarian clergyman of his time.

2. "The Rule of Life" (1867–1871), in *The Later Lectures of Ralph Waldo Emerson, 1843–1871*, ed. Ronald A. Bosco & Joel Myerson, 2 vols. (Athens: University of Georgia Press, 2001), 2:388.

3. Waldo to Thomas Carlyle, 17 September 1836, in *Correspondence of Emerson and Carlyle*, ed. Joseph Slater (New York: Columbia University Press, 1964), p. 148, written after Charles Chauncy Emerson's death in May 1836.

4. To the best of our knowledge, John Hanson Mitchell is the first scholar of Concord and, by extension, Emerson family history, to introduce the idea publicly that Bulkeley suffered from Tourette's Syndrome.

5. Grindall Reynolds (1822–1894), pastor of the First Church in Concord.

6. Details that follow have been drawn from a variety of sources, including the Emerson brothers' letters. In addition to the letters, see Haven Emerson, "Five Generations of Tuberculosis: A Family History," in *Selected Papers of Haven Emerson* (Battle Creek, Mich.: W. K. Kellogg Foundation, 1949), pp. 487–494. For a general treatment of the disease, see Rene & Jean Dubos, *The White Plague: Tuberculosis, Man and Society* (Boston: Little, Brown, 1952), which also provides a brief overview of the disease in the Emerson family (pp. 39–41); for a more recent treatment of the disease in the Emerson family, see Janet M. Anderson, "Ellen Emerson and the Tubercular Muse," *Literature and Medicine,* 18 (Spring 1999): 39–59.

7. William Emerson died on 13 September 1868, after suffering over several months from a wasting disease. In addition to pneumonia, which is usually given as the cause of William's death, he may also have had a form of cancer, for as soon as he died, his body was sealed in a lead coffin and shipped overnight to Concord for immediate burial (see Waldo to Lidian Emerson, 13 September 1868, *L*, 6:33–34). In the midst of making plans to escape from New York to Minnesota—which was then believed to be a good environment for tubercular patients—for his health, young William Emerson died on 29 February 1864. On the day his son died, William wrote the news to Waldo, asking that preparations be made for his burial in Concord, and stating that the boy, who had only recently married, was "our chiefest jewel. His mother [Susan Haven Emerson] had long since made up her mind that he could not stay in this world, & bears the bereavement as well as possible for a mother to do" (MHi, Ms N-251 [636]).

8. Haven Emerson, "Five Generations of Tuberculosis: A Family History," p. 495.

9. Possibly because within their familial circle the Emerson brothers knew all too well the symptoms of tuberculosis, their letters often appear to us to be circumspect in their descriptions of health crises within the family. It is clear that brother William's son "Willie" had tuberculosis; however, Waldo was never explicit in naming his own son's particular ailment. In a letter to his brother William, Waldo wrote only that Edward "showed himself so feeble when shut up in a college room & routine, that I have had him at home now for a fortnight & have almost decided to withdraw him [from Harvard] altogether for this year & let him enter Freshman again next July" (6 November 1861, *L,* 5:256–257). But the two brothers undoubtedly knew exactly what each was talking about. In letters they exchanged for the next several months, both discussed the desirability of Edward joining his cousin Willie in Curaçao, where he had been since May 1861. In the end, however, Edward, who did not return to Harvard in July 1862 as his father had earlier hoped he would, decided to journey to California to restore his health, and he left Concord on 12 May 1862 and did not return home until the following October (see *L,* 5:271n, and *JMN,* 15:251–252).

10. MH, bMS Am 1280.220 (126).

11. For more on Waldo as a letter-writer, see the introduction to *The Selected Letters of Ralph Waldo Emerson,* ed. Joel Myerson (New York: Columbia University Press, 1997).

12. William Shakespeare, *Hamlet,* Act III, Scene 1.

13. Possibly a vague allusion to Exodus 33:11–13 (see *L,* 1:191n).

14. MH, bMS Am 1280.220 (52), folder 34.

15. MH, bMS Am 1280.226 (165). For Charles's letter to Mary, see MH, bMS Am 1280.220 (49).

16. Probably Samuel Ripley (1783–1847), Mary Moody Emerson's step-brother and the brothers' half-uncle, a Unitarian minister in Waltham, Massachusetts, from 1809 to 1846, where he operated the "Ripley school," which prepared boys for entrance to Harvard; in 1818, he married the learned Sarah Alden Bradford (1793–1867), one of Mary's favorite confidantes.

17. 9–15 February 1833, MH, bMS Am 1280.226 (105).

18. "ama, si vis amari": love if you want to be loved, from Epistles 9.6.6 by Seneca the Elder (ca. 54 B.C.E.–39 C.E.), Roman writer and rhetorician.

19. MH, bMS Am 1280.226 (218).

20. In addition to being known as an orator, Everett (1794–1865) was a Unitarian minister, Harvard professor, and politician.

21. For more on Squire Samuel Hoar (1778–1856), see chapter 5.

22. "Character" (1865), in *The Complete Works of Ralph Waldo Emerson,* ed. Edward Waldo Emerson, 12 vols. (Boston: Houghton Mifflin, 1903–1904), 10:100–101.

23. For comprehensive genealogical treatments of the Emerson and Haskins lines through the time the Emerson brothers were born, see Benjamin Kendall Emerson, *The Ipswich Emersons A.D. 1636–1900: A Genealogy of the Descendants of Thomas Emerson of Ipswich, Mass. with Some Account of His English Ancestry* (Boston: David Clapp & Son, 1900), and David Greene Haskins, *Ralph Waldo Emerson: His Maternal Ancestors with Some Reminiscences of Him* (Boston: Cupples, Upham, 1887). Genealogical information

relating to the Emerson and Haskins families developed here has been drawn primarily from these two sources.

24. Writing to his brother William about their mother's funeral and burial in November 1853, which illness had prevented William from attending in Concord, Waldo reported that he had arranged for a Congregational service presided over by Barzillai Frost, who "uniformly held Mother in veneration." He wrote, "Every thing yesterday [18 November] was well & properly done. I could have gladly asked, had it been anywise practicable, that the English liturgy should have been read at her burial; for she was born a subject of King George, had been, in her childhood, so versed in that service, that, in her old age, it seemed still most natural to her, & the Common Prayer Book was on her bureau" (19 November 1853, *L,* 4:401).

25. Printed in Haskins, *Ralph Waldo Emerson: His Maternal Ancestors,* p. 27.

26. *Ralph Waldo Emerson: His Maternal Ancestors,* pp. 26–27.

27. Plato (428/7–348/7 B.C.E..), the most famous of the Greek philosophers, believed that actual objects are copies of transcendent ideas; the followers of John Calvin (1509–1564), a Protestant reformer and theologian, believed in the depravity of mankind and the doctrine of predestination.

28. Michelangelo Buonarroti (1475–1564), Italian painter, sculptor, and poet, often called "Aneglo" by Waldo.

29. MHi, Ms N-251 (334).

30. 25 September [1834], MH, bMS Am 1280.220 (52), folder 21.

31. Abolitionists were the antislavery people; the Non-Resistance Society preached passive resistance to authority; temperance reformers advocated the avoidance of alcohol.

32. "The Burial of Sir John Moore" (1817), 11. 11–12, by Charles Wolfe (1791–1823), Irish clergyman.

33. For "Ezra Ripley, D. D.," which first appeared in the *Atlantic Monthly,* 52 (November 1883): 592–596, see *Complete Works,* 10:381–395.

34. 7 April 1809, MHi, Ms N-251 (16).

35. 30 October 1831, MH, bMS Am 1280.226 (259).

36. 12–15 June [1831], MH, bMS Am 1280.226 (56).

37. 16 June 1831, MH, bMS Am 1280.226 (7).

38. 17 June 1831, MH, bMS Am 1280.226 (158).

39. With his wife, the Reverend Benajah Root attended William Emerson during his last hours. On 21 October 1776, he wrote to William's congregation in Concord, describing his illness, death, and burial "with honors of war" (see *L,* 7:129).

40. Peter Barrett (b. 1755), the son of Col. James Barrett of Concord.

41. Shakespeare, *Othello,* Act IV, Scene 2.

42. MH, bMS Am 1280.226 (56).

43. Edward worked in Sidney Mason's establishment when he moved to Puerto Rico; see chapter 3.

44. "en avant": continuing to move onwards.

45. The Freemason's were a powerful secret society in which members communicated with each in public by means of secret symbols.

46. MH, bMS Am 1280.226 (7).

47. Waldo preached Sermons X and LXIV on 5 June in Burlington.

48. James Marsh (1794–1842), president of the University of Vermont and American editor of *Aids to Reflection* (1829), by Samuel Taylor Coleridge (1772–1834), English poet and philosopher.

49. Waldo preached Sermons XCIII and XCV on 12 June in Northampton.

50. Judge Joseph W. Lyman, Sr. (1767–1847), and Anne Jean Robbins (1789–1867), his second wife, were friends of the Emerson family and the parents of Charles's close friend, Joseph W. Lyman, Jr. (1812–1871).

51. MH, bMS Am 1280.226 (158).

52. MH, bMS Am 1280.226 (163).

53. 29 October [1832], MHi, Ms N-251 (268).

54. Possibly a reference to 1 Samuel 17: "And David girded his sword upon his armour, and he assayed to go; for he had not proved it. And David said unto Saul, I cannot go with these; for I have not proved them. And David put them off him."

55. [March 1828], MH, bMS Am 1280.226 (139).

56. The manuscripts for both essays are at the Harvard Archives: "Whether the Moral Influence of Poetry Has Been on the Whole Beneficial to Mankind" (HU 89.165.69) and "Publick Opinion" (HU 6828.54)

57. 25 April [1828], *MMEL*, pp. 239–240.

58. MH, bMS Am 1280.226 (101).

59. MH, bMS Am 1280.226 (148).

60. Charles may be thinking of the hymn, "We Give You But Your Own," which contains this line.

61. MHi, Ms N-251 (177).

62. For more on the family's finances, see chapter 6.

63. 14 July 1828, MHi, Ms N-251 (114).

64. 1-[4] October 1815, MHi, Ms N-251 (20).

65. 12 September [1817], MHi, Ms N-251 (23), and 5–19 December 1817, MH, bMS Am 1280.226 (3050), respectively.

66. 1–10 January 1818, MHi, Ms N-251 (26).

67. 23 July 1818, MHi, Ms N-251 (28).

68. 10 July 1831, MHi, Ms N-251 (196).

69. 4–8 July 1831, MH, bMS Am 1280.226 (2960).

70. John Thornton Kirkland (1770–1840), Congregationalist minister and president of Harvard at this time.

71. No one named James Blanchard graduated from Harvard; William Duncan Lamb (d. 1819) was graduated, along with Charles, in the Class of 1818.

72. Francis Jenks (1798–1832), Harvard Class of 1817, graduated from the Harvard Divinity School in 1820.

73. Joseph Green Cogswell (1786–1871), teacher, educator, and librarian, was graduated from Harvard in 1806 and served as a tutor 1813–1815.

74. Hugo Grotius (1583–1645), Dutch jurist, poet, and playwright, wrote *De veritate religionis Christianae [True Religion]* (1632).

75. Nathaniel Langdon Frothingham (1793–1870), instructor in rhetoric and oratory from 1812 to 1815 and later a Unitarian clergyman in Boston

76. Willard Phillips (1784–1873), tutor in Latin, arithmetic, and natural philosophy from 1811 to 1815.

77. Livy (59 B.C.E.–17 C.E.), Roman historian.

78. MHi, Ms N-251 (20).

79. MHi, Ms N-251 (23).

80. Virgil (70–19 B.C.E.), Roman epic poet and author of the *Aeneid*.

81. MH, bMS Am 1280.226 (3050).

82. *The Traveller* (1764), ll. 8–9, by Oliver Goldsmith (ca. 1730–1774), multifaceted English writer, changed by William from the original "My heart untravelled, fondly turns to thee; /Still to my brother turns. . . ."

83. MHi, Ms N-251 (26).

84. Jean Pierre Claris de Florian (1755–1794), French romancer, dramatist, and writer of fables.

85. MHi, Ms N-251 (28).

86. MHi, Ms N-251 (31).

87. Monadnoc, a mountain in New Hampshire.

88. MHi, Ms N-251 (195).

89. MHi, Ms N-251 (196).

90. Writing to William on 30 April 1828, after learning that his brother had spent the better part of the spring in ill heath, Waldo remarked, "Have you forgotten that all the Emersons overdo themselves? Don't you die of the leprosy of your race—ill-weaved ambition." The cure, Waldo told William, was in walking out in nature and relaxing in the comfortable surroundings of one's own home. He concluded, adding, "I can't persuade that wilful brother Edward of mine to use the same sovereign nostrum" (*L,* 1:233).

91. In spite of the extraordinary volume of his lifelong correspondence, Waldo did not always enjoy writing letters. He considered them an obligation, and as such, he believed the necessity to write them intruded on his freedom. For his attitude toward letter writing, see Myerson's introduction to *Selected Letters* and Ronald A. Bosco, "'Good Society is such an optical illusion': Ralph Waldo Emerson and His Correspondents," *Manuscripts,* 55 (Spring 2003): 117–134.

92. MH, bMS Am 1280.226 (243).

93. MH, bMS Am 1280.226 (244).

94. MH, bMS Am 1280.226 (244).

95. John Adams (1772–1863), principal of the Phillips Academy from 1810 to 1833.

96. The Theological Seminary at Phillips Academy was known for its conservative religious views; Eliphalet Pearson (1752–1826) was professor of sacred literature there.

97. While attending Phillips Academy, Edward boarded first at the home of Mrs. Phebe Abbot of Andover, and then he later moved to the home of Ezra Abbot, a local farmer.

98. MH, bMS Am 1280.226 (224).

99. Gordon Hall (1784–1826), a Congregational minister and former president of Andover Theological Seminary, became a missionary in Calcutta and Bombay, where he served from 1813 until his death from cholera.

100. MH, bMS Am 1280.226 (226).

101. Edward had been home in Boston, where he extended his visit in order to help Ruth and William pack the belongings his oldest brother intended to carry with him to his new teaching job in Kennebunk, Maine.

102. MH, bMS Am 1280.226 (227).

103. Elm Vale, Mary's farm in Waterville, Maine.

104. MH, bMS Am 1280.226 (231).

105. See Edward to Ruth, 24 March 1818, above.

106. Ebenezer Porter (1772–1834), first president of Andover Theological Seminary.

107. MH, bMS Am 1280.226 (232).

108. MH, bMS Am 1280.226 (233).

109. MH, bMS Am 1280.226 (234).

110. Evidently, Ruth had written a letter granting her permission that Edward be allowed to study in his room when he felt too indisposed to attend classes.

111. MH, bMS Am 1280.226 (236).

112. William Bartlet (1748–1841), Newburyport merchant and one of the four founders of the Theological Seminary at Phillips Academy, paid for the building of a chapel there, which was dedicated on 22 September 1818 and named for him.

113. MH, bMS Am 1280.226 (237).

114. MH, bMS Am 1280.226 (242).

115. The Quakers or Society of Friends, English sect founded in the seventeenth century known for its pacifism and belief in a inner spiritual voice

116. MH, bMS Am 1280.226 (243).

117. Francis Bacon (1561-1626), English essayist, statesman, and philosopher.

118. MH, bMS Am 1280.226 (244).

119. For more on this institution, see Pauline Holmes, *A Tercentenary History of the Boston Public Latin School 1635–1935* (Cambridge, Mass.: Harvard University Press, 1935).

120. 22 February 1813, *MMEL*, p. 70.

121. For Waldo's paper on Socrates, see *Two Unpublished Essays,* ed. Edward Everett Hale (Boston: Lamson, Wolffe, 1896).

122. See Ronald A. Bosco, "His Lectures Were Poetry, His Teaching the Music of the Spheres: Annie Adams Fields and Francis Greenwood Peabody on Emerson's 'Natural History of the Intellect' University Lectures at Harvard in 1870," *Harvard Library Bulletin,* n.s. 8 (Summer 1997): 1–79.

123. Ecclesiastes 12:6.

124. "vox et preterea nihil": fine words without meaning or significance.

125. MH, bMS Am 1280.226 (174).

126. Elizabeth Palmer Peabody, "Emerson as Preacher," in *The Genius and Character of Emerson: Lectures at the Concord School of Philosophy,* ed. F. B. Sanborn (Boston: James R. Osgood, 1885), p. 146.

127. See Charles to Mary, 14 March 1829, MH, bMS Am 1280.220 (49).

128. For a recent collection of reminiscences of Waldo, many of which were published after his death and remark at some length on his early years at Harvard, see *Emerson in His Own Time: A Biographical Chronicle of His Life, Drawn from Recollections, Interviews, and Memoirs by His Family, Friends, and Associates,* ed. Ronald A. Bosco & Joel Myerson (Iowa City: University of Iowa Press, 2003).

129. Margaret Fuller (1810–1850), author, feminist, and friend of Waldo's, also published "Lines . . . on the Death of C. C. E." in the 17 May 1835 *Boston Daily Centinel & Gazette.* David Hatch Barlow (1803–1864), one of Edward's former classmates and oldest friends, was as devastated as Edward's brothers were by the news of his death. On 24 October 1824, Waldo acknowledged Barlow's "kind & elegant tribute to the memory of your friend & my brother" (*L,* 1:422). Barlow's "Lines to the Memory of Edward Bliss Emerson, who died in Porto Rico, October 1834, Aged 29," appeared on 8 November 1834 in the *Christian Register,* where Fuller first encountered them.

130. Fuller to Frederic Henry Hedge, 9 November 1834, in *The Letters of Margaret Fuller,* ed. Robert N. Hudspeth, 6 vols. (Ithaca, N.Y.: Cornell University Press, 1983–1994), 1:211–212.

131. Joseph Story (1779–1845), lawyer and politician.

132. Shakespeare, *Hamlet,* Act III, Scene 1.

133. This text was enclosed in a letter from Edward Everett to Waldo, 22 November 1855, Edward Everett's Letterbook, MHi.

134. Frederic Henry Hedge (1805–1890), Unitarian minister and long-time friend of Waldo's. Hedge's letters were among the many that James Elliot Cabot (1821–1903), Waldo's literary executor, was collecting for his *A Memoir of Ralph Waldo Emerson,* 2 vols. (Boston: Houghton Mifflin, 1887).

135. The Marquise de Lafayette (1757–1834), a hero of the American Revolution, had participated in a triumphal march through Boston in 1825

136. Frederic Henry Hedge to James Elliot Cabot, 14 September 1882 and 30 September 1882, in Mathew Fisher, "Emerson Remembered: Nine Letters by Frederic Henry Hedge," in *Studies in the American Renaissance 1989,* ed. Joel Myerson (Charlottesville: University Press of Virginia, 1989), pp. 318–319, 322–323.

137. Oliver Wendell Holmes (1809–1894), author and physician.

138. "To The Pious Memory Of The Accomplished Young Lady Mrs. Anne Killigrew" (1686), ll. 23–25, by John Dryden (1631–1700), English metaphysical poet and dramatist.

139. *Paradise Lost* (1667), Book IV, l. 820, by John Milton (1608–1674), English poet and political writer.

140. Oliver Wendell Holmes, *Ralph Waldo Emerson* (Boston: Houghton Mifflin, 1885), pp. 20–21, 23–24.

141. Edward Waldo Emerson, *Emerson in Concord: A Memoir* (Boston: Houghton Mifflin, 1888), pp. 51–52.

142. George Frisbie Hoar (1826-1904), American lawyer and legislator, was Waldo's neighbor in Concord.

143. Samuel May (1810–1899), Harvard Divinity School graduate, minister at Leicester, Massachusetts, and abolitionist.

144. Joseph Warren Cross (1808–1906), minister at Boxborough and West Boylston, Massachusetts.

145. George F. Hoar, *Autobiography of Seventy Years,* 2 vols. (New York: Scribner's, 1903), 1:62–69.

CHAPTER 2

1. See Conrad Wright, "The Early Period (1811–1840)," in *The Harvard Divinity School: Its Place in Harvard University and in American Culture,* ed. George Hunston Williams (Boston: Beacon, 1954), pp. 23–27. Later, Ware's son was replaced by Waldo as pastor of the Second Church, and Norton attacked Waldo's Divinity School Address, calling it "the latest form of infidelity."

2. George Ripley to his mother, 30 September 1823, in Octavius Brooks Frothingham, *George Ripley* (Boston: Houghton Mifflin, 1882), pp. 20–21.

3. Henry A. Pochmann, *German Culture in America, 1600–1900* (Madison: University of Wisconsin Press, 1957), p. 63.

4. For information on Göttingen, see Cynthia Stokes Brown, "The American Discovery of the German University: Four Students at Göttingen, 1815–1822" (Ph.D. diss., Johns Hopkins University, 1964); [George Henry Calvert], "Göttingen in 1824," *Putnam's Monthly Magazine,* 8 (December 1856): 595–607, and *First Years in Europe* (Boston: William V. Spencer, 1866); Thomas Wentworth Higginson, "Göttingen and Harvard a Century Ago," in *Carlyle's Laugh and Other Surprises* (Boston: Houghton Mifflin, 1909), pp. 327–348; William Howitt, *The Student-Life of Germany* (Philadelphia: Carey & Hart, 1842); and John Russell, *A Tour in Germany, and Some of the Southern Provinces of the Austrian Empire, in the Years 1820, 1821, 1822,* 2 vols. (Edinburgh, Scotland: Archibald Constable, 1824).

For studies of the theological issues current at Göttingen, see Jerry Wayne Brown, *The Rise of Biblical Criticism in America, 1800–1870: The New England Scholars* (Middletown, Conn.: Wesleyan University Press, 1969); Carl Diehl, *Americans and German Scholarship 1770–1870* (New Haven, Conn.: Yale University Press, 1978); Elisabeth Hurth, "Sowing the Seeds of 'Subversion': Harvard's Early Göttingen Students," in *Studies in the American Renaissance 1992,* ed. Joel Myerson (Charlottesville: University Press of Virginia, 1992), pp. 91–106, and "William and Ralph Waldo Emerson and the Problem of the Lord's Supper: The Influence of German 'Historical Speculators,'" *Church History,* 62 (June 1993): 190–206; Karen Kalinevitch, "Ralph Waldo Emerson's Older Brother: The Letters and Journal of William Emerson" (Ph.D. diss., University of Tennessee, 1982); and Stanley M. Vogel, *German Literary Influences on the American Transcendentalists* (New Haven, Conn.: Yale University Press, 1955).

5. In general, see Brown, "American Discovery of the German University," and Orie William Long, *Literary Pioneers: Early American Explorers of European Culture* (Cambridge, Mass.: Harvard University Press, 1935). Concerning William's predecessors to Göttingen, for George Bancroft (1800–1891), see *The Life and Letters of George Bancroft,*

ed. M. A. DeWolfe Howe (New York: Scribner's, 1908), and Russel B. Nye, *George Bancroft: Brahmin Rebel* (New York: Knopf, 1944); for Joseph Green Cogswell (1786–1871), see *Life of Joseph Green Cogswell as Sketched in His Letters,* [ed. Anna E. Ticknor] (Cambridge, Mass.: Riverside Press, 1874); for Edward Everett, see Paul Revere Frothingham, *Edward Everett, Orator and Statesman* (Boston: Houghton Mifflin, 1925); for George Ticknor (1791–1871), see *Life, Letters, and Journals of George Ticknor,* ed. George S. Hillard et al., 2 vols. (Boston: James R. Osgood, 1876), and David B. Tyack, *George Ticknor and the Boston Brahmins* (Cambridge, Mass.: Harvard University Press, 1967).

6. Brown, "American Discovery of the German University," p. 270.

7. Hurth, "Harvard's Early Göttingen Students," p. 93.

8. Tyack, *George Ticknor and the Boston Brahmins,* p. 61.

9. Brown, "American Discovery of the German University," pp. 36, 43, 66; Calvert, "Göttingen in 1824," 596.

10. Bancroft's journal, 26 October 1818, in Long, *Literary Pioneers,* pp. 111–112.

11. Bancroft's journal, in *Life and Letters,* 1:58.

12. Ticknor, *Life, Letters, and Journals,* 1:79–80. In the following year he wrote that he visited Cogswell for half an hour after dinner each night and three times a week spent "from nine to ten in the evening with him, so that I feel I am doing quite right and quite as little as I ought to do in giving up the remaining thirteen hours of the day to study, especially as I gave fourteen to it last winter without injury" (letter of 30 November 1816, in Higginson, "Göttingen and Harvard a Century Ago," p. 337).

13. Cogswell, letter of 8 March 1817, in Higginson, "Göttingen and Harvard a Century Ago," p. 333. A few months later, Cogswell decided that all this was "rather too much for me, ten hours a day in the lecture room and seven or eight more for study," calling it "rather beyond my powers." But, he concluded, "I am too proud to give up" (*Life of Joseph Green Cogswell,* p. 62).

14. Ticknor's journal, 6 August 1815, in Brown, "American Discovery of the German University," p. 110; Nye, *George Bancroft,* p. 37.

15. Bancroft to Andrews Norton, 19 August 1820, in Long, *Literary Pioneers,* p. 127.

16. Cogswell, letter of 13 July 1817, in Higginson, "Göttingen and Harvard a Century Ago," p. 338.

17. Bancroft's journal, 10 September 1818, in Brown, "American Discovery of the German University," pp. 140–141.

18. Ticknor's journal, 4 October 1815, in Brown, "American Discovery of the German University," pp. 106–107.

19. Bancroft to John Thornton Kirkland, 2 April 1820, in Long, *Literary Pioneers,* pp. 120–121.

20. Bancroft to Andrews Norton, 7 February 1820, and to John Thornton Kirkland, 17 September 1820, in Long, *Literary Pioneers,* pp. 120, 131.

21. Bancroft to William, [n.d.], written on the back of William to Bancroft, [May 1823], and 3 May 1823, MHi, MS N-251 (40), (42). After settling in at Göttingen, William was pleased to find that his expenses corresponded "exactly with our calculations at home, founded upon Mr. Bancroft's information. I cannot yet exactly estimate what the other items will amount to (viz. Learning German—other instruction—Clothes—

Walking—Firewood and Stationery) but as nearly as I can calculate, they will not exceed our estimate; so that I believe without any books a year's expenses would be fully covered by $400" (letter to Waldo, 1 April 1824, MHi, Ms N-251 [51]). In this he was probably lucky, as other estimates of expenses varied widely. An English visitor, John Russell, wrote that the "lowest cost I ever heard mentioned as sufficient to bring a young man respectably through at Göttingen is three hundred rix-dollars yearly," and using William's calculation ("suppose the Rix-dol. to be 70 cts"—letter to Waldo, 1 April 1824, cited above) this would make the annual amount $210; Calvert later stated that the "average total annual expenditure of a native student is about three hundred dollars"; and Everett placed the amount at five hundred dollars, which "would be an allowance one half as large again as that of the majority of common students & two thirds as large as that of a Count" (Russell, *A Tour in Germany*, 1:370; Calvert, "Göttingen in 1824," 601; Everett to John Thornton Kirkland, [n.d.], in Brown, "American Discovery of the German University," p. 64).

22. Mother Carey's Chickens, a sailors' name for storm petrels, being a corruption of Mater Cara, one of the epithets of Maria, the mother of Christ, used by the Spanish and Portuguese sailors who were the first westerners in the southern seas.

23. Wells and Greene served as William's bankers, and posted and forwarded his letters.

24. MHi, Ms N-251 (47).

25. William began this paragraph at the top of the second page.

26. Raphael (1483–1520), Italian painter whose works adorn the Vatican; Titian (ca. 1477–1576), Venetian painter and courtier; Corregio (1494–1534), who founded a school of painting at Parma.

27. Because photography had not yet been invented, visitors to museums abroad returned with copies of paintings and statues as mementoes of their trip, thus keeping many otherwise unemployed artists busy in the trade of copying.

28. Louis xiv (1638–1715), King of France during a period in which art flowered, was known for the magnificence of his court; Napoleon Bonaparte (1769–1821), French general and ruler, was banished for life to St. Helena after his defeat at Waterloo during his attempt to regain his rule.

29. Surtout: an overcoat.

30. Thomas Wentworth Storrow (1779–1862), a successful merchant who lived in France during the 1820s.

31. MHi, Ms N-251 (48).

32. The writer Washington Irving (1783–1859) does not mention meeting William in either his letters or journals.

33. François de Saignac de La Motte-Fénelon (1651–1715), French archbishop and man of letters; the Treaty of Cambray, conducted by Margaret of Austria (1480–1530) and Louise of Savoy (1476–ca. 1531) at Cambray in 1529, restored peace between France and Spain.

34. Edward Everett's brother Alexander (1790–1847) was serving as *chargé d'affaires* at the Hague. Waldo wrote William that "Thro' E. Everett, heard you dined with his brother" (*L*, 1:142n).

35. MHi, Ms N-251 (50).

36. Georg Friedrich Benecke (1762–1844), a professor of philology.

37. Arnold Hermann Ludwig Heeren (1760–1842), a professor of philosophy and history.

38. Possibly George Barrell Emerson (1797–1881), naturalist and educational reformer who was the brothers' second cousin.

39. Calvert estimated the expenses of a student thus: "For furnished lodgings he pays from two to ten dollars a month, two or three for a single room, four to six for two, and eight to ten for a suite of three. Breakfast is furnished, and also tea, if required, by the landlord at a stipulated price. For his dinner he sends to a *traiteur,* or dines at one of the hotels, the charge varying, according to quality, from three to ten dollars a month" ("Göttingen in 1824," 600).

40. MHi, Ms N-251 (51).

41. Walter the Doubter (Walter van Twiller), a governor of New York during the period it was ruled by the Dutch in the early 1600s, and a character in Washington Irving's satirical *A History of New York* (1809).

42. MHi, Ms N-251 (52).

43. Brown, "American Discovery of the German University," pp. 308–309.

44. Nye, *George Bancroft,* p. 36.

45. George Henry Calvert (1803–1889), William's fellow student, who would later become a poet and essayist, had left America for England in 1823, arriving in Göttingen in January 1824. In later years, he wrote that in William's "mind and character, I found that support and comfort which—especially in the remote isolation of a foreign land—make a friend so valuable" ("Göttingen in 1824," 602).

46. MHi, Ms N-251 (56).

47. A reference either to the insanity of Caligula (12–41 c.e.), the third Roman emperor, or to the Roman practice of vomitoria, the regurgitating of food or drink in order to ingest even more.

48. Students at Göttingen lived under the legal jurisdiction of the university and their professors sat as judges, a privilege they had received because "they were under age, not engaged in trade, and in need of a quick decision" (Brown, "American Discovery of the German University," p. 218).

49. MHi, Ms N-251 (58). In his letterbook (draft?) version of this letter, William wrote "As is commonly the case, my love for my own profession increases everyday. The character of God, the just and immutable laws of the moral world, which in my solitude I am trying to examine in my own heart, are subjects sublime and attractive. The more I contemplate them, the greater cause of admiration I find. I deplore my past days of blindness, and fear lest the occurrences of every day should again fasten the scales upon my eyes. I do not find it needful to seek for proofs of the being and omnipresence of God in my metaphysical subtleties, for I find them in my own thoughts, in my own moral history. I feel little concerned for the result of my future inquiries into the nature and offices of the Saviour. In the perfection of his example, in the divine character of his instruction there is a sublimity, which seems to communicate itself to my own soul when I think of them and to convince me that I too am a Son of God, and that I need

but throw off my shackles, these bonds of habit, and early perverted nature, to attest my religion to the Divinity" (MHi, N-251 [713]).

50. Following this is a passage cancelled by William: 'there is a principle of perfect justice in ever in operation; and [cancelled 'you'] man errs, he ['errs, he' inserted] needs not to wait for punishment in the calamities of this world or the sufferings of another; he finds it [cancelled 'th' and 'in the history of his own feelings'] every day in his own history . . . '

51. Rede: counsel, advice; the quotation is from Shakespeare's *Hamlet,* Act I, Scene 3.

52. Manuscript copy in William Emerson's letterbook, MHi, Ms N-251 (713).

53. Manuscript copy in William Emerson's letterbook, MHi, Ms N-251 (713).

54. Manuscript copy in William Emerson's letterbook, MHI, Ms N-251 (713).

55. William Paley (1743–1805), English cleric and Utilitarian philosopher.

56. Charlemagne (ca. 742-814), conqueor of the Holy Roman Empire.

57. MHi Ms N-251 (63).

58. Minerva, Roman goddess of wisdom.

59. William Emerson's "Journal of a Tour from Göttingen to Dresden," MHi, MS N-251 (714). Goethe wrote of this visit on 19 September 1824: "Will. Emerson aus Boston, Nordamerika, in Göttingen studirend, protestantischer Theolog. Blieb für mich" (*L,* 1:162n).

60. From *The Task* (1785), Book 4, "The Winter Evening," by William Cowper (1731–1806), English poet and satirist.

61. Shakespeare, *As You Like It,* Act II, Scene 7.

62. Three golden lions were on the royal standard of Hanover.

63. Hottentots: a pejorative name given to the people in southern Africa found by the first white settlers.

64. MHi, Ms N-251 (69).

65. William to Waldo and Edward, 10 January 1825, MHi, Ms N-251 (71).

66. Objections to a marriage could be made when the banns (or public announcement of the event) were published, but, obviously, not after the wedding ceremony itself.

67. MHi, Ms N-251 (73).

68. Charles wrote William on 16 September 1824: "Perhaps you do not know that I was so fortunate as to get the 1st prize for latin Poem, at the P[ublic]. L[atin]. S[school]. wh. I now send you in the Prize book—" (MHi, Ms N-251 [62]).

69. Shakespeare, *Troilus and Cressida,* Act III, Scene 3.

70. Hermes, Greek messenger of the gods (called Mercury by the Romans).

71. 27 January 1825, MHi, Ms N-251 (74). From "Rob Roy's Grave" (1807) by William Wordsworth (1770–1850), British Romantic poet.

72. Two books by Eichhorn were in Waldo's library (see *L,* 1:250n). In 1830, when Waldo was formulating his objections against administering the rite of the Lord's Supper, and when he knew William had written Ezra Ripley about his own objections to the service (see 4 April 1830, printed below), Waldo wrote William to send him "th

leading objections to th Evidence of Xty as they strike yr mind—just mark th books of Eichhorn or others chap. & verse as near as may be that ought to have weight with a seeker of truth to remove his belief in th divine authority of th New Testament" (5 April 1830, *L,* 7:192–193). For an extended discussion of William's influence on Waldo in this respect, see Hurth, "William and Ralph Waldo Emerson and the Problem of the Lord's Supper."

73. 29 March 1825, MHi, Ms N-251 (78).

74. MHi, Ms N-251 (58).

75. William is in fact listed in the Harvard catalogue as having received the M.A. degree.

76. Bancroft to Andrews Norton, 10 July 1819, in Brown, "American Discovery of the German University," p. 183. Bancroft's description of enduring a more than two-hour examination is in Brown, pp. 184–185, and is summarized in Nye, *George Bancroft,* pp. 45–46.

77. Brown, "American Discovery of the German University," pp. 182–183.

78. Calvert, "Göttingen in 1824," 607.

79. William to Edward, 14–24 June 1825, MHi, Ms N-251 (81).

80. William is probably quoting from a now-lost letter from his mother.

81. MHi, Ms N-251 (82).

82. Bacchus, the Roman god of wine.

83. MHi, Ms N-251 (83).

84. MHi, Ms N-251 (84).

85. Quoted in Evelyn Barish, *Emerson: The Roots of Prophesy* (Princeton, N.J.: Princeton University Press, 1989), p. 161. Edward Waldo Emerson described the circumstances thus: "William's mind was exact and judicial and his conscience active. The German philosophy and the Biblical criticism shook his belief in the forms and teachings of the religion in which he had been brought up. . . . To William, beset by distressing doubts at Göttingen, it occurred that, but eighty miles away at Weimar, lived the wisest man of the age. He forthwith sought him out, was kindly received, and laid his doubts before him. He hoped, no doubt, that Goethe could clear these up, and show some way in which he could honorably and sincerely exercise the priestly office. The counsel which he received was in effect—for unhappily there is no written record and the story rests on family tradition—to persevere in his profession, comply with the usual forms, preach as best he could, and not trouble his family and his hearers with his doubts. Happily [William followed] . . . the inward voice. . . . He was an honorable and successful practitioner [of law], but his standard of work, and the sacrifices and heroic asceticism of his early life made him a sufferer all his days" (*The Complete Works of Ralph Waldo Emerson,* ed. Edward Waldo Emerson, 12 vols. [Boston: Houghton Mifflin, 1903–1904], 4:367–368n).

86. MH, bMS Am 1280.226 (3054).

CHAPTER 3

1. William to Ruth Haskins Emerson, 3–5 June 1828, MHi, Ms N-251 (108).

2. Charles to Ruth Haskins Emerson, [January 1828?], MH, bMS Am 1280.226 (134).

3. Charles to Ruth Haskins Emerson, [22? February 1828], MH, bMS Am 1280.226 (137).

4. See William to Ruth Haskins Emerson, 12 January 1828 and 27 March–1 April 1828, MHi, Ms N-251 (94), (98).

5. William to Ruth Haskins Emerson and Waldo, 13 May 1828, MHi, Ms N-251 (103).

6. 13 May 1828, MHi, Ms N-251 (104).

7. [March 1828?], MH, bMS Am 1280.220 (50).

8. MH, bMS Am 1280.226 (245).

9. MHi, Ms N-251 (105).

10. See Waldo to William, 3 July 1828, where Waldo mentions that "Dr Haskins" is an inmate at the McLean Asylum and his presence along with Bulkeley's caused concern for Edward's recovery among the hospital staff (L, 7:173). Although in his diary Jarvis refers to this person as an "uncle" of the Emerson brothers, he has never been identified.

11. Dr. James Jackson (1777–1867), physician to the Emerson family.

12. MHi, Ms N-251 (107).

13. MHi, Ms N-251 (108).

14. Henry Ware, Jr. (1794–1843), Unitarian minister and Waldo's predecessor at the Second Church in Boston, where Waldo had agreed to replace him, as needed, beginning on 13 July; he received sixty dollars in payment for his services (L, 1:236–237n).

15. On 3 July, Charles received the Bowdoin Prize for his dissertation; Charles's manuscript to which Waldo refers in this letter was a draft of what turned out to be his Harvard Class Day's Valedictory Oration.

16. Dr. Rufus Wyman (d. 1842), superintendent of the McLean Asylum.

17. Kenneth Walter Cameron, "The Emersons in the Jarvis Notebooks," in The Transcendentalists and Minerva, 3 vols. (Hartford, Conn.: Transcendental Books, 1958), 2:490–491.

18. MHi, Ms N-251 (112).

19. MH, bMS Am 1280.226 (141).

20. MHi, Ms N-251 (113).

21. This may be a reference to Mary Moody Emerson.

22. MHi, Ms N-251 (113).

23. MMEL, p. 244.

24. According to Rusk, "Before [Waldo] discoverd his mistake he had written at the bottom: 'Divinity Hall / Dear William, / Tis as well if one has a brother now'" (L, 1:248n).

25. MH, bMS Am 1280.226 (41).

26. MHi, Ms N-251 (125).

27. Presumably, Waldo is referring to his engagement to Ellen.

28. "While thee I seek, protecting Power" (1790), a hymn by Helen Maria Williams (1762-1827), British poet, letter writer, and novelist (*L*, 7:177n).

29. 4–8 July 1831, MH, bMS Am 1280.226 (2960); emphasis added.

30. [5? September 1828], MH, bMS Am 1280.226 (94).

31. 23 November [1828], MHi, Ms N-251 (125).

32. See Waldo to William, 5 December 1830, where Waldo states, "We [at home] have talked over the matter a great deal & are all pretty strongly of one mind—that [Edward] ought to come here," and Waldo to Ezra Ripley, 15 December 1830, where Waldo reports William's news that Ruth Haskins Emerson arrived in New York half an hour before Edward's ship set sail (*L*, 1:312, 313).

33. An alumnus of Dartmouth College and a friend of William's, the New York physician Cyrus Perkins also treated Charles during his last illness.

34. MH, bMS Am 1280.220 (54).

35. MHi, Ms N-251 (181).

36. Dr. Channing was in St. Croix for his health.

37. Congress had voted on 28 May 1830 for the removal of Indians to lands west of the Mississippi.

38. George Ashmun (1804–1870), Massachusetts politician; probably Nehemiah Adams (1806–1878), a graduate of the conservative Andover Theological Seminary in 1829, and pastor at the First Church of Cambridge; probably Richard Henry Dana, Sr. (1787–1879), poet, essayist, and founder of the *North American Review;* Calvin Ellis Stowe (1802–1886), clergyman, was professor of Greek in Dartmouth at this time (he would marry the aspiring author Harriet Beecher in 1836); George Stillman Hillard (1808–1879), Boston lawyer and reformer.

39. William Gray Swett (1808–1843), a Harvard classmate of Charles, was graduated from the Harvard Divinity School in 1831.

40. MH, bMS Am 1280.226 (5).

41. "ad libitum": done at the discretion of the performer.

42. MHi, Ms N-251 (189).

43. Waldo printed Edward's "The Last Farewell" in the first number (July 1840) of the *Dial*. The six stanzas of the poem have the definite ring of finality about them, as Edward reveals in the recurring refrain, "Far away, far away," his awareness that this is the last time he will view Boston's "lofty spires" and the life they represent receding in the distance. In the poem he devotes the fourth stanza to thoughts of his brothers:

> Farewell, my brothers true,
> My betters, yet my peers;
> How desert without you
> My few and evil years!
> But though aye one in heart,
> Together sad or gay,
> Rude ocean doth us part;

> We separate to-day,
> Far away, far away.

For the entire poem, see "The Last Farewell: Lines Written by the Author's Brother, Edward Bliss Emerson, Whilst Sailing out of Boston Harbor, Bound for the Island of Porto Rico, in 1832," in *The Complete Works of Ralph Waldo Emerson,* ed. Edward Waldo Emerson, 12 vols. (Boston: Houghton Mifflin, 1903–1904), 9:258–260.

44. 26 January 1833, MH, bMS Am 1280.226 (72).

45. Shakespeare, *Richard II,* Act III, Scene 1.

46. Shakespeare, "Sonnet 33," l. 2.

47. Epictetus, second century Greek Stoic philosopher.

48. Whigs, conservative politicians, often representing monied interests.

49. MHi, Ms N-251 (199).

50. MH, bMS Am 1280.226 (173).

51. Christopher Columbus (ca. 1446–1506), known as the discoverer of America.

52. Waldo, who had sailed for Europe on 25 December 1832, arrived in New York on 7 October and in Boston on 9 October 1833.

53. MH, bMS Am 1280.226 (220).

54. MHi, Ms N-251 (315).

55. Wordsworth, *The Excursion* (1814), Book I, 1: 501.

56. MH, bMS Am 1280.226 (19).

57. For Waldo's letter to Edward of 12 April 1834, see *L,* 1:408–409.

58. MH, bMS Am 1280.226 (221).

59. MHi, MS N-251 (338).

60. See Waldo to William, 8 October 1834, where Waldo asks his brother if he can board with him in New York for a few days prior to settling in to Concord, which he planned to do by the end of the month (*L,* 1:421).

61. *The Death of Wallenstein,* (1799), Act V, Scene 1, by Johann Christoph Friedrich von Schiller (1759–1805), German playwright and romantic philosopher.

62. "caput mortuum": a worthless residue.

63. Epicurus (341–270 B.C.E.), Greek philosopher and founder of the school of Epicureanism, which held that emotional calm was the highest good and that intellectual pleasures were superior to momentary sensualism; Stoics, philosophical school founded in 308 B.C.E. known for their belief in submitting to necessity.

64. Shakespeare, *Much Ado about Nothing,* Act V, Scene 1, ll. 34–38.

65. Francis George Shaw (1809–1882), reformer and translator.

66. MHi, Ms N-251 (340).

67. 19 October 1834, *MMEL,* p. 352.

68. 23 October 1834, *MMEL,* pp. 352–354.

69. MH, bMS Am 1280.220 (52), folder 23.

70. The letter referred to here apparently does not survive; see the editor's commentary, *L,* 7:229.

71. 29 October [1834], MH, bMS Am 1280.226 (123).

72. MHi, Ms N-251 (370).

73. Sylvester Baxter never completed work on his biography, the typescript of which is deposited among the Emerson family papers in the Houghton Library: "The Other Emersons: Being an Account of the Three Brilliant and Scholarly Brothers *William, Edward Bliss, and Charles Chauncy Emerson*," Introduction, p. 7, where Baxter also translated the church record of Edward's death and burial quoted here (MH, bMS Am 1220.235 [709]).

74. "He who has faith in me, although he be dead, will live" (see John 11:25: "Jesus said unto her, I am the resurrection, and the life: he that believeth in me, though he were dead, yet shall he live").

75. MHi, Ms N-251 (354).

76. Francis Armstrong to William, 5 February 1835, MH, bMS Am 1280.226 (3109).

77. MH, bMS Am 1280.226 (3849).

78. MH, bMS Am 1280.226 (2967).

79. Baxter, "The Other Emersons," Notes told to Mr. Forbes by His Mother in the Summer of 1926, n.p. (MH, bMS Am 1220.235 [709]).

80. For Charles's secret diary, which he kept from 1831 to 1836, see MH, bMS Am 1280.220 (119), folders 1–5. Selections from this are printed in chapter 4.

81. Isaiah 52:11: "Depart ye, depart ye, go ye out from thence, touch no unclean thing; go ye out of the midst of here; be ye clean, that bear the vessels of the Lord."

82. 24 July [1830], MH, bMS Am 1280.220 (53), folder 6.

83. 25 September 1831 and 27 September 1831, *L,* 1:332 (both).

84. John Ware (1795–1864), Boston physician and brother of Henry Ware, Jr.

85. MHi, Ms N-251 (207).

86. MH, bMS Am 1280.226 (12).

87. MH, bMS Am 1280.226 (62).

88. [January? 1832], MH, bMS Am 1280.220 (54).

89. MH, bMS Am 1280.220 (53), folder 8.

90. MH, bMS Am 1280.226 (62).

91. In Roman mythology, Pygmalion was a sculptor who fell in love with a statue of a woman that he had carved, and, in response to his prayer, Aphrodite brought it to life and named her Galatea.

92. Napoleon Bonaparte (1769–1821), French general and ruler.

93. Solomon (ca. 973–ca. 933 B.C.E.), king of Israel known for his impartial justice.

94. Shakespeare, *King Lear,* Act II, Scene 4: "Thou art the thing itself: unaccommodated man is no more but such a poor bare, forked animal as thou art."

95. James Cook (1728–1779), English mariner and explorer.

96. Francisco Pizarro (ca. 1471–1541), Spanish conquistador who defeated the Incas.

97. MH, bMS Am 1280.226 (62).

98. John Mason was Sidney Mason's brother and successor.

99. Washington Allston (1779–1843), historical painter and novelist.

100. MH, bMS Am 1280.226 (100).

101. cordillera: parallel mountain ranges.

102. MH, bMS Am 1280.220 (53), folder 8.

103. MHi, Ms N-251 (218).

104. Possibly a reference to Jaquith Pond in Maine.

105. MH, bMS Am 1280.226 (101).

106. MH, bMS Am 1280.226 (161).

107. Hannah Emerson Farnham (1770–1807), the brothers' paternal aunt, was married to William Farnham, a bookseller from Newburyport.

108. A paraphrase of "The Wife of Bath's Tale" in *The Canterbury Tales,* 1. 874, by Geoffrey Chaucer (ca. 1343/1344–1400), English poet.

109. Shakespeare, *Antony and Cleopatra,* Act IV, Scene 13.

110. Cleopatra (69–30 B.C.E.), ruler of Egypt, and Gaius Julius Caesar (100–44 B.C.E.), Roman general and statesman, formed both a political and personal union, having a son together; Gnaeus Marcius Coriolanus, fifth-century B.C.E. Roman patrician who led an unsuccessful revolt against Rome.

111. Titian (ca. 1477–1576), Venetian painter and courtier.

112. In the Bible, the inhabitants of Gibeon, a village near Jerusalem, were condemned by Joshua to serve as manual laborers for the Israelites.

113. MH, bMS Am 1280.220 (49).

114. "stultus ego putavi": "I, fool that I am, thought" from Virgil's Eclogue 1.19-20.

115. MHi, Ms N-251 (219).

116. That is, from royalty to commoners who deal with horses.

117. Wordsworth, "The Rainbow" (1802), 1. 7.

118. Enoch, Old Testament patriarch and father of Methuselah; Elijah, ninth-century B.C.E. Hebrew prophet.

119. Emanuel Swedenborg (1688–1772), Swedish scientist, theologian, and mystic, published *The Doctrine of the New Jerusalem Concerning the Lord* (1833).

120. MH, bMS Am 1280.226 (102).

121. 14 March [1832], copy in Waldo's hand, MH, bMS Am 1280.226 (151).

122. MH, bMS Am 1280.226 (162).

123. MHi, Ms N-251 (290).

124. MHi, Ms N-251 (355).

125. MHi, Ms N-251 (356). Edmund Burke (1729–1797), Irish politician and natural philosopher.

126. MHi, Ms N-251 (357).

127. Edward Everett, *An Address Delivered at Lexington, on the 19th (20th) of April, 1835* (Charlestown, Mass.: W. W. Wheildon, 1835).

128. 7 April 1835, MHi, Ms N-251 (359).

129. 29 April [1835], MHi, Ms N-251 (361).

130. Musketaquit or Musketaquid, a river in Concord.

131. The voyages of Ulysses are chronicled in *The Odyssey* by Homer.

132. 18 August 1835, MHi, Ms N-251 (369).

133. Charles to William, 7 July [1835], MHi, Ms N-251 (366).

134. [18? July 1835], MH, bMS Am 1280.226 (129).

135. 9 August 1835, MH, bMS Am 1280.226 (2968).

136. Charles to Joseph Lyman, 8 October 1835, MH, bMS Am 1280.220 (53), folder 13.

137. Socrates (ca. 470–399 B.C.E.), one of the most famous Greek philosophers, known for his dialogic method of teaching, which gained many adherents.

138. Entry for 13 February 1836, MH, bMS Am 1280.220 (119), folders 1–5.

139. MH, bMS Am 1280.220 (53), folder 14.

140. MHi, Ms N-251 (377).

141. 6-[7] March 1836, MH, bMS Am 1280.220 (52), folder 36.

142. MH, bMS Am 1280.220 (52), folder 39.

143. 10 April 1836, MH, bMS Am 1280.220 (52), folder 40.

144. MH, bMS Am 1280.220 (52), folder 40.

145. MH, bMS Am 1280.226 (2975).

146. The New York physician Cyrus Perkins, who was now treating Charles during his last illness, had previously treated Edward in New York in 1830 and recommended that he seek a "cure" by relocating to the Caribbean.

147. MH, bMS Am 1280.226 (2976).

148. MH, bMS Am 1280.226 (132).

149. MH, bMS Am 1280.220 (52), folder 42.

150. MH, bMS Am 1280.226 (2979).

151. MH, bMS Am 1280.220 (52), folder 43.

152. 10 May 1836, MH, bMS Am 1280.226 (2956).

153. The Griswolds are in-laws of Joseph Woodward Haven, Susan Haven Emerson's brother, who married a Cornelia Griswold in 1833 (L, 2:19n).

154. Sylvester Baxter, "The Other Emersons," Notes told to Mr. Forbes by His Mother in the Summer of 1926, n.p. (MH, bMS Am 1220.235 [709]).

155. Eventually, when William and Waldo were approaching their old age, the dream was partially fulfilled. From 1864 until Susan Haven Emerson's death in 1868, William and his wife resided in Concord, where they rented the home of Col. William Whiting. Although Bulkeley had died in 1859, their presence made, as Lidian had predicted it would in a letter written to her daughter Edith on 18 January 1864, "a good time" for all (*The Selected Letters of Lidian Jackson Emerson*, ed. Delores Bird Carpenter [Columbia: University of Missouri Press, 1987], p. 227). After his wife's death in February 1868, William returned to New York, where he died on 13 September 1868.

156. 28 July 1842, MHi, Ms N-251 (397).

157. *Complete Works,* 9:128–129.

158. For the complete text of the poem, see *Complete Works,* 9:261–265.

159. "Notes from the Journal of a Scholar," *Dial,* 1 (July 1840): 13–16, and 4 (July 1843): 88–92; "A Leaf from 'A Voyage to Porto Rico,'" *Dial,* 3 (April 1843): 522–526.

160. *Complete Works,* 9:145–147, stanzas 1–13, 15.

CHAPTER 4

1. Edward Young (1683–1765), English poet, critic, and dramatist, best known for his poem *Night Thoughts* (1742–1745).

2. George Gordon, Lord Byron (1788–1824), English Romantic poet.

3. Ralph Waldo Emerson, Journal MME 4, MH, MS Am 1280H (140), entry copied from a passage in Mary's writings dated "1821. Concord, 11 Feb."

4. The editors of the *JMN* call this notebook "Charles C. Emerson"; for the complete notebook, see *JMN*, 6:255–286.

5. "History," in *The Collected Works of Ralph Waldo Emerson*, ed. Alfred R. Ferguson, Joseph Slater, & Douglas Emory Wilson, 6 vols. to date (Cambridge, Mass.: Harvard University Press, 1971), 2:6.

6. See *JMN*, 7:443–446.

7. Waldo to Thomas Carlyle, 17 September 1836, in *The Correspondence of Emerson and Carlyle*, ed. Joseph Slater (New York: Columbia University Press, 1964), p. 148.

8. See Evelyn Barish, *Emerson: The Roots of Prophecy* (Princeton, N.J.: Princeton University Press, 1989); David R. Williams "The Wilderness Rapture of Mary Moody Emerson: One Calvinist Link to Transcendentalism," in *Studies in the American Renaissance 1986*, ed. Joel Myerson (Charlottesville: University Press of Virginia), pp. 1–16; *MMEL*; and, especially, Phyllis Cole, *Mary Moody Emerson and the Origins of Transcendentalism* (New York: Oxford University Press, 1998).

9. See Simmons's commentary in *MMEL*, pp. 127–128, 133. In addition to Mary's letters, her unpublished "Almanack"—a spiritual diary of over one-thousand pages which she kept from 1802 to 1855—survives at the Houghton Library; see MH, bMS Am 1280.235. Mary's "Almanack" is presently being edited by Phyllis Cole, Sandra Harbert Petrulionis, and Noelle Baker.

10. 26 July 1822, *MMEL*, p. 166. Charles was two-and-a-half years old at the time of his father's death in 1811; most likely, then, he had little, if any, memory either of his father or of the scene that Mary described for him here.

11. "Mary Moody Emerson," in *The Complete Works of Ralph Waldo Emerson*, ed. Edward Waldo Emerson, 12 vols. (Boston: Houghton Mifflin, 1903–1904), 10:403, 432; 402; 403, 411; 408; 432–433. The essay first appeared in the *Atlantic Monthly*, 52 (December 1883), 733–745. With respect to his tendency to translate the lives of his intimates into models of Greek or Roman heroes, see also "Samuel Hoar," in *Complete Works*, 10:437–448, where Waldo celebrates Elizabeth's late father as "our old Roman," "born under a Christian and humane star, full of mansuetude and nobleness, honor, and charity" (10:437).

12. The character descriptions of Mary by Sarah Ripley and Peabody are quoted from *MMEL*, pp. 408–409.

13. Robert D. Richardson, Jr., *Emerson: The Mind on Fire* (Berkeley: University of California Press, 1995), p. 36.

14. Indeed, Cole calls her the boys' "female stepfather" (*Mary Moody Emerson*, p. 139).

15. 7 July 1812, MHi, Ms N-251 (18).

16. 25 February 1815, MH, bMS Am 1220.226 (1064).

17. Although the precise source of trouble that occasioned William's apology to Mary is unknown, it likely had something to do with his continuing the play on his "profound erudition." On 8 June, William had traveled to Charlestown to be examined by the learned Sarah Alden Bradford, one of Mary's favorite confidantes, in preparation for his entrance to Harvard.

18. Rebecca Haskins (b. 1799), the daughter of Robert (1773–1855) and Rebecca Emerson Haskins (1776–1845), was Mary's niece. During the early months of 1813, Mary paid for Rebecca to attend school in Boston and board with the Emersons. Her brother Caspar Lavater Haskins had recently died.

19. Reverend Mase Shepard, of Little Compton, Rhode Island, married Ruth Haskins Emerson's sister Deborah (1765–1841) in 1788.

20. John Lovejoy Abbot (1783–1814) was installed as minister of the First Church on 14 July 1813.

21. Probably Charles Rollin, *The Ancient History of the Egyptians, Carthaginians, Assyrians, Babylonians, Medes and Persians, Macedonians, and Grecians* (first American edition, 1805), and John Melish, *Travels in the United States of America, in the Years 1806 and 1807, and 1809, 1810, and 1811* (1812).

22. François-René, vicomte de Chateaubriand, *Travels in Greece, Palestine, Egypt and Barbary: During the Years 1806 and 1807* (first American edition, 1813).

23. MHi, Ms N-251 (19).

24. Père-Lachaise, the largest cemetery in Paris, is named for François d'Aix de La Chaise (1624–1709), French Jesuit priest and confessor of Louis XIV. Originally part of a medieval cemetery and open fields before the Jesuits purchased it in 1626 for the order's provincial estate, the entire property was acquired by Paris in 1803.

25. Molière (1622–1673), French dramatist and actor best known for his comedies.

26. Peter Abelard (1079–1142), French philosopher and theologian, secretly married Héloïse (Eloisa), whose outraged family mutilated him. He eventually withdrew to a monastery and she to a convent. At his death, she was given his body, and at hers in 1164, they were buried beside each other. Their bodies were entombed together in Paris in 1817.

27. William was in Dublin in January 1824, having stayed in Ireland for a month before sailing from Dublin to Havre, France, on his way to Göttingen.

28. Manuscript copy, MHi, in William Emerson's letterbook, Ms N-251 (713).

29. For Mary's of 13 June 1840, see *MMEL*, pp. 418–419.

30. George Ripley (1802–1880), member of the Transcendental Club, a founder of Brook Farm, literary critic of the *New York Tribune*, and editor; Martin Luther (1483–1546), famous German prelate; and John Calvin (1509–1564), Protetstant reformer and theologian.

31. Thomas Hobbes (1588–1679), English philosopher; Sir Isaac Newton (1642–1727), English natural philosopher and mathematician; John Flamsteed (1646–1719), English astronomer.

32. *Essay on Man* (1733), "Epistle III," by Alexander Pope (1688–1744), poet who championed the heroic couplet.

33. John Haven Emerson was born on 15 April; his brother was William.

34. The plaster portrait medallion of Charles, done by Sophia Peabody (later Mrs. Nathaniel Hawthorne), is reproduced as the frontispiece to *Studies in the American Renaissance 1984,* ed. Joel Myerson (Charlottesville: University Press of Virginia, 1984).

35. Orville Dewey (1794–1882), minister at the Second Unitarian church of New York.

36. Thomas Babington Macaulay (1800-1859), English author and frequent contributor to the *Edinburgh Review.* The reference is to his *Critical and Miscellaneous Essays* (1840).

37. Thomas Carlyle (1795–1881), prolific Scottish writer who was Emerson's lifelong friend and correspondent.

38. Ebenezer Elliott (1781–1849), English poet known as the Corn Law Rhymer because of his verses attacking that law and describing the poverty of the rural countryside; Thomas Campbell (1777–1844), English poet and critic; Samuel Rogers (1763–1855), English poet.

39. The *Dial,* the unofficial journal of the Transcendentalists, published its first quarterly issue in July 1840. Margaret Fuller was the editor, assisted by Emerson, and the journal ran for four years. William critiques it in a number of his letters to Waldo.

40. MHi, Ms N-251 (388).

41. William's son Charles was born on 15 December 1841; Waldo's son, Waldo, died on 27 January 1842.

42. Emerson's lecture series in New York during March 1842 was on "The Times."

43. Samuel and Sarah Alden Bradford Ripley would move into the Old Manse after the death of Ezra Ripley.

44. Elizabeth's father, Squire Samuel Hoar (1778–1856), had been chosen to represent the Seneca Indians.

45. MHi, Ms N-251 (397).

46. Samuel Moody Haskins (b. 1813), son of Rebecca Emerson Haskins, who died on 16 August 1845. Apparently her health that spring was very bad, and there were premature announcements of her death, such as William's here (see *MMEL,* p. 460).

47. This phrase does not appear in *Nature* (1836).

48. "ex cathedra": literally, "from the chair," or speaking from a position of authority.

49. Martha, goddess of the household and symbol of the active life.

50. The American edition of Carlyle's *Past and Present,* which Waldo edited, was published in 1843; Waldo's *Essays: Second Series* appeared in 1844.

51. Texas was officially granted statehood on 29 December 1845; Henry Clay (1777–1852), U.S. secretary of state, attempted to purchase Texas and later was instrumental in preparing the legislation that included the Fugitive Slave Law; James G. Birney (1792–1857), abolitionist who ran as the Liberty Party's candidate for president in 1844.

52. Thomas Jefferson (1743–1826), third U.S. president (1801–1809) and founder of the University of Virginia.

53. John Adams (1735–1826), second U.S. president (1797–1801), or his son, John Quincy Adams (1767–1848), sixth U.S. president (1825–1829).

54. Charles never received a middle name.

55. MHi, Ms N-251 (418).

56. Samuel Ripley, husband of Mary's friend Sarah Alden Bradford Ripley, had died on 24 November.

57. Waldo had sailed for England on 5 October 1847, where he met, among many others, Harriet Martineau (1802–1876), English novelist and religious and economic writer, and her brother, James Martineau (1805–1900), English Unitarian minister, theologian, and philosopher.

58. MHi, Ms N-251 (437).

59. MHi, Ms N-251 (523).

60. William Henry Furness (1802–1896), Philadelphia Unitarian minister and childhood friend of Waldo's.

61. Amos Bronson Alcott (1799–1888), Emerson's longtime friend and Concord neighbor.

62. For details of Mary's transfer of her life's writings to Ellen Emerson, see Simmons's commentary in *MMEL,* pp. 543–549; Ellen's letters of 10 January and 15 January 1861 to her sister Edith and that of 26 January 1861 to her aunt Susan Haven Emerson, in *The Letters of Ellen Tucker Emerson,* ed. Edith E. W. Gregg, 2 vols. (Kent, Ohio: Kent State University Press, 1982), 1:221–227; and Waldo's brief remarks on the event, *JMN,* 15:496.

63. 16–17 March 1862, MHi, Ms N-251 (612).

64. Hannah Parsons tried several times to have a photograph taken of Mary suitable to keep for posterity, but as in the failed attempt described here by William, she was never successful.

65. MHi, Ms N-251 (615).

66. Sarah Ripley Ansley (b. 1816), the daughter of Robert and Rebecca Moody Haskins, was Mary's niece.

67. Samuel Moody Haskins (b. 1813), the son of Robert and Rebecca Moody Haskins, was the pastor of Saint Mark's Episcopal Church in Williamsburgh, New York; it is likely that Mr. Clapp was also an Episcopal minister.

68. MH, bMS Am 1280.226 (3047).

69. 3–4 May 1863, MHi, Ms N-251 (626).

70. 30 October 1863, MHi, Ms N-251 (631).

71. Sylvester Baxter, "The Other Emersons: Being an Account of the Three Brilliant and Scholarly Brothers *William, Edward Bliss, and Charles Chauncy Emerson,*" version 1, chapter 1, section 3 (MH, bMS Am 1220.235 [709]). See also O. W. Firkins, *Ralph Waldo Emerson* (Boston: Houghton Mifflin, 1915), pp. 4, 9, 57. Interestingly, in both Baxter's and Firkins's accounts of Waldo and his brothers, William remains largely on the periphery except for each writer's extensive discussion of the effect of his studies in Germany.

72. William, then a senior at Harvard, spent his winter break teaching at Kennebunk.

73. For Mary's letter to Waldo, see *MMEL,* pp. 104–105.

74. Benjamin Apthorp Gould (1787–1859), headmaster of the Boston Latin School from 1814 to 1828.

75. Thomas Haskins (b. 1801), son of Ruth's sister Rebecca and Robert Haskins; Charles Shepard, son of Ruth's sister Deborah and Mase Shepard; and William Ladd (d. 1850) married Ruth's sister Mary Haskins (1766–1839).

76. Hannah Upham Haskins (b. 1734) had suffered a paralytic stoke in 1814; she died in Boston on 18 September 1819.

77. MH, bMS Am 1280.226 (175).

78. Although mentioned by Mary in her letter to Edward of 1 January 1818 as a "trifle . . . [to] be accepted for the sake of your Aunt," neither party ever identifies the "favour"; for Mary's letter, see *MMEL,* pp. 106–107.

79. Waldo used "Ralph" as his name through 1821.

80. For Waldo's accounts of teaching at Waltham, see *L,* 1:55–58.

81. MH, bMS Am 1280.226 (176).

82. By 1820 William was operating a private school in Boston. All evidence suggests that he was successful at teaching as well as at recruiting students; see *L,* 1:90n3.

83. Possibly Samuel Blagge, listed in *The Boston Directory* for 1820 as "Swedish Council, notary public"; see *L,* 1:94n21.

84. Lemuel Shaw (1781–1861), jurist and Herman Melville's father-in-law.

85. John Haskins Ladd and his wife Eliza Smith Wyer lived in Alexandria and were cousins of the Emerson brothers. John was the son of William G. Ladd—possibly the William Ladd mentioned here—and Ruth's sister Mary Haskins.

86. 15 and 31 January 1820, MH, bMS Am 1280.226 (3).

87. MHi, Ms N-251 (73)

88. MHi, Ms N-251 (105).

89. MHi, Ms N-251 (106).

90. Quotations are from Edward to Mary, 11 March 1831, printed below.

91. Isaac Hurd (1785–1856), a Concord physician.

92. The Reverend William Ellery Channing had delivered his sermon on "Likeness to God" on 10 September 1828 and it was published that year (see also *MMEL,* p. 250n).

93. Waldo was ordained junior pastor at the Second Church on 11 March 1829 and became pastor on 1 July of that year.

94. Isaiah 30:10: "Prophesy not unto us right things, speak unto us smooth things, prophesy deceits."

95. MH, bMS Am 1280.226 (177).

96. According to the published *Order of Services at the Ordination of Mr Ralph Waldo Emerson, as Junior Pastor of the Second Church and Society in Boston, on Wednesday, March 11, 1829* (Boston: Isaac R. Butts, 1829), John Pierce offered the introductory prayer; Samuel Ripley delivered the ordination sermon; Francis Parkman offered the ordaining prayer; David Hatch Barlow led the hymn; Ezra Ripley delivered the ministerial charge; Nathaniel Langdon Frothingham presided over the Right Hand of Fellowship; Ezra Stiles Gannett delivered the address to the Society; Charles Upham offered a concluding prayer; and Waldo offered the closing Benediction (see MH, *pAB85.Em345.N8290 [A]).

97. For texts of the first two sermons Waldo preached as pastor at the Second Church,

see Sermon XXVIII (the sermon he preached in the morning) and its sequel, Sermon XXIX (preached in the afternoon), in *The Complete Sermons of Ralph Waldo Emerson*, ed. Albert J. von Frank et al., 4 vols. (Columbia: University of Missouri Press, 1989–1994), 1:231–247. In these sermons, he discusses his conception of the duties of a Christian minister and pastor.

98. MH, bMS Am 1280.220 (49).

99. MH, bMS Am 1280.226 (178).

100. 14–17 March 1829, MH, bMS Am 1280.220 (49). Aeschylus (525–456 B.C.E.), Athenian tragic dramatist.

101. Baxter, "The Other Emersons," version 6, chapter 5, section 7 (MH, bMS Am 1220.235 [709]).

102. 30 November 1830, MH, bMS Am 1280.220 (49).

103. William Emerson Haskins (b. 1806) had married Frances Maria Hodges in 1830. Edward did not go with them.

104. MH, bMS Am 1280.226 (50).

105. The druggist Sampson Reed (1800–1880) promoted the ideas of Emanuel Swedenborg and, through his writings, helped Waldo to develop the ideas of correspondence and organic form.

106. Giordano Bruno (ca. 1548–1600), Italian pantheistic philosopher.

107. MH, bMS Am 1280.226 (1639).

108. "Winter: A Dirge" (1781), ll. 17–20, by Robert Burns (1759–1796), Scotland's most famous poet.

109. Numerous popular revolts against monarchies took place in Europe in 1830.

110. This was a controversy between the north and south over tariffs and protectionism.

111. Richard Henry Lee (1732–1794) presented the Continental Congress in 1776 with a resolution calling for independence of the American colonies from Britain; Alexander Hamilton (1755?–1804) believed in the establishment of a strong central government; Fisher Ames (1758–1808) also championed strong central government.

112. MH, bMS Am 1280.226 (4).

113. *MMEL*, pp. 309–310. Simmons dates this letter from Mary to Edward [June? 1831]; the letter is endorsed "M. M. Emerson / 21 Dec^r / 1831 / A 11 March—." Given Mary's references in the letter to Edward's illness and his "removal" to St. Croix, which occurred on 14 December 1830, and Edward's notation "A 11 March—." which provides the date of his response, Mary's letter had to have been written in late December 1830. For another discussion of the dating of this letter, see Baxter, "The Other Emersons," version 7, chapter 2, section 17 (MH, bMS Am 1220.235 [709]).

114. 11 March 1831, MH, bMS Am 1280.226 (180).

115. Sir Walter Scott (1771–1832), prolific Scottish novelist.

116. 5 and [28?] April 1834, MH, bMS Am 1280.226 (182).

117. François de Saignac de La Motte-Fénelon (1651–1715), prelate and author of an early utopian novel.

118. MH, bMS Am 1280.226 (55).

119. Shakespeare, *King Lear,* Act II, Scene 4.

120. MH, bMS Am 1280.226 (89).

121. In the text that follows, Charles's dates are preserved as he inscribed them; for those entries that include a day of the week plus the month and date but lack the year, years have been editorially supplied and explained in a note when necessary. Internal evidence indicates that, as Charles kept the Diary irregularly over a five-year period, he did not always add new entries in true chronological order. Whether dated or not, entries that appear to have been made on separate occasions are separated from each other by a horizontal space.

122. "The Young American," in *The Collected Works of Ralph Waldo Emerson,* ed. Alfred R. Ferguson, Joseph Slater, & Douglas Emory Wilson, 6 vols. to date (Cambridge, Mass.: Harvard University Press, 1971-), 1:230.

123. Charles means "cession," a yielding to another.

124. Ptolemy of Alexandria (fl. 127–145), astronomer, geographer, and mathematician who believed that Earth was the center of the universe.

125. Between 1831 and Charles's death on 9 May 1836, 24 May occurred on a Sunday only in 1835.

126. That is, Charles could not define it as he would a land survey, where "mites and bounds" is a type of measurement.

127. Possibly a reference to Psalm 84:3: "Yea, the sparrow hath found an house, and the swallow a nest for herself, where she may lay her young, even thine altars, O Lord of hosts, my King, and my God."

128. Charles could be referring to Cato the Younger (95–46 B.C.E.), Roman military man and philosopher, who committed suicide after his unsuccessful opposition to Caesar, or Marcus Porcius Cato (234–149 B.C.E.), Roman statesman and prosodist.

129. "The Young American," in *Collected Works,* 1:226, quoting an unlocated source.

130. Charles obviously had the day of the week wrong, since between 1831 and his death on 9 May 1836, 22 August never occurred on a Sunday; 22 August occurred on a Monday in 1831 and a Saturday in 1835.

131. Between 1831 and 1836, 9 November occurred on a Monday only in 1835.

132. A paraphrase of Milton, *Comus* (1637), l. 298.

133. Psalm 23:4.

134. John 8:32.

135. Atlas, Greek mythological figure who bore the world on his shoulders.

136. Between 1831 and 1836, 10 June occurred on a Wednesday only in 1835.

137. MH, bMS Am 1280.220 (119), folders 1–5.

138. Mercury, Roman god of commerce and rhetoric; chyrography or chirography: handwriting.

139. Manuscript torn; word editorially supplied.

140. Manuscript torn; word editorially supplied.

141. Goldsmith, "The Traveller" (1764), ll. 7–8, 10.

142. MH, bMS Am 1280.226 (25).

143. The brackets are Charles's.

144. Joseph Stevens Buckminster (1784–1812), liberal Boston Unitarian minister and man of letters.

145. MH, bMS Am 1280.226 (32).

146. Charles is now nearly 17 years old.

147. Matthew 6:24.

148. MH, bMS Am 1280.226 (33). Marcus Tullius Cicero (106–43 B.C.E.), Roman philosopher and statesman.

149. MHi, Ms N-251 (93).

150. MHi, Ms N-251 (122).

151. 14 December [1828], MH, bMS Am 1280.226 (96).

152. 12-28 January [1828], MH, bMS Am 1280.226 (38).

153. 14 November 1829, MH, bMS Am 1280.226 (45).

154. From "The Omnipresent," quoted from a review of "Klopstock's *Life and Odes*," by Friedrich Gottlieb Klopstock (1724-1803), German poet, in *Foreign Review and Continental Miscellany*, 3 (1829): 373 (see *MMEL*, p. 270n).

155. 1841, *JMN*, 7:444, quoted above.

156. Edward Thompson Taylor (1793–1871), Methodist preacher at the Seamen's Bethel in Boston, is mentioned in Waldo's journals.

157. John 16:33: "I have told you these things, so that in me you may have peace. In this world you will have trouble. But take heart! I have overcome the world."

158. Demosthenes (b. ca. 384–322 B.C.E.), the most famous of the Greek orators.

159. Jean Louis Lefebvre de Cheverus (1768–1836), French Roman Catholic prelate who fled to America during the French Revolution, was consecrated the first Roman Catholic bishop of Boston in 1810, and returned to France in 1823.

160. St. John was exiled on the island of Patmos, near Greece; see Revelations 1:9.

161. MH, bMS Am 1280.220 (49).

162. 7 December [1823], MH, bMS Am 1280.226 (29).

163. 28 January [1825], MH, bMS Am 1280.226 (31).

164. MH, bMS Am 1280.226 (37).

165. Wordsworth, "The Excursion" (1814), Book 4, 1. 1264.

166. MH, bMS Am 1280.226 (49).

167. Charles to Mary, [ca. 14 March 1832], fragmentary copy in Waldo's hand, on the same sheet with his copy of Charles to Elizabeth Hoar, 29 March [n.y.], MH, bMS Am 1280.220 (49).

168. Copy in an unknown hand, together with Charles to Ruth Haskins Emerson, 14 March [1832], MH, bMS Am 1280.226 (151).

CHAPTER 5

1. For more information, see *One First Love: The Letters of Ellen Louisa Tucker to Ralph Waldo Emerson,* ed. Edith W. Gregg (Cambridge, Mass.: Harvard University Press,

1962), and Henry F. Pommer, *Emerson's First Marriage* (Carbondale: Southern Illinois University Press, 1967). Information on Emerson's preaching engagements is from *The Complete Sermons of Ralph Waldo Emerson,* ed. Albert J. von Frank et al., 4 vols. (Columbia: University of Missouri Press, 1989–1992).

2. He preached there from 23 December through 6 January 1828, then again on one Sunday in May, two Sundays in June, and three Sundays in December 1828. Waldo also preached there on two Sundays in June 1829.

3. *One First Love,* ed. Gregg, pp. 137–138.

4. MH, bMS Am 1280.226 (42).

5. Charles to William, 27 January 1829, MHi, Ms N-251 (128).

6. The section begins " Let not your heart be troubled: ye believe in God, believe also in me. In my Father's house are many mansions: if it were not so, I would have told you. I go to prepare a place for you. And if I go and prepare a place for you, I will come again, and receive you unto myself; that where I am, there ye may be also."

7. Charles to Mary, [6 February 1831], MH, bMS Am 1280.226 (54).

8. Charles to William, 6 February [1831], MHi, Ms N-251 (182).

9. Charles to William, 6–8 February [1831], MHi, Ms N-251 (183).

10. John McAleer, *Ralph Waldo Emerson: Days of Encounter* (Boston: Little, Brown, 1984), p. 107.

11. Charles to Elizabeth, 7 December 1833, copy by Waldo in *The Poetry Notebooks of Ralph Waldo Emerson,* ed. Ralph H. Orth et al. (Columbia: University of Missouri Press, 1986), p. 584.

12. McAleer, *Ralph Waldo Emerson,* p. 103.

13. Robert D. Richardson, Jr., *Emerson: The Mind on Fire* (Berkeley: University of California Press, 1995), p. 109.

14. A color reproduction of the miniature is in Ronald A. Bosco & Joel Myerson, "Ralph Waldo Emerson: A Bicentennial Exhibition at Houghton Library of the Harvard College Library," *Harvard Library Bulletin,* 13, nos. 3–4 (Fall–Winter 2003): 20; for the rocking chair, see Ellen Tucker Emerson, *The Life of Lidian Jackson Emerson,* ed. Delores Bird Carpenter (Boston: Twayne, 1980), p. 60.

15. Emerson, *The Life of Lidian Jackson Emerson,* pp. 47, 56.

16. Richardson, *Emerson,* p. 191; the quotation from Emerson is from *JMN,* 5:8.

17. John Eliot (1604-1690), Puritan minister, contributed to the *Bay Psalm Book* (1640).

18. Peter Bulkeley (1583–1659) and Simon Willard (1605–1676), the founders of Concord, Massachusetts.

19. This may have been a familiar Native American lament: a similar version appears in *A Red Man's Greetings* (1893), by Simon Pokagon (1830-99), known as the "Longfellow of the Indians."

20. Charles to William, 14–18 September 1838, MHi, Ms N-251 (371).

21. Ralph L. Rusk, *The Life of Ralph Waldo Emerson* (New York: Scribner's, 1949), p. 220.

22. Once, when Waldo gave her a ring "recording the death of his great-uncle Waldo, and said 'Perhaps if you will look in it you will find the name you should call

me by,'" Lidian "looked, smiled, and said 'I do! It says *Mr* Waldo Emerson!'" (Emerson, *Life of Lidian Jackson Emerson,* p. 51). Compare this to Ellen's nicknames for Waldo of "Grandpa" and then "King," and his for her of "Ellinelli" and then "Queen" (Richardson, *Emerson,* p. 84).

23. Emerson, *Life of Lidian Jackson Emerson,* p. 48.

24. Emerson, *Life of Lidian Jackson Emerson,* pp. 77, 157; the quotation is loosely summarized from *JMN,* 5:456, which in turn was used by Waldo in his essay on "Love."

25. Emerson, *Life of Lidian Jackson Emerson,* pp. 77, 104.

26. Charles to William, 14–18 September 1835, MHi, Ms N-251 (371).

27. Charles to William, 12 February [1835], MHi, Ms N-251 (355).

28. Charles to William, 3 March 1835, MHi, Ms N-251 (356).

29. *The Selected Letters of Lidian Jackson Emerson,* ed. Delores Bird Carpenter (Columbia: University of Missouri Press, 1987), p. 27.

30. William to Waldo, 9 February 1835, MH, bMS Am 1280.226 (2965).

31. Emerson, *Life of Lidian Jackson Emerson,* pp. 50–51.

32. "It isnt seeing William, who came yesterday nor my mother dear, nor the preparation (part of which I am) for William's wedding,—that can make me feel light hearted"; see Charles to Elizabeth, [30 November 1833], MH, bMS Am 1280.220 (52), folder 5.

33. For more on William and his family, see chapter 6.

34. In Deuteronomy 25:17–18, Amalek is described thus: "Remember what Amalek did unto thee by the way, when ye were come forth out of Egypt; How he met thee by the way, and smote the hindmost of thee, even all that were feeble behind thee, when thou wast faint and weary; and he feared not God." In the Hebrew tradition, Amalek "represents intellectual doubt, the kind that erodes one's sense of belief" (http://tckillian.com/greg/amalek.html#_Toc34574848).

35. These lines are not in *One First Love,* ed. Gregg.

36. MH, bMS Am 1280.226 (82).

37. MH, bMS Am 1280.226 (110).

38. James Walker (1794–1874), Unitarian pastor in Charlestown, Massachusetts, and later president of Harvard.

39. [14 April 1822], MH, bMS Am 1280.226 (25).

40. Charles to Mary, 8–10 October 1832, MH, bMS Am 1280.226 (69).

41. 25 July 1824, manuscript copy in William Emerson's letterbook, MHi, Ms–251 (713).

42. [March 1828], MH, bMS Am 1280.226 (139).

43. 12 September [1825], MH, bMS Am 1280.226 (32).

44. Charles to Mary, 11 October [1825], MH, bMS Am 1280.226 (33).

45. Charles to Mary, 12–28 January [1828], MH, bMS Am 1280.226 (38).

46. 25 November [1826], MH, bMS Am 1280.226 (91); Waldo's reply is in *L,* 1:181–183.

47. Manuscript notes for 11 May and 8 October 1835, and 27 February [n.y.], MH, bMS Am 1280.220 (52), folder 31.

48. 15 August 1831, MH, bMS Am 1280.226 (57).

49. 5 June 1829, MH, bMS Am 1280.226 (44).

50. 14 August 1830, MHi, Ms N-251 (166).

51. 9 November 1828, MHi, Ms N-251 (122).

52. Charles to Waldo, 2 February 1832, MH, bMS Am 1280.226 (102).

53. 27 October 1831, MH, bMS Am 1280.226 (60).

54. 3 July [1835], MH, bMS Am 1280.226 (89).

55. Charles to Joseph Lyman, 11 August 1830, MH, bMS Am 1280.220 (53), folder 6.

56. Charles to William, 4 October [1829], MHi, Ms N-251 (151).

57. 12 September 1830, MH, bMS Am 1280.226 (49).

58. Charles to Edward and William, 30 October 1830, MHi, Ms N-251 (175).

59. 26 July [1834], MH, bMS Am 1280.226 (85).

60. Charles to Joseph Lyman, 7 April 1829, MH, bMS Am 1280.220 (53), folder 2.

61. Information on Elizabeth Hoar's life comes from Elizabeth Maxfield-Miller, "Elizabeth of Concord: Selected Letters of Elizabeth Sherman Hoar to the Emersons, Family, and the Emerson Circle" (Parts I–III)," in *Studies in the American Renaissance 1984–1986*, ed. Joel Myerson (Charlottesville: University Press of Virginia, 1984–1986), pp. 229–298, 95–156, 113–198; and Paula Ivaska Robbins, *The Royal Family of Concord: Samuel, Elizabeth, and Rockwood Hoar and Their Friendship with Ralph Waldo Emerson* ([n. p.]: Xlibris, 2003).

62. Maxfield-Miller, "Elizabeth of Concord" (1984), p. 239.

63. Kenneth Walter Cameron, *The Massachusetts Lyceum During the American Renaissance* (Hartford, Conn.: Transcendental Books, 1969), p. 118.

64. Charles to Joseph Lyman, 10 March 1832, fragmentary manuscript copy, MH, bMS Am 1280.226 (156).

65. Squire Hoar had also offered Edward a position in his office; see Edward to Samuel Hoar, 26 November 1829, Concord Free Public Library.

66. 9 August 1832, MH, bMS Am 1280.226 (162).

67. 13 September 1832, MH, bMS Am 1280.226 (67).

68. Charles to William, 2 November [1833], MHi, Ms N-251 (304).

69. shealing: a small cottage in a quiet place.

70. Charles to James Jackson, Jr., 8 January 1833, MHi.

71. Maxfield-Miller, "Elizabeth of Concord" (1984), p. 243, and see Charles to Elizabeth, 20 August 1833 ("Ellen, that "noble violet flower""), MH bMS Am 1280.220 [52], folder 2); "The Violet," *One First Love,* ed. Gregg, p. 149

72. Gay Wilson Allen erroneously prints a letter of Charles as being by Elizabeth in his *Waldo Emerson: A Biography* (New York: Viking, 1981), p. 266. In fact, it is Charles to Elizabeth, 23 April [1834], MH, bMS Am 1280.220 (52), folder 9, published in Maxfield-Miller (1995), p. 116, and copied by Waldo into *JMN,* 5:156.

73. *Letters of Lidian Jackson Emerson,* ed. Carpenter, p. 38.

74. Nancy Craig Simmons, in *MMEL,* p. 277.

75. A reference to their engagement the previous weekend.

76. There are too many biblical references similar to this to ascertain exactly which one Charles means.

77. Charles had visited Edward in Puerto Rico from December 1831 to April 1832.

78. Charles was still waiting for Squire Hoar's reply to his request to marry his daughter.

79. "The Passionate Man's Pilgrimage" (1603), by Sir Walter Raleigh (1554–1618), English adventurer, historian, and poet.

80. Charles regularly returned to Boston to work on his law practice.

81. MH, bMS Am 1280.220 (52), folder 1. Squire Hoar had given his approval for their marriage. This is probably the first letter in their correspondence.

82. MH, bMS Am 1280.220 (52), folder 2.

83. Shakespeare, *Hamlet,* Act V, Scene 2.

84. Medea, Greek sorceress who gained immortality for refusing the advances of the god Zeus.

85. aweel: Scottish phrase meaning "ah well!"

86. MH, bMS Am 1280.220 (52), folder 3.

87. MH, bMS Am 1280.220 (52), folder 3.

88. MH, bMS Am 1280.220 (52), folder 5.

89. Ariel, the god of the air, occasionally portrayed as an elf.

90. MH, bMS Am 1280.220 (52), folder 5.

91. Shakespeare, *Macbeth,* Act V, Scene 3.

92. Shakespeare, *Romeo and Juliet,* Act III, Scene 5.

93. MH, bMS Am 1280.220 (52), folder 6.

94. Ilium or Troy, where the events of Homer's *Iliad* took place.

95. Halbert Glendinning and Mary Avenel, characters in Scott's novel, *The Monastery* (1820).

96. The character Crito and Socrates appear in Plato's *Crito* (ca. 360 B.C.E.).

97. MH, bMS Am 1280.220 (52), folder 6.

98. In *Hamlet,* when Ophelia goes mad, she sings wildly and plays her lute.

99. MH, bMS Am 1280.220 (52), folder 7.

100. Portia, quoted from Shakespeare, *The Merchant of Venice,* Act III, Scene 2.

101. *Undine, or, The Water Spirit* by Friedrich Heinrich de la Motte-Fouque (1777–1843), French prelate, was first published in German in 1811 and first translated into English in 1818.

102. "casus omissus": an event or occasion.

103. MH, bMS Am 1280.220 (52), folder 8.

104. Waldo later used this quote from an unidentified source in his lecture "The Tendencies and Duties of Men of Thought" (see *The Later Lectures of Ralph Waldo Emerson, 1843–1871,* ed. Ronald A. Bosco & Joel Myerson, 2 vols. (Athens: University of Georgia Press, 2001), 1:189.

105. Shakespeare, *As You Like It,* Act II, Scene 7.

106. Shakespeare, *King Lear,* Act I, Scene 1.

107. MH, bMS Am 1280.220 (52), folder 8.

108. MH, bMS Am 1280.220 (52), folder 8.

109. Shakespeare, *Henry IV, Part Two,* Act II, Scene 2.

110. This phrase was used in Carlyle's *Sartor Resartus* (1834), then appearing serially in *Fraser's Magazine.*

111. MH, bMS Am 1280.220 (52), folder 9.

112. Waldo delivered a poem at the Phi Beta Kappa society's ceremonies on 28 Au-

gust, which Charles commented on in his letter to Elizabeth of 27–[28] August: "Waldo did not speak his verses as I would have had him—I could have delivered his poem better than he did—But it was too good to be otherwise than popular with those who had wit to apprehend it" (MH, bMS Am 1280.220 [52], folder 18).

113. A comment on Shakespeare by Ben Jonson (1573–1637), an English dramatist, in *Timber; or, Discoveries* (1640).

114. eclaircissement: explanation.

115. MH, bMS Am 1280.220 (52), folder 9.

116. "hic labor": this toil.

117. MH, bMS Am 1280.220 (52), folder 11.

118. dree our weird: suffer our fate.

119. MH, bMS Am 1280.220 (52), folder 13.

120. Shakespeare, *Hamlet,* Act V, Scene 1.

121. MH, bMS Am 1280.220 (52), folder 14. From the *Journal* of Reginald Heber (1783-1826), British cleric and hymn writer.

122. These lines are not in *One First Love,* ed. Gregg.

123. MH, bMS Am 1280.220 (52), folder 15.

124. Cybele, a goddess of nature and fertility whose temple was on Mount Ida in Asia Minor.

125. Araby or Arabia.

126. Shakespeare, *Henry VI,* Act III, Scene 2.

127. Psyche, princess in classical mythology whose exceptional beauty aroused Venus's jealousy and Cupid's love.

128. Portia, in Shakespeare, *The Merchant of Venice,* is both wealthy and ends the play with the man who loves her.

129. MH, bMS Am 1280.220 (52), folder 17.

130. MH, bMS Am 1280.220 (52), folder 18.

131. MH, bMS Am 1280.220 (52), folder 19.

132. Benjamin Franklin (1706–1790), statesman, scientist, and philosopher. Charles had written Elizabeth on 11 September "But as Dr. Franklin said, ''Tis other peoples' eyes that ruin me'" (MH, bMS Am 1280.220 [52], folder 20).

133. Matthew 16:24: "Then Jesus said to His disciples, 'If anyone desires to come after Me, let him deny himself, and take up his cross, and follow Me'"; Lamentations 3:27: "It is good for a man to bear The yoke in his youth"; possibly Mark 10:21: "Then Jesus, looking at him, loved him, and said to him, 'One thing you lack: Go your way, sell whatever you have and give to the poor, and you will have treasure in heaven; and come, take up the cross, and follow Me.'"

134. MH, bMS Am 1280.220 (52), folder 20.

135. "merum vinum": unmixed wine. Because Italian wine was very strong and usually mixed with water, Charles's citation means he wants his religion strong and undiluted.

136. Coleridge, "The Good, Great Man" (1802), 1. 13.

137. MH, bMS Am 1280.220 (52), folder 21.

138. "The sun to me is dark / And silent as the moon, / When she deserts the night / Hid in her vacant interlunar cave" from Milton's *Samson Agonistes* (1671).

139. MH, bMS Am 1280.220 (52), folder 21.

140. Shakespeare, *Richard II,* Act II, Scene 1, where it appears as "must I ravel out / My weav'd-up follies?"

141. Cassandra, in Greek myth, was given the gift of prophesy by Apollo, but when she refused his advances, he cursed her by having no one believe her predictions.

142. MH, bMS Am 1280.220 (52), folder 24.

143. "A primrose by a river's brim / A yellow primrose was to him, / And it was nothing more" from Wordsworth's "Peter Bell" (1819), 11. 247–250.

144. Charles may be thinking of *The History of the Indian Wars in New England* (1677) or *General History of New England* (1815) by William Hubbard (ca. 1621–1704); possibly *The New English Canaan* (1637) or *Manners and Customs of the Indians* (of New England) (1637) by Thomas Morton (ca. 1575/9–1647).

145. Charles I (1600–1649), king of England (1625–1649), engaged parliament in a Civil War (1639–1646), which resulted in his execution.

146. Orion, Greek mythological hunter whose name is used for a constellation.

147. Roger Williams (ca. 1603–1683), the founder of Rhode Island.

148. MH, bMS Am 1280.220 (52), folder 25.

149. "mundus sensibilis": the world of the senses.

150. A reference to Shakespeare's play of that title.

151. MH, bMS Am 1280.220 (52), folder 27.

152. From the traditional British ballad, "The Blind Beggar's Daughter of Bednall-Green."

153. MH, bMS Am 1280.220 (52), folder 28.

154. Philip van Artevelde (1340–1382), captain general of Ghent, Belgium, led an unsuccessful revolt of weavers against the wealthy and died in the process.

155. "quousque tandem": all the way to what point? This is short for "Quousque tandem abutere, Catilina, patientia nostra" ("How far then, Catiline, will you abuse our patience"), the first words of Cicero's "First Oration Against Catiline."

156. MH, bMS Am 1280.220 (52), folder 29.

157. Sibyl, a prophetess.

158. Charles is undoubtedly referring to pages from his journal.

159. Waldo printed an extract from the journal Charles kept while he was in Puerto Rico in the *Dial* as "A Leaf from 'A Voyage to Porto Rico.'"

160. Despite Charles's inference, this line does not appear in *Hamlet.*

161. MH, bMS Am 1280.220 (52), folder 30.

162. MH, bMS Am 1280.220 (52), folder 33.

163. aroint ye: "begone you!"

164. Matthew 6:34: "Take therefore no thought for the morrow: for the morrow shall take thought for the things of itself. Sufficient unto the day is the evil thereof."

165. MH, bMS Am 1280.220 (52), folder 35.

166. Emerson, *Life of Lidian Jackson Emerson,* pp. 56–60.

167. *Letters of Lidian Jackson Emerson,* ed. Carpenter, pp. 26, 36.

168. Charles to Joseph Lyman, 19 January 1836, MH, bMS Am 1280.220 (53), folder 14.

169. Emerson, *Life of Lidian Jackson Emerson,* p. 66.

170. Typescript copy, MH, bMS Am 1280.220 (117), folder 10.

171. Eliza Rotch Farrar (1791–1870), wife of a Harvard professor and a special friend of Fuller's.

172. MH, bMS Am 1280.220 (52), folder 36.

173. MH, bMS Am 1280.200 (52), folder 37.

174. MH, bMS Am 1280.220 (52), folder 38.

175. MH, bMS Am 1280.220 (52), folder 41.

176. catarrh: generally speaking, a cold.

177. MH, bMS Am 1280.220 (52), folder 41.

178. MH, bMS Am 1280.226 (2975).

179. MH, bMS Am 1280.226 (2976).

180. MH, bMS Am 1280.220 (52), folder 42. On the same day, William reported to Waldo that "Charles certainly seems better; his cough has been much softened, & he is less drowsy, has more cheerfulness; but his feet have swelled somewhat, & his breathing is about as short as before. . . . Charles walked yesterday morning & rode about an hour in a carriage with mother yesterday afternoon, & enjoyed the airing" (MH, bMS Am 1280.226 [2977]).

181. William also commented on this to Waldo: "He was stronger yesterday than for two days before; his color & looks more natural, his voice & cheerfulness much restored, & the bowel looseness lessened somewhat. I place no reliance on his conviction that he is getting better" (6 May 1836, MH, bMS Am 1280.226 [2978]).

182. MH, bMS Am 1280.220 (52), folder 42.

183. MH, bMS Am 1280.226 (2979).

184. MH, bMS Am 1280.220 (52), folder 43.

185. MH, bMS Am 1280.226 (2955).

186. MH, bMS Am 1280.226 (2956).

187. *Letters of Elizabeth Palmer Peabody, American Renaissance Woman,* ed. Bruce A. Ronda (Middletown, Conn.: Wesleyan University Press, 1984), pp. 164–165, 167.

188. *The Correspondence of Emerson and Carlyle,* ed. Joseph Slater (New York: Columbia University Press, 1963), p. 148.

189. Waldo did prepare a journal comprised of extracts from Charles's manuscripts (see *JMN,* 6:255–286) and later edited three items from Charles's journal for publication in the *Dial:* two installments of "Notes from the Journal of a Scholar" and "A Leaf from 'A Voyage to Porto Rico.'"

190. *Selected Letters of Lidian Jackson Emerson,* ed. Carpenter, pp. 47–48. Lidian added that "make her worthy" were Elizabeth's words, not hers.

191. Maxfield-Miller, "Elizabeth of Concord" (1985), p. 147.

192. Ruth Haskins Emerson's will, Middlesex County Register of Probate, First Series, no. 31346.

193. *The American Notebooks,* ed. Claude M. Simpson (Columbus: Ohio State University Press, 1972), p. 316.

194. Elizabeth Oakes Smith, "Recollections of Emerson, His Household and Friends," in *Selections from the Autobiography of Elizabeth Oakes Smith,* ed. Mary Alice Wyman

(Lewiston, Me.: Lewiston Journal, 1924); rpt. in *Emerson in His Own Time,* ed. Ronald A. Bosco & Joel Myerson (Iowa City: University of Iowa Press, 2003), p. 249.

195. Joel Myerson, "Margaret Fuller's 1842 Journal: At Concord with the Emersons," *Harvard Library Bulletin,* 21 (July 1973); rpt. in *Emerson in His Own Time,* ed. Bosco & Myerson, p. 25.

196. *The Letters of Ellen Tucker Emerson,* ed. Edith E. W. Gregg, 2 vols. (Kent, Ohio: Kent State University Press, 1982), 2:294.

197. *Poetry Notebooks,* p. 420.

198. In Maxfield-Miller, "Emerson and Elizabeth of Concord," *Harvard Library Bulletin,* 19 (July 1971): 290–306.

199. F. B. Sanborn, "A Concord Note-Book: Ellery Channing and His Table-Talk. Second Paper," *Critic,* 27 (August 1905): 122.

200. Maxfield-Miller, "Elizabeth of Concord" (1984), pp. 248–249.

CHAPTER 6

1. Beginning in 1852, they used the telegraph for important and immediate communication, such as when Ruth Haskins Emerson died (see, for example, *L,* 4:309, 397).

2. As William wrote Waldo early in their financial correspondence, "I am glad to hear of your resolutions of economy. I too have made them; & like you, have had the best of reasons for breaking them. The consequence, of course, is perpetual slavery. So that I am pretty much come to the conclusion that slavery is the only state of civilized man" ([ca. 6]–9 April 1847, MHi, Ms N-251 [433]).

3. *L,* 7:110n, which also notes that Henry David Thoreau later received it.

4. MHi, Ms N-251 (51); see chapter 2, where it is quoted at length.

5. MHi, Ms N-251 (66). This prudent investment, overseen by Waldo and William, was still returning value three decades later (see *L,* 5:164–165).

6. MHi, Ms N-251 (71).

7. In his letter to William of 1 November 1824, Edward wrote "Advertisements. The La Fayette hotel, having 35 rooms &c. built opposite the Boylston market-house to let" (MHi, Ms N-251 [66]). Rusk notes that the name was "a timely choice in the year of La Fayette's visit to Boston," and that the *Boston Courier* of 5 January 1825 "reported that this tavern had been rented; and the writer described, with some enthusiasm, the newly-painted sign showing the beloved general, in uniform on one side of the board, in citizen's clothes on the other" (*L,* 1:158–159n).

8. Soon afterwards, Waldo made a long entry on compensation in his journal (see *JMN,* 3:265–268).

9. Information about Waldo's lawsuit and the settlement of Ellen's estate is drawn from Ralph L. Rusk, *The Life of Ralph Waldo Emerson* (New York: Scribner's, 1949), pp. 157, 200, 250–251, and John McAleer, *Ralph Waldo Emerson: Days of Encounter* (Boston: Little, Brown, 1984), p. 108.

10. After Ashmun's death, a monument was raised to his memory on which was an inscription written by Charles (*L*, 10:223–224).

11. Possibly Abiel Washburn, Ellen Louisa Tucker's uncle.

12. 4–5 April [1833], MH, bMS Am 1280.226 (106).

13. 27 June 1833, MH, bMS Am 1280.226 (112).

14. 25 January 1834, MHi, Ms N-251 (310).

15. 13 May [1834], MHi, Ms N-251 (321).

16. Charles wrote to William on 22–23 May [1834] that their mother has "an annual stipend of about 80 or 90 dollars from the LaFayette Estate—& she now lives at the rate of $6. per week, & I suppose that sum will not for the present vary much from a true estimate of her expenses. By & by when we are richer it may be $10 or 12. We may count the excess therefore of her expenses above her income to be about $225" (MHi, Ms N-251 [324]).

17. Information on Mary Moody Emerson's real estate transactions comes from *MMEL*, and Phyllis Cole, *Mary Moody Emerson and the Origins of Transcendentalism: A Family History* (New York: Oxford University Press, 1998).

18. Simmons, in *MMEL*, p. 412.

19. William wrote Waldo on 10 May 1863 about "the little property" Mary had left. Elizabeth Hoar possessed "two or three wills" and he held one, which he would not present for probate until Waldo had compared it with Elizabeth's copies. William had "made two or three wills at her request, one of which, at least, she signed; but she was very mutable, & hard to please about it" (MHi, Ms N-251 [627]).

20. 16 October 1853, MHi, Ms N-251 (523).

21. Mary to William, 3 October 1853, manuscript copy, MH, bMS Am 1280.220 (117), folder 27.

22. William to Waldo, 16–17 March 1862, MHi, Ms N-251 (615).

23. William had telegraphed Waldo who reported on the burial service to William on 5 May 1863:

> It was a pleasant misty day such as Aunt would have chosen,—and the rain waited till we had laid her in the ground an hour. I brought all our friends home with me, telling them I would produce all the memorabilia of the Sibyl, if they desired; They came, but did not ask for memories, and I reserved them. The present is ever too strong for the past, & in so many late years she has been only a wreck, & in all years could so readily be repulsive, that few know or care for her genius. Yet I who cling always to her writings, forget every thing else very fast, though her behaviour, when I saw it, was intolerable. Her genius was the purest and though I have learned to discriminate & drop what a huge alloy of theology & metaphysics, her letters & journals still charm me still as thirty years ago, & honor the American air. (*L*, 5:326)

24. MH, bMS Am 1280.226 (2963).

25. Kenneth Walter Cameron, *The Transcendentalists and Minerva*, 3 vols. (Hartford, Conn.: Transcendental Books, 1958), 1:6–10, and "Charles Chauncy Emerson's Library," *Emerson Society Quarterly*, no. 10 (1st Quarter 1958): 48. Charles's most valuable

possession was a church organ worth $300. His major creditors were Emersons: $49.86 to William, $100 to Mary Moody Emerson, $103.25 to Ruth Haskins Emerson, and $446.10 to Edward's estate—which suggests how complicated and intertwined were the Emerson family finances.

26. Information on Charles's temporary burial in New York is in chapter 3.

27. John Gorham Palfrey (1796–1881), minister, Harvard Divinity School professor, editor, and historian.

28. A typical expense account for Bulkeley is in *L,* 3:162–163. For Waldo's description of his death and burial, see *L,* 5:148–150. William was unable to come to Concord for the funeral.

29. Samuel Bradford, *Some Incidents in the Life of Samuel Bradford, Senior* (Philadelphia: Privately published, 1880), pp. 63–64.

30. William to Waldo, 4 March 1838, MH, bMS Am 1280.226 (2994). This move was also dictated by his growing law practice: according to Margaret Fuller, William's practice was generating about $4,800 annually (see 31 March 1839, in *The Letters of Margaret Fuller,* ed. Robert N. Hudspeth, 6 vols. [Ithaca, N.Y.: Cornell University Press, 1983–1995], 2:63).

31. *Nelson's Guide to the City of New York and Its Neighbourhood* (London: T. Nelson, 1858), pp. 13–14. Staten Island retained its rural charm throughout William's time there and, indeed, it was "the most remote of all the boroughs [of New York], and the least urban" even in the 1990s (see Eric Homberger, *The Historical Atlas of New York City* [New York: Henry Holt, 1994], p. 125).

32. Information on Staten Island is from the entry on it by Charles L. Sachs in *The Encyclopedia of New York City,* ed. Kenneth L. Jackson (New Haven, Conn.: Yale University Press; New York: New York Historical Society, 1995), pp. 1112–1118.

33. George W. Hilton, *The Staten Island Ferry* (Berkeley, Calif.: Howell-North Books, 1964), p. 19.

34. David Schuyler, *Apostle of Taste: Andrew Jackson Downing 1815–1852* (Baltimore, Md.: Johns Hopkins University Press, 1996), pp. 32–34.

35. "The Snuggery. Home of the Emersons on Staten Island," *New York Tribune,* 24 May 1903, part 2, p. 16, and Richard J. Turk, Jr., "Emerson Hill," *Staten Island Historian,* 21 (April–June 1960): 13–14.

36. William to Waldo, 29 December 1852, MHi, Ms N-251 (502). There is a picture of Helvellyn in "The Snuggery," p. 16. The hill near it became known as "Emerson Hill."

37. William to Waldo, 18 October 1854, MHi, Ms N-251 (541).

38. The Emersons had rechristened the nearby settlement of Dutch Farms as "Concord" (Charles W. Leng & William T. Davis, *Staten Island and Its People: A History 1609–1929,* 5 vols. [New York: Lewis Historical Publishing, 1930–1933], 2:810).

39. William to Waldo, 28 December 1854, MHi, Ms N-251 (544).

40. William to Waldo, 4 March 1860 and 3–4 May 1863, MHi, Ms N-251 (591), (626). William even provided directions to Waldo about how to get to their new house: "So if you give your baggage on board the Norwich boat to an express man, you have only to walk up Vestry & Canal Streets to the corner of Canal & Varick, & then take

the next 6th Avenue horse car to 22d Street, & then you have only 2/3 of a block to 109, where you will arrive in time for breakfast at 7 ½ o'clock" (22–23 May 1863, MHi, Ms N-251 [628]).

41. 7 April 1837, MH, bMS Am 1280.226 (2987).

42. Abel Adams (1792–1867), Waldo's longtime friend and financial advisor.

43. Lucy Cotton Jackson Brown (1798–1868), Waldo's sister-in-law.

44. When he bought the house in 1835, Charles had written a friend that "Waldo bought him a house, (Coolidge's at the head of the Turnpike, a naked white establishment you may remember) for $3500, a tolerably good bargain as the building is well finished & cost nearly 8000 seven years ago. He will have land enough for garden & orchard—2 acres, 6 rods" (24 July [1835] to Joseph Lyman, MH, bMS Am 1280.220 [53], folder 12).

45. According to Rusk, Lidian's property was "already confided to the hands of her dishonest cousin Abraham Jackson, who was eventually detected and punished but only after a long career as an embezzler" (*Emerson*, p. 251).

46. A. Forbes & J. W. Greene, *The Rich Men of Massachusetts* (Boston: W. V. Spencer, 1851), p. 101.

47. In doing this, we rely on the Economic History Services' "What Is Its Relative Value" Web site (http://www.eh.net/hmit/compare) and take the average of the two figures derived from the Consumer Price Index and the Gross Domestic Product Deflator. The site is current only through equivalencies in 2002.

48. 29 April–2 May 1838, MH, bMS Am 1280.226 (2998).

49. John Milton Cheney (1797–1869), Waldo's college classmate and cashier of the Middlesex Institution for Savings in Concord.

50. "peculium": a special fund for private and personal uses.

51. Regan and Goneril, characters in Shakeapeare's *King Lear* who fight for their father's lands.

52. MH, bMS Am 1280.226 (3001).

53. "ad libitum": in accordance with desire.

54. 17 February 1839, MH, bMS Am 1280.226 (3010).

55. William regularly borrowed money during this period using Waldo's Atlantic Bank stock as collateral; see, for example, Waldo to William, 22 July 1840, *L*, 2:317.

56. William often assigned his life insurance policy to Waldo as guarantee against loans; see, for example, William to Waldo, 12 July 1840, MHi, Ms N-251 (386).

57. 1 July 1839, MH, bMS Am 1280.226 (3017). In 2002 dollars, William's net debt of $2,100 would equal $38,000.

58. Waldo lectured in New York on "The Philosophy of History" (10 March), "The Character of the Present Age" (13 March), and "The Literature of the Present Age" (17 March).

59. MHi, Ms N-251 (382); see also *L*, 2:272–273.

60. MHi, Ms N-251 (383).

61. MH, bMS Am 1280.226 (3028).

62. Job 3:3: "Let the day perish wherein I was born, and the night in which it was said, There is a man child conceived."

63. MH, bMS Am 1280.226 (2985).

64. Jean Fréderic Oberlin (1740–1826), French cleric noted for his success in improving agriculture, industry, and morals in his pastorate.

65. MH, bMS Am 1280.226 (3031). For Waldo's letter, see *L*, 2:452–453.

66. Writing Mary Moody Emerson on 28 July 1842 about visiting the Concord Emersons, William comments "Waldo is always the same to us, Elizabeth, a spectacle worthy of all good angels; mother unfortunately was a little lame; Lidian is always kind & conscientious. But that is a great void which the little boy's death has made. He was the hope of the house, its particular jewel" (MHi, Ms N-251 [397]).

67. MH, bMS Am 1280.226 (3032).

68. The first page of the letter is filled with figures showing that William had paid Waldo $450 between 7 May 1840 and 30 August 1841.

69. MHi, Ms N-251 (412).

70. MH, bMS Am 1280.226 (3033).

71. Fuller held a number of "Conversations" upon various topics in Boston to support herself; most were open only to women.

72. Mount Lebanon, New York, home to a community of Shakers, an English communal order whose leaders came to America in 1774, known for its pacifism and furniture making; New Harmony, a utopian community in Indiana.

73. MH, bMS Am 1280.226 (3030).

74. See Waldo's letter to George Ripley, 15 December 1840, *L*, 2:368–371, 7:435–437.

75. Prytaneum, a Greek public building in which official hospitality was extended to distinguished citizens and strangers.

76. 19 August 1856, MHi, Ms N-251 (577). In his reply of 2 September, Waldo said

I must say a word to the notes you sent me on "English Traits." p. 113 Fauriel the Belgian biographer of Wellington represents him as such a dear stupid good creature, that he chose to consider himself responsible for the army debts, & would not stir abroad for fear of bailiffs; which I call the family-man carried to the sublime. On p. 212, I find no difficulty. For p. 103, I own *solidarity* is not yet a good English word; but Fourier & Socialism have made it so common in French books, that it has become inevitable in English. But it means responsibleness, as when Alfred divided his people into Hundreds, & each Hundred responsible for a crime committed by any man belonging to it.—I spelled sirloin, but my "corrector" printed *surloin*, & I rarely defy him. (*L*, 5:34)

77. 28 August 1840, MHi, Ms N-251 (387). William is referring to Alcott's "Orphic Sayings"; see Joel Myerson, "'In the Transcendental Emporium': Bronson Alcott's 'Orphic Sayings' in the *Dial*," *English Language Notes*, 10 (September 1972): 31-38.

78. William Emerson, Jr. married Sarah H. Gibbons on 25 November 1863.

79. 17 April 1858, MHi, Ms N-251 (584).

80. 22 January 1864, MHi, Ms N-251 (633).

81. 14 March 1865, MH, bMS Am 1280.226 (3048).

82. This letter is lost; see William to Waldo, 30 March 1843, MHi, Ms N-251 (403).

83. MHi, Ms N-251 (407).

84. MHi, Ms N-251 (409).

85. Letter to Waldo, 8 June 1843, in *The Correspondence of Henry David Thoreau,* ed. Walter Harding and Carl Bode (New York: New York University Press, 1957), p. 112.

86. *Journal, Volume 1: 1837–1844,* ed. Elizabeth Hall Witherell at al. (Princeton, N.J.: Princeton University Press, 1981), p. 478.

87. *The Personality of Emerson* (Boston: George E. Goodspeed, 1903), p. 22.

88. 22 March, quoted in Walter Harding, *The Days of Henry Thoreau,* enl. ed. (Princeton, N.J.: Princeton University Press, 1982), p. 155; for a detailed picture of this time, see pp. 145–156.

89. 31 March 1839, Fuller, *Letters,* 2:62–63.

90. Raymond R. Borst, *The Thoreau Log* (Boston: G. K. Hall, 1992), p. 483.

91. The likely candidate is a reprinting of "Walt Whitman and His Poems" from the September *United States Review* in either the 24 August *Evening Post* of New York or the 8 September *Albion.*

92. William to Waldo, 15 September [1855], MHi, Ms N-251 (563), and 14 March 1865, MH, bMS Am 1280.226 (3048). The article from the *New York Times* is "News from Washington," 12 March 1865, p. 5.

93. Unfortunately, Waldo's assumption proved correct. While he made money on all his books, it was not until 1860, when he signed with Ticknor & Fields (later Houghton Mifflin), who were booksellers *and* distributors, and took standard royalties on all his works, did his sales really take off and provide him with a steady income from his books. William foresaw this, writing to Waldo that Munroe "will cramp the circulation of your book" (28 September [1846], MHi, Ms N-251 [425]).

94. Between 1836 and 1881, Waldo, working with various American publishers, sold over 300,000 copies of his books, from which he received an income of over $70,000; see Joel Myerson, "Ralph Waldo Emerson's Income from His Books," in *The Professions of Authorship: Essays in Honor of Matthew J. Bruccoli,* ed. Richard Layman and Myerson (Columbia: University of South Carolina Press, 1996), pp. 135–149.

95. Information about Carlyle's publications comes from the "Bibliopoly 1835–1847" chapter of *The Correspondence of Emerson and Carlyle,* ed. Joseph Slater (New York: Columbia University Press, 1964), pp. 16–29, and Rodger L. Tarr, *Thomas Carlyle: A Descriptive Bibliography* (Pittsburgh, Pa.: University of Pittsburgh Press, 1989).

96. Reproduced in Joel Myerson, *Ralph Waldo Emerson: A Descriptive Bibliography* (Pittsburgh, Pa.: University of Pittsburgh Press, 1982), p. 29.

97. See *L,* 2:104–105. William replied that he had received two copies, one for himself and the other for Orville Dewey. The other eight copies would go to, among others, William Cullen Bryant at the *New York Evening Post,* "Mr McCrackan (for the Am. Monthly) & Dr Hawks (for the N.Y. Review)" (19 January 1838, MH, bMS Am 1280.226 [2993]).

98. Reproduced in Myerson, *Ralph Waldo Emerson: A Descriptive Bibliography,* p. 39.

99. William proposed to D. Appleton that they publish *Poems* and give Waldo 15% of the retail price for each copy sold. He also volunteered to speak to Harper & Brothers. Waldo declined, invoking his practice of paying publishers to distribute his books

rather than his taking a traditional royalty (see William to Waldo, 19 August [1846], MHi, Ms N-251 [424]; *L,* 3:350–351).

100. See *L,* 3:315ff, and *Emerson-Carlyle Correspondence,* pp. 386ff.

101. MH, bMS Am 1280.226 (3035).

102. Waldo lectured in New York from "The Times" series on 3, 5, 7, 9, 12, and 14 March.

103. Charles Eames (1812–1867), historical lecturer.

104. Horace Greeley (1811–1872), editor of the *New-York Tribune.*

105. MHi, Ms N-251 (401).

106. For more on the "New England" series, which Waldo delivered between 7 and 22 February in New York, see *The Later Lectures of Ralph Waldo Emerson, 1843–1871,* ed. Ronald A. Bosco & Joel Myerson, 2 vols. (Athens: University of Georgia Press, 2001), 1:6 and passim.

107. Thomas Delf worked for the English publisher D. Appleton.

108. 31 January [1847], MHi, Ms N-251 (426).

109. MHi, Ms N-251 (487).

110. MHi, Ms N-251 (506).

111. *Later Lectures,* 1:320.

112. For more on this untitled lecture, see *L,* 5:219.

113. William to Waldo, 1 May 1860, MHi, Ms N-251 (599).

114. For example, for the *Le Courrier des Etats-Unis,* see William to Waldo, 8 December 1850, MHi, Ms N-251 (472), and Waldo to William, 12 July 1852, *L,* 4:300.

115. For example, for a trip in 1862 William sent money and a detailed accounting to Waldo for the expenses incurred during a visit to Concord; see William to Waldo, 3 September 1862 and 2 October 1862, MHi Ms N-251 (618), (619).

116. See also Waldo to William, 8 June 1853, in which he draws on William for monies to slate and tin his roof (*L,* 4:363).

117. MH, bMS Am 1280.226 (3043).

118. 8 October 1844, MHi Ms N-251 (417).

119. See *The Ice King: Frederic Tudor and His Circle,* ed. Alan Seaburg, Carl Seaburg, & Stanley Paterson (Mystic, Conn.: Mystic Seaport Museum, 2003).

120. 7 March 1847, *L,* 3:383; 19–20 March 1847, MHi, Ms N-251 (429).

121. Franklin Benjamin Sanborn (1831–1917), reporter, author, and Concord resident.

122. Luke 9:60.

123. MHi, Ms N-251 (564).

124. The brothers' father seems to have been the first in the line to have been afflicted with tuberculosis. It subsequently affected William, Waldo, and Edward Waldo Emerson, and killed Edward, Charles, and William's son, William, Jr. (see Haven Emerson, "Five Generations of Tuberculosis: A Family Story," in *Selected Papers of Haven Emerson* [Battle Creek, Mich.: W. K. Kellogg Foundation, 1949], pp. 487–494).

125. 31 August–[1 September 1852], MHi, Ms N-251 (494).

126. 2 September [1852], MHi, Ms N-251 (495).

127. See William to Waldo, 1 February 1855, MHi, Ms N-251 (548).

128. 10–11 January 1862, MHi, Ms N-251 (614).

129. MHi, Ms N-251 (636). The funeral service took place in Concord and Willie was buried in the family plot at Sleepy Hollow, as were William's other children and their wives. A longtime family friend, Sarah Ripley, commented, "What a succession of beautiful and talented young men the fiend consumption has taken from their list" (Joan W. Goodwin, *The Remarkable Mrs. Ripley: The Life of Sarah Alden Bradford Ripley* [Boston: Northeastern University Press, 1998], p. 326).

130. See Waldo to William, 17 April 1855, *L*, 4:502; William to Waldo, 3 May [1855], MHi, Ms N-251 (554); Waldo to William, 6 May 1855, *L*, 4:506.

131. 17 June 1868, MHi, Ms N-251 (662).

132. 17 February 1839, MH, bMS Am 1280.226 (3010).

133. Moncure Daniel Conway (1832–1907), abolitionist, historian, and biographer.

134. MHi, Ms N-251 (625).

135. *L*, 5:348. Lidian was "in a state of great delight," and she hoped they would buy the house after renting it (18 January 1864, *The Selected Letters of Lidian Jackson Emerson*, ed. Delores Bird Carpenter [Columbia: University of Missouri Press, 1987], p. 227).

136. *L*, 5:380–381. William wrote Waldo on 24 April 1864, "Our household stuff will probably be sent forward towards Concord by a freight train tomorrow eveg; when it shall arrive there rests in the womb of fate" (MHi, Ms N-251 [639]).

137. See *L*, 6:4–13 passim; *The Letters of Ellen Tucker Emerson*, ed. Edith E. W. Gregg, 2 vols. (Kent, Ohio: Kent State University Press, 1982), 1:458–460; Ellen Tucker Emerson, *The Life of Lidian Jackson Emerson*, ed. Delores Bird Carpenter (Boston: Twayne, 1980), p. 154.

138. William to Waldo, 5 May 1868, MHi, Ms N-251 (658). Haven married Susan Tompkins on 2 June 1868.

139. MHi, Ms N-251 (666). This is the last letter from William in a correspondence that lasted for over fifty years.

140. Information in this paragraph is drawn from *L*, 6:33–50 passim, and *Letters of Ellen Tucker Emerson*, ed. Gregg, 1:533.

Index